A COMPLETE GUIDE
TO THE
FUTURES MARKET

The Wiley Trading series features books by traders who have survived the market's ever changing temperament and have prospered—some by reinventing systems, others by getting back to basics. Whether a novice trader, professional or some-where in-between, these books will provide the advice and strategies needed to prosper today and well into the future. For more on this series, visit our website at www.WileyTrading.com.

Founded in 1807, John Wiley & Sons is the oldest independent publishing company in the United States. With offices in North America, Europe, Australia and Asia, Wiley is globally committed to developing and marketing print and electronic products and services for our customers' professional and personal knowledge and understanding.

A COMPLETE GUIDE TO THE FUTURES MARKET

Technical Analysis, Trading Systems,
Fundamental Analysis, Options, Spreads, and
Trading Principles

SECOND EDITION

Jack D. Schwager

Mark Etzkorn

WILEY

Published by John Wiley & Sons, Inc., Hoboken, New Jersey.
The first edition of *A Complete Guide to the Futures Market* was published by John Wiley & Sons in 1984.
Published simultaneously in Canada.

Library of Congress Cataloging-in-Publication Data:

Names: Schwager, Jack D., 1948- author.
Title: A complete guide to the futures market : fundamental analysis,
   technical analysis, trading, spreads and options / Jack D. Schwager.
Description: Second edition. | Hoboken, New Jersey : John Wiley & Sons, Inc.,
   [2017] | Series: Wiley trading series | Includes index.
Identifiers: LCCN 2016034802 (print) | LCCN 2016047999 (ebook) | ISBN
   9781118853757 (pbk.) | ISBN 9781118859599 (pdf) | ISBN 9781118859544 (epub)
Subjects: LCSH: Futures market. | Commodity exchanges. | Hedging (Finance)
Classification: LCC HG6046 .S39 2017 (print) | LCC HG6046 (ebook) | DDC
   332.64/52-dc23
LC record available at https://lccn.loc.gov/2016034802

Printed in the United States of America.
SKY10050102_070723

In memory of Stephen Chronowitz, my mentor and friend.

CONTENTS

xii

CONTENTS

Jack Schwager is a co-founder and Chief Research Officer of FundSeeder, a firm that seeks to find undiscovered trading talent worldwide via its trader platform (FundSeeder.com), and a co-founder of FundSeeder Investments (FundSeederinvest.com), which seeks to connect properly regulated traders with sources of investment capital. Mr. Schwager is a recognized industry expert in futures and hedge funds and the author of a number of widely acclaimed financial books. Previously, Mr. Schwager was a partner in the Fortune Group (2001–2010), a London-based hedge fund advisory firm. His prior experience also includes 22 years as Director of Futures research for some of Wall Street's leading firms, most recently Prudential Securities.

Mr. Schwager has written extensively on the futures industry and great traders in all financial markets. He is perhaps best known for his best-selling series of interviews with the greatest hedge fund managers of the last three decades: *Market Wizards* (1989), *The New Market Wizards* (1992), *Stock Market Wizards* (2001), *Hedge Fund Market Wizards* (2012), and *The Little Book of Market Wizards* (2014). His other books include *Market Sense and Nonsense* (2012), a compendium of investment misconceptions, and the three-volume series *Schwager on Futures*, consisting of *Fundamental Analysis* (1995), *Technical Analysis* (1996), and *Managed Trading* (1996). He is also the author of *Getting Started in Technical Analysis* (1999), part of Wiley's popular *Getting Started* series.

Mr. Schwager is a frequent seminar speaker and has lectured on a range of analytical topics including the characteristics of great traders, investment fallacies, hedge fund portfolios, managed accounts, technical analysis, and trading system evaluation. He holds a BA in Economics from Brooklyn College (1970) and an MA in Economics from Brown University (1971).

Mark Etzkorn is founder of FinCom Media. He was formerly Editor-in-Chief of *Active Trader* magazine, editor at *Futures* magazine, and a member of the Chicago Mercantile Exchange. He has authored, edited, and contributed to more than 10 books on the financial markets.

PART I

PRELIMINARIES

CHAPTER 1

For Beginners Only

If a little knowledge is dangerous, where is the man who has so much as to be out of danger?

—Thomas Henry Huxley

■ Purpose of This Chapter

The focus of this book is on analysis and trading. Although these subjects are explored in far greater depth than in most general commodity texts, the presentation in the following chapters does not assume any prior knowledge except for a familiarity with the basic concepts of futures markets. This chapter is intended to provide a sketch of the background information necessary to make this book accessible to the novice reader. The title of this chapter should be taken literally. Traders who are already familiar with futures markets should proceed directly to Chapter 2.

The introductory discussion provided by this chapter is deliberately brief and does not purport to cover all background subjects. Topics such as the history of exchanges, choosing a broker, and operation of the clearinghouse are not covered because a familiarity with these subjects is unnecessary for the analysis and trading of futures markets. Readers who desire a more detailed discussion of commodity market basics can refer to a wide range of introductory commodity texts.

■ The Nature of Futures Markets

A futures contract is a commitment to deliver or receive a standardized quantity and quality of a commodity or financial instrument at a specified future date. The price associated with this commitment is the trade entry level.

The essence of a futures market is in its name: Trading involves a commodity or financial instrument for a future delivery date, as opposed to the present time. Thus, if a cotton farmer wished to make a current sale, he would sell his crop in the local cash market. However, if the same farmer wanted to lock in a price for an anticipated future sale (e.g., the marketing of a still unharvested crop), he would have two options: He could locate an interested buyer and negotiate a contract specifying the price and other details (quantity, quality, delivery time, location, etc.). Alternatively, he could sell futures. Some of the major advantages of the latter approach are the following:

1. The futures contract is standardized; hence, the farmer does not have to find a specific buyer.
2. The transaction can be executed virtually instantaneously online.
3. The cost of the trade (commissions) is minimal compared with the cost of an individualized forward contract.
4. The farmer can offset his sale at any time between the original transaction date and the final trading day of the contract. The reasons this may be desirable are discussed later in this chapter.
5. The futures contract is guaranteed by the exchange.

Until the early 1970s, futures markets were restricted to commodities (e.g., wheat, sugar, copper, cattle). Since that time, the futures area has expanded to incorporate additional market sectors, most significantly stock indexes, interest rates, and currencies (foreign exchange). The same basic principles apply to these financial futures markets. Trading quotes represent prices for a future expiration date rather than current market prices. For example, the quote for December 10-year T-note futures implies a specific price for a $100,000, 10-year U.S. Treasury note to be delivered in December. Financial markets have experienced spectacular growth since their introduction, and today trading volume in these contracts dwarfs that in commodities. Nevertheless, futures markets are still commonly, albeit erroneously, referred to as commodity markets, and these terms are synonymous.

■ Delivery

Shorts who maintain their positions in deliverable futures contracts after the last trading day are obligated to deliver the given commodity or financial instrument against the contract. Similarly, longs who maintain their positions after the last trading day must accept delivery. In the commodity markets, the number of open long contracts is always equal to the number of open short contracts (see section Volume and Open Interest). Most traders have no intention of making or accepting delivery, and hence will offset their positions before the last trading day. (The long offsets his position by entering a sell order, the short by entering a buy order.) It has been estimated that fewer than 3 percent of open contracts actually result in delivery. Some futures contracts (e.g., stock indexes, eurodollar) use a *cash settlement* process whereby outstanding long and short positions are offset at the prevailing price level at expiration instead of being physically delivered.

Contract Specifications

Futures contracts are traded for a wide variety of markets on a number of exchanges both in the United States and abroad. The specifications for these contracts, especially details such as daily price limits, trading hours, and ticker symbols, can change over time; exchange web sites should be consulted for up-to-date information. Table 1.1 provides the following representative trading details for six futures markets (E-mini S&P 500, 10-year T-note, euro, Brent crude oil, corn, and gold):

1. **Exchange.** Note that some markets are traded on more than one exchange. In some cases, different contracts for the same commodity (or financial instrument) may even be traded on the same exchange.

2. **Ticker symbol.** The quote symbol is the letter code that identifies each market (e.g., ES for the E-mini S&P 500, C for corn, EC for the euro), combined with an alphanumeric suffix to represent the month and year.

3. **Contract size.** The specification of a uniform quantity per contract is one of the key ways in which a futures contract is standardized. By multiplying the contract size by the price, the trader can determine the dollar value of a contract. For example, if corn is trading at $4.00/bushel (bu), the contract value equals $20,000 ($4 × 5,000 bu per contract). If Brent crude oil is trading at $48.30, the contract value is $48,300 ($48.30 × 1,000 barrels). Although there are many important exceptions, very roughly speaking, higher per-contract dollar values will imply a greater potential/risk level. (The concept of contract value has no meaning for interest rate contracts.)

4. **Price quoted in.** This row indicates the relevant unit of measure for the given market.

5. **Minimum price fluctuation ("tick") size and value.** This row indicates the minimum increment in which prices can trade, and the dollar value of that move. For example, the minimum fluctuation for the E-mini S&P 500 contract is 0.25 index points. Thus, you can enter an order to buy December E-mini S&P futures at 1,870.25 or 1,870.50, but not 1,870.30. The minimum fluctuation for corn is $\frac{1}{4}$ ¢/bu, which means you can enter an order to buy December corn at $4.01 $\frac{1}{2}$ or $4.01 $\frac{3}{4}$, but not $4.01 $\frac{5}{8}$ per bushel. The tick value is obtained by multiplying the minimum fluctuation by the contract size. For example, for Brent crude oil, one cent ($0.01) per barrel × 1,000 barrels = $10. For corn, $\frac{1}{4}$ ¢/bu × 5,000 = $12.50.

6. **Contract months.** Each market is traded for specific months. For example, the E-mini S&P 500 futures contract is traded for March, June, September, and December. Corn is traded for March, May, July, September, and December. Table 1.2 shows the letter designations for each month of the year, which are added (along with the contract year) to a market's base ticker symbol to create a contract-specific ticker symbol. For example, December 2017 E-mini S&P 500 futures have a ticker symbol of ESZ17, while the symbol for the March 2018 contract is ESH18. The symbol for May 2017 corn is CK17. The last trading day for a contract typically occurs on a specified date in the contract month, although in some markets (such as crude oil), the last trading day falls in the month preceding the contract month. For most markets, futures are listed for contract months at least one year forward from the current date. However, trading activity is normally heavily concentrated in the nearest two contracts.

TABLE 1.1 Sample Futures Contract Specifications

	E-Mini S&P 500	10-Year T-Note	Euro FX	Brent Crude Oil	Corn	Gold
Exchange	CME Group	CME Group/CBOT	CME Group	Intercontinental Exchange (ICE Futures Europe)	CME Group/CBOT	CME Group/NYMEX
Ticker Symbol	ES	TY	EC	B	C	GC
Contract Size	$50 × S&P 500 Index	U.S. Treasury note with a face value at maturity of $100,000.	125,000 euros	1,000 barrels	5,000 bushels (~ 127 metric tons)	100 troy ounces
Price Quoted In	Index points	Points ($1,000) and halves of 1/32 of a point (e.g., 126-16 represents 126 16/32 and 126-165 represents 126 16.5/32).	U.S. dollars per euro	U.S. dollars and cents	Cents per bushel	U.S. dollars and cents per troy ounce
Minimum Price Fluctuation ("tick") Size and Value	0.25 index points = $12.50	One-half of 1/32 of one point ($15.625, rounded to the nearest cent per contract).	$0.00005 per euro increments ($6.25/contract)	One cent ($0.01) per barrel = $10	1/4 cent per bushel = $12.50	$0.10 per troy ounce = $10
Contract Months	Mar, Jun, Sep, Dec	Mar, Jun, Sep, Dec	Mar, Jun, Sep, Dec	All months of the year	Mar, May, Jul, Sep, Dec	The current month; the next two months; any Feb, Apr, Aug, and Oct within a 23-month period; and any June and Dec within a 72-month period beginning with the current month.
Trading Hours	Mon–Fri, 5:00 p.m. previous day to 4:15 p.m.; trading halt from 3:15 p.m. to 3:30 p.m.	5:00 p.m. to 4:00 p.m., Sun–Fri.	Sun–Fri. 5 p.m. to 4 p.m. CT with a 60-min. break each day beginning at 4:00 p.m.	1 a.m. to 11 p.m. London time	Sun–Fri, 7:00 p.m. to 7:45 a.m. CT and Mon–Fri, 8:30 a.m. to 1:20 p.m. CT.	Sun–Fri, 6:00 p.m. to 5:00 p.m. (5:00 p.m. to 4:00 p.m. Chicago time/CT) with a 60-minute break each day beginning at 5:00 p.m. (4:00 p.m. CT).

Daily Price Limit	7%, 13%, and 20% limits are applied to the futures fixing price, effective 8:30 a.m. to 3 p.m. CT, Mon–Fri.	7%, 13%, and 20% limits are applied to the futures fixing price, effective 8:30 a.m. to 3 p.m. CT, Mon–Fri. (See exchange for specifics.)	N/A	N/A	N/A	$0.25	N/A
Settlement Type	Cash settlement	Deliverable	Deliverable	Physical delivery based on EFP delivery, with an option to cash settle against the ICE Brent Index price for the last trading day of the futures contract.	Deliverable	Deliverable	Deliverable
First Notice Day	N/A	Final business day of the month preceding the contract month.	N/A	N/A	N/A	Last business day of month preceding contract month.	The last business day of the month preceding the delivery month.
Last Notice Day	N/A	Final business day of the contract month.	N/A	N/A	N/A	The business day after the last contract's last trading day.	The second-to-last business day of the delivery month.
Last Trading Day	Until 8:30 a.m. on the 3rd Friday of the contract month.	12:01 p.m. on the 7th business day preceding the last business day of the delivery month.	9:16 a.m. CT on the second business day immediately preceding the third Wed of the contract month.	The last business day of the second month preceding the relevant contract month.	The business day after the last contract's last trading day.	Business day prior to the 15th calendar day of the contract month.	The third-to-last business day of the delivery month.
Deliverable Grade	N/A	U.S. T-notes with a remaining term to maturity of 6.5 to 10 years from the first day of the delivery month.	N/A	N/A	N/A	#2 Yellow at contract price, #1 Yellow at a 1.5 cent/bushel premium, #3 Yellow at a 1.5 cent/bushel discount.	Gold delivered under this contract shall assay to a minimum of 995 fineness.

TABLE 1.2	Contract Month Designations
Month	Ticker Designation
January	F
February	G
March	H
April	J
May	K
June	M
July	N
August	Q
September	U
October	V
November	X
December	Z

7. **Trading hours.** Trading hours are listed in terms of the local times for the given exchange. (All U.S. exchanges are currently located in either the Eastern or Central time zones.)

8. **Daily price limit.** Exchanges normally specify a maximum amount by which the contract price can change on a given day. For example, if the December corn contract closed at $4.10 on the previous day, and the daily price limit is 25¢/bu, corn cannot trade above $4.35 or below $3.85. Some markets employ formulas for increasing the daily limit after a specified number of consecutive limit days.

In cases in which free market forces would normally seek an equilibrium price outside the range boundaries implied by the limit, the market will simply move to the limit and virtually cease to trade. For example, if after the market close the U.S. Department of Agriculture (USDA) releases a very bullish corn crop production estimate, which hypothetically would result in an immediate 30¢/bu price rise in an unrestricted market, prices will be *locked limit up* (25¢/bu) the next day. This means that the market will open and stay at the limit, with virtually no trading taking place. The reason for the absence of trading activity is that the limit rule restriction maintains an artificially low price, leading to a deluge of buy orders at that price but few if any sell orders.

In the case of a very severe surprise event (e.g., sudden major crop damage), a market could move several limits in succession, although such moves are less common than in the days before near-24-hour electronic trading. In such situations, traders on the wrong side of the fence might not be able to liquidate their positions until the market trades freely. The new trader should be aware of, but not be overly frightened by, this possibility, since such events of extreme volatility rarely come as a complete surprise. In most cases, markets vulnerable to such volatile price action can be identified. Some examples of such markets would include commodities in which the USDA is scheduled to release a major report, coffee or frozen concentrated orange juice during their respective freeze seasons, and markets that have exhibited recent extreme trading volatility. For some markets, the limit on the nearby contract is removed at some point approaching expiration (frequently *first notice day*—see item 10). Daily price limits can change frequently, so traders should consult the exchange on which their products trade to ensure they are aware of current thresholds.

9. **Settlement type.** Markets are designated either as physically deliverable or cash settled. In Table 1.1, the E-mini S&P 500 futures are cash settled, while all the other markets can be physically delivered.

10. **First notice day.** This is the first day on which a long can receive a delivery notice. First notice day presents no problem for shorts, since they are not obligated to issue a notice until after the last trading day. Furthermore, in some markets, first notice day occurs after last trading day, presenting no problem to the long either, since all remaining longs at that point presumably wish to take delivery. However, in markets in which first notice day precedes last trading day, longs who do not wish to take delivery should be sure to offset their positions in time to avoid receiving a delivery notice. (Brokerage firms routinely supply their clients with a list of these important dates.) Although longs can pass on an undesired delivery notice by liquidating their position, this transaction will incur extra transaction costs and should be avoided. *Last notice day* is the final day a long can receive a delivery notice.

11. **Last trading day.** This is the last day on which positions can be offset before delivery becomes obligatory for shorts and the acceptance of delivery obligatory for longs. As indicated previously, the vast majority of traders will liquidate their positions before this day.

12. **Deliverable grade.** This is the specific quality and type of the underlying commodity or financial instrument that is acceptable for delivery.

■ Volume and Open Interest

Volume is the total number of contracts traded on a given day. Volume figures are available for each traded month in a market, but most traders focus on the total volume of all traded months.

Open interest is the total number of outstanding long contracts, or equivalently, the total number of outstanding short contracts—in futures, the two are always the same. When a new contract begins trading (typically about 12 to 18 months before its expiration date), its open interest is equal to zero. If a buy order and sell order are matched, then the open interest increases to 1. Basically, open interest increases when a new buyer purchases from a new seller and decreases when an existing long sells to an existing short. The open interest will remain unchanged if a new buyer purchases from an existing long or a new seller sells to an existing short.

Volume and open interest are very useful as indicators of a market's liquidity. Not all listed futures markets are actively traded. Some are virtually dormant, while others are borderline cases in terms of trading activity. Illiquid markets should be avoided, because the lack of an adequate order flow will mean that the trader will often have to accept very poor trade execution prices if he wants to get in or out of a position.

Generally speaking, markets with open interest levels below 5,000 contracts, or average daily volume levels below 1,000 contracts, should be avoided, or at least approached very cautiously. New markets will usually exhibit volume and open interest figures below these levels during their initial months (and sometimes even years) of trading. By monitoring the volume and open interest figures, a trader can determine when the market's level of liquidity is sufficient to warrant participation. Figure 1.1 shows February 2016 gold (top) and April 2016 gold (bottom) prices, along with their respective daily volume figures. February gold's volume is negligible until November 2015, at which point it increases rapidly into December and maintains a high level through January (the February contract expires in late February). Meanwhile, April gold's volume is minimal until January, at which point it increases steadily and becomes the more actively traded contract in the last two days of January—even though the February gold contract is still a month from expiration at that point.

The breakdown of volume and open interest figures by contract month can be very useful in determining whether a specific month is sufficiently liquid. For example, a trader who prefers to initiate a long position in a nine-month forward futures contract rather than in more nearby contracts because of an assessment that it is relatively underpriced may be concerned whether its level of trading activity is sufficient to avoid liquidity problems. In this case, the breakdown of volume and open interest figures by contract month can help the trader decide whether it is reasonable to enter the position in the more forward contract or whether it is better to restrict trading to the nearby contracts.

Traders with short-term time horizons (e.g., intraday to a few days) should limit trading to the most liquid contract, which is usually the nearby contract month.

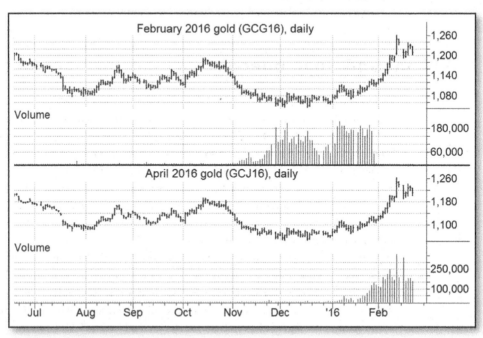

FIGURE 1.1   Volume Shift in Gold Futures
Chart created using TradeStation. ©TradeStation Technologies, Inc. All rights reserved.

■ Hedging

A sell hedge is the sale of a futures contract as a temporary substitute for an anticipated future sale of the cash commodity.[1] Similarly, a buy hedge is a temporary substitute for an anticipated forward purchase of the cash commodity. In essence, the goal of the hedger is to lock in an approximate future price in order to eliminate exposure to interim price fluctuations. The concept of hedging is perhaps best explained through illustration. Let's look at several examples of hedging.

Hedging Examples for a Commodity

Cotton Producer Sell Hedge   The date is April 1. A cotton farmer estimates his potential production at approximately 200,000 lbs, assuming average yields. The current cash price is 95¢/lb—an extremely attractive price, but one the producer cannot take advantage of, since his crop will not be harvested until November. December futures are trading at 85¢/lb, reflecting market expectations for an interim price decline. The producer believes the December price may actually be overly optimistic. He expects that a large increase in U.S. production, in response to high prices, will result in a major price collapse by the time the new crop is harvested. Given his bearish expectations, the producer is eager to lock in a price on his anticipated production.

Historical comparisons indicate the November–December cash prices in the producer's region tend to average approximately 2–4¢ below the December futures price. (The difference between cash and futures is called the *basis*. In this case, the November–December basis is said to be "2–4¢ under.") Thus, by selling December futures at the current price of 85¢/lb, the farmer can lock in an approximate cash price of 81–83¢. Because the producer believes prices will be significantly below 80¢/lb by harvest time, he decides to sell three December futures contracts against the expected post-harvest sale of his crop. This is called a *sell hedge*.

Note that three contracts represent 150,000 lbs of cotton, an amount equivalent to three-quarters of the producer's anticipated crop. The farmer does not hedge his entire crop, because his eventual output is still open to considerable uncertainty. If weather conditions are extremely poor, his yields could be reduced by more than 25 percent. Consequently, to avoid the possibility of overhedging his crop, an action that would leave him with a net short position, he prudently decides to sell only three contracts.

Table 1.3 illustrates two hypothetical outcomes of this hedge. In case 1, the producer is entirely correct in his expectations, and cash prices decline to 72¢/lb by December 1. In line with the normal historical basis relationship, December futures are simultaneously trading at 75¢/lb. The producer sells his cash crop at 72¢/lb, but also realizes a profit of 10¢/lb on his futures position. Thus, on the 150,000 lbs of crop that he has hedged, his effective price is 82¢/lb. (Commissions have not been included in this or the following illustrations in order to keep exposition as simple as possible. The adjustment for commissions would not meaningfully alter the results.) As a result of hedging, the

---

[1] The sell hedge may also be used as a proxy for temporary inventory reduction (see example of stock portfolio manager later in this section).

TABLE 1.3 Cotton Producer Sell Hedge

Case 1: Severely Weakening Cash Price		Case 2: Relatively Firm Cash Price	
Apr. 1	**Dec. 1**	**Apr. 1**	**Dec. 1**
Cash price 95¢	72¢	Cash price 95¢	92¢
Futures price 85¢	75¢	Futures price 85¢	95¢
Results:		Results:	
Cash sale price: 72¢		Cash sale price: 92¢	
Profit on futures: 10¢		Loss on futures: 10¢	
Effective sale price: 82¢		Effective sale price: 82¢	

farmer has locked in a much better price than he would have realized had he waited until his crop was harvested before taking any marketing action. In dollar terms, the producer's income is $15,000 higher than it would have been without the hedge:

$$3 \times 10¢/lb \times 50,000 \text{ lbs} = \$15,000$$

A hedge will not always be profitable. In the situation illustrated by case 2, Table 1.3, the producer's projections proved wrong as cash prices remained firm, declining a mere 3¢/lb from their lofty April 1 levels. In this case, the farmer is able to sell his crop at a much better than expected 92¢/lb, but he experiences a loss of 10¢/lb on his futures position. His effective sales price is once again 82¢/lb. Of course, in this instance, with the benefit of hindsight, the producer would have been much better off had he had not hedged. Nonetheless, note that even though he has sacrificed the opportunity for a windfall profit by hedging, he still realizes his target sales price of 82¢/lb.

The value of hedging is that it provides the producer with a much wider range of marketing strategies. Remember, if he prefers to take his chances and wait until after the harvest to market his crop, he can do so. Futures widen the range of possibilities by allowing the producer to lock in any futures-implied price during the interim. Thus, although he will not always make the right choice, presumably, over the long run, the increased marketing flexibility provided by futures should prove advantageous.

Cotton Mill Buy Hedge   The date is June 1. A cotton mill has forward contracted to supply a fabric order for the following March. To meet this production order, the mill will need 1 million lbs of cotton on hand by December.

The current cash price is 77¢/lb, and December futures are trading at 80¢/lb. Assuming the same −3¢/lb basis established in the aforementioned cotton producer example, the December futures price quote implies cash prices will be unchanged in December relative to their current levels.

Although the mill has plenty of time to purchase the actual cotton, it is concerned that cash prices will rise significantly in the coming months. Since the end-product sales price has already been negotiated, the company must lock in its input price in order to guarantee a satisfactory profit margin. Given this scenario, the mill has two choices:

1. Increase its inventory sufficiently to cover its anticipated December–March requirements.
2. Hedge its forward requirements by buying December cotton futures.

Given the price structure in this example, the mill will be much better off buying futures. Why? Because the purchase of futures covers the forward commitment without incurring any storage costs. (This is true since the December futures price implies an unchanged cash price relative to current levels.) In contrast, the purchase of actual cotton would incur storage-related costs for the six-month period. The most important of these expenses would be borrowing costs, or lost interest, if the firm was using its own funds.

Table 1.4 illustrates two alternative outcomes for this hedge. In both cases, it is assumed the firm purchases the actual cotton on December 1, simultaneously offsetting its long hedge position in futures. In the first situation, cash prices increase between June and December, and the actual cash market purchase price on December 1 is 87¢/lb. However, as a result of a 10¢/lb profit on the futures hedge, the effective price to the firm is 77¢ (the cash price on June 1). In the second illustration, cash prices decline, and the firm's actual purchase price is 67¢/lb. However, as a result of a 10¢/lb loss in futures, the effective price is once again 77¢/lb. Although in this case the mill would have been better off not hedging, it is still purchasing the cotton at the previously desired locked-in price.

Since most companies will be more concerned about locking in adequate profit margins than about giving up windfall profits, hedging should provide a useful tool for business management. Furthermore, it should be emphasized that the firm always has the option not to hedge if, for any reason, the price implied by futures is not considered attractive. In short, users of commodities who incorporate hedging should have an advantage over their competitors, because they have a much wider range of purchasing strategies.

Hedging in Financial Futures

The previous examples illustrate the buy-and-sell hedge for a commodity. The same basic principles apply to the financial markets, as shown by the following examples.

A corporation expecting the need for a loan in six months and concerned about rising borrowing costs in the interim could lock in an approximate fixed rate by selling short-term interest rate futures (e.g., eurodollars). (An increase in interest rates will cause the *price* of interest rate instruments to decline.)

TABLE 1.4	Cotton Mill Buy Hedge		
Case 1: Rising Cash Price		**Case 2: Declining Cash Price**	
June 1	Dec. 1	June 1	Dec. 1
Cash price 77¢	87¢	Cash price 77¢	67¢
Futures price 80¢	90¢	Futures price 80¢	70¢
Results:		Results:	
Cash purchase price: 87¢		Cash purchase price: 67¢	
Profit on futures: 10¢		Loss on futures: 10¢	
Effective purchase price: 77¢		Effective purchase price: 77¢	

A bond fund manager anticipating a cash influx in three months and an imminent decline in interest rates could lock in a rate of return by going long T-note futures.

A stock portfolio manager concerned about the possibility of a sharp, temporary break in stock prices could reduce market exposure by selling stock index futures (E-mini S&P 500, E-mini Nasdaq 100, Russell 2000 Index Mini). Such action would be far more cost effective (i.e., would incur much lower commission costs) than liquidating part or all of his portfolio and reinstating the position at a later date.

A U.S. company that knew it would require 10 million euros in three months to pay for an import transaction could lock in the exchange rate by purchasing euro futures.

General Observations Regarding Hedging

1. In all the preceding examples, the hedger offsets either an anticipated future transaction in the actual market or a current position with an equal but opposite transaction in futures. Thus, for the hedger, participation in futures can reduce risks associated with price changes. In effect, the true speculators among producers and users of commodities (or the financial markets) are those who do not hedge. For example, the farmer who does not hedge is speculating on the direction of prices during the interim before his crop is harvested.

2. Some written discussions of hedging almost seem to imply that producers and users of exchange-traded commodities should automatically hedge. This is ridiculous—hedging should be considered only if the futures-implied price is desirable. Otherwise, one is merely exchanging the futures-implied price for the subsequent actual cash price. Over the long run, this type of hedging should be a break-even process in terms of trades and a net loss generator because of commissions.

3. Hedging should be viewed as an important marketing tool, because it provides the producer and user with a wide range of purchase and sale strategies. Hedgers can always choose not to hedge, but nonhedgers eliminate the possibility of enhancing their profits through futures-related opportunities.

4. The hedger need not wait until the time of the actual transaction to lift the hedge. For example, reconsider the case of the cotton producer who sells December futures at 85¢/lb. If by October, futures have declined to 70¢/lb, the hedger might very well decide to cover his short hedge position. Although at a price of 85¢/lb the farmer was eager to protect against the possibility of declining prices, at a price of 70¢/lb he might well prefer to take his chances. If prices were subsequently to rally, the producer might decide to reinstate his hedge. In fact, sophisticated hedgers will often use such a trading approach in hedging. The key point is that, contrary to most textbook illustrations, a hedge should be maintained only as long as the implied price protection is deemed desirable.

5. It is important to keep the time differential and expectations in mind when comparing a current cash price with the cash price implied by futures. For example, in the hedge illustrated in case 1, Table 1.3, the futures-implied cash price is 13¢/lb below the current cash price. Yet, despite

this wide discount, the hedge is still very profitable because the price differential is ultimately far outweighed by the intervening price decline. Thus, the relevant question is not whether the futures-implied cash price is attractive relative to the *current* cash price, but rather whether it is attractive relative to the *expected future* cash price.

6. The hedger does not precisely lock in a transaction price. His effective price will depend on the basis. For example, if the cotton producer sells futures at 85¢/lb, assuming a −3¢ basis, his effective sales price will be 80¢/lb, rather than the anticipated 82¢/lb, if the actual basis at the time of offset is −5¢. However, it should be emphasized that this basis-price uncertainty is far smaller than the outright price uncertainty in an unhedged position. Furthermore, by using reasonably conservative basis assumptions the hedger can increase the likelihood of achieving, or bettering, the assumed locked-in price.

7. Although a hedger plans to buy or sell the actual commodity, it will usually be far more efficient to offset the futures position and use the local cash market for the actual transaction. Futures should be viewed as a pricing tool, not as a vehicle for making or taking delivery.

8. Most standard discussions of hedging make no mention whatsoever of price forecasting. This omission seems to imply that hedgers need not be concerned about the direction of prices. Although this conclusion may be valid for some hedgers (e.g., a middleman seeking to lock in a profit margin between the purchase and sales price), it is erroneous for most hedgers. There is little sense in following an automatic hedging program. Rather, the hedger should evaluate the relative attractiveness of the price protection offered by futures. Price forecasting would be a key element in making such an evaluation. In this respect, it can easily be argued that price forecasting is as important to many hedgers as it is to speculators.

■ Trading

The trader seeks to profit by anticipating price changes. For example, if the price of December gold is $1,150/oz, a trader who expects the price to rise above $1,250/oz will go long. The trader has no intention of actually taking delivery of the gold in December. Right or wrong, the trader will offset the position sometime before expiration. For example, if the price rises to $1,275 and the trader decides to take profits, the gain on the trade will be $12,500 per contract (100 oz × $125/oz). If, on the other hand, the trader's forecast is wrong and prices decline to $1,075/oz, with the expiration date drawing near, the trader has little choice but to liquidate. In this situation, the loss would be equal to $7,500 per contract. Note that the trader would not take delivery even given a desire to maintain the long gold position. In this case, the trader would liquidate the December contract and simultaneously go long in a more forward contract. (This type of transaction is called a *rollover* and would be implemented with a *spread* order—defined in the next section.) Traders should avoid taking delivery, since it can often result in substantial extra costs without any compensating benefits.

Novice traders should caution against the securities-based bias of trading only from the long side. In futures trading, there is no distinction between going short and going long.[2] Since prices can go down as well as up, the trader who takes only long positions will eliminate approximately half the potential trading opportunities. Also, it should be noted that futures frequently command a premium to current prices; consequently, the inflation argument for a long-side bias is frequently erroneous.

The successful trader must employ some method for forecasting prices. The two basic analytical approaches are:

1. **Technical analysis.** The technical analyst bases projections on non-economic data. Price data are by far the most important—and often only—input in technical analysis. The basic assumption of technical analysis is that prices exhibit repetitive patterns and that the recognition of these patterns can be used to identify trading opportunities. Technical analysis can also include other data, such as volume, open interest, and sentiment measures.

2. **Fundamental analysis.** The fundamental analyst uses economic data (e.g., production, consumption, exports) to forecast prices. In essence, the fundamentalist seeks to uncover trading opportunities by identifying potential transitions to significantly more ample or tighter supply-demand balances.

As discussed in Chapter 2, technical and fundamental analysis are not mutually exclusive approaches. Many traders use both in the decision-making process or as components of automated trading systems.

■ Types of Orders

Day versus Good Till Canceled (GTC)

Unless specified otherwise, orders are assumed to be good only for the day of entry. If the trader wants the order to remain open until canceled, he must specify that it is a good-till-canceled (GTC) order.

Market

This instruction directs the broker to execute the order upon receipt at the prevailing price level. Market orders are used when the trader is more concerned with initiating or liquidating a position immediately than with trying to achieve a specific execution price. Market orders ensure the trade will be executed unless prices are locked in at the daily limit or the order is entered too close to the end of the trading session.

---

[2] Some beginners are confused about how it is possible for a trader to sell a commodity he does not own. The key to the answer lies in the fact that the trader is selling a *futures* contract, not the cash commodity. Even though the trader who stays short past the last trading day must acquire the actual commodity to fulfill his contractual obligation, there is no need for him to own the commodity before that time. The short sale is simply a bet that prices will go down before the last trading day. Right or wrong, the trader will offset his short position before the last trading day, eliminating any need for actual ownership of the commodity.

Limit

The limit order, also called an *or-better* order, is used when the trader wants to ensure that the execution price will be no worse than a certain level. For example, an order to buy December gold at a $1,150/ounce limit can only be executed at a price equal to or below $1,150.

If the market is trading higher than that level when the brokerage receives the order, it must wait for the price to decline to $1,150 before it can execute the trade. If the price fails to return to that level, the brokerage is unable to fill the order. Similarly, an order to sell December gold at a $1,190/ounce limit would indicate that the order can only be filled at a price equal to or above $1,190. Limit orders will normally provide better fills than will market orders, but the trade-off is that they may not be executed. A trader whose primary concern is to get the order filled, particularly if it is an order to liquidate a losing position, should not use a limit order.

Stop

A stop order is not executed until the market reaches the given price level. The indicated price on a buy stop must always be above the market, while the indicated price on a sell stop must always be below the market.

In effect, a stop order will always be filled at a price worse than the market price. Why then would a trader use a stop order? There are two very important reasons: First, stop orders are used to limit losses or protect open profits. For example, a trader who buys March sugar at 14.50¢/lb might place an order to sell March sugar at 13.50¢/lb stop, GTC. If the market subsequently declines to 13.50¢/lb or lower, the stop order becomes a market order. In this way, the trader limits his risk on the trade to approximately 100 points. The reason for the word *approximately* is that markets often move beyond the stop price before the order can be executed. In the case of a short position, the protective stop order would be placed at a higher price. For example, if the trader went short March sugar at 14.50¢/lb, an order might be placed to buy March sugar at 15.50¢/lb stop, GTC.

Second, a stop order may be used if a trader views the market's ability to reach a certain level as a price signal. For example, if March sugar has been trading between 12.00¢ and 15.00¢/lb for several months, a trader might believe that the ability of the market to significantly penetrate the high of this range would be a sign of strength, suggesting a potential bull move. In this case, the trader might enter an order to buy March sugar at 15.50¢/lb stop. Thus, even though March sugar can be purchased more cheaply at the current price, the trader prefers to use the stop order because he only wants to be long if the market is able to demonstrate a specified degree of strength.

Stop-Limit

A stop-limit order is a stop order in which the actual execution price is limited. For example, an order to "buy March 10-year T-notes at 124'16 stop, 124'24 limit, GTC" means that if March 10-year T-note futures advance to 124'16, the buy order is activated but cannot be executed at a price above 124'24. Similarly, an order to "sell March T-notes at 122 stop, 121'22 limit, GTC" is a sell stop that is activated if the market declines to 122, but which cannot be filled at a price below 121'22. The stop and limit portions of the order need not necessarily be at different prices.

Stop Close-Only

A stop close-only is a stop order that is activated only if any portion of the closing price range is beyond the indicated price. (This type of order is not accepted on all exchanges.)

Market If Touched

A market-if-touched (MIT) order is similar to a limit order except that it becomes a market order anytime the limit price is reached. For example, given the following sequence of prices—79.40, 79.35, 79.25, 79.20, 79.25, 79.30, 79.40, 79.50 . . .—a 79.20 MIT buy order would become a market order once 79.20 was reached, but a 79.20 limit order could be filled only at a price of 79.20 or better. In this illustration, the market decline to 79.20 is so fleeting that the limit order might very well not be filled, while the MIT order would be executed (probably at some price above 79.20). The MIT is a hairsplitting type of order that is largely superfluous. Over the long run, a trader will achieve equivalent results by using slightly higher buy limits (lower sell limits) instead of MIT orders.

Fill or Kill

As the name implies, a fill-or-kill (FOK) order is a limit order that must be filled immediately or canceled.

Scale

A scale order is used for multicontract positions in which the trader wants to enter different contracts at different prices. For example, if June British pound futures are trading at 153.00, a trader who wants to sell 10 contracts on a possible rally to the 155.00–157.00 zone might enter a scale order to sell 10 June British pound contracts, one at 155.20 limit and one contract every 0.20 points higher, with the last contract having a limit price of 157.00.

One Cancels Other

The one-cancels-other (OCO) order is a two-sided order in which the execution of one side cancels the other. For example, a trader who is long February live cattle at 117.00, with an objective of 125.00 and a stop point at 109.00, might enter the following order: sell 1 February cattle 125.00 limit/109.00 stop, OCO, GTC.

Contingent

In this type of order the execution instruction for one contract is contingent on another contract. An example would be: Sell October sugar at the market if March sugar trades at 13.00 or lower. (This type of order is not accepted on all exchanges.)

Spread

A spread involves the simultaneous purchase of one futures contract against the sale of another futures contract, either in the same market or in a related market. In essence, a spread trader is primarily concerned with the *difference* between prices rather than the *direction* of price. An example of a spread trade would be: Buy 1 July cotton/sell 1 December cotton, July 200 points premium December. This order would be executed if July could be bought at a price 200 points or less above the level at which December is sold. Such an order would be placed if the trader expected July cotton to widen its premium relative to December cotton.

Not all brokerages will accept all the order types in this section (and may offer others not listed here). Traders should consult with their brokerage to determine which types of orders are available to them.

■ Commissions and Margins

In futures trading, commissions are typically charged on a per-contract basis. In most cases, large traders will be able to negotiate a reduced commission rate. Although commodity commissions are relatively moderate, commission costs can prove substantial for the active trader—an important reason why position trading is preferable unless one has developed a very effective short-term trading method.

Futures margins are basically good-faith deposits and represent only a small percentage of the contract value (roughly 5 percent with some significant variability around this level). Futures exchanges will set minimum margin requirements for each of their contracts, but many brokerage houses will frequently require higher margin deposits. Since the initial margin represents only a small portion of the contract value, traders will be required to provide additional margin funds if the market moves against their positions. These additional margin payments are referred to as *maintenance*.

Many traders tend to be overly concerned with the minimum margin rate charged by a brokerage house. If a trader is adhering to prudent money management principles, the actual margin level should be all but irrelevant. As a general rule, the trader should allocate at least three to five times the minimum margin requirement to each trade. Trading an account anywhere near the full margin allowance greatly increases the chances of experiencing a severe loss. Traders who do not maintain at least several multiples of margin requirements in their accounts are clearly overtrading.

■ Tax Considerations

Tax laws change over time, but for the average speculator in the United States, the essential elements of the futures contract tax regulations can be summarized in three basic points:

1. There is no holding period for futures trades (i.e., all trades are treated equally, regardless of the length of time a position is held, or whether a position is long or short).

2. Sixty percent of futures trading gains are treated as long-term capital gains, and the remaining 40 percent are treated as short-term capital gains. Since current maximum tax rates on long- and short-term capital gains are 20 percent and 50 percent, respectively, this formula suggests a maximum tax rate of 32 percent on futures trades.

3. Gain (loss) in a given year is calculated as the total of realized gain (loss) plus unrealized gain (loss) as of December 31.

CHAPTER 2

The Great Fundamental versus Technical Analysis Debate

Curiously, however, the broken technician is never apologetic about his method. If anything, he is more enthusiastic than ever. If you commit the social error of asking him why he is broke, he will tell you quite ingeniously that he made the all-too-human error of not believing his own charts. To my great embarrassment, I once choked conspicuously at the dinner table of a chartist friend of mine when he made such a comment. I have since made it a rule never to eat with a chartist. It's bad for digestion.

—Burton G. Malkiel

One evening, while having dinner with a fundamentalist, I accidentally knocked a sharp knife off the edge of the table. He watched the knife twirl through the air, as it came to rest with the pointed end sticking into his shoe. "Why didn't you move your foot?" I exclaimed. "I was waiting for it to come back up," he replied.

—Ed Seykota (an avowed technician)

Fundamental analysis involves the use of economic data (e.g., production, consumption, disposable income) to forecast prices, whereas technical analysis is based primarily (and often solely) on the study of patterns in the price data itself. Which method is better? This question is the subject of great debate. Interestingly, the experts are no less divided on this matter than are novices. In a series of books in which I interviewed some of the world's best traders,[1] I was struck by the sharply divergent views on this issue.

Jim Rogers was characteristic of one extreme of the spectrum. During the 1970s, Jim Rogers and George Soros were the two principals of the Quantum Fund, perhaps the most successful Wall Street fund of its day. In 1980, Rogers left the fund to escape managerial responsibilities and devote all his time to managing his own investments—an endeavor at which he again proved spectacularly successful. (The Quantum Fund maintained its excellent performance in the ensuing years under George Soros's directorship.) Over the years, Rogers has been on record with a high percentage of accurate market forecasts. As but one example, in my 1988 interview with him, Rogers correctly predicted both the massive collapse in the Japanese stock market and the continued multiyear downtrend in gold prices. Clearly, Jim Rogers is a man whose opinion merits serious attention.

When I queried Rogers about his opinion on chart reading (the classic method of technical analysis), he replied: "I haven't met a rich technician. Excluding, of course, the technicians who sell their services and make a lot of money." That cynical response succinctly summarized Rogers's views about technical analysis.

Marty Schwartz is a trader whose opinion lies at the other extreme. At the time of our interview, Schwartz, an independent stock index futures trader, was considering managing outside money. In conjunction with this undertaking, he had just had his personal track record audited, and he allowed me to view the results. During the prior 10-year period, he had achieved an average return of 25 percent—monthly! Equally impressive, during this 120-month period, he witnessed only two losing months—minuscule declines of 2 percent and 3 percent. Again, here was an individual whose opinion on the market warranted serious respect.

Although I did not mention Rogers's comments to Schwartz, when I asked Schwartz whether he had made a complete transition from fundamental to technical analysis (Schwartz had started his financial career as a stock analyst), his response almost sounded like a direct rebuttal to Jim Rogers: "Absolutely. I always laugh at people who say, 'I've never met a rich technician.' I love that! It is such an arrogant, nonsensical response. I used fundamentals for nine years and got rich as a technician."

There you have it. Two extraordinarily successful market participants holding polar-opposite views regarding the efficacy of fundamental versus technical analysis. Whom do you believe?

In my own assessment, both Rogers's and Schwartz's viewpoints contain elements of truth. It is possible to succeed as a trader by being a pure fundamentalist, a pure technician, or a hybrid of the two. The two methods are certainly not mutually exclusive. In fact, many of the world's most successful traders use fundamental analysis to determine the direction to trade a market and technical analysis to time the entry and exit of such trades.

One virtually universal trait I found among successful traders was that they had gravitated to an approach that best fit their personality. Some traders prefer very long-term approaches, while others

---

[1] *Market Wizards* (Hoboken, NJ: John Wiley & Sons, 2012 [orig. pub. 1989]); *The New Market Wizards* (Hoboken, NJ: John Wiley & Sons, 2008); *Stock Market Wizards* (New York, NY: HarperBusiness, 2003); and *Hedge Fund Market Wizards* (Hoboken, NJ: John Wiley & Sons, 2012).

are inclined toward day trading; some traders feel comfortable only when following signals gener-ated by an automated system, while others find such a mechanical method anathema; some traders thrive in the near-bedlam atmosphere of a trading room, while others succeed only if their decisions are made in the calm of a quiet office; and some traders find fundamental analysis a natural approach, while others instinctively lean to technical methods, and still others a blend of the two.

Essentially, then, there is no universal answer to the question, which is better, fundamental analy-sis or technical analysis? Quite simply, it depends on the individual, who must determine his or her natural approach.

The relative popularity of fundamental analysis versus technical analysis tends to wax and wane in broad cyclical fashion. When I first became a market analyst in the 1970s, fundamental analysis was considered a solid approach, while technical analysis was regarded by most as some sort of hocus-pocus or black magic.

The situation changed, however, because the huge price trends that developed during the com-modity inflation period of the 1970s were ideally suited to the trend-following techniques widely favored by technical analysts. Even the simplest trend-following strategies tended to perform extremely well during this period, while sophisticated fundamental methodologies often proved to be highly misleading. In this environment, the popularity of technical analysis grew enormously, while fundamental analysis declined in favor. This basic trend extended into the 1980s, as technical analysis became the primary method of choice and fundamental analysis a minority technique. By the end of the 1980s, a significant majority of money managers in the futures industry (known as commodity trading advisors, or CTAs) employed technical analysis exclusively or at least for the bulk of their trading decisions. Thus, whereas at the beginning of the 1970s few market participants would even consider technical analysis, by the late 1980s few would consider fundamental analysis.

By this time, however, general market behavior had become increasingly erratic, with fewer sus-tained trends and an increasing percentage of false price breakouts (i.e., price moves above or below trading ranges that are followed by price reversals rather than price extensions). Simultaneously, the spectacular performance of some technical trend followers deteriorated substantially, or at the very least their results exhibited periodic deep equity retracements. At the same time, it appeared that many of the traders and money managers with the best performance were those who were primar-ily fundamentally oriented, or at least relied on fundamentals as a significant input in their trading decisions.

To summarize, there is no "right" side to the great fundamental versus technical debate: the appro-priate method depends on the individual. Moreover, even for individual traders, the perceived answer may change dramatically, or even completely reverse, over the years. Also, combining fundamental analysis with technical analysis can provide a particularly effective approach and is indeed descriptive of the general methodology used by some of the world's most successful traders. The bottom line is that each trader must explore both approaches and select the methodology or blend that feels the most comfortable and appropriate.

The relative pros and cons of using fundamental and technical analysis for trading, as well as practical considerations about combining the two methods, are examined in greater detail in Chapter 29.

PART II

Chart Analysis and Technical Indicators

CHAPTER 3

Charts: Forecasting Tool or Folklore?

Common sense is not so common.

—Voltaire

There is a story about a speculator whose desire to be a winner was intensified by each successive failure. Initially he tried basing his trading decisions on fundamental analysis. He constructed intricate models that provided price forecasts based on an array of supply/demand statistics. Unfortunately, his models' predictions were invariably upset by some unexpected event, such as a drought or a surprise export sale.

Ultimately, in exasperation, he gave up on the fundamental approach and turned to chart analysis. He scrutinized price charts, searching for patterns that would reveal the secrets of trading success. He was the first to discover such unusual formations as shark-tooth bottoms and Grand Teton tops. But alas, the patterns always seemed reliable until he started basing his trades on them. When he went short, top formations proved to be nothing more than pauses in towering bull markets. Equally distressing, steady uptrends had an uncanny tendency to reverse course abruptly soon after he went long.

"The problem," he reasoned, "is that chart analysis is too inexact. What I need is a computerized trading system." So he began testing various schemes to see if any would have been profitable as a trading system in the past. After exhaustive research, he found that buying cattle, cocoa, and eurodollars on the first Tuesday of months with an odd number of days and then liquidating these positions on the third Thursday of the month would have yielded extremely profitable results during the preceding five years. Inexplicably, this carefully researched pattern failed to hold once he began trading. Another stroke of bad luck.

The speculator tried many other approaches—Elliott waves, Fibonacci numbers, Gann squares, the phases of the moon—but all proved equally unsuccessful. It was at this point that he heard of a famous guru who lived on a remote mountain in the Himalayas and who answered the questions of all pilgrims who sought him out. The trader boarded a plane to Nepal, hired guides, and set out on a two-month trek. Finally, completely exhausted, he reached the famous guru.

"Oh, Wise One," he said, "I am a frustrated man. For many years I have sought the key to successful trading, but everything I have tried has failed. What is the secret?"

The guru paused for only a moment, and, staring at his visitor intently, answered, "BLASH." He said no more.

"Blash?" The trader did not understand the answer. It filled his mind every waking moment, but he could not fathom its meaning. He repeated the story to many, until finally one listener interpreted the guru's response.

"It's quite simple," he said. "Buy low and sell high."

The guru's message is apt to be disappointing to readers seeking the profound key to trading wisdom. BLASH does not satisfy our concept of an insight because it appears to be a matter of common sense. However, if, as Voltaire suggested, "Common sense is not so common," neither is it obvious. For example, consider the following question: What are the trading implications of a market reaching new highs? The "common-sense" BLASH theory would unambiguously indicate that subsequent trading activity should be confined to the short side.

Very likely, a large percentage of speculators would be comfortable with this interpretation. Perhaps the appeal of the BLASH approach is tied to the desire of most traders to demonstrate their brilliance. After all, any fool can buy the market after a long uptrend, but it takes genius to fade the trend and pick a top. In any case, few trading responses are as instinctive as the bias toward buying when prices are low and selling when prices are high.

As a result, many speculators have a strong predilection toward favoring the short side when a market trades in new high ground. There is only one thing wrong with this approach: it doesn't work. A plausible explanation is readily available. A market's ability to reach and sustain new highs is usually evidence of powerful underlying forces that often push prices much higher. Common sense? Certainly. But note that the trading implications are exactly opposite to those of the "common-sense" BLASH approach.

The key point of all of this is that many of our common-sense instincts about market behavior are wrong. Chart analysis provides a means of acquiring common sense in trading—a goal far more elusive than it sounds. For example, if prior to beginning trading an individual exhaustively researched historical price charts to determine the consequences of a market's reaching new highs, he would have a strong advantage in avoiding one of the common pitfalls that await the novice trader. Similarly, other market truths can be gleaned through a careful study of historical price patterns.

It must be acknowledged, however, that the usefulness of charts as an indicator of future price direction is a fiercely contested subject. Rather than list the pros and cons of this argument, we found an episode of a financial markets TV series that was very popular in the 1980s and 1990s, which succinctly highlighted some of the key issues in this debate. The transcript from this program is presented:

MODERATOR: Hello, I'm Louis Puneyser of *Wallet Street Week*. Tonight we will depart from our normal interview format to provide a forum for a debate on the usefulness of commodity price charts. Can all those wiggly lines and patterns really predict the future? Or is Shakespeare's description of life also appropriate to chart analysis: ". . . a tale told by an idiot, full of sound and fury, signifying nothing"? Our guests tonight are Faith N. Trend, a renowned technical analyst with the Wall Street firm of Churnum & Burnum, and Phillip A. Coin, a professor at Ivory Tower University and the author of *The Only Way to Beat the Market—Become a Broker*. Mr. Coin, you belong to a group called the Random Walkers. Is that some sort of hiking club that decides its destinations by throwing darts at a trail map? (*He smiles smugly into the camera.*)

PROFESSOR COIN: Well, no, Mr. Puneyser. The Random Walkers are a group of economists who believe that market price movements are random. That is, one can no more devise a system to predict market prices than one can devise a system to predict the sequence of colors that will turn up on a roulette wheel. Both events are strictly a matter of chance. Prices have no memory, and what happened yesterday has nothing to do with what will happen tomorrow. In other words, charts can only tell you what has happened in the past; they are useless in predicting the future.

MS. TREND: Professor, you overlook a very important fact: daily prices are not drawn out of a bowl, but rather are the consequence of the collective activity of all market participants. Human behavior may not be as predictable as the motion of planets as governed by the laws of physics, but neither is it totally random. If this is not the case, your profession—economics—is doomed to the same fate as alchemy. (*Professor Coin squirms uncomfortably in his seat upon this reference.*) Charts reveal basic behavioral patterns. Insofar as similar interactions between buyers and sellers will result in similar price patterns, the past can indeed be used as a guideline for the future.

PROFESSOR COIN: If past prices can be used to predict future prices, why have a myriad of academic studies concluded that tested technical rules failed to outperform a simple buy-and-hold policy once commissions were taken into account?

MS. TREND: The rules used in those studies are generally oversimplified. The studies demonstrate that those particular rules don't work. They don't prove that a richer synthesis of price information, such as chart analysis, or a more complex technical system, cannot be successfully exploited for making trading decisions.

PROFESSOR COIN: Why then are there no studies that conclusively demonstrate the viability of chart analysis as a forecasting tool?

MS. TREND: Your argument merely reflects the difficulties of quantifying chart theories rather than the deficiencies of the chartist approach. One man's top formation is another man's congestion area. An attempt to define anything but the simplest chart pattern mathematically will be unavoidably arbitrary. The problems become even more tangled when one realizes that at any given time, the chart picture may exhibit conflicting patterns. Thus, in a sense, it is not really possible to test many chart theories objectively.

PROFESSOR COIN: That's rather convenient for you, isn't it? If these theories can't be rigorously tested, of what use are they? How do you know that trading on charts will lead to better than a 50/50 success rate—that is, before commissions?

MS. TREND: If you mean that blindly following every chart signal will only make your broker rich, I don't disagree. However, my point is that chart analysis is an art, not a science. A familiarity with basic chart theories is only the starting point. The true usefulness of charts depends on the individual trader's ability to synthesize successfully his own experience with standard concepts. In the right hands, charts can be extremely valuable in anticipating major market trends. There are many successful traders who base their decisions primarily on charts. What would you attribute their success to—a lucky streak?

PROFESSOR COIN: Yes. Exactly that, a lucky streak. If there are enough traders, some of them will be winners, whether they reach their decisions by reading charts or throwing darts at the commodity price page. It's not the method, just the laws of probability. Even in a casino, some percentage of the people are winners. You wouldn't say that their success is due to any insights or system.

MS. TREND: All that proves is that superior performance by some chartists *could* be due to chance. It doesn't disprove the contention that the skillful chartist is onto something that gives him an edge.

MODERATOR: I sense a lot of resistance here, and I think we could use some more support. Have either of you brought any evidence along that would tend to substantiate your positions?

PROFESSOR COIN: Yes! (*At this point, Professor Coin pulls a thick manuscript from his briefcase and thrusts it into Mr. Puneyser's hands. The moderator flips through the pages and shakes his head as he notices a profusion of funny little Greek letters.*)

MODERATOR: I had something a little less mathematical in mind. Even educational TV is not ready for this.

PROFESSOR COIN: Well, I also have this. (*He pulls out a sheet of paper and hands it to Ms. Trend.*) How would you interpret this chart, Ms. Trend? (*He unsuccessfully attempts to suppress a smirk.*)

MS. TREND: I'd say this looks like a chart based on a series of coin tosses. You know, heads one box up, tails one box down.

PROFESSOR COIN: (*Whose smirk has turned into a very visible frown.*) How did you know that?

MS. TREND: Lucky guess.

PROFESSOR COIN: Well, anyway, that doesn't affect my argument. Look at this chart. Here's a trend. And this here—isn't that what you people call a head-and-shoulders formation?

MODERATOR: Speaking of head and shoulders, do either of you have an opinion on Procter & Gamble?

PROFESSOR COIN: (*Continuing.*) The same chart patterns you are so quick to point to on your price charts also show up in obviously random series.

MS. TREND: Yes, but that line of reasoning can lead to some odd conclusions. For instance, would you agree that the fact that working economists tend to have advanced degrees is not a chance occurrence?

PROFESSOR COIN: Of course.

MS. TREND: Well then, a random sample of the population is also likely to turn up some people with advanced degrees. Do you then conclude that the fact that an economist has an advanced degree is a coincidence?

PROFESSOR COIN: I still don't see any difference between price charts and my randomly generated chart.

MS. TREND: You don't? Does this look like a randomly generated chart? *(Ms. Trend holds up a July 1980 silver chart—see Figure 3.1.)*

PROFESSOR COIN: Well, not exactly, but . . .

MS. TREND: *(On the attack.)* Or this. *(She holds up the December 1994 coffee chart—see Figure 3.2.)* I could go on.

MODERATOR: *(To Professor Coin.)* Ms. Trend really seems to be percolating. Are there any grounds for dismissing her examples?

PROFESSOR COIN: Well, I admit those examples are pretty extreme, but they still don't prove that past prices can predict future prices.

MODERATOR: Before our time reaches limit-up, so to speak, I would like to rechart our course. I wonder what your opinions are about fundamental analysts?

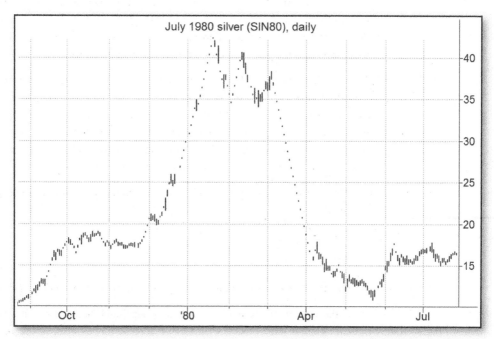

FIGURE 3.1 July 1980 Silver

Chart created using TradeStation. ©TradeStation Technologies, Inc. All rights reserved.

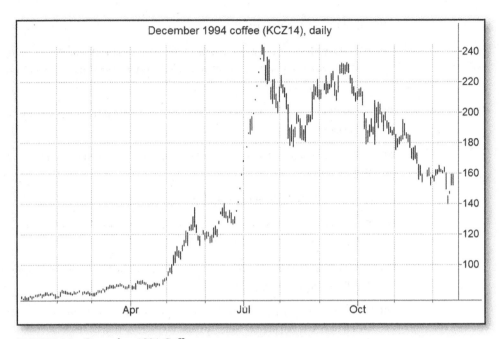

FIGURE 3.2 December 1994 Coffee

Chart created using TradeStation. ©TradeStation Technologies, Inc. All rights reserved.

PROFESSOR COIN: Well, they're better than chartists since they can at least *explain* price moves. But I'm afraid their attempts to *forecast* prices are equally futile. You see, at any given moment, the market discounts all known information, so there is no way they can project prices unless they can anticipate unforeseen future developments such as droughts or export embargoes.

MS. TREND: Well, first I would like to address the implication that chart analysts ignore fundamentals. Actually we believe that the price chart provides an unambiguous and immediate summary of the net impact of all fundamental and psychological factors. In contrast, accurate fundamental models, if they could be constructed at all, would be extremely complex. Furthermore, the fundamental data for the forecast period would have to be estimated, thereby making the price projections extremely vulnerable to error.

MODERATOR: Then you might say you both agree with the statement that fundamentalists end up with holes in their shoes.

MS. TREND: Yes.

PROFESSOR COIN: Yes.

MODERATOR: Well, on that upbeat note of agreement, we end tonight's program.

In a sense, the argument between the "random walkers" and the chartists can never be clearly resolved. It must be understood that it is impossible to prove randomness; all that one can prove is that a given pattern does not exist. Since there is no consensus as to the precise mathematical definition of many chart patterns, the viability of these patterns as price indicators can be neither proven nor disproven.

For example, if one wanted to test the contention that breakouts from trading ranges represent valid trade signals, the first requirement would be to formulate concise definitions of a trading range and a breakout. Assume that the following definitions are adopted: (1) that the trading range is a price band that completely encloses all daily price changes during the past six-week period and that is no wider than 5 percent of the median price during that period,[1] and (2) that a breakout is a closing price above or below the six-week trading range. Although the validity of breakouts as trading signals could be tested for these specific definitions, the definitions themselves will be challenged by many. Some of the objections might be the following:

1. The price band is too narrow.
2. The price band is too wide.
3. The six-week period is too long.
4. The six-week period is too short.
5. No allowance is made for isolated days beyond the confines of the range—an event that most chart analysts would agree does not disturb the basic pattern.
6. The direction of the trend prior to the trading range is not considered—a factor many chartists would view as a critical input in interpreting the reliability of a breakout.
7. The breakout should be required to exceed the boundary of the trading range by a minimum amount (e.g., 1 percent of the price level) in order to be viewed as valid.
8. Several closes above the trading range should be required to indicate a breakout.
9. A time lag should be used to test the validity of the breakout; for example, are prices still beyond the trading range one week after the initial penetration of the range?

The preceding list represents only a partial itemization of the possible objections to our hypothetical definitions of a trading range and breakout, and all of this for one of the most basic chart patterns. Imagine the ambiguities and complications in specifically defining a pattern such as a confirmed head and shoulders.

For their part, the chartists cannot win the argument, either. Although chart analysis is based on general principles, its application depends on individual interpretation. The successful chart-oriented trader might not have any doubts about the viability of chart analysis, but the "random walk" theoreticians would dismiss his success as a consequence of the laws of probability, since even a totally random trade selection process would yield a percentage of winners. In short, the debate is not about to be concluded.

It is also important to realize that even if conclusive tests were possible, the conflicting claims of the random walkers and the chartists need not necessarily be contradictory. One way of viewing the situation is that markets may witness extended periods of random fluctuation, interspersed with shorter periods of nonrandom behavior. Thus, even if the price series as a whole appears random, it

---

[1] The specification of maximum price width is deliberately intended to exclude periods of wide-swinging prices from being defined as trading ranges.

is entirely possible that there are periods within the data that exhibit definite patterns. The goal of the chart analyst is to identify those periods (i.e., major trends).

The time has come to admit my own biases. Personal experience has convinced me that charts are a valuable, if not essential, trading tool. However, such perceptions do not prove anything. The random walkers would argue that my conclusions could be based on selective memory—that is, a tendency to remember the successes of chart analysis and forget the failures—or just pure luck. And they are right. Such explanations *could* indeed be correct.

The bottom line is that each trader must evaluate chart analysis independently and draw his own conclusions. However, it should be strongly emphasized that charts are considered to be an extremely valuable trading tool by many successful traders, and therefore the new trader should be wary of rejecting this approach simply on the basis of intuitive skepticism. The following are some of the principal potential benefits of using charts. Note that a number of these uses remain valid even if one totally rejects the possibility that charts can be used to forecast prices.

1. Charts provide a concise price history—essential information for any trader.
2. Charts can provide the trader with a good sense of the market's volatility—an important consideration in assessing risk.
3. Charts are a very useful tool to the fundamental analyst. Long-term price charts enable the fundamentalist to isolate quickly the periods of major price moves. By determining the fundamental conditions or events that were peculiar to those periods, the fundamentalist can identify the key price-influencing factors. This information can then be used to construct a price behavior model.
4. Charts can be used as a timing tool, even by traders who formulate their trading decisions on the basis of other information (e.g., fundamentals).
5. Charts can be used as a money management tool by helping to define meaningful and realistic stop points.
6. Charts reflect market behavior that is subject to certain repetitive patterns. Given sufficient experience, some traders will uncover an innate ability to use charts successfully as a method of anticipating price moves.
7. An understanding of chart concepts is probably an essential prerequisite for developing profitable technical trading systems.
8. Cynics take notice: under specific circumstances, a contrarian approach to classical chart signals can lead to very profitable trading opportunities. The specifics of this approach are detailed in Chapter 15.

In short, charts have something to offer everyone, from cynics to believers. The remaining chapters of Part II review and evaluate the key concepts of classical chart theory, as well as addressing the all-important question of how charts can be used as an effective trading tool.

CHAPTER 4

Types of Charts

You don't need a weatherman to know which way the wind blows.

—Bob Dylan

■ Bar Charts

Bar charts are by far the most common type of price chart. In a daily bar chart, each day is represented by a vertical line that ranges from the daily low to the daily high. The day's closing value is indicated by a horizontal protrusion to the right of the bar, while the opening price is represented by a protrusion to the left of the bar. Figure 4.1 is a daily bar chart of the July 2015 soybean contract.

The daily (or intraday for short-term traders) bar chart is most useful for trading purposes, but bar charts for longer data periods provide extremely important perspective. These longer-period bar charts (e.g., weekly, monthly) are entirely analogous to the daily bar chart, with each vertical line representing the price range and final price level for the period. Figure 4.2 is a weekly bar chart for soybean futures. The segment within the rectangle corresponds to the period depicted in Figure 4.1. Figure 4.3 is a monthly bar chart for soybean futures, and the two rectangles enclose the periods depicted in Figures 4.2 and 4.1.

The change in time perspective can go in the other direction as well; intraday charts can provide greater detail of the price action than daily charts. Figure 4.4 is a 30-minute chart of the July soybean futures that covers the same time period as the last eight daily bars in Figure 4.1.

Used in combination, the monthly, weekly, daily, and intraday bar charts provide a telephoto-type effect. The monthly and weekly charts would be used to provide a broad market perspective and to formulate a technical opinion regarding the potential long-term trend. The daily chart—and, for

FIGURE 4.1 Daily Bar Chart: July 2015 Soybeans

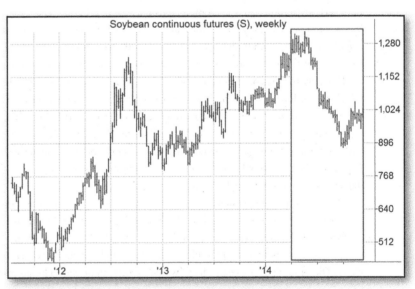

FIGURE 4.2 Weekly Bar Chart: Soybeans (Continuous Futures)
Note: Continuous futures will be defined in the next section.

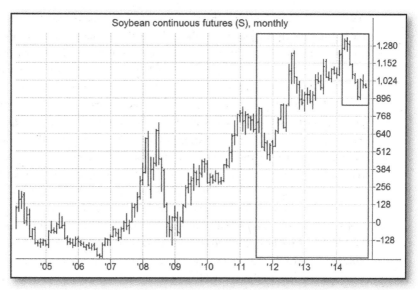

FIGURE 4.3 Monthly Bar Chart: Soybeans (Continuous Futures)
Chart created using TradeStation. ©TradeStation Technologies, Inc. All rights reserved.

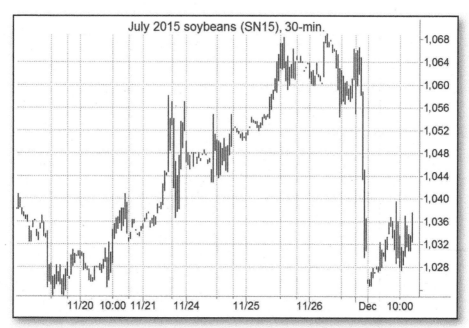

FIGURE 4.4 30-Minute Bar Chart: July 2015 Soybeans
Chart created using TradeStation. ©TradeStation Technologies, Inc. All rights reserved.

shorter-term traders, intraday charts—would then be employed to determine the timing of trades. If the long-term technical picture is sufficiently decisive, by the time the trader gets to the daily or intraday charts, he may already have a strong market bias. For example, if a trader interprets the monthly and weekly charts as suggesting the likelihood that the market has witnessed a major long-term top, he will only monitor the daily and intraday charts for sell signals.

The difference in perspective between short-term and long-term charts can be striking. For example, in the daily bar chart shown in Figure 4.5, the technical picture for coffee seemed quite bearish, with prices in late October 2013 having just pushed below a period of sideways price action while in the midst of a longer-term downtrend that showed no evidence of abating. The weekly futures chart (Figure 4.6), however, provided a strikingly different perspective. Although this multiyear chart also showed the market in an unbroken downtrend, it revealed that prices had fallen to the vicinity of the 2008 and 2009 lows—a significant price level that had supported the market in the past, and which, in late 2013, implied the potential for a major trend reversal in that vicinity. Indeed, as the inset chart for the December 2014 coffee contract shows, prices subsequently embarked on a huge rally from November 2013 into early October 2014. Although in late October 2013 it may not have been apparent which of these conflicting interpretations would prevail, the basic point is that longer-term charts may suggest very different interpretations of price patterns than those indicated by daily charts. Hence, both types of charts should be examined.

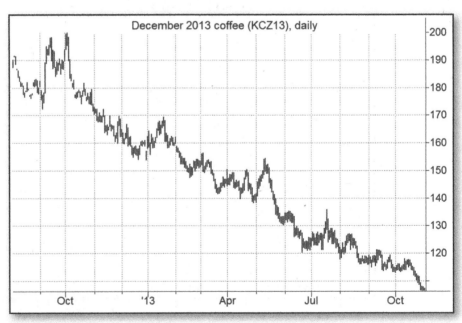

FIGURE 4.5   Daily Bar Chart Perspective: December 2013 Coffee
Chart created using TradeStation. ©TradeStation Technologies, Inc. All rights reserved.

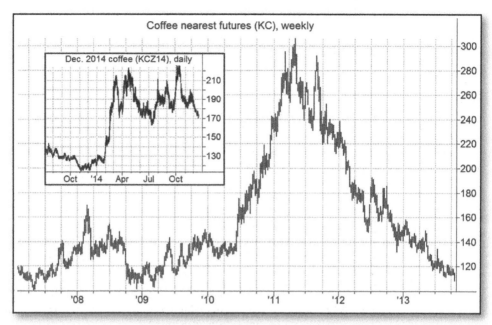

FIGURE 4.6 Weekly Bar Chart Perspective: Coffee Nearest Futures

Chart created using TradeStation. ©TradeStation Technologies, Inc. All rights reserved.

Linked Contract Series: Nearest Futures versus Continuous Futures

The time period covered by the typical weekly or monthly bar chart requires the use of a series of contracts. Normally, these contracts are combined using the *nearest futures* approach: a contract is plotted until its expiration and then the subsequent contract is plotted until its expiration, and so on. Traders should be aware that a nearest futures chart may reflect significant distortions due to the price gaps between the expiring month and the subsequent contract.

Figure 4.7 provides two clear examples of this type of distortion. The top chart is a live cattle weekly nearest futures chart; the bottom chart is a live cattle weekly *continuous* futures chart, which will be defined momentarily. The nearest futures chart implies a large 7.175-cent (6 percent) one-week gain in the price of cattle from the August 31 close to the September 7, 2012 close. However, this price jump never really took place because the price gap represented nothing more than the expiration of the lower-priced August 2012 cattle contract and the switch to the higher-priced October 2012 cattle contract. In contrast, the continuous futures chart, which, as will be explained shortly, reflects actual price movements, showed that price had rallied only 0.45 cents from August 31 to September 7, 2012. Almost exactly a year later the same relationship between the prices in different contract months produced an even more noteworthy discrepancy: While the nearest futures chart showed a 3.15-cent gain from August 30 to September 6, 2013, the continuous futures chart shows cattle prices actually *declined* 1.125 cents between these dates.

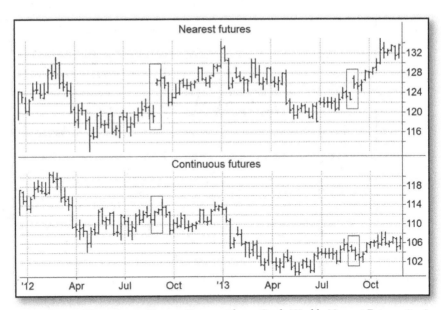

FIGURE 4.7 Distortion in Nearest Futures Chart: Cattle Weekly Nearest Futures (top) and Cattle Weekly Continuous Futures (bottom)

The fact that a nearest futures chart is vulnerable to great distortion, in the sense that price moves depicted in the chart may contrast dramatically with the results realized by an actual trader (as was the case in the cattle example), makes it necessary to consider an alternate linked-contract representation that does not share this defect. The continuous futures chart provides such an alternative approach.

Continuous futures is a series that links together successive contracts in such a way that price gaps are eliminated at rollover points. Although continuous futures will precisely reflect price *swings,* past continuous levels will not match actual historical *levels.* (In contrast, nearest futures will accurately reflect actual historical levels, but not price swings.) The appropriate series depends on the intended purpose. Nearest futures should be used to indicate the actual price levels at which a market traded in the past. However, continuous futures should be used to illustrate the results that would have been realized by a trader. Continuous futures will be discussed in greater detail in Chapters 5 and 18.

■ Close-Only ("Line") Charts

As the name implies, close-only charts ignore high and low price information and reflect only closing values. Some price series can be depicted only in close-only chart formats because intraday data are not readily available. Two examples are cash price series (Figure 4.8) and spreads (Figure 4.9), which represent the price *difference* between two contracts, in this case the July 2015 and November 2015 soybean futures prices.

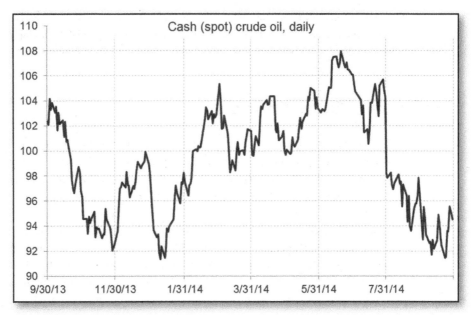

FIGURE 4.8 Cash Price Chart: Crude Oil

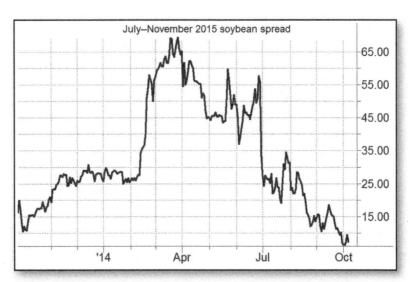

FIGURE 4.9 Spread Chart: July–November 2015 Soybeans
Chart created using TradeStation. ©TradeStation Technologies, Inc. All rights reserved.

Some chart traders may prefer close-only charts even when high/low/close data are available because they feel a clearer price picture can be obtained by using only the close. In their view, the inclusion of high/low data only serves to obfuscate the price chart. There is much to be said for the emphasis on the closing value as the embodiment of the day's essential price information. Nevertheless, many important chart patterns depend on the availability of high/low data, and one should think twice before ignoring this information.

■ Point-and-Figure Charts

The essential characteristic of the point-and-figure chart is that it views all trading as a single continuous stream and hence ignores time. A point-and-figure chart is illustrated in Figure 4.10. As can be seen, a point-and-figure chart consists of a series of columns of X's and O's. Each X represents a price move of a given magnitude called the *box size*. As long as prices continue to rise, X's are added to a column for each increment equal to the box size. However, if prices decline by an amount equal to or greater than the *reversal size* (usually quoted as a multiple of the box size), a new column of O's is initiated and plotted in descending fashion. The number of O's will depend on the magnitude of the reversal, but by definition must at least equal the reversal size. By convention, the first O in a column is always plotted one box below the last X in the preceding column. An analogous description would apply to price declines and upside reversals. The choice of box and reversal size is arbitrary.

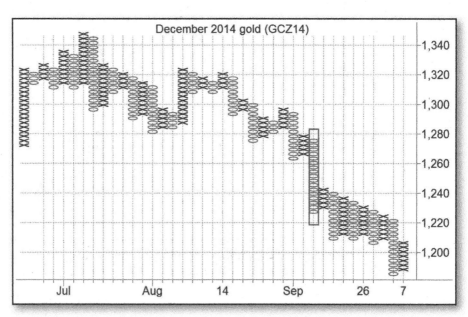

FIGURE 4.10 Point-and-Figure Chart: December 2014 Gold

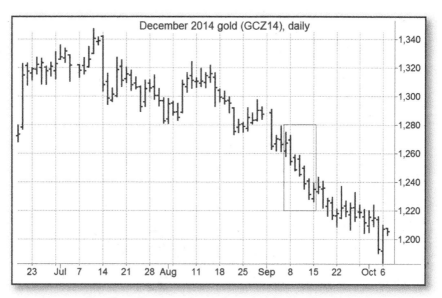

FIGURE 4.11 Bar Chart Corresponding to Point-and-Figure Chart in Figure 4.10: December 2014 Gold

Figure 4.10 is a point-and-figure chart of December 2014 gold futures with a box size of $3 and a reversal size of three boxes, or $9. In other words, as long as a price decline of $9 or more does not occur, X's continue to be added in a single column. When a price decline of $9 or more occurs, a new column of O's is begun, with the first O placed one box below the last X.

As stated previously, the point-and-figure chart does not reflect time. One column may represent one day or two months. For example, Figure 4.11 is a bar chart corresponding to the point-and-figure chart in Figure 4.10. The period captured in the rectangle corresponds to the similarly highlighted column in the point-and-figure chart. Note that this seven-day period occupies only one column on the point-and-figure chart.

■ Candlestick Charts

Candlestick charts add dimension and color to the simple bar chart. The segment of the bar that represents the range between the open and close is represented by a two-dimensional "real body," while the extensions beyond this range to the high and low are shown as lines (called "shadows"). A day on which the open and close are near opposite extremes of the daily range will have a large real body, whereas a day on which there is little net change between the open and close will have a small real body. The color of the real body indicates whether the close was higher than the open (white—Figure 4.12) or lower than the open (black—Figure 4.13). Figure 4.14 shows a daily candlestick chart corresponding to the price action displayed in Figures 4.10 and 4.11.

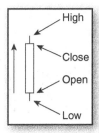

FIGURE 4.12   Candlestick Chart: White Real Body

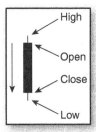

FIGURE 4.13   Candlestick Chart: Black Real Body

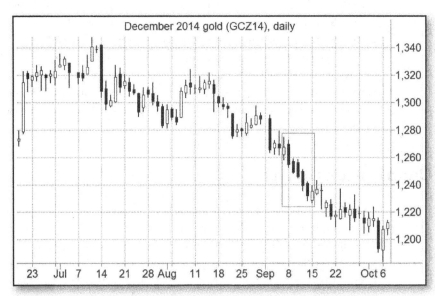

FIGURE 4.14   Candlestick Chart Corresponding to Figures 4.10 and 4.11: December 2014 Gold

Chart created using TradeStation. ©TradeStation Technologies, Inc. All rights reserved.

Linking Contracts for Long-Term Chart Analysis: Nearest versus Continuous Futures

45

■ The Necessity of Linked-Contract Charts

Many of the chart analysis patterns and techniques detailed in Chapters 6 through 9 require long-term charts—often charts of multiyear duration. This is particularly true for the identification of top and bottom formations, as well as the determination of support and resistance levels.

A major problem facing the chart analyst in the futures markets is that most futures contracts have relatively limited life spans and even shorter periods in which these contracts have significant trading activity. For many futures contracts (e.g., currencies, stock indexes) trading activity is almost totally concentrated in the nearest one or two contract months. For example, in Figure 5.1, there were only about two months of liquid data available for the March 2016 Russell 2000 Index Mini futures contract when it became the most liquid contract in this market as the December 2015 contract expiration approached. This market is not particularly unusual in this respect. In many futures markets, almost all trading is concentrated in the nearest contract, which will have only a few months (or weeks) of liquid trading history when the prior contract approaches expiration.

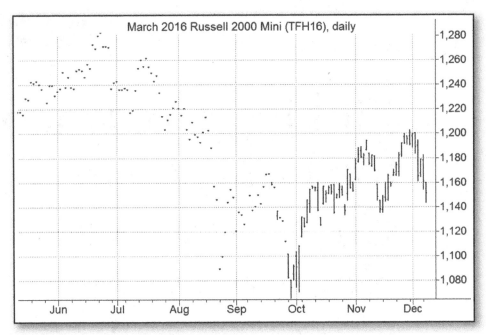

FIGURE 5.1 March 2016 Russell 2000 Mini Futures

Chart created using TradeStation. ©TradeStation Technologies, Inc. All rights reserved.

The limited price data available for many futures contracts—even those that are the most actively traded contracts in their respective markets—makes it virtually impossible to apply most chart analysis techniques to individual contract charts. Even in those markets in which the individual contracts have a year or more of liquid data, part of a thorough chart study would still encompass analyzing multiyear weekly and monthly charts. Thus, the application of chart analysis unavoidably requires linking successive futures contracts into a single chart. In markets with very limited individual contract data, such linked charts will be a necessity in order to perform *any* meaningful chart analysis. In other markets, linked charts will still be required for analyzing multiyear chart patterns.

■ Methods of Creating Linked-Contract Charts

Nearest Futures

The most common approach for creating linked-contract charts is typically termed *nearest futures*. This type of price series is constructed by taking each individual contract series until its expiration and then continuing with the next contract until its expiration, and so on.

Although, at surface glance, this approach appears to be a reasonable method for constructing linked-contract charts, the problem with a nearest futures chart is that there are price gaps between expiring and new contracts—and quite frequently, these gaps can be very substantial. For example, assume the September coffee contract expires at 132.50 cents/lb and the next nearest contract (December) closes at 138.50 cents/lb on the same day. Further assume that on the next day

December coffee falls 5 cents/lb to 133.50—a 3.6 percent drop. A nearest futures price series will show the following closing levels on these two successive days: 132.50 cents, 133.50 cents. In other words, the nearest futures contract would show a one-cent (0.75 percent) gain on a day on which longs would actually have experienced a huge loss. This example is by no means artificial. Such distortions—and indeed more extreme ones—are quite common at contract rollovers in nearest futures charts.

The vulnerability of nearest futures charts to distortions at contract rollover points makes it desirable to derive alternative methods of constructing linked-contract price charts. One such approach is detailed in the next section.

Continuous (Spread-Adjusted) Price Series

The spread-adjusted price series known as "continuous futures" is constructed by adding the cumulative difference between the old and new contracts at rollover points to the new contract series.[1] An example should help clarify this method. Assume we are constructing a spread-adjusted continuous price series for gold using the June and December contracts.[2] If the price series begins at the start of the calendar year, initially the values in the series will be identical to the prices of the June contract expiring in that year. Assume that on the rollover date (which need not necessarily be the last trading day) June gold closes at $1,200 and December gold closes at $1,205. In this case, all subsequent prices based on the December contract would be adjusted downward by $5—the difference between the December and June contracts on the rollover date.

Assume that at the next rollover date December gold is trading at $1,350 and the subsequent June contract is trading at $1,354. The December contract price of $1,350 implies that the spread-adjusted continuous price is $1,345. Thus, on this second rollover date, the June contract is trading $9 above the adjusted series. Consequently, all subsequent prices based on the second June contract would be adjusted downward by $9. This procedure would continue, with the adjustment for each contract dependent on the cumulative total of the present and prior transition point price differences. The resulting price series would be free of the distortions due to spread differences that exist at the rollover points between contracts.

The construction of a continuous futures series can be thought of as the mathematical equivalent of taking a nearest futures chart, cutting out each individual contract series contained in the chart, and pasting the ends together (assuming a continuous series employing all contracts and using the same rollover dates as the nearest futures chart). Typically, as a last step, it is convenient to shift the scale of the entire series by the cumulative adjustment factor, a step that will set the current price of the series equal to the price of the current contract without changing the shape of the series. The construction of a continuous futures chart is discussed in greater detail in Chapter 18.

---

[1] To avoid confusion, readers should note that some data services use the term *continuous futures* to refer to linking together contracts of the same month (e.g., linking from March 2015 corn when it expires to March 2016 corn, and so on). Such charts are really only a variation of nearest futures charts—one in which only a single contract month is used—and will be as prone to wide price gaps at rollovers as nearest futures charts, if not more so. These types of charts have absolutely nothing in common with the spread-adjusted continuous futures series described in this section—that is, nothing but the name. It is unfortunate that some data services have decided to use this same term to describe an entirely different price series than the original meaning described here.

[2] The choice of a combination of contracts is arbitrary. One can use any combination of actively traded months in the given market.

Comparing the Series

It is important to understand that a linked futures price series can only accurately reflect either price *levels*, as does nearest futures, or price *moves*, as does continuous futures, but not both—much as a coin can land on either heads or tails, but not both. The adjustment process used to construct continuous series means that past prices in a continuous series will not match the actual historical prices that prevailed at the time. However, a continuous series will accurately reflect the actual price movements of the market and will exactly parallel the equity fluctuations experienced by a trader who is continually long (rolling over positions on the same rollover dates used to construct the continuous series), whereas a nearest futures price series can be extremely misleading in these respects.

■ Nearest versus Continuous Futures in Chart Analysis

Given the significant differences between nearest and continuous futures price series, the obvious question in the reader's mind is probably: Which series—nearest futures or continuous futures—would be more appropriate for chart analysis? To some extent, this is like asking which factor a consumer should consider before purchasing a new car: price or quality. The obvious answer is both—each factor provides important information about a characteristic that is not measured by the other. In terms of price series, considering nearest futures versus continuous futures, each series provides information that the other doesn't. Specifically, a nearest futures price series provides accurate information about past price *levels*, but not price *swings*, whereas the exact reverse statement applies to a continuous futures series.

Consider, for example, Figure 5.2. What catastrophic event caused the instantaneous 165-cent (24 percent) collapse in the nearest futures chart for corn from July 12 to July 15, 2013? Answer: absolutely nothing. This "phantom" price move reflected nothing more than a transition from the old crop July contract to the new crop December contract. Figure 5.3, which depicts the continuous futures price for the same market (and by definition eliminates price gaps at contract rollovers), shows that no such price move existed—corn was actually little changed from July 12 to July 15. Clearly, the susceptibility of nearest futures charts to distortions caused by wide gaps at rollovers can make it difficult to use nearest futures for chart analysis that focuses on price swings.

On the other hand, the continuous futures chart achieves accuracy in depicting price swings at the sacrifice of accuracy in reflecting price levels. In order to accurately show the magnitude of past price swings, historical continuous futures prices can end up being very far removed from the actual historical price levels. In fact, it is not even unusual for historical continuous futures prices to be negative (see Figure 5.4). Obviously, such "impossible" historical prices can have no relevance as guidelines to prospective support and resistance levels.

The fact that each type of price chart—nearest and continuous—has certain significant intrinsic weaknesses argues for combining both types of charts in a more complete analysis. Often these two types of charts will provide entirely different price pictures. For example, consider the nearest futures chart for lean hogs depicted in Figure 5.5. Looking at this chart, it would be tempting to

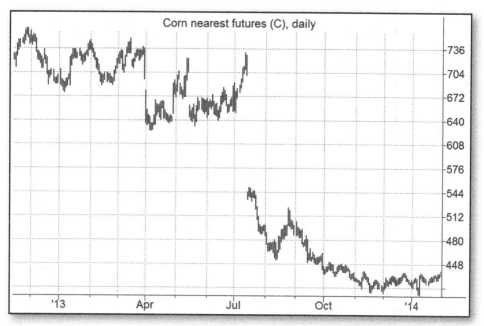

FIGURE 5.2 Corn Nearest Futures

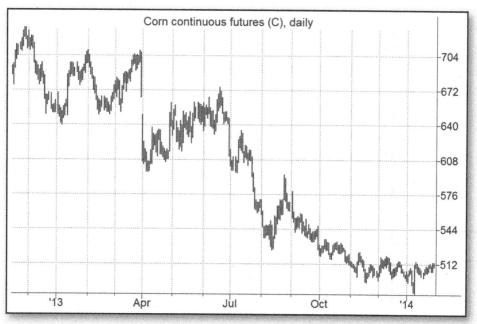

FIGURE 5.3 Corn Continuous Futures

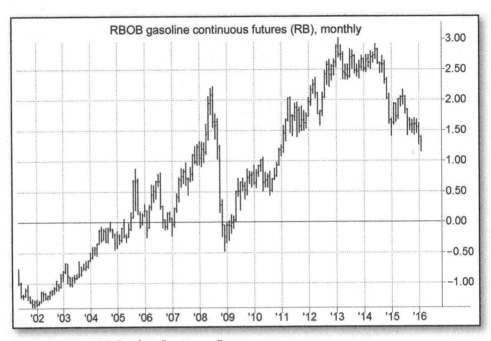

FIGURE 5.4 RBOB Gasoline Continuous Futures

Chart created using TradeStation. ©TradeStation Technologies, Inc. All rights reserved.

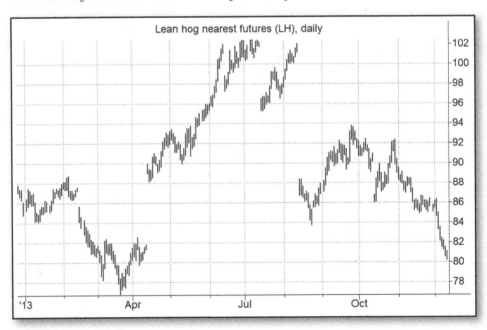

FIGURE 5.5 Lean Hog Nearest Futures

Chart created using TradeStation. ©TradeStation Technologies, Inc. All rights reserved.

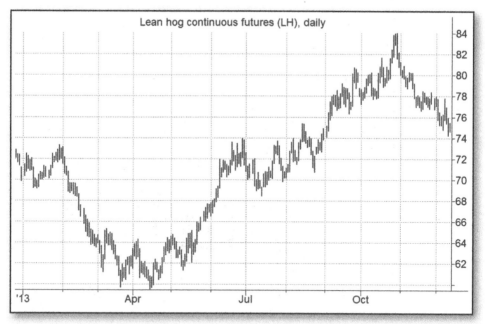

FIGURE 5.6 Lean Hog Continuous Futures
Chart created using TradeStation. ©TradeStation Technologies, Inc. All rights reserved.

conclude that hogs were experiencing a period of severe price dislocation and volatility in 2013, peaking sometime in early July. Now look at Figure 5.6, which shows the continuous version of the same market. This chart shows that hog prices were in a consistent uptrend that began in April and peaked at the end of October. It is no exaggeration to say that, without the benefit of the chart labels, it would be virtually impossible to recognize that Figures 5.5 and 5.6 depict the same market.

◼ Conclusion

In summary, the brevity of liquid trading periods for futures contracts in many markets makes the use of linked-contract charts essential. Continuous futures charts, which remove the distortions caused by price gaps at contract rollovers, are probably the most meaningful type of longer-term chart and, on balance, are far preferable to the more conventional nearest futures chart—although the latter can still be a useful supplement in identifying long-term support and resistance levels. Continuous futures are even more critical for testing trading systems—a topic that will be discussed in Chapter 18. Figures 5.7 through 5.16 provide comparisons between long-term nearest and continuous charts for various futures markets. Note how strikingly different nearest and continuous futures charts for the same market can be. Readers are reminded that continuous futures charts generated in the future will show different price scales than those shown in the following pages (although the price moves will remain the same), since it is assumed that the scales will be adjusted to match the prevailing current contract.

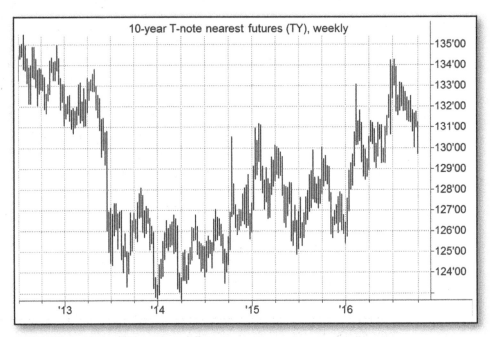

FIGURE 5.7   10-Year T-Note Nearest Futures

Chart created using TradeStation. ©TradeStation Technologies, Inc. All rights reserved.

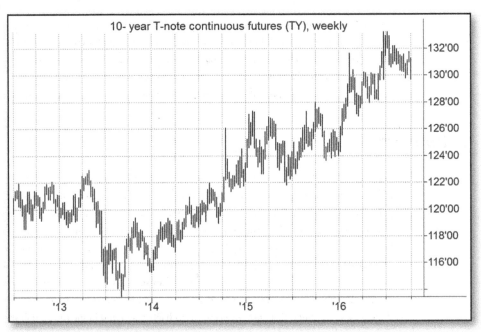

FIGURE 5.8   10-Year T-Note Continuous Futures

Chart created using TradeStation. ©TradeStation Technologies, Inc. All rights reserved.

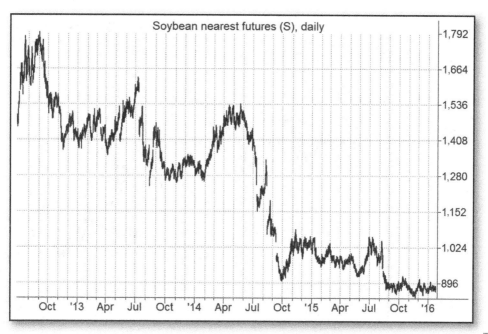

FIGURE 5.9 Soybean Nearest Futures

Chart created using TradeStation. ©TradeStation Technologies, Inc. All rights reserved.

53

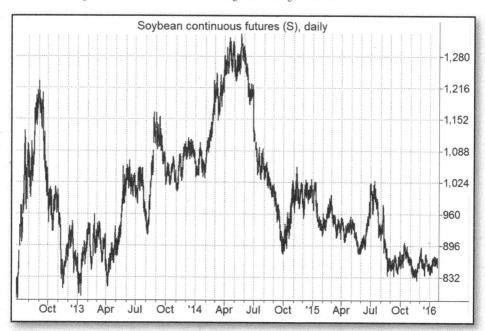

FIGURE 5.10 Soybean Continuous Futures

Chart created using TradeStation. ©TradeStation Technologies, Inc. All rights reserved.

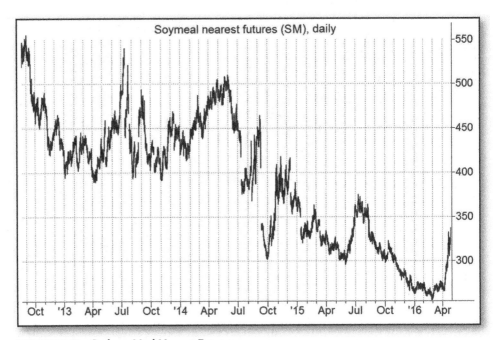

FIGURE 5.11   Soybean Meal Nearest Futures

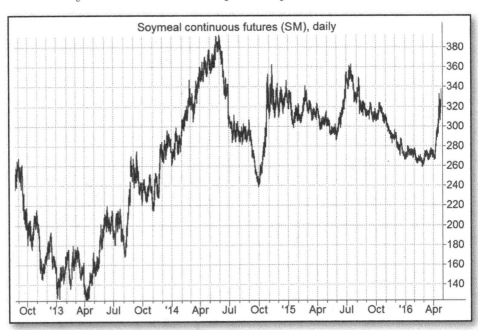

FIGURE 5.12   Soybean Meal Continuous Futures

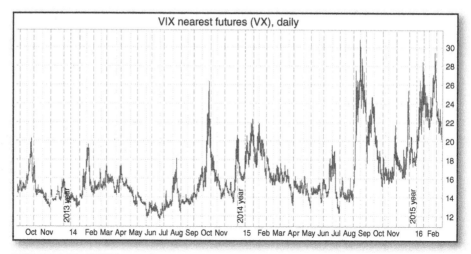

FIGURE 5.13 VIX Nearest Futures

Chart created using TD Ameritrade's thinkorswim.

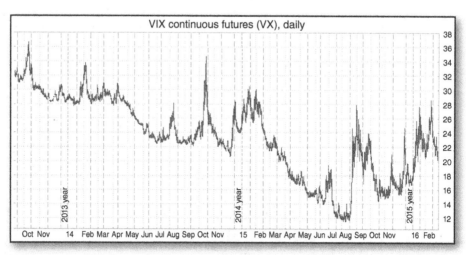

FIGURE 5.14 VIX Continuous Futures

Chart created using TD Ameritrade's thinkorswim.

LINKING CONTRACTS FOR LONG-TERM CHART ANALYSIS

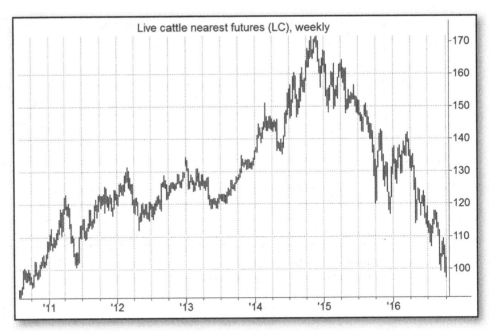

FIGURE 5.15 Live Cattle Nearest Futures

Chart created using TradeStation. ©TradeStation Technologies, Inc. All rights reserved.

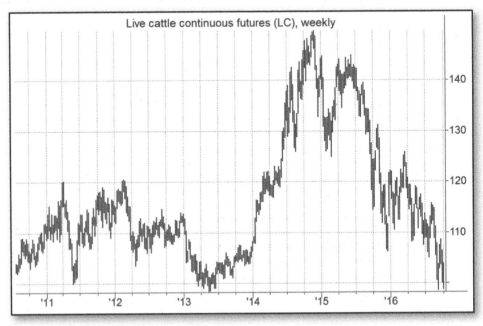

FIGURE 5.16 Live Cattle Continuous Futures

Chart created using TradeStation. ©TradeStation Technologies, Inc. All rights reserved.

CHAPTER 6

Trends

The trend is your friend except at the end when it bends.

—Ed Seykota

■ Defining Trends by Highs and Lows

One standard definition of an uptrend is a succession of higher highs and higher lows. For example, during the May 2014–March 2015 period in Figure 6.1, each relative high (RH) is higher than the preceding high, and each relative low (RL) is higher than the preceding low. In essence, an uptrend can be considered intact until a previous reaction low point is broken. A violation of this condition serves as a warning signal that the trend may be over. For example, in Figure 6.1, the late April penetration of the early April relative low confirmed the end of the nearly yearlong rally, after which the market entered an extended trading range (see weekly chart inset). Figure 6.2 provides an intraday example of an uptrend defined by successively higher highs and higher lows. It should be emphasized, however, that the disruption of the pattern of higher highs and higher lows (or lower highs and lower lows) should be viewed as a clue, not a conclusive indicator, of a possible long-term trend reversal.

In similar fashion, a downtrend can be defined as a succession of lower lows and lower highs (see Figure 6.3). A downtrend can be considered intact until a previous reaction high is exceeded.

Uptrends and downtrends are also often defined in terms of trend lines. An uptrend line is a line that connects a series of higher lows (see Figures 6.4 through 6.6); a downtrend line is a line that connects a series of lower highs (see Figure 6.7). Trend lines can sometimes extend for many years. For example, Figure 6.8 is a weekly chart with a trend line reflecting a multiyear uptrend in the E-mini Nasdaq 100 futures that included the daily timeframe uptrend from Figure 6.4. Figure 6.9 illustrates a trend line defining a 33-year uptrend in 10-year U.S. T-note futures.

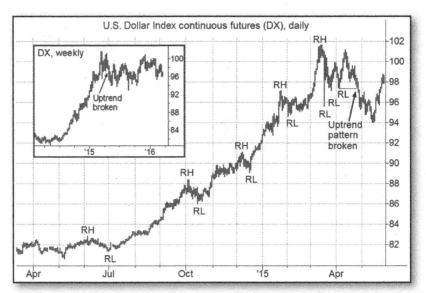

FIGURE 6.1 Uptrend as Succession of Higher Highs and Higher Lows: Dollar Index Continuous Futures

Note: RH = relative high; RL = relative low.

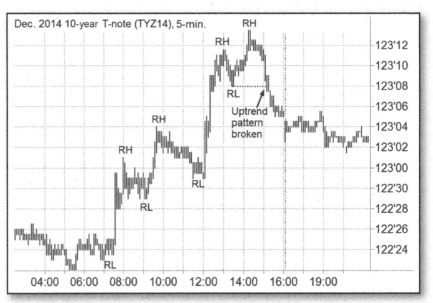

FIGURE 6.2 Uptrend as Succession of Higher Highs and Higher Lows: December 2014 10-Year T-Note

Note: RH = relative high; RL = relative low.

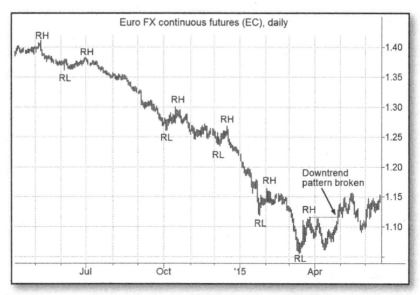

FIGURE 6.3 Downtrend as Succession of Lower Highs and Lower Lows: Euro Continuous Futures

Note: RH = relative high; RL = relative low.

FIGURE 6.4 Uptrend Line: E-Mini Nasdaq 100 Continuous Futures

FIGURE 6.5 Uptrend Line: Copper Continuous Futures

FIGURE 6.6 Uptrend Line: June 2016 E-Mini Dow Futures

FIGURE 6.7   Downtrend Line: WTI Crude Oil Continuous Futures

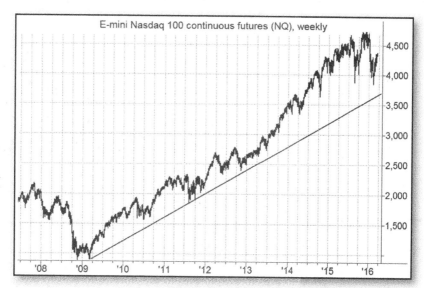

FIGURE 6.8   Uptrend Line: E-Mini Nasdaq 100 Continuous Futures

FIGURE 6.9   Uptrend Line: 10-Year U.S. T-Note Continuous Futures

It is not uncommon for reactions against a major trend to begin near a line parallel to the trend line. Sets of parallel lines that enclose a trend are called *trend channels*. Figure 6.10 shows an uptrend channel on a daily chart, while Figure 6.11 shows a downtrend channel on a weekly chart.

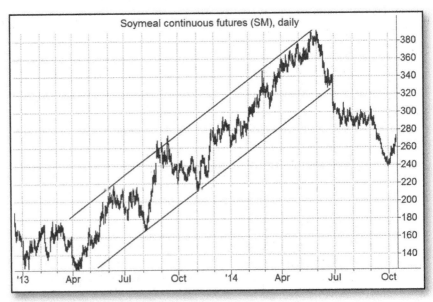

FIGURE 6.10   Uptrend Channel: Soymeal Continuous Futures

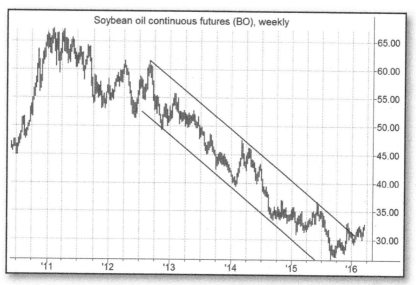

FIGURE 6.11 Downtrend Channel: Soybean Oil Continuous Futures
Chart created using TradeStation. ©TradeStation Technologies, Inc. All rights reserved.

The following rules are usually applied to trend lines and channels:

1. Declines approaching an uptrend line and rallies approaching a downtrend line are often good opportunities to initiate positions in the direction of the major trend.
2. The penetration of an uptrend line (particularly on a closing basis) is a sell signal; the penetration of a downtrend line is a buy signal. Normally, a minimum percentage price move or a minimum number of closes beyond the trend line is required to confirm a penetration.
3. The lower end of a downtrend channel and the upper end of an uptrend channel represent potential profit-taking zones for short-term traders.

Trend lines and channels are useful, but their importance is often overstated. It is easy to overestimate the reliability of trend lines when they are drawn with the benefit of hindsight. A consideration that is frequently overlooked is that trend lines often need to be redrawn as a bull or bear market is extended. Thus, although the penetration of a trend line will sometimes offer an early warning signal of a trend reversal, it is also common that such a development will merely require a redrawing of the trend line. For example, Figure 6.12 shows an uptrend line connecting the November and December 2012 lows in the Russell 2000 Mini futures. Prices remained above this line until February 2013, when prices closed below it, signaling an end to this move. Figure 6.13 extends Figure 6.12 by two months and shows that the February penetration of the original (dashed) trend line was a pullback that preceded a rally to a higher high. Prices remained above the revised (solid) trend line connecting the November and February lows until early April, at which point the market posted a more significant correction. Figure 6.14, however, shows the larger uptrend extended for almost another year, prompting three additional revisions to the uptrend line, each of which was necessitated by a closing penetration of the preceding trend line.

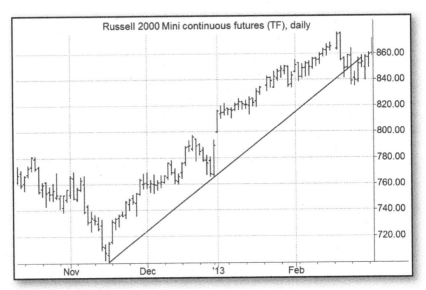

FIGURE 6.12 Uptrend Line: Russell 2000 Mini Continuous Futures

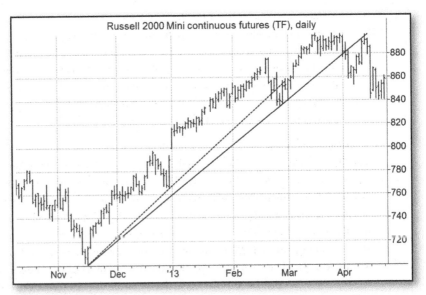

FIGURE 6.13 Uptrend Line Redefined: Russell 2000 Mini Continuous Futures

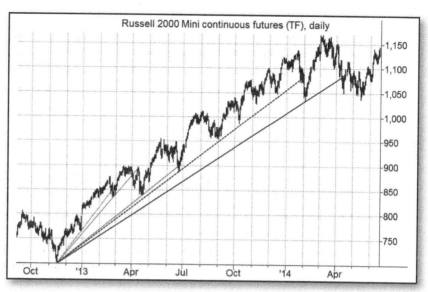

FIGURE 6.14   Uptrend Line Redefined: Russell 2000 Mini Continuous Futures
Chart created using TradeStation. ©TradeStation Technologies, Inc. All rights reserved.

Figure 6.15 provides a similar example for a downtrend. The initial downtrend line connecting the December 2014 and March 2015 highs (gray dotted line) was penetrated to the upside in June, but after a few weeks of sideways price action, the market resumed its decline. The revised trend line (thicker dashed line) connecting the December 2014 and June 2015 highs extended until November 2015, when prices again pushed higher—enough to require a third revision to the downtrend line (solid line), but not enough to end the longer-term downtrend.

FIGURE 6.15   Downtrend Line Redefined: Oat Continuous Futures
Chart created using TradeStation. ©TradeStation Technologies, Inc. All rights reserved.

The preceding examples are meant to drive home the point that the penetration of trend lines is more the rule than the exception. The simple fact is that trend lines tend to be penetrated, sometimes repeatedly, during their evolution, which is equivalent to saying that trend lines are frequently redefined as they extend. The important implications of this observation are that trend lines work much better in hindsight than in real time and that penetrations of trend lines often prove to be false signals.

■ TD Lines

In his book *The New Science of Technical Analysis*,[1] Thomas DeMark accurately notes that the drawing of trend lines is a highly arbitrary process. Presented with the same chart, different people will draw different trend lines. In fact, presented with the same chart at different times, even the same person might well draw the trend line differently.

It is easy to see the reason for this lack of precision. A trend line is typically intended to connect several relative highs or relative lows. If there are only two such points, the trend line can be drawn precisely. If, however, the trend line is intended to connect three or more points—as is frequently the case—a precise line will exist in only the rare circumstance that the relationship between all the points is exactly linear. In most cases, the trend line that is drawn will exactly touch at most one or two of the relative highs (or lows), while bisecting or missing the other such points. The trend line that provides the best fit is truly in the eye of the beholder.

DeMark recognizes that in order for a trend line to be defined precisely and unambiguously, it must be based on exactly two points. DeMark also notes that, contrary to convention, trend lines should be drawn from right to left because "recent price activity is more significant than historical movement." These concepts underlie his approach of drawing trend lines. DeMark's TD methodology for defining trend lines is explained by the following definitions:[2]

Relative high. A daily high that is higher than the high on the N prior and N succeeding days, where N is a parameter value that must be defined. For example, if $N = 5$, the relative high is defined as a high that is higher than any high in the prior five days and succeeding five days. (An analogous definition could be applied for data expressed in any time interval. For example, in a 60-minute bar chart, the relative high would be a high that is higher than the high on the prior or succeeding N 60-minute bars.)

Relative low. A daily low that is lower than the low on the N prior and N succeeding days.

TD downtrend line. The prevailing downtrend line is defined as the line connecting the most recent relative high and the most recent preceding relative high that is *also* higher than the most recent relative high. The latter condition is essential to assure the trend line connecting the two relative highs slopes down. Figure 6.16 illustrates the prevailing TD downtrend line, assuming an $N = 5$ parameter value is used to define relative highs.

---

[1] Thomas DeMark, *The New Science of Technical Analysis* (New York, NY: John Wiley & Sons, 1994).
[2] The following definitions and terminology differ from those used by DeMark, but the implied method of identifying trend lines is equivalent. I simply find the following approach clearer and more succinct than DeMark's presentation of the same concept.

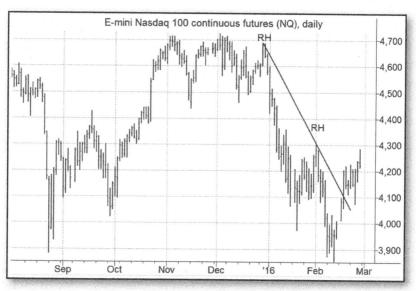

FIGURE 6.16 TD Downtrend Line ($N = 5$): E-Mini Nasdaq 100 Continuous Futures

TD uptrend line. The prevailing uptrend line is defined as the line connecting the most recent relative low and the most recent preceding relative low that is *also* lower than the most recent relative low. Figure 6.17 illustrates the prevailing TD uptrend line, assuming an $N = 8$ parameter value is used to define relative lows.

By basing trend line definitions on the most recent relative highs and relative lows, trend lines will be continually redefined as new relative highs and relative lows are defined. For example, Figure 6.18

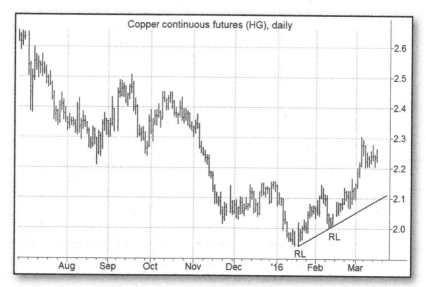

FIGURE 6.17 TD Uptrend Line ($N = 8$): Copper Continuous Futures

FIGURE 6.18 Succession of TD Uptrend Lines ($N = 10$): U.S. Dollar Index Continuous Futures

Note: Lines 1–3 are successive TD uptrend lines that use $N = 10$ to define relative lows (RL).

shows the succession of TD uptrend lines that would be implied as new relative lows are defined ($N = 10$) until a trend reversal signal is received. In this chart it is assumed that a trend reversal signal is defined as three consecutive closes below the prevailing uptrend line. In similar fashion, Figure 6.19

FIGURE 6.19 Succession of TD Downtrend Lines ($N = 10$): June 2015 Euro Futures

Note: Lines 1 and 2 are successive TD downtrend lines that use $N = 10$ to define relative highs (RH).

illustrates TD downtrend lines that would be implied as new relative highs are defined ($N = 10$) until a trend reversal signal is received (again, based on three consecutive closes beyond the trend line).

Different values for N will yield very different trend lines. For example, Figures 6.20 through 6.22 contrast the TD uptrend lines implied by three different values of N for the same chart. The lower the value of N, the more frequently the trend line is redefined and the more sensitive the line is to penetration. For example, contrast the 21 trend lines generated by the $N = 2$ definition in Figure 6.22, versus the mere three trend lines that result when an $N = 10$ definition is used in Figure 6.20.

In analogous fashion, Figures 6.23 through 6.25 contrast the TD downtrend lines implied by three different values of N for the same chart. Similar to Figures 6.20 through 6.22, these charts also show that when the value of N is low, the prevailing downtrend line is redefined frequently and tends to be very sensitive. In Figure 6.23, which shows TD lines for $N = 10$, there are only three downtrend lines. For $N = 5$ the number of trend lines increases to five during the same period (Figure 6.24). Finally, for $N = 2$, 18 different trend lines are generated (Figure 6.25). As these illustrations make clear, the choice of a value for N will make a tremendous difference in the trend lines that are generated and the resulting trading implications.

DeMark's basic definition of trend lines is equivalent to the aforementioned definitions with $N = 1$. Although he acknowledges that trend lines can be defined using higher values of N—"TD lines of higher magnitude," in his terminology—his stated preference is for trend lines drawn using the basic definition. Personally, my own preference is quite the opposite. Although it is a truism that

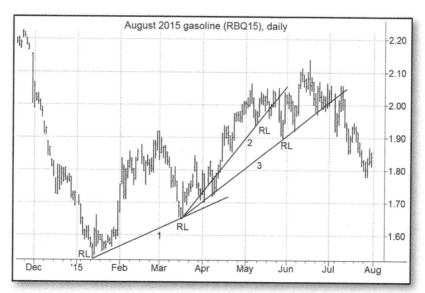

FIGURE 6.20 Succession of TD Uptrend Lines ($N = 10$): August 2015 Gasoline
Note: Lines 1–3 are successive TD uptrend lines, using $N = 10$ to define relative lows (RL).

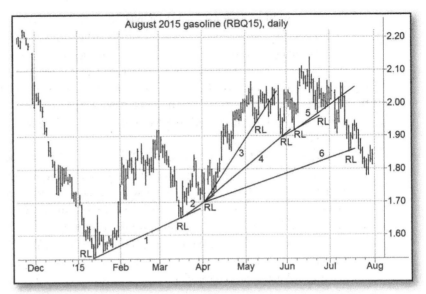

FIGURE 6.21 Succession of TD Uptrend Lines ($N = 5$): August 2015 Gasoline
Note: Lines 1–6 are successive TD uptrend lines, using $N = 5$ to define relative lows (RL).

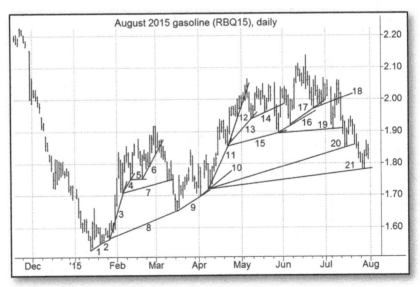

FIGURE 6.22 Succession of TD Uptrend Lines ($N = 2$): August 2015 Gasoline
Note: Lines 1–21 are successive TD uptrend lines, using $N = 2$ to define relative lows (RL).

FIGURE 6.23 Succession of TD Downtrend Lines ($N = 10$): Gold Continuous Futures
Note: Lines 1–3 are successive TD downtrend lines, using $N = 10$ to define relative highs (RH).

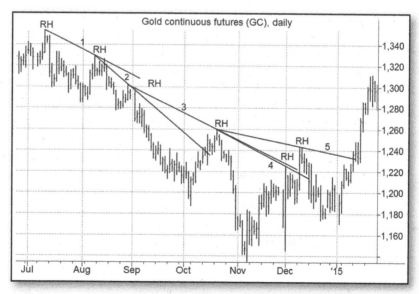

FIGURE 6.24 Succession of TD Downtrend Lines ($N = 5$): Gold Continuous Futures
Note: Lines 1–5 are successive TD downtrend lines, using $N = 5$ to define relative highs (RH)

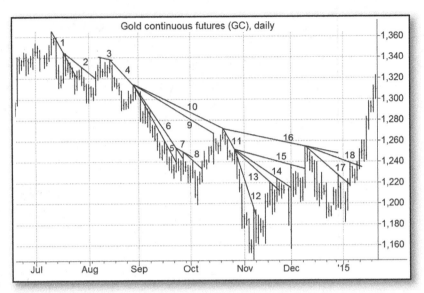

FIGURE 6.25 Succession of TD Downtrend Lines ($N = 2$): Gold Continuous Futures
Note: Lines 1–18 are successive TD downtrend lines, using $N = 2$ to define relative highs (RH).
Chart created using TradeStation. ©TradeStation Technologies, Inc. All rights reserved.

using an $N = 1$ definition for trend lines will yield earlier signals for valid trend line breakouts, the critical trade-off is that such an approach will tend to provide very tight trend lines that are prone to far more false breakout signals. As a general principle, I think it is far more critical to avoid bad signals than to get the jump on good signals; hence, I strongly favor using higher values of N (e.g., $N = 3$ to $N = 12$) to define trend lines.

There is, however, no "right" or "wrong" choice for a value for N; it is strictly a matter of subjective preference. The reader is encouraged to experiment drawing trend lines using different values of N. Each trader will feel comfortable with certain values of N and uncomfortable with others. Generally speaking, short-term traders will gravitate to low values of N and long-term traders to higher values.

As a fine-tuning point, which becomes particularly important if trend lines are defined using $N = 1$, it is preferable to define relative highs and relative lows based on true highs and true lows rather than nominal highs and lows. These terms are defined as:

> **True high.** The high or previous close, whichever is higher.
> **True low.** The low or previous close, whichever is lower.

For most days, the true high will be identical to the high and the true low will be identical to the low. The differences will occur on downside gap days (days on which the entire trading range is below the previous day's close) and upside gap days (days on which the entire trading range is above the previous day's close). Although such gaps are much rarer (and, generally, smaller) than in the days

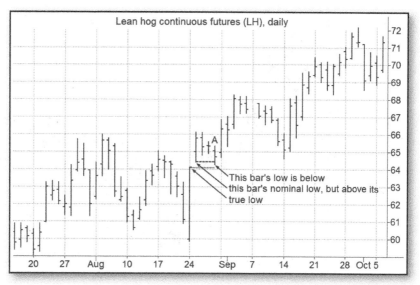

FIGURE 6.26 Nominal Low versus True Low: Lean Hog Continuous Futures
Chart created using TradeStation. ©TradeStation Technologies, Inc. All rights reserved.

before nearly 24-hour electronic trading, they do occasionally still occur, and can thus impact the identification of relative highs and lows. The use of true highs and true lows yields relative highs and relative lows that are more in line with our intuitive concept of what these points should represent.

For example, in Figure 6.26, using an $N = 3$ definition, bar A would be identified as a relative low based on the nominal low. This point is identified as a relative low, however, only because of the upside gap that occurred three days earlier; it hardly fits the intuitive concept of a relative low. In this case, using the true low instead of the nominal low would eliminate the low of Bar A as a relative low.

■ Internal Trend Lines

Conventional trend lines are typically drawn to encompass extreme highs and lows. An argument can be made, however, that extreme highs and lows are aberrations resulting from emotional excesses in the market, and that, as such, these points may be unrepresentative of the dominant trend in the market. An internal trend line does away with the implicit requirement of having to draw trend lines based on extreme price excursions. An internal trend line is a trend line drawn so as to best approximate the majority of relative highs or relative lows without any special consideration being given to extreme points. In a rough sense, an internal trend line can be thought of as an approximate best-fit line of relative highs and relative lows. Figures 6.27 through 6.34 provide a wide range of examples of internal uptrend and downtrend lines. For comparison, most of these charts also depict conventional trend lines, which are shown as dashed lines. (To avoid cluttering the charts, only one or two of the conventional trend lines that would have been implied in the course of a price move are shown.)

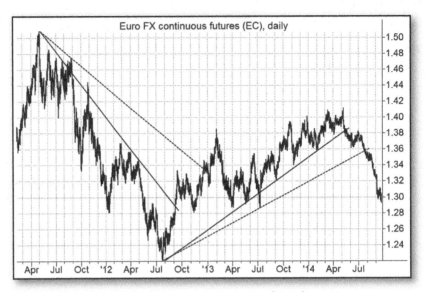

FIGURE 6.27   Internal Trend Line versus Conventional Trend Line: Euro
Continuous Futures

Chart created using TradeStation. ©TradeStation Technologies, Inc. All rights reserved.

FIGURE 6.28   Internal Trend Line versus Conventional Trend Line: E-Mini S&P 500
Index Continuous Futures

Chart created using TradeStation. ©TradeStation Technologies, Inc. All rights reserved.

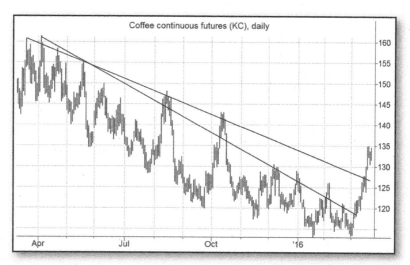

FIGURE 6.29 Alternate Internal Trend Lines: Coffee Continuous Futures

Chart created using TradeStation. ©TradeStation Technologies, Inc. All rights reserved.

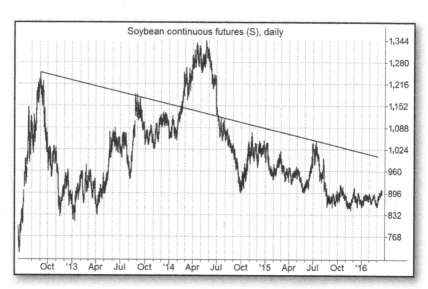

FIGURE 6.30 Internal Trend Line: Soybean Continuous Futures

Chart created using TradeStation. ©TradeStation Technologies, Inc. All rights reserved.

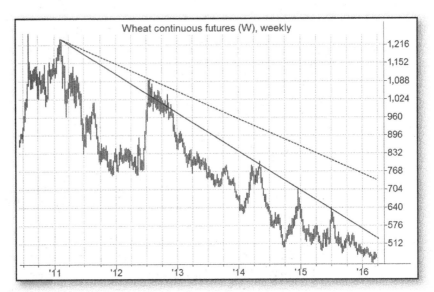

FIGURE 6.31 Internal Trend Line versus Conventional Trend Line: Wheat Continuous Futures

FIGURE 6.32 Internal Trend Line versus Conventional Trend Line: Live Cattle Continuous Futures

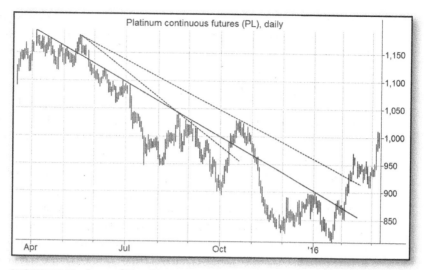

FIGURE 6.33 Internal Trend Line versus Conventional Trend Lines: Platinum Continuous Futures

Chart created using TradeStation. ©TradeStation Technologies, Inc. All rights reserved.

FIGURE 6.34 Internal Trend Line versus Conventional Trend Lines: Soybean Oil Continuous Futures

Chart created using TradeStation. ©TradeStation Technologies, Inc. All rights reserved.

One shortcoming of internal trend lines is that they are unavoidably arbitrary, perhaps even more so than conventional trend lines, which at least are anchored by the extreme highs or lows. In fact, there is often more than one plausible internal trend line that can be drawn on a chart—see, for example, Figure 6.29. Nevertheless, in my experience, internal trend lines are far more useful than conventional trend lines in defining potential support and resistance areas. An examination of Figures 6.27 through 6.34 will reveal the internal trend lines depicted in these charts generally provided a better indication of where the market would hold in declines and stall in advances than did the conventional trend lines. Of course, this sample of illustrations does not prove the superiority of internal trend lines over conventional trend lines, since it is always possible to find charts that appear to validate virtually any contention, and such a proof is certainly not intended or implied. Rather, the comparisons in these charts are intended only to give the reader a sense of how internal trend lines *might* provide a better indication of potential support and resistance areas.

The fact that I personally find internal trend lines far more useful than conventional trend lines proves nothing—the anecdotal observation of a single individual hardly represents scientific proof. In fact, given the subjective nature of internal trend lines, a scientific test of their validity would be very difficult to construct. My point, however, is that internal trend lines are a concept that should certainly be explored by the serious chart analyst. I am sure that by doing so many readers will also find internal trend lines more effective than conventional trend lines, or at least a worthwhile addition to the chart analyst's tool kit.

■ Moving Averages

Moving averages provide a very simple means of smoothing a price series and making any trends more discernible. A simple moving average is defined as the average close of the past N days, ending with the current day. For example, a 40-day moving average would be equal to the average of the past 40 closes, including the current day. (Typically, moving averages are calculated using daily closes. However, moving averages can also be based on opens, highs, lows, or an average of the daily open, high, low, and close. Also, moving averages can be calculated for time intervals of data other than daily, in which case the "close" would refer to the final price quote in the given time interval.) The term *moving average* refers to the fact that the set of numbers being averaged is continuously moving through time. Figure 6.35 illustrates a 40-day moving average superimposed on a price series. Note that the moving average clearly reflects the trend in the price series and smooths the meaningless fluctuations in the data. In choppy markets moving averages will tend to oscillate in a general sideways pattern, as illustrated in Figure 6.36.

One very simple method of using moving averages to define trends is based on the direction of change in a moving average's value relative to the previous day. For example, a moving average (and by implication the trend) would be considered to be *rising* if today's value was higher than yesterday's value and *declining* if today's value was lower.

Note that the basic definition of a rising moving average is equivalent to the simple condition that today's close is higher than the close N days ago. Why? Because yesterday's moving average is identical

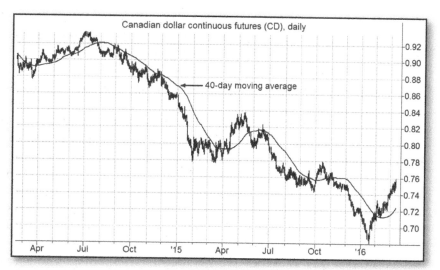

FIGURE 6.35 Moving Average (40-Day) in Trending Market: Canadian Dollar Continuous Futures

Chart created using TradeStation. ©TradeStation Technologies, Inc. All rights reserved.

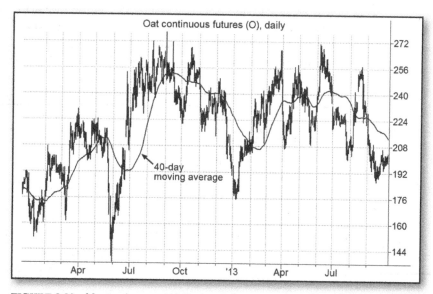

FIGURE 6.36 Moving Average (40-Day) in Sideways Market: Oat Continuous Futures

Chart created using TradeStation. ©TradeStation Technologies, Inc. All rights reserved.

to today's moving average with the exception that yesterday's moving average includes the close N days ago and does not include today's close. Therefore, if today's close is higher than the close of N days ago, then today's moving average will be higher than yesterday's moving average. Similarly, a declining moving average is equivalent to the condition that today's close is lower than the close N days ago.

The smoothing properties of moving averages are achieved at the expense of introducing lags in the data. By definition, since moving averages are based on an average of past prices, turning points in moving averages will always lag the corresponding transitions in the raw price series. This characteristic is readily evident in both Figures 6.35 and 6.36.

In trending markets, moving averages can provide a very simple and effective method of identifying trends. Figure 6.37 duplicates Figure 6.35, denoting buy signals at points at which the moving average reversed to the upside by at least 10 ticks and sell signals at points at which the moving average turned down by the same minimum amount. (The reason for using a minimum threshold reversal to define turns in the moving average is to keep trend signals from flipping back and forth—"whipsawing"—repeatedly at times when the moving average is near zero.) As Figure 6.37 shows, this extremely simple technique generated good trading signals. During the 24-month period shown, this method generated only seven signals. The first signal (long) was exited with a small profit in August. The short position triggered at this point captured a significant portion of the July 2014–March 2015 decline. The April 2015 buy was exited with a small loss in June 2015, but the ensuing short trade was exited profitably in October. The subsequent buy was reversed in late November at a loss, and the final short trade was exited with a profit in February 2016.

The problem is that while moving averages will do well in trending markets, in choppy, sideways markets they are apt to generate many false signals. For example, Figure 6.38 duplicates Figure 6.36, indicating buy signals at points where the moving average turned up by at least 10 ticks and sell signals at points witnessing equivalent downside reversals in the moving average. The same method that worked so well in Figure 6.37—buying on upturns in the moving average and selling on downturns in the moving average—proves to be a disastrous strategy in this market, yielding six losses and one essentially break-even trade.

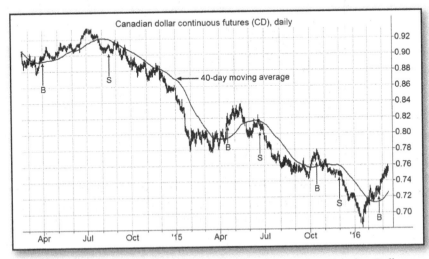

FIGURE 6.37 Moving-Average-Based Signals in Trending Market: Canadian Dollar Continuous Futures
Notes: Buy (B) = 10-tick rise in moving average off its low. Sell (S) = 10-tick decline in moving average off its high.
Chart created using TradeStation. ©TradeStation Technologies, Inc. All rights reserved.

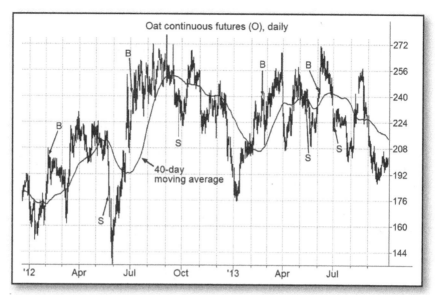

FIGURE 6.38 Moving-Average-Based Signals in Sideways Market: Oat Continuous Futures

Notes: Buy (B) = 10-tick rise in moving average off its low. Sell (S) = 10-tick decline in moving average off its high.

Chart created using TradeStation. ©TradeStation Technologies, Inc. All rights reserved.

There are many other ways of calculating a moving average besides the simple moving average described in this section. Some of these other methods, as well as the application of moving averages in trading systems, are discussed in Chapter 16.

CHAPTER 7

Trading Ranges

There is the plain fool, who does the wrong thing at all times everywhere, but there is the Wall Street fool, who thinks he must trade all the time.

—Edwin Lefèvre

■ Trading Ranges: Trading Considerations

A trading range is a horizontal corridor that contains price fluctuations for an extended period. Generally speaking, markets tend to spend most of their time in trading ranges. Unfortunately, however, trading ranges are very difficult to trade profitably. In fact, most technical traders will probably find that the best strategy they can employ for trading ranges is to minimize their participation in such markets—a procedure that is easier said than done.

Although there are methodologies that can be profitable in trading ranges, the problem is that these same approaches are disastrous for trending markets, and while trading ranges are easily identifiable for the past, they are nearly impossible to predict. Also, it should be noted that most chart patterns (e.g., flags, pennants) are relatively meaningless if they occur within a trading range. (Chart patterns are discussed in Chapter 9.)

Trading ranges can often last for years. For example, the silver market remained in a trading range for much of the 1990s (see Figure 7.1). Figures 7.2, 7.3, and 7.4 show a multiyear crude oil trading range represented in continuous futures, nearest futures, and the December 2014 contract. These three charts illustrate that the trading range boundaries and periods will differ depending on whether depicted as continuous futures, nearest futures, or an individual contract, although there will typically be significant overlap between these alternative representations. Trading ranges also show up in shorter-term charts. Figure 7.5 shows an example on a 15-minute chart of euro futures.

FIGURE 7.1 Multiyear Trading Range: Silver Continuous Futures
Chart created using TradeStation. ©TradeStation Technologies, Inc. All rights reserved.

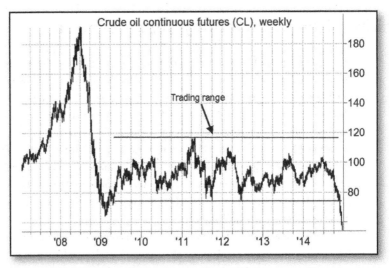

FIGURE 7.2 Multiyear Trading Range: Crude Oil Continuous Futures
Chart created using TradeStation. ©TradeStation Technologies, Inc. All rights reserved.

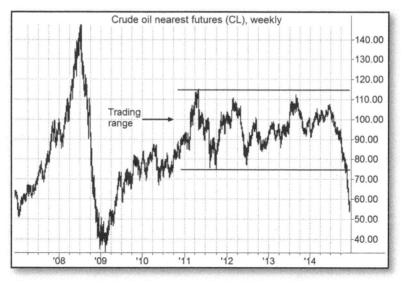

FIGURE 7.3 Multiyear Trading Range: Crude Oil Nearest Futures
Chart created using TradeStation. ©TradeStation Technologies, Inc. All rights reserved.

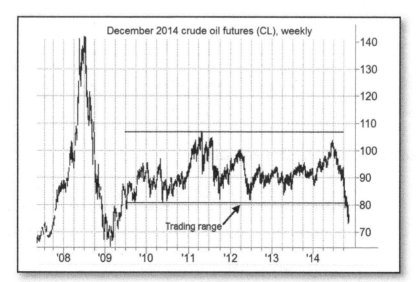

FIGURE 7.4 Multiyear Trading Range: December 2014 Crude Oil Futures
Chart created using TradeStation. ©TradeStation Technologies, Inc. All rights reserved.

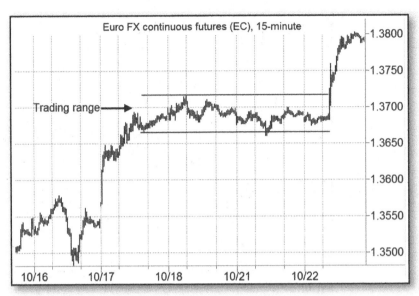

FIGURE 7.5   Intraday Trading Range: December 2013 Euro Futures

Once a trading range is established, the upper and lower boundaries tend to define *support* and *resistance* areas. This topic is discussed in greater detail in the next chapter. Breakouts from trading ranges can provide important trading signals—an observation that is the subject of the next section.

■ Trading Range Breakouts

A *breakout* from a trading range suggests an impending price move in the direction of the breakout. The significance and reliability of a breakout are often enhanced by the following three factors:

1. **Duration of the trading range.** The longer the duration of a trading range, the more potentially significant the eventual breakout. This point is illustrated using a weekly chart example in Figure 7.6 and a daily chart example in Figure 7.7.

2. **Narrowness of range.** Breakouts from narrow ranges tend to provide particularly reliable trade signals (see Figures 7.8, 7.9, and 7.10). Furthermore, such trades can be especially attractive since the meaningful stop point implies a relatively low dollar risk.

3. **Confirmation of breakout.** It is rather common for prices to break out from a trading range by only a small amount, or for only a few days, and then fall back into the range. One reason for this tendency is that stop orders are frequently clustered in the region beyond a

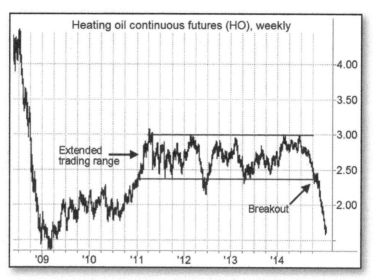

FIGURE 7.6 Downside Breakout from Extended Trading Range: Weekly Heating Oil Continuous Futures

trading range. Consequently, a move slightly beyond the range can sometimes trigger a string of stops. Once this initial flurry of orders is filled, the breakout will fail unless there are solid fundamental reasons and underlying buying (or overhead selling in the case of a downside breakout) to sustain the trend.

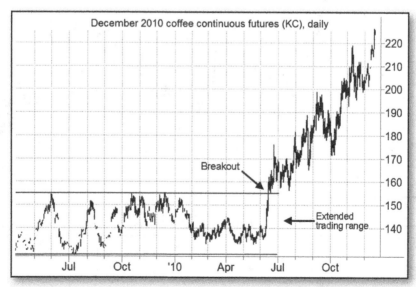

FIGURE 7.7 Upside Breakout from Extended Trading Range: December 2010 Coffee Continuous Futures

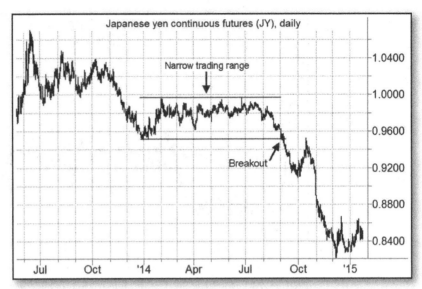

FIGURE 7.8 Downside Breakout from Narrow Trading Range: Japanese Yen Continuous Futures

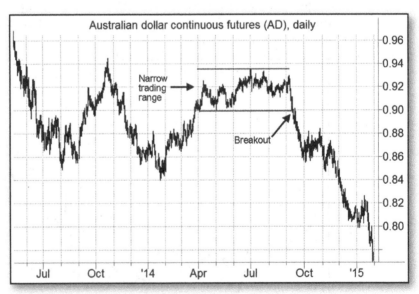

FIGURE 7.9 Downside Breakout from Narrow Trading Range: Australian Dollar Continuous Futures

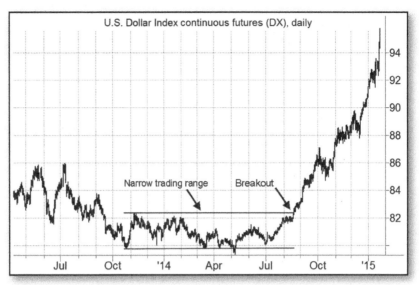

FIGURE 7.10 Upside Breakout from Narrow Trading Range: U.S. Dollar Index
Continuous Futures

In view of these behavioral considerations, the reliability of a breakout from a trading range as a signal for an impending trend is significantly improved if prices are still beyond the range after a number of days (e.g., five). Other types of confirmation can also be used—minimum percent penetration, a given number of *thrust days* (discussed in Chapter 9), and so on. Although waiting for a confirmation following breakouts will lead to worse fills on some valid signals, it will help avoid many "false" signals. The net balance of this trade-off will depend on the confirmation condition used and must be evaluated by the individual trader. The key point, however, is that the trader should experiment with different confirmation conditions, rather than blindly follow all breakouts.

CHAPTER 8

Support and Resistance

In a narrow market, when prices are not getting anywhere to speak of but move in a narrow range, there is no sense in trying to anticipate what the next big movement is going to be—up or down.

—Edwin Lefèvre

■ Nearest Futures or Continuous Futures?

For any application of technical analysis in which the accurate representation of price *moves* is essential, continuous futures, as opposed to nearest futures, are the only viable choice for depicting price series that extend across multiple contracts. However, in the case of support and resistance, actual past price *levels*, which are accurately represented by only the nearest futures, are also important. This consideration raises the question of which type of longer-term chart—nearest or continuous futures—should be used to determine support and resistance levels. There is no correct answer. Insofar as the accurate measurement of prior price *moves* is important in determining support and resistance, continuous futures charts should be used. Insofar as past actual price *levels* are important in determining support and resistance, nearest futures charts should be used. Essentially, strong arguments can be made for using both types of charts for defining support and resistance levels. Traders need to experiment with whether they find nearest or continuous futures charts more useful in identifying support and resistance levels, or, for that matter, if they find consulting both of these charts the most effective method.

■ Trading Ranges

Once a trading range is established (at least one to two months of sideways price movement on the daily time frame), prices will tend to meet resistance at the upper end of the range and support at the lower end of the range. Although chart analysis is best suited as a tool to signal trend-following trades, some agile traders adopt a strategy of selling rallies and buying declines in a trading range situation. Generally speaking, such a trading approach is difficult to pull off successfully. Furthermore, it should be emphasized that fading minor trends within a trading range can lead to disaster unless losses are limited (e.g., by liquidating the position if prices penetrate the range boundary by a specified minimum amount, or the market trades beyond the range for a minimum number of bars, or both).

After prices break out from a trading range, the interpretation of support and resistance is turned on its head. Specifically, once prices witness a sustained breakout above a trading range, the upper boundary of that range becomes a zone of price support. The extended lines in Figures 8.1 and 8.2 indicate the support levels implied by the upper boundaries of the prior trading ranges. In the case of a sustained breakout below a trading range, the lower boundary of that range becomes a zone of price resistance. The extended lines in Figures 8.3 and 8.4 indicate the resistance levels implied by the lower boundaries of preceding trading ranges.

FIGURE 8.1   Support Near Top of Prior Trading Range: Euro Stoxx 50 Continuous Futures

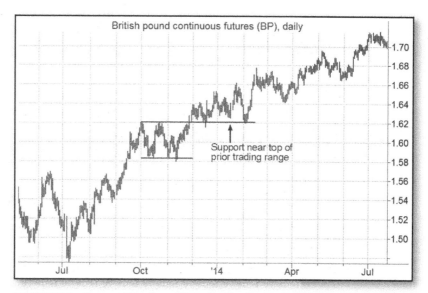

FIGURE 8.2 Support Near Top of Prior Trading Range: British Pound Continuous Futures

Chart created using TradeStation. ©TradeStation Technologies, Inc. All rights reserved.

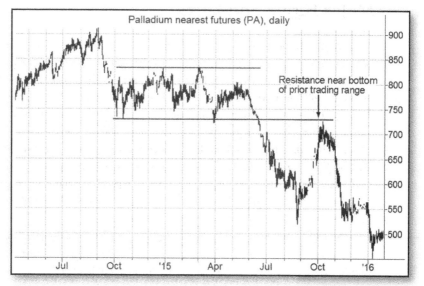

FIGURE 8.3 Resistance Near Bottom of Prior Trading Range: Palladium Nearest Futures

Chart created using TradeStation. ©TradeStation Technologies, Inc. All rights reserved.

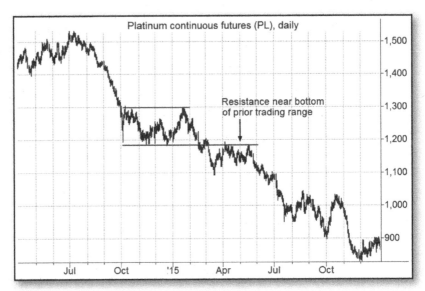

FIGURE 8.4 Resistance Near Bottom of Prior Trading Range: Platinum Continuous
Futures

Chart created using TradeStation. ©TradeStation Technologies, Inc. All rights reserved.

■ Prior Major Highs and Lows

Normally, resistance will be encountered in the vicinity of previous major highs and support in the
vicinity of major lows. Figures 8.5, 8.6, and 8.7 illustrate both behavioral patterns. For example, in
Figure 8.5 the late 2003 low acted as a support level for subsequent lows in 2004, 2007, and 2008,
while the 2005 high provided a resistance level for the 2009 highs. In Figure 8.6 the late 2009 and
early 2010 highs formed near the resistance level of the 2008 high, while the late 2011 low provided
support for the 2012 and 2013 lows. Subsequently, the 2014 high functioned as resistance for the
2015 highs, while the early 2016 low formed just above the support level of the early 2015 low.
Although the concept of resistance near prior peaks and support near prior lows is perhaps most
important for weekly or monthly charts, such as Figures 8.5 and 8.6, the principle also applies to
daily charts, such as Figure 8.7. In this chart, the June and August 2013 highs occurred near the March
2013 peak.

It should be emphasized that a prior high does not imply subsequent rallies will fail *at or below*
that point, but rather that resistance can be anticipated in the *general vicinity* of that point. Similarly,
a prior low does not imply that subsequent declines will hold *at or above* that point, but rather that
support can be anticipated in the *general vicinity* of that point. Some practitioners of technical analysis
treat prior highs and lows as points endowed with sacrosanct significance: If a prior high was 1,078,
then they consider 1,078 to be major resistance, and if, for example, the market rallies to 1,085,
they consider resistance to be broken. This is nonsense. Support and resistance should be considered
approximate areas, not precise points. Note that although prior major highs and lows proved highly

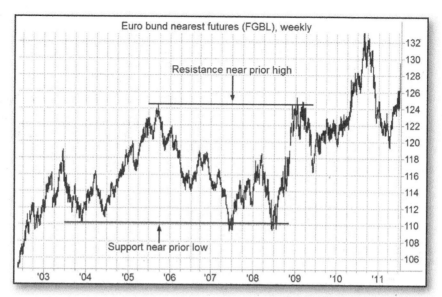

FIGURE 8.5 Resistance at Prior High and Support at Prior Low: Euro Bund Nearest Futures

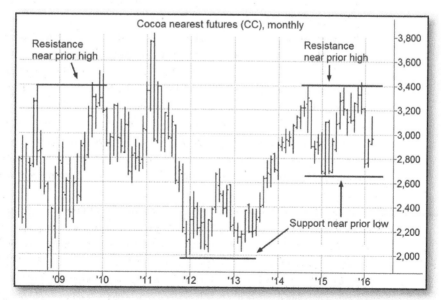

FIGURE 8.6 Resistance at Prior Highs and Support at Prior Lows: Cocoa Nearest Futures

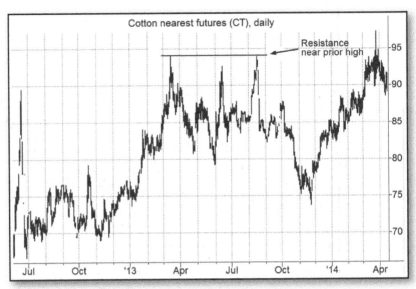

FIGURE 8.7   Resistance at Prior High: Cotton Nearest Futures

significant as resistance and support in all three of the preceding charts, reversals mostly occurred before price reached a given level or after penetrating it by a notable amount (although usually not closing beyond it); reversals that occur very near the precise levels of prior highs or lows are the exception rather than the rule.

The penetration of a previous high can be viewed as a buy signal, and the penetration of a prior low can be viewed as a sell signal. Similar to the case of breakouts from trading ranges, to be viewed as trading signals penetrations of highs and lows should be significant in terms of price magnitude, time duration, or both. Thus, for example, as should be clear from the preceding discussion regarding Figures 8.6 and 8.7, a one-period (one-day for daily chart, one-week for weekly chart, etc.) penetration of a prior high or low would not prove anything. A stronger confirmation than a mere penetration of a prior high or low should be required before assuming such an event represents a buy or sell signal. Some examples of possible confirmation conditions include a minimum number of closes beyond the prior high or low, a minimum percent price penetration, or both requirements.

Figures 8.8 and 8.9 illustrate examples of penetrations of previous highs as buy signals, assuming a confirmation condition of three closes above the high. Similarly, Figures 8.10 and 8.11 provide examples of penetrations of previous lows as sell signals, using an analogous confirmation condition. In Figure 8.9 price turned lower in late 2012 a little above the resistance level of the early 2012 high. In January 2014 the market posted its third weekly close above the late 2012 high (dashed line), triggering a buy signal. Incidentally, this chart also provides a good example of a prior low (formed in 2013) holding as support more than two years later.

Following a *sustained* penetration of a prior high or low, the interpretation of support and resistance is turned on its head. In other words, the area of a prior high becomes support and the area of

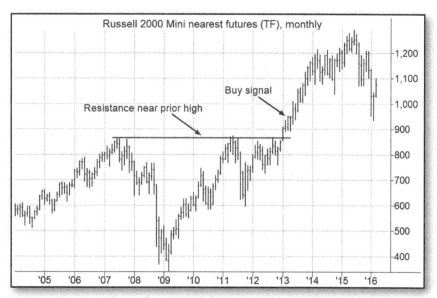

FIGURE 8.8 Penetration of Previous High as Buy Signal: Russell 2000 Mini Nearest Futures

Chart created using TradeStation. ©TradeStation Technologies, Inc. All rights reserved.

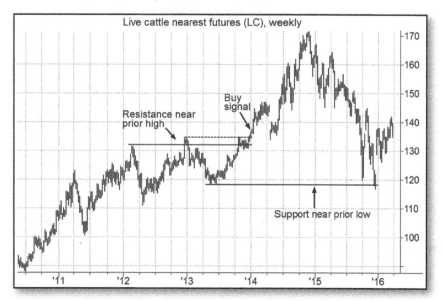

FIGURE 8.9 Penetration of Previous High as Buy Signal: Live Cattle Nearest Futures

Chart created using TradeStation. ©TradeStation Technologies, Inc. All rights reserved.

a previous low becomes resistance. For example, in Figure 8.12 the resistance level from Figure 8.9 subsequently became support in April 2014 when the market pulled back temporarily before rallying to new highs. In Figure 8.13, which extends the support line of Figure 8.10, the September 2011

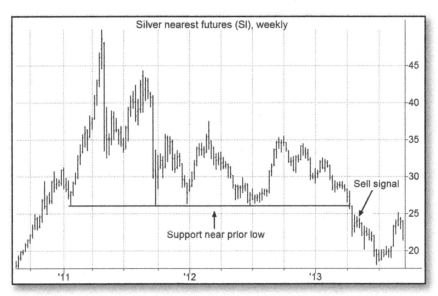

FIGURE 8.10 Penetration of Previous Low as Sell Signal: Silver Nearest Futures

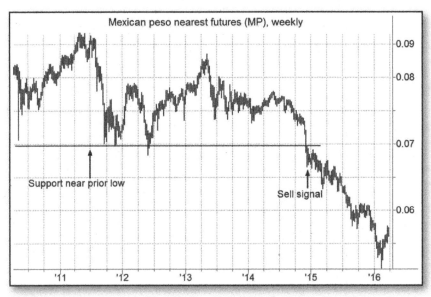

FIGURE 8.11 Penetration of Previous Low as Sell Signal: Mexican Peso Nearest Futures

low provides a support area for the December 2011 and June 2012 lows. When this support level is subsequently penetrated in April 2013, this same level then proves to be a resistance area for the June–August 2013 rebound. Figure 8.14 shows a remarkably similar pattern unfolding on the daily silver chart: The late June 2013 low provided support for subsequent lows between November 2013

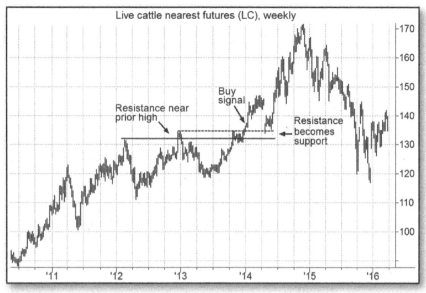

FIGURE 8.12 Previous Resistance Becomes Support: Live Cattle Nearest Futures
Chart created using TradeStation. ©TradeStation Technologies, Inc. All rights reserved.

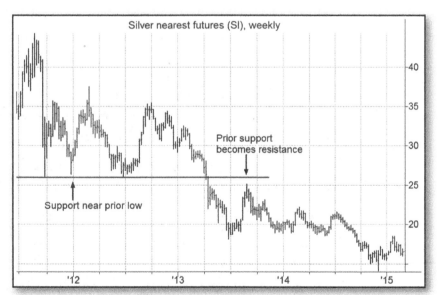

FIGURE 8.13 Previous Support Becomes Resistance: Silver Nearest Futures
Chart created using TradeStation. ©TradeStation Technologies, Inc. All rights reserved.

and June 2014. This support level subsequently functioned as resistance in January and May 2015 after the market rallied off its late 2014 lows. In Figure 8.15, the support level that was penetrated to the downside in August 2015 functioned as resistance for the October 2015 rebound as well as the rally that peaked in March 2016.

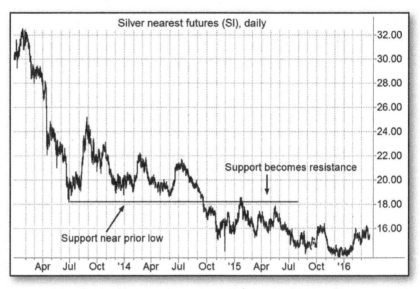

FIGURE 8.14 Previous Support Becomes Resistance: Silver Nearest Futures

FIGURE 8.15 Previous Support Becomes Resistance: Live Cattle Nearest Futures

Concentrations of Relative Highs and Relative Lows

The previous section dealt with support and resistance at prior major highs and lows—single peaks and nadirs. In this section we are concerned with support and resistance at price zones with concentrations of relative highs and relative lows rather than absolute tops and bottoms. Specifically, there is often a tendency for relative highs and relative lows to be concentrated in relatively narrow zones. These zones imply support regions if current prices are higher and resistance areas if current prices are lower. This approach is particularly useful for anticipating support and resistance areas in long-term nearest futures charts, which, as the reader will recall, accurately reflect past price *levels* (in contrast to continuous futures, which accurately reflect past price *swings*). Figures 8.16 through 8.21 provide weekly chart examples of support or resistance occurring at prior concentrations of relative lows and relative highs (or relative lows alone). In Figure 8.21, a support zone initially defined by multiple relative highs from 2007 to 2010 subsequently functions as a resistance zone in 2013–2014 after the market sells off.

The approach of using concentrations of prior relative highs and lows to define support and resistance can also be applied to daily continuous or nearest futures charts of sufficient duration—for example, two years. (The life span of most individual futures contracts is too short for this method to be effectively applied on such charts.) Figures 8.22 through 8.24 provide daily chart examples of support and resistance occurring at prior concentrations of relative highs and relative lows. Figure 8.24 is similar to Figure 8.21 in that a support zone transforms into a resistance zone.

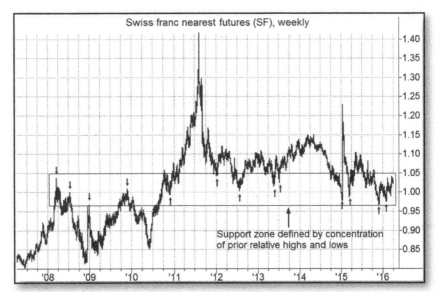

FIGURE 8.16 Support Zone Defined by Concentration of Prior Relative Lows and Highs: Swiss Franc Nearest Futures
Note: ↑ = relative low; ↓ = relative high.
Chart created using TradeStation. ©TradeStation Technologies, Inc. All rights reserved.

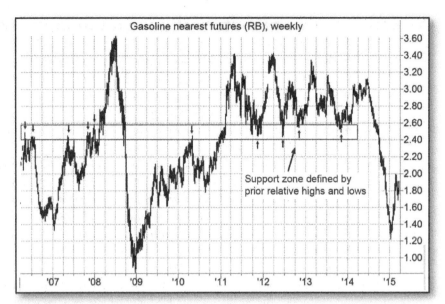

FIGURE 8.17 Support Zone Defined by Concentration of Prior Relative Lows and Highs: Gasoline Nearest Futures

Note: ↑ = relative low; ↓ = relative high.

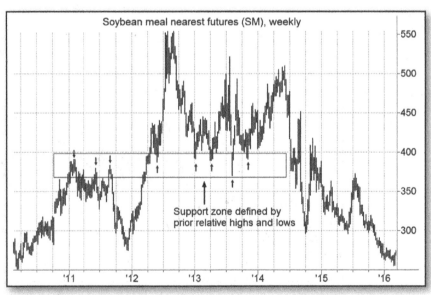

FIGURE 8.18 Support Zone Defined by Concentration of Prior Relative Highs and Lows: Soybean Meal Nearest Futures

Note: ↑ = relative low; ↓ = relative high.

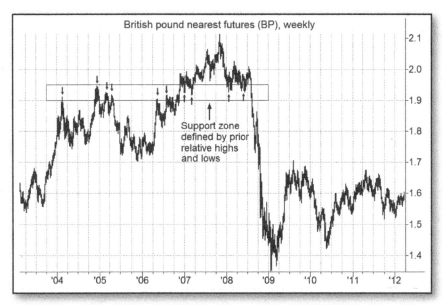

FIGURE 8.19 Support Zone Defined by Concentration of Prior Relative Highs and Lows: British Pound Nearest Futures

Note: ↑ = relative low; ↓ = relative high.

Chart created using TradeStation. ©TradeStation Technologies, Inc. All rights reserved.

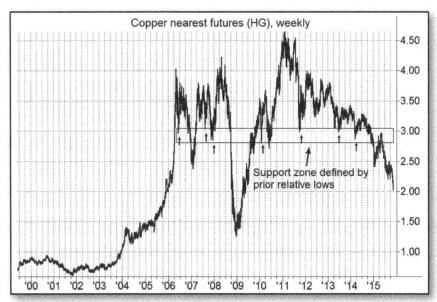

FIGURE 8.20 Support Zone Defined by Concentration of Prior Relative Lows: Copper Nearest Futures

Note: ↑ = relative low.

Chart created using TradeStation. ©TradeStation Technologies, Inc. All rights reserved.

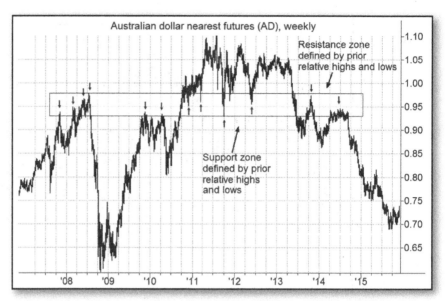

FIGURE 8.21   Support and Resistance Zones Defined by Concentration of Prior Relative Highs and Lows: Australian Dollar Nearest Futures

Note: ↑ = relative low; ↓ = relative high.

Chart created using TradeStation. ©TradeStation Technologies, Inc. All rights reserved.

FIGURE 8.22   Support Zone Defined by Concentration of Prior Relative Lows and Highs: Cocoa Nearest Futures

Note: ↑ = relative low; ↓ = relative high.

Chart created using TradeStation. ©TradeStation Technologies, Inc. All rights reserved.

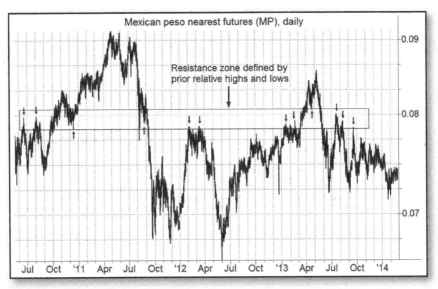

FIGURE 8.23 Resistance Zone Defined by Concentration of Prior Relative Highs and Lows: Mexican Peso Nearest Futures

Note: ↑ = relative low; ↓ = relative high.

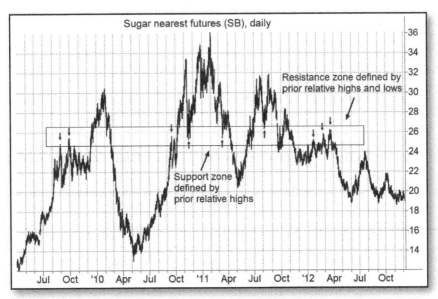

FIGURE 8.24 Support and Resistance Zones Defined by Concentration of Prior Relative Highs and Lows: Sugar Nearest Futures

Note: ↑ = relative low; ↓ = relative high.

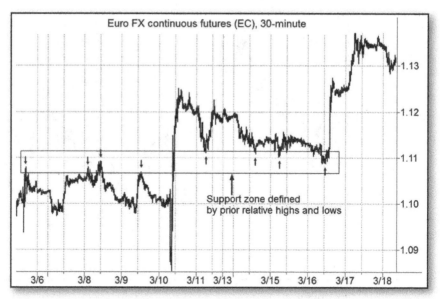

FIGURE 8.25   Support Zone Defined by Concentration of Prior Relative Highs and Lows: Euro Continuous Futures
Note: ↑ = relative low; ↓ = relative high.
Chart created using TradeStation. ©TradeStation Technologies, Inc. All rights reserved.

Although best suited to longer-term charts, the technique of using prior concentrations of relative highs and lows as support and resistance zones can also be applied to shorter-term charts. Figure 8.25 provides an intraday example: a support zone defined by a series of prior relative highs and lows on a 30-minute chart.

■ Trend Lines, Channels, and Internal Trend Lines

The concept that trend lines, channel lines, and internal trend lines indicate areas of potential support and resistance was detailed in Chapter 6. Again, as previously discussed, based on personal experience, I believe that internal trend lines are more reliable in this regard than conventional trend lines. However, the question of which type of trend line is a better indicator is a highly subjective matter, and some readers may well reach the opposite conclusion. In fact, there is not even a mathematically precise definition of a trend line or an internal trend line, and how these lines are drawn will vary from individual to individual.

■ Price Envelope Bands

A price envelope band can be derived from a moving average. The upper band of the price envelope is defined as the moving average plus a given percentage of the moving average. Similarly, the lower band of the price envelope is defined as the moving average minus a given percentage of the moving average. For example, if the current moving average value is 600 and the percentage value is defined as 3 percent, the upper band value would be 618 and the lower band value would be 582. By selecting an appropriate percent boundary for a given moving average, a trader can define an envelope band so that it encompasses most of the price activity, with the upper boundary approximately coinciding with relative highs and the lower boundary approximately coinciding with relative lows.

Figure 8.26 illustrates a price envelope band for the Australian dollar continuous futures using a 20-day moving average and a 2.5 percent value. The price envelope provides a good indication of support and resistance for much of the period captured in the chart, especially when the market is moving sideways (e.g., February–April 2015 and September 2015–January 2016). An alternative way of expressing the same concept is that the price envelope indicates "overbought" and "oversold" levels. Price envelope bands can also be applied to data for other than daily time intervals. For example, Figure 8.27 illustrates a 1.25 percent price envelope band applied to 60-minute bars of the March 2016 E-mini S&P 500 contract.

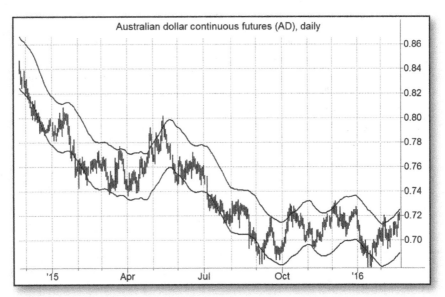

FIGURE 8.26 Price Envelope Band as Indication of Support and Resistance in Daily Bar Chart: Australian Dollar Continuous Futures

Chart created using TradeStation. ©TradeStation Technologies, Inc. All rights reserved.

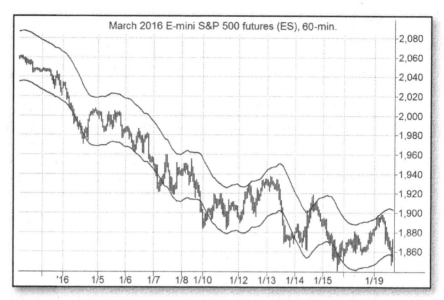

FIGURE 8.27 Price Envelope Band as Indication of Support and Resistance on 60-Minute Bar Chart: March 2016 E-Mini S&P 500 Futures

It should be noted, however, that the price envelope is not as effective a tool as it might appear to be. Although it provides a reasonably good indication of when the market may be nearing a turning point, prices can continue to hug one end of the price envelope during extended trends. This pattern, for example, is evident at the beginning of Figure 8.26 (November–December 2014), as well as the middle of the chart (July and August–September 2015). Thus, while it is true that price excursions beyond the price envelope band tend to be limited and temporary, the fact that prices are near one of the boundaries of the envelope does not necessarily mean that a price turning point is imminent. On balance, the price envelope provides one means of gauging potential areas of support and resistance, but it is also susceptible to multiple false signals.

CHAPTER 9

Chart Patterns

Never confuse brilliance with a bull market.

—Paul Rubink

■ One-Day Patterns

Spikes

A spike high is a day whose high is sharply above the highs of the preceding and succeeding days. Frequently, the closing price of a spike high day will be near the lower end of the day's trading range. A spike high is meaningful only if it occurs after a price advance, in which case it can often signify at least a temporary climax in buying pressure, and hence can be viewed as a potential relative high. Sometimes spike highs will prove to be major tops.

Generally speaking, the significance of a spike high will be enhanced by the following factors:

1. A wide difference between the spike high and the highs of the preceding and succeeding days.
2. A close near the low of the day's range.
3. A substantial price advance preceding the spike's formation.

The more extreme each of these conditions, the greater the likelihood that a spike high will prove to be an important relative high or even a major top.

In analogous fashion, a spike low is a day whose low is sharply below the lows of the preceding and succeeding days. Frequently, the closing price on a spike low day will be near the upper end of the day's trading range. A spike low is meaningful only if it occurs after a price decline, in which case it can often signify at least a temporary climax in selling pressure and hence can be viewed as a potential relative low. Sometimes spike lows will prove to be a major bottom.

Generally speaking, the significance of a spike low will be enhanced by these three factors:

1. A wide difference between the lows of the preceding and succeeding days and the spike low.
2. A close near the high of the day's range.
3. A substantial price decline preceding the spike's formation.

The more extreme each of these conditions, the greater the likelihood that a spike low will prove to be an important relative low or even a major bottom.

Figures 9.1 through 9.4 contain several examples of spike highs and spike lows on daily and weekly charts. The massive spike high in Figure 9.3 marked a multiyear top in the Swiss franc futures. Figure 9.4 contains two examples of spike lows that marked swing bottoms.

The preceding descriptions of spike highs and lows listed three essential characteristics that typify such days. However, the definition of these conditions was somewhat imprecise. Specifically, how great must the difference be between a day's high (low) and the highs (lows) of the preceding and succeeding days in order for it to qualify as a spike high (low)? How close must the close be to the low (high) for a day to be considered a spike high (low)? How large must a preceding advance (decline) be for a day to be viewed as a possible spike high (low)? The answer to these questions is that there are no precise specifications; in each case, the choice of a qualifying condition is a subjective one. However, Figures 9.1 through 9.4 should provide an intuitive sense of the types of days that qualify as spikes.

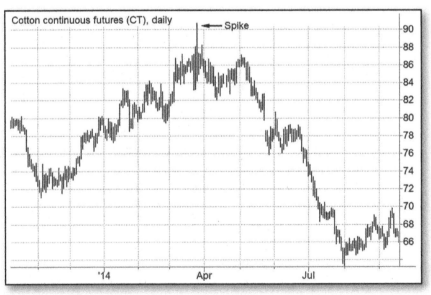

FIGURE 9.1 Spike High: Cotton Continuous Futures

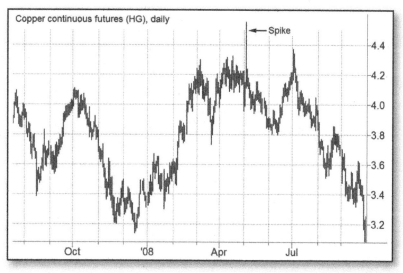

FIGURE 9.2 Spike High: Copper Continuous Futures
Chart created using TradeStation. ©TradeStation Technologies, Inc. All rights reserved.

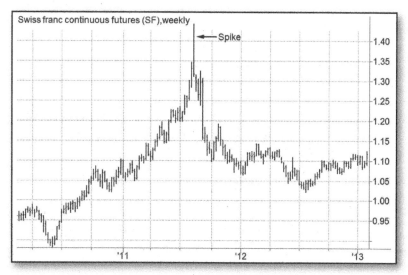

FIGURE 9.3 Spike High: Swiss Franc Continuous Futures
Chart created using TradeStation. ©TradeStation Technologies, Inc. All rights reserved.

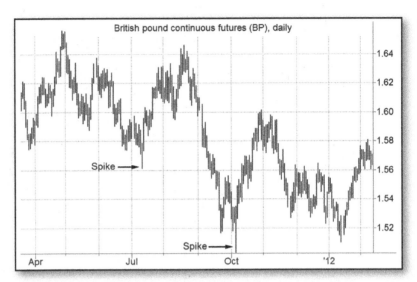

FIGURE 9.4 Spike Lows: British Pound Continuous Futures

Chart created using TradeStation. ©TradeStation Technologies, Inc. All rights reserved.

It is possible, though, to construct a mathematically precise definition for spike days. An example of such a definition for a spike high might be a day that fulfilled all three of the following conditions (the definition for a spike low day would be analogous):

1. $H_t - \text{Max}(H_{t-1}, H_{t+1}) > k \cdot \text{ADTR}_{10}$,

   where H_t = high on given day

              H_{t-1} = high on preceding day

              H_{t+1} = high on succeeding day

              k = multiplicative factor that must be defined (e.g., $k = 0.75$)

              ADTR_{10} = average daily true range during past 10 days[1]

2. $H_t - C_t > 3 \cdot (C_t - L_t)$,

   where C_t = close on given day

              L_t = low on given day

3. $H_t >$ maximum high during past N days, where N = constant that must be defined (e.g., $N = 50$)

The first of the preceding conditions assures us that the spike high will exceed the surrounding highs by an amount at least equal to three-quarters of the past 10-day average true range (assuming the value of k is defined as 0.75). The second condition assures us that the spike day's close will be in the lower quartile of its range. The third condition, which requires that the spike day's high exceed the highest high during the past 50 days (assuming $N = 50$), guarantees that

---

[1] The true range is equal to the true high minus the true low. The true high is the maximum of the current day's high and the previous day's close. The true low is the minimum of the current day's low and the previous day's close.

the day was preceded by an upswing. (Generally speaking, higher values of N will require larger prior advances.)

The three-part definition just provided for a spike high day is only intended to offer an example of how a mathematically precise definition can be constructed. Many other definitions are possible.

Reversal Days

The standard definition of a reversal high day is a day that makes a new high in an upmove and then reverses to close below the preceding day's close. Analogously, a reversal low day is a day that makes a new low in a decline and then reverses to close above the preceding day's close. The following discussion focuses on reversal high days, but mirror-image comments would apply to reversal low days.

Similar to spike highs, a reversal high day is generally interpreted as suggesting a buying climax and hence a relative high. However, the condition required for a reversal high day by the standard definition is a relatively weak one, meaning that reversal high days are fairly common. Hence, while many market highs are reversal days, the problem is that the majority of reversal high days are not market highs. Figure 9.5, which illustrates this point, is fairly typical. It shows the final leg of the crude oil market's historic rally to its all-time high in July 2008 and its equally impressive sell-off in the following months. Note that although a reversal high day occurred just a few days before the July top, it had been preceded by eight other reversal days since late February, only one of which (the seventh, in late

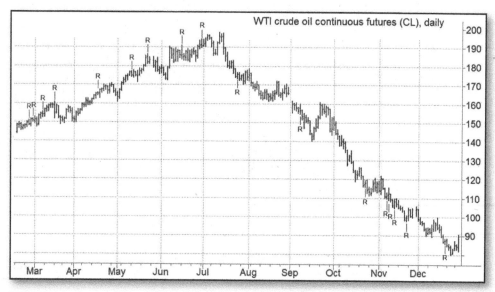

FIGURE 9.5 Reversal Days: WTI Crude Oil Continuous Futures
Note: R = reversal day.
Chart created using TradeStation. ©TradeStation Technologies, Inc. All rights reserved.

May) was followed by a downswing of any significance. The reversal low days that occurred from late July to December paint a similar picture: Given crude oil futures fell another $20 before bottoming in February 2009 (not shown), even the final signal in December 2008 was extremely premature. Figure 9.6 depicts another example of the commonplaceness of premature reversal day signals. In this case, a reversal day actually occurred at the exact peak of a major rally dating back to the beginning of 2009. This incredible sell signal, however, was preceded by eight other reversal days, the majority of which occurred far earlier in the advance. Anyone who might have traded this market based on reversal signals would probably have thrown in the towel well before the valid signal finally materialized.

In the examples just provided, at least a reversal day signal occurred at or near the actual high. Frequently, however, an uptrend will witness a number of reversal highs that prove to be false signals and then fail to register a reversal high near the actual top. It can be said that reversal high days successfully call 100 out of every 10 highs. In other words, reversal days provide occasional excellent signals, but far more frequent false signals.

In my opinion, the standard definition of reversal days is so prone to generating false signals that it is worthless as a trading indicator. The problem with the standard definition is that merely requiring a close below the prior day's close is much too weak a condition. Instead, I suggest defining a reversal high day as a day that witnesses a new high in an upmove and then reverses to close below the preceding day's *low*. (If desired, the condition can be made even stronger by requiring that the close be below the low of the prior two days.) This more restrictive definition will greatly reduce the number of false reversal signals, but it will also knock out some valid signals. For example, this

FIGURE 9.6 Reversal Days. Copper Continuous Futures

Note: R = reversal day.

Chart created using TradeStation. ©TradeStation Technologies, Inc. All rights reserved.

revised definition would have eliminated all but the fourth signal in Figure 9.5. In Figure 9.6 the more restrictive definition for a reversal day would have avoided all but the fourth signal and the ninth (final and valid) signal.

A reversal day may sound somewhat similar to a spike day, but the two patterns are not equivalent. A spike day will not necessarily be a reversal day, and a reversal day will not necessarily be a spike day. For example, a spike high day may not close below the previous day's low (or even below the previous day's close, as specified by the standard definition), even if the close is at the day's low. As an example of the reverse case, a reversal high day may not *significantly* exceed the prior day's high, as required by the spike high definition, or exceed the subsequent day's high at all, since the subsequent day's price action is not part of the reversal day definition. Also, it is possible that a reversal day's close may not be near the low, a standard characteristic of a spike day, even if it is below the previous day's close.

Occasionally, a day will be both a reversal day and a spike day. Such days are far more significant than days that are only reversal days. An alternative to using the more restrictive definition for a reversal day is using the standard definition, but requiring that the day also fulfill spike day conditions. (Although a day that met both the strong reversal day condition and the spike day conditions would be most meaningful of all, such days are fairly rare.) Figure 9.7 provides an example of a day that met both spike and reversal low day conditions. Figure 9.8 highlights three days: a spike and reversal high day that marked the high of the rally, a spike and reversal low day several days later that was followed by a few days of sideways price action, and a spike and reversal low day that was followed by a correction within the prevailing downtrend.

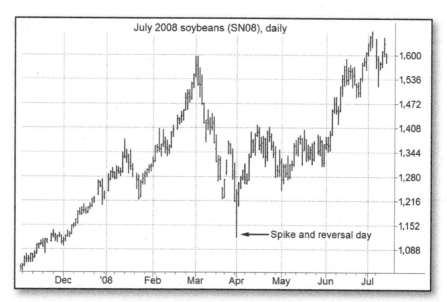

FIGURE 9.7 Spike and Reversal Day: July 2008 Soybeans
Chart created using TradeStation. ©TradeStation Technologies, Inc. All rights reserved.

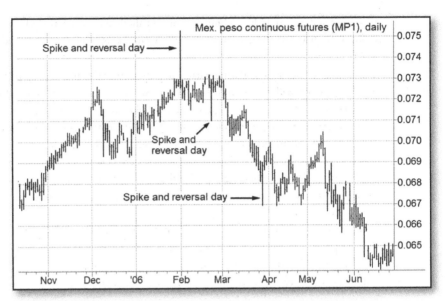

FIGURE 9.8 Spike and Reversal Days: Mexican Peso Continuous Futures
Chart created using TradeStation. ©TradeStation Technologies, Inc. All rights reserved.

Thrust Days

An upthrust day is a day with a close above the previous day's high, while a downthrust day is a day with a close below the previous day's low. The significance of thrust days is tied to the concept that the close is by far the most important price of the day. A single thrust day is not particularly meaningful, since thrust days are quite common. However, a series of upthrust days (not necessarily consecutive) would reflect pronounced strength. Similarly, a series of downthrust days would reflect pronounced market weakness.

During bull markets upthrust days significantly outnumber downthrust days—see, for example, the especially bullish mid-May to early July period in Figure 9.9. Conversely, in bear markets downthrust days significantly outnumber upthrust days—see the July–September period in Figure 9.10. And, as should come as no surprise, in sideways markets, upthrust and downthrust days tend to be in rough balance—for example, the March to mid-April period in Figure 9.9 and the October–November period in Figure 9.10.

Run Days

A run day is a strongly trending day. Essentially, a run day is a more powerful version of a thrust day (although it is possible for a run day to fail to meet the thrust day condition). Run days are defined as follows:

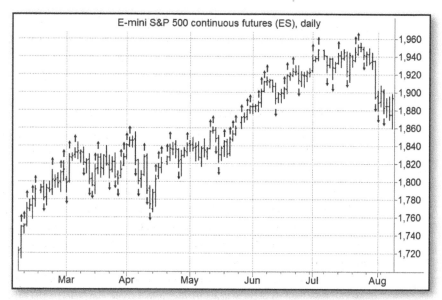

FIGURE 9.9 Upthrust and Downthrust Days in Bull Market: E-Mini S&P 500 Continuous Futures

Note: ↑ = upthrust day; ↓ = downthrust day.

Chart created using TradeStation. ©TradeStation Technologies, Inc. All rights reserved.

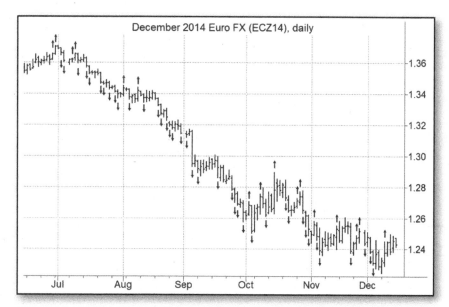

FIGURE 9.10 Upthrust and Downthrust Days in Bear Market: December 2014 Euro

Note: ↑ = upthrust day; ↓ = downthrust day.

Chart created using TradeStation. ©TradeStation Technologies, Inc. All rights reserved.

Up run day. A day that meets the following two conditions:

1. The true high of the run day is greater than the maximum true high of the past N days (e.g., N = 5).
2. The true low on the run day is less than the minimum true low on the subsequent N days.

Down run day. A day that meets the following two conditions:

1. The true low of the run day is less than the minimum true low of the past N days.
2. The true high on the run day is greater than the maximum true high on the subsequent N days.

As can be seen by these definitions, run days cannot be defined until N days after their occurrence. Also, note that although most run days are also thrust days, it is possible for the run day conditions to be met on a day that is not a thrust day. For example, it is entirely possible for a day's low to be lower than the past five-day low, its high to be higher than the subsequent five-day high, and its close to be *higher* than the previous day's low.

Figures 9.11 and 9.12 provide examples of run days (based on a definition of N = 5). As these charts show, run days tend to occur when a market is in a trend run—hence the name. The materialization of up run days, particularly in clusters, can be viewed as evidence the market is in a bullish phase (see Figure 9.11). Similarly, a predominance of down run days provides evidence the market is in a bearish state (see Figure 9.12). In Chapter 17, we use the concept of run days to construct trading systems.

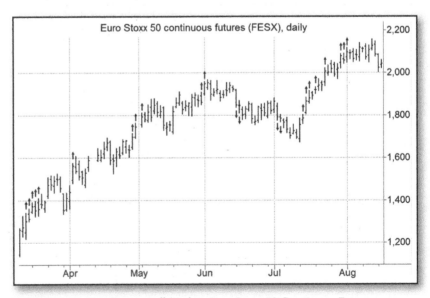

FIGURE 9.11 Run Days in Bull Market: Euro Stoxx 50 Continuous Futures
Note: ↑ up run day; ↓ down run day.
Chart created using TradeStation. ©TradeStation Technologies, Inc. All rights reserved.

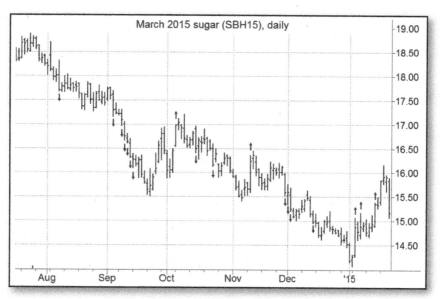

FIGURE 9.12 Run Days in Bear Market: March 2015 Sugar

Note: ↑ = up run day; ↓ = down run day.

Chart created using TradeStation. ©TradeStation Technologies, Inc. All rights reserved.

Note: Although the basic premise of thrust days and run days would apply to longer time frames, it does not hold on intraday charts. The closing prices of intraday bars—especially on very short time frames, such as one or two minutes—do not carry the same weight as the closing prices of daily and weekly bars, which mark the end of significant trading periods.

Wide-Ranging Days

A wide-ranging day is a day whose volatility significantly exceeds the average volatility of recent trading days. Wide-ranging days are defined as follows:

> **Wide-ranging day.** A day the *volatility ratio* (VR) is greater than k (e.g., $k = 2.0$). The VR is equal to today's true range divided by the average true range of the past N-day period (e.g., $N = 15$).

Wide-ranging days can have special significance. For example, a wide-ranging day with a strong close that materializes after an extended decline often signals an upside trend reversal. Similarly, a wide-ranging day with a weak close that occurs after an extended advance can signal a downside reversal. In Figure 9.13, strong-closing wide-ranging days marked the reversals of two downswings in euro futures. (Note that although the back-to-back wide-ranging days in July did not close in the upper reaches of their respective ranges, both closed near or above the previous days' highs.) Figure 9.14 features two sets of consecutive weak-closing wide-ranging days that

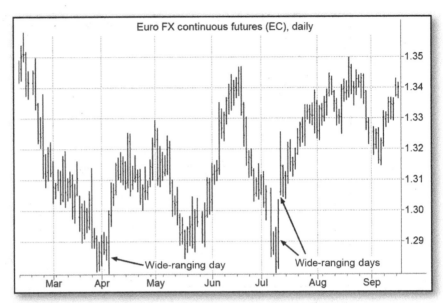

FIGURE 9.13 Wide-Ranging Up Days: Euro Continuous Futures

FIGURE 9.14 Wide-Ranging Down Days: Silver Continuous Futures

ended rallies in silver in dramatic fashion. The weekly chart inset shows these events marked the effective end of the market's longer-term uptrend, ushering in an extended period of sideways-to-lower price action.

Figures 9.15 and 9.16 highlight days that satisfy the previously described example of wide-ranging day criteria: The true range of each wide-ranging day is greater than twice the average true range of the preceding 15 days. In Figure 9.15, the first of these days, a weak-closing wide-ranging day in May 2012 marked the definitive end of a WTI crude oil rally following the consolidation that had formed near the market highs. The second downside wide-ranging day had no special significance, as it formed after a large decline had already occurred. The third (strong-closing) wide-ranging day signaled a major market reversal to the upside.

In Figure 9.16 there are four wide-ranging days, the first three of which were the start of major trend reversals; the fourth failed to witness any follow-through price action. However, there is an important caveat: The "wide-ranging day" in early May, which signaled a reversal near the market top, did not, in fact, strictly meet the wide-ranging day criteria based on the parameters we used as an example (2.0 multiple and 15 days)—its true range was only 1.94 times the size of the 15-day average true range. Had we instead chosen a multiple of 1.9 instead of 2.0 to define wide-ranging days, this day would have represented a wide-ranging day without any qualification. There is nothing special about the parameter values of 2.0 and 15 days chosen in our example. Moderate shifts of these values up or down would still preserve the spirit of the wide-ranging day, as was indeed the case with the early May wide-ranging day, which had a larger-than-normal range with a very weak close following a major uptrend. There is a trade-off in choosing the parameter value for the multiple: The lower the multiple chosen to define wide-ranging days, the greater the probability of capturing valid wide-ranging day reversal signals, but the greater the chance of identifying wide-ranging days that are meaningless. In this context, it may make sense for a trader to use more than one set of parameter values to define wide-ranging days to be aware of days that just miss the selected definition. Of course, days defined by higher multiples would carry greater weight.

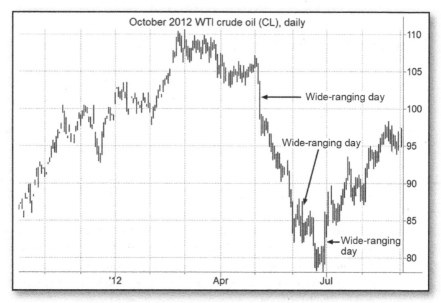

FIGURE 9.15 Wide-Ranging Up and Down Days: October 2012 WTI Crude Oil
Chart created using TradeStation. ©TradeStation Technologies, Inc. All rights reserved.

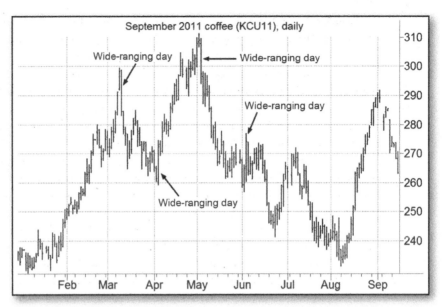

FIGURE 9.16 Wide-Ranging Up and Down Days: September 2011 Coffee
Chart created using TradeStation. ©TradeStation Technologies, Inc. All rights reserved.`

Figures 9.17 and 9.18 show instances of wide-ranging bars on different timeframes. The wide-ranging weeks in Figure 9.17 marked the beginning of an uptrend in Japanese yen futures that extended into early 2012, as shown in the monthly chart inset. In Figure 9.18 the weak-closing wide-ranging hourly bar reversed a seven-day advance. In Chapter 17, we will use the concept of wide-ranging days as the primary element in constructing a sample trading system.

■ Continuation Patterns

Continuation patterns are various types of congestion phases that materialize within long-term trends. As the name implies, a continuation pattern is expected to be resolved by a price swing in the same direction that preceded its formation.

Triangles

There are three basic types of triangle patterns: symmetrical (see Figures 9.19 through 9.21), ascending (Figures 9.22 and 9.23), and descending (Figures 9.24 and 9.25). A symmetrical triangle is usually followed by a continuation of the trend that preceded it, as in Figures 9.19 through 9.21. Conventional chart wisdom suggests that nonsymmetrical triangles will yield to a trend in the direction of the slope of the hypotenuse, as is the case in Figures 9.22 through 9.25. However, the direction of the breakout from a triangle formation is more important than the type. For example, in Figure 9.26, although the two congestion patterns are descending triangles—and the second is preceded by a price decline—both break out to the upside and are followed by rallies.

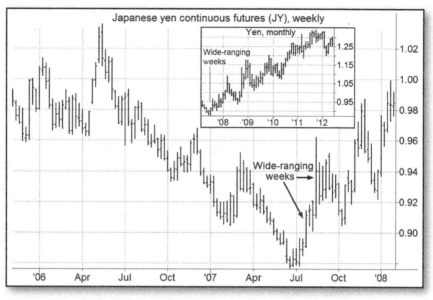

FIGURE 9.17 Wide-Ranging Up Weeks: Japanese Yen Continuous Futures
Chart created using TradeStation. ©TradeStation Technologies, Inc. All rights reserved.

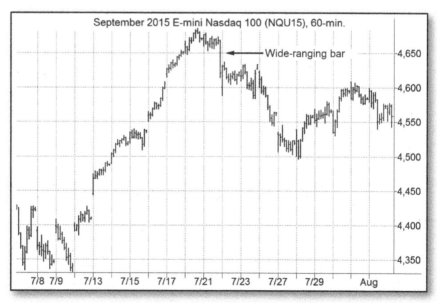

FIGURE 9.18 Wide-Ranging Down Bar: September 2015 E-Mini Nasdaq 100 Futures
Chart created using TradeStation. ©TradeStation Technologies, Inc. All rights reserved.

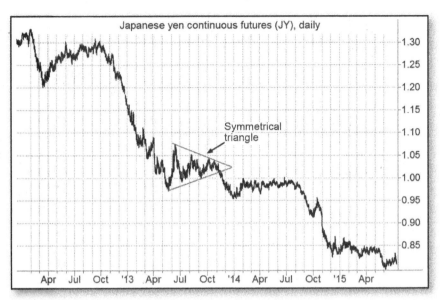

FIGURE 9.19 Symmetrical Triangle: Japanese Yen Continuous Futures
Chart created using TradeStation. ©TradeStation Technologies, Inc. All rights reserved.

FIGURE 9.20 Symmetrical Triangle: March 2015 DAX
Chart created using TradeStation. ©TradeStation Technologies, Inc. All rights reserved.

FIGURE 9.21 Symmetrical Triangle: Copper Continuous Futures

Chart created using TradeStation. ©TradeStation Technologies, Inc. All rights reserved.

FIGURE 9.22 Ascending Triangle: Euro Stoxx 50 Continuous Futures

Chart created using TradeStation. ©TradeStation Technologies, Inc. All rights reserved.

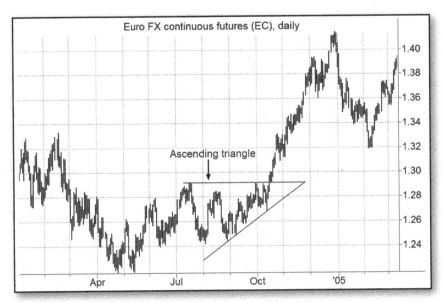

FIGURE 9.23 Ascending Triangle: Euro Continuous Futures

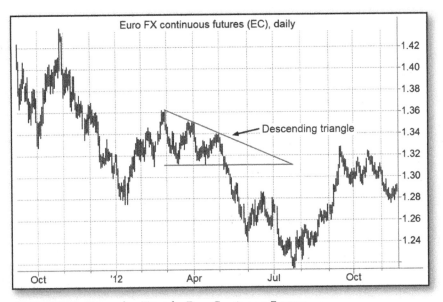

FIGURE 9.24 Descending Triangle: Euro Continuous Futures

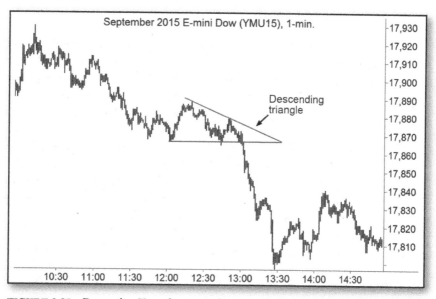

FIGURE 9.25 Descending Triangle: September 2015 E-Mini Dow

Chart created using TradeStation. ©TradeStation Technologies, Inc. All rights reserved.

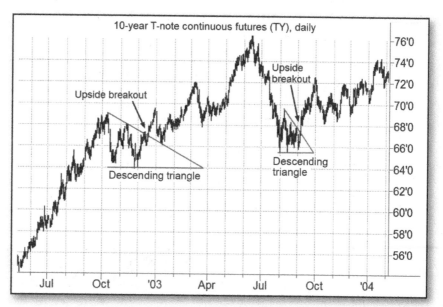

FIGURE 9.26 Descending Triangles with Upside Breakouts: 10-Year T-Note Continuous Futures

Chart created using TradeStation. ©TradeStation Technologies, Inc. All rights reserved.

Flags and Pennants

Flags and pennants are narrow-band, short-duration (e.g., one to three weeks) congestion phases within trends. The formation is called a flag when it is enclosed by parallel lines and a pennant when the lines converge. Figures 9.27 through 9.31 illustrate both types of patterns. Figure 9.29 shows flags forming on a weekly chart, while Figure 9.30 shows flags and pennants on an intraday chart.

Pennants may appear to be similar to triangles, but they differ in terms of time: the triangle has a longer duration. Similarly, the difference between a horizontal flag and a trading range is a matter of duration. Among the many flags and pennants in Figure 9.27, for example, there are two congestion patterns (in August–September 2011 and January–February 2012) that could be classified as either long flags or pennants or short trading ranges or triangles. Regardless of which name these patterns are given, their implication is the same: flags and pennants typically represent pauses in a major trend. In other words, these patterns are usually followed by price swings in the same direction as the price swings that preceded their formation.

A breakout from a flag or pennant can be viewed as a confirmation the trend is continuing and a trading signal in the direction of the trend. Since breakouts are usually in the direction of the main trend, however, I prefer to enter positions during the formation of the flag or pennant, anticipating the probable direction of the breakout. This approach allows for more advantageous trade entries, without a significant deterioration in the percentage of correct trades, since reversals following breakouts from flags and pennants are about as common as breakouts in the counter-to-anticipated direction. Following a breakout from a flag or pennant, the opposite extreme of the formation can be used as an approximate stop-loss point.

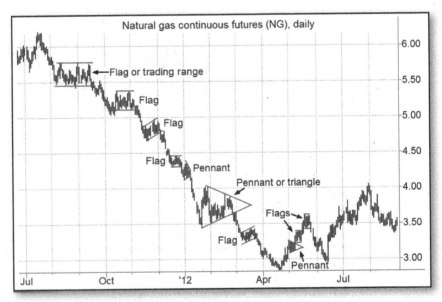

FIGURE 9.27 Flags and Pennants: Natural Gas Continuous Futures

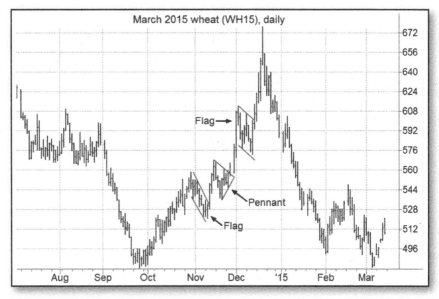

FIGURE 9.28 Flags and Pennants: March 2015 Wheat
Chart created using TradeStation. ©TradeStation Technologies, Inc. All rights reserved.

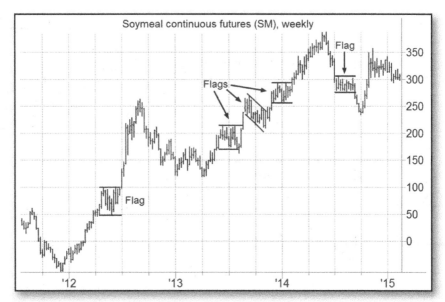

FIGURE 9.29 Flags and Pennants: Soymeal Continuous Futures
Chart created using TradeStation. ©TradeStation Technologies, Inc. All rights reserved.

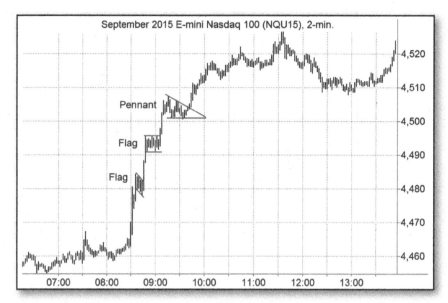

FIGURE 9.30 Flags and Pennants: September E-Mini Nasdaq 100

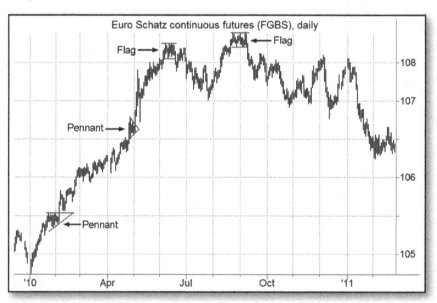

FIGURE 9.31 Flags and Pennants: Euro Schatz Continuous Futures

A significant penetration of a flag or pennant in the opposite-to-anticipated direction—that is, counter to the main trend—can be viewed as a signal of a potential trend reversal. For example, in Figure 9.31 note that after a strong rally that included pennant breakouts in the direction of the main trend, downside breakouts from the two flags that formed in June and August–September marked short-term and longer-term highs.

Flags and pennants typically point in the opposite direction of the main trend. This characteristic is exhibited by the majority of flags and pennants illustrated in Figures 9.27 through 9.31. The direction in which a flag or pennant points, however, is not an important consideration. In my experience, I have not found any significant difference in reliability between flags and pennants that point in the same direction as the main trend as opposed to the more usual opposite slope.

Flags or pennants that form near the top or just above a trading range can be particularly potent bullish signals. In the case where a flag or pennant forms near the top of a trading range, it indicates that the market is not backing off despite having reached a major resistance area—the top of the range. Such price action has bullish implications and suggests that the market is gathering strength for an eventual upside breakout. In the case where the flag or pennant forms above the trading range, it indicates that prices are holding above a breakout point, thereby lending strong confirmation to the breakout. Generally speaking, the more extended the trading range, the greater the potential significance of a flag or pennant that forms near or above its top. Figures 9.32 through 9.34 provide examples of flags or pennants that materialized near the top or above trading ranges and proved to be precursors of price advances.

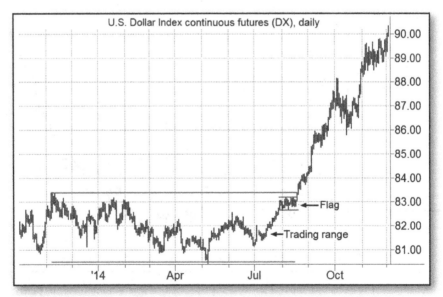

FIGURE 9.32 Flag Near Top of Trading Range as Bullish Signal: U.S. Dollar Index Continuous Futures
Chart created using TradeStation. ©TradeStation Technologies, Inc. All rights reserved.

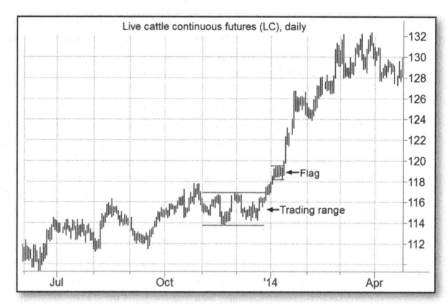

FIGURE 9.33 Flag Above Top of Trading Range as Bullish Signal: Live Cattle Continuous Futures

Chart created using TradeStation. ©TradeStation Technologies, Inc. All rights reserved.

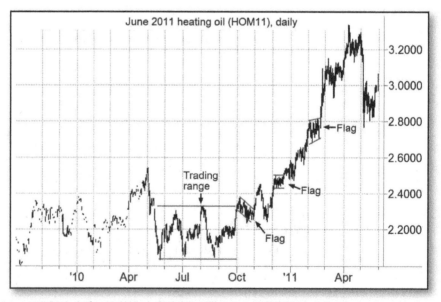

FIGURE 9.34 Flag Near Top of Trading Range as Bullish Signal: June 2011 Heating Oil

Chart created using TradeStation. ©TradeStation Technologies, Inc. All rights reserved.

For similar reasons, flags or pennants that form near the bottom or just below trading ranges are particularly bearish patterns. Figures 9.35 through 9.37 provide examples of flags or pennants that materialized near the bottom or below trading ranges and proved to be harbingers of price declines.

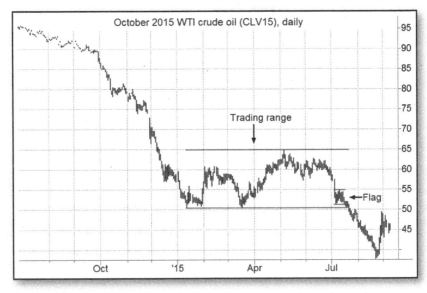

FIGURE 9.35 Flag Near Bottom of Trading Range as Bearish Signal: October 2015 WTI Crude Oil

Chart created using TradeStation. ©TradeStation Technologies, Inc. All rights reserved.

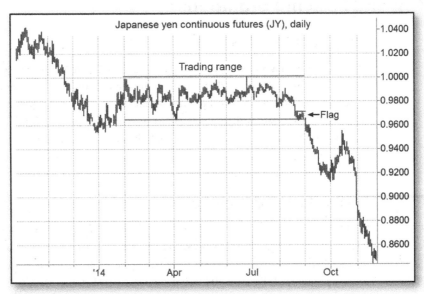

FIGURE 9.36 Flag Near Bottom of Trading Range as Bearish Signal: Japanese Yen Continuous Futures

Chart created using TradeStation. ©TradeStation Technologies, Inc. All rights reserved.

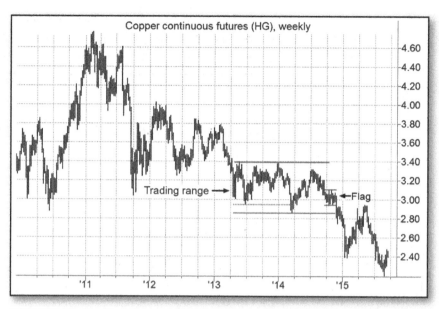

FIGURE 9.37 Flag Near Bottom of Trading Range as Bearish Signal: Copper Continuous Futures

Chart created using TradeStation. ©TradeStation Technologies, Inc. All rights reserved.

■ Top and Bottom Formations

V Tops and Bottoms

The "V" formation is a turn-on-a-dime type of top (see Figure 9.38) or bottom (see Figure 9.39). One problem with a V top or bottom is that it is frequently difficult to distinguish from a sharp correction unless accompanied by other technical indicators (e.g., prominent spike, significant reversal day, wide gap, wide-ranging day). The V top in Figure 9.38 did contain such a clue—a spike day—whereas the V bottom in Figure 9.39 was unaccompanied by any other evidence of a trend reversal.

Double Tops and Bottoms

Double tops and bottoms are exactly what their names imply. Of course, the two tops (or bottoms) that make up the pattern need not be exactly the same, only in the same general price vicinity. Double tops and bottoms that materialize after large price moves should be viewed as strong indicators of a major trend reversal. Figure 9.40 illustrates a major double top in weekly Euro Bobl futures, while Figure 9.41 shows a double top on the daily chart for Canadian dollar futures. (Continuous futures are used for most of the charts illustrating double tops and bottoms because the liquid trading period for most individual contracts is usually not long enough to display the time span encompassing these

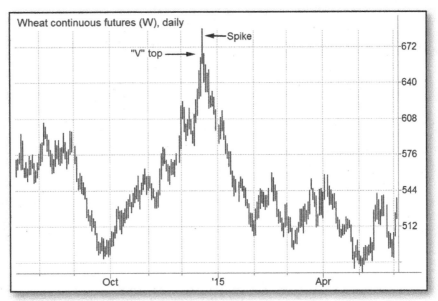

FIGURE 9.38 "V" Top: Wheat Continuous Futures
Chart created using TradeStation. ©TradeStation Technologies, Inc. All rights reserved.

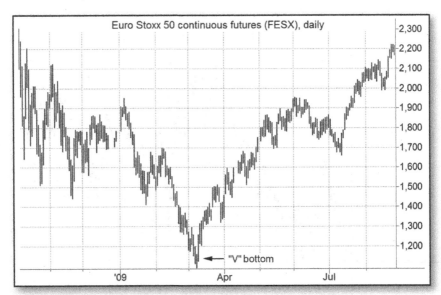

FIGURE 9.39 "V" Bottom: Euro Stoxx 50 Continuous Futures
Chart created using TradeStation. ©TradeStation Technologies, Inc. All rights reserved.

patterns and the preceding and succeeding trends.) Figure 9.42 shows a major double bottom in the E-mini Nasdaq 100 futures. Figure 9.43 depicts a double bottom on a two-minute chart: In this case the pattern preceded an explosive upmove (nearly 1 percent in less than an hour) in the June 2015 Mini Russell 2000 futures.

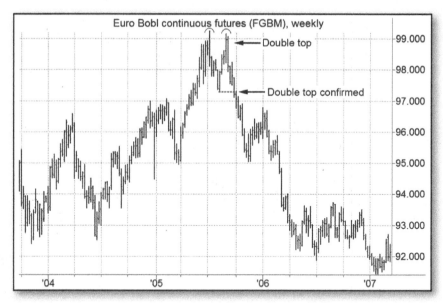

FIGURE 9.40 Double Top: Euro Bobl Weekly Continuous Futures
Chart created using TradeStation. ©TradeStation Technologies, Inc. All rights reserved.

FIGURE 9.41 Double Top: Canadian Dollar Continuous Futures
Chart created using TradeStation. ©TradeStation Technologies, Inc. All rights reserved.

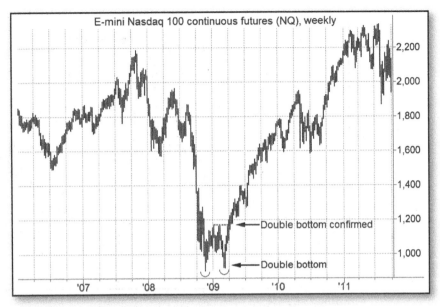

FIGURE 9.42 Double Bottom: E-Mini Nasdaq 100 Continuous Futures

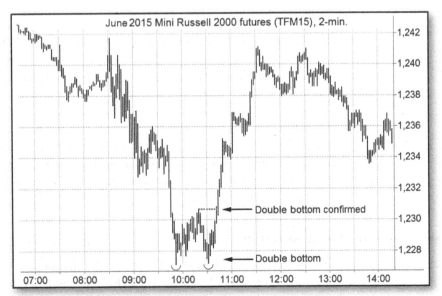

FIGURE 9.43 Double Bottom: June 2015 Mini Russell 2000 Futures

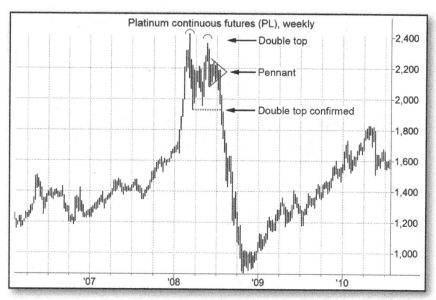

FIGURE 9.44 Double Top: Platinum Continuous Futures

Chart created using TradeStation. ©TradeStation Technologies, Inc. All rights reserved.

As illustrated in Figures 9.40 through 9.43, a double top (bottom) is considered completed when prices move below (above) the reaction low (high) between the two tops (bottoms) of the formation. When the intervening reaction is relatively deep, as for example in Figure 9.44, it is impractical to wait for such an "official" confirmation, and a trader may have to anticipate that the pattern has formed based on other evidence. For example, in Figure 9.44, the confirmation of the double top did not occur until the market had dropped nearly 20 percent from the May 2008 high (the second peak of the double top). However, the pennant pattern that formed after the initial downswing from that high implied the next price swing would also be down. Based on this clue, a trader could have reasonably concluded a double top was in place, even though the pattern had not yet been completed according to the standard definition. Top and bottom formations with more repetitions (e.g., triple top or bottom) occur rather infrequently but would be interpreted in the same fashion. Figure 9.45 shows a triple top in weekly DAX futures.

Head and Shoulders

The head-and-shoulders pattern is one of the best-known chart formations. The head-and-shoulders top is a three-part formation in which the middle high is above the high points on either side (see Figure 9.46). Similarly, the head-and-shoulders bottom is a three-part formation in which the middle low is below the low point on either side (see Figures 9.47 and 9.48). Perhaps one of the most common mistakes made by novice chartists is the premature anticipation of the head-and-shoulders formation. The head-and-shoulders pattern is not considered complete until the neckline—a line

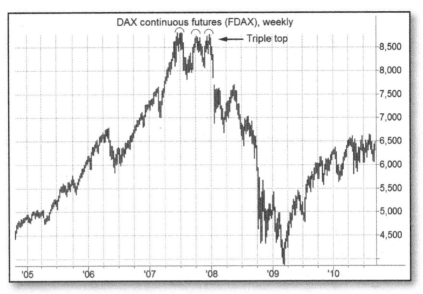

FIGURE 9.45 Triple Top: DAX Continuous Futures

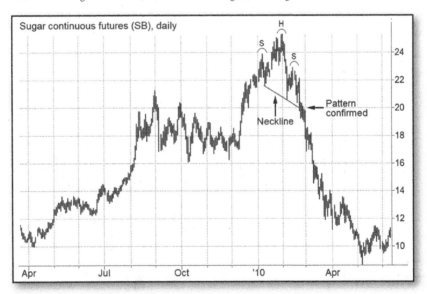

FIGURE 9.46 Head-and-Shoulders Top: Sugar Continuous Futures

connecting the reaction lows or highs separating the shoulders from the head—is penetrated, as illustrated in these charts. Furthermore, a valid head-and-shoulders pattern is formed only after a major price move has occurred. Patterns that bear the shape of a head-and-shoulders formation but lack this requirement can be misleading.

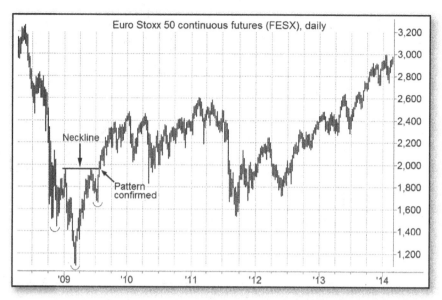

FIGURE 9.47   Head-and-Shoulders Bottom: Euro Stoxx 50 Continuous Futures
Chart created using TradeStation. ©TradeStation Technologies, Inc. All rights reserved.

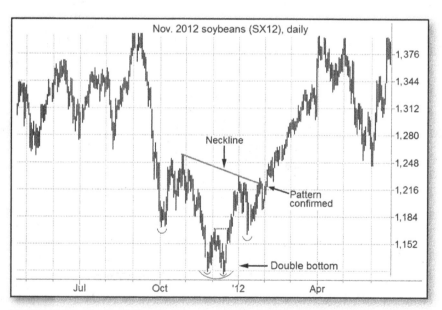

FIGURE 9.48   Head-and-Shoulders Bottom: November 2012 Soybeans
Chart created using TradeStation. ©TradeStation Technologies, Inc. All rights reserved.

Figure 9.48 is noteworthy in that the "head" of the head-and-shoulders bottom consists of twin lows that constitute a double bottom, a pattern that would have been confirmed when price traded above the early December high (short dashed line), as discussed in the previous section. The penetration of the head-and-shoulders neckline occurred approximately six weeks later.

Sometimes the distinction between a head-and-shoulders pattern and a triple top (or bottom) pattern is not clear-cut. For example, Figure 9.49 shows a major long-term top in the U.S. Dollar Index futures in which the ultimate high has slightly lower highs on either side. This formation could reasonably be categorized as either pattern—regardless, its implication as a top pattern is the same.

Rounding Tops and Bottoms

Rounding tops and bottoms (also called *saucers*) occur somewhat infrequently, but are among the most reliable top and bottom formations. Figure 9.50 shows a Nikkei 225 continuous futures chart with a rounding top that formed at the apex of a multiyear high and was followed by a sharp sell-off. Ideally, the pattern would not contain any "jags," as this chart does (e.g., the sharply lower low in late June); however, I consider the main criterion to be whether the outer perimeter conforms to a rounding shape. Figure 9.51 depicts a rounding top pattern that formed a major peak in soybean continuous futures in 2014. Although the late-April to early-May price dip prevented a perfect rounding top pattern, the outer boundary of the March–May price action conformed well to a rounding pattern.

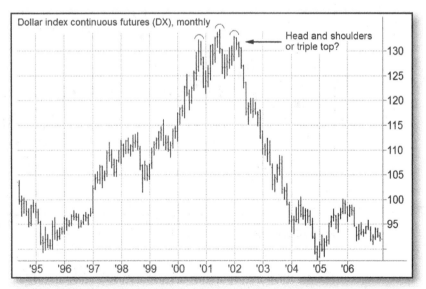

FIGURE 9.49 Head-and-Shoulders or Triple Top? Dollar Index Continuous Futures

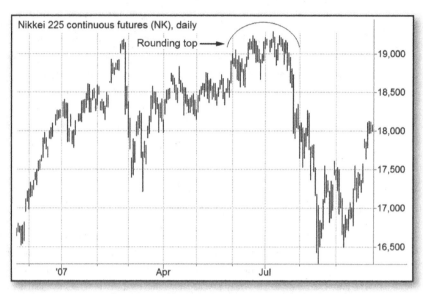

FIGURE 9.50   Rounding Top: Nikkei 225 Continuous Futures

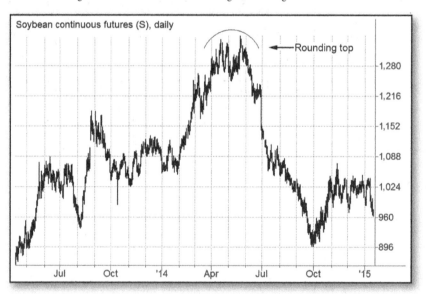

FIGURE 9.51   Rounding Top: Soybean Continuous Futures

Figure 9.52 provides a textbook instance of a rounding bottom pattern in lean hog continuous futures. Notice that in this example the price action during the bottoming process was relatively smooth and mostly free of the occasional jagged moves that were present in the previous examples. This rounding bottom was followed by an explosive upmove that began in mid-February 2014. Figure 9.53 shows a briefer rounding bottom in the Swiss franc that marked the transition from a downturn to an uptrend.

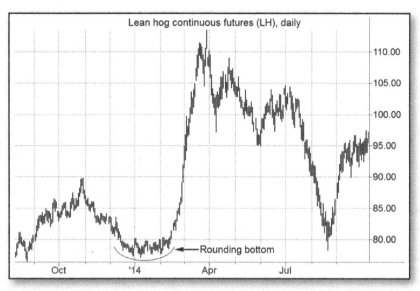

FIGURE 9.52 Rounding Bottom: Lean Hog Continuous Futures

Chart created using TradeStation. ©TradeStation Technologies, Inc. All rights reserved.

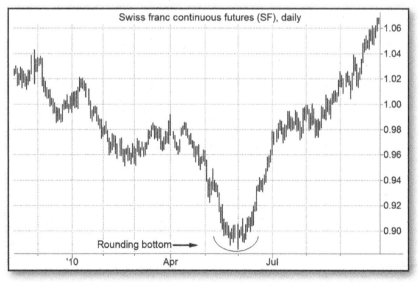

FIGURE 9.53 Rounding Bottom: Swiss Franc Continuous Futures

Chart created using TradeStation. ©TradeStation Technologies, Inc. All rights reserved.

Triangles

Triangles, which are among the most common continuation patterns, can be top and bottom formations as well. Figures 9.54 through 9.57 illustrate triangle tops and bottoms. As in the case of the continuation pattern, the key consideration is the direction of the breakout from the triangle.

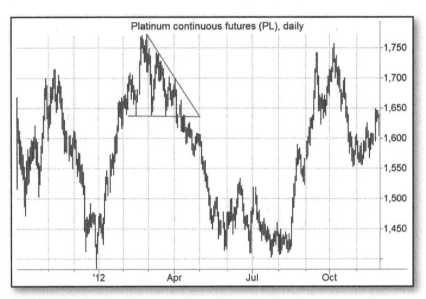

FIGURE 9.54 Triangle Top: Platinum Continuous Futures
Chart created using TradeStation. ©TradeStation Technologies, Inc. All rights reserved.

FIGURE 9.55 Triangle Top: Orange Juice Continuous Futures
Chart created using TradeStation. ©TradeStation Technologies, Inc. All rights reserved.

FIGURE 9.56 Triangle Bottom: DAX Continuous Futures

Chart created using TradeStation. ©TradeStation Technologies, Inc. All rights reserved.

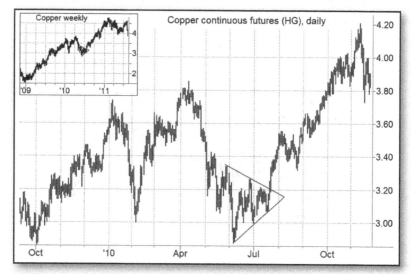

FIGURE 9.57 Triangle Bottom: Copper Continuous Futures

Chart created using TradeStation. ©TradeStation Technologies, Inc. All rights reserved.

The tops in Figures 9.54 and 9.55 took the form of large descending triangles. The downside breakouts out of both patterns were followed by energetic sell-offs. (Notice also in Figure 9.55 the two flags that formed during the March–May downtrend that followed the penetration of the triangle's lower boundary. Each would have given traders who missed the initial breakout a chance to capture at least some of the downmove.) Figure 9.56 shows a triangle bottom in DAX continuous futures that was followed by a major uptrend. The symmetrical triangle bottom that formed on the daily copper chart in 2010 (Figure 9.57) is shown in the weekly inset to be part of a correction in the market's longer-term uptrend.

Major tops and bottoms may often be consistent with more than one type of pattern. For example, a case could have been made for defining the preceding triangular tops and bottoms as head-and-shoulders formations with, generally speaking, similar pattern confirmation points.

Wedge

In a rising wedge, prices edge steadily higher in a converging pattern (see Figure 9.58). In instances when the successive highs form in a relative tight band, as they do here, the inability of prices to accelerate on the upside, despite continued probes into new high ground, suggests the existence of strong scale-up selling pressure. A sell signal occurs when prices break below the lower wedge line. Figure 9.59 provides an example of a declining wedge. Wedge patterns can sometimes take an extremely long time to complete. The wedge in Figure 9.59 formed over the course of a year, and even longer-term wedges have been known to occur.

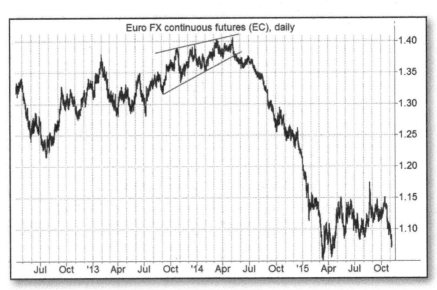

FIGURE 9.58   Rising Wedge: Euro Continuous Futures
Chart created using TradeStation. ©TradeStation Technologies, Inc. All rights reserved.

FIGURE 9.59 Declining Wedge: Sugar Continuous Futures
Chart created using TradeStation. ©TradeStation Technologies, Inc. All rights reserved.

Spikes and Reversal Days

These one-day patterns, which often mark relative highs and relative lows, and sometimes major peaks and bottoms, were discussed in an earlier section of this chapter.

CHAPTER 10

Is Chart Analysis Still Valid?

I always laugh at people who say, "I've never met a rich technician." I love that! It is such an arrogant, nonsensical response. I used fundamentals for nine years and got rich as a technician.

—Marty Schwartz

Most traders who have never used chart analysis (and even some who have) are quite skeptical about this approach. Some of the commonly raised objections include: "How can such a simple analytical approach work?" "Since key chart points are hardly a secret, won't large professional traders sometimes push the market enough to trigger chart stops artificially?" "Even if chart analysis worked before it was detailed in scores of websites, books, and magazines, isn't the method too well publicized to still be effective?"

Although the points raised by these questions are basically valid, a number of factors explain why chart analysis remains an effective trading approach:

1. Trading success does not depend on being right more than half the time—or, for that matter, even half the time—as long as losses are rigidly controlled and profitable trades are permitted to run their course. For example, consider a trader who in March 1991 assumed that September 1992 eurodollars had entered another trading range (see Figure 10.1) and decided to trade in the direction of any subsequent closing breakout. Figure 10.2 shows the initial trade signals and liquidation points that would have been realized as a result of this strategy. The implicit assumption is that stops are placed at the midpoint of the trading range. (The relevant considerations in choosing a stop point are discussed in detail in Chapter 13.) As can be seen in Figure 10.2, the first two trades would have resulted in immediate losses. Figure 10.3, however, shows the third signal was the real thing—a long position that would have occurred in time to benefit from a major price advance that far exceeded the combined price swings on the prior two adverse trades. (Note the relevant trading range is redefined— that is, widened—after each of the false breakouts.)

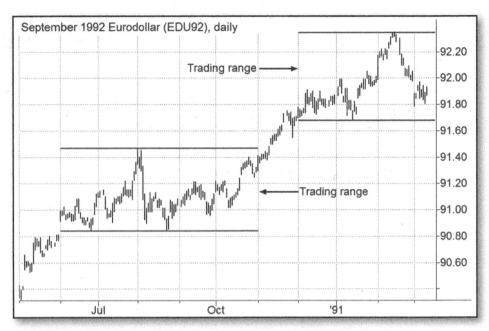

FIGURE 10.1   Trading Range Market: September 1992 Eurodollar
Chart created using TradeStation. ©TradeStation Technologies, Inc. All rights reserved.

It is noteworthy that although two out of three trades were losers, on balance the trader would have realized a large net profit. The key point is that a disciplined adherence to money management principles is an essential ingredient in the successful application of chart analysis.

2. Chart analysis can be made much more effective by requiring confirmation conditions for trade entry, rather than blindly following all technical signals. There is a natural trade-off in the choice of confirmation rules: the less restrictive the conditions, the greater the number of false signals; the more restrictive the conditions, the greater the potential surrendered profit due to late entry. Some of the key methods that can be used to construct confirmation conditions might include the following: time delays, minimum percent penetration, and specific chart patterns (e.g., the trade must be confirmed by two subsequent thrust days in the direction of the signal).

There is no such thing as a best set of confirmation conditions. In any list of tested alternatives, the indicated best strategy will vary from market to market as well as over time. Thus, the ultimate choice of confirmation rules will depend on the trader's analysis and experience. In fact, the specific choice of confirmation conditions is one of the pivotal ways in which chart analysis is individualized.

As an illustration of how confirmation conditions might be used, consider the following set of rules:

a.   Wait three days after signal is received.

b.   For a buy signal, enter trade if the close is above the high since signal was received, or on the first subsequent day fulfilling this condition. An analogous condition would apply to sell signals.

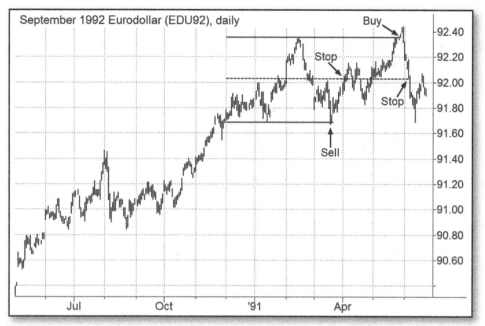

FIGURE 10.2 False Breakout Signals: September 1992 Eurodollar

Chart created using TradeStation. ©TradeStation Technologies, Inc. All rights reserved.

As can be seen in Figure 10.2, these rules would have filtered out the losing March and May signals while only modestly delaying the entry point for the subsequent highly profitable buy signal. Of course, one could also construct examples in which the use of confirmation conditions is detrimental to the trading results. However, the key point is that the use of confirmation rules is one of the primary means of transforming classical chart concepts into a more powerful trading approach.

3. Chart analysis is more than just the recognition and interpretation of individual patterns. One of the earmarks of the successful chart trader is an ability to synthesize the various components of the overall picture. For example, the trader who recognizes just a trading range in September 1992 Eurodollars (see Figure 10.1) would treat upside and downside breakouts equivalently. However, the more experienced chartist will also consider the broader picture. For example, by examining the long-term weekly continuous futures chart in early 1991 (see Figure 10.4), the analyst could have noted that the market had just formed a flag pattern near the top of a five-year trading range. This extremely bullish long-term chart picture would have strongly cautioned against accepting any apparent sell signals on the daily chart. Such a more comprehensive chart analysis could therefore have helped the analyst avert the false sell signal in March (see Figure 10.2) and adopt a much more aggressive trading stance from the long side than would have been warranted if the situation were viewed as just another trading range.

Figures 10.5 and 10.6 illustrate a similar example in June 2012 natural gas futures. In early 2011 a trader who decided to trade in the direction of a breakout of the October 2010–January 2011 trading range (again, assuming a stop point in the middle of the range) would have

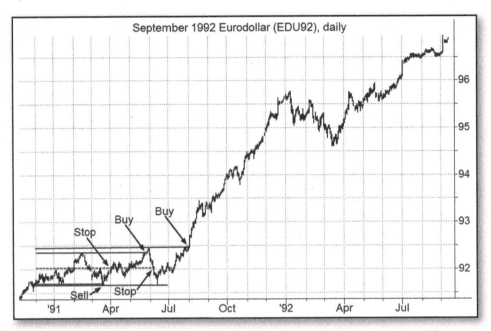

FIGURE 10.3 Winning Breakout Signal after Two False Signals: September 1992 Eurodollar
Chart created using TradeStation. ©TradeStation Technologies, Inc. All rights reserved.

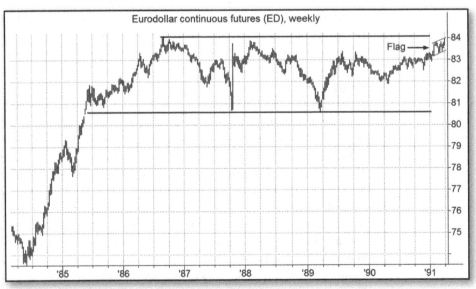

FIGURE 10.4 Long-Term Chart as Part of Comprehensive Analysis: Eurodollar Continuous Futures
Chart created using TradeStation. ©TradeStation Technologies, Inc. All rights reserved.

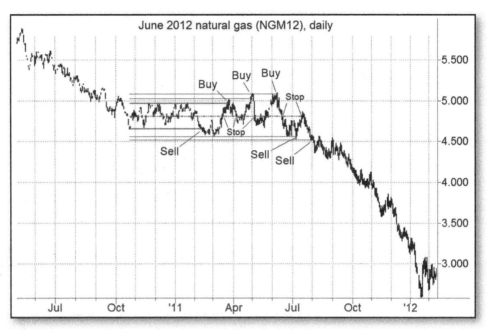

FIGURE 10.5 False and Winning Breakout Signals: June 2012 Natural Gas Futures
Chart created using TradeStation. ©TradeStation Technologies, Inc. All rights reserved.

experienced five losing trades (three buys and two sells) before the August 2011 sell signal that was followed by an extended downmove. The context provided by the weekly chart (Figure 10.6), however, suggests a trader who was aware of the longer-term downtrend that preceded the consolidation could have reasonably chosen to ignore upside breakouts and focus exclusively on downside breakouts in expectation of a continuation of that trend.

Of course, the preceding examples benefit from hindsight. However, the point is not to prove the application of chart analysis would have conclusively indicated the probable continuation of a long-term bull market in eurodollar futures in early 1991 or the likely perpetuation of the extended downtrend in natural gas futures in 2011, but rather to illustrate the multifaceted analytical process of the experienced chart trader. It should be clear that the skill and subjectivity implied in this approach place chart analysis in the realm of an art that cannot be mimicked by merely following a set of textbook rules. This is a crucial point in understanding how the chartist approach can remain valid despite widespread publicity.

4. Assuming some skill in fundamental forecasting (i.e., a better than 50/50 accuracy rate), chart analysis can be combined with fundamental projections *to provide a more effective approach.* Specifically, if the long-term fundamental forecast indicates the probability of much higher (lower) prices, only bullish (bearish) chart signals would be accepted. If the fundamental projection was neutral, both buy and sell signals would be accepted. Thus, the chart analyst who is also a competent fundamental analyst would have a decided edge over the majority of traders basing their trading decisions solely on chart-oriented input.

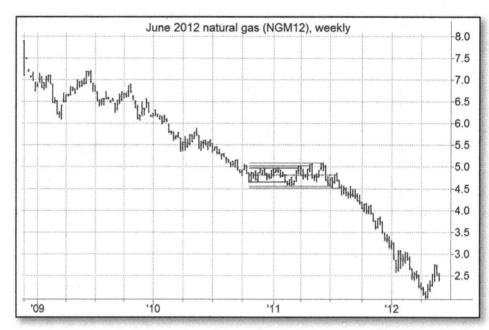

FIGURE 10.6 Long-Term Chart as Part of Comprehensive Analysis: June 2012 Weekly Natural Gas Futures

Chart created using TradeStation. ©TradeStation Technologies, Inc. All rights reserved.

5. The failure of a market to follow through in the direction of a key chart signal is a crucial item of information often overlooked by novice chartists. Recognizing and acting on these situations can greatly enhance the effectiveness of the chartist approach. This subject is discussed in detail in Chapter 15.

In conclusion, the skeptics are probably correct in claiming that a Pavlovian response to chart signals will not lead to trading success. However, this assertion in no way contradicts the contention that a more sophisticated utilization of charts, as suggested by the cited factors, can indeed provide the core of an effective trading plan. In any case, chart analysis remains a highly individualistic approach, with success or failure critically dependent on the trader's skill and experience. It would be unreasonable to expect to play the violin well without some degree of practice and innate talent. Chart analysis is no different—the sour notes of novice practitioners notwithstanding.

CHAPTER 11

Technical Indicators

Any intelligent fool can make things bigger, more complex, and more violent. It takes a touch of genius—and a lot of courage to move in the opposite direction.

— Ernst F. Schumacher

■ What Is an Indicator?

Technical indicators are mathematical formulas based on market data—most often prices, but also occasionally volume and open interest. (In the equity market, other data, such as the number of advancing or declining issues, are sometimes incorporated in these calculations.) The implicit goal of most technical indicators is to signal potential changes in market direction that might not be apparent through direct price analysis or fundamental analysis. The implicit *assumption* underlying this approach is that indicators extract or distill useful forecasting information from market data.

Most indicators attempt to translate price action into directional signals in one of two ways:

1. Comparing current price levels to past price levels to determine the prevailing direction and magnitude of price change.
2. Using a smoothing function, such as a moving average, to filter out what are deemed to be random fluctuations ("noise"), thus revealing a market's prevailing trend.

There are any number of ways to accomplish either of these goals, or to combine them. Consider the simple case of comparing today's closing price with the most recent 20 days of price action to determine how much price has changed and whether the close is relatively strong or weak. The following are only some of the possible approaches:

1. Calculate the difference between the current close and the close 20 days ago.
2. Calculate the percentage change (ratio) of the current close and the close 20 days ago.

3. Determine the current closing price's position within the 20-day high-low range, or its position within the range of the highest and lowest closing prices of the past 20 days.
4. Measure how much the current closing price varies from the "typical" price of the past 20 days by comparing it (as either a difference or a ratio) to the average (or median) of the other closing prices during this period.
5. Alternatively, a shorter-term moving average (or median) value could be substituted for the closing price in the previous calculation, in which case the indicator would become the difference between (or ratio of), say, a 3-day moving average and the 20-day moving average.
6. Use a statistical measurement, such as percentile rank, to determine where the current close places among the 20 most recent closes, or within the 20-day range.
7. Rather than using the most recent closing price as the reference point, the direction and pace of price changes over the past 20 days could alternatively be measured by comparing the period's aggregate (or average) gains to its aggregate (or average) losses. One example: Divide the sum (or average) of the positive close-to-close changes over the past 20 days by the sum (or average) of the absolute negative close-to-close changes over the past 20 days.

All these calculations provide some gauge of how far, and in what direction, a market has moved over the past 20 days. Moreover, any of the foregoing indicators could be based on values other than 20, expanding the list of possible indicators by another dimension. If this list of possible indicators seems excessive (or redundant), peruse any trading website, app, or analysis platform, and you are likely to be confronted by dozens—sometimes in excess of 100—technical indicators, all purportedly designed to help interpret and forecast market activity. Grappling with the sheer number of indicators, and their often cryptic formulas and names, can be a daunting prospect for the new trader or analyst, who might understandably assume each of these tools has unique properties and specific purposes.

The truth, however, is that despite the wide array of indicators and the properties ascribed to them by various proponents and followers, the majority of these tools are based on a handful of basic mathematical formulas. In fact, variations and combinations of the previously listed seven calculations provide the basis for a surprisingly large percentage of the most widely referenced technical tools. One critical consequence of this observation is that there is a high degree of correlation among technical indicators, even if they might seem to be unrelated at a glance.

Rather than risking a descent down the rabbit hole of comparing the supposed applications and idiosyncrasies of dozens of technical indicators, the following discussion instead focuses on the basic types of calculations underlying these indicators and what they can and cannot convey about market behavior. The goal is to provide the reader with a logical foundation for objectively interpreting and analyzing technical indicators. In short, readers looking for answers to questions such as "What's the best technical indicator?" or "What are the best settings for indicator *xyz*?" or "Which indicators are best for trading currency (or grain, or stock index) futures?" should look elsewhere. These are, in fact, meaningless questions because they presuppose a degree of differentiation among indicators that does not exist and assume a stability in the performance of individual indicators that is unsupported by empirical evidence.

◼ The Basic Indicator Calculations

Most technical indicators incorporate one or more of the following five calculations:

1. A smoothing function, such as a moving average or moving median.
2. A comparison of the current data point to a specific past data point, as either a difference (e.g., today's close minus the close 10 days ago) or a ratio (today's close divided by the close 10 days ago).
3. A comparison of the current data point to an average (e.g., today's close minus the average close of the past 10 days).
4. A comparison of an average to another average of a different length (e.g., the 10-day moving average minus the 30-day moving average).
5. A comparison of the current data point to a past range (e.g., the difference between today's close and the lowest low of the past 10 days divided by the difference between the highest high of the past 10 days and the lowest low of the past 10 days).

Beyond the number of price bars used (the "look-back period"), these calculations allow for a great deal of variation without altering the basic characteristics of the indicator. For example, a smoothing function could take the form of a simple moving average, a weighted moving average, an exponential moving average, or an "adaptive average" that adjusts its length according to changes in market volatility. Moreover, any of these averages could be based on a bar's closing price, high, low, open, or midpoint.

◼ Comparing Indicators

Figures 11.1 through 11.5 illustrate the five types of indicator calculations defined in the previous section and highlight the relationships between them. For reference, we'll use the following shorthand to identify these formulas:

> **Indicator 1: MA** (moving average).
> **Indicator 2: Close – Close** (difference) or **Close/Close** (ratio).
> **Indicator 3: Close – MA** (difference between close and moving average) or **Close/MA** (ratio of close and moving average).
> **Indicator 4: MA – MA** (difference between two moving averages) or **MA/MA** (ratio of two moving averages).
> **Indicator 5: CS** (closing strength).

In all cases, subscripts are used to denote the look-back period—for example, "MA_{30}" refers to a 30-bar moving average, "$Close - Close_{10}$" refers to the difference between the current close and the close 10 bars ago, and so on.

In Figure 11.1, a daily price chart of WTI crude oil from August 2015 to May 2016 is overlaid with 10- and 30-day simple moving averages (thin and thick lines, respectively). The lower portion of the chart contains two indicators. The first is the difference between the most recent close and the close

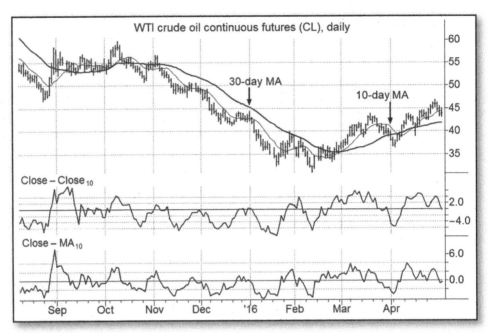

FIGURE 11.1 Difference Indicators: Close – Close vs. Close – MA

10 days earlier (Close – Close_{10}), while the second is the difference between the close and the 10-day moving average (Close – MA_{10}). Both calculations provide a snapshot of the price movement over the most recent 10 days—how much price has moved relative to each indicator's respective reference price. For the first indicator, positive values occur when the current close is above the close 10 days ago; negative values occur when the current close is below the close 10 days ago. For the second indicator, positive or negative values reflect closing prices above or below the 10-day average price. Notice that although the two indicators have minor differences, their fluctuations closely mirror each other.

The indicators in Figure 11.2 are the ratio versions of the indicators in Figure 11.1—that is, the result of dividing the current close by the close 10 days ago (Close/Close_{10}), and dividing the current close by the 10-day moving average (Close/MA_{10}). Note that they appear to be the same as the indicators in Figure 11.1 except for their scaling. In fact, the indicators in Figure 11.2 are perfectly correlated to their counterparts in Figure 11.1. In other words, in terms of trading signal generation, there is absolutely no difference between the two sets of indicators.

Figure 11.3 returns to the difference calculations used in Figure 11.1, except the look-back period for both is 30 days instead of 10 days. Again, the indicators appear very similar, although each is significantly different from its counterpart in Figure 11.1 because of the longer look-back period: The 30-day indicators in Figure 11.3 highlight far fewer of the shorter-term price highs and lows and instead trace the contour of the intermediate-term price action. For example, during the

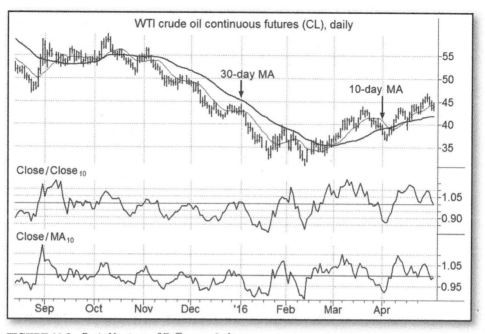

FIGURE 11.2 Ratio Versions of Difference Indicators

Chart created using TradeStation. ©TradeStation Technologies, Inc. All rights reserved.

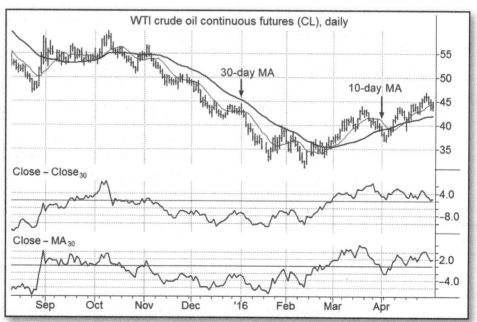

FIGURE 11.3 30-Day Versions of Close − Close and Close − MA Indicators

Chart created using TradeStation. ©TradeStation Technologies, Inc. All rights reserved.

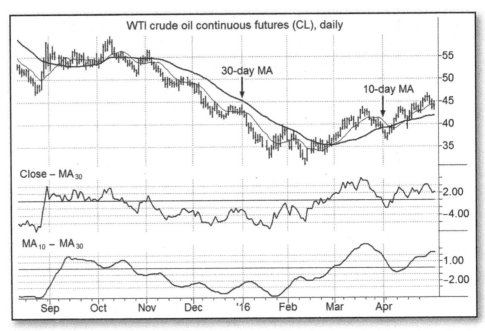

FIGURE 11.4 Price – MA vs. MA – MA Indicators

Chart created using TradeStation. ©TradeStation Technologies, Inc. All rights reserved.

October–December 2015 period, both indicators are smoother and have a more pronounced downward bias than their 10-day counterparts in Figure 11.1.

Figure 11.4 compares the Close – MA_{30} indicator from Figure 11.3 with the $MA_{10} - MA_{30}$ indicator, which represents the difference between the 10-day moving average and 30-day moving average. The use of two moving averages produces an indicator that is closely related to the Close − MA indicator, but is smoother and a bit less timely (e.g., note the delay between the $MA_{10} - MA_{30}$ and the Close – MA_{30} indicator in reflecting the early-April price low).

Finally, Figure 11.5 compares the Close/$Close_{10}$ indicator from Figure 11.2 with the CS_{10} indicator, which shows where the current close falls within the range (high–low) of the most recent 10 days (e.g., if the close is the highest price of the most recent 10 days, the indicator reading is 1.00, or 100 percent).

The similarities between the indicators in Figures 11.1 through 11.5 are substantial and not specific to the time window represented in these charts. Table 11.1 shows the correlation coefficients[1] for all six pair combinations of the four 10-day indicator calculations (Close – Close, Close – MA, CS, and MA – MA[2])

---

[1] The correlation coefficient, which measures the linear relationship between two data samples, ranges from −1.00 to +1.00, with −1.00 representing a perfect negative correlation (values moving in exact opposition) and +1.00 representing perfect positive correlation (values moving exactly in tandem).

[2] The MA – MA calculations in Table 11.1 use three days for the short-term moving average and 10 days for the long-term moving average.

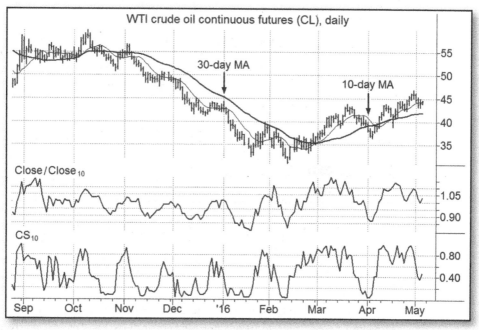

FIGURE 11.5 Close/Close vs. Closing Strength Indicators
Chart created using TradeStation. ©TradeStation Technologies, Inc. All rights reserved.

during two periods: August 14, 2015 through May 5, 2016 (the period shown in Figures 11.1 through 11.5); and a much longer period, May 5, 2005 through May 5, 2016. The lowest correlation between any two indicators during the August 2015–May 2016 period was 0.81. The correlations for the 2005–2016 period were similar, with some pairs registering modestly higher correlations and other pairs modestly lower correlations. Even the lowest figure in Table 11.1 (0.77, for the May 2005–May 2016 Close – Close vs. CS indicator comparison) reflects a significant level of positive correlation.

TABLE 11.1 10-Day Indicator Correlations, Crude Oil

	Close – Close vs. Close – MA	Close – Close vs. MA – MA	Close – Close vs. CS	Close – MA vs. MA – MA	Close – MA vs. CS	MA – MA vs. CS
Aug. 2015–May 2016	0.81	0.83	0.81	0.89	0.93	0.83
May 2005–May 2016	0.84	0.86	0.77	0.90	0.87	0.78

TABLE 11.2 20-Day Indicator Correlations

		Close – Close vs. Close – MA	Close – Close vs. MA – MA	Close – Close vs. CS	Close – Close vs. U/D Avg.	Close – MA vs. MA – MA	Close – MA vs. CS	Close – MA vs. U/D Avg.	MA – MA vs. CS	MA – MA vs. U/D Avg.	CS vs. U/D Avg.
Crude oil	Aug. '15–May '16	0.84	0.81	0.84	0.88	0.72	0.95	0.72	0.68	0.69	0.72
	May '05–May '16	0.88	0.88	0.79	0.57	0.80	0.87	0.52	0.69	0.51	0.53
Corn	Aug. '15–May '16	0.77	0.84	0.71	0.33	0.53	0.91	0.15	0.45	0.34	0.19
	May '05–May '16	0.86	0.90	0.71	0.59	0.69	0.80	0.52	0.55	0.53	0.51
S&P 500	Aug. '15–May '16	0.90	0.84	0.81	0.81	0.71	0.68	0.79	0.90	0.64	0.66
	May '05–May '16	0.88	0.84	0.74	0.51	0.67	0.57	0.44	0.86	0.43	0.48
Euro	Aug. '15–May '16	0.80	0.86	0.77	0.77	0.58	0.90	0.74	0.55	0.61	0.75
	May '05–May '16	0.86	0.90	0.76	0.65	0.70	0.87	0.59	0.61	0.57	0.62
	Average:	*0.85*	*0.86*	*0.77*	*0.64*	*0.68*	*0.82*	*0.56*	*0.66*	*0.54*	*0.56*
	Median:	*0.86*	*0.85*	*0.77*	*0.62*	*0.69*	*0.87*	*0.55*	*0.64*	*0.55*	*0.58*

Table 11.2 extends the same analysis to three additional markets—corn, E-mini S&P 500, and euro futures—and from 6 to 10 indicator-pair combinations, based on adding a sixth calculation: the Up/Down Average ("U/D Avg."), which is defined as the average positive close-to-close change over the past N days divided by the average (absolute) negative close-to-close change over the past N days, normalized so that it fluctuates in a range from zero to 1.00.[3] Table 11.2 also differs from Table 11.1 in that it is based on 20-day look-back periods (instead of 10), except for the MA – MA indicator, which uses a short-term moving average length of 10 days and a long-term moving average length of 30 days.

Although Table 11.2 contains some readings well below the lowest correlation figure in Table 11.1 (mostly for pairs involving the Up/Down Average indicator), the average and median correlations for the ten indicator combinations shown are still uniformly strong, ranging from a low of 0.54 to a high of 0.87. Table 11.3, which replicates the analysis of Table 11.2 using 60-day look-back periods instead of 20 (and 20-day and 60-day moving average lengths for the MA – MA indicator), demonstrates very similar results, with the average/median correlations ranging from a low of 0.49 to a high of 0.90.

The significance of the similarity between the indicator formulas discussed thus far is that they are the building blocks of a host of popular indicators, especially those known as momentum indicators, or "oscillators." This group includes, but is by no means limited to, momentum, rate-of-change (ROC), the stochastic oscillator, the relative strength index (RSI), %R, moving average

---

[3] The formula for normalizing the indicator values between 0 and 1.00 is: $1 - \{1/[1 + (UA/DA)]\}$, where UA is the average positive close-to-close change over the past n bars and DA is the absolute value of the average negative close-to-close change over the past n bars.

TABLE 11.3	60-Day Indicator Correlations										
		Close – Close vs. Close – MA	Close – Close vs. MA – MA	Close – Close vs. CS	Close – Close vs. U/D Avg	Close – MA vs. MA – MA	Close – MA vs. CS	Close – MA vs. U/D Avg	MA – MA vs. CS	MA – MA vs. U/D Avg	CS vs. U/D Avg
Crude oil	Aug. '15–May '16	0.85	0.90	0.82	0.60	0.88	0.95	0.83	0.83	0.67	0.75
	May '05–May '16	0.91	0.92	0.76	0.27	0.90	0.86	0.43	0.74	0.26	0.50
Corn	Aug. '15–May '16	0.23	0.05	0.42	0.53	0.56	0.90	0.07	0.46	0.22	0.22
	May '05–May '16	0.87	0.85	0.76	0.68	0.84	0.82	0.61	0.66	0.59	0.58
S&P 500	Aug. '15–May '16	0.62	0.13	0.57	0.22	0.82	0.96	0.70	0.81	0.77	0.66
	May '05–May '16	0.64	0.18	0.60	0.24	0.83	0.88	0.44	0.70	0.40	0.41
Euro	Aug. '15–May '16	0.80	0.74	0.78	0.79	0.70	0.93	0.90	0.60	0.73	0.85
	May '05–May '16	0.85	0.86	0.78	0.62	0.84	0.88	0.59	0.72	0.53	0.64
	Average:	0.72	0.58	0.69	0.49	0.80	0.90	0.57	0.69	0.52	0.58
	Median:	0.82	0.80	0.76	0.56	0.84	0.89	0.60	0.71	0.56	0.61

convergence-divergence (MACD), the price (or moving average) oscillator, the commodity channel index (CCI), and the money flow index (MFI). (*Note:* There is little consistency in the technical indicator lexicon, especially with regard to more generic indicators. Terms such as *momentum, rate of change,* and *price oscillator* sometimes refer to different calculations in different sources. The names used here are widely applied, but may conflict with other sources. The calculations, not the names, are what are important.)

Figure 11.6 compares five popular indicators: momentum, the "fast" stochastic oscillator, CCI, RSI, and the MFI. "Momentum" is simply the Close – Close indicator. The fast stochastic is a three-day moving average of the CS indicator. (The second, thinner line in the stochastic plot in Figure 11.6 is a three-day moving average of the primary indicator line.) The CCI divides the difference between price and a moving average (similar to the Close – MA indicator) by a measure of the absolute total price deviation during the look-back period. The RSI is essentially the U/D Average indicator, except it uses an exponential smoothing function instead of a simple moving average and is scaled from zero to 100 instead of zero to 1. The MFI is basically a volume-weighted version of the RSI that magnifies indicator readings that are accompanied by high trade volume. The precise formulas for these indicators (which are readily available online) are less important than the fact that they are all derived from our basic indicator calculations and are all highly correlated to each other. Table 11.4 summarizes the average correlations for 20-day versions of the 10 pair combinations of these five common indicators for the same periods shown in Tables 11.2 and 11.3. As Table 11.4 clearly demonstrates, these five popular indicators are all highly correlated, with correlations ranging from a low of 0.67 to a high of 0.94.

The takeaway from this analysis is that all technical indicators that measure the magnitude and direction of prices over a given time period must inevitably compare at least two price points or

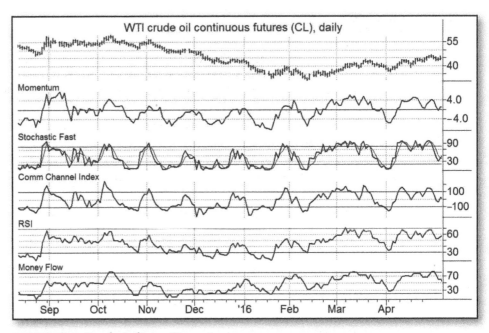

FIGURE 11.6 Popular Indicator Comparison

Chart created using TradeStation. ©TradeStation Technologies, Inc. All rights reserved.

groups of prices, which means they must incorporate at least one of the indicator formulas we have outlined, or a closely related calculation. Figures 11.1 through 11.6 and Tables 11.1 through 11.4 suggest the specific type of calculation used is far less important than the time period it surveys in terms of differentiating one indicator from another. This characteristic of indicators is starkly illustrated in Figure 11.7, which compares three indicator calculations (top to bottom): $Close - Close_{10}$, $MA_3 - MA_{10}$, and $MA_{20} - MA_{100}$. Although the upper and middle indicators use a different type of calculation, they are very similar. In contrast, the middle and lower indicators use the same type of calculation but are radically different. The key point is that the upper and middle indicators are similar because they both track a similar trend length, while the middle and lower indicators are very different because the time length surveyed by the lower indicator is much longer. *In short, it's the time length, not the indicator, that matters.*

TABLE 11.4 Correlations of Common Indicators, Daily Crude Oil

	Mom vs. Stoch	Mom vs. CCI	Mom vs. RSI	Mom vs. MFI	Stoch vs. CCI	Stoch vs. RSI	Stoch vs. MFI	CCI vs. RSI	CCI vs. MFI	RSI vs. MFI
Aug. '15–May '16	0.81	0.77	0.87	0.82	0.94	0.87	0.68	0.86	0.69	0.82
May '05–May '16	0.78	0.71	0.84	0.82	0.93	0.87	0.72	0.83	0.67	0.81

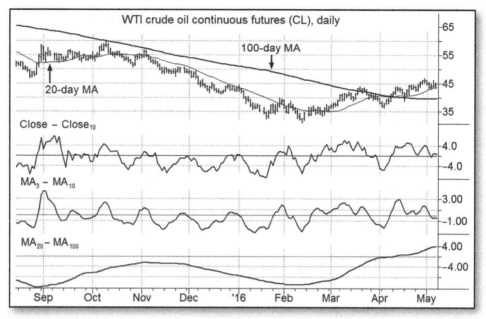

FIGURE 11.7 Indicator Length vs. Calculation Type

Chart created using TradeStation. ©TradeStation Technologies, Inc. All rights reserved.

■ Moving Average Types

Moving averages, which are incorporated in many indicators, can be calculated in different ways. Whereas a simple moving average (SMA) weights all prices equally (i.e., a 10-day average is the sum of the closing prices of the past 10 days divided by 10), the weighted moving average (WMA) and exponential moving average (EMA) use multipliers to increase the influence of more recent data in the calculation (see Chapter 16 for details). The logic behind weighting a moving average is based on an implicit assumption (not necessarily true) that recent price action is more important than more distant price action when attempting to forecast future price direction. The intent of weighting a moving average is to reduce lag by creating an indicator that is more responsive to directional changes—a seemingly logical goal, but one that can have drawbacks as well as advantages.

Table 11.5 shows the results of testing the same basic trading system using simple, weighted, and exponential moving averages. The system goes long when prices close above the moving average and goes short when prices close below the moving average. The system was tested on three markets: the E-mini S&P 500 futures (ES), WTI crude oil futures (CL), and euro futures (EC), using daily data from January 30, 2006, through January 28, 2016. In all cases, one contract was traded per signal, and the moving average length was set to 60 days.

The results, while based on a small sample of markets, are illustrative. In each market, a different type of moving average produced the highest net profit and highest profit factor (gross profit/gross loss).

TABLE 11.5 Simple, Weighted, and Exponential Moving Average Signals

	Net Profit[a]	No. Trades	Win %	Profit Factor[b]
ES				
Exponential	$5,440	163	23.31%	0.98
Simple	−$1,635	163	19.63%	0.92
Weighted	−$30,860	209	23.44%	0.76
CL				
Simple	$175,050	161	24.22%	1.87
Exponential	$113,870	178	23.03%	1.42
Weighted	$102,010	225	20.44%	1.3
EC				
Weighted	$59,763	186	24.19%	1.36
Exponential	$46,350	202	21.78%	1.29
Simple	$29,325	154	21.43%	1.18

[a]Closed trades plus open trade profit/loss (P/L) at end of test period.
[b]Reflects closed trades only.

The implication is that the search for the "best" smoothing approach is likely to be a fruitless one. Over time, applied across multiple markets and parameter values, a particular smoothing calculation is unlikely to demonstrate a meaningful advantage over another. Figure 11.8 helps illustrate why. The daily crude oil prices in this chart are overlaid with 60-day simple (dashed line), weighted (thick solid line), and exponential (thin solid line) moving averages. In just a single roughly six-month period, there are multiple instances of the varying degrees of lag among the three moving averages helping or

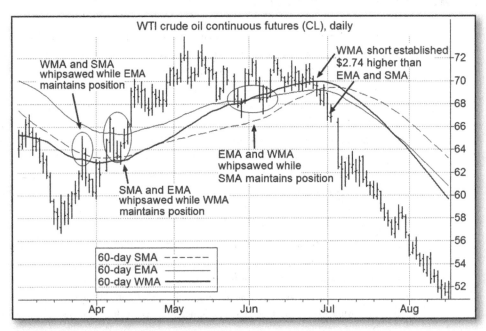

FIGURE 11.8 Moving Average Comparison

Chart created using TradeStation. ©TradeStation Technologies, Inc. All rights reserved.

hurting performance. For example, in March 2015, the market closed above both the WMA and SMA (triggering long positions) before reversing to close below both averages the next day (triggering short positions)—a classic example of a "whipsaw" loss that occurs in trend-following strategies during congested or volatile market conditions. The EMA escaped this loss. However, in other instances of whipsaw trades evident in the chart, it was the WMA or SMA that avoided the losing trade, while the other two averages did not. Also, note that after the WMA suffered a whipsaw loss in early June while the SMA did not, in late June the WMA then provided a better short entry as the market turned sharply lower. Multiply the offsetting benefits and drawbacks illustrated in this chart by similar occurrences in multiple markets over many years, and it is easy to see why one smoothing approach is unlikely to significantly outperform another, other than by chance.

Ultimately, the look-back period will be more important than the particular smoothing technique. Over time, the difference between using a 40-period EMA and a 40-period SMA will be much less significant than the difference between using a 40-period EMA and an 80-period EMA. Once again, it is the time length used in the calculation rather than the calculation type that matters.

■ Oscillators and Trading Signals

The most common type of indicator by far is the one commonly referred to as the *momentum indicator* or *oscillator,* which is a calculation designed to highlight shorter-term swing points and so-called overbought and oversold levels. All the basic calculations and indicators in Figures 11.1 through 11.7 (using shorter-term look-back periods) could be placed in this category. The popularity of oscillators is probably driven by the desire of many traders to capture as many of a market's twists and turns as possible. The popularity of oscillators, however, is arguably inversely correlated to their usefulness. To see why, let's examine a few examples of applying oscillators as trading tools.

Figure 11.9 depicts the 10-year T-note futures with a 10-day fast stochastic oscillator line (i.e., a three-day moving average of the CS calculation). The indicator's two horizontal lines at 80 and 20 are default overbought and oversold levels that, according to oscillator conventional wisdom, are used to indicate points at which price moves are overextended and likely to correct. Thus, overbought readings (above 80) signal selling opportunities, and oversold readings (below 20) signal buying opportunities. Although the oscillator does seem to signal all the price turning points, it does so prematurely.

The astute reader might argue that the simplistic use of the oscillator to signal trades whenever it enters overbought/oversold zones may be a suboptimal application of the indicator. What if, instead, we waited for the indicated reversal to be confirmed before generating a trade signal? For example, a buy signal might be triggered by the following dual conditions:

1. The oscillator declines into oversold territory (<20), suggesting an environment potentially conducive to long positions.
2. The oscillator then rises back above the oversold threshold (>20), confirming the anticipated trend reversal from down to up.

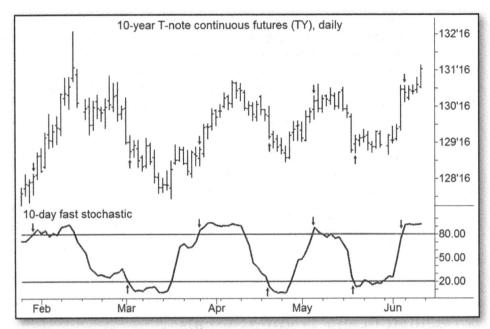

FIGURE 11.9   Oscillator Signals: Initial Penetration

Chart created using TradeStation. ©TradeStation Technologies, Inc. All rights reserved.

A trade would be signaled only after the second condition is met. An analogous set of dual conditions would apply to sell signals. Figure 11.10 is the same chart as Figure 11.9 except it illustrates signals based on adding the confirmation condition. Now, the oscillator seems to perform spectacularly well as a trading tool, generating sells near relative highs and buys near relative lows! Many novice traders will see a chart such as Figure 11.10 and think they have discovered the perfect trading system. In fact, it is not uncommon for some vendors to market systems using similar approaches, illustrating the purported wonderful performance of their system with charts that look very much like Figure 11.10.

So what is wrong with such a dual-condition oscillator application for generating trading signals? Nothing, as long as you can predict that the market will stay in a trading range *in the future*. The period shown in Figure 11.10 (late January to mid-June 2016) represents nearly ideal conditions for short-term indicators such as oscillators to track price swings: the market moved sideways and the price swings were relatively similar in magnitude. In such environments oscillators can appear to be almost foolproof trading tools. If, however, the same approach is applied to a trending market—and keep in mind it's impossible to know whether a trending or trading range market will prevail in the future—the results can be disastrous. Figure 11.11 shows the signals that would have resulted from applying the same dual-condition trade rules in a trending market. In this case, during an eight-month period when the euro futures declined approximately 16 percent, the same oscillator triggered exactly one sell signal while issuing nine buy signals, including seven consecutive losing buys from August 2014 to January 2015.

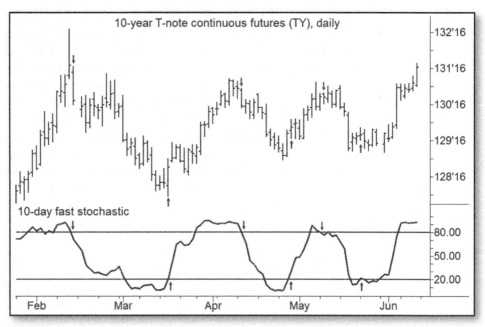

FIGURE 11.10   Oscillator Dual-Condition Signals

Chart created using TradeStation. ©TradeStation Technologies, Inc. All rights reserved.

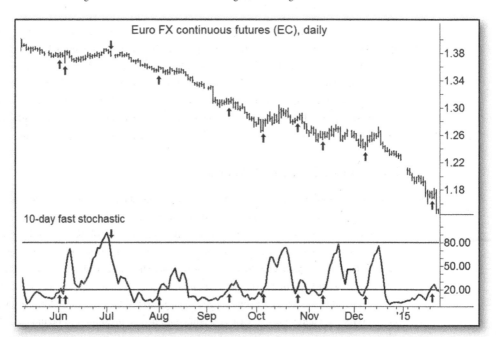

FIGURE 11.11   Oscillator Signals in Trending Market

Chart created using TradeStation. ©TradeStation Technologies, Inc. All rights reserved.

The bottom line is that oscillators will work well as contrarian trading tools if we can assume the market will move in a trading range. If the market instead embarks on an extended trend, oscillator-based signals can lead to huge losses. And while it is easy to identify past trading ranges for which an oscillator-based trading strategy will produce magnificent hypothetical results, we don't know whether a trading range or trending market will prevail in the immediate future. In other words, we don't know whether the upcoming market environment will be conducive or adverse to the use of oscillators. As a subjective observation, on balance, oscillators have probably harmed traders more than helped them. However, if a trader fully understands their limitations, these tools could still provide reasonable trading signals. For example, if a trader has good reason to expect that a trading range market is more likely to prevail—and uses rigorous risk management to control losses if this projection proves wrong—then an oscillator could be used as a trading tool.

■ Indicator Myths

Through repetition over decades, certain bits of "common wisdom" regarding technical indicators have become entrenched in trading literature, despite the ability of traders to disprove such misleading ideas through testing. The following list is far from exhaustive, but it touches upon some of the most dangerously misleading, and easily refutable, examples of such myths.

The Confirmation Myth

Traders are often exhorted to consult multiple technical indicators to "confirm" a potential trade signal. This advice may sound sensible, but given the high correlation among so many indicators, such confirmation is often an illusion. Unless the indicators being consulted are uncorrelated—say, if they use radically different look-back periods (which is usually not the case)—they are probably simply repeating the same information, with any apparent variations between the indicators likely meaningless. The similarities between the indicators shown in Figures 11.1 through 11.7 illustrate how easy it is to generate false "confirmation" from calculations that are, more or less, the same indicator.

The "Magic Number" Myth

This misconception revolves around the belief that a specific indicator parameter (typically, the look-back period) provides universally optimal performance or otherwise possesses special properties. Popular examples include the nearly ubiquitous use of a 14-day look-back period as the default setting for short-term countertrend indicators and references in the financial media regarding the importance of the penetration of a 200-day moving average. The reality is that such parameter values will be optimal only in isolated markets as a function of chance. The question of what values work best for a specific portfolio over a specific time range can be answered only by computer testing. And even then, the answer would apply only to past data and could not be presumed to be indicative of the optimal values for the future. Chapter 19, which addresses the issue of optimization, provides a more in-depth discussion of this point.

The Leading Indicator Myth

Some technical tools are commonly referred to as "leading" indicators for their supposed ability to signal a market move before the price series itself gives any indication of a change in direction. Although it might be fair to say that a price-based indicator could (to some eyes) highlight an aspect of price action with predictive properties, the inescapable fact is that an indicator can never "lead" price action because, by definition, it is based on historical prices. If a certain indicator reading or pattern proves (through testing) to have predictive value, that information *must* be present in the price series itself.

The Divergence Signal Myth

This belief is a subset of the leading indicator myth. Divergence is most commonly used to describe the phenomenon of an indicator (usually one designated as a "countertrend" tool) moving in opposition to a price series, and thus supposedly giving advance warning of vulnerability in the prevailing price trend. For example, prices might make a new high in an uptrend, while the countertrend indicator makes a lower high, suggesting the new price peak has been established on weaker momentum, which in turn implies that a correction or reversal is imminent. Such patterns are, in fact, quite common at market turning points. Unfortunately, though, they are also quite common at other times as well, often generating one false reversal signal after another during extended market trends. Figure 11.12, which depicts crude oil prices during the market's extended sell-off in 2014 and into early 2015, highlights

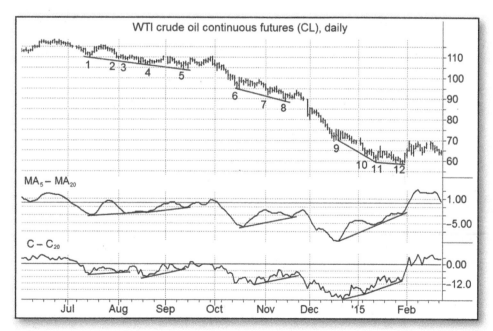

FIGURE 11.12 Price-Indicator Divergences

Chart created using TradeStation. ©TradeStation Technologies, Inc. All rights reserved.

a series of successive price lows that were accompanied by higher lows in the $MA_5 - MA_{20}$ and Close $- Close_{20}$ indicators. These divergences between price and the indicators began signaling the potential for a significant correction or reversal as soon as the trend began—approximately six months and $50/bl. before the market staged a modest bounce in late January 2015. The situation is even worse than it looks because Figure 11.12 omits some smaller false divergences that were left unmarked to avoid cluttering the chart.

■ Indicator "Types"

Indicators are typically categorized according to whether they are intended to identify longer-term trends or emphasize shorter-term price swings and countertrend moves. While it is true that smoothing functions, such as moving averages, lend themselves to trend analysis because they simplify price action, such classifications usually have more to do with an indicator's look-back period than any inherent characteristic of the calculation. For example, although moving average crossovers are "classic" trend-following signals, an $MA_3 - MA_{10}$ calculation (three-day moving average minus 10-day moving average), which conforms to the standard moving-average crossover form, could hardly be described as a long-term trend-following indicator (see Figure 11.13). By contrast, the basic C – C momentum calculation, most often used to highlight short-term price swings, will nonetheless reflect longer-term trends as its look-back period increases, as evidenced by the $C - C_{100}$ calculation shown in Figure 11.13.

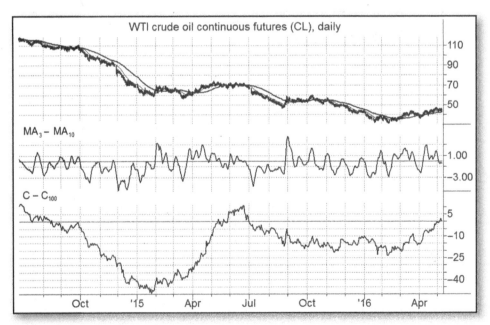

FIGURE 11.13   Length vs. Indicator Type

■ Conclusion

Because they are derivatives of price, it can be argued that technical indicators—when used to generate trading signals—actually distance traders and analysts from the data they are attempting to understand. Although indicators can, perhaps, highlight certain aspects of market action that might not be immediately evident by looking at a chart or a spreadsheet, they cannot create information that is not already present in the market data itself.

Simplicity is generally a virtue with regard to technical indicators. There are only so many ways to measure the direction and magnitude of price changes, and the slight differences between approaches are unlikely to produce meaningful differences in trading signals. The more inputs an indicator has (and the more arcane those inputs are), the more likely that either it is obscuring, rather than clarifying, the market action it is intended to interpret, or it is merely a more complex version of a simpler calculation.

Perhaps the most important insight the reader can take away from this chapter is that indicators that tend to work well in nontrending conditions will unavoidably perform miserably in trending conditions, whereas tools designed for trends will fare poorly in trendless markets. Unfortunately, markets do not ring bells when they are switching from one phase to the other. As a result, no single indicator or parameter input (such as the look-back period) can be expected to perform consistently well across multiple markets and time frames.

PART III

APPLYING CHART
ANALYSIS TO TRADING

CHAPTER 12

Midtrend Entry and Pyramiding

Nobody can catch all the fluctuations.

—Edwin Lefèvre

For many reasons, you may find yourself considering whether to enter a new position after the market has already made a substantial price move. Examples include: (1) you were not previously following the market; (2) in an effort to get a better price, you futilely waited for a price correction that never developed; (3) you were previously skeptical about the sustainability of the trend, but have now changed your opinion.

Faced with such a situation, many traders will be extremely reluctant to trade the market. This attitude can be easily explained in psychological terms. The act of entering a new position after a trend is already well underway in a sense represents an admission of failure. Even if the trade is profitable, traders know their gains would have been much greater if they had acted earlier. Thus, even when you have a strong sense of probable market direction, you might be tempted to think: "I've missed so much of the move, why bother?"

As an example, consider chart-oriented traders examining the coffee market in mid-February 2014 (see Figure 12.1) after not having participated in the sharp price advance prior to that time. Such traders would have noted the market had broken out above the resistance level defined by the January 2014 and October 2013 highs, with prices remaining in new high ground for two weeks—a very bullish chart configuration. In addition, prices had just formed a flag pattern after an upmove— price action indicative of another imminent upswing. However, observing that prices had already advanced more than 37 percent since the November 2013 low (and more than 25 percent in just seven days in late January and early February), traders might have been reluctant to enter a new long position belatedly, reasoning the market was overextended.

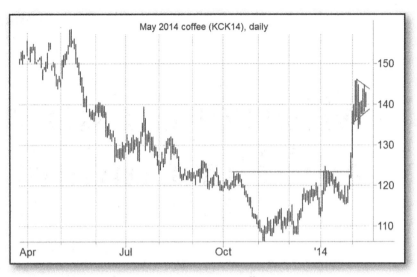

FIGURE 12.1 Missed Price Move? (May 2014 Coffee)

Figure 12.2 vividly illustrates the folly of this conclusion. Incredibly, as of mid-February 2014, coffee prices had completed only about 35 percent of their ultimate advance to the March high. The moral of this tale is provided by an observation in *Reminiscences of a Stock Operator* by Edwin Lefèvre: "[Prices] are never too high to begin buying or too low to begin selling."

The key question is how one enters the market in the midst of a major trend. Actually, the goals in implementing a midtrend position are the same as those for initiating any position: favorable timing

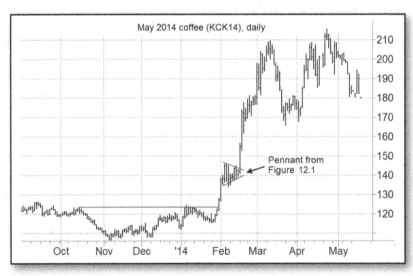

FIGURE 12.2 How It Turned Out (May 2014 Coffee)

of entry and risk control. The following are four key strategies that could be employed to achieve these objectives:

1. **Percent retracement.** This approach attempts to capitalize on the natural tendency of a market to partially retrace prior price swings. Generally speaking, one might initiate the position anytime the market retraces a given percentage of the price swing from the last relative low or relative high. A reasonable choice for this percentage would be a figure in the 35 to 65 percent range. Figure 12.3 illustrates the entry points using this approach, assuming a 50 percent retracement criterion. Notice two of these retracements are based on rallies (A–D and C–D, respectively) that are defined by the same relative high but different relative lows. The main advantage of this method is that it is capable of providing superior entry points. However, it is also subject to a major disadvantage: frequently, the necessary retracement condition may not be fulfilled until the trend has carried much further, or possibly even reversed.

2. **Reversal of minor reaction.** This approach is based on waiting for a minor reaction to materialize and then entering on the first signs of a resumption of the major trend. Of course, the precise method would depend on how a reaction and trend resumption were defined. The choices are virtually limitless. For illustration purposes, we will provide one possible set of definitions.

   A "reaction" is identified whenever the *reaction count* reaches 4. The reaction count is initially set to 0. In a rising market, the count would be raised to 1 any day in which the high and low were equal or lower than the corresponding points on the day on which the high of the move was set. The count would be increased by 1 each day the high and low are equal to or lower than the high

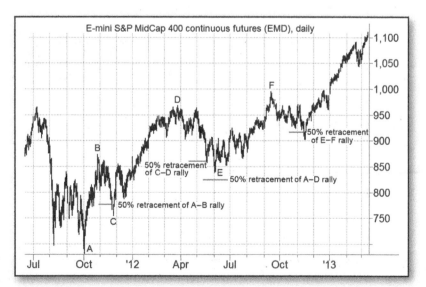

FIGURE 12.3 Buy Signals on 50 Percent Retracements (E-Mini S&P MidCap 400 Continuous Futures)

and low of the most recent day on which the count was increased. The count would be reset to 0 anytime the market moved to new highs. Analogous conditions would apply to a declining market.

The resumption of the major trend would be indicated whenever the *thrust count* reached 3. The thrust count would initially be set to 0 and would begin being monitored after a reaction was defined. In the case of a reaction in a rising market, the thrust count would increase by 1 on each upthrust day and would be reset to 0 anytime the reaction low was penetrated. (Thrust days were defined in Chapter 9.) Once a signal was received, the reaction low could be used as a stop-loss reference point. For example, the position might be liquidated anytime the market closed below the reaction low. Once again, an analogous set of conditions could be used for defining a resumption of the trend in a declining market.

Figure 12.4 illustrates the reversal of minor reaction approach using the specific definitions just detailed. The points at which reactions are defined are denoted by the symbol *RD*, with the numbers prior to these points indicating the reaction count values. Buy signals are indicated at the points at which the thrust count equals 3, with the letters prior to these points indicating the thrust count values. For any given entry point, stop-loss liquidation would be signaled by a close below the most recent stop level, which in this case is the lowest relative low between the identification of the reaction and the completion of the thrust count.

3. **Continuation pattern and trading range breakouts.** The use of continuation patterns and trading ranges for entry signals was discussed in Chapter 9. Since to some extent chart patterns are in the eye of the beholder, this approach will reflect a degree of subjectivity. Figure 12.5 offers one interpretation of continuation patterns (implicit assumption:

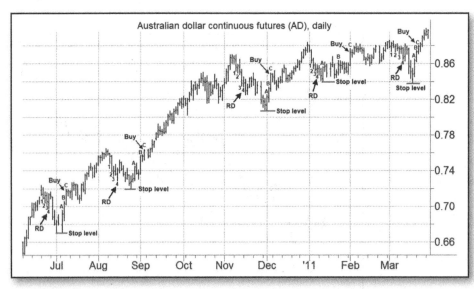

FIGURE 12.4 Reversal of Minor Reaction (Australian Dollar Continuous Futures)

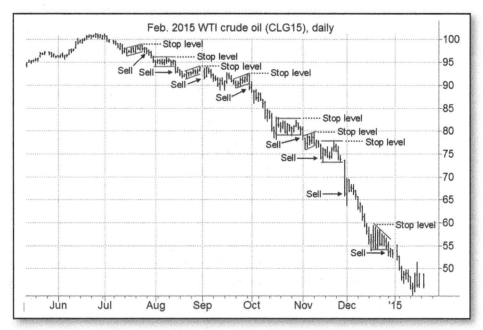

FIGURE 12.5 Continuation Pattern Breakouts as Entry Signals (February WTI Crude Oil)
Chart created using TradeStation. ©TradeStation Technologies, Inc. All rights reserved.

at least five trading days are required to form a continuation pattern), and the corresponding sell points reflect closes below these consolidations. It should be noted, however, that once a trend is considered established, it is not absolutely necessary to wait for penetrations of continuation patterns as confirmation of trade entry signals. By definition, these patterns are expected to be resolved by price swings in the same direction as the price moves that preceded their formation. Thus, for example, in a downtrend, short positions could be established within consolidation patterns based on an expectation of an eventual downside breakout. The high prices in the patterns depicted in Figure 12.5 could be used as reference points for the placement of protective stops (as marked on the chart) following the downside breakouts of these patterns.

4. **Reaction to long-term moving average.** Price retracements to a moving average of the price series can be viewed as signals that the reaction to the main trend is near an end. Specifically, if a trader believed that an uptrend was in place, long positions could be entered anytime prices declined to below a specified moving average. Similarly, if a downtrend were believed to be in effect, short positions could be initiated on rallies above the moving average. Figure 12.6, which superimposes a 40-day moving average over continuous E-mini S&P 500 futures, provides an illustration of this approach. For example, traders who were bullish on the stock market during the period depicted and looking to enter on a correction could have used price pullbacks below the 40-day moving average as entry signals for long positions. The arrows in Figure 12.6 indicate potential buy entry levels based on this approach.

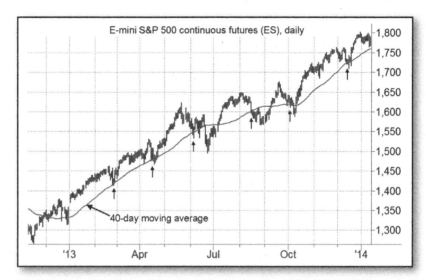

FIGURE 12.6 Reaction to Long-Term Moving Average (E-Mini S&P 500 Futures)
Note: ↑ = buy entry signal based on a reaction to below the 40-day moving average.
Chart created using TradeStation. ©TradeStation Technologies, Inc. All rights reserved.

Chapter 16 illustrates how crossovers of moving averages can be used as *trend-reversal* signals. In the application just described, we have used moving average crossover points to signal *countertrend* trade entry signals. There is no contradiction. When moving average crossovers are employed for generating trend reversal signals, typically, two moving averages are used so that the smoothing of both data series will reduce false trend-reversal signals. In the method just detailed, we deliberately defined crossover points based on the price series itself, which is more sensitive than a moving average since it contains no smoothing of the data, and one moving average. In other words, we would use more sensitive definitions of moving average crossovers for countertrend applications than we would for trend-identification applications.

It should be noted that the problem of midtrend entry is identical to the problem of *pyramiding*, which is the implementation of additional units to an existing position. Both transactions involve implementing a position after the market has already witnessed a substantial move in a given direction. Consequently, the strategies discussed in this chapter for a midtrend entry could also be applied to the timing of pyramid positions.

A few additional guidelines are necessary for pyramiding. First, one should not add to any existing position unless the last unit placed shows a profit. Second, one should not add to an existing position if the intended stop point would imply a net loss for the entire position. Third, pyramid units should be no greater than the base (initial) position size.

CHAPTER 13

Choosing Stop-Loss Points

It was the same with all. They would not take a small loss at first but had held on,
in the hope of a recovery that would "let them out even." And prices had sunk and
sunk until the loss was so great that it seemed only proper to hold on, if need be a year,
for sooner or later prices must come back. But the break "shook them out," and prices just
went so much lower because so many people had to sell, whether they would or not.

—Edwin Lefèvre

The success of chart-oriented trading is critically dependent on the effective control of losses. A precise stop-loss liquidation point should be determined *before* initiating a trade. The most disciplined approach would be to enter a good-till-canceled (GTC) stop order at the same time the trade is implemented. However, if the trader knows he can trust himself, he could predetermine the stop point and then enter a day order at any time this price is within the permissible daily limit.

How should stop points be determined? A basic principle is that the position should be liquidated at or before the point at which price movement causes a transition in the technical picture. For example, assume a trader decides to sell September natural gas after the mid-October downside breakout has remained intact for five days (see Figure 13.1). In this case, the protective buy stop should be placed no higher than the upper boundary of the July–October trading range, since the realization of such a price would totally transform the chart picture. Some of the technical reference points commonly used for placing protective stops include:

1. **Trend lines.** A sell stop can be placed below an uptrend line; a buy stop can be placed above a downtrend line. One advantage of this approach is that the penetration of a trend line will

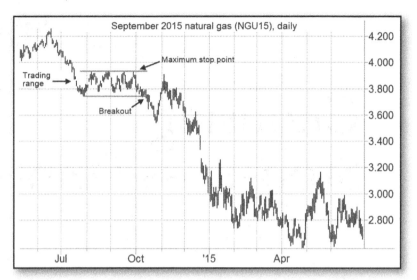

FIGURE 13.1 Stop Placement Following Trading Range Breakout: September 2015 Natural Gas

Chart created using TradeStation. ©TradeStation Technologies, Inc. All rights reserved.

usually be one of the first technical signals in a trend reversal. Thus, this type of stop point will strongly limit the magnitude of the loss or the surrendered open profit. However, this attribute comes at a steep price: trend line penetrations are prone to false signals. As discussed in Chapter 6, it is common for trend lines to be redefined in the course of a bull or bear market.

2. **Trading range.** As illustrated in the preceding natural gas example, the opposite side of a trading range can be used as a stop point. Frequently, the stop can be placed closer (particularly in the case of broader trading ranges) because if the breakout is a valid signal, prices should not retreat too deeply into the range. Thus, the stop might be placed somewhere in the zone between the midpoint and the more distant boundary of the range. The near end of the trading range, however, would not be a meaningful stop point. In fact, retracements to this area are so common that many traders prefer to wait for such a reaction before initiating a position. (The advisability of this delayed entry strategy following breakouts is a matter of personal choice. In many instances it will provide better fills, but it will also cause the trader to miss some major moves.)

3. **Flags and pennants.** After a breakout in one direction of a flag or pennant formation, the return to the opposite end (or some point beyond) can be used as a signal of a price reversal, and by implication a point for placing stops. For example, in Figure 13.2 the downside penetration of a flag pattern in mid-August was quickly followed by a rebound above the same formation. This price action proved to be a precursor of a significant price advance.

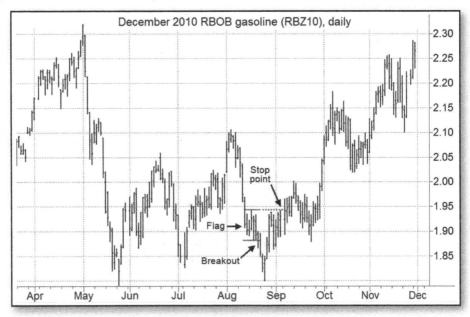

FIGURE 13.2 Stop Placement Following Flag Pattern Breakout: December 2010 RBOB Gasoline

Chart created using TradeStation. ©TradeStation Technologies, Inc. All rights reserved.

4. **Wide-ranging days.** Similar to flags and pennants, after a breakout in one direction, the return to the opposite end can be used as a signal of a price reversal, and hence a point for placing stops. For example, in Figure 13.3 note how the return of prices back above the true high of the wide-ranging down day that formed in mid-March (after initially trading below this pattern) led to a strong rally.

5. **Relative highs and relative lows.** If the implied risk is not too great, the most recent relative high or relative low can be used as a stop point.[1] For example, assume a trader initiated a long position in December corn in response to the breakout above resistance in June (see Figure 13.4). In this case, the sell stop could be placed below either the May low or the June low.

Sometimes the risk implied by even the closest technically significant points may be excessive. In this case, the trader may decide to use a *money stop*—that is, a protective stop-loss point with no technical significance that is determined by the desired dollar risk level. For example, consider the plight of a trader in July 2008 who after the swift, steep (nearly $18/barrel) price break during the week ending July 18 is convinced the crude oil market has put in a major top (see Figure 13.5). The closest

---

[1] The specific definition of a relative low or relative high is somewhat arbitrary. (The following description is in terms of the relative low, but analogous commentary would apply to the relative high.) The general definition of a relative low is a day whose low is below the lows of the preceding and succeeding N days. The specific definition of a relative low will depend on the choice of N. A reasonable range for N is 5 to 15.

FIGURE 13.3 Stop Placement Following Wide-Ranging Day Breakout: June 2012 10-Year T-Note

Chart created using TradeStation. ©TradeStation Technologies, Inc. All rights reserved.

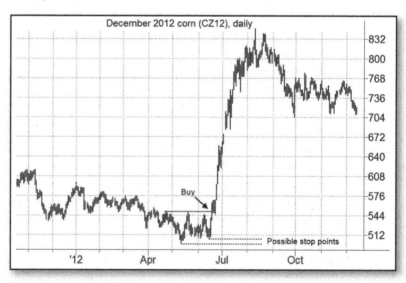

FIGURE 13.4 Stop Placement at Relative Lows: December 2012 Corn

Chart created using TradeStation. ©TradeStation Technologies, Inc. All rights reserved.

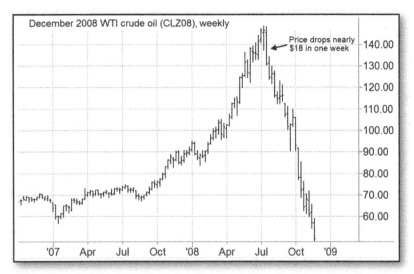

FIGURE 13.5 Example of Market Where Money Stop Is Appropriate: December 2008 WTI Crude Oil

Chart created using TradeStation. ©TradeStation Technologies, Inc. All rights reserved.

meaningful stop point—the contract high (which is the nearest relative high)—would imply a risk of $17,850 per contract (assuming entry at the July 18 closing price)! Although risk can sometimes be reduced if the trader waits for a reaction before entering the market, such a retracement may not occur until the market moves substantially lower. Thus, in a situation in which the nearest meaningful stop point implies a very large risk, a market order accompanied by a money stop may represent the most viable trading approach.

Stops should be used not only to limit losses but also to protect profits. In the case of a long position, the stop should be raised intermittently as the market rises. Similarly, in a declining market, the stop should be lowered as the market declines. This type of stop is called a *trailing stop*.

Figure 13.6 illustrates the use of a trailing stop. Assume a trader implements a long position on the breakout above the upper boundary of the trading range, with a stop-loss liquidation plan keyed to relative lows. Specifically, the trader plans to liquidate the long position following a close below the most recent relative low with the reference point being revised each time the market moves to new high ground. (Of course, the stop condition may often be more restrictive. For example, the trader might require a specified number of closes below a previous low, or a minimum penetration of that low to activate the stop.) The initial stop-loss point would be a close below Stop 1, which is set at a level in the lower half of the trading range—a point that represents less risk than a stop at the more distant March 2009 relative low. Following the early June 2009 advance to new highs, the stop-loss reference point would be raised to the May low (Stop 2). Similarly, the stop reference points would be raised successively to the levels indicated by Stops 3 to 11. The position would have been stopped out on the decline below Stop 11 in March 2010.

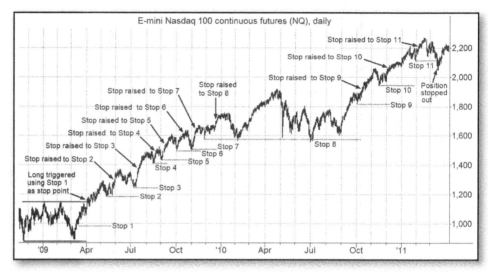

FIGURE 13.6 Trailing Stop: E-Mini Nasdaq 100 Continuous Futures
Chart created using TradeStation. ©TradeStation Technologies, Inc. All rights reserved.

As a general rule, stops should be changed only to reduce risk. Some traders who can't stand the thought of getting stopped out at the bottom of a move (top if short) may be diligent in placing a GTC stop order upon initiating the position, but then cancel the order when the market gets within range. This type of order has been derisively, albeit appropriately, referred to as a CIC (cancel if close) order. Revising the stop to allow greater risk defeats the entire purpose of the stop.

CHAPTER 14

Setting Objectives and Other Position Exit Criteria

It never was my thinking that made the big money for me. It was always my sitting. Got that? My sitting tight! It is no trick at all to be right on the market.

—Edwin Lefèvre

A trade is like the army—getting in is a lot easier than getting out. Provided the trader is adhering to money management principles, a losing trade presents little ambiguity; that is, liquidation would be indicated by a predetermined stop point. However, the profitable trade presents a problem (albeit a desirable one). How should the trader decide when to take profits? Myriad solutions have been proposed to this dilemma. The following sections explore some of the primary approaches.

▪ Chart-Based Objectives

Many chart patterns are believed to provide clues regarding the magnitude of the potential price move. For example, conventional chart wisdom suggests that once prices penetrate the neckline of a head-and-shoulders formation, the ensuing price move will at least equal the distance from the top (or bottom) of the head to the neckline. As another example, many point-and-figure chartists claim that the number of columns that compose a trading range provides an indication of the potential number of boxes in a subsequent trend. (See discussion in Chapter 4 for an explanation of point-and-figure charting.) Generally speaking, chart patterns are probably considerably less reliable as indicators of price objectives than as trade signals.

■ Measured Move

This method is the essence of simplicity. The underlying premise is that markets will move in approximately equal-size price swings. Thus, if a market rallies 30 cents and then reacts, the implication is that the rally from the reaction low will approximate 30 cents. Although the measured move concept is so simple that it strains credibility, the approach offers reasonable guidelines more frequently than one might expect. When two or more of these objectives nearly coincide, it tends to enhance the reliability of the price area as an important objective zone.

Since price swings often span several contracts, it is useful to apply the measured move technique to longer-term price charts that link several contracts. Generally speaking, continuous futures charts are more appropriate than nearest futures charts for measured move analysis because, as was noted in Chapter 4 and further detailed in Chapter 5, continuous futures accurately reflect price swings, whereas nearest futures do not.

In Figure 14.1, the measured move objective that was fulfilled in July 2012 was the result of adding the amount of the December 2011–May 2012 rally (404.75¢) to the early June 2012 low of 667.25¢. Figure 14.2 shows two measured moves on a weekly chart. The first measured move target at 0.2711 (MM1), which was very close to the March 2015 relative low, was derived by subtracting the June–December 2014 decline of 0.0752 from the January 2015 high of 0.3462. The second measured move objective at 0.2297 (MM2), which was fairly close to the September 2015 low, was obtained by subtracting the January–March 2015 decline of 0.0818 from the late April high of

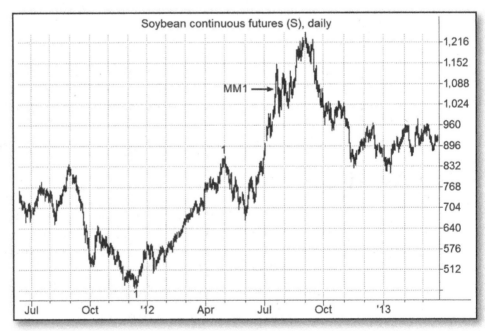

FIGURE 14.1 Measured Move: Soybean Continuous Futures

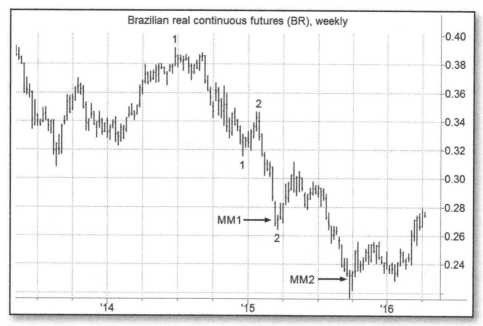

FIGURE 14.2 Measured Moves: Brazilian Real Continuous Futures
Chart created using TradeStation. ©TradeStation Technologies, Inc. All rights reserved.

0.3115. Figure 14.3 shows four measured move targets, three of which (MM1, MM3, and MM4) implied targets very near swing point highs.

Figure 14.4 illustrates a series of reasonably accurate measured move targets in frozen orange juice futures from mid-2012 to late 2013. Price didn't reach three of the targets (MM2, MM6, and MM9, represented by dashed lines), but missed only MM2 by a notable margin. Of the other six targets, all but MM4 represented quite advantageous exit points. Also, note that MM3 and MM5 signaled exit points at around the same level, reinforcing the target objective in that price vicinity.

Figure 14.5 provides another example of successive reasonably accurate measured move targets over a roughly two-year period. Note that the same price point can serve as the terminus of two different price swings (see October 2014 high with stacked 8 and 4), which can lead to two different measured move objectives based on that point (MM4 and MM8). This chart also provides an example of coincident measured move objectives: MM6, which is a projection based on the January–March 2014 upswing off the May low, occurred one tick away from MM8, which was the result of adding the June–October 2013 rally to the November low. MM4 and MM5 also signaled exits at approximately the same price level.

As Figures 14.4 and 14.5 illustrate, when there is more than one relevant price swing for deriving a measured move objective, there will be more than one measured move objective for the same projected low or high. When two or more of these objectives nearly coincide, it tends to enhance the reliability of the projected price area as an important target zone. Figure 14.6 provides a perfect example of two coinciding measured move price targets. The measured move objectives implied by the July 2014–March 2015 decline (MM5) and the May–October 2015 decline (MM6) coincided just above the actual market bottom formed in January 2016.

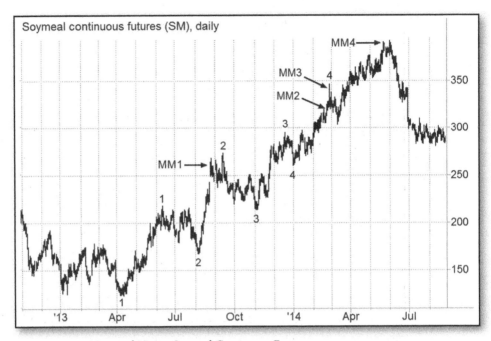

FIGURE 14.3 Measured Moves: Soymeal Continuous Futures
Chart created using TradeStation. ©TradeStation Technologies, Inc. All rights reserved.

FIGURE 14.4 Measured Moves: Orange Juice Continuous Futures
Chart created using TradeStation. ©TradeStation Technologies, Inc. All rights reserved.

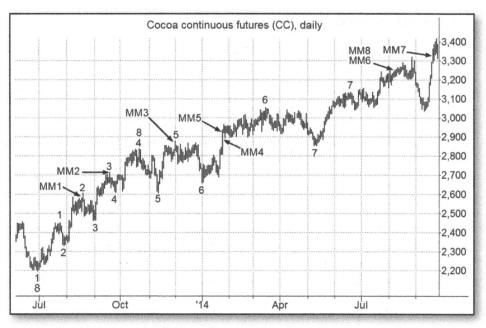

FIGURE 14.5 Concentration of Measured Move Targets: Cocoa Continuous Futures
Chart created using TradeStation. ©TradeStation Technologies, Inc. All rights reserved.

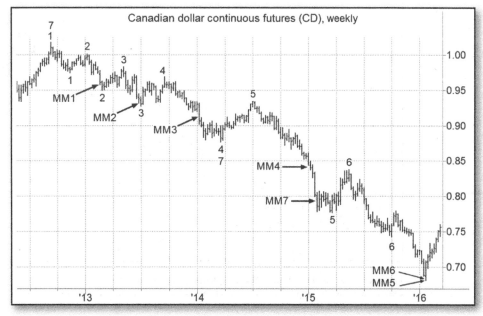

FIGURE 14.6 Concentration of Measured Move Targets: Canadian Dollar Continuous Futures
Chart created using TradeStation. ©TradeStation Technologies, Inc. All rights reserved.

■ Rule of Seven

This method of setting objectives is an interesting and easy-to-use approach detailed in *Techniques of a Professional Commodity Chart Analyst* by Arthur Sklarew (Windsor Books, 1980). The rule of seven refers to a common set of multipliers used to determine objectives, which are derived by dividing 7 by 5, 4, 3, and 2, respectively. Thus, the multipliers are: $7 \div 5 = 1.4$, $7 \div 4 = 1.75$, $7 \div 3 = 2.33$, and $7 \div 2 = 3.5$. The products of each of these multipliers and the magnitude of the first price swing in a bull market are added to the low to obtain a set of price objectives. In a bear market, the products are subtracted from the high.

Sklarew suggests using the latter three multipliers (1.75, 2.33, and 3.5) for finding objectives in bull markets and the first three multipliers (1.4, 1.75, and 2.33) for deriving objectives in a bear market. In addition, he indicates objectives based on the lower multipliers are more meaningful if the reference price move (the price swing multiplied by the multipliers) is of extended duration (i.e., several months) and objectives based on the higher multipliers are more significant if a short-term price swing is used in the calculations. Of course, there will be some degree of subjectivity in this approach, since the perception of what constitutes the first price swing in a trend could vary from trader to trader.

The rule of seven is illustrated in Figure 14.7. (Note that this is the same chart that was used as Figure 14.3 to illustrate measured move objectives. Readers may find it instructive to compare the

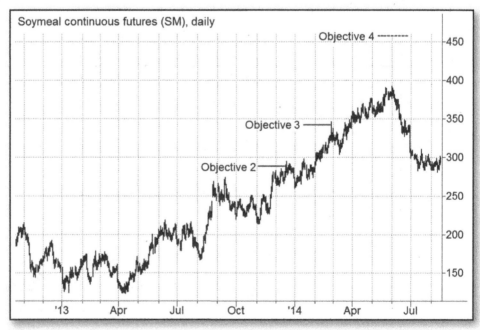

FIGURE 14.7 Rule of Seven: Soymeal Continuous Futures

Chart created using TradeStation. ©TradeStation Technologies, Inc. All rights reserved.

implications of these two approaches.) The first wave of the bull market that began in April 2013 was 94.30 points, measured from the April low to the June high. Following Sklarew's guidelines, because this is a bull market, we skip the first objective and use the second through fourth objectives, obtained using the multipliers 1.75, 2.33, and 3.5. The April 11 low, which is used to calculate all the objectives, was 123.90. The second objective is 288.90 [123.90 + (1.75 × 94.30)]. The third objective is 343.60 [123.90 + (2.33 × 94.30)]. The fourth objective is 454 [123.90 + (3.5 × 94.30)]. Note that objective 2 was just below the December 2013 relative high of 294.80, while objective 3 was just below the February 27 relative high of 346.10. The market failed to reach objective 4.

Figure 14.8 (which repeats Figure 14.6) illustrates the rule of seven for an extended bear market in Canadian dollar continuous futures. The chart intentionally shows two sets of objectives based on using different lows (A and B) to define the initial leg of the downtrend. In both cases, the September 2012 high was used as the initial high reference price. The first wave of this bear market using low A in March 2013 was 0.0674 points, while using low B in March 2014 the first wave was 0.1407 points. Following Sklarew's guidelines, since this is a bear market, we use the first through third objectives (obtained using the multipliers 1.4, 1.75, and 2.33). The products of these three multipliers and the two initial price swings are subtracted from the high of the move to obtain the two sets of downside objectives. Of the three objectives that referenced low A, only Objective 2 was

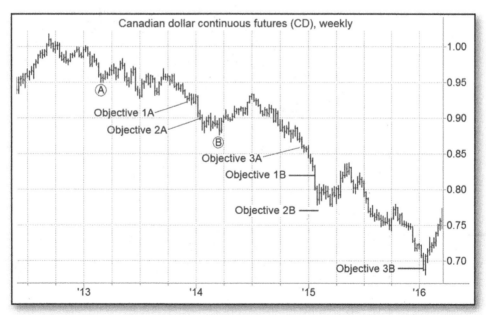

FIGURE 14.8 Rule of Seven: Canadian Dollar Continuous Futures
Chart created using TradeStation. ©TradeStation Technologies, Inc. All rights reserved.

fairly close to a relative low (during the January–March 2014 consolidation). Among the objectives using low B, Objective 2 was just below the March 2015 relative low, while Objective 3 was just above the January 2016 low.

■ Support and Resistance Levels

Points near support levels provide a reasonable choice for setting initial objectives on short positions. For example, the indicated objective zone in Figure 14.9 is based on support anticipated in the area of two prior relative lows. Similarly, prices near resistance levels can be used for setting initial objectives on long positions. For example, the indicated objective in Figure 14.10 is based on resistance implied by the two previous highs in late 2009 and early 2010. In Figure 14.11, an upside objective for British pound prices after the early 2009 bottom was implied by the late 2005 relative low, a level that continued to function as a ceiling for prices over the next several years (a case of former support becoming resistance, as discussed in Chapter 8).

Generally speaking, support and resistance levels usually represent only temporary rather than major objectives. Consequently, in using this approach, it is advisable to seek to reenter the position at a better price if a reaction does develop.

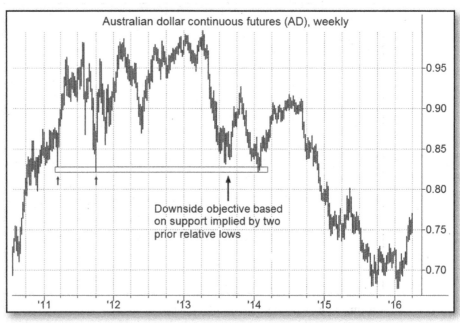

FIGURE 14.9 Downside Objective at Support Zone: Australian Dollar Continuous Futures
Chart created using TradeStation. ©TradeStation Technologies, Inc. All rights reserved.

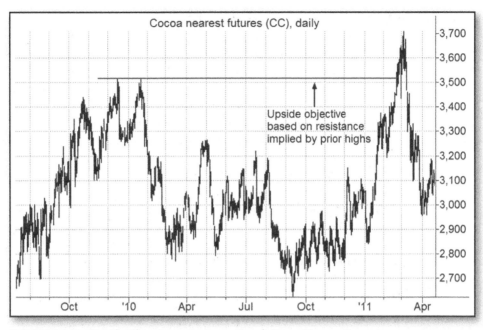

FIGURE 14.10   Upside Objective at Resistance Level: Cocoa Nearest Futures
Chart created using TradeStation. ©TradeStation Technologies, Inc. All rights reserved.

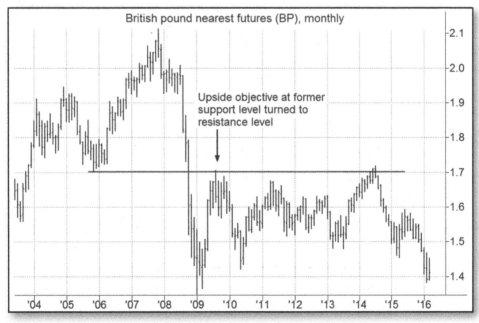

FIGURE 14.11   Upside Objective at Former Support Turned Resistance: British Pound Nearest Futures
Chart created using TradeStation. ©TradeStation Technologies, Inc. All rights reserved.

■ Overbought/Oversold Indicators

Overbought/oversold indicators are technical measures intended to reflect when prices have risen or fallen too sharply and are thus vulnerable to a reaction. Figure 14.12 illustrates the relative strength index (RSI), which provides an example of an overbought/oversold indicator.[1] The RSI has a range of values between 0 and 100. Based on the standard interpretation, levels above 70 suggest an overbought condition, while levels below 30 suggest an oversold condition.

The choice of specific overbought/oversold boundaries is a subjective one. For example, instead of 70 and 30, one might use 75 and 25, or 80 and 20. The more extreme the selected threshold levels, the closer the overbought/oversold signals will be to market turning points, but the greater the number of such points that will be missed.

The buy (up) arrows in Figure 14.12 denote points at which the RSI crosses below 30—that is, reaches an oversold condition that can be viewed as a signal to liquidate short positions. The sell (down) arrows denote points at which the RSI crosses above 70—that is, reaches an overbought condition that can be viewed as a signal to liquidate long positions.

Although the overbought/oversold signals in Figure 14.12 provide some reasonably good position liquidation signals in the latter half of the chart (mid-April 2015 forward), the signals before that

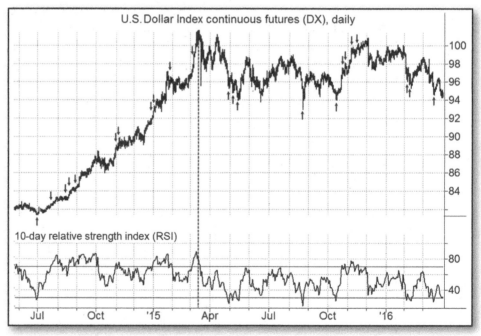

FIGURE 14.12 Relative Strength Index in Trend and Trading Range Conditions: U.S. Dollar Index Continuous Futures

Chart created using TradeStation. ©TradeStation Technologies, Inc. All rights reserved.

---

[1] The RSI was originally introduced in J. Welles Wilder, Jr., *New Concepts in Technical Trading Systems* (Winston-Salem, NC: Hunter Publishing, 1978).

point—when the market was in a strong uptrend—were almost all terrible. The 27 percent rally off the July 2014 low that ultimately extended into March 2015 generated 10 overbought signals, four of which occurred in rapid succession in the first two months of the rally. Only the final two signals during this period, in late January and early March 2015, could be considered relatively timely. This example hints at both the benefits and drawbacks of using overbought/oversold indicators as liquidation signals. The approach will usually work well when the market is in a trading range, but will fail miserably during strong trending phases.

The derivation and interpretation of various technical indicators are discussed in detail in Chapter 11.

■ DeMark Sequential

As discussed in Chapter 11, all the popular overbought/oversold indicators (e.g., RSI, moving average convergence-divergence [MACD], stochastic) are very highly correlated with each other. Tom DeMark's sequential, which is intended to signal points where the market is fully extended and vulnerable to a major trend reversal, represents a completely different and original overbought/oversold indicator. The sequential methodology falls within the domain of pattern recognition. The sequential is fully described in a 48-page chapter in Tom DeMark's book *The New Science of Technical Analysis* (John Wiley & Sons, 1994). The following brief summary of the technique is intended to give a general sense of the approach. Readers interested in a fully detailed explanation of the sequential, which includes several additional qualifying conditions and a discussion of various alternative trade entry and exit rules, are referred to DeMark's text.

The fulfillment of the sequential *buy* condition involves three basic stages:

1. **Setup.** The setup requires nine or more consecutive closes that are lower than the corresponding closes four trading days earlier.
2. **Intersection.** This condition requires that the high of any day on or after the eighth day of the setup exceed the low of any day three or more trading days earlier. Essentially, this is a minimal qualifying condition that ensures that the buy setup will not be deemed complete in a "waterfall" price slide.
3. **Countdown.** The countdown stage begins once the previous two conditions have been fulfilled. Starting from 0, the countdown increases by one on each day with a close lower than the low two days earlier. A sequential buy signal is generated once the countdown reaches 13. In contrast to the setup stage, countdown days do not need to be consecutive. The countdown is canceled if any of the following three conditions arise:
   a. There is a close that exceeds the highest intraday high during the setup stage.
   b. A *sell* setup occurs (i.e., nine consecutive closes above the corresponding closes four days earlier).
   c. Another buy setup occurs before the buy countdown is complete. In this situation, the new buy setup takes precedence, and the countdown restarts from 0 once the intersection condition is met.

The fulfillment of the sequential *sell* conditions are analogous:

1. **Setup.** The setup requires nine or more consecutive closes that are higher than the corresponding closes four trading day earlier.

2. **Intersection.** This condition requires that the low of any day on or after the eighth day of the setup is lower than the high of any day three or more trading days earlier. Essentially, this is a minimal qualifying condition that ensures that the sell setup will not be deemed complete in a "runaway" rally.

3. **Countdown.** The countdown stage begins once the previous two conditions have been fulfilled. Starting from 0, the countdown increases by one on each day with a close higher than the high two days earlier. A sequential sell signal is generated once the countdown reaches 13. In contrast to the setup stage, countdown days do not need to be consecutive. The countdown is canceled if any of the following three conditions arise:

   a. There is a close that is below the lowest intraday low during the setup stage.

   b. A *buy* setup occurs (i.e., nine consecutive closes below the corresponding closes four days earlier).

   c. Another sell setup occurs before the sell countdown is complete. In this situation, the new sell setup takes precedence, and the countdown restarts from 0 once the intersection condition is met.

Figures 14.13 through 14.17 provide illustrations of markets that fulfilled the complete sequential process. In each case, the setup, intersection, and countdown stages are marked on the charts; the final bar of the setup stage is highlighted with a boldfaced **9,** while the final bar of the countdown phase is marked with a boldfaced **13.** The preceding description will be clearer if read in conjunction with an examination of these charts.

Figure 14.13 provides an illustration of a sequential sell signal in June 2016 10-year T-note futures. Note that in this case, the first day of the countdown stage (which occurred three days after the end of the setup stage) also fulfilled the intersection requirement (a bar with a low below the high of a day three or more days earlier). The countdown phase completed on February 11, the day that marked the highest high and close of the upmove. Figure 14.14, which shows the June 2016 gold contract, provides an example of a sequential buy. As was the case in Figure 14.13, the first day of the countdown stage also marked the fulfillment of the intersection requirement. The completion of the countdown stage coincided with the mid-December 2015 low.

Figure 14.15 provides another example of a sequential buy, this time in the May 2016 soybean contract. In this case the intersection requirement occurred on the eighth bar of the setup phase, while the countdown phase didn't begin until nine days after the end of the setup phase. The countdown completed in early March 2016, the day with the lowest low of the move and one day after the lowest close. (*Note:* Figures 14.14 and 14.15 reflect day-session-only data.)

The sequential rules can also be applied to bar charts for time periods other than daily. Figure 14.16 illustrates a sequential sell on a monthly copper continuous futures chart. Here, the end of the setup stage, the beginning of the countdown stage, and the fulfillment of the intersection requirement all occur on the same bar (month). The market peaked at month 11 of the countdown phase, but the real

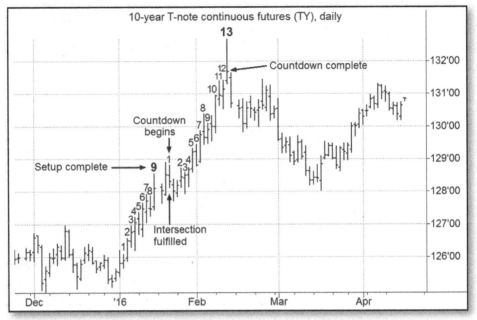

FIGURE 14.13 DeMark Sequential: June 2016 10-Year T-Note Continuous Futures

Source for sequential signals: DeMark Analytics (www.demark.com)

Chart created using TradeStation. ©TradeStation Technologies, Inc. All rights reserved.

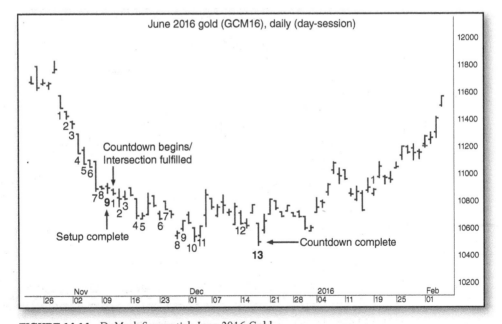

FIGURE 14.14 DeMark Sequential: June 2016 Gold

Source for sequential signals: Copyright 2016, DeMark for CQG, www.demark.com

Chart from CQG, Inc. © 2017 All rights reserved worldwide. Signal from Demark Analytics.

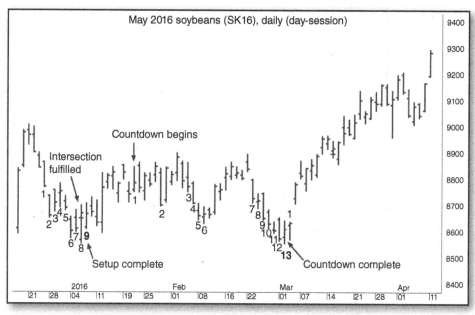

FIGURE 14.15 DeMark Sequential: May 2016 Soybeans

Source for sequential signals: Copyright 2016, DeMark for CQG, www.demark.com
Chart from CQG, Inc. © 2017 All rights reserved worldwide. Signal from Demark Analytics.

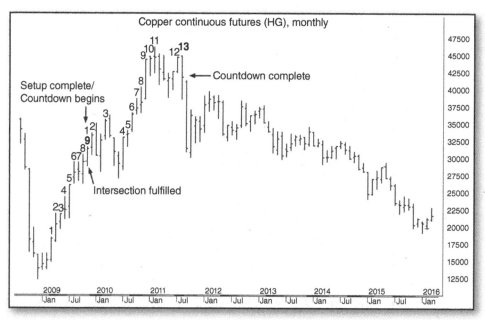

FIGURE 14.16 DeMark Sequential: Copper Continuous Futures

Source for sequential signals: Copyright 2016, DeMark for CQG, www.demark.com
Chart from CQG, Inc. © 2017 All rights reserved worldwide. Signal from Demark Analytics.

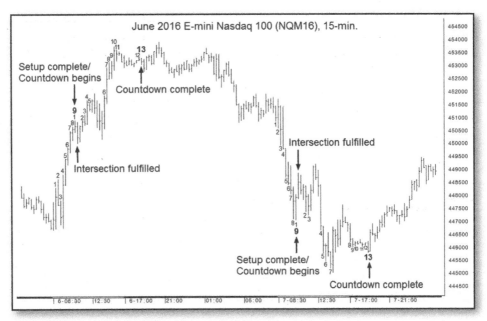

FIGURE 14.17 DeMark Sequential: June 2016 E-Mini Nasdaq 100

Source for sequential signals: Copyright 2016, DeMark for CQG, www.demark.com
Chart from CQG, Inc. © 2017 All rights reserved worldwide. Signal from Demark Analytics.

reversal did not occur until after the completion of countdown six months later. Figure 14.17 shows completed sequential sell and buy setups on an intraday chart (15-minute bars). The sell setup completed during a consolidation near the top of the rally, while the buy setup completed a bit above the low of the subsequent decline, but right at the start of the first extended rally after the low.

The preceding examples were obviously selected with hindsight to illustrate the methodology. Of course, in real-life trading, the accuracy of the DeMark sequential approach will not approach the uniformly near-perfect signals provided by the previous set of examples. If it did, all anyone would need to do would be to trade all sequential signals and retire a multimillionaire. Nevertheless, these examples should demonstrate that sequential can be a very powerful tool, with the capability of providing extraordinary timing signals. Sequential also has the advantage of being inversely correlated to trend-following approaches that typically dominate the technical tool bag. For these reasons, many traders might find DeMark's sequential a very useful addition to their overall trading methodology.

■ Contrary Opinion

The theory of contrary opinion suggests that whenever a large majority of speculators are bullish, those who want to be long are already long. Consequently, there will be a paucity of potential new buyers, and the market will be vulnerable to a downside reaction. An analogous interpretation would apply when the majority of traders are bearish. Contrary opinion measures are based on either surveys of market advisory recommendations or surveys of traders and implicitly assume these opinions represent a reasonable proxy for overall market sentiment. The overbought and oversold thresholds in contrary opinion indexes will vary with the source.

Although contrary opinion is undoubtedly a sound theoretical concept, the Achilles' heel of this approach is the difficulty of measuring market sentiment accurately. Contrary opinion measures provided by existing services have frequently signaled major turning points. On the other hand, it is also not unusual for a contrary opinion index to stay high while the market continues to climb, or to stay low as the market continues to slide. On balance, this method provides useful information as long as it is not used as the sole trading guideline.

■ Trailing Stops

The use of trailing stops may be among the least glamorous, but most sensible, methods of determining a trade exit point. Although one will never sell the high or buy the low using this method, the approach comes closest to the ideal of permitting a profitable trade to run its course. Trailing stops were detailed in Chapter 13.

■ Change of Market Opinion

This method of exiting trades represents another approach with very little flash, but lots of common sense. In this case, the trader sets no predetermined objectives at all, but rather maintains the position until her market opinion changes to at least neutral.

CHAPTER 15

The Most Important Rule in Chart Analysis

The market is like a flu virus—as soon as you think you have it pegged, it mutates into something else.

—Wayne H. Wagner

■ Failed Signals

A failed signal is among the most reliable of all chart signals. When a market fails to follow through in the direction of a chart signal, it very strongly suggests the possibility of a significant move in the opposite direction. For example, in Figure 15.1 note how the market abruptly reversed course after breaking out above the high of the July–August 2013 consolidation in WTI crude oil. If the upside penetration signal were valid, the market should not have retreated back to the lower portion of the consolidation and certainly not below its lower boundary. The fact that such a retracement occurs almost immediately following the breakout strongly suggests a "bull trap." Such price action is consistent with the market's rising just enough to activate stop orders lying beyond the boundary of the range, but uncovering no additional buying support after the breakout—an indication of a very weak underlying technical picture. In effect, the immediate failure of the apparent buy signal can be viewed as a strong indication the market should be sold.

Now that we have established the critical importance of failed signals, the following sections detail various types of failed signals, along with guidelines as to their interpretation and trading implications.

■ Bull and Bear Traps

Bull and bear traps are major breakouts that are soon followed by abrupt, sharp price reversals, in stark contrast to the price follow-through that is expected to follow breakouts. In my experience, this type of counter-to-anticipated price action is among the most reliable indicators of major tops and bottoms.

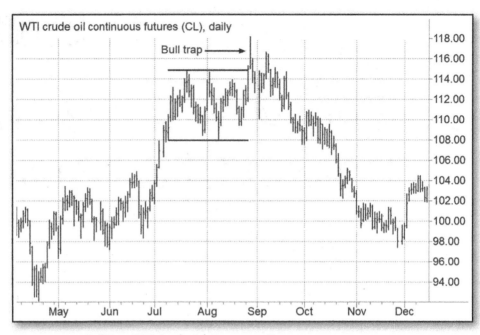

FIGURE 15.1   Bull Trap: WTI Crude Oil Continuous Futures
Chart created using TradeStation. ©TradeStation Technologies, Inc. All rights reserved.

An example of a bull trap was provided in the previous section (Figure 15.1). Another instance of a bull trap was the June 2015 peak in RBOB gasoline (see Figure 15.2). After rallying from January to May 2015, the market consolidated for roughly one month before breaking out to new highs in mid-June. However, the market quickly reversed back into the trading range, and by mid-July prices had broken below the range's lower boundary, setting the stage for a multimonth downtrend.

Analogous to the bull trap, in the case of a bear trap, the market falls just enough to trigger resting stops below the low end of a trading range, but fails to uncover any additional selling pressure after the breakout—an indication of substantial underlying strength. In effect, the immediate failure of a sell signal can be viewed as a signal the market should be bought.

Figure 15.3 shows a bear trap that marked the 2014 low in U.S. Dollar Index futures. In May the market broke below the lower boundary of a long-standing trading range but reversed two days later to close back above that threshold. This price action proved to be the beginning of the market's largest rally in more than a decade.

Figure 15.4 provides another example of a bear trap. Corn prices, which had been trending lower since late summer 2012, entered a trading range in November–December 2013. The market broke below the downside of the range in early January 2014, falling more than 2 percent over the next two days before reversing sharply and returning to the midpoint of the range. May corn futures subsequently surged approximately 25 percent over the next three months.

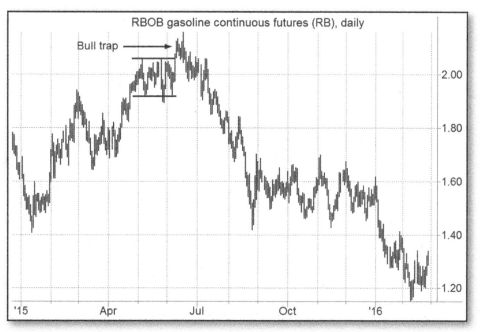

FIGURE 15.2 Bull Trap: RBOB Gasoline Futures
Chart created using TradeStation. ©TradeStation Technologies, Inc. All rights reserved.

FIGURE 15.3 Bear Trap: U.S. Dollar Index Futures
Chart created using TradeStation. ©TradeStation Technologies, Inc. All rights reserved.

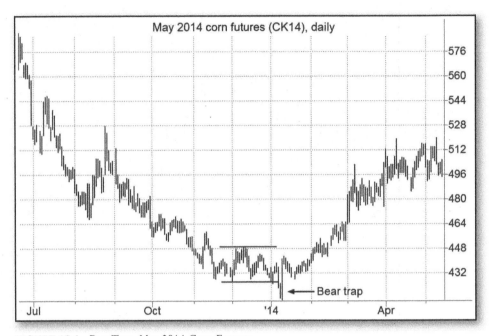

FIGURE 15.4   Bear Trap: May 2014 Corn Futures

How much of a pullback is required to indicate a bull or bear trap has occurred? The following are several possible confirmation conditions:

Initial price confirmation. A price retracement to the midpoint of the consolidation that preceded the breakout.

Strong price confirmation. A price retracement to the more distant boundary (lower for bull trap; upper for bear trap) of the consolidation that preceded the breakout.

Time confirmation. The failure of the market to return to the extreme price witnessed following the breakout within a specified amount of time (e.g., four weeks).

The trade-off between initial and strong price confirmations is that the former will provide better entry levels in trading bull and bear traps, whereas the latter will provide more reliable signals. The time confirmation condition can be used on its own or in conjunction with the two price confirmation conditions. Figures 15.5 through 15.8 repeat Figures 15.1 through 15.4, adding each of the three confirmation conditions (using four weeks for the time confirmation condition). Note the time confirmation can occur before both price confirmation conditions, after both price confirmation conditions (as is the case in Figures 15.6 and 15.8), or between the price confirmations (Figures 15.5 and 15.7).

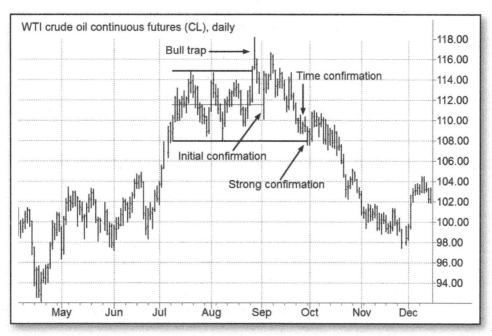

FIGURE 15.5 Bull Trap Confirmation Conditions: WTI Crude Oil Continuous Futures
Chart created using TradeStation. ©TradeStation Technologies, Inc. All rights reserved.

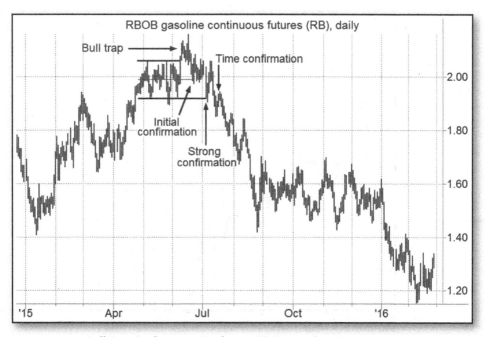

FIGURE 15.6 Bull Trap Confirmation Conditions: RBOB Gasoline Continuous Futures
Chart created using TradeStation. ©TradeStation Technologies, Inc. All rights reserved.

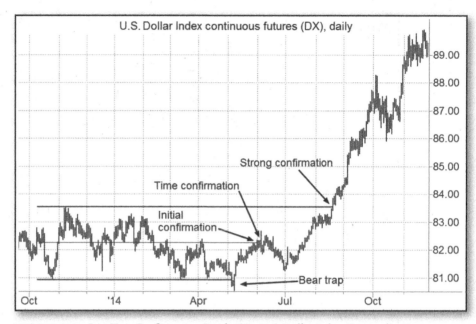

FIGURE 15.7 Bear Trap Confirmation Conditions: U.S. Dollar Index Continuous Futures
Chart created using TradeStation. ©TradeStation Technologies, Inc. All rights reserved.

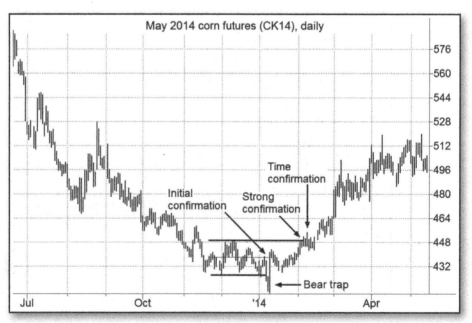

FIGURE 15.8 Bear Trap Confirmation Conditions: May 2014 Corn Futures
Chart created using TradeStation. ©TradeStation Technologies, Inc. All rights reserved.

A bull trap signal would be invalidated if the market returned to the breakout high. Similarly, a bear trap signal would be invalidated if the market returned to the breakout low. More sensitive conditions could be used to invalidate bull or bear trap signals once the market has moved sufficiently in the direction of the signal or a specified amount of time has elapsed. An example of such a condition would be the return of prices to the opposite boundary of a consolidation once a strong price confirmation signal was received (e.g., in the case of a bull trap, a return to the top of the consolidation after prices broke to below the low end of the consolidation). An example of a more sensitive combined price/time invalidation signal would be the return of prices to the median of a consolidation (i.e., the initial *price* confirmation point for bull and bear trap signals) at any time four or more weeks after a strong price confirmation was received. The more sensitive the selected invalidation condition, the smaller the loss on an incorrect call of a bull or bear trap, but the greater the chance that a correct trade will be abandoned prematurely.

If the selected invalidation condition does not occur, a trade implemented on a bull or bear trap signal would be held until a price objective or other trade liquidation condition was met or until there was evidence of an opposite direction trend reversal.

■ False Trend Line Breakouts

As discussed in Chapter 6, trend lines are particularly prone to false breakouts. Such false breakouts can be used as signals for trading in the direction opposite to the breakout. In fact, in my opinion, false trend line breakout signals are considerably more reliable than conventional trend line breakout signals. In the case of a downtrend, a false trend line breakout would be confirmed if the market closed below the trend line a specified number of times (e.g., two, three) following an upside breakout. Similarly, in the case of an uptrend, a false trend line breakout would be confirmed if the market closed above the trend line a specified number of times following a downside breakout.

Figure 15.9 provides an example of a false breakout of an uptrend line in 10-year T-note futures. The September downside breakout of the uptrend line was soon followed by a break above the line. The indicated failure signal is based on an assumed requirement of two closes above the line for confirmation. Figure 15.10 provides a similar example in the E-mini Nasdaq 100 futures.

It is quite possible for a chart to yield multiple successive false trend breakout signals in the process of a trend line being redefined. In Figure 15.11 the initial upside penetration of the prevailing downtrend line occurred in mid-March. Prices quickly retreated back below the line, with the indicated failure signal assumed to be triggered by the second close below the line. Another false breakout occurred about a month later based on the redefined trend line using the March relative high. Prices retreated below this downtrend line several days later, yielding another false trend breakout signal.

FIGURE 15.9 False Breakout of Uptrend Line: 10-Year T-Note Continuous Futures
Chart created using TradeStation. ©TradeStation Technologies, Inc. All rights reserved.

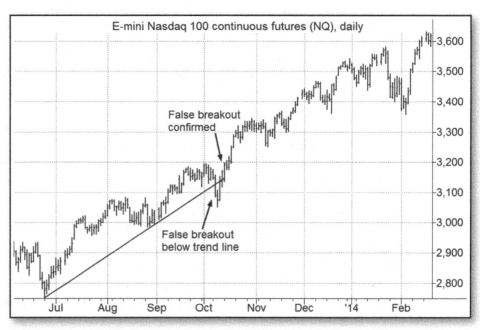

FIGURE 15.10 False Breakout of Uptrend Line: E-Mini Nasdaq Continuous Futures
Chart created using TradeStation. ©TradeStation Technologies, Inc. All rights reserved.

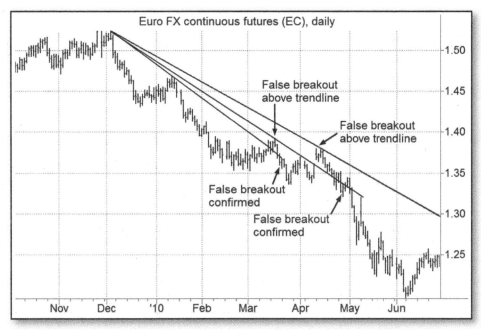

Euro FX continuous futures (EC), daily

False breakout
above trendline

False breakout
above trendline

False breakout
confirmed

False breakout
confirmed

FIGURE 15.11 Multiple False Breakouts of Downtrend Lines: Euro Continuous Futures

■ Return to Spike Extremes

As was detailed in Chapter 9, price spikes frequently occur at important price reversals. Consequently, the return of prices to a prior spike extreme can be viewed as transforming the original spike into a failed signal. The more extreme the spike (i.e., the greater the magnitude by which the spike high or low exceeds the highs or lows on the prior and subsequent days), the more significant its penetration. The significance of such failed signals is also enhanced if at least several weeks, and preferably several months, have elapsed since the original spike.

In Figure 15.12, the January 2016 return to both the August and October 2015 spike highs was followed by a sharp rally well above the prior spike highs. In Figure 15.13, the October 2010 penetration of the early 2008 spike high was followed by a sharp rally. Figures 15.14 and 15.15 provide two illustrations of downside penetrations of spike lows being followed by steep sell-offs.

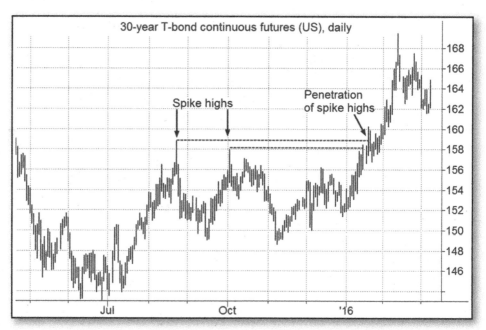

FIGURE 15.12 Penetration of Spike Highs: 30-Year T-Bond Continuous Futures
Chart created using TradeStation. ©TradeStation Technologies, Inc. All rights reserved.

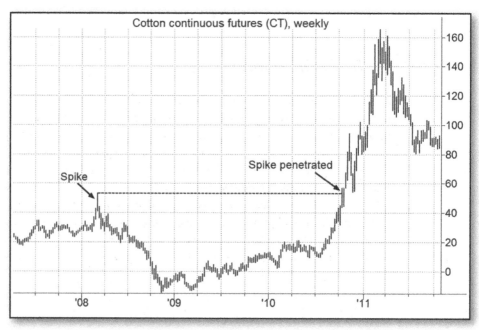

FIGURE 15.13 Penetration of Spike High: Cotton Continuous Futures
Chart created using TradeStation. ©TradeStation Technologies, Inc. All rights reserved.

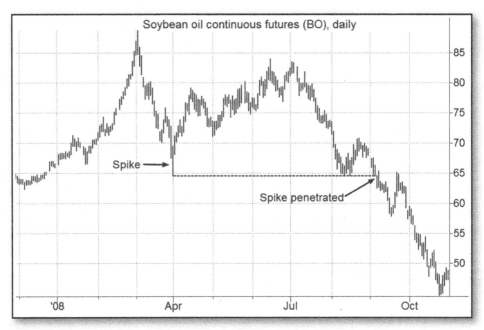

FIGURE 15.14 Penetration of Spike Highs: Soybean Oil Continuous Futures

Chart created using TradeStation. ©TradeStation Technologies, Inc. All rights reserved.

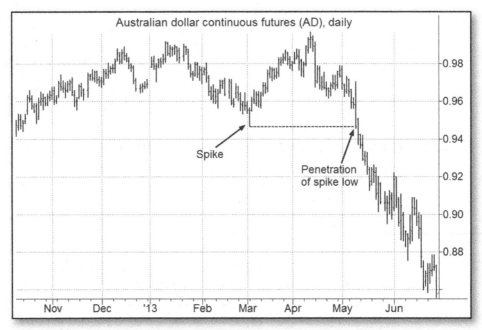

FIGURE 15.15 Penetration of Spike Low: Australian Dollar Continuous Futures

Chart created using TradeStation. ©TradeStation Technologies, Inc. All rights reserved.

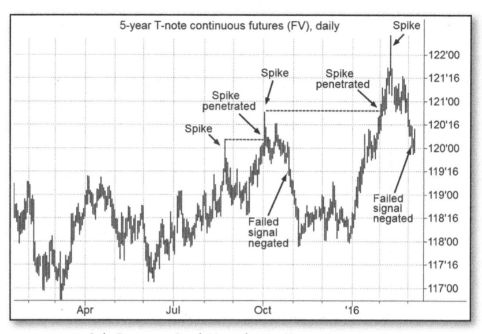

FIGURE 15.16 Spike Penetration Signals Negated: 5-Year T-Note Continuous Futures
Chart created using TradeStation. ©TradeStation Technologies, Inc. All rights reserved.

Generally speaking, a close beyond the opposite extreme of the spike can be viewed as negating the failed signal. For example, in Figure 15.16 the price briefly exceeded the August spike high, forming a second spike high in early October, but then immediately retreated, falling below the low of the August spike day—a *failed* failed signal, so to speak. This pattern repeated itself in early 2016 when the market penetrated the October spike, rallied for about a week (forming a spike high in the process), but then reversed to close below the low of the October spike day in early March.

■ Return to Wide-Ranging Day Extremes

As explained in Chapter 9, wide-ranging days (WRDs) with particularly strong or weak closes tend to lead to price extensions in the same direction. Consequently, a close above the high price of a downside WRD or below the low price of an upside WRD can be viewed as confirming such days as failed signals.

In Figure 15.17 the WRD that formed in mid-April 2015 is penetrated to the downside about 10 weeks later, leading to a significant decline. In Figure 15.18 a huge WRD formed in early July 2013 in the vicinity of the May swing high. Three days later, the uptrend was reversed by a downside WRD, which was followed three days later by a close below the low of the first WRD, confirming a failed signal and leading to an extended market slide.

Figure 15.19 shows an example of an up-closing WRD in late April that was reversed by a down-closing WRD 12 days later. A closing penetration of the April WRD occurred four days later and was followed by a large, sustained downtrend. Figure 15.20 shows a massive down-closing WRD that was eclipsed to the upside a little more than a month later and followed by a strong rally to new high ground.

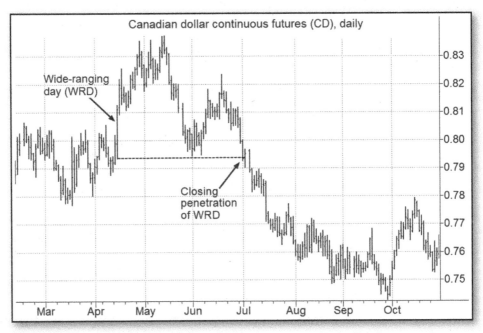

FIGURE 15.17 Penetration of Upside Wide-Ranging Day: Canadian Dollar Continuous Futures

Chart created using TradeStation. ©TradeStation Technologies, Inc. All rights reserved.

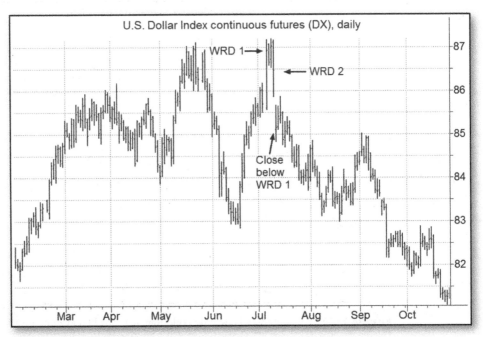

FIGURE 15.18 Penetration of Upside Wide-Ranging Day: U.S. Dollar Index Continuous Futures

Chart created using TradeStation. ©TradeStation Technologies, Inc. All rights reserved.

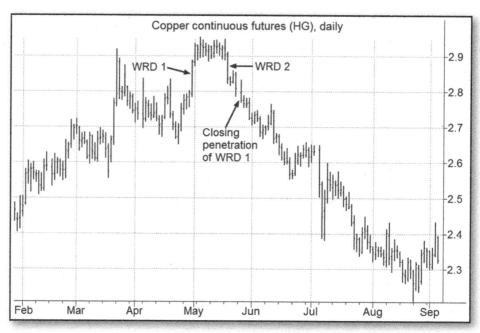

FIGURE 15.19 Penetration of Upside Wide-Ranging Day: Copper Continuous Futures
Chart created using TradeStation. ©TradeStation Technologies, Inc. All rights reserved.

FIGURE 15.20 Penetration of Downside Wide-Ranging Day: Bund Continuous Futures
Chart created using TradeStation. ©TradeStation Technologies, Inc. All rights reserved.

■ Counter-to-Anticipated Breakout of Flag or Pennant

As was explained in Chapter 9, typically, flag or pennant consolidations tend to be followed by price swings in the same direction as the price swings that preceded their formation. Therefore, if a flag or pennant formation is followed by a breakout in the opposite direction of the preceding price swing, it would qualify the pattern as a failed signal.

In Figure 15.21, just as would have been implied by the chart interpretation guidelines presented in Chapter 9, the flag formations that evolved during the 2014 downtrend in soybean prices were generally followed by downswings. The one exception, however, was the flag that formed in late September and early October. In this instance, the flag was followed by an upside breakout. This counter-to-anticipated price action was followed by a rally of more than 13 percent to the mid-November high. Figures 15.22, 15.23, and 15.24 provide three examples where counter-to-anticipated downside breakouts of flag patterns signaled major trend reversals. Note that Figure 15.24 is, in fact, the same reversal depicted in Figure 15.19, which focused on the downside penetration of the strong-closing WRD that immediately preceded the flag. In Figure 15.25 heating oil prices rallied more than 33 percent in one month after the counter-to-anticipated upside breakout of the flag that formed in early 2015.

A counter-to-anticipated breakout does not need to be followed by an immediate extension of the price move in order to be a valid confirmation of a failed signal. How much of a retracement can be allowed before the interpretation of a failed signal is abandoned? One reasonable approach is to

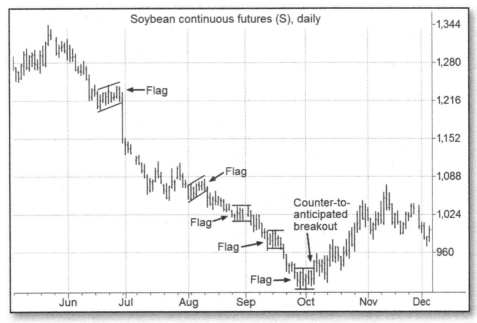

FIGURE 15.21 Counter-to-Anticipated Breakout of Flag Pattern: Soybean Continuous Futures
Chart created using TradeStation. ©TradeStation Technologies, Inc. All rights reserved.

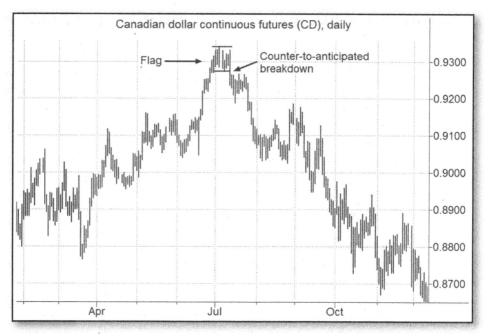

FIGURE 15.22 Counter-to-Anticipated Breakout of Flag Pattern: Canadian Dollar Continuous Futures
Chart created using TradeStation. ©TradeStation Technologies, Inc. All rights reserved.

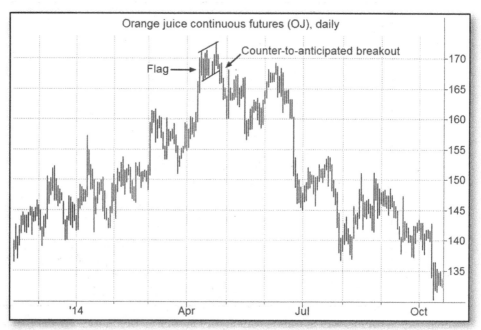

FIGURE 15.23 Counter-to-Anticipated Breakout of Flag Pattern: Orange Juice Continuous Futures
Chart created using TradeStation. ©TradeStation Technologies, Inc. All rights reserved.

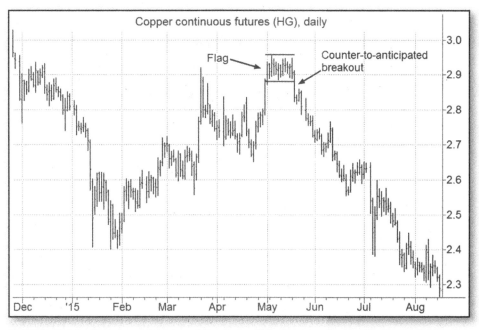

FIGURE 15.24 Counter-to-Anticipated Breakout of Flag Pattern: Copper Continuous Futures
Chart created using TradeStation. ©TradeStation Technologies, Inc. All rights reserved.

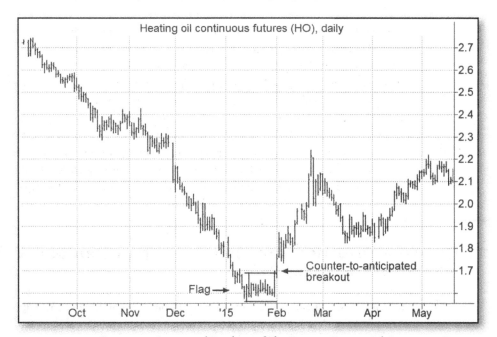

FIGURE 15.25 Counter-to-Anticipated Breakout of Flag Pattern: Heating Oil Continuous Futures
Chart created using TradeStation. ©TradeStation Technologies, Inc. All rights reserved.

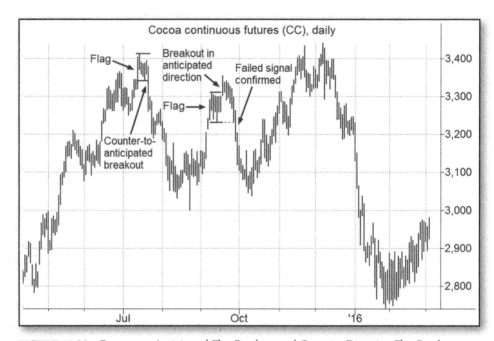

FIGURE 15.26 Counter-to-Anticipated Flag Breakout and Opposite Direction Flag Breakout Following Normal Breakout: Cocoa Continuous Futures

consider the confirmation of a failed signal in force as long as prices do not close beyond the opposite end of the relevant flag or pennant. The retracement in Figure 15.21 provides a good example: after the breakout above the top of the September–October flag, prices pulled back but held at the approximate midpoint of the flag before pushing higher, thereby leaving the failed signal intact.

Figure 15.26 highlights two flag patterns. The first formed in July when prices were rallying and was followed by a sharp sell-off after a counter-to-anticipated breakout to the downside. The second flag occurred in September when the market was rebounding. The market initially broke out of this flag in the expected direction—to the upside—but after a few days prices dropped back into the flag's range and, eventually, penetrated the bottom of the flag, confirming a failed signal pattern. The market subsequently dropped more than 5 percent over the next two weeks. This type of reversal after a normal breakout is the subject of the next section.

■ Opposite Direction Breakout of Flag or Pennant Following a Normal Breakout

In some cases, flags and pennants are followed by breakouts in the anticipated direction, but prices then reverse to close beyond the opposite extreme of the flag or pennant, as was the case with the September 2015 pattern in Figure 15.26. This combined price action provides another example of

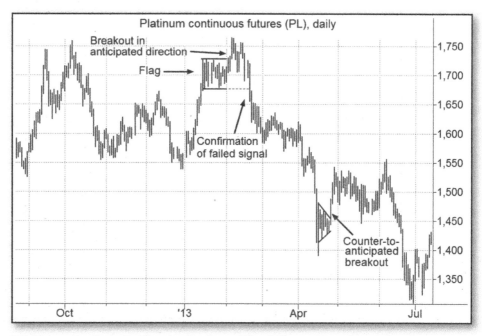

FIGURE 15.27 Opposite Direction Breakout of Flag Following Normal Breakout: Platinum Continuous Futures

a failed signal, since the anticipated breakout of the flag or pennant is followed by a price reversal instead of a price follow-through. Note that a *close* beyond the opposite end of the flag or pennant is required to confirm a failed signal, rather than a mere intraday penetration. Although this more restrictive condition will yield slightly less timely confirmations of failed signals in cases when such a conclusion proves valid, it will reduce the number of inaccurate calls of failed signals.

In Figure 15.27 the flag consolidation that formed in January–February 2013 after an upswing off support near the November–December lows was followed by an upside breakout, as might have been anticipated. Instead of witnessing a further sustained advance, however, prices moved higher for only two days, and less than two weeks later the market had retreated to below the low end of the flag consolidation. This price action qualified the earlier upside breakout above the flag pattern as a failed signal. (Note this type of signal could also be termed a bull or bear trap if it occurs at a major high or low.) In April a counter-to-anticipated upside breakout of a pennant formation was followed by a sharp bounce and consolidation before the market dropped to new lows in June.

In Figure 15.28 the flag that formed during an upswing in natural gas prices was also followed by an upside breakout and then a retreat below the low end of the flag. In this instance, the market pushed back into the flag's range several days later but did not reach the pattern's upper boundary, leaving the failed signal confirmation intact.

Figure 15.29 illustrates a flag pattern that formed during an extended downtrend in sugar futures. The market first broke out of the flag in the anticipated direction but reversed in a few days after

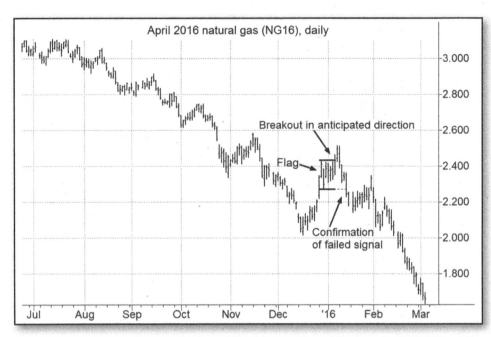

FIGURE 15.28 Opposite Direction Breakout of Flag Following Normal Breakout: April 2016 Natural Gas
Chart created using TradeStation. ©TradeStation Technologies, Inc. All rights reserved.

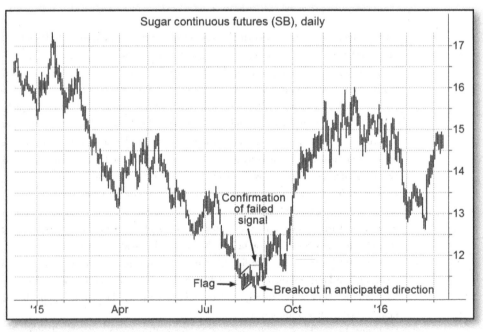

FIGURE 15.29 Opposite Direction Breakout of Flag Following Normal Breakout: Sugar
Continuous Futures
Chart created using TradeStation. ©TradeStation Technologies, Inc. All rights reserved.

FIGURE 15.30   Opposite Direction Breakout of Flag Following Normal Breakout: Euro Continuous Futures

forming a spike low. The subsequent upside penetration of the flag confirmed the failed signal. After a partial pullback toward the middle of this upward-sloping flag, prices staged a huge upmove. Note this failed signal is also a perfect example of a bear trap bottom.

In Figure 15.30 an expected downside breakout of the flag was followed by an upswing above its upper boundary, confirming a failed flag signal that was followed by a brisk rally.

■ Penetration of Top and Bottom Formations

The penetration of patterns that are normally associated with major tops and bottoms represents another important type of failed signal. For example, Figure 15.31 illustrates the double top that formed in U.S. 30-year T-bond futures in late 2010 and the penetration of this top several months later. The monthly chart inset shows the extent of the market's subsequent rally. Penetrations of double tops and double bottoms can be significant failure signals even if the top or bottom formation is not confirmed. For example, Figure 15.32 shows the downside penetration of an unconfirmed double bottom—that is, prices did not exceed the pattern's October 2013 intermediate high. Nonetheless, penetration of the pattern's July 2013 and January 2014 lows represented the violation of an important support level, as evidenced by the continued sell-off that followed.

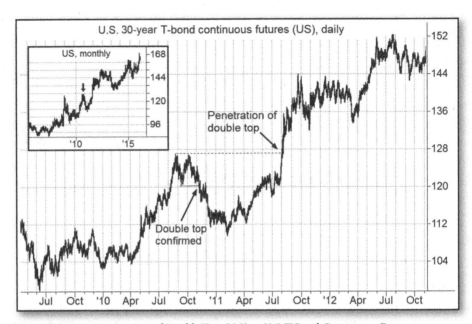

FIGURE 15.31 Penetration of Double Top: 30-Year U.S. T-Bond Continuous Futures
Chart created using TradeStation. ©TradeStation Technologies, Inc. All rights reserved.

FIGURE 15.32 Penetration of Double Bottom: Australian Dollar Continuous Futures
Chart created using TradeStation. ©TradeStation Technologies, Inc. All rights reserved.

FIGURE 15.33 Failed Head-and-Shoulders Top Pattern: Soymeal Continuous Futures

Penetrations of double-top and double-bottom patterns provide good signals but are relatively rare. Failed signals involving head-and-shoulders patterns are more common and often provide excellent trading indicators. Although the choice of what condition constitutes a confirmation of a failed head-and-shoulders pattern is somewhat arbitrary, I would use the criterion of prices exceeding the most recent shoulder. For example, in Figure 15.33 the rebound above the shoulder that peaked at the beginning of November 2012 would represent a confirmation of a failed head-and-shoulders top pattern. Sometimes prices will first dip back after penetrating the shoulder, even when a substantial advance ultimately ensues, as is the case in Figure 15.34, which shows a long-term example on a weekly chart of the E-mini S&P 500 futures. As long as prices don't close below the relative low formed between the head and right shoulder, the failed signal would remain intact. Figure 15.35 provides another example of a strong rally following a failed head-and-shoulders top.

Figure 15.36 illustrates a failed head-and-shoulders bottom pattern. In analogous fashion to the head-and-shoulders top case, the downside penetration of the more recent shoulder is used as the confirmation condition of a failed signal.

The trader may often benefit by waiting for a retracement before implementing a position based on the confirmation of a failed head-and-shoulders pattern, as illustrated by Figure 15.34. The trade-off is that such a strategy will result in missing very profitable trades in those cases where there is no retracement or only a very modest retracement (e.g., Figures 15.35 and 15.36).

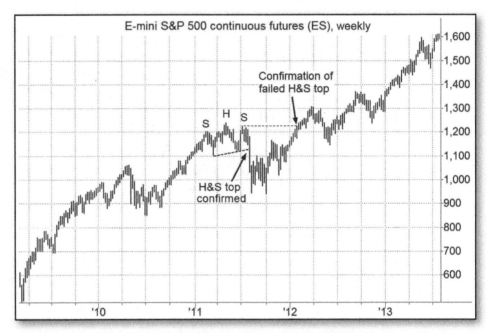

FIGURE 15.34 Failed Head-and-Shoulders Top Pattern: E-Mini S&P 500 Continuous Futures

Chart created using TradeStation. ©TradeStation Technologies, Inc. All rights reserved.

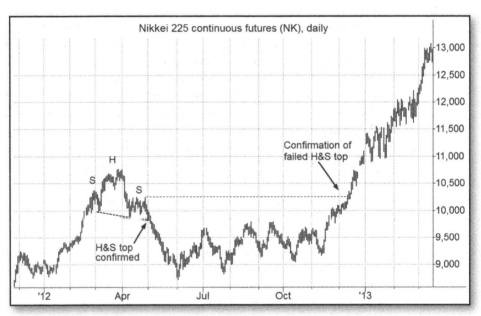

FIGURE 15.35 Failed Head-and-Shoulders Top Pattern: Nikkei 225 Continuous Futures

Chart created using TradeStation. ©TradeStation Technologies, Inc. All rights reserved.

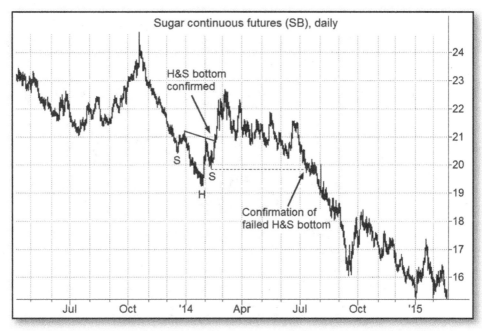

FIGURE 15.36 Failed Head-and-Shoulders Bottom Pattern: Sugar Continuous Futures

Chart created using TradeStation. ©TradeStation Technologies, Inc. All rights reserved.

■ Breaking of Curvature

As was discussed in Chapter 9, rounding patterns often provide very reliable trading signals. In this sense, the breaking of a curved price pattern can be viewed as transforming the pattern into a failed signal. Figure 15.37 actually contains two examples where the breaking of the curvature of what had been an apparent rounding-top pattern represented a bullish signal. In Figure 15.38, the breaking of the curvature of an apparent rounding-bottom pattern led to a steep decline in corn prices in 2014. Note the downthrust in January 2014 (the low of the curved pattern) was the bear trap illustrated in Figures 15.4 and 15.8. So, in effect, this chart illustrates two successive failure patterns, the first signaling a near-two-month rebound, and the second the subsequent reversal into a major downtrend.

■ The Future Reliability of Failed Signals

There is an inverse relationship between the popularity of an indicator and its efficiency. For example, decades ago, when technical analysis was used by fewer market practitioners, chart breakouts (price moves above or below prior trading ranges) tended to work relatively well, providing many excellent signals without an abundance of false signals. In my observation, as technical analysis became increasingly popular and breakouts a commonly used tool, the efficiency of this pattern seemed to deteriorate. In fact, it now seems that price *reversals* following breakouts may more often be the rule than the exception.

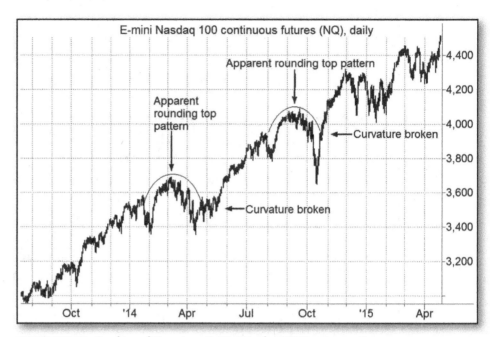

FIGURE 15.37 Breaking of Curvature: E-Mini Nasdaq 100 Continuous Futures

Chart created using TradeStation. ©TradeStation Technologies, Inc. All rights reserved.

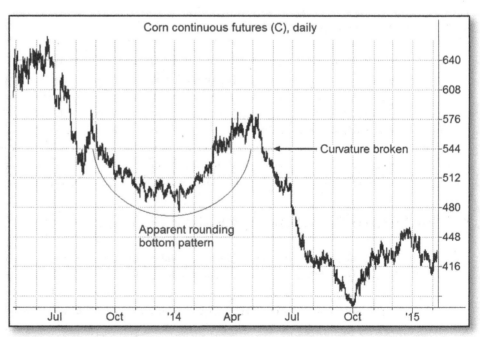

FIGURE 15.38 Breaking of Curvature: Corn Continuous Futures

Chart created using TradeStation. ©TradeStation Technologies, Inc. All rights reserved.

As stated earlier, I find failed signals considerably more reliable than conventional chart patterns. Although the concept of failed signals is certainly not new, I don't believe its usage is widely emphasized. If the use of failed signals were to become significantly more widespread, however, their long-term reliability could be adversely affected.

As a final comment, it should be emphasized that the concept of failed signals in this chapter has been presented in the context of conventional chart analysis as it exists today. In the future—particularly the distant future—what passes for popular chart interpretation may well change. The concept of failed signals, however, can be made dynamic by pegging it to the conventional wisdom. In other words, if a new chart pattern became popular as a technical signal in the future (e.g., in the way breakouts are widely used today), a failure of the pattern could be viewed as more significant than the pattern itself. In this more general sense, the concept of failed signals could prove timeless.

◼ Conclusion

The novice trader will ignore a failed signal, riding a position into a large loss while hoping for the best. More experienced traders, having learned the importance of money management, will exit quickly once it is apparent they have made a bad trade. However, the truly skilled trader will be able to do a 180-degree turn, reversing a position at a loss if market behavior (e.g., confirmation of a failed signal) points to such a course of action. In other words, it takes great discipline to capitalize on failed signals, but such flexibility is essential to the effective synthesis of chart analysis and trading.

PART IV

TRADING SYSTEMS AND PERFORMANCE MEASUREMENT

CHAPTER 16

Technical Trading Systems: Structure and Design

There are only two types of trend-following systems: fast and slow.

—Jim Orcutt

B e forewarned. If you are expecting to find the blueprint for a heretofore secret trading system that *consistently* makes 100 percent plus per year *in real-life trading* with minimal risk, you'll have to look elsewhere. For one thing, I have not yet discovered such a "sure thing" money machine. But, in a sense, that is beside the point. Quite frankly, I have always been somewhat puzzled by advertisements for books or computer software promising to reveal the secrets of systems that make 100 percent, 200 percent, and more! Why are they selling such valuable information for $99, or even $2,999?

The primary goal of this chapter is to provide readers with the background knowledge necessary to develop their own trading systems. The discussion focuses on the following five areas:

1. An overview of some basic trend-following systems
2. The key weaknesses of these systems
3. Guidelines for transforming "generic" systems into more powerful systems
4. Countertrend systems
5. Diversification as a means of improving performance

Chapter 17 provides additional examples of trading systems, using original systems as illustrations. The essential issues of appropriate data selection, system testing procedures, and performance measurement are discussed in Chapters 18, 19, and 20.

The Benefits of a Mechanical Trading System

Is paper trading easier than real trading? Most speculators would answer yes, even though both tasks require an equivalent decision process. This difference is explained by a single factor: emotion. Overtrading, premature liquidation of good positions because of rumors, jumping the gun on market entry to get a better price, riding a losing position—these are but a few of the negative manifestations of emotion in actual trading. Perhaps the greatest value of a mechanical system is that it eliminates emotion from trading. In so doing, it allows the speculator to avoid many of the common errors that often impede trading performance. Furthermore, removing the implied need for constant decision making substantially reduces trading-related stress and anxiety.

Another benefit of a mechanical system is that it ensures a consistent approach—that is, the trader follows all signals indicated by a common set of conditions. This is important, since even profitable trading strategies can lose money if applied selectively. To illustrate this point, consider the example of a market advisory whose recommendations yield a net profit over the long run (after allowances for commissions and poor executions). Will the advisory's subscribers make money if they only implement trades in line with its recommendations? Not necessarily. Some people will pick and choose trades, invariably missing some of the biggest winners. Others will stop following the recommendations after the advisor has a losing streak, and as a result may miss a string of profitable trades. The point is that a good trading strategy is not sufficient; success also depends on consistency.

A third advantage of mechanical trading systems is they normally provide the trader with a method for controlling risk. Money management is an essential ingredient of trading success. Without a plan for limiting losses, a single bad trade can lead to disaster. Any properly constructed mechanical system will either contain explicit stop-loss rules or specify conditions for reversing a position given a sufficient adverse price move. As a result, following signals generated by a mechanical trading system will normally prevent the possibility of huge losses on individual trades (except in extreme circumstances when one is unable to liquidate a position because the market is in the midst of a string of locked-limit moves). Thus, the speculator using a mechanical system may end up losing money due to the cumulative effect of a number of negative trades, but at least his account will not be decimated by one or two bad trades.

Of course, money management does not necessarily require the use of a trading system. Risk control can also be achieved by initiating a good-till-canceled stop order whenever a new position is taken, or by predetermining the exit point upon entering a trade and sticking to that decision. However, many traders lack sufficient discipline and will be tempted to give the market just a little more time once too often.

Three Basic Types of Systems

The categories used to classify trading systems are completely arbitrary. The following three-division classification is intended to emphasize a subjective interpretation of the key conceptual differences in possible trading approaches:

Trend-following. A trend-following system waits for a specified price move and then initiates a position in the same direction based on the implicit assumption that the trend will continue.

Countertrend. A countertrend system waits for a significant price move and then initiates a position in the opposite direction on the assumption that the market is due for a correction.

Pattern recognition. In a sense, all systems can be classified as pattern recognition systems. After all, the conditions that signal a trend or a countertrend trade are a type of pattern (e.g., close beyond the 20-day high or low). However, the implication here is that the chosen patterns are not based primarily on directional moves, as is the case in trend-following and countertrend systems. For example, a pattern-recognition system might generate signals on the basis of "spike days" (see Chapter 9). In this case, the key consideration is the pattern itself (e.g., spike) rather than the extent of any preceding price move. Of course, this example is overly simplistic. In practice, the patterns used for determining trading signals will be more complex, and several patterns may be incorporated into a single system.

Systems of this type may sometimes employ probability models in making trading decisions. In this case the researcher would try to identify patterns that appeared to act as precursors of price advances or declines in the past. An underlying assumption in this approach is that such past behavioral patterns can be used to estimate current probabilities for rising or declining markets given certain specified conditions. This chapter does not elaborate on this approach of trading system design since it lies beyond the scope of the overall discussion.

It should be emphasized that the lines dividing the preceding categories are not always clear-cut. As modifications are incorporated, a system of one type may begin to more closely approximate the behavioral pattern of a different system category.

Trend-Following Systems

By definition, trend-following systems never sell near the high or buy near the low, because a meaningful opposite price move is required to signal a trade. Thus, in using this type of system, the trader will always miss the first part of a price move and may surrender a significant portion of profits before an opposite signal is received (assuming the system is always in the market). There is a basic trade-off involved in the choice of the sensitivity, or speed, of a trend-following system. A sensitive system, which responds quickly to signs of a trend reversal, will tend to maximize profits on valid signals, but it will also generate far more false signals. A nonsensitive, or slow, system will reflect the reverse set of characteristics.

Many traders become obsessed with trying to catch every market wiggle. Such a predilection leads them toward faster and faster trend-following systems. Although in some markets fast systems consistently outperform slow systems, in most markets the reverse is true, as the minimization of losing trades and commission costs in slow systems more than offsets the reduced profits in the good trades. This observation is only intended as a cautionary note against the natural tendency toward seeking out more sensitive systems. However, in all cases, the choice between fast and slow systems must be determined on the basis of empirical observation and the trader's subjective preferences.

There is a wide variety of possible approaches in constructing a trend-following system. In this chapter we focus on two of the most basic methods: moving average systems and breakout systems.

Moving Average Systems

The moving average for a given day is equal to the average of that day's closing price and the closing prices on the preceding $N - 1$ days, where N is equal to the number of days in the moving average.

For example, in a 10-day moving average, the appropriate value for a given day would be the average of the 10 closing prices culminating with that day. The term *moving average* refers to the fact that the set of numbers being averaged is continuously moving through time.

Because the moving average is based on past prices, in a rising market the moving average will be below the price, while in a declining market the moving average will be above the price. Thus, when a price trend reverses from up to down, prices must cross the moving average from above. Similarly, when the trend reverses from down to up, prices must cross the moving average from below. In the most basic type of moving average system, these crossover points are viewed as trade signals: a buy signal is indicated when prices cross the moving average from below; a sell signal is indicated when prices cross the moving average from above. The crossover should be determined based on closing prices. Table 16.1 illustrates the calculation of a 10-day simple moving average and indicates the corresponding crossover signal points.

TABLE 16.1	Calculating a Moving Average		
Day	Closing Price	10-Day Moving Average	Crossover Signal
1	80.50		
2	81.00		
3	81.90		
4	81.40		
5	83.10		
6	82.60		
7	82.20		
8	83.10		
9	84.40		
10	85.20	82.54	
11	84.60	82.95	
12	83.90	83.24	
13	84.40	83.49	
14	85.20	83.87	
15	86.10	84.17	
16	85.40	84.45	
17	84.10	84.64	Sell
18	83.50	84.68	
19	83.90	84.63	
20	83.10	84.42	
21	82.50	84.21	
22	81.90	84.01	
23	81.20	83.69	
24	81.60	83.33	
25	82.20	82.94	
26	82.80	82.68	Buy
27	83.40	82.61	
28	83.80	82.64	
29	83.90	82.64	
30	83.50	82.68	

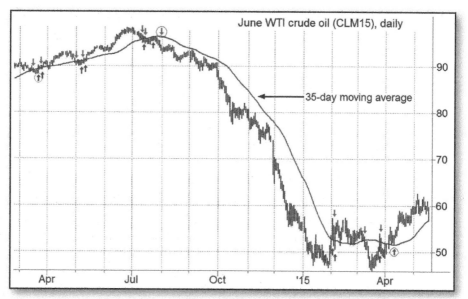

FIGURE 16.1 June 2015 WTI Crude Oil and 35-Day Moving Average

Note: ↑ = buy signal: prices cross moving average from below and close above line; ↓ = sell signal: prices cross moving average from above and close below line; ⬆ = buy signal not eliminated by filter; ⬇ = sell signal not eliminated by filter.

Chart created using TradeStation. ©TradeStation Technologies, Inc. All rights reserved.

Figure 16.1 shows the June 2015 WTI crude oil contract with a 35-day moving average. The non-circled buy and sell signals on the chart are based on the simple moving average system just described. (For now ignore the circled signals; they are explained later.) Note that although the system catches the major downtrend, it also generates several false signals. Of course, this problem can be mitigated by increasing the length of the moving average, but the tendency toward excessive false signals is a characteristic of the simple moving average system. The reason for this is that temporary, sharp price fluctuations, sufficient to trigger trade signals, are commonplace events in futures markets.

One school of thought suggests the problem with the simple moving average system is that it weights all days equally, whereas more recent days are more important and hence should be weighted more heavily. Many different weighting schemes have been proposed for constructing moving averages. Two of the most common weighting approaches are the *linearly weighted moving average* (LWMA) and the *exponentially weighted moving average* (EWMA).[1]

The LWMA assigns the oldest price in the moving average a weight of 1, the second oldest price a weight of 2, and so on. The weight of the most recent price would be equal to the number of days

[1] The following two sources were used as reference for the remainder of this section: (1) Perry Kaufman, *Trading Systems and Methods* (Hoboken, NJ: John Wiley & Sons, 2013), and (2) *Technical Analysis of Stocks & Commodities,* bonus issue 1995, sidebar, page 66.

TECHNICAL TRADING SYSTEMS: STRUCTURE AND DESIGN

in the moving average. The LWMA is equal to the sum of the weighted prices divided by the sum of the weights:

$$LWMA = \frac{\sum_{t=1}^{n} P_t \cdot t}{\sum_{t=1}^{n} t}$$

where t = time indicator (oldest day = 1, second oldest = 2, etc.)

P_t = price at time t

n = number of days in moving average

For example, for a 10-day LWMA, the price of 10 days ago would be multiplied by 1, the price of 9 days ago by 2, and so on through the most recent price, which would be multiplied by 10. The sum of these weighted prices would then be divided by 55 (the sum of 1 through 10) to obtain the LWMA.

The EWMA is calculated as the sum of the current price multiplied by a *smoothing constant* between 0 and 1, denoted by the symbol a, and the previous day's EWMA multiplied by $1 - a$:

$$EWMA_t = aP_t + (1 - a)EWMA_{t-1}$$

This linked calculation wherein each day's value of the EWMA is based on the previous day's value means that *all* prior prices will have some weight, but the weight of each day drops exponentially the further back in time it is. The weight of any individual day would be:

$$a(1 - a)^k$$

where k = number of days prior to current day (for current day, $k = 0$ and term reduces to a).

Since a is a value between 0 and 1, the weight of each given day drops sharply moving back in time. For example, if $a = 0.1$, yesterday's price would have a weight of 0.09, the price two days ago would have a weight of 0.081, the price 10 days ago would have a weight of 0.035, and the price 30 days ago would have a weight of 0.004.

An EWMA with a smoothing constant, a, corresponds roughly to a simple moving average of length n, where a and n are related by the following formula:

$$a = 2/(n + 1)$$

or

$$n = (2 - a)/a$$

Thus, for example, an EWMA with a smoothing constant equal to 0.1 would correspond roughly to a 19-day simple moving average. As another example, a 40-day simple moving average would correspond roughly to an EWMA with a smoothing constant equal to 0.04878.

In my view, there is no strong empirical evidence to support the idea that linearly or exponentially weighted moving averages provide a substantive and consistent improvement over simple moving averages. Sometimes weighted moving averages will do better; sometimes simple moving averages will do better. (See Chapter 11 for an illustration of this point.) The question of which method will yield better results will be entirely dependent on the markets and time periods selected, with no reason to assume that *past* relative superiority will be indicative of the probable *future* pattern. In short, experimentation with different weighted moving averages probably does not represent a particularly fruitful path for trying to improve the simple moving average system.

A far more meaningful improvement is provided by the crossover moving average approach. In this system, trade signals are based on the interaction of two moving averages, as opposed to the interaction between a single moving average and price. The trading rules are very similar to those of the simple moving average system: a buy signal is generated when the shorter moving average crosses above the longer moving average; a sell signal is generated when the shorter moving average crosses below the longer moving average. (In a sense, the simple moving average system can be thought of as a special case of the crossover moving average system, in which the short-term moving average is equal to 1.) Because trade signals for the crossover system are based upon two smoothed series (as opposed to one smoothed series and price), the number of false signals is substantially reduced. Figures 16.2, 16.3, and 16.4 compare trade signals generated by a simple 12-day moving average system, a simple 48-day moving average system, and the crossover system based on these two averages. Generally speaking, the crossover moving average system is far superior to the simple moving average. (However, it should be noted that

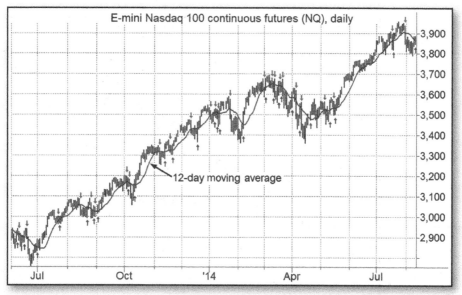

FIGURE 16.2 E-Mini Nasdaq 100 Continuous Futures with 12-Day Moving Average
Note: ↑ = buy signal: prices cross moving average from below and close above line; ↓ = sell signal: prices cross moving average from above and close below line.
Chart created using TradeStation. ©TradeStation Technologies, Inc. All rights reserved.

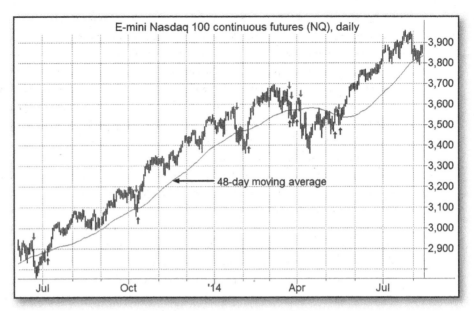

FIGURE 16.3 E-Mini Nasdaq 100 Continuous Futures with 48-Day Moving Average

Note: ↑ = buy signal: prices cross moving average from below and close above line; ↓ = sell signal: prices cross moving average from above and close below line.

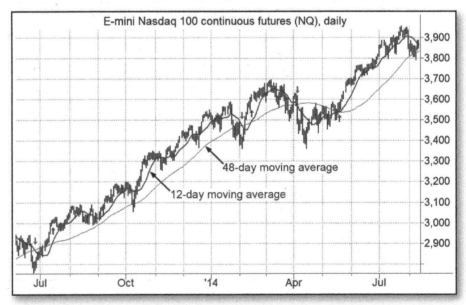

FIGURE 16.4 E-Mini Nasdaq 100 Continuous Futures with Moving Average Crossover

Note: ↑ = buy signal: short-term moving average (12-day) crosses long-term moving average (48-day) from below; ↓ = sell signal: short-term moving average crosses long-term moving average from above.

by including some of the trend-following-system modifications discussed in a later section, even the simple moving average system can provide the core for a viable trading approach.) The weaknesses of the crossover moving average system and possible improvements are discussed later.

Breakout Systems

The basic concept underlying breakout systems is very simple: the ability of a market to move to a new high or low indicates the potential for a continued trend in the direction of the breakout. The following set of rules provides an example of a simple breakout system:

1. Cover short and go long if today's close exceeds the prior N-day high.
2. Cover long and go short if today's close is below the prior N-day low.

The value chosen for N will define the sensitivity of the system. If a short-duration period is used for comparison to the current price (e.g., $N = 7$), the system will indicate trend reversals fairly quickly, but will also generate many false signals. In contrast, the choice of a longer-duration period (e.g., $N = 40$) will reduce false signals, but at the cost of slower entry.

Figure 16.5 compares the trade signals generated by the preceding simple breakout system in silver continuous futures using $N = 7$ and $N = 40$. The following three observations, which are evidenced in Figure 16.5, are also valid as generalizations describing the trade-offs between fast and slow breakout systems:

1. A fast system will provide an earlier signal of a major trend transition (e.g., the October 2012 sell signal).

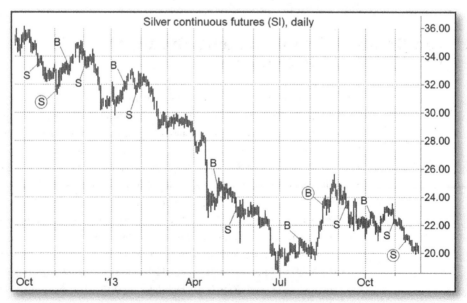

FIGURE 16.5 Breakout System Signals, Fast versus Slow Systems: Silver Continuous Futures
Note: B, S = signals for $N = 7$; Ⓑ, Ⓢ = signals for $N = 40$.
Chart created using TradeStation. ©TradeStation Technologies, Inc. All rights reserved.

2. A fast system will generate far more false signals.

3. The loss per trade in the slower system will be greater than the loss for the corresponding trade in the faster system. In some cases, a fast system might even realize a small profit on a minor trend that results in a loss in a slower system. For example, the $N = 40$ system's August buy signal that was liquidated in November resulted in a net loss of approximately $2.54 (excluding commissions). The corresponding buy signal for the $N = 7$ version—triggered in July and exited in September—resulted in a net *gain* of around $2.46.

As indicated by the preceding illustration, fast and slow systems will each work better under different circumstances. In the case of the chosen illustration, on balance, the slow system was much more successful. Of course, one could just as easily have chosen an example in which the reverse observation was true. However, empirical evidence suggests that, in most markets, slower systems tend to work better. In any case, the choice between a fast and a slow system must be based on up-to-date empirical testing.

The previous example of a breakout system was based on the current day's close and prior period's high and low. It should be noted that these choices were arbitrary. Other alternative combinations might include current day's high or low versus prior period's high or low; current day's close versus prior period's high close or low close; and current day's high or low versus prior period's high close or low close. Although the choice of the condition that defines a breakout will affect the results, the differences between the variations just given (for the same value of N) will be largely random and not overwhelming. Thus, while each of these definitions might be tested, it probably makes more sense to focus research efforts on more meaningful modifications of the basic system.

The pitfalls of breakout-type systems are basically the same as those of moving average systems and are detailed in the following section.

■ Ten Common Problems with Standard Trend-Following Systems

1. **Too many similar systems.** Many different trend-following systems will generate similar signals. Thus, it is not unusual for a number of trend-following systems to signal a trade during the same one- to five-day period. Because many speculators and futures funds base their decisions on basic trend-following systems, their common action can result in a flood of similar orders. Under such circumstances, traders using these systems may find their market and stop orders filled well beyond the intended price, if there is a paucity of offsetting orders.

2. **Whipsaws.** Trend-following systems will signal all major trends; the problem is that they will also generate many false signals. A major frustration experienced by traders using trend-following systems is that markets will frequently move far enough to trigger a signal and then reverse direction. This unpleasant event can even occur several times in succession; hence, the term *whipsaw*. For example, Figure 16.6, which indicates the trade signals generated by a breakout system (close beyond prior N-day high-low) for $N = 10$, provides a vivid illustration of the dark side of trend-following systems.

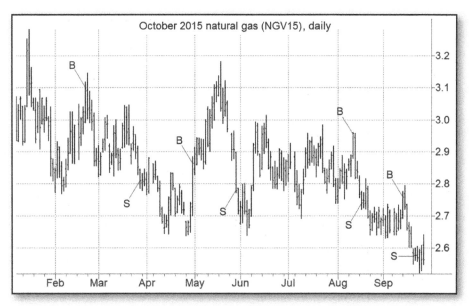

FIGURE 16.6 Breakout Signals in Trading Range Market: October 2015 Natural Gas Futures
Note: B = buy signal: close above prior 10-day high; S = sell signal: close below 10-day low.
Chart created using TradeStation. ©TradeStation Technologies, Inc. All rights reserved.

3. **Failure to exploit major price moves.** Basic trend-following systems always assume an equal-unit-size position. As a result, given an extended trend, the best such a system can do is to indicate a one-unit position in the direction of the trend. For example, in Figure 16.7 a breakout system with $N = 40$ would signal a long position in December 2012 and remain long throughout the entire uptrend until February 2014. Although this outcome is hardly unfavorable, profitability could be enhanced if the trend-following system were able to take advantage of such extended trends by generating signals indicating increases in the base position size.

4. **Nonsensitive (slow) systems can surrender a large percentage of profits.** Although slow variations of trend-following systems may often work best, one disturbing feature of such systems is that they may sometimes surrender a large portion of open profits. In Figure 16.8, for example, a breakout system with $N = 40$ catches a major portion of the October–December 2014 price advance in silver, but then surrenders more than the entire gain before an opposite signal occurs. The June buy signal is initially profitable, but then realizes a much larger loss by the time a sell signal is received.

5. **Cannot make money in trading range markets.** The best any trend-following system can do during a period of sideways price action is to break even—that is, generate no new trade signals. In most cases, however, trading range markets will be characterized by whipsaw losses. This is a particularly significant consideration since sideways price action represents the predominant state of most markets.

6. **Temporary large losses.** Even an excellent trend-following system may witness transitory periods of sharp equity retracement. Such events can be distressing to the trader who enjoys a profit cushion, but they can be disastrous to the trader who has just begun following the system's signals.

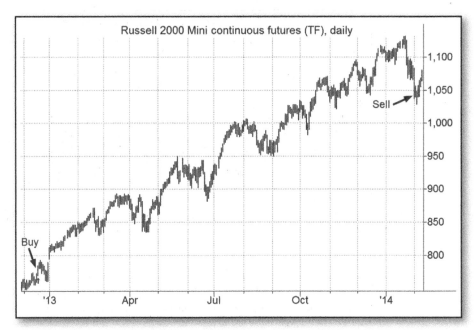

FIGURE 16.7 Failure of System to Exploit Major Price Move: Russell 2000 Mini Futures

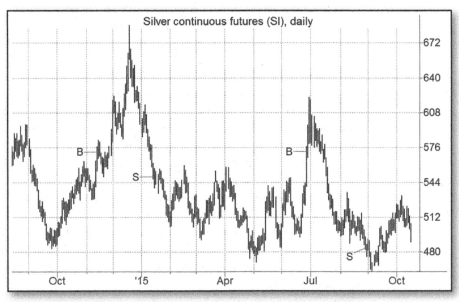

FIGURE 16.8 Surrender of Profits by Nonsensitive System: Silver Continuous Futures

Note: B = buy signal: close above prior 40-day high; S = sell signal: close below 40-day low.

7. **Extreme volatility in best-performing systems.** In some cases, the trader may find that the most profitable trend-following systems are also subject to particularly sharp retracements, thereby implying an unacceptable level of risk.

8. **System works well in testing but then bombs.** This scenario is perhaps the most common tale of woe among traders who have used mechanical trading systems.

9. **Parameter shift.**[2] Frequently, the trader may perform an exhaustive search to find the best variation of a system based on past data (e.g., the optimum value of N in a breakout system), only to find that the same variation performs poorly (relative to other variations) in the ensuing period.

10. **Slippage.** Another common experience: the system generates profits on paper, but *simultaneously* loses money in actual trading. Slippage is discussed in Chapter 19.

■ Possible Modifications for Basic Trend-Following Systems

Even simple systems, such as moving average or breakout systems, will probably prove profitable if traded consistently over a broad range of markets for a sufficient length of time (e.g., three to five years or longer). However, the simplicity of these systems is a vice as well as a virtue. In essence, the rules of these systems are perhaps too simple to adequately account for the wide variety of possible market situations. Even if net profitable over the long run, simple trend-following systems will typically leave the trader exposed to periodic sharp losses. In fact, the natural proclivity of many, if not most, users of such systems to abandon the approach during a losing period will lead them to experience a net loss even if the system proves profitable over the longer run.

In this section, we discuss some of the primary ways to modify basic trend-following systems in an effort to improve their performance. For simplicity, most of the examples will use the previously described simple breakout system. However, the same types of modifications could also be applied to other basic trend-following systems (e.g., crossover moving average).

Confirmation Conditions

An important modification that can be made to a basic trend-following system is the requirement for additional conditions to be met before a signal is accepted. If these conditions are not realized before an opposite direction signal is received, no trade occurs. Confirmation rules are designed specifically to deal with the nemesis of trend-following systems: false signals. The idea is that valid signals will fulfill the confirmation conditions, while false signals generally will not. The range of possible

---

[2]The meaning of the term *parameter* as it is used in trading systems is detailed in Chapter 19.

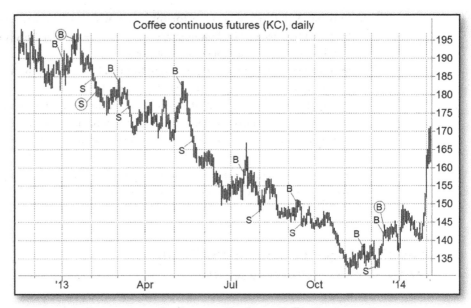

FIGURE 16.9 Penetration as Confirmation Condition: Coffee Continuous Futures
Note: B, S = signals for breakout system with $N = 12$; Ⓑ, Ⓢ = signals for breakout system
with $N = 12$ and 3 percent closing penetration confirmation.

choices for confirmation conditions is limited only by the imagination of the system designer. Here
are three examples:

1. **Penetration.** A trade signal is accepted only if the market moves a specified minimum amount
   beyond a given reference level (e.g., signal price). This confirming price move can be measured
   in either nominal or percentage terms. Figure 16.9 compares the trade signals generated by a
   standard breakout system with $N = 12$ and the corresponding system with a confirmation rule
   requiring a close that exceeds the prior N-day high or low by at least 3 percent.[3] Note that in
   this example, although the confirmation rule results in moderately worse entry levels for valid
   signals, it eliminates five of six losing buy signals. (The sell signals following the nonconfirmed
   buy signals are also eliminated, since the system is already short at these points.)

2. **Time delay.** In this approach, a specified time delay is required, at the end of which the signal is
   reevaluated. For example, a confirmation rule may specify that a trade signal is taken if the market closes beyond the signal price (higher for a buy, lower for a sell) at any time six or more days
   beyond the original signal date. Figure 16.10 compares the signals generated by a basic breakout
   system with $N = 12$, and the corresponding system with the six-day time delay confirmation
   condition. Again, the confirmation rule eliminates five of the six losing buy signals.

---

[3] Because Figure 16.9 depicts a continuous futures series, percentage price changes would be equal to the
price changes shown on this chart divided by the corresponding nearest futures price, which is not shown.
Recall from Chapter 5 that continuous futures accurately reflect price *swings* but not price *levels*. Consequently, continuous futures cannot be used as the divisor to calculate percentage changes.

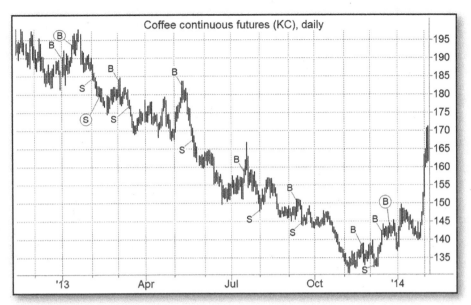

FIGURE 16.10 Time Delay as a Confirmation Condition: Coffee Continuous Futures
Note: B, S = signals for breakout system with $N = 12$; Ⓑ, Ⓢ = signals for breakout system with
$N = 12$ and six-day time delay confirmation.

3. **Pattern.** This is a catch-all term for a wide variety of confirmation rules. In this approach, a specified pattern is required to validate the basic system signal. For example, the confirmation rule might require three subsequent thrust days beyond the signal price.[4] Figure 16.11 compares the signals generated by the basic breakout system, with $N = 12$ and the signals based upon the corresponding system using the three-thrust-day validation condition. The thrust-day count at confirmed signals is indicated by the numbers on the chart. Here, too, the confirmation rule eliminates five of six losing buy signals.

The design of trading systems is a matter of constant trade-offs. The advantage of confirmation conditions is that they will greatly reduce whipsaw losses. However, it should be noted that confirmation rules also have an undesirable side effect—they will delay entry on valid signals, thereby reducing gains on profitable trades. For example, in Figures 16.9 through 16.11, note that the confirmation rules result in worse entry prices for all the valid trade signals. The confirmation condition will be beneficial as long as reduced profits due to delayed entry are more than offset by avoided losses. A system that includes confirmation conditions will not always outperform its basic system counterpart, but if properly designed it will perform significantly better over the long run.

---

[4] A thrust day, which was originally defined in Chapter 9, is a day with a close above the previous day's high or below the previous day's low.

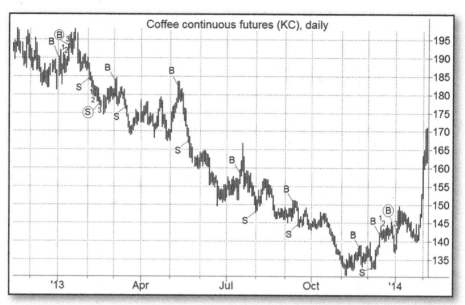

FIGURE 16.11 Example of a Pattern Confirmation Condition: Coffee Continuous Futures
Note: B, S = signals for breakout system with $N = 12$; Ⓑ, Ⓢ = signals for breakout system with $N = 12$ and three-thrust-day confirmation.
Chart created using TradeStation. ©TradeStation Technologies, Inc. All rights reserved.

Filter

The purpose of a filter is to eliminate those trades that are deemed to have a lower probability of success. For example, the technical system might be combined with a fundamental model that classifies the market as bullish, bearish, or neutral. Technical signals would then be accepted only if they were in agreement with the fundamental model's market designation. In cases of disagreement, a neutral position would be indicated. In most cases, however, the filter condition(s) will also be technical in nature. For example, if one could derive a set of rules that had some accuracy in defining the presence of a trading range market, signals that were received when a trading range market was indicated would not be accepted. In essence, in developing a filter, the system designer is trying to find a common denominator applicable to the majority of losing trades.

We will use the frequently unsatisfactory simple moving average system to provide a specific example of a filter condition. The noncircled signals in Figure 16.1 illustrate the typical tendency of the simple moving average system to generate many false signals—even in trending markets. These whipsaw trades can be substantially reduced by applying a filter rule that requires trade signals to be consistent with the trend of the moving average. For example, price crossing the moving average from below and closing above the moving average would be accepted as a buy signal only if the moving average was up relative to the previous day's level. This filter condition makes intuitive sense because it adheres to the basic technical concept of trading with the major trend.

Two points should be clarified regarding the application of this rule:

1. A rejected signal could be activated later if the moving average subsequently turned in the direction of the signal *before* an opposite-direction crossover of the price and moving average.
2. Signals that occur after rejected signals are ignored because the net position is already consistent with the implied trade. This observation is true because the simple moving average system is always in the market.

The circled signals in Figure 16.1 indicate the trades that would have been accepted if the filter rule just described were applied. (In both instances these trades occurred after delays, as previously described, rather than upon immediate penetration of the moving average.) As can be seen, the rule substantially reduces the number of false signals. Although in some cases the application of the filter condition results in adversely delayed trade entries (for example, the July sell signal), on balance the benefits clearly outweigh the disadvantages. Of course, a single illustration doesn't prove anything. However, the implication of Figure 16.1 does have a more general applicability. Most empirical testing would reveal that, more often than not, the inclusion of the type of filter rule depicted in Figure 16.1 tends to improve performance.

In fact, a crossover between price and the moving average that is opposite to the direction of the moving average trend can often provide a good signal to *add to rather than reverse* the original position. For example, in Figure 16.1 the March and May 2014 downside penetrations of the moving average could be viewed as buy rather than sell signals because the moving average trend was still up in those instances. The rationale behind this interpretation is that in a trending market, reactions often carry to the vicinity of a moving average before prices resume their longer-term trend (see Chapter 12). Thus, in effect, such rejected signals could actually provide the basis for a method of pyramiding.

It should be noted that, in a sense, the confirmation conditions detailed in the previous section represent one type of filter, insofar as signals that fulfill a subsequent set of conditions are accepted, while those that do not are eliminated. However, the distinction here is that a filter implies a set of screening rules applied *at the time* the base system signal is received. In other words, the sorting procedure occurs without any dependency on subsequent developments (although, to be perfectly accurate, subsequent developments could still permit a delayed acceptance of a rejected signal). Consequently, as we have defined the terms, a system can include both a filter and a confirmation rule. In such a system, only signals that were accepted based on the filter definition and subsequently validated by the confirmation rule(s) would actually result in trades.

Market Characteristic Adjustments

One criticism of simple trend-following systems is that they treat all markets alike. For example, in a breakout system, with $N = 20$, both highly volatile and very quiet markets will require the same conditions for a buy signal—a 20-day high. Market characteristic adjustments seek to compensate for the fact that a system's optimum parameter value settings will depend on market conditions. For example, in the case of a breakout system, instead of using a constant value for N, the relevant value for N might be contingent on the market's volatility classification. As a specific illustration, the average two-day price range during the past 50-day period might be used to place the market into one of five volatility classifications.[5] The value of N used to generate signals on any given day would then depend on the prevailing volatility classification.

Volatility appears to be the most logical choice for classifying market states, although other criteria could also be tested (e.g., fundamentally based conditions, average volume level). In essence, this type of modification seeks to transform a basic trend-following system from a static to a dynamic trading method.

Differentiation between Buy and Sell Signals

Basic trend-following systems typically assume analogous conditions for buy and sell signals (e.g., buy on close above 20-day high, sell on close below 20-day low). However, there is no reason to make this assumption automatically. It can be argued that bull and bear markets behave differently. For example, a survey of a broad spectrum of historical price data would reveal that price breaks from major tops tend to be more rapid than price rallies from major bottoms.[6] This observation suggests a rationale for using more sensitive conditions to generate sell signals than those used to generate buy signals. However, the system designer using such an approach should be particularly sensitive to the danger of overfitting the system—a pitfall discussed in detail in Chapter 19.

Pyramiding

One inherent weakness in basic trend-following systems is that they automatically assume a constant unit position size for all market conditions. It would seem desirable to allow for the possibility of larger position sizes in the case of major trends, which are almost entirely responsible for the success of any trend-following system. One reasonable approach for adding units to a base position in a major trend is to wait for a specified reaction and then initiate the additional unit(s) on evidence of a resumption of the trend. Such an approach seeks to optimize the timing of pyramid units, as well as to provide exit rules that reasonably limit the potential losses that could be incurred by such added positions. An

---

[5] A two-day price range is used as a volatility measure instead of a one-day range since the latter can easily yield a distorted image of true market volatility. For example, on a limit day, the one-day range would equal zero, in extreme contrast to the fact that limit days reflect highly volatile conditions. Of course, many other measures could be used to define volatility.

[6] The reverse statement would apply to short-term interest rate markets, which are quoted in terms of the instrument price, a value that varies inversely with the interest rate level. In the interest rate markets, interest rates rather than instrument prices are analogous to prices in standard markets. For example, there is no upper limit to a commodity's price or interest rates, but the downside for both of these items is theoretically limited. As another example, commodity markets tend to be more volatile when prices are high, while short-term interest rate markets tend to be more volatile when interest rates are high (instrument prices are low). The situation for long-term (i.e., bond) markets is ambiguous since although interest rates can fall no lower than approximately zero, the pricing mathematics underlying these instruments result in an accelerated price advance (for equal interest rate changes) as interest rates fall.

example of this type of approach was detailed in Chapter 12. Another example of a possible pyramid strategy would be provided by the following set of rules:

Buy Case

1. A reaction is defined when the net position is long and the market closes below the prior 10-day low.
2. Once a reaction is defined, an additional long position is initiated on any subsequent 10-day high if the following conditions are met:
   a. The pyramid signal price is above the price at which the most recent long position was initiated.
   b. The net position size is less than three units. (This condition implies that there is a limit of two pyramid units.)

Sell Case

1. A reaction is defined when the net position is short and the market closes above the prior 10-day high.
2. Once a reaction is defined, an additional short position is initiated on any subsequent 10-day low if the following conditions are met:
   a. The pyramid signal price is below the price at which the most recent short position was initiated.
   b. The net position size is less than three units. (This condition implies that there is a limit of two pyramid units.)

Figure 16.12 illustrates the addition of this pyramid plan to a breakout system with $N = 40$ applied to the 2012–2013 gold market. (For now, ignore the "stop level" signals; they are explained shortly.)

Risk control becomes especially important if a pyramiding component is added to a system. Generally speaking, it is usually advisable to use a more sensitive condition for liquidating a pyramid position than the condition required to generate an opposite signal. The following is one example of a set of stop rules that might be employed in a system that uses pyramiding. Liquidate all pyramid positions whenever either condition is fulfilled:

1. An opposite trend-following signal is received.
2. The market closes above (below) the high (low) price since the most recently defined reaction that was followed by a pyramid sell (buy). Figure 16.12 illustrates the stop levels implied by this rule in the case of the 2012–2013 gold market.

Trade Exit

The existence of a trade exit rule in a system (e.g., a stop rule) would permit the liquidation of a position prior to receiving an opposite trend-following signal. Such a rule would serve to limit losses

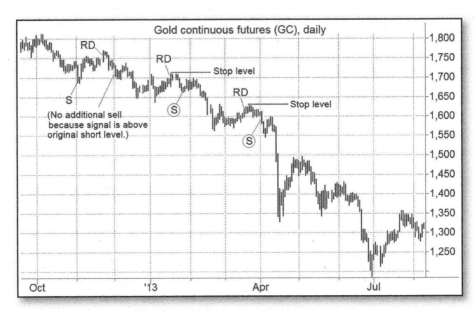

FIGURE 16.12   Pyramid Signals: Gold Continuous Futures
Note: S = base position sell signal; Ⓢ = pyramid sell signal; RD = reaction defined.
Chart created using TradeStation. ©TradeStation Technologies, Inc. All rights reserved.

on losing trades as well as limit the amount of open profits surrendered on winning trades. Although these are highly desirable goals, the trade-off implied by using a trade exit rule is relatively severe. If a trade exit rule is used, rules must be specified for reentering the position; otherwise, the system will be vulnerable to missing major trends.

The danger in using a trade exit rule is that it may result in the premature liquidation of a good trade. Although the reentry rule will serve as a backstop, the combination of an activated trade exit rule and a subsequent reentry is a whipsaw loss. Thus, it will not be at all uncommon for the addition of a trade exit rule (and implied reentry rule) to have a negative impact on performance. Nevertheless, although it is not easy, for some systems it will be possible to structure trade exit rules that improve performance on balance. (In terms of return, and usually in terms of return/risk measures as well, if a trade exit rule helps performance, the use of the trade exit rule as a reversal signal—as opposed to just a liquidation signal—will help performance even more.) Trade exit rules can also be made dynamic. For example, the trade exit condition can be made increasingly sensitive as a price move becomes more extended in either magnitude or duration.

■ Countertrend Systems

General Considerations Regarding Countertrend Systems

Countertrend systems often appeal to many traders because their ultimate goal is to buy low and sell high. Unfortunately, the difficulty of achieving this goal is inversely proportional to its desirability.

A critical distinction to keep in mind is that whereas a trend-following system is basically self-correcting, a countertrend system implies unlimited losses. Therefore, it is essential to include some stop-loss conditions in any countertrend system (unless it is traded simultaneously with trend-following systems). Otherwise, the system could end up being long for the duration of a major downtrend or short for the duration of a major uptrend. (Stop-loss conditions are optional for most trend-following systems, since an opposite signal will usually be received before the loss on a position becomes extreme.[7])

One important advantage of using a countertrend system is that it provides the opportunity for excellent diversification with simultaneously employed trend-following systems. In this regard, it should be noted that a countertrend system might be desirable even if it was a modest net loser, the reason being that if the countertrend system was inversely correlated to a simultaneously traded trend-following system, trading both systems might imply less risk than trading the trend-following system alone. Therefore, it is entirely possible that the two systems combined might yield a higher percent return (at the same risk level), even if the countertrend system alone lost money.

Types of Countertrend Systems

The following are some types of approaches that can be used to try to construct a countertrend system:

Fading minimum move. This is perhaps the most straightforward countertrend approach. A sell signal is indicated each time the market rallies by a certain minimum amount above the low point since the last countertrend buy signal. Similarly, a buy signal is indicated whenever the market declines by a minimum amount below the high point since the last countertrend sell signal. The magnitude of the price move required to generate a trade signal can be expressed in either nominal or percentage terms. Figure 16.13 illustrates the trade signals that would be generated by this type of countertrend system for a 7.5 percent threshold level in the January–September 2015 natural gas market. It is no accident this chart depicts the same market that was previously used in this chapter to illustrate whipsaw losses for a sensitive trend-following system (see Figure 16.6). Countertrend systems will tend to work best under those types of market conditions in which trend-following systems fare poorly.

Fading minimum move with confirmation delay. This is similar to the preceding countertrend system, with the exception that some minimum indication of a trend reversal is required before the countertrend trade is initiated. For example, a one-thrust-day confirmation might be required to validate countertrend signals based on fading a given percent price move.

Oscillators. A countertrend system could use oscillators to generate trade signals. However, as discussed in Chapters 11 and 12, although using oscillators to signal countertrend trades may work well in a trading-range market, in a trending market such an approach can be disastrous.

---

[7] Stop-loss rules, however, might be mandatory for an extremely nonsensitive trend-following system—for example, a breakout system with $N = 150$.

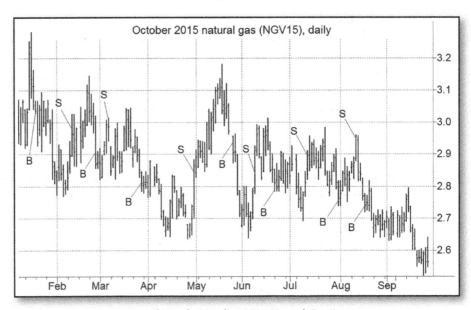

FIGURE 16.13 Countertrend Signals: October 2015 Natural Gas Futures

Note: Percentages are calculated as price changes in continuous futures divided by corresponding *nearest* futures price levels. B = buy signal: 7.5% decline from prior high; S = sell signal: 7.5% advance from prior low.

Chart created using TradeStation. ©TradeStation Technologies, Inc. All rights reserved.

Contrary opinion. A countertrend system might use contrary opinion as an input in timing trades. For example, once the contrary opinion rose above a specified level, a short position would be indicated contingent on confirmation by a very sensitive technical indicator. (Contrary opinion was discussed in Chapter 14.)

■ Diversification

The standard interpretation attached to the term *diversification* is that trading is spread across a broad range of markets. Although this is the single most important type of diversification, assuming the availability of sufficient funds, there are two additional levels of possible diversification. First, each market can be traded with several systems. Second, several variations of each system can be used. For example, if two contracts of cocoa are being traded using the breakout system, each contract can be traded using a different value of N (i.e., the number of days whose high or low must be penetrated to trigger a signal).

In the following discussion, the term *single market system variation (SMSV)* will refer to the concept of a specific variation of a given system traded in a single market. Thus, the simple breakout system, with $N = 20$, traded in the cocoa market would be an example of an SMSV. In the simplest case in which a single system is used for all markets, and a single system variation is used in each market, there would be only one SMSV for each market traded. This simplified case represents the typical application of trading systems and employs only the standard diversification across markets. However, if sufficient funds are available, additional benefits can be obtained by also diversifying across different systems and different variations of each system.

There are three important benefits to diversification:

1. **Dampened equity retracements.** Different SMSVs will not witness their losses at precisely the same periods. Thus, by trading a wide variety of SMSVs, the trader can achieve a smoother equity curve. This observation implies that trading 10 SMSVs with equivalent profit/risk characteristics could provide lower risk at the same return level than trading 10 units of a single SMSV. Or, alternatively, by trading larger size, 10 SMSVs with equivalent profit/risk characteristics could provide higher return at the same risk level than trading 10 units of a single SMSV. Up to a point, diversification would be beneficial even if the portfolio included SMSVs with poorer expected performance. A key consideration would be a given SMSV's correlation with the other SMSVs in the portfolio.

2. **Ensured participation in major trends.** Typically, only a few of the actively traded futures markets will witness substantial price trends in any given year. Because the majority of trades in most trend-following systems will lose money,[8] it is essential that the trader participate in the large-profit trades—that is, major trends. This is a key reason for the importance of diversification across markets.

3. **Bad luck insurance.** Futures systems trading, like baseball, is a game of inches. Given the right combination of circumstances, even a minute difference in the price movement on a single day could have an extraordinary impact on the profitability of a specific SMSV. To illustrate this point, we consider a breakout system ($N = 20$) with a confirmation rule requiring a single thrust day that penetrates the previous day's high or low by a minimum amount. In system A this amount is 0.05 cents; in system B it is 0.10 cents. This is the only difference between the two systems.

Figure 16.14 compares these two systems for the December 1981 coffee market and represents the most striking instance I have ever encountered of the sensitivity of system performance to minute changes in system values. The basic system buy signal (i.e., close above the 20-day high) was received on July 16. This buy was confirmed by system A on July 17 as the close was 0.09 cents above the previous day's high (point A1). System B, however, which required a 0.10-cent penetration, did not confirm the signal until the following day (point B1).

The buy signal for system A would have been executed at approximately $0.97 (point A2). However, due to the ensuing string of limit moves, the buy signal for system B could not be filled until prices surpassed $1.22 (point B2). Thus, during this short interim, system A gained

---

[8] Such systems can still be profitable because the average gain significantly exceeds the average loss.

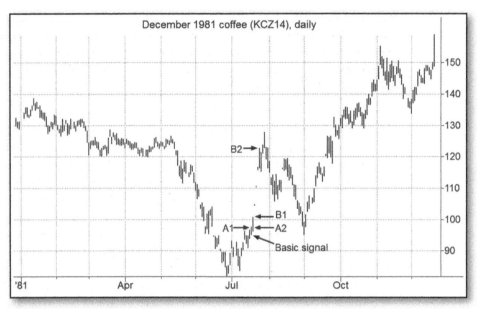

FIGURE 16.14 System Trading: A Game of Inches (December 1981 Coffee)
Chart created using TradeStation. ©TradeStation Technologies, Inc. All rights reserved.

25¢/lb ($9,375 per contract), while system B, which was unable to reverse its short position, lost a similar amount. The failure of the market to close 0.01 cent higher on a given day (a price move equivalent to less than $4) resulted in an incredible $18,750 per contract difference in the performance of the two nearly identical system variations! It should be emphasized this example reflects the randomness in commodity price movements rather than the instability of the tested system. Any system, other than a day trading system, could reflect the same degree of instability, since the performance difference was due to just a single trade in which the signals were separated by only one day.

This example should explain how it is possible for a trader to lose money in a given market using a system that generally performs well—he may just have chosen a specific variation that does much worse than most other variations (even very similar ones). By trading several variations of a system, the speculator could mitigate the impact of such isolated, abnormally poor results.[9] Of course, in so doing, the trader would also eliminate the possibility of gains far exceeding the average performance of the system. On balance, however, this prospect represents a desirable trade-off, since it is assumed that the basic trading goal is consistent performance rather than windfall profits.

---

[9] In the preceding example, system A and system B were deliberately chosen to be nearly identical in order to make the point about the potential impact of chance in its strongest possible form. However, in practice, the trader should choose system variations that are substantially more differentiated.

Ten Common Problems with Trend-Following Systems Revisited

We are now ready to consider possible solutions to the previously enumerated problems with standard trend-following systems. The problems and the possible solutions are summarized in Table 16.2.

TABLE 16.2   Problems with Standard Trend-Following Systems and Possible Solutions

Problems with Standard Trend-Following Systems		Possible Solutions
1.	Too many similar systems	1a.	Try to construct original systems in order to avoid the problem of "trading with the crowd."
		1b.	If trading more than one contract, spread out entry.
2.	Whipsaws	2a.	Employ confirmation conditions.
		2b.	Develop filter rules.
		2c.	Employ diversification.
3.	Failure to exploit major price moves	3.	Add pyramiding component.
4.	Nonsensitive (slow) systems can surrender a large percentage of profits.	4.	Employ trade exit rules.
5.	Cannot make money in trading-range markets	5.	Trade trend-following systems in conjunction with countertrend systems.
6.	Temporary large losses	6a.	If funds permit, trade more than one system in each market.
		6b.	When beginning to trade a system, trade more lightly if entering positions at a point after the signal has been received.
7.	Extreme volatility in best-performing systems	7.	By employing diversification, the trader can allocate some funds to a high-profit-potential system that is too risky to trade on its own.
8.	System works well in testing but then bombs.	8.	The danger of such a development can be reduced if systems are properly tested. This subject is discussed in detail in Chapter 19.
9.	Parameter shift	9a.	If funds permit, diversify by trading several variations of each system.
		9b.	Experiment with systems that incorporate market characteristic adjustments.
10.	Slippage	10.	Use realistic assumptions (discussed in Chapter 19).

Examples of Original Trading Systems

261

Nothing works at all times in all kinds of markets.

—Adam Smith

The previous chapter provided two examples of generic trading systems—moving averages and breakouts. This chapter details several original trading systems that are based on some of the patterns introduced in Chapter 9. Although the systems detailed here represent fully automated trading strategies, the primary goal of this chapter is not to offer specific trading systems, but rather to give readers a feel for how technical concepts can be utilized to construct a mechanical trading approach. Studying these examples should provide readers with ideas as to how to design their own trading systems.

■ Wide-Ranging-Day System

Basic Concept

A wide-ranging day, which was introduced in Chapter 9, is a day with a much wider *true range*[1] than recent trading sessions. The high volatility inherent in wide-ranging days gives these days special significance. Typically, the market will tend to extend in the direction of the initial price move beyond

---

[1] The *true range* is equal to the *true high* minus the *true low*. The *true high* is the maximum of the current day's high and the previous day's close. The *true low* is the minimum of the current day's low and the previous day's close.

the boundaries of the wide-ranging day. However, situations in which the market originally penetrates one side of the wide-ranging day and then reverses to penetrate the other side also have significance.

The wide-ranging-day system defines trading ranges based on wide-ranging days. Signals are generated when prices close above or below these trading ranges. In the simplest case, the trading range is defined as the wide-ranging day itself. However, we make the system more general by defining the trading range as the price range encompassing all the true highs and true lows during the period extending from $N1$ days before the wide-ranging day to $N2$ days after, where $N1$ and $N2$ are parameter values that must be defined. For example, if both $N1$ and $N2$ equal 0, the trading range would be defined by the wide-ranging day itself (i.e., the range between the true high and true low of the wide-ranging day). If $N1 = 2$ and $N2 = 4$, the trading range would be defined as the range between the highest true high and lowest true low in the interval beginning two days before the wide-ranging day and ending four days after it.

Definitions

Wide-ranging day. A day on which the *volatility ratio* (VR) is greater than k (e.g., $k = 2$). The VR is equal to today's true range divided by the average true range of the past N-day period (e.g., $N = 10$).

Price trigger range (PTR). The range defined by the highest true high and lowest true low in the interval between $N1$ days before the most recent wide-ranging day to $N2$ days after. Note that the PTR cannot be defined until $N2$ days after a wide-ranging day. (If $N2 = 0$, the PTR would be defined as of the close of the wide-ranging day itself.) The PTR will be redefined each time there is a new wide-ranging day (i.e., $N2$ days after such an event).

Trading Signals

Buy case. On a close above the high of the PTR, reverse from short to long.

Sell case. On a close below the low of the PTR, reverse from long to short.

Daily Checklist

To generate trading signals, perform the following steps each day:

1. If short and today's close is above the high of the PTR, liquidate short and go long.
2. If long and today's close is below the low of the PTR, liquidate long and go short.
3. Check whether exactly $N2$ days have elapsed since the most recent wide-ranging day. If this condition is met, redefine the PTR.

The order of these steps is very important. Note that the check for new trading signals *precedes* the check whether the PTR should be redefined. Thus, if the day a new PTR is defined also signals a trade based on the prevailing PTR going into that day, a signal would be generated. If step 3 preceded steps 1 and 2, trade signals could get delayed each time a signal occurred on the day a new PTR is defined ($N2$ days after the most recent wide-ranging day, which would be the wide-ranging day itself when $N2 = 0$). For example, assume the system is long, $N2 = 0$, and the close on a new wide-ranging day is below the low of the preceding wide-ranging day. According to the listed step order, the new wide-ranging day would signal a reversal from long to short. If steps 1 and 2 followed step 3, no signal would occur, since the PTR would be redefined, and the market would have to close below the *new* wide-ranging day to trigger a signal.

System Parameters

N1. The number of days prior to the wide-ranging day included in the PTR period.

N2. The number of days after the wide-ranging day included in the PTR period.

k. The value the volatility ratio (VR) must exceed in order to define a wide-ranging day.

Note: N, the number of past days used to calculate the VR, is assumed to be fixed (e.g., N = 10).

Parameter Set List

Table 17.1 provides a sample parameter set list. Readers can use this list as is or adjust it as desired. The subject of testing multiple parameter sets and deciding which one to use in actual trading is addressed in Chapter 19.

TABLE 17.1	Parameter Set List		
	k	*N1*	*N2*
1.	1.6	0	0
2.	1.6	2	0
3.	1.6	4	0
4.	1.6	0	2
5.	1.6	2	2
6.	1.6	4	2
7.	1.6	0	4
8.	1.6	2	4
9.	1.6	4	4
10.	2.0	0	0
11.	2.0	2	0
12.	2.0	4	0
13.	2.0	0	2
14.	2.0	2	2
15.	2.0	4	2
16.	2.0	0	4
17.	2.0	2	4
18.	2.0	4	4
19.	2.4	0	0
20.	2.4	2	0
21.	2.4	4	0
22.	2.4	0	2
23.	2.4	2	2
24.	2.4	4	2
25.	2.4	0	4
26.	2.4	2	4
27.	2.4	4	4

An Illustrated Example

To illustrate how the system works, Figures 17.1 through 17.5 superimpose trading signals on copper charts spanning late October 2013 to November 2015, a period the weekly chart inset in Figure 17.1 shows consisted mostly of a choppy, longer-term price descent, interspersed with short-term uptrends in mid-2014 and early 2015. Note these charts are continuous futures to coincide with the price series used to generate signals. As will be fully detailed in the next two chapters, continuous futures are usually the most suitable price series to use in trading systems. To help provide continuity between charts, each chart overlaps one to two months of the preceding chart.

Two types of signals are indicated on the accompanying charts:

1. The noncircled signals are generated by the system when both $N1$ and $N2$ are set to zero. In other words, the PTR is defined by the true high and true low of the wide-ranging day.
2. The circled signals are generated by the system when $N1 = 2$ and $N2 = 4$. (In other words, the PTR is defined by the true price range encompassing the interval beginning two days before the wide-ranging day and ending four days after it.)

Occasionally, both sets of parameter values will yield identical signals. In most cases, however, the second system version will trigger signals later or not at all. (The reverse can never occur, since the PTR based on $N1 = 2$ and $N2 = 4$ must be at least as wide as the PTR based on $N1 = 0$ and $N2 = 0$. Therefore any penetration of the former PTR must also be a penetration of the latter PTR, but not vice versa.)

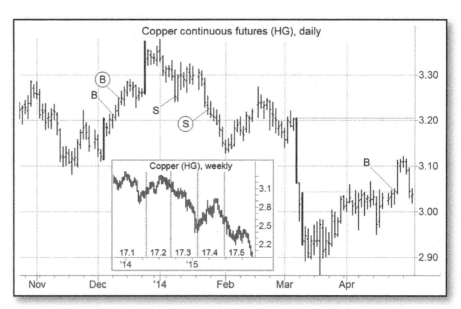

FIGURE 17.1   Wide-Ranging Day System, Chart 1: Copper Continuous Futures
Note: Thicker bars are wide-ranging days. B, S = buy and sell signals for $N1 = 0$ and $N2 = 0$; Ⓑ, Ⓢ = buy and sell signals for $N1 = 2$ and $N2 = 4$.

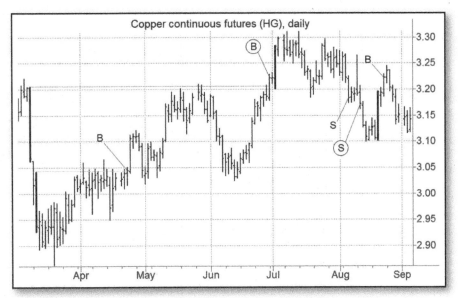

FIGURE 17.2 Wide-Ranging Day System, Chart 2: Copper Continuous Futures
Note: Thicker bars are wide-ranging days. B, S = buy and sell signals for $N1 = 0$ and $N2 = 0$; Ⓑ, Ⓢ = buy and sell signals for $N1 = 2$ and $N2 = 4$.
Chart created using TradeStation. ©TradeStation Technologies, Inc. All rights reserved.

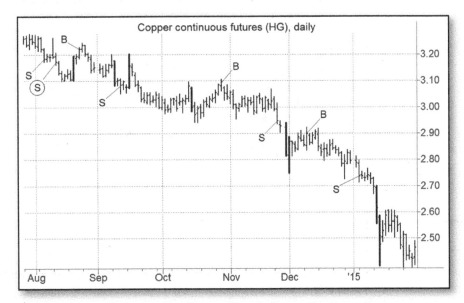

FIGURE 17.3 Wide-Ranging Day System, Chart 3: Copper Continuous Futures
Note: Thicker bars are wide-ranging days. B, S = buy and sell signals for $N1 = 0$ and $N2 = 0$; Ⓑ, Ⓢ = buy and sell signals for $N1 = 2$ and $N2 = 4$.
Chart created using TradeStation. ©TradeStation Technologies, Inc. All rights reserved.

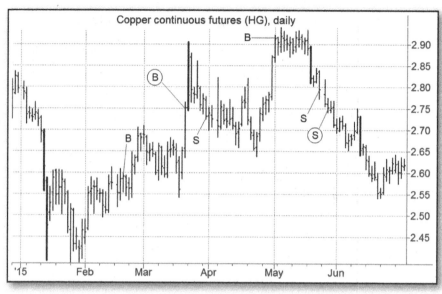

FIGURE 17.4 Wide-Ranging Day System, Chart 4: Copper Continuous Futures
Note: Thicker bars are wide-ranging days. B, S = buy and sell signals for *N1* = 0 and
N2 = 0; Ⓑ, Ⓢ = buy and sell signals for *N1* = 2 and *N2* = 4.

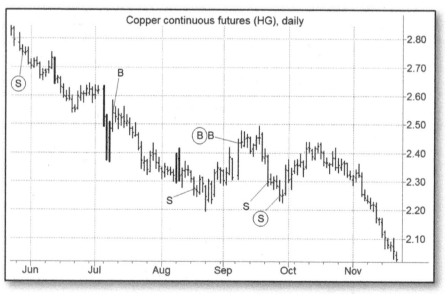

FIGURE 17.5 Wide-Ranging Day System, Chart 5: Copper Continuous Futures
Note: Thicker bars are wide-ranging days. B, S = buy and sell signals for *N1* = 0 and
N2 = 0; Ⓑ, Ⓢ = buy and sell signals for *N1* = 2 and *N2* = 4.

First, we examine the trading signals generated for the system version when both $N1$ and $N2$ equal zero (the noncircled signals). Therefore, for now, ignore the circled signals, which are based on the parameter set consisting of $N1 = 2$ and $N2 = 4$. We will subsequently examine the instances in which the two parameter sets yield different signals.

The first signal occurs in December 2013 when a close above the high of the December 4 wide-ranging day triggers a buy (Figure 17.1). The system then reverses to short modestly higher in January 2014 when the market closes below the low of the wide-ranging day formed in late December. The January short position profits from the ensuing downtrend and remains intact until late April when the market closes above the high of the second wide-ranging day that formed in March, triggering a buy signal.

The April 2014 long position remains intact for several months, capturing a portion of the ensuing uptrend, until it is reversed in early August when the market closes below the low of the early July wide-ranging day (Figure 17.2). The early August short position is short-lived and results in the first losing trade when a subsequent market bounce forms a wide-ranging day that is exceeded by a closing price two days later, triggering a buy signal. This August buy signal proves to be a whipsaw trade as the system reverses back to short in September 2014 (Figure 17.3).

The next buy signal materializes near the same level in late October 2014 when the market closes above the true high of the October wide-ranging day. This buy signal proves to be another whipsaw loss as the market immediately turns lower and eventually closes below the same October wide-ranging day, triggering a sell signal in November. Note, as is the case here, a single wide-ranging day can trigger multiple trades (in opposite directions) in the absence of intervening wide-ranging days. The November sell signal yields a small profit before leading to a third successive losing buy signal in December 2014. The January 2015 sell signal is exited at a profit in February 2015 when the market closes above the high of the second wide-ranging day formed in January (Figure 17.4). Additional trades are shown in Figures 17.4 and 17.5.

Next we examine how the signals generated by the second parameter set ($N1 = 2$, $N2 = 4$; circled on charts) differ from those that result from the first parameter set ($N1 = 0$, $N2 = 0$). One pattern the reader will notice is that whenever both parameter sets had signals in the same cycle—a signal in the same direction before the first parameter set triggered an opposite signal—the delay caused by using the second parameter set almost invariably resulted in a less favorable entry level. In most cases the differences in entry levels were moderate (e.g., the signals shown in Figure 17.1). In some instances, however, the difference in entry levels was quite substantial. For example, in Figure 17.2, the second parameter set went long in late June, more than two months after the first parameter set, because prices needed to close not just above the high of the March 11 wide-ranging day, but above the high of the two days preceding that day. Occasionally, both parameter sets may trigger signals on the same day (e.g., the September 2015 buy in Figure 17.5), but there are no instances where the second parameter set has a better entry. The poorer entry levels generated by the second parameter set are no accident, since the wider PTRs defined by the nonzero $N1$ and $N2$ values will always result in equal or higher buy signals and equal or lower sell signals.

The reader might well wonder why one would ever want to use nonzero values for $N1$ and $N2$, since the resulting delayed entries are invariably equal to or worse than entries based on keeping $N1$ and $N2$ equal to zero. The answer lies in the fact that the broader PTRs that result from nonzero $N1$ and $N2$ values will tend to filter out some losing signals—a characteristic that can have a major impact on the system's profitability. For example, following the August 2014 sell signal, the second parameter set avoids the three successive losing buy signals generated by the first parameter set (Figure 17.3). As a result, the second parameter set generates a substantial profit during this period while the series of trades generated by the first parameter set results in a net loss, despite the prevailing major downtrend.

On balance, in the market example illustrated in Figures 17.1 through 17.5, the benefit of filtering out some losing trades far outweighs the cumulative negative impact of the worse entries that result from using nonzero values for $N1$ and $N2$: For the entire period, the second parameter set generates a cumulative profit of $0.488 per pound ($12,200 per contract) versus a cumulative loss of –$0.379 per pound (–$9,475 per contract) for the first parameter set.

Although in some cases parameter sets with more sensitive entry conditions will experience the better performance, the outcome in our example is more typical. Generally speaking, the parameter sets with more restrictive entry conditions will do better, as the benefit of reducing whipsaw trades outweighs the disadvantage of worse entries. Ironically, human nature will lead most traders, especially novices, to choose more sensitive parameter sets because they will be attracted by the better entries and smaller surrender of open profits on individual trades offered by these sets, failing to fully appreciate the cumulative impact of reduced bad trades—a trait characteristic of more restrictive parameter sets.

It should be emphasized the selected example was intended to illustrate the mechanics of the wide-ranging day system across varied market conditions, not to put the system in the best light. Therefore, this example deliberately contained both intervals of strong wins as well as whipsaw losses. Note that I could easily have made the system look much more impressive by selecting a market and time period with much smoother trends. Such cherry-picked illustrations are all too common in trading books, articles, web sites, and—especially—advertisements. We return to this subject in the discussion of "the well-chosen example" in Chapter 19.

■ Run-Day Breakout System

Basic Concept

Up and *down run days* were defined in Chapter 9. As was explained, run days tend to occur in strongly trending markets. In this system, buy reversal signals are generated when the market closes above the maximum true high of a specified number of prior down run days. Similarly, sell reversal signals are generated when the market closes below the minimum true low of a specified number of prior up run days. The idea is that the ability of the market to close opposite the extreme point defined by one or more such strongly trending days implies a trend reversal has occurred.

Trading Signals

Buy case. Reverse to long whenever *both* of the following two conditions are met:

1. The close is above the maximum true high of the most recent $N2$ down run days. (*Note:* Only the run day true highs are considered, not the true highs on the interim days.)
2. The most recent run day is an *up* run day. (Without this second condition, in some cases, the first condition in the sell case would result in an automatic reversal back to a short position.)

Sell case. Reverse to short whenever *both* of the following two conditions are met:

1. The close is below the minimum true low of the most recent $N2$ up run days. (*Note:* Only the run day true lows are considered, not the true lows on the interim days.)
2. The most recent run day is a *down* run day. (Without this second condition, in some cases, the first condition in the buy case would result in an automatic reversal back to a long position.)

Daily Checklist

To generate trading signals, perform the following three steps each day:

1. Check whether the trading day $N1$ days prior to the current day can be defined as an up or a down run day.[2] (Recall that a run day cannot be defined until the close $N1$ days after the run day.) Keep track of all run days and their true highs and true lows.
2. If short, check whether today's close is above the maximum true high of the past $N2$ down run days. If it is, check whether the most recent run day was an up run day. If it was, reverse from short to long.
3. If long, check whether today's close is below the minimum true low of the past $N2$ up run days. If it is, check whether the most recent run day was a down run day. If it was, reverse from long to short.

Parameters

$N1$. The parameter used to define run days. For example, if $N = 3$, a day would be defined as an up run day if its true high was greater than the maximum true high of the prior three days and its true low was less than the minimum true low of the following three days.

$N2$. The number of prior down run days used to compute the maximum true high that must be exceeded by a close for a buy signal. (Also, the number of prior up run days used to compute the minimum true low that must be penetrated by a close for a sell signal.)

---

[2] Although uncommon, a day can be *both* an up run day and down run day. This unusual situation will occur if a day's true high is greater than the true highs during the prior and subsequent $N1$ days, and its true low is lower than the true lows during the prior and subsequent $N1$ days. Days that fulfill both the up and down run day definitions are not considered run days.

	N1	N2
TABLE 17.2 Parameter Set List		
1.	3	2
2.	3	3
3.	3	4
4.	3	5
5.	5	2
6.	5	3
7.	5	4
8.	7	2
9.	7	3
10.	7	4

Parameter Set List

Table 17.2 provides a sample parameter set list. Readers can use this list as is or adjust it as desired.

An Illustrated Example

To illustrate the mechanics of the run-day breakout system, Figures 17.6 through 17.9 show the buy and sell signals generated by the system for the parameter set $N1 = 5$ and $N2 = 4$ in the WTI crude oil market. Down run days are denoted by downward-pointing arrows and up run days by upward-pointing arrows.

A close below the minimum true low of the four most recent up run days triggers a sell signal in January 2014 (Figure 17.6). Note the second condition for a sell signal—that is, the most recent run day is a down run day—was fulfilled on the day of the signal. Had the signal occurred one day earlier, no trade would have been taken because the December 31, 2013, down run day (the first in the string of four) would not yet have been confirmed, and the most recent run day would have been the December 19 up run day. (Remember that each run day marked with an arrow can be confirmed only after five days have passed.)

A buy signal occurs in February 2014 when the market closes above the true high of the December 31 down run day (the maximum true high of that string of four down run days). The second condition is also met as the most recent run day is an up run day.

The market drifts higher into June (note the predominance of up run days versus down run days) and then begins to sag into July (Figure 17.7). The system next goes short in July when the market closes below the minimum true low of the prior four up run days. The system stays short through the entire ensuing downtrend, which is characterized by a tremendous predominance of down run days, eventually reversing nearly nine months later (in April 2015) on the close above the true high of the cluster of down run days in March (Figure 17.8). The system holds this position through June as the market moves sideways to slightly higher. The downturn in July generates a flurry of down run days, and the system turns short on July 22 with a close below the March 25 low (Figure 17.9). Note that

FIGURE 17.6 Run-Day Breakout System ($N1 = 5$; $N2 = 4$), Chart 1: WTI Crude Oil Continuous Futures

Note: The direction of the arrows indicates the direction of the run day.

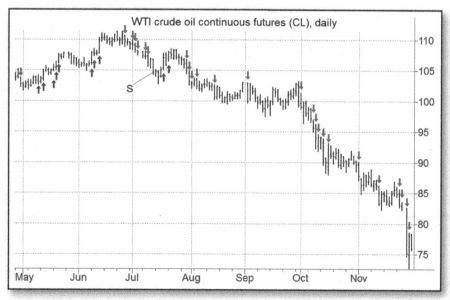

FIGURE 17.7 Run-Day Breakout System ($N1 = 5$; $N2 = 4$), Chart 2: WTI Crude Oil Continuous Futures

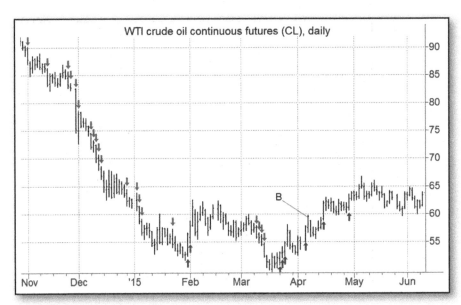

FIGURE 17.8 Run-Day Breakout System ($N1 = 5$; $N2 = 4$), Chart 3: WTI Crude Oil Continuous Futures

Chart created using TradeStation. ©TradeStation Technologies, Inc. All rights reserved.

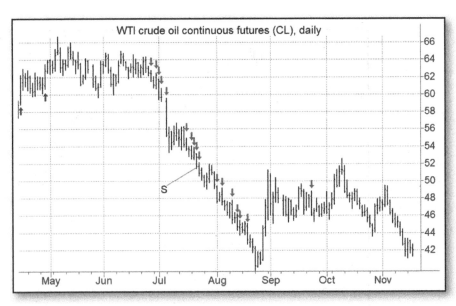

FIGURE 17.9 Run-Day Breakout System ($N1 = 5$, $N2 = 4$), Chart 4: WTI Crude Oil Continuous Futures

Chart created using TradeStation. ©TradeStation Technologies, Inc. All rights reserved.

although the sharp rebound in late August is large enough to rally the market above the maximum true high of the four most recent down run days, there is no buy signal because there is no intervening up run day.

Overall, the system successfully exploits the major downtrend (July 2014 to August 2015) that occurs during the two-year survey period, capturing about half of the total profit that would be realized by a hypothetical trader who goes short at the high of the two-year period and covers the position at the low of the period. Readers, however, are cautioned against generalizing the system's performance based on this single market/single parameter set example. In most cases, the system will not attain the level of performance exhibited in this illustration.

■ Run-Day Consecutive Count System

Basic Concept

This system also uses run days as the key input in generating trading signals. In this system, reversal signals occur whenever there are a specified number of up run days without any intervening down run days, or vice versa.

Definitions

The system uses the following definitions:

Buy count. The buy count is activated whenever a sell signal is received. The count starts at zero and increases by one whenever a new up run day is defined. The count is reset to zero whenever there is a down run day. In effect, the buy count represents the number of up run days that occur without any intervening down run days. The buy count is closed when a buy signal is received.

Sell count. The sell count is activated whenever a buy signal is received. The count starts at zero and increases by one whenever a new down run day is defined. The count is reset to zero whenever there is an up run day. In effect, the sell count represents the number of down run days that occur without any intervening up run days. The sell count is closed when a sell signal is received.

Trading Signals

Buy case. Reverse to long whenever the buy count reaches $N2$. Keep in mind that the fulfillment of this condition will not be known until $N1$ days after the $N2$th *consecutive* up run day. (Consecutive here means that there are no intervening down run days, not that the up run days occur on consecutive days.)

Sell case. Reverse to short whenever the sell count reaches N2. Keep in mind that the fulfillment of this condition will not be known until N1 days after the N2th *consecutive* down run day. (Consecutive here means that there are no intervening up run days, not that the down run days occur on consecutive days.)

Daily Checklist

To generate trading signals, perform the following three steps each day:

1. Check whether the trading day N1 days prior to the current day can be defined as an up or a down run day. (Recall that a run day cannot be defined until the close N1 days after the run day.) If the day is an up run day, increase the buy count by one if the buy count is active (i.e., if the current position is short); otherwise, reset the sell count to zero. (Either the buy or sell count is always active, depending on whether the current position is short or long.) If the day is defined as a down run day, increase the sell count by one if the sell count is active (i.e., if current position is long); otherwise, reset the buy count to zero.
2. If the buy count is active, check whether it is equal to N2 after step 1. If it is, cover short, go long, close buy count, and activate sell count.
3. If the sell count is active, check whether it is equal to N2 after step 1. If it is, cover long, go short, close sell count, and activate buy count.

Parameters

N1. The parameter used to define run days.
N2. The number of *consecutive* run days required for a signal.

Parameter Set List

Table 17.3 provides a sample parameter set list. Readers can use this list as is or adjust it as desired.

TABLE 17.3	Parameter Set List	
	N1	N2
1.	3	1
2.	3	2
3.	3	3
4.	3	4
5.	5	1
6.	5	2
7.	5	3
8.	7	1
9.	7	2
10.	7	3

An Illustrated Example

Figures 17.10 through 17.14 illustrate the signals generated by the run day consecutive count system for $N1 = 5$ and $N2 = 3$. In other words, the system reverses from long to short whenever there are three consecutive down run days and from short to long whenever there are three consecutive up run days. (Consecutive here means that there are no intervening run days in the opposite direction; not consecutive days.) *Keep in mind that the actual trade signal will not be received until the fifth close after the third consecutive run day, since a run day is not defined until N1 days after its occurrence ($N1 = 5$ in this example).*

The first signal in Figure 17.10—a buy in December 2013—occurs during a brief trading range and is reversed by a sell signal that occurs near the January 2014 low—a good example of how even profitable systems can generate terrible individual trade signals. The three consecutive up run days that start off February trigger a long position on February 12 (five days after the third up run day). Figure 17.11 shows this position remains intact until June 12, when the system reverses to short. Note that although the signal occurs on the fifth consecutive down run day in the sequence, it is the fact that this day is five days after the third consecutive down run day that triggers the trade. The downtrend that begins in June witnesses 18 down run days with no intervening up run days. In contrast, the preceding February–May uptrend contained 12 up run days and only one down run day.

The system reverses to the upside at the start of November 2014 (Figure 17.12), one week into a two-and-a-half-month trading range. The three consecutive down run days, which lead to the downside breakout of this range, turn the system short in January 2015. The next signal is the worst trade in the survey period, as the system reverses to long in February, shortly before the March 2 relative

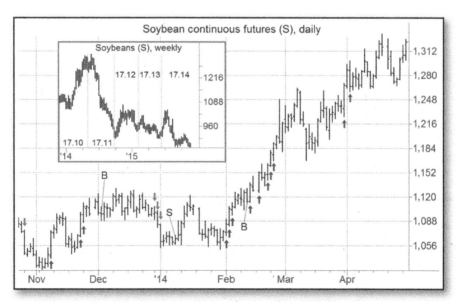

FIGURE 17.10 Run-Day Consecutive Count System, Chart 1: Soybean Continuous Futures

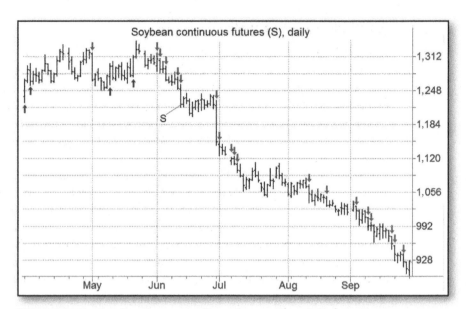

FIGURE 17.11 Run-Day Consecutive Count System, Chart 2: Soybean Continuous
Futures

Chart created using TradeStation. ©TradeStation Technologies, Inc. All rights reserved.

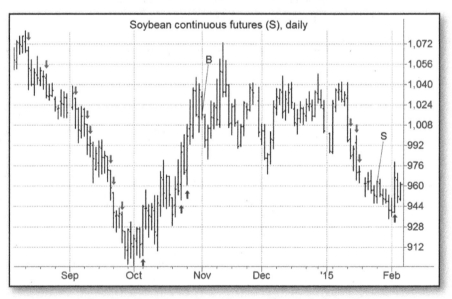

FIGURE 17.12 Run-Day Consecutive Count System, Chart 3: Soybean Continuous
Futures

Chart created using TradeStation. ©TradeStation Technologies, Inc. All rights reserved.

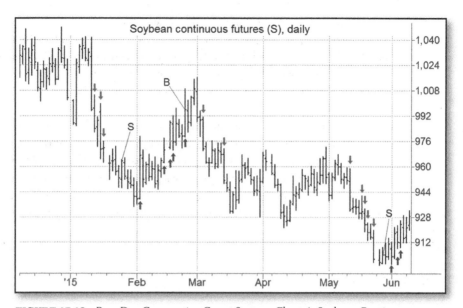

FIGURE 17.13 Run-Day Consecutive Count System, Chart 4: Soybean Continuous Futures

Chart created using TradeStation. ©TradeStation Technologies, Inc. All rights reserved.

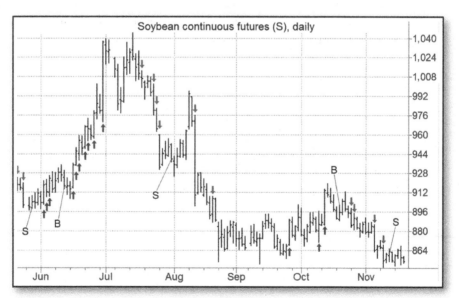

FIGURE 17.14 Run-Day Consecutive Count System, Chart 5: Soybean Continuous Futures

Chart created using TradeStation. ©TradeStation Technologies, Inc. All rights reserved.

high (Figure 17.13). The system does not generate a sell signal until late May, just before a relative low. Fortunately, the system reverses back to long two weeks later in June 2015 just before a sharp, but short-lived, rally (Figure 17.14). The subsequent downside reversal is equally abrupt, and the system surrenders most of its profit on the long position by the time the next sell signal is generated in July. The final two signals occur in October and November 2015 within a relatively narrow consolidation phase.

It should be noted that our intention was to select a realistic market illustration of the system and not to cherrypick an example in which the system performed particularly well, as is typical in most books on trading. The foregoing example provided a market with both favorable (two 4-month trends) and unfavorable (a more than yearlong wide-swing trading range) price environments. On balance, the system was net profitable (a cumulative gain of 76.25 cents per bushel, or $3,812.50 per contract) as the profits during the two trending periods outweighed the losses during the extended trading range period.

■ Conclusion

In this chapter we have introduced some original trading systems. Although they are viable as described, readers may wish to experiment with modifications that use the concepts of these systems as the core of more complex approaches. The ultimate goal of this chapter was not to present specific trading systems, but rather to illustrate how basic chart concepts can be transformed into trading systems. The number of possible systems that can be constructed from the technical patterns and concepts already discussed in this volume are limited only by the imagination of the reader.

CHAPTER 18

Selecting the Best Futures Price Series for System Testing

Garbage in, garbage out.

—Anonymous

System traders wishing to test their ideas on futures prices have always faced a major obstacle: the transitory life span of futures contracts. In contrast to the equities market, where a given stock is represented by a single price series spanning the entire test period, in futures each market is represented by a string of expiring contracts. Proposed solutions to this problem have been the subject of many articles and a great deal of discussion. In the process, substantial confusion has been generated, as evidenced by the use of identical terms to describe different types of price series. Even worse, so much misinformation has been provided on this subject that many market participants now believe the equivalent of "the earth is flat" theory.

There are four basic types of price series that can be used. The definition, advantages, and disadvantages of each are discussed in turn.

■ Actual Contract Series

At a surface glance, the best route might seem to be simply to use the actual contract series. However, there are two major problems with this approach. First, if you are testing a system over a meaningful length of time, each market simulation will require a large number of individual price series. For example, a 15-year test run for a typical market would require using approximately 60 to 90 individual contract price series. Moreover, using the individual contract series requires an algorithm for determining what action to take at the rollover points. As an example of the type of problem that may be encountered, it is entirely possible for a given system to be long in the old contract and short in the new contract or vice versa. These problems are hardly insurmountable, but they make the use of individual contract series a somewhat unwieldy approach.

The awkwardness involved in using a multitude of individual contracts is not, however, the main problem. The primary drawback in using individual contract series is that the period of meaningful liquidity in most contracts is very short—much shorter than the already limited contract life spans. To see the scope of this problem, examine a cross section of futures price charts depicting the price action in the one-year period prior to expiration. In many markets, contracts don't achieve meaningful liquidity until the final five or six months of trading, and sometimes even less. This problem was illustrated in Chapter 5. The limited time span of liquid trading in individual contracts means that any technical system or method that requires looking back at more than about six months of data—as would be true for a whole spectrum of longer-term approaches—cannot be applied to individual contract series. Thus, with the exception of short-term system traders, the use of individual contract series is not a viable alternative. It's not merely a matter of the approach being difficult but, rather, its being impossible because the necessary data simply do not exist.

■ Nearest Futures

The problems in using individual contract series as just described has led to the construction of various linked price series. The most common approach is almost universally known as *nearest futures*. This price series is constructed by taking each individual contract series until its expiration and then continuing with the next contract until its expiration, and so on. This approach may be useful for constructing long-term price charts for purposes of chart analysis, but it is worthless for providing a series that can be used in the computer testing of trading systems.

The problem in using a nearest futures series is that there are price gaps between expiring and new contracts—and quite frequently these gaps can be very substantial. For example, assume the July corn contract expires at $4 and that the next nearest contract (September) closes at $3.50 on the same day. Assume that on the next day September corn moves from $3.50 to $3.62. A nearest futures price series will show the following closing levels on these two successive days: $4, $3.62. In other words, the nearest futures contract would imply a 38-cent loss on a day on which longs would have enjoyed (or shorts would have suffered) a price gain of 12 cents. This example is by no means artificial. In fact, it would be easy to find a plethora of similarly extreme situations in actual price histories. Moreover, even if the typical distortion at rollover is considerably less extreme, the point is that there is virtually always some distortion, and the cumulative effect of these errors would destroy the validity of any computer test.

Fortunately, few traders are naive enough to use the nearest futures type of price series for computer testing. The two alternative linked price series described in the next sections have become the approaches employed by most traders wishing to use a single price series for each market in computer testing.

■ Constant-Forward ("Perpetual") Series

The constant-forward (also known as "perpetual") price series consists of quotes for prices a constant amount of time forward. The interbank currency market offers actual examples of constant-forward price series. For example, the three-month forward price series for the euro represents the quote for the euro three months forward from each given day in the series. This is in contrast to the standard U.S. futures contract, which specifies a fixed expiration date.

A constant-forward series can be constructed from futures price data through interpolation. For example, if we were calculating a 90-day constant-forward (or perpetual) series and the 90-day forward date fell exactly one-third of the way between the expirations of the nearest two contracts, the constant-forward price would be calculated as the sum of two-thirds of the nearest contract price and one-third of the subsequent contract price. As we moved forward in time, the nearer contract would be weighted less, and the weighting of the subsequent contract would increase proportionately. Eventually, the nearest contract would expire and drop out of the calculation, and the constant-forward price would be based on an interpolation between the subsequent two contracts.

As a more detailed example, assume you want to generate a 100-day forward price series based on euro futures, which are traded in March, June, September, and December contracts. To illustrate the method for deriving the 100-day constant-forward price, assume the current date is January 20. In this case, the date 100 days forward is April 30. This date falls between the March and June contracts. Assume the last trading dates for these two contracts are March 14 and June 13, respectively. Thus, April 30 is 47 days after the last trading day for the March contract and 44 days before the last trading day for the June contract. To calculate the 100-day forward price for January 20, an average price would be calculated using the quotes for March and June euro futures on January 20, weighting each quote in inverse proportion to its distance from the 100-day forward date (April 30). Thus, if on January 20 the closing price of March futures is 130.04 and the closing price of June futures is 130.77, the closing price for the 100-day forward series would be:

$$\frac{44}{91}(130.04) + \frac{47}{91}(130.77) = 130.42$$

Note that the general formula for the weighting factor used for each contract price is:

$$W_1 = \frac{C_2 - F}{C_2 - C_1} \qquad W_2 = \frac{F - C_1}{C_2 - C_1}$$

where C_1 = number of days until the nearby contract expiration
C_2 = number of days until the forward contract expiration
F = number of days until forward quote date
W_1 = weighting for nearby contract price quote
W_2 = weighting for forward contract price quote

So, for example, the weightings of the March and June quotes that would be used to derive a 100-day forward quote on March 2 would be as follows:

$$\text{Weighting for March quote} = \frac{103 - 100}{103 - 12} = \frac{3}{91}$$

$$\text{Weighting for June quote} = \frac{100 - 12}{103 - 12} = \frac{88}{91}$$

As we move forward in time, the nearer contract is weighted less and less, but the weighting for the subsequent contract increases proportionately. When the number of days remaining until the expiration of the forward contract equals the constant-forward time (100 days in this example), the quote for the constant-forward series would simply be equal to the quote for the forward contract (June). Subsequent price quotes would then be based on a weighted average of the June and September prices. In this manner, one continuous price series could be derived.

The constant-forward price series eliminates the problem of huge price gaps at rollover points and is certainly a significant improvement over a nearest futures price series. However, this type of series still has major drawbacks. To begin, it must be stressed that one cannot literally trade a constant-forward series, since the series does not correspond to any real contract. An even more serious deficiency of the constant-forward series is that it fails to reflect the effect of the evaporation of time that exists in actual futures contracts. This deficiency can lead to major distortions—particularly in carrying-charge markets.

To illustrate this point, consider a hypothetical situation in which spot gold prices remain stable at approximately $1,200/ounce for a one-year period, while forward futures maintain a constant premium of 1 percent per two-month spread. Given these assumptions, futures would experience a steady downtrend, declining $73.82/ounce[1] ($7,382 per contract) over the one-year period (the equivalent of the cumulative carrying-charge premiums). Note, however, the constant-forward series would completely fail to reflect this bear trend because it would register an approximate constant price. For example, a two-month constant-forward series would remain stable at approximately $1,212/ounce ($1.01 \times \$1,200 = \$1,212$). Thus, the price pattern of a constant-forward series can easily deviate substantially from the pattern exhibited by the actual traded contracts—a highly undesirable feature.

■ Continuous (Spread-Adjusted) Price Series

The spread-adjusted futures series, commonly known as *continuous futures*, is constructed to eliminate the distortions caused by the price gaps between consecutive futures contracts at their transition points. In effect, the continuous futures price will precisely reflect the fluctuations of a futures position that is continuously rolled over to the subsequent contract N days before the last trading day, where N is a parameter that needs to be defined. If constructing their own continuous futures data series, traders should select a value of N that corresponds to their actual trading practices.

---

[1] This is true since, given the assumptions, the one-year forward futures price would be approximately $1,273.82 ($1.01^6 \times \$1,200 = \$1,273.82$) and would decline to the spot price ($1,200) by expiration.

For example, if a trader normally rolls a position over to a new contract approximately 20 days before the last trading day, N would be defined as 20. The scale of the continuous futures series is adjusted so the current price corresponds to a currently traded futures contract.

Table 18.1 illustrates the construction of a continuous futures price for the soybean market. For simplicity, this example uses only two contract months, July and November; however, a continuous price could be formed using any number of traded contract months. For example, the continuous futures price could be constructed using the January, March, May, July, August, September, and November soybean contracts.

TABLE 18.1 **Construction of a Continuous Futures Price Using July and November Soybeans (cents/bushel)***

Date	Contract	Actual Price	Spread at Rollover (Nearby Forward)	Cumulative Adjustment Factor	Unadjusted Continuous Futures (Col. 3 + Col. 5)	Continuous Futures Price (Col. 6 − 772.5)
6/27/12	Jul-12	1,471			1,471	698.5
6/28/12	Jul-12	1,466			1,466	693.5
6/29/12	Jul-12	1,512.75			1,512.75	740.25
7/2/12	Nov-12	1,438	85	85	1,523	750.5
7/3/12	Nov-12	1,474.75		85	1,559.75	787.25
⁑						
10/30/12	Nov-12	1,533.75		85	1,618.75	846.25
10/31/12	Nov-12	1,547		85	1,632	859.5
11/1/12	Jul-13	1,474	86.25	171.25	1,645.25	872.75
11/2/12	Jul-13	1,454		171.25	1,625.25	852.75
⁑						
6/27/13	Jul-13	1,548.5		171.25	1,719.75	947.25
6/28/13	Jul-13	1,564.5		171.25	1,735.75	963.25
7/1/13	Nov-13	1,243.25	312.5	483.75	1,727	954.5
7/2/13	Nov-13	1,242.5		483.75	1,726.25	953.75
⁑						
10/30/13	Nov-13	1,287.5		483.75	1,771.25	998.75
10/31/13	Nov-13	1,280.25		483.75	1,764	991.5
11/1/13	Jul-14	1,224.5	45.5	529.25	1,753.75	981.25
11/4/13	Jul-14	1,227.75		529.25	1,757	984.5
⁑						
6/27/14	Jul-14	1,432		529.25	1,961.25	1,188.75
6/30/14	Jul-14	1,400.5		529.25	1,929.75	1,157.25
7/1/14	Nov-14	1,147.5	243.25	772.5	1,920	1,147.5
7/2/14	Nov-14	1,141.5		772.5	1,914	1,141.5

*Assumes rollover on last day of the month preceding the contract month.

For the moment, ignore the last column in Table 18.1 and focus instead on the unadjusted continuous futures price (column 6). At the start of the period, the actual price and the unadjusted continuous futures price are identical. At the first rollover point, the forward contract (November 2012) is trading at an 85-cent discount to the nearby contract (July 2012). All subsequent prices of the November 2012 contract are then adjusted upward by this amount (the addition of a positive nearby/forward spread), yielding the unadjusted continuous futures prices shown in column 6. At the next rollover point, the forward contract (July 2013) is trading at an 86.25-cent discount to the nearby contract (November 2012). As a result, all subsequent actual prices of the July 2013 contract must now be adjusted by the cumulative adjustment factor—the total of all rollover gaps up to that point (171.25 cents)—in order to avoid any artificial price gaps at the rollover point. This cumulative adjustment factor is indicated in column 5. The unadjusted continuous futures price is obtained by adding the cumulative adjustment factor to the actual price.

The preceding process is continued until the current date is reached. At this point, the final cumulative adjustment factor is subtracted from all the unadjusted continuous futures prices (column 6), a step that sets the current price of the series equal to the price of the current contract (November 2014 in our example) without changing the shape of the series. This continuous futures price is indicated in column 7 of Table 18.1. Note that although actual prices seem to imply a net price decline of 329.50 cents during the surveyed period, the continuous futures price indicates a 443-cent *increase*—the actual price change that would have been realized by a constant long futures position.

In effect, the construction of the continuous series can be thought of as the mathematical equivalent of taking a nearest futures chart, cutting out each individual contract series contained in the chart, and pasting the ends together (assuming a continuous series employing all contracts and using the same rollover dates as the nearest futures chart).

In some markets, the spreads between nearby and forward contracts will range from premiums to discounts (e.g., cattle). However, in other markets, the spread differences will be unidirectional. For example, in the gold market, the forward month always trades at a premium to the nearby month.[2] In these types of markets, the spread-adjusted continuous price series can become increasingly disparate from actual prices.

It should be noted that when nearby premiums at contract rollovers tend to swamp nearby discounts, it is entirely possible for the series to eventually include negative prices for some past periods as cumulative adjustments mount, as illustrated in the soybean continuous futures chart in Figure 18.1. The price gain that would have been realized by a continuously held futures position during this period

---

[2] The reason for this behavioral pattern in gold spreads is related to the fact that world gold inventories exceed annual usage by many multiples, perhaps even by as much as a hundredfold. Consequently, there can never actually be a "shortage" of gold—and a shortage of nearby supplies is the only reason why a storable commodity would reflect a premium for the nearby contract. (Typically, for storable commodities, the fact that the forward contracts embed carrying costs will result in these contracts trading at a premium to more nearby months.) Gold prices fluctuate in response to shifting perceptions of gold's value among buyers and sellers. Even when gold prices are at extremely lofty levels, it does not imply any actual shortage, but rather an upward shift in the market's perception of gold's value. Supplies of virtually any level are still available—at some price. This is not true for most commodities, in which there is a definite relevant limit in total supplies.

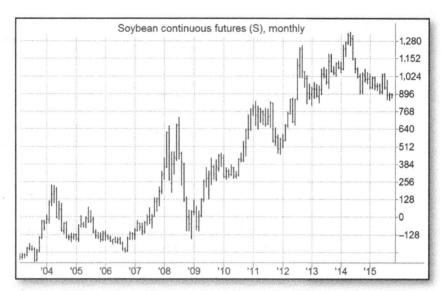

FIGURE 18.1 "Negative" Prices in a Continuous Futures Chart: Soybean Continuous Futures
Chart created using TradeStation. ©TradeStation Technologies, Inc. All rights reserved.

far exceeded the net price gain implied by nearest futures, and the subtraction of the cumulative adjustment factor from the most recent (2015) prices would result in negative prices for the majority of the time before 2009. Such an outcome is unavoidable if the continuous futures price series is to reflect the net gain in a continually held long position and if the series is shifted by the constant factor necessary to set the current continuous futures price equal to the current contract actual price.

Although the fact that a continuous futures price series could include negative prices may sound disconcerting, it does not present any problems in using the series for testing systems. The reason for this is that in measuring the profits or losses of trades, it is critical that the price series employed accurately reflects price *changes,* not price *levels.* However, it also will often be useful to generate the actual prices that correspond to the continuous futures prices in order to facilitate such applications as checking trading signals against actual contract charts.

It should also be noted that the transition between contracts need not occur on the last trading day, as is the conventional assumption in the nearest futures price series. In fact, because physically delivered contracts are particularly vulnerable to distortions in their final weeks of trading due to technical concerns regarding delivery, it probably makes sense to avoid these prices in constructing a continuous series. It follows, then, that one should use a rollover date before the last trading day (e.g., 20 days prior to the last trading day).

■ Comparing the Series

It is important to understand that a linked futures price series can only accurately reflect either price *levels,* as do nearest futures, or price *moves,* as do continuous futures, but not both—much as a coin can land on either heads or tails but not both. The adjustment process used to construct continuous series means that past prices in a continuous series will not match the actual historical prices that prevailed at the time. However, the essential point is that the continuous series is the only linked futures series that will exactly reflect price swings and hence equity fluctuations in an actual trading account. Consequently, it is the only linked series that can be used to generate accurate simulations in computer testing of trading systems.

The preceding point is absolutely critical! Mathematics is not a matter of opinion. There is one right answer and there are many wrong answers. The simple fact is that if a continuous futures price series is defined so that rollovers occur on days consistent with rollovers in actual trading, results implied by using this series will precisely match results in actual trading (assuming, of course, accurate commission and slippage cost estimates). In other words, the continuous series will exactly parallel the fluctuations of a constantly held (i.e., rolled over) long position. All other types of linked series will not match actual market price movements.

To illustrate this statement, we compare the implications of various price series using the sideways gold market example cited earlier in this chapter (i.e., gold hovering near $1,200 and a forward/nearby contract premium equal to 1 percent per two-month spread). A trader buying a one-year forward futures contract would therefore pay approximately $1,273.82 ($1.01^6 \times \$1,200 = \$1,273.82$). The spot price would reflect a sideways pattern near $1,200. As previously seen, a 60-day constant-forward price would reflect a sideways pattern near $1,212 ($1.01 \times \$1,200$). A nearest futures price series would exhibit a general sideways pattern, characterized by extended minor downtrends (reflecting the gradual evaporation of the carrying charge time premium as each nearby contract approached expiration), interspersed with upward gaps at rollovers between expiring and subsequent futures contracts.

Thus the spot, constant-forward, and nearest futures price series would all suggest that a long position would have resulted in a break-even trade for the year. In reality, however, the buyer of the futures contract pays $1,273.82 for a contract that eventually expires at $1,200. Thus, from a trading or real-world viewpoint, the market actually witnesses a downtrend. The continuous futures price is the only price series that reflects the market decline—and real dollar loss—a trader would actually have experienced.

I have often seen comments or articles by industry "experts" arguing for the use of constant-forward (perpetual) series instead of continuous series in order to avoid distortions. This argument has it exactly backwards. Whether these proponents of constant-forward series adopt their stance because of naïveté or self-interest (i.e., they are vendors of constant-forward-type data), they are simply wrong. This is not a matter of opinion. If you have any doubts, try matching up fluctuations in an actual trading account with those that would be implied by constant-forward-type price series. You will soon be a believer.

Are there any drawbacks to the continuous futures time series? Of course. It may be the best solution to the linked series problem, but it is not a perfect answer. A perfect alternative simply does not exist. One potential drawback, which is a consequence of the fact that continuous futures accurately reflect only price swings, not price levels, is that continuous futures cannot be used for any type of percentage calculations. This situation, however, can be easily remedied. If a system requires the calculation of a percentage change figure, use continuous futures to calculate the nominal price change and nearest futures for the divisor. Also, there is some unavoidable arbitrariness involved in constructing a continuous series, since one must decide which contracts to use and on what dates the rollovers should occur. However, this issue is not really a problem since these choices should merely mirror the contracts and rollover dates used in actual trading. Moreover, there is arbitrariness involved in the use of any of the price series discussed. Finally, in some markets, the contracts being linked together may have very different past price patterns (as is often the case in livestock markets). However, this problem would exist in any kind of linked series.

■ Conclusion

For the purpose of computer testing of trading systems, there are only two types of valid price series: (1) individual contract series and (2) continuous futures series. Individual contract series are a viable approach only if the methodologies employed do not require looking back more than four or five months in time (a restriction that rules out a vast number of technical approaches). In addition, the use of individual contract series is far clumsier. Thus, for most purposes, the continuous futures price series provides the best alternative. As long as one avoids using continuous prices for percentage calculations, this type of price series will yield accurate results (i.e., results that parallel actual trading) as well as provide the efficiency of a single series per market. Again, I would strongly caution data users to avoid being misled by those who argue for the use of constant-forward-type series in computer testing applications. If your goal is a price series that will accurately reflect futures trading, the constant-forward series will create distortions rather than avoid them.

Over the years more—but not all—data vendors and system-testing platforms have embraced the continuous futures series described here as the default data type for long-term analysis and system testing. Traders should nonetheless confirm with the vendor that long-term futures data series linking different contracts are indeed constructed using the continuous futures (i.e., spread-adjusted) methodology. Traders should also be cognizant of the contracts and rollover dates used by the vendor so that they can match their contract selection and rollover dates accordingly. Vendors should be able to provide a clear explanation of the methodology they employ for constructing long-term (i.e., linked-contract) futures data series.

CHAPTER 19

Testing and Optimizing Trading Systems

Every decade has its characteristic folly, but the basic cause is the same: people persist in believing that what has happened in the recent past will go on happening into the indefinite future, even while the ground is shifting under their feet.

—George J. Church

■ The Well-Chosen Example[1]

You've plunked down your $895 to attend the 10th annual "Secret of the Millionaires" futures trading seminar. At that price, you figure the speakers will be revealing some very valuable information.

The current speaker is explaining the Super-Razzle-Dazzle (SRD) commodity trading system. The slide on the huge screen reveals a price chart with "B" and "S" symbols representing buy and sell points. The slide is impressive: All of the buys seem to be lower than the sells.

This point is brought home even more dramatically in the next slide, which reveals the equity stream that would have been realized trading this system—a near-perfect uptrend. Not only that but the system is also very easy to keep up.

As the speaker says, "All it takes is 10 minutes a day and a knowledge of simple arithmetic."

You never realized making money in futures could be so simple. You could kick yourself for not having attended the first through ninth annual seminars.

---

[1] The following section is adapted from an article that first appeared in *Futures* magazine in September 1984.

Once you get home, you select 10 diversified markets and begin trading the SRD system. Each day you plot your equity. As the months go by, you notice a strange development. Although the equity in your account exhibits a very steady trend, just as the seminar example did, there is one small difference: The trend on your equity chart is down. What went wrong?

The fact is you can find a favorable illustration for almost any trading system. The mistake is in extrapolating probable future performance on the basis of an isolated and well-chosen example from the past.

A true-life example may help illustrate this point. Back in 1983, when I had been working on trading systems for only a couple of years, I read an article in a trade magazine that presented the following very simple trading system:

1. If the six-day moving average is higher than the previous day's corresponding value, cover short and go long.
2. If the six-day moving average is lower than the previous day's corresponding value, cover long and go short.

The article used the Swiss franc in 1980 as an illustration. Without going into the details, suffice it to say that applying this system to the Swiss franc in 1980 would have resulted in a profit of $17,235 per contract after transaction costs. Even allowing for a conservative fund allocation of $6,000 per contract, this implied an annual gain of 287 percent! Not bad for a system that can be summarized in two sentences. It is easy to see how traders, presented with such an example, might eagerly abandon their other trading approaches for this apparent money machine.

I couldn't believe such a simple system could do so well. So I decided to test the system over a broader period—1976 to mid-1983[2]—and a wide group of markets.

Beginning with the Swiss franc, I found that the total profit during this period was $20,473. In other words, excluding 1980, the system made only $3,238 during the remaining 6½ years. Thus, assuming that you allocated $6,000 to trade this approach, the average annual percent return for those years was a meager 8 percent—quite a comedown from 287 percent in 1980.

But wait. It gets worse. Much worse.

When I applied the system to a group of 25 markets from 1976 through mid-1983, the system lost money in 19 of the 25 markets. In 13 of the markets—more than half of the total survey—the loss exceeded $22,500, or $3,000 per year, per contract! In five markets, the loss exceeded $45,000, equivalent to $6,000 per year, per contract! Also, it should be noted that, even in the markets where the system was profitable, its performance was well below gains exhibited for these markets during the same period by most other trend-following systems.

There was no question about it. This was truly a bad system. Yet if you looked only at the well-chosen example, you might think you had stumbled upon the trading system Jesse Livermore used in his good years. Talk about a gap between perception and reality.

This system witnessed such large, broadly based losses that you may well wonder why fading the signals of such a system might not provide an attractive trading strategy. The reason is that most of the

---

[2] The start date was chosen to avoid the distortion of the extreme trends witnessed by many commodity markets during 1973–1975. The end date merely reflected the date on which I tested this particular system.

losses are the result of the system being so sensitive that it generates large transaction costs. (Transaction costs include commission costs *plus* slippage. The concept of slippage is discussed later in this chapter.) This sensitivity of the system occasionally is beneficial, as was the case for the Swiss franc in 1980. However, on balance, it is the system's major weakness.

Losses due to transaction costs would not be realized as gains by fading the system. Moreover, doing the opposite of all signals would generate equivalent transaction costs. Thus, once transaction costs are incorporated, the apparent attractiveness of a contrarian approach to using the system evaporates.

Because the related episode and the system testing it inspired occurred many years ago, some readers might justifiably wonder whether the system has been a viable strategy in more recent years. To answer this question, we tested the same system on a portfolio of 31 U.S. futures contracts for the 10 years ending November 30, 2015, and produced similar results: Only 12 of the 31 markets generated a net gross profit—that is, a profit before accounting for commissions or slippage. Incorporating a $25 commission and slippage assessment reduced the number of profitable markets to nine, and the total losses of the unprofitable markets outweighed the profits of the winning markets by a factor of more than 4 to 1, with a total cumulative loss of −$940,612 for the entire 10-year period (assuming a trade size of one contract per market).

The moral is simple: Don't draw any conclusions about a system (or indicator) on the basis of isolated examples. The only way you can determine if a system has any value is by testing it (without benefit of hindsight) over an extended time period for a broad range of markets.

■ Basic Concepts and Definitions

A *trading system* is a set of rules that can be used to generate trade signals. A *parameter* is a value that can be freely assigned in a trading system in order to vary the timing of signals. For example, in the basic breakout system, N (the number of prior days whose high or low must be exceeded to indicate a signal) is a parameter. Although the operation of the rules in the system will be identical whether $N = 7$ or $N = 40$, the timing of the signals will be vastly different. (For an example, see Figure 16.5 in Chapter 16.)

Most trading systems will have more than one parameter. For example, in the crossover moving average system there are two parameters: the length of the short-term moving average and the length of the long-term moving average. Any combination of parameter values is called a *parameter set*. For example, in a crossover moving average system, moving averages of 10 and 40 would represent a specific parameter set. Any other combination of moving average values would represent another parameter set. In systems with only one parameter (e.g., breakout), the parameter set would consist of only one element.[3]

---

[3] Note that the terms *parameter set* and *system variation* (the latter was used in Chapter 16) refer to identical concepts. The introduction of the term *parameter set* was merely deferred until this chapter because doing so allowed for a more logically ordered presentation of the material.

Most "generic" systems are limited to one or two parameters. However, the design of more creative and flexible systems, or the addition of modifications to basic systems, will usually imply the need for three or more parameters. For example, adding a confirmation time delay rule to the cross-over moving average system would imply a third parameter: the number of days in the time delay.

As a general principle, it is wise to use the simplest form of a system (i.e., the least number of parameters) that does not imply any substantial deterioration in performance relative to the more complex versions. However, one should not drop parameters that are deemed important simply to reduce the number of implied parameter sets. In this case, a more reasonable approach would be to limit the number of parameter sets actually tested.

It should be noted that even for a simple one- or two-parameter-set system, it is not necessary to test all possible combinations. For example, in a simple breakout system in which one wishes to test the performance for values of $N = 1$ to $N = 100$, it is not necessary to test each integer in this range. A more efficient approach would be to first test the system using spaced values for N (e.g., 10, 20, 30, . . . , 100), and then, if desired, the trader could focus on any areas that appeared to be of particular interest. For example, if the system exhibited particularly favorable performance for the parameter values $N = 40$ and $N = 50$, the trader might want to also test some other values of N in this narrower range. Such an additional step, however, is probably unnecessary, since, as is discussed later in this chapter, performance differences in parameter set values—particularly values in such close proximity—are probably a matter of chance and lack any significance.

As a more practical real-life example, assume we wish to test a crossover moving average system that includes a time-delay confirmation rule. If we were interested in the performance of the system for parameter values 1 to 50 for the shorter-term moving average, 2 to 100 for the longer-term moving average, and 1 to 20 for the time delay, there would be a total of 74,500 parameter sets.[4] Note that we cannot reduce the number of parameters without severely damaging the basic structure of the system. However, we can test a far more limited number of parameter sets and still produce a very good approximation of the system's overall performance. Specifically, we might use increments of 10 for the shorter-term moving average (10, 20, 30, 40, and 50), increments of 20 for the longer-term moving average (20, 40, 60, 80, and 100), and three selected values for the time delay (e.g., 5, 10, and 20). This approach would limit the number of parameter sets to be tested to 57.[5] Once these parameter sets are tested, the results would be analyzed, and a moderate number of additional parameter sets might be tested as suggested by this evaluation. For example, if a time delay of 5—the smallest value tested—seemed to work best for most favorably performing parameter sets, it would also be reasonable to test smaller values for the time delay.

Conceptually, it might be useful to define four types of parameters:

Continuous parameter. A continuous parameter can assume any value within a given range. A percentage price penetration would be an example of a continuous parameter. Because a

---

[4] To avoid double counting, each "short-term" moving average can only be combined with a "long-term" moving average for a longer period. Thus, the total number of combinations is given by (99 + 98 + 97 + ... + 50) (20) = 74,500.

[5] (5 + 4 + 4 + 3 + 3)(3) = 57.

continuous parameter can assume an infinite number of values, it is necessary to specify some interval spacing in testing such a parameter. For example, a percent penetration parameter might be tested over a range of 0.05 percent to 0.50 percent, at intervals of 0.05 (i.e., 0.05, 0.10, . . . , 0.50). It is reasonable to expect performance results to change only moderately for an incremental change in the parameter value (assuming a sufficiently long test period).

Discrete parameter. A discrete parameter can assume only integer values. For example, the number of days in a breakout system is a discrete parameter. Although one can test a discrete parameter for every integer value within the specified range, such detail is often unnecessary, and wider spacing is frequently employed. As with continuous parameters, it is reasonable to expect performance results to change only moderately for a small change in the parameter value.

Code parameter. A code parameter is used to represent a definitional classification. Thus, there is no significance to the cardinal value of a code parameter. For example, assume we wish to test a simple breakout system using three different definitions of a breakout (buy case): *close* above previous N-day *high, high* above previous N-day *high,* and *close* above previous N-day *high close.* We could test each of these systems separately, but it might be more efficient to use a parameter to specify the intended definition. Thus, a parameter value of 0 would indicate the first definition, a value of 1 the second definition, and a value of 2 the third definition. Note that there are only three possible values for this parameter, and that there is no significance to incremental changes in parameter values.

Fixed or nonoptimized parameter. Normally, any type of parameter will be allowed to assume different values in testing a system. However, in systems with a large number of parameters, it may be necessary to fix some parameter values in order to avoid an excessive number of parameter sets. Such parameters are called *nonoptimized parameters.* For example, in a nonsensitive (slow) trend-following system, we might wish to include a backup stop rule to prevent catastrophic losses. By definition, in this situation, the stop rule would be activated on only a few occasions. Consequently, any parameters implicit in the stop rule could be fixed, since variation in these parameter values would not greatly affect the results.

Choosing the Price Series

The first step in testing a system in a given market is choosing the appropriate price series. The issues related to this selection were fully detailed in Chapter 18. Generally speaking, a continuous futures series is the preferred choice, although actual contract data could be used for short-term trading systems.

Choosing the Time Period

Generally speaking, the longer the test period, the more reliable the results. If the time period is too short, the test will not reflect the system's performance for a reasonable range of market situations. For example, a test of a trend-following system on the Canadian dollar market that used only the three

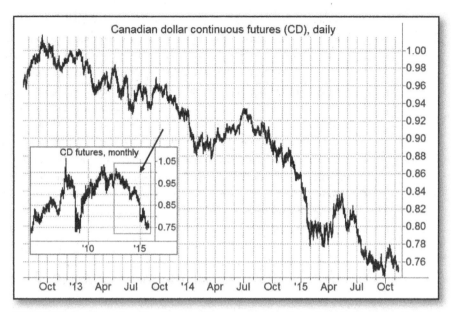

FIGURE 19.1 Major Trending Phase as Unrepresentative Price Sample: Canadian Dollar Continuous Futures

Chart created using TradeStation. ©TradeStation Technologies, Inc. All rights reserved.

years of data from roughly October 2012 to October 2015—a period dominated by a sustained bear market (see Figure 19.1)—would yield highly misleading results in terms of the system's probable long-term performance, as evidenced by the monthly chart inset, which shows the market's price action dating back to 2004. Although testing over only the recent past is almost always undesirable, longer periods are not always necessarily better for testing than shorter ones. In some markets, if too long a period is used for testing a system, the earlier years in the survey period might be extremely unrepresentative of current market conditions.

Although it is impossible to provide a decisive answer as to the optimum number of years to be used in testing, 10 to 20 years is a reasonable range. For short-term trading systems (average duration of trades equal to a few weeks or less), a shorter test period (e.g., 5 to 10 years) would probably be sufficient. Trading system test results based on time periods significantly shorter than these guidelines should be suspect. In fact, it is rather incredible that some published studies on trading systems are based on test periods of two years or less.

Trading systems that use intraday data do not need to be tested over as long a time period as is the case for daily data because any time period will contain far more data points. For example, in the case of five-minute bars, a stock-index futures contract—just during the stock market's cash trading session—will generate the equivalent of a year's worth of daily price bars (252) in a little more than three days. A year's worth of this five-minute data would contain approximately as many price bars as 78 years of daily data.

However, the far greater amount of data inherent in intraday data does not mean the test period can be reduced proportionally—not even close. The governing principle will always be to select enough data to expose the system to a wide range of market conditions. A trader testing a system based on five-minute bars should run the test on far more than 30 days of data, even though this data contains more bars than 10 years of daily price bars, since the larger-scale market conditions can often be relatively static over such brief time periods. For example, the intraday price action during a very strong 30-day trending period will likely differ dramatically from the typical intraday price action during a 30-day trading range. The necessity that any meaningful system test span bull, bear, and sideways markets means that even intraday systems will need to be tested over a period of at least several years, if not more. In fact, given the current speed of computer processing, if the data are available, there is no compelling reason to run intraday systems tests for significantly shorter periods than daily systems. Sure, such tests will include dramatically more data, but that is a good thing.

Ideally, one should test a system using a longer time period (e.g., 15 years) and then evaluate the results for the period as a whole and various shorter time intervals (e.g., individual years). Such an approach is important in determining the system's degree of *time stability*—the relative performance consistency from one period to the next. Time stability is important because it enhances confidence regarding a system's potential for maintaining consistently favorable performance in the future. Most people would be quite hesitant about using a system that generated significant net profits over a 15-year period due to three spectacularly performing years but then witnessed losses or near break-even results in the remaining 12 years—and rightly so. In contrast, a system that registered moderate net gains during the 15-year period and was profitable in 14 of the 15 years would undoubtedly be viewed as more attractive by most traders.

■ Realistic Assumptions

System traders often discover that their actual results are substantially worse than the paper trading results implied by the system. In fact, this situation is so common that it even has its own name: *slippage*. Assuming that the divergence in the results is not due to errors in the program, slippage is basically a consequence of a failure to use realistic assumptions in testing the system. Basically, there are two types of such faulty assumptions:

1. **Transaction costs.** Most traders don't realize that merely adjusting for actual commission costs in testing a system is not a sufficiently rigid assumption. The reason for this is that commissions account for only a portion—and usually a minor portion—of transaction costs. Another less tangible, but no less real, cost is the difference between the theoretical execution price and the actual fill price. For example, if one is testing a system assuming order entry on the close, the use of the midpoint of the closing range might not be a realistic assumption. For some reason, buys near the upper end of the closing range and sells near the lower end of the closing range seem to be far more common than their reverse counterparts. There are two ways of addressing this problem. First, use the worst possible fill price (e.g., high of the closing range for buys). Second, use a transaction cost per trade assumption much greater than the actual

historical commission costs (e.g., $25 per side, per trade). The latter approach is preferable because it is more general. For example, how would one decide the worst possible fill price for an intraday stop order?

2. **Limit days.** Unless it is programmed otherwise, an automated trading system will indicate executions on the receipt of each signal. However, in the real world, things are not quite so simple. Occasionally, execution will not be possible because the market is locked at the daily permissible limit. Or even if execution is possible, it could occur at a much worse level than the intended price because the market gaps far beyond the signal trigger price. Although nearly continuous trading hours have made these events less common than in decades past, they still occur, especially in less liquid markets. If one assumes execution in such a situation, the paper results may dramatically overstate actual performance. Figure 19.2 illustrates the difference even a single locked-limit day can have on trade results. September 2011 corn futures closed limit down at 648 cents on June 30. A trader who wanted—or worse, needed—to sell on this close but did not receive a fill would have had to wait for the next session to execute the trade. The market opened 41.25 cents lower the next day, representing a $2,062.50 loss per contract, assuming the trade was filled exactly at the opening price.

The potential systems trader may discover that seemingly attractive trading systems disintegrate once realistic assumptions are employed. This characteristic is particularly true for very active systems, which generate very large transaction costs. However, it is far better to make this discovery in the analytical testing stage than in actual trading.

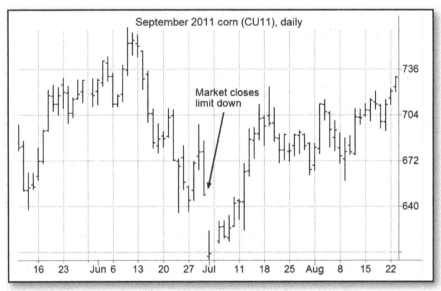

FIGURE 19.2 Wide Gap between Signal Price and Actual Entry: Impact of Limit Days (September 2011 Corn)

■ Optimizing Systems

Optimization refers to the process of finding the best-performing parameter set(s) for a given system applied to a specific market. The underlying premise of optimization is that parameter sets that worked best in the past have a greater probability of superior performance in the future. (The question of whether this assumption is valid is addressed in the next section.)

A basic question that must be considered in optimization is what criteria should be used for defining best performance. Frequently, best performance is simply interpreted as largest equity gain. However, such a definition is incomplete. Ideally, four factors should be considered in performance comparisons:

1. **Percent return.** Return measured relative to funds needed to trade the system. The importance of using percent return rather than nominal gain is detailed in Chapter 20.

2. **Risk measure.** In addition to percent gain, it is also important to employ some measure of equity fluctuations (e.g., variability in rate of gain, retracements in equity). Besides the obvious psychological reasons for wishing to avoid parameter sets and systems with high volatility, a risk measure is particularly significant because one might pick an unfavorable starting date for trading the system. Chapter 20 discusses several performance measures that incorporate both percent return and risk.

3. **Parameter stability.** It is not sufficient to find a parameter set that performs well. It is also necessary to ascertain the parameter set does not reflect a fluke in the system. In other words, we wish to determine that similar parameter sets also exhibit favorable performance. In fact, the goal of optimization should be to find broad regions of good performance rather than the single best-performing parameter set.

   For example, if in testing a simple breakout system one found that the parameter set $N = 7$ exhibited the best percent return/risk characteristics but that performance dropped off very sharply for parameter sets $N < 5$ and $N > 9$, while all sets in the range $N = 25$ to $N = 54$ performed relatively well, it would make much more sense to choose a parameter set from the latter range. Why? Because the exceptional performance of the set $N = 7$ appears to be a peculiarity of the historical price data, which is not likely to be repeated. The fact that surrounding parameter sets performed poorly suggests that there is no basis for confidence in trading the parameter set $N = 7$. In contrast, the broad range of performance stability for sets in the region $N = 25$ to $N = 54$ suggests that a set drawn from the center of this range would have a better prospect for success.

4. **Time stability.** As detailed in a previous section, it is important to ascertain that favorable performance for the period as a whole is truly representative of the total period rather than a reflection of a few isolated intervals of extraordinary performance.

For comparisons involving different parameter sets for the *same* system, the preceding factors tend to be highly correlated. Generally, the parameter sets with the best gains will also be the sets that exhibit the smallest equity retracements. Consequently, for the optimization of a single system, the use of a basic return/risk measure (e.g., the Sharpe ratio or the gain-to-pain ratio) will usually yield similar results to a complex performance evaluation that incorporates multiple performance measures. Thus, although the multifactor performance evaluation is theoretically preferable, it is often not essential. However, if one is comparing parameter sets from completely different systems, the explicit consideration of risk, parameter stability, and time stability is more important.

The foregoing represents a theoretical discussion of optimization concepts and procedures, and implicitly assumes that optimization enhances a system's *future* performance. As discussed in the next section, however, the viability of optimization is open to serious question.

■ The Optimization Myth

It is ironic that optimization receives so much attention while its underlying premise is rarely considered. In other words, do the better performing parameter sets of the *past* continue to exhibit above-average performance in the *future?*

As an empirical test of the validity of optimization we examine the historical rankings of a range of parameter set values for a breakout system: reverse from short to long if today's close is higher than the highest close during the past *N* days; reverse from long to short if today's close is lower than the lowest close during the past *N* days. Nine values of *N* for this system were tested: 20, 30, 40, 50, 60, 70, 80, 90, and 100.

Tables 19.1 to 19.10 compare the profit/loss rankings of these parameter sets in 10 markets for three 2-year test periods (2009–2010, 2011–2012, and 2013–2014), with parameter sets listed in the order of their performance during the respective *prior* eight-year periods. (All markets were traded with one contract per signal.) In other words, the top-performing parameter set of the prior eight-year period (2001–2008, 2003–2010, or 2005–2012) is listed first, the second-best parameter set of the prior period is listed second, and so on. For example, if the top number in a column is 6, it means that the best-performing parameter set for that market in the prior eight-year period was the sixth-ranked parameter set (out of nine) during the given test period.

TABLE 19.1 Breakout System (10-Year T-Notes): Comparison of Parameter Set Rankings in Two-Year Test Periods vs. Rankings in Prior Eight-Year Periods

Parameter Set Rank Prior Eight-Year Period	Rank of Same Parameter Set in 2009–2010	Rank of Same Parameter Set in 2011–2012	Rank of Same Parameter Set in 2013–2014
1	9	9	7
2	8	6	5
3	7	7	3
4	2	8	1
5	5	4	4
6	6	5	6
7	1	3	2
8	3	1	9
9	4	2	8

TABLE 19.2 Breakout System (Euro): Comparison of Parameter Set Rankings in Two-Year Test Periods vs. Rankings in Prior Eight-Year Periods

Parameter Set Rank Prior Eight-Year Period	Rank of Same Parameter Set in 2009–2010	Rank of Same Parameter Set in 2011–2012	Rank of Same Parameter Set in 2013–2014
1	4	2	1
2	9	1	7
3	5	4	2
4	6	5	5
5	7	6	8
6	3	3	3
7	8	7	9
8	2	8	6
9	1	9	4

TABLE 19.3 Breakout System (Japanese Yen): Comparison of Parameter Set Rankings in Two-Year Test Periods vs. Rankings in Prior Eight-Year Periods

Parameter Set Rank Prior Eight-Year Period	Rank of Same Parameter Set in 2009–2010	Rank of Same Parameter Set in 2011–2012	Rank of Same Parameter Set in 2013–2014
1	9	5	4
2	2	3	1
3	8	7	6
4	1	6	2
5	3	1	7
6	4	4	8
7	7	9	9
8	6	2	5
9	5	8	3

TABLE 19.4 Breakout System (Gold): Comparison of Parameter Set Rankings in Two-Year Test Periods vs. Rankings in Prior Eight-Year Periods

Parameter Set Rank Prior Eight-Year Period	Rank of Same Parameter Set in 2009–2010	Rank of Same Parameter Set in 2011–2012	Rank of Same Parameter Set in 2013–2014
1	7	2	2
2	3	4	3
3	4	5	4
4	9	1	9
5	6	6	1
6	8	9	7
7	1	8	5
8	2	7	6
9	5	3	8

TABLE 19.5 Breakout System (Natural Gas): Comparison of Parameter Set Rankings in Two-Year Test Periods vs. Rankings in Prior Eight-Year Periods

Parameter Set Rank Prior Eight-Year Period	Rank of Same Parameter Set in 2009–2010	Rank of Same Parameter Set in 2011–2012	Rank of Same Parameter Set in 2013–2014
1	8	3	1
2	4	5	4
3	5	1	2
4	1	6	3
5	6	8	9
6	2	9	5
7	9	4	8
8	7	7	6
9	3	2	7

TABLE 19.6 Breakout System (WTI Crude Oil): Comparison of Parameter Set Rankings in Two-Year Test Periods vs. Rankings in Prior Eight-Year Periods

Parameter Set Rank Prior Eight-Year Period	Rank of Same Parameter Set in 2009–2010	Rank of Same Parameter Set in 2011–2012	Rank of Same Parameter Set in 2013–2014
1	3	6	1
2	2	7	6
3	7	9	8
4	4	1	2
5	5	3	5
6	1	5	4
7	9	8	9
8	6	2	3
9	8	4	7

TABLE 19.7 Breakout System (Corn): Comparison of Parameter Set Rankings in Two-Year Test Periods vs. Rankings in Prior Eight-Year Periods

Parameter Set Rank Prior Eight-Year Period	Rank of Same Parameter Set in 2009–2010	Rank of Same Parameter Set in 2011–2012	Rank of Same Parameter Set in 2013–2014
1	3	7	3
2	4	1	7
3	2	3	5
4	1	8	8
5	9	4	1
6	5	9	6
7	6	2	2
8	8	5	4
9	7	6	9

TABLE 19.8 Breakout System (Soybeans): Comparison of Parameter Set Rankings in Two-Year Test Periods vs. Rankings in Prior Eight-Year Periods

Parameter Set Rank Prior Eight-Year Period	Rank of Same Parameter Set in 2009–2010	Rank of Same Parameter Set in 2011–2012	Rank of Same Parameter Set in 2013–2014
1	6	4	5
2	3	5	3
3	4	7	1
4	1	2	4
5	2	3	2
6	8	1	7
7	7	6	6
8	9	8	8
9	5	9	9

TABLE 19.9 Breakout System (Coffee): Comparison of Parameter Set Rankings in Two-Year Test Periods vs. Rankings in Prior Eight-Year Periods

Parameter Set Rank Prior Eight-Year Period	Rank of Same Parameter Set in 2009–2010	Rank of Same Parameter Set in 2011–2012	Rank of Same Parameter Set in 2013–2014
1	3	1	9
2	8	2	1
3	1	6	6
4	7	8	3
5	9	9	2
6	2	5	4
7	6	7	8
8	5	4	7
9	4	3	5

TABLE 19.10 Breakout System (E-Mini Nasdaq 100): Comparison of Parameter Set Rankings in Two-Year Test Periods vs. Rankings in Prior Eight-Year Periods

Parameter Set Rank Prior Eight-Year Period	Rank of Same Parameter Set in 2009–2010	Rank of Same Parameter Set in 2011–2012	Rank of Same Parameter Set in 2013–2014
1	5	3	9
2	7	1	7
3	4	2	8
4	2	8	4
5	6	6	6
6	9	5	1
7	3	9	2
8	8	4	5
9	1	7	3

As a visual aid to help see if there is any consistency between past and future performance, the two top-performing parameter sets in each test period are denoted by circles and the two bottom parameter sets by squares. If the basic premise of optimization were valid—that is, that the best-performing parameter sets of the *past were* likely to be the best-performing parameter sets in the *future*—then Tables 19.1 through 19.10 should reflect a pattern of circles consistently near column tops and squares consistently near column bottoms. However, this is not the case. Both circles and squares are sometimes near column tops, sometimes near column bottoms, and sometimes near column midpoints. The apparent randomness in the vertical placement of the circles and squares in Tables 19.1 through 19.10 implies the correlation between past and future performance is highly tenuous.

Table 19.11 further highlights the weakness of the relationship between past and future performance. In addition to showing the average rank of the best-performing parameter sets from the eight-year sample periods in the subsequent two-year test periods (second column), Table 19.11 also shows how often the best- and worst-performing sets in a prior eight-year period repeated their positions in the subsequent two-year period versus completely reversing their rank order. Note the initially best- and worst-performing parameter sets repeated in subsequent two-year periods a total of eight times, which is only one time more than the number of times the best set became the worst set or the worst set became the best set. Also notice that the best-performing parameter set became the worst-performing set one more time (5) than the best-performing set repeated as the top set.

This instability in the values of the best-performing parameter sets from period to period means gauging a system's performance by the best *past* parameter sets will grossly overstate the system's performance potential. To illustrate this point, Tables 19.12 through 19.15 compare the performance of the best parameter set in each test period versus the average of all parameter sets and the performance of the parameter sets that had the best and worst results in the

TABLE 19.11 Stability of Best- and Worst-Performing Parameter Sets

Market	Avg. Rank of Best Parameter Set	Best Parameter Set Repeated	Worst Parameter Set Repeated	Best Set Becomes Worst Set	Worst Set Becomes Best Set
10-yr. T-note	4.70	0	0	2	0
Euro	4.30	1	1	0	1
Japanese yen	4.77	0	0	1	0
Gold	4.27	0	0	0	0
Natural gas	5.10	1	0	0	0
WTI crude oil	5.13	1	0	0	0
Corn	6.00	0	1	0	0
Soybeans	5.43	0	2	0	0
Coffee	5.30	1	0	1	0
E-mini Nasdaq 100	4.70	0	0	1	1
Total		4	4	5	2

prior period. In this example, based on the all-market totals, selecting the worst parameter set in the prior period would have outperformed a strategy of picking the best past parameter set in one of the three test periods (see Table 19.12), as well as the three-period total (see Table 19.15). The penultimate column of these tables marks the instances the worst-performing parameter set in a prior eight-year period outperformed the prior best-performing set in the subsequent two-year period. The final column shows how often the average parameter set performance in the subsequent two-year period outperformed the best-performing set of the prior eight-year period.

TABLE 19.12 Profit/Loss ($) Comparisons for 2009–2010 Test Period: Actual Best Parameter Set vs. Period Average and Best and Worst Parameter Sets in Prior Period

Market	Best Parameter Set in Period	Best Parameter Set in Prior Period	Worst Parameter Set in Prior Period	Avg. of all Parameter Sets	Worst Prior > Best Prior	Avg. > Best Prior
10-yr. T-note	$7,453	−$7,188	$2,391	$253	X	X
Euro	$47,575	$18,963	$47,575	$22,511	X	X
Japanese yen	$5,438	−$23,825	−$9,638	−$8,967	X	X
Gold	$50,740	$7,420	$19,020	$25,084	X	X
Natural gas	$46,960	−$7,360	$34,120	$16,522	X	X
WTI crude oil	−$11,670	−$26,030	−$45,150	−$33,041		
Corn	$8,875	$6,913	−$338	$3,188		
Soybeans	$34,188	$11,875	$22,350	$16,944	X	X
Coffee	$25,650	$12,075	$11,963	$6,713		
E-Mini Nasdaq 100	$12,330	$4,820	$12,330	$5,417	X	X
Total	**$227,538**	**−$2,338**	**$94,623**	**$54,625**	**7**	**7**

TABLE 19.13 Profit/Loss ($) Comparisons for 2011–2012 Test Period: Actual Best Parameter Set vs. Period Average and Best and Worst Parameter Sets in Prior Period

Market	Best Parameter Set in Period	Best Parameter Set in Prior Period	Worst Parameter Set in Prior Period	Avg. of All Parameter Sets	Worst Prior > Best Prior	Avg. > Best Prior
10-yr. T-note	$13,172	−$3,750	$9,234	$3,516	X	X
Euro	$10,900	$10,900	−$11,550	$1,938		
Japanese yen	−$1,538	−$7,963	−$12,913	−$8,157		
Gold	$16,310	$7,300	$3,170	−$5,672		
Natural gas	$16,050	$2,590	$10,930	−$712	X	
WTI crude oil	$12,330	−$30,950	−$11,920	−$19,537	X	X
Corn	−$963	−$8,563	−$8,538	−$9,138	X	
Soybeans	$24,013	−$3,113	−$16,413	−$2,590		X
Coffee	$48,563	$48,563	$20,963	$8,308		
E-Mini Nasdaq 100	$1,540	−$7,630	−$20,870	−$13,506		
Total	**$140,377**	**$7,385**	**−$37,906**	**−$45,550**	**4**	**3**

TABLE 19.14 Profit/Loss ($) Comparisons for 2013–2014 Test Period: Actual Best Parameter Set vs. Period Average and Best and Worst Parameter Sets in Prior Period

Market	Best Parameter Set in Period	Best Parameter Set in Prior Period	Worst Parameter Set in Prior Period	Avg. of All Parameter Sets	Worst Prior > Best Prior	Avg. > Best Prior
10-yr. T-note	$2,922	−$2,328	−$3,359	−$1,557		X
Euro	$19,963	$19,963	$5,013	$2,568		
Japanese yen	$39,713	$38,138	$39,713	$27,339	X	
Gold	$25,840	$21,160	−$4,340	$11,042		
Natural gas	$6,250	$6,250	−$1,590	−$2,077		
WTI crude oil	$39,060	$39,060	$18,070	$23,379		
Corn	$9,750	$3,675	−$1,150	$2,661		
Soybeans	$8,663	$488	−$12,863	$1,211		X
Coffee	$28,313	−$9,113	$2,963	$7,677	X	X
E-Mini Nasdaq 100	$29,640	−$8,780	$16,505	$10,635	X	X
Total	**$210,112**	**$108,512**	**$58,961**	**$82,878**	**3**	**4**

TABLE 19.15 Profit/Loss ($) Comparisons for Three Test Periods Combined: Actual Best Parameter Sets vs. Period Averages and Best and Worst Parameter Sets in Prior Periods

Market	Best Parameter Set in Period Total	Best Parameter Set in Prior Period Total	Worst Parameter Set in Prior Period Total	Avg. of All Parameter Sets Total	Worst Prior > Best Prior	Avg. > Best Prior
10-yr. T-note	$23,547	−$13,266	$8,266	$2,212	X	X
Euro	$78,438	$49,825	$41,038	$27,017		
Japanese yen	$43,613	$6,350	$17,163	$10,215	X	X
Gold	$92,890	$35,880	$17,850	$30,454		
Natural gas	$69,260	$1,480	$43,460	$13,733	X	X
WTI crude oil	$39,720	−$17,920	−$39,000	−$29,199		
Corn	$17,663	$2,025	−$10,025	−$3,289		
Soybeans	$66,863	$9,250	−$6,925	$15,565		X
Coffee	$102,525	$51,525	$35,888	$22,698		
E-Mini Nasdaq 100	$43,510	−$11,590	$7,965	$2,546	X	X
Total	**$578,027**	**$113,559**	**$115,678**	**$91,953**	**4**	**5**

Our example used a very small list of only nine parameter sets. Many system developers run optimizations across hundreds or even thousands of parameter sets. Imagine the degree of performance overstatement that would occur by representing a system's performance by the best parameter sets in these cases!

For comparison, Tables 19.16 through 19.19 show the same information as Tables 19.12 through 19.15 except they reflect tests of the same system conducted 20 years earlier on a slightly different portio (30-year U.S. T-bonds, Deutsche marks, Japanese yen, gold, silver, heating oil, corn, soybeans, live cattle, and sugar). In this case, the three 8-year sample periods were 1981–1988, 1983–1990, and 1985–1992 and the three 2-year test periods were 1989–1990, 1991–1992, and 1993–1994.

TABLE 19.16 Profit/Loss ($) Comparisons for 1989–1990 Test Period: Actual Best Parameter Set vs. Period Average and Best and Worst Parameter Sets in Prior Period

Market	Best Parameter Set in Period	Best Parameter Set in Prior Period	Worst Parameter Set in Prior Period	Avg. of All Parameter Sets	Worst Prior > Best Prior	Avg. > Best Prior
T-bond	6,670	−9,090	1,420	−2,180	X	X
Deutsche mark	7,780	3,020	6,340	5,390	X	X
Japanese yen	11,840	9,240	8,420	8,130		
Gold	3,390	1,700	−320	1,080		
Silver	5,850	5,330	1,630	3,050		
Heating oil	7,650	1,760	6,430	3,380	X	X
Corn	1,640	−2,190	−2,730	−590		X
Soybeans	4,970	−7,160	4,740	−740	X	X
Cattle	2,090	850	−3,290	−20		
Sugar	4,240	4,170	−5,560	−840		
Total	56,120	7,630	17,080	16,030	4	5

TABLE 19.17 Profit/Loss ($) Comparisons for 1991–1992 Test Period: Actual Best Parameter Set vs. Period Average and Best and Worst Parameter Sets in Prior Period

Market	Best Parameter Set in Period	Best Parameter Set in Prior Period	Worst Parameter Set in Prior Period	Avg. of All Parameter Sets	Worst Prior > Best Prior	Avg. > Best Prior
T-bond	3,710	−1,820	−2,920	−420		X
Deutsche mark	9,180	1,680	9,180	4,770	X	X
Japanese yen	3,340	−240	−3,620	−1,670		
Gold	1,370	90	1,370	−1,050	X	
Silver	−720	−1,890	−1,780	−1,640	X	X
Heating oil	5,510	−980	4,290	1,540	X	X
Corn	560	−480	340	−440	X	X
Soybeans	−2,420	−6,090	−3,190	−4,650	X	X
Cattle	1,380	−160	1,380	−340	X	
Sugar	810	−1,690	−1,850	−1,410		X
Total	22,700	−11,570	3,200	−5,010	7	7

TABLE 19.18 Profit/Loss ($) Comparisons for 1993–1994 Test Period: Actual Best Parameter Set vs. Period Average and Best and Worst Parameter Sets in Prior Period

Market	Best Parameter Set in Period	Best Parameter Set in Prior Period	Worst Parameter Set in Prior Period	Avg. of All Parameter Sets	Worst Prior > Best Prior	Avg. > Best Prior
T-bond	11,600	3,500	7,910	7,180	X	X
Deutsche mark	6,210	−3,660	−1,410	−3,300	X	X
Japanese yen	3,620	2,460	−3,060	260		
Gold	490	−1,900	−930	−1,460	X	X
Silver	1,600	−3,650	−790	−2,690	X	X
Heating oil	2,200	2,200	−890	−1,700		
Corn	1,910	1,910	−1,030	640		
Soybeans	2,120	1,570	−2,060	−240		
Cattle	1,600	950	1,600	500	X	
Sugar	880	570	−240	−550		
Total	32,230	3,950	−900	−1,360	5	4

TABLE 19.19 Profit/Loss ($) Comparisons for Three Test Periods Combined: Actual Best Parameter Sets vs. Period Averages and Best and Worst Parameter Sets in Prior Periods

Market	Best Parameter Sets in Test Periods Total	Best Parameter Sets in Prior Periods Total	Worst Parameter Sets in Prior Periods Total	Period Parameter Set Averages Total	Worst Prior > Best Prior	Avg. > Best Prior
T-bond	21,980	−7,410	6,410	3,950	X	X
Deutsche mark	23,170	1,040	14,110	6,860	X	X
Japanese yen	18,800	11,460	1,740	6,720		
Gold	5,250	−110	120	−1,430	X	
Silver	6,730	−210	−940	−1,280		
Heating oil	15,360	2,980	9,830	3,220	X	X
Corn	4,110	−760	−3,420	−390		X
Soybeans	4,670	−11,680	−510	−5,330	X	X
Cattle	5,070	1,640	−310	140		
Sugar	5,930	3,060	−7,650	−2,800		
Total	111,070	10	19,380	9,660	5	5

Based on the combined three-period, all-market totals from this second set of tests, selecting the worst parameter set in the prior period actually would have outperformed a strategy of picking the best past parameter set in two of the three test periods, as well as the three-period total!

This observation is not intended to imply that the prior-period worst-performing parameter set is likely to outperform the prior-period best-performing set. If similar empirical tests were conducted for other systems, the prior-period best-performing parameter set would probably outperform the prior-period worst-performing set more often than the other way around (although the types of results witnessed in our example are far from uncommon). The key point, however, is that invariably, as was the case in Tables 19.12 through 19.15 and 19.16 through 19.19, the prior-period best-performing parameter sets would fall far short of the actual best-performing parameter sets for the given periods and would often fail to provide any statistically significant improvement over the average of all parameter sets.

Although optimization seemed to have little, if any, value when applied market by market, optimization does appear to be a bit more useful if applied to a portfolio. In other words, instead of picking the best past parameter set for each market, the best past single parameter set applied across all markets is selected. Table 19.20 shows the two-year test period parameter set rankings for a portfolio consisting of the 10 markets that provided the results for Tables 19.16 through 19.19.[6] The one striking correlation between past and future performance is that the worst parameter set in the prior eight-year period is also the worst parameter set in the subsequent two-year period in all three test intervals!

Although the worst past parameter set also seems likely to be the worst future parameter set, other past ranking placements seem to imply little predictive value. The average ranking for all three test periods of the remaining eight prior-period ranking placements (i.e., all rankings excluding the worst one) is 4.5. While the average test period ranking of the best parameter set in the prior eight-year period (3.3) is somewhat better than this average, the fourth-ranked parameter set in the prior period has by far the best average ranking in the future test periods (2.3). Also note that the second-best prior-period parameter set has an average test period rank almost identical to the corresponding average for the second worst prior-period parameter set (4.7 vs. 5.0).

To gain some insight as to why the worst prior-period ranking seems to be such an excellent predictor of future performance (namely, continued poor performance for that parameter set), while other ranking placements seem to have little predictive value, we examine performance rankings based on parameter set value. Table 19.21 indicates parameter set rankings in each of the three tests periods based on parameter set values (as opposed to prior-period rankings as was the case in Table 19.20). The parameter set values are listed in ascending order.

TABLE 19.20	Breakout System (Portfolio): Comparison of Parameter Set Rankings in Two-Year Test Periods vs. Rankings in Prior Eight-Year Periods			
Parameter Set Rank Prior Eight-Year Period	Rank of Same Parameter Set in 1989–1990	Rank of Same Parameter Set in 1991–1992	Rank of Same Parameter Set in 1993–1994	Avg. Rank
1	1	7	2	3.3
2	5	1	8	4.7
3	3	6	4	4.3
4	2	4	1	2.3
5	4	8	6	6.0
6	6	3	7	5.3
7	7	5	3	5.0
8	8	2	5	5.0
9	9	9	9	9.0

---

[6] In this case the portfolio consisted of one contract in each market, with the exception of corn, which was traded with two contracts because of its low volatility.

TABLE 19.21	Breakout System (Portfolio): Comparison of Parameter Set Rankings in Two-Year Test Periods Based on N-Values			
Parameter Set N-Value	Rank of Parameter Set in 1989–1990	Rank of Parameter Set in 1991–1992	Rank of Parameter Set in 1993–1994	Avg. Rank
20	9	9	9	9.0
30	8	2	5	5.0
40	7	5	3	5.0
50	6	3	1	3.3
60	4	6	6	5.3
70	5	7	8	6.7
80	1	1	2	1.3
90	2	4	4	3.3
100	3	8	7	6.0

Table 19.21 reveals that the worst-performing parameter set in each of the test periods was actually the same parameter set! (Since Table 19.20 indicated the test period worst parameter set was the same as the prior-period worst parameter set in all three cases, the implication is that this same parameter set was also the worst-performing parameter set in all three prior eight-year periods.) This consistently worst-performing parameter set is at one extreme end of the parameter set range tested: $N = 20$.

Although $N = 20$—the most sensitive parameter set value tested—is consistently the worst performer (when applied across a portfolio), the other values tested ($N = 30$ to $N = 100$) show no consistent pattern. It is true that the parameter set $N = 80$ was by far the best-performing set with an incredible average rank of 1.3. However, the average rankings of the two surrounding N-values (6.7 and 3.3) suggest that the stellar performance of $N = 80$ was probably a statistical fluke. As was explained earlier in this chapter, a lack of *parameter stability* suggests that the past superior performance of a parameter set probably reflects a peculiarity in the historical data tested rather than a pattern that is likely to be repeated in the future.

Tables 19.22 and 19.23 show analogous portfolio optimization statistics for the portfolios in the more recent test periods that were reviewed in Tables 19.12 through 19.15. Note in Table 19.23 that the same $N = 20$ parameter set once again exhibited inferior performance, registering as the worst-performing set in two of the three periods.

It is instructive to review the observations revealed by the foregoing optimization experiments:

■ Optimization appeared to have no value whatsoever when applied on a market-by-market basis.

■ When applied to a portfolio, however, optimization in the earlier (1981–1994) example appeared useful in predicting the parameter set most likely to witness inferior future performance, although it still showed no reliable pattern in predicting the parameter set most likely to witness superior future performance.

■ Upon closer examination it appeared this pattern of consistent inferior performance was not so much a consequence of the prior-period ranking as the parameter value. In other words, the

TABLE 19.22 Breakout System (Portfolio): Comparison of Parameter Set Rankings in Two-Year Test Periods vs. Rankings in Prior Eight-Year Periods (2000–2014)

Parameter Set Rank Prior Eight-Year Period	Parameter Set Rank in 2009–2010	Parameter Set Rank in 2011–2012	Parameter Set Rank in 2013–2014	Average Rank
1	9	1	1	3.7
2	2	7	5	4.7
3	3	2	3	2.7
4	7	3	9	6.3
5	6	4	4	4.7
6	8	5	8	7.0
7	4	8	2	4.7
8	5	6	7	6.0
9	1	9	6	5.3

TABLE 19.23 Breakout System (Portfolio): Comparison of Parameter Set Rankings in Two-Year Test Periods Based on N-Values (2000–2014)

Parameter Set N-Value	Rank of Parameter Set in 2009–2010	Rank of Parameter Set in 2011–2012	Rank of Parameter Set in 2013–2014	Average Rank
20	9	3	9	7.0
30	7	5	8	6.7
40	6	8	7	7.0
50	8	9	6	7.7
60	5	6	2	4.3
70	3	7	3	4.3
80	4	4	4	4.0
90	1	2	5	2.7
100	2	1	1	1.3

parameter set range tested began at a value that was clearly suboptimal for the given system: $N = 20$. This same parameter value remained suboptimal, on average, in the more recent test period as well. Although not indicated in the parameter set ranking tables, lower values of N would have shown even worse performance—in fact, strikingly worse—as the value of N was decreased.

These observations, which are consistent with the results of other similar empirical tests I have conducted in the past, suggest the following five key conclusions regarding optimization:[7]

---

[7]Although a single empirical experiment cannot be used to draw broad generalizations, I am willing to do so here because the results of the optimization test just described are fairly typical of many similar tests I have conducted in the past. In this sense, the optimization tests detailed in the text are not intended as a *proof* of the severe limitations of optimization, but rather as *illustrations* of this point.

1. Any system—repeat, any system—can be made to be very profitable through optimization (i.e., over its past performance). If you ever find a system that can't be optimized to show good profits in the past, congratulations, you have just discovered a money machine (by doing the opposite, unless transaction costs are exorbitant). Therefore, a wonderful past performance for a system that has been optimized may be nice to look at, but it doesn't mean very much.

2. Optimization will always, repeat always, overstate the potential future performance of a system—usually by a wide margin (say, three trailer trucks' worth). Therefore, optimized results should never, repeat never, be used to evaluate a system's merit.

3. For many if not most systems, optimization will improve *future* performance only marginally, if at all.

4. If optimization has any value, it is usually in defining the broad boundaries for the ranges from which parameter set values in the system should be chosen. Fine-tuning of optimization is at best a waste of time and at worst self-delusion.

5. In view of the preceding items, sophisticated and complex optimization procedures are a waste of time. The simplest optimization procedure will provide as much meaningful information (assuming that there is any meaningful information to be derived).

In summary, contrary to widespread belief, there is some reasonable question as to whether optimization will yield meaningfully better results over the long run than randomly picking the parameter sets to be traded. Lest there be any confusion, let me explicitly state that this statement is not intended to imply that optimization is never of any value. First, as indicated previously, optimization can be useful in defining the suboptimal extreme ranges that should be excluded from the selection of parameter set values (e.g., $N \leq 20$ in our breakout system example). Also, it is possible that, for some systems, optimization may provide some edge in parameter set selection, even after suboptimal extreme ranges are excluded. However, I do mean to imply that the degree of improvement provided by optimization is far less than generally perceived and that traders would probably save a lot of money by first proving any assumptions they are making about optimization rather than taking such assumptions on blind faith.

■ Testing versus Fitting

Perhaps the most critical error made by users of futures trading systems is the assumption the performance of the optimized parameter sets during the test period provides an approximation of the potential performance of those sets in the future. As was demonstrated in the previous section, such assumptions will lead to grossly overstated evaluations of a system's true potential. It must be understood that futures market price fluctuations are subject to a great deal of randomness. Thus, the "ugly truth" is that the question of which parameter sets will perform best during any given period is largely a matter of chance. The laws of probability indicate that if enough parameter sets are tested, even a meaningless trading system will yield some sets with favorable past performance. Evaluating a system based on the optimized parameter sets (i.e., the best-performing sets during the survey period) would be best described as fitting the system to past results rather than testing the system. If optimization can't be used to gauge performance, how then do you evaluate a system? The following sections describe two meaningful approaches.

Blind Simulation

In the blind simulation approach the system is optimized using data for a time period that deliberately excludes the most recent years. The performance of the system is then tested using the selected parameter sets for subsequent years. Ideally, this process should be repeated several times.

Note that the error of fitting results is avoided because the parameter sets used to measure performance in any given period are selected entirely on the basis of prior rather than concurrent data. In a sense, this testing approach mimics real life (i.e., one must decide which parameter sets to trade on the basis of past data).

The optimization tests of the previous section used this type of procedure, stepping through time in two-year intervals. Specifically, system results for the 2001–2008 period were used to select the best-performing parameter sets, which were then tested for the 2009–2010 period. Next, the system results for the 2003–2010 period were used to select the best-performing parameter sets, which were then tested for the 2011–2012 period. Finally, the system results for the 2005–2012 period were used to select the best-performing parameter sets, which were then tested for the 2013–2014 period.

The essential point is that simulation and optimization periods should not be allowed to overlap. Simulations that are run over the same period as the optimization are worthless.

Average Parameter Set Performance

Finding the average parameter set performance requires defining a complete list of all parameter sets you wish to test *before* running any simulations. Simulations are then run for all the parameter sets selected, and the average of all sets tested is used as an indication of the system's potential performance. This approach is valid because you could always throw a dart to pick a parameter from a broad range of parameter set values. If you throw enough darts, the net result will be the average. The important point is that this average should be calculated across all parameter sets, not just those sets that prove profitable. Note that the trader might still choose to trade the optimized parameter sets for the future (instead of randomly selected ones), but the evaluation of the system's performance should be based on the average of all sets tested (which is equivalent to a random selection process).

The blind simulation approach probably comes closest to duplicating real-life trading circumstances. However, the average parameter set performance is probably as conservative and has the advantage of requiring far less calculation. Both approaches represent valid procedures for testing a system.

One important caveat: In the advertised claims for given systems, the term *simulated results* is often used loosely as a euphemism for optimized results (instead of implying the results are based on a blind simulation process). If this is the case, the weight attached to the results should equal the amount of money invested in the system: zero. The commonplace misuse and distortion of simulated results is examined in detail in the next section.

■ The Truth about Simulated Results

Although the value of optimization in improving a system's future performance is open to debate, there is absolutely no question the use of optimized results will greatly distort the implied future performance of a system. As was demonstrated earlier in this chapter, there is very little, if any, correlation between the best-performing parameters in a system for one period and the best-performing parameters in a subsequent period. Hence, assuming that the performance implied by the best-performing parameters could have been achieved in the past is totally unrealistic.

After years of experience, my attitude toward simulated results is summarized by what I call Schwager's simulations corollary to Gresham's law of money. As readers may recall from Economics 101, Gresham's proposition was that "bad money drives out good." Gresham's contention was that if two types of money were in circulation (e.g., gold and silver) at some arbitrarily defined ratio (e.g., 16:1), the bad money (i.e., the money overvalued at the fixed rate of exchange) would drive out the good. Thus, if gold were worth more than 16 ounces of silver, a 16:1 ratio would result in silver driving gold out of circulation (as people would tend to hoard it).

My corollary is "bad simulations drive out good." The term *bad* means simulations derived based on highly tenuous assumptions, not bad in terms of indicated performance. On the contrary, truly "bad" simulations will show eye-popping results.

I frequently see ads hawking systems that supposedly make 200 percent, 400 percent, or even 600 percent a year. Let's be conservative—and I use the term loosely—and assume a return of *only* 100 percent per year. At this level of return, $100,000 would grow to over $1 *billion* in just over 13 years! How can such claims possibly be true, then? The answer is they can't. The point is that, given enough hindsight, it is possible to construct virtually any type of past-performance results. If anyone tried to sell a system or a trading program based on truly realistic simulations, the results would appear laughably puny relative to the normal promotional fare. It is in this sense that I believe that bad (unrealistic) simulations drive out good (realistic) simulations.

How are simulated results distorted? Let us count the ways:

1. **The well-chosen example (revisited).** In constructing a well-chosen example, the system promoter selects the best market, in the best time period, using the best parameter set. Assuming a system is tested on 25 markets for 15 years and uses 100 parameter set variations, there would be a total of 37,500 (25 × 15 × 100) one-year results. It would be difficult to construct a system in which not one of these 37,500 possible outcomes showed superlative results. For example, if you tossed a group of 10 coins 37,500 times, don't you think you would get 10 out of 10 heads sometimes? Absolutely. In fact, you would get 10 out of 10 heads on the average of one out of 1,024 times.

2. **Kitchen sink approach.** By using hindsight to add parameters and create additional system rules that conveniently take care of past losing periods, it is possible to generate virtually any level of past performance.

3. **Ignoring risk.** Advertised system results frequently calculate return as a percent of margin or as a percent of an unrealistically low multiple of margin. This return measurement approach

alone can multiply the implied returns severalfold. Of course, the risk would increase commensurately, but the ads don't provide those details.

4. **Overlooking losing trades.** It is hardly uncommon for charts in system websites or advertisements to indicate buy and sell signals at the points at which some specified rules were met, but fail to indicate other points on the same chart where the same conditions were met and the resulting trades were losers.

5. **Optimize, optimize, optimize.** Optimization (i.e., selecting the best-performing parameter sets for the *past*) can tremendously magnify the past performance of a system. Virtually any system ever conceived by man would look great if the results were based on the best parameter set (i.e., the parameter set that had the best past performance) for each market. The more parameter sets tested, the wider the selection of past results, and the greater the potential simulated return.

6. **Unrealistic transaction costs.** Frequently, simulated results only include commissions but not slippage (the difference between the assumed entry level and the actual fill that would be realized by using a market or stop order). For short-term systems (e.g., those using intraday data), ignoring slippage can make a system that would wipe out an account in real life look like a money machine.

7. **Fabrication.** Even though it is remarkably easy to construct system rules with great performance for the past, some promoters don't even bother doing this much. For example, one infamous individual for years repeatedly promoted $299 systems that were outright frauds.

The preceding is not intended to indict all system promoters or those using simulated results. Certainly, there are many individuals who construct simulated results in appropriately rigorous fashion. However, the sad truth is that the extraordinary misuse of simulations over many years has made simulated results virtually worthless. Advertised simulated results are very much like restaurant reviews written by the proprietors—you would hardly expect to ever see a bad review. I can assure you that you will never see any simulated results for a system that show the system long the S&P as of the close of October 16, 1987, September 10, 2001, or March 5, 2010. Can simulated results ever be used? Yes, if you are the system developer *and* you know what you're doing (e.g., use the simulation methods detailed in the previous section), or, equivalently, if you have absolute faith in the integrity and competence of the system developer.

■ Multimarket System Testing

Although it is probably unrealistic to expect any single system to work in all markets, generally speaking, a good system should demonstrate profitability in a large majority of actively traded markets (e.g., 85 percent or more). There are, of course, some important exceptions. A system employing fundamental input would, by definition, be applicable to only a single market. In addition, the behavior of some markets is so atypical (e.g., stock indexes) that systems designed for trading such markets might well perform poorly over the broad range of markets.

In testing a system for a multimarket portfolio, it is necessary to predetermine the relative number of contracts to be traded in each market. This problem is frequently handled by simply assuming the system will trade one contract in each market. However, this is a rather naive approach, for two reasons. First, some markets are far more volatile than other markets. For example, a portfolio that included one contract of coffee and one contract of corn would be far more dependent on the trading results in coffee. Second, it may be desirable to downgrade the relative weightings of some markets because they are highly correlated with other markets (e.g., 10-year T-notes and 30-year T-bonds).[8]

In any case, the percentage allocation of available funds to each market should be determined prior to testing a system. These relative weightings can then be used to establish the number of contracts to be traded in each market.

■ Negative Results

One should not overlook the potential value of negative results. Analyzing the conditions under which a system performs poorly can sometimes reveal important weaknesses in the system that have been overlooked and thus provide clues as to how the system can be improved. Of course, the fact that the implied rule changes improve results in the poorly performing case does not prove anything. However, the validity of any suggested rule changes would be confirmed if such revisions generally tended to improve the results for other parameter sets and markets as well. The potential value of negative results as a source of ideas for how a system can be improved cannot be overstated. The concept that disorder is a catalyst for thought is a general truth that was perfectly expressed by the late novelist John Gardner: "In a perfect world, there would be no need for thought. We think because something goes wrong."

The idea of learning from poor results is basically applicable to a system that works in most markets and for most parameter sets but performs badly in isolated cases. However, systems that exhibit disappointing results over a broad range of markets and parameter sets are likely to be lost causes, unless the results are spectacularly poor. In the latter case, a system that exactly reverses the trade signals of the original system might be attractive. For example, if tests of a new trend-following system reveal that the system consistently loses money in most markets, the implication is that one might have accidently stumbled upon an effective countertrend system. Such discoveries may be difficult on the ego, but they should not be ignored.

Of course, the fact that a system exhibits stable poor performance does not imply that the reverse system would perform favorably, since transaction costs may account for a significant portion of losses. Thus, the reverse system might also perform badly once these costs are taken into account, as was the case for the aforementioned well-chosen example described at the start of

---

[8] For purposes of future trading (as opposed to historical testing), historical performance might be a third relevant factor in determining contract weightings. However, this factor cannot be included as an input in the testing procedure because it would bias the results.

this chapter. As another example, at surface glance, reversing the signals generated by a system that loses an average of $3,000 per year may appear to be an attractive strategy. If, however, two-thirds of the loss can be attributed to transaction costs, fading the signals of this system will result in a loss of $1,000 per year, assuming a continuation of the same performance. (The preceding assumptions imply that transaction costs equal $2,000 per year and that the trades lose $1,000 per year net of these costs. Thus, reversing the signals would imply a $1,000-per-year gain on the trades, but the $2,000-per year transaction costs would imply a net loss of $1,000 per year.) Moral: If you are going to design a bad system, it should be truly terrible if it is to be of value.

Ten Steps in Constructing and Testing a Trading System

1. Obtain all data needed for testing. Again, with the exception of short-term trading systems, which may be able to use actual contract data, the use of continuous futures (not to be confused with nearest futures or perpetual prices) is highly recommended.
2. Define the system concept.
3. Program rules to generate trades in accordance with this concept.
4. Select a small subset of markets and a subset of years for these markets.
5. Generate system trading signals for this subset of markets and time for a given parameter set.
6. Check to see that the system is doing what was intended. Almost invariably, a careful check will reveal some inconsistencies due to either or both of the following reasons:
   a. There are errors in the program.
   b. Rules in program do not anticipate some circumstances, or they create unforeseen repercussions.

   Some examples of the latter might include the system failing to generate a signal, given an event at which a signal is intended; system generating a signal when no signal is intended; system rules inadvertently creating a situation in which no new signals can be generated or in which a position is held indefinitely. In essence, these types of situations arise because there will often be some missed nuances.

   The system rules need to be modified to correct both programming errors as well as unforeseen inconsistencies. It should be emphasized that corrections of the latter type are only concerned with making the system operate consistently with the intended concept and should be made *without any regard as to whether the changes help or hurt performance in the sample cases used in the developmental process.*
7. After making necessary corrections, repeat step 6. Pay particular attention to changes in the indicated signals versus those from previous runs for two reasons:
   a. To check whether the program changes achieved the desired fix.
   b. To make sure the changes did not have unintended effects.
8. Once the system is working as intended, and all rules and contingencies have been fully defined, *and only after such a point,* test the system on the entire defined parameter set list across the full database. Be sure the intended trading portfolio has been defined before this test is run.

9. As detailed earlier in this chapter, evaluate performance based on the average of all parameter sets tested or a blind simulation process. (The former involves far less work.)
10. Compare these results with the results of a generic system (e.g., breakout, crossover moving average) for the corresponding portfolio and test period. The return/risk of the system should be *measurably* better than that of the generic system if it is to be deemed to have any real value.

The preceding steps represent a rigorous procedure that is designed to avoid generating results that are upwardly biased by hindsight. As such, expect most system ideas to fail the test of merit in step 10. Designing a system with a truly superior performance is more difficult than most people think.

■ Observations about Trading Systems

1. In trend-following systems, the basic method used to identify trends (e.g., breakout, crossover moving average) may well be the least important component of the system. In a sense, this contention is merely a restatement of Jim Orcutt's observation that "There are only two types of trend-following systems: fast and slow." Thus, in designing trend-following systems, it may make more sense to concentrate on modifications (e.g., filters and confirmation rules to reduce bad trades, market characteristic adjustments, pyramiding rules, stop rules) than on trying to discover a better method for defining trends.
2. Complexity for its own sake is no virtue. Use the simplest form of a system that does not imply a meaningful sacrifice in performance relative to more complex versions.
3. The well-publicized and very valid reason for trading a broad range of markets is risk control through diversification. However, there is a very important additional reason for trading as many markets as possible: insurance against missing any of the sporadic giant price moves in the futures markets. The importance of catching all such major trends cannot be overstressed—it can make the difference between mediocre performance and great performance. The 2008–2011 gold market and the 2007–2009 and 2014–2016 crude oil markets are three spectacular examples of markets that were critical to portfolio performance.
4. If trading funds are sufficient, diversification should be extended to systems as well as markets. Trading several systems rather than a single system could help smooth overall performance. Ideally, the greatest degree of diversification would be achieved if the mix of systems included countertrend and pattern-recognition systems as well as trend-following systems. (However, this goal may be difficult to achieve because countertrend and pattern-recognition systems are generally significantly harder to design than trend-following systems.)
5. If sufficient funds are available, it is better to trade a number of diversified parameter sets than to trade a single optimized set.
6. Generally speaking, the value of parameter optimization is far overstated.
7. The previous observation strongly suggests that optimized results should never be used for evaluating the relative performance of a system. Two meaningful methods for testing systems were discussed in the text.

8. So-called *simulated* results are frequently *optimized* results (i.e., derived with the benefit of hindsight) and, as such, virtually meaningless. This caveat is particularly pertinent in regard to promotions for trading systems, which invariably use very well-chosen examples.

9. An analysis of the results of successful systems will almost invariably reveal the presence of many markets with one or more years of very large profits, but few instances of very large single-year losses. The implication is that a key reason for the success of these systems is that their rules adhere to the critical, albeit clichéd principle of letting profits run and cutting losses short.

10. A market should not be avoided because its volatility increases sharply. In fact, the most volatile markets are often the most profitable.

11. Isolating negative results for a system that performs well on balance can provide valuable clues as to how the system can be improved.

12. A frequently overlooked fact is that trading results may often reflect more information about the market than the system. For example, in Figure 19.3, the fact that a trend-following system that was short in mid-January 2015 would have witnessed the transformation of a large open profit into a large loss before the system provided a liquidation or reversal signal would not necessarily reflect inadequate risk control. Virtually any trend-following system would have experienced the same fate.

This example illustrates how the value of a system cannot be judged in a vacuum. In some cases, poor performance may reflect nothing more than the fact that market conditions would have resulted in poor results for the vast majority of systems. Similarly, favorable results may also reflect the conditions of the market rather than any degree of superiority in the tested

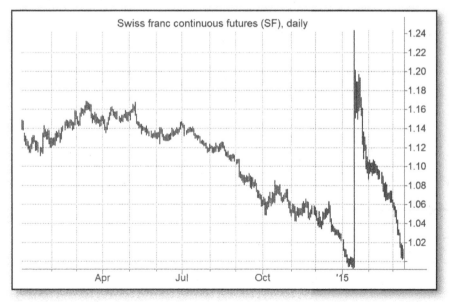

FIGURE 19.3 Trading Results Reflect Market, Not System: Short Swiss Franc Continuous Futures

system. These considerations suggest that a meaningful assessment of a new system's performance should include a comparison to a benchmark (e.g., the corresponding performance of standard systems, such as a crossover moving average or a simple breakout, during the same period for the same markets).

13. Use continuous futures prices for testing systems.
14. Use only a small portion of the database (i.e., some markets for only a segment of the full time period) for developing and debugging a system.
15. Use charts with superimposed signal annotations as an aid to debugging systems.
16. In checking the accuracy and completeness of the signals generated by a system, make changes dictated by deviations from the intended operation of the system (due to oversights related to the full implications of the rules employed or unforeseen situations) with complete disregard for whether such changes increase or decrease profits in the sample tests.

CHAPTER 20

How to Evaluate Past Performance*

Why Return Alone Is Meaningless

You are looking for a London hotel room on the Internet. You find the same hotel room at two different sites (both including taxes) at two different prices:

- Site A: 300

- Site B: 250

Which is the better deal? The answer may seem obvious, but it's not. On one occasion, when I posed this question to a conference audience, one attendee shouted the response, "It depends whether they both include breakfast." "That would have to be a very expensive breakfast," I answered. But at least he had the right idea. The question I posed contained incomplete information. I didn't specify what currency the prices were quoted in. What if the 300 price was in dollars and the 250 price was in pounds (let's say when the pound was at $1.40)? Changes everything, doesn't it?

"Well," you are probably thinking, "no rational person will ignore the currency denomination in comparing two prices, so what's the point?" The point is that investors make this type of error all the time when selecting investments by focusing only on returns. Comparing returns without risk is as meaningless as comparing international hotel prices without the currency denomination. Risk is the denomination of return.

---

*This chapter is adapted from Jack D. Schwager, *Market Sense and Nonsense: How the Markets Really Work (and How They Don't)* (Hoboken, NJ: John Wiley & Sons, 2012).

TABLE 20.1	A Comparison of Two Managers		
	Return	Risk (Standard Deviation)	Return/Risk Ratio
Manager A	10%	5	2:1
Manager B	25%	25	1:1

Consider the two managers in Table 20.1. Assuming the two managers are considered qualitatively equivalent, which is the better-performing manager?[1] Many investors would opt for Manager B, reasoning, "I am willing to accept the higher risk to get the higher return potential." But is this reasoning rational? In Table 20.2 we add a third investment alternative—leveraging an investment with Manager A at 300 percent.[2] The leveraged investment with Manager A now has both a higher return and lower risk than Manager B. So even risk-seeking investors should prefer Manager A, using a leverage factor that raises return to the desired level.

One can picture risk as a hole—the deeper the hole, the greater the risk—and return as a pile of sand. Leverage is the shovel that, if desired, allows transferring some of the sand from the risk hole to the return pile, thereby increasing return in exchange for accepting greater risk—a trade-off that may be preferred if the risk level is lower than desired. Continuing the analogy, by using negative leverage (i.e., holding more cash), it is also possible to transfer sand from the return pile to the risk hole, thereby reducing risk in exchange for accepting lower return. In this sense, risk and return are entirely interchangeable through leverage (that is, through varying exposure).

TABLE 20.2	A Comparison of Two Managers Revisited		
	Return	Risk (Standard Deviation)	Return/Risk Ratio
Manager A	10%	5	2:1
Manager B	25%	25	1:1
Manager A 3×	30%	15	2:1

---

[1] Although this chapter is written from the perspective of an investor comparing investments with two different managers, exactly analogous comments would apply to a trader comparing two different systems or two different trading strategies.

[2] For strategies that use margin (e.g., futures, foreign exchange, options), managers need only a small percentage of the nominal investment to meet margin requirements. In these instances, investors can often use notional funding—that is, funding an account with a smaller amount of cash than the nominal level. For example, an investor might notionally fund an account with $300,000 cash to be traded as a $900,000 investment, implicitly leveraging the cash investment 300 percent vis-à-vis an investment that is not notionally funded. Technically speaking, although notional funding increases the exposure per dollar invested, it does not actually imply leverage, since there is no borrowing involved. Our example assumes notional funding. Nevertheless, in the ensuing discussion, we use the term leverage to indicate increased exposure (even if there is no borrowing involved). For strategies that must be fully funded, the leveraged portion of returns would have to be reduced by borrowing costs.

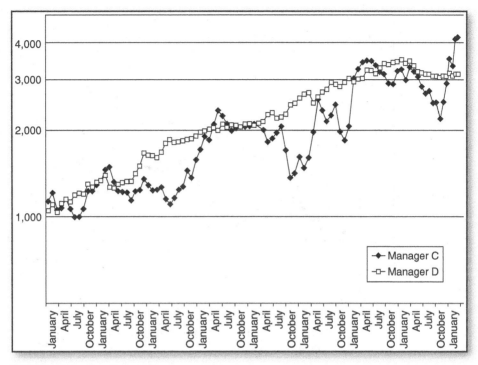

FIGURE 20.1 Two Paths to Return

As a practical example to illustrate this concept, in Figure 20.1 we compare two actual managers. Assuming we consider past performance indicative of potential future performance—at least in a relative sense—which manager provides a better investment? It would appear the answer is indeterminate: Manager C clearly achieves a superior return, but Manager D displays considerably lower risk, as evidenced by much smaller equity drawdowns throughout the track record. The seeming inability to determine which manager exhibits better performance is true only in a superficial sense, however. In Figure 20.2, we again compare Managers C and D, but this time we assume the exposure to Manager D is doubled.[3] Now it is clear that Manager D is superior in terms of both return and risk, achieving a significantly higher ending net asset value (NAV) and still doing so with visibly lower equity drawdowns (despite the doubling of exposure). Even though Manager C ended up with a higher return in Figure 20.1, investors could have achieved an even higher return with a 2× investment in Manager D while still maintaining less risk. The lesson is that return is a faulty gauge; it is the return/risk ratio that matters.

---

[3] Managers C and D are commodity trading advisors (CTAs) who trade futures, so increased exposure could have been achieved through notional funding (i.e., without leverage through borrowing). The returns depicted in Figure 20.1 were adjusted to remove interest income, so that doubling exposure (whether through notional funding or through borrowed leverage) would multiply all the returns by a near-exact factor of 2.0. (If returns included interest income, then doubling the exposure would not fully double the returns because there would be no interest income on the additional exposure.)

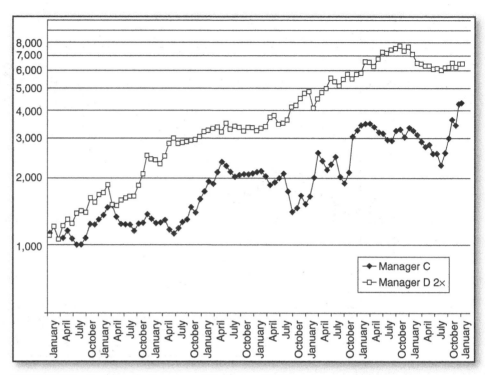

FIGURE 20.2 Doubling the Exposure of the Lower-Risk Manager

What if leverage is not available as a tool? For example, what if investors have a choice between Managers C and D in Figure 20.1 but there are practical impediments to increasing the exposure of Manager D? Now return and risk are inextricably bundled, and investors must choose between the higher-return/higher-risk profile of Manager C and the lower-return/lower-risk profile of Manager D. It might seem that risk-tolerant investors would always be better off with Manager C. Such investors might say, "I don't care if Manager C is riskier, as long as the end return is higher." The flaw in this premise is that investors who start with Manager C at the wrong time—and that is easy to do—may actually experience significant losses rather than gains, even if they maintain the investment, and especially if they don't. The more volatile the path of returns, the more likely investors will abandon the investment during one of the equity plunges and, as a result, never realize the higher return. After all, investors in real time do not know the investment will eventually recover. Thus, even though Manager C ends up ahead of Manager D, many investors will never survive the ride to see the eventual successful outcome (and even those who do may have initiated their investment on an upside excursion, reducing or even eliminating their net return). The greater the volatility, the larger the percentage of investors who will close out their investments at a loss.

Clearly, there is a need to use risk-adjusted returns rather than returns alone to make valid performance comparisons. In the next section we consider some alternative risk-adjusted return measures.

Risk-Adjusted Return Measures

Sharpe Ratio

The Sharpe ratio is the most widely used risk-adjusted return measure. The Sharpe ratio is defined as the average *excess return* divided by the standard deviation. Excess return is the return above the risk-free return (e.g., the Treasury bill rate). For example, if the average return is 8 percent per year and the T-bill rate is 3 percent, the excess return would be 5 percent. (It should be noted that during certain periods, such as the years following the 2008 financial crisis, zero, or near-zero, interest rates can effectively eliminate the expectation of a meaningful "risk-free" return. For reference, the average three-month T-bill rate from 2009 through 2015 was only 0.08 percent. In contrast, from 2002 to 2008 the average three-month T-bill rate was 2.58 percent, and during 1995–2001 it was 5.03 percent.) The standard deviation is a measure of the variability of return. In essence, the Sharpe ratio is the average excess return normalized by the volatility of returns:

$$SR = \frac{AR - RF}{SD}$$

where SR = Sharpe ratio

$\quad AR$ = average return (used as proxy for expected return)

$\quad RF$ = risk-free interest rate (e.g., Treasury bill return)

$\quad SD$ = standard deviation

The standard deviation is calculated as follows:

$$SD = \sqrt{\frac{\sum_I^N (X_i - \bar{X})^2}{N - 1}}$$

where $\bar{X}$ = mean

$\quad X_i$ = individual returns

$\quad N$ = number of returns

Assuming monthly data is used to calculate the Sharpe ratio, as is most common, the Sharpe ratio would be annualized by multiplying by the square root of 12. Note that the return is an arithmetic average return, not the compounded return.

There are two basic problems with the Sharpe ratio:

1. **The return measure is based on average rather than compounded return.** The return an investor realizes is the compounded return, not the average return. The more volatile the return series, the more the average return will deviate from the actual (i.e., compounded) return. For example, a two-year period with a 50 percent gain in one year and a 50 percent loss in the other would represent a zero percent average return, but the investor would actually realize a 25 percent loss (150% × 50% = 75%). The average annual compounded return of −13.4 percent, however, would reflect the reality (86.6% × 86.6% = 75%).

2. **The Sharpe ratio does not distinguish between upside and downside volatility.**
The risk measure inherent in the Sharpe ratio—the standard deviation—does not reflect the way most investors perceive risk. Investors care about loss, not volatility. They are averse to downside volatility, but actually like upside volatility. I have yet to meet any investors who complained because their managers made too much money in a month. The standard deviation, and by inference the Sharpe ratio, however, makes no distinction between upside and downside volatility. This characteristic of the Sharpe ratio can result in rankings that would contradict most investors' perceptions and preferences.[4]

Figure 20.3 compares two hypothetical managers that have identical returns over the period depicted, but very different return profiles. Which manager appears riskier? Decide on an answer before reading on.

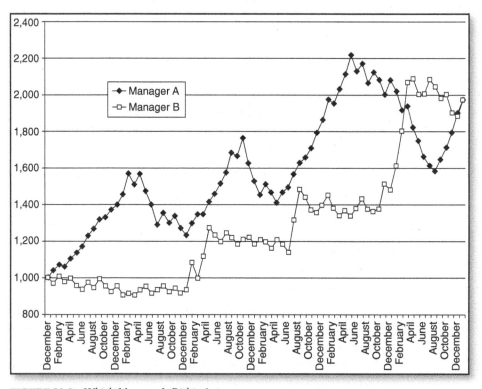

FIGURE 20.3   Which Manager Is Riskier?

---

[4]To be fair, in some cases, high upside volatility can be indicative of a greater potential for downside volatility, and in these instances the Sharpe ratio will be an appropriate measure. The Sharpe ratio, however, will be particularly misleading in evaluating strategies that are designed to achieve sporadic large gains while strictly controlling downside risk (that is, "right-skewed" strategies).

Most likely you chose Manager A as being riskier. Manager A has three drawdown episodes in excess of 20 percent, with the largest being 28 percent. In contrast, Manager B's worst peak-to-valley decline is a rather moderate 11 percent. Yet the standard deviation—the risk component of the Sharpe ratio—is 30 percent higher for Manager B. As a result, even though both Managers A and B have equal cumulative returns and Manager A has much larger equity retracements, Manager A also has a significantly higher Sharpe ratio: 0.71 versus 0.58 (assuming a 2 percent risk-free rate). Why does this occur? Because Manager B has a number of very large gain months, and it is these months that strongly push up Manager B's standard deviation, thereby reducing the Sharpe ratio. Although most investors would clearly prefer the return profile of Manager B, the Sharpe ratio decisively indicates the reverse ranking.

The potential for a mismatch between Sharpe ratio rankings and investor preferences has led to the creation of other return/risk measures that seek to address the flaws of the Sharpe ratio. Before we review some of these alternative measures, we first consider the question: What are the implications of a negative Sharpe ratio?

Although it is commonplace to see negative Sharpe ratios reported for managers whose returns are less than the risk-free return, negative Sharpe ratios are absolutely meaningless. When the Sharpe ratio is positive, greater volatility (as measured by the standard deviation), a negative characteristic, will reduce the Sharpe ratio, as it logically should. When the Sharpe ratio is negative, however, greater volatility will actually increase its value—that is, the division of a negative return by a larger number will make it less negative. Comparisons involving negative Sharpe ratios can lead to absurd results. Table 20.3 provides an example. Manager B has a negative excess return twice the size of Manager A's (−10 percent versus −5 percent) and four times the volatility of Manager A. Even though Manager B is much worse than Manager A in terms of both return and volatility, Manager B has a higher (less negative) Sharpe ratio. This preposterous result is a direct consequence of higher volatility resulting in higher (less negative) Sharpe ratios when the Sharpe ratio is in negative territory. What should be done with negative Sharpe ratios? Ignore them.[5] They are always worthless and frequently misleading.

Sortino Ratio

The Sortino ratio addresses both of the Sharpe ratio's previously cited problems. First, it uses the compounded return, which is representative of the actual realized return over any period of time,

TABLE 20.3 A Comparison of Two Managers with Negative Sharpe Ratios

	Average Annual Return	Risk-Free Return	Excess Return	Annualized Standard Deviation	Sharpe Ratio
Manager A	−3%	2%	−5%	5	−1.0
Manager B	−8%	2%	−10%	20	−0.5

[5] What if some value must be used, as in an application such as ranking a list of managers based on the ratio? In this case, a dual rank criterion makes much more sense: ranking managers based on the Sharpe ratio when excess returns are positive and on excess returns when Sharpe ratios are negative.

instead of the arithmetic return. Second, and most important, the Sortino ratio focuses on defining risk in terms of downside deviation, considering only deviations below a specified minimum acceptable return (MAR) instead of a standard deviation (used in the Sharpe ratio), which includes all deviations, upside as well as downside. Specifically, the Sortino ratio is defined as the compounded return in excess of the MAR divided by the downside deviation, as follows:

$$SR = \frac{ACR - MAR}{DD}$$

where SR = Sortino ratio

ACR = annual compounded return

MAR = minimum acceptable return (e.g., zero, risk-free, average)

DD = downside deviation

where DD is defined as:

$$DD = \sqrt{\frac{\sum_i^N (min(X_i - MAR, 0))^2}{N}}$$

where X_i = individual returns

MAR = minimum acceptable return (e.g., zero, risk-free, average)

N = number of data values

For example, if we define $MAR = 0$, then DD calculations will include only deviations for months with negative returns (the other months will equal zero).

The MAR in the Sortino ratio can be set to any level, but one of the following three definitions is normally used for the MAR:

1. **Zero.** Deviations are calculated for all negative returns.
2. **Risk-free return.** Deviations are calculated for all returns below the risk-free return.
3. **Average return.** Deviations are calculated for all returns below the average of the series being analyzed. This formulation is closest to the standard deviation, but considers deviations for only the lower half of returns.

Frequently, the fact that a manager has a higher Sortino ratio than Sharpe ratio is cited as evidence that returns are positively skewed—that is, there is a tendency for larger deviations on the upside than on the downside. This type of comparison is incorrect. The Sortino and Sharpe ratios cannot be compared, and as formulated, the Sortino ratio will invariably be higher, even for managers whose worst losses tend to be larger than their best gains. The reason for the upward bias in the Sortino ratio is that it calculates deviations for only a portion of returns—those returns below the MAR—but uses a divisor based on the number of *all* returns to calculate the downside deviation. Because it distinguishes between upside and downside deviations, the Sortino ratio probably comes closer to reflecting investor preferences than does the Sharpe ratio and, in this sense, may be a better tool for comparing managers. But the Sortino ratio should be compared only with other Sortino ratios and never with Sharpe ratios.

Symmetric Downside-Risk Sharpe Ratio

The symmetric downside-risk (SDR) Sharpe ratio, which was introduced by William T. Ziemba,[6] is similar in intent and construction to the Sortino ratio, but makes a critical adjustment to remove the inherent upward bias in the Sortino ratio vis-à-vis the Sharpe ratio. The SDR Sharpe ratio is defined as the compounded return minus the risk-free return divided by the downside deviation. The downside deviation is calculated similarly to the downside deviation in the Sortino ratio with one critical exception: a multiplier of 2.0 is used to compensate for the fact that only returns below a specified benchmark contribute to the deviation calculation.[7] The benchmark used for calculating the downside deviation can be set to any level, but the same three choices listed for the MAR in the Sortino ratio would apply here as well: zero, risk-free return, and average return. (In his article, Ziemba uses zero as the benchmark value.) Unlike the Sortino ratio, the SDR Sharpe ratio (with the benchmark set to the average) can be directly compared with the Sharpe ratio.[8]

$$SDRSR = \frac{ACR - RF}{\sqrt{2} \times DD}$$

where $SDRSR$ = symmetric downside-risk Sharpe ratio

ACR = annual compounded return

RF = risk-free interest rate (e.g., T-bill return)

DD = downside deviation

---

[6] William T. Ziemba, "The Symmetric Downside-Risk Sharpe Ratio," *Journal of Portfolio Management* (Fall 2005): 108–121.

[7] Ziemba used the term *benchmark* instead of MAR in defining downside deviation. If the median were used as the benchmark, only half the returns would be used to calculate the downside deviation, and a multiplier of 2.0 would then provide an exact compensating adjustment. For other choices for the benchmark (e.g., zero, risk-free return, average), the number of points below the benchmark would not necessarily be exactly half, and a multiplier of 2.0 would provide an approximate adjustment.

[8] To be perfectly precise, there would be a tendency for the SDR Sharpe ratio to be slightly lower for a symmetric distribution of returns because the SDR Sharpe ratio uses the compounded return rather than the arithmetic return used in the Sharpe ratio, and the arithmetic return will always be equal to or higher than the compounded return. If, however, zero or the risk-free return is used as the benchmark in the downside deviation calculation, assuming the manager's average return is greater than the risk-free return, there would be a tendency for the SDR Sharpe ratio to be higher than the Sharpe ratio for a symmetric distribution of returns for two reasons:

1. There will be fewer than half the returns below the benchmark, so the multiplication by 2.0 will not fully compensate.

2. Downside deviations from the risk-free return (and especially zero) would be smaller than deviations from the average.

These two factors would cause the downside deviation to be smaller than the standard deviation, implying a higher SDR Sharpe ratio than Sharpe ratio.

where *DD* is defined as:

$$DD = \sqrt{\frac{\sum_i^N (\min(X_i - \overline{X}, 0))^2}{N - 1}}$$

where X_i = individual returns

$\overline{X}$ = benchmark return (e.g., mean, zero, risk-free)

Since the SDR Sharpe ratio includes only the downside deviation, multiplying by the square root of 2 (a consequence of doubling the squared deviations) is equivalent to assuming the upside deviation is equal (i.e., symmetric) to the downside deviation. This proxy replacement of the upside deviation is what makes it possible to compare SDR Sharpe ratio values with Sharpe ratio values.

The SDR Sharpe ratio (with any of the standard choices for a benchmark value) is preferable to the Sharpe ratio because it accounts for the very significant difference between the risk implications of downside deviations versus upside deviations as viewed from the perspective of the investor. The SDR Sharpe ratio is also preferable to the Sortino ratio because it is an almost identical calculation,[9] but with the important advantage of being directly comparable with the widely used Sharpe ratio. Also, by comparing a manager's SDR Sharpe ratio versus the Sharpe ratio, an investor can get a sense of whether the manager's returns are positively or negatively skewed.

Gain-to-Pain Ratio

The gain-to-pain ratio (GPR) is the sum of all monthly returns divided by the absolute value of the sum of all monthly losses.[10] This performance measure indicates the ratio of cumulative net gain to the cumulative loss realized to achieve that gain. For example, a GPR of 1.0 would imply that, on average, an investor has to experience an amount of monthly losses equal to the net amount gained. The GPR penalizes all losses in proportion to their size, and upside volatility is beneficial since it impacts only the return portion of the ratio.

---

[9] Besides the essential introduction of the 2.0 multiplier term, which allows unbiased comparisons between the SDR Sharpe ratio and the Sharpe ratio, the only difference between the SDR Sharpe ratio and the Sortino ratio is that it subtracts the risk-free return from the compounded return instead of the MAR (which may or may not be the risk-free return).

[10] The gain-to-pain ratio (GPR) is a performance statistic I have been using for many years. I am not aware of any prior use of this statistic, although the term is sometimes used as a generic reference for return/risk measures or a return/drawdown measure. The GPR is similar to the profit factor, which is a commonly used statistic in evaluating trading systems. The profit factor is defined as the sum of all profitable trades divided by the absolute value of the sum of all losing trades. The profit factor is applied to trades, whereas the GPR is applied to interval (e.g., monthly) returns. Algebraically, it can easily be shown that if the profit factor calculation were applied to monthly returns, the profit factor would equal GPR + 1 and would provide the same performance ordering as the GPR. For quantitatively oriented readers familiar with the omega function, note that the omega function evaluated at zero is also equal to GPR + 1.

$$GPR = \frac{\sum_{i=1}^{N} X_i}{\left| \sum_{i}^{N} \min(X_i, 0) \right|}$$

where X_i = individual returns

A key difference between the GPR and measures such as the Sharpe ratio, the SDR Sharpe ratio, and the Sortino ratio is that the GPR will be indifferent between five 2 percent losses and one 10 percent loss, whereas the other ratios discussed so far will be impacted far more by the single larger loss. This difference results because the standard deviation and downside deviation calculations used for the other ratios involve squaring the deviation between the reference return level (e.g., average, zero, risk-free) and the loss. For example, if the reference return is zero percent, the squared deviation for one 10 percent loss would be five times greater than the squared deviation for five 2 percent losses ($10^2 = 100$; $5 \times 2^2 = 20$). In the GPR calculation, by contrast, both cases will add 10 percent to the denominator. If an investor is indifferent as to whether a given magnitude of loss is experienced over multiple months or in a single month, then the GPR would be a more appropriate measure than the SDR Sharpe ratio and Sortino ratio. However, an investor who considers a single larger loss worse than multiple losses totaling the same amount would have the opposite preference.

Although the GPR would typically be applied to monthly data, it can also be calculated for other time intervals. If daily data are available, the GPR can provide a statistically very significant measure because of the large amount of sample data. The longer the time frame, the higher the GPR because many of the losses visible on a shorter time interval will be smoothed out over a longer period. In my experience, *on average*, daily GPR values tend to be about one-sixth as large as the monthly GPR for the same manager, although the ratio between daily and monthly GPR values can range widely. For monthly data, roughly speaking, GPRs greater than 1.0 are good and those above 1.5 are very good. For daily data, the corresponding numbers would be approximately 0.17 and 0.25.

One advantage of the GPR over the other ratios is that rankings remain consistent even for negative returns—that is, a smaller negative GPR is always better than a larger negative GPR (a relationship that is not necessarily true for the other ratios). A GPR of zero means that the sum of all wins is equal to the sum of all losses. The theoretical minimum GPR value is −1.0 and would occur if there were no winning months. The closer the GPR is to −1.0, the smaller the ratio of the sum of all wins to the sum of all losses.[11]

Tail Ratio

An important question for the investor is whether a manager's extreme returns tend to be larger on the upside or the downside. Managers with frequent small gains and occasional large losses (negatively skewed managers) are more risky and less desirable than managers with frequent small

---

[11] The ratio of the sum of wins to the sum of losses is equal to GPR + 1. So, for example, a GPR of −0.25 would imply that the ratio of the sum of wins to the sum of losses is 0.75.

losses and occasional large gains (positively skewed managers). Although there is a statistic that measures skewness—the degree to which a return distribution has longer tails (extreme events) on the right (positive) or left (negative) side than the symmetric normal distribution—it is difficult to attach intuitive meaning to specific values (beyond the value of the sign).

The tail ratio measures the tendency for extreme returns to be skewed to the positive or negative side in a statistic whose value is intuitively clear.

$$TR = \frac{\dfrac{\sum_{p=0}^{p=T} X_p}{N_{p<T}}}{\left| \dfrac{\sum_{p=100-T}^{p=100} X_p}{N_{p>100-T}} \right|}$$

where X_p = return at percentile p
   T = threshold percentile to calculate numerator of tail ratio (Implicit assumption: Lower percentile rankings represent higher return. For example, the top 10% of returns would be all returns less than T, where $T = 10$.)
   $N_{p<T}$ = number of returns below percentile
   $N_{p>100-T}$ = number of returns above percentile $100-T$

The tail ratio requires one parameter input: the upper and lower percentile threshold used to calculate the statistic. If the threshold is set to 10, for example, the tail ratio would be equal to the average of all returns in the top decile of returns divided by the absolute value of the average of all returns in the bottom decile of returns. (*Note:* If the average of bottom decile returns is positive, the tail ratio would have no meaning and cannot be calculated.) If returns were normally distributed, the tail ratio would equal 1.0. A ratio significantly less than 1.0 would indicate a tendency for the largest losses to be of greater magnitude than the largest gains, while a ratio significantly greater than 1.0 would indicate the reverse tendency. For example, if the tail ratio was equal to 0.5, it would imply that the magnitude of the average loss in the bottom decile was twice as large as the average gain in the top decile—a reading indicative of a potentially very risky manager.

MAR and Calmar Ratios

The MAR ratio is the annualized compounded return divided by the maximum drawdown.

$$MAR = \frac{ACR}{1 - \min\left(\dfrac{NAV_j}{NAV_i}\right)}$$

where ACR = annual compounded return (expressed in decimal form)
   NAV = net asset value
   $j > i$

The Calmar ratio is exactly the same except the calculation is specifically restricted to the past three years of data. Although these ratios are useful in that they are based on a past worst-case situation, the fact that the risk measure divisor is based on only a single event impedes their statistical significance. Also, if applied over entire track records, the MAR will be strongly biased against managers with longer records, because the longer the record, the greater the potential maximum drawdown. (This bias does not exist in the Calmar ratio because, by definition, it is based on only the past three years of data.) Manager comparisons should be limited to common time periods, a restriction that is especially critical when using the MAR ratio.

Return Retracement Ratio

The return retracement ratio (RRR) is similar to the MAR and Calmar ratios in that it is a measure of the average annual compounded return divided by a retracement measure. The key difference, however, is that instead of being based on a single retracement (the maximum retracement), the RRR divides return by the average maximum retracement (AMR), which is based on a maximum retracement calculation for each month. The maximum retracement for each month is equal to the greater of the following two numbers:

1. The largest possible cumulative loss that could have been experienced by any existing investor in that month (the percentage decline from the prior peak NAV to the current month-end NAV).
2. The largest loss that could have been experienced by any new investor starting at the end of that month (the percentage decline from the current month-end NAV to the subsequent lowest NAV).

$$RRR = \frac{ACR - RF}{AMR}$$

where ACR = annual compounded return

RF = risk-free return

AMR = average maximum retracement = MR_i / N

where N = number of months

MR_i = max($MRPNH_i$, $MRSNL_i$)

where $MRPNH_i$ is the maximum retracement from prior NAV high, and is defined as:

$$MRPNH_i = (PNH_i - NAV_i) / PNH_i$$

where PNH_i = prior NAV high (prior to month i)

NAV_i = NAV at end of month i

$MRSNL_i$ is the maximum retracement to a subsequent NAV low, and is defined as:

$$MRSNL_i = (NAV_i - SNL_i) / NAV_i$$

where SNL_i is the subsequent NAV low (subsequent to month i).

The reason for using both metrics to determine a maximum retracement for each month is that each of the two conditions would be biased to show small retracement levels during a segment of the track record. The first condition would invariably show small retracements for the early months in the track record because there would not have been an opportunity for any large retracements to develop. Similarly, the second condition would inevitably show small retracements during the latter months of the track record for analogous reasons. By using the maximum of both conditions, we assure a true worst-case number for each month. The average maximum retracement is the average of all these monthly maximum retracements. The return retracement ratio is statistically far more meaningful than the MAR and Calmar ratios because it is based on multiple data points (one for each month) as opposed to a single statistic (the maximum drawdown in the entire record).

Comparing the Risk-Adjusted Return Performance Measures

Table 20.4 compares Managers A and B shown in Figure 20.3 in terms of each of the risk-adjusted return performance measures we discussed. Interestingly, the Sharpe ratio, which is by far the most widely used return/risk measure, leads to exactly the opposite conclusion indicated by all the other measures. Whereas the Sharpe ratio implies that Manager A is significantly superior in return/risk terms, all the other performance measures rank Manager B higher—many by wide margins. Recall that both Managers A and B had identical cumulative returns, so the only difference between the two was the riskiness implied by their return paths. The Sharpe ratio, which uses the standard deviation as its risk metric, judged Manager B as being riskier because of higher volatility, as measured across all months. Most of Manager B's volatility, however, was on the upside—a

TABLE 20.4 A Comparison of Risk-Adjusted Return Measures

	Manager A	Manager B	B as Percent of A
Sharpe ratio	0.71	0.58	82%
Sortino ratio (zero)	1.27	1.44	113%
Sortino ratio (risk-free)	1.03	1.15	112%
Sortino ratio (average)	0.87	0.94	107%
SDR Sharpe ratio (zero)	0.75	0.85	113%
SDR Sharpe ratio (risk-free)	0.73	0.81	112%
SDR Sharpe ratio (average)	0.62	0.66	107%
Gain-to-pain ratio (GPR)	0.70	0.71	101%
Tail ratio (10%)	1.13	2.86	253%
Tail ratio (5%)	1.10	2.72	247%
MAR ratio	0.41	1.09	265%
Calmar ratio	0.33	1.70	515%
Return retracement ratio (RRR)	0.77	1.67	218%

characteristic most investors would consider an attribute, not a fault. Although Manager A had lower volatility overall, the downside volatility was significantly greater than Manager B's—a characteristic that is consistent with most investors' intuitive sense of greater risk. The Sharpe ratio does not distinguish between downside and upside volatility, while the other risk-adjusted return measures do.

Although all the risk-adjusted return measures besides the Sharpe ratio penalize only downside volatility, they do so in different ways that have different implications:

- **Sortino ratio and SDR Sharpe ratio.** These ratios penalize returns below a specified level (e.g., zero) with the weight assigned to downside deviations increasing more than proportionately as their magnitude increases. Thus, one larger downside deviation will reduce the ratio more than multiple smaller deviations that sum to the same amount. These ratios are unaffected by the order of losing months. Two widely separated losses of 10 percent will have the same effect as two consecutive 10 percent losses, even though the latter results in a larger equity retracement.

- **GPR.** The GPR penalizes downside deviations in direct proportion to their magnitude. In contrast to the Sortino and SDR Sharpe ratios, one large deviation will have exactly the same effect as multiple smaller deviations that sum to the same amount. This difference explains why Managers A and B are nearly equivalent based on the GPR, but Manager A is significantly worse based on the Sortino and SDR Sharpe ratios: Manager A has both larger and fewer losses, but the sum of the losses is nearly the same for both managers. The GPR is similar to the Sortino and SDR Sharpe ratios in terms of being indifferent to the order of losses; that is, it does not penalize for consecutive or proximate losses.

- **Tail ratio.** The tail ratio focuses specifically on the most extreme gains and losses. The tail ratio will be very effective in highlighting managers whose worst losses tend to be larger than their best gains. In terms of the tail ratio, Manager B, who achieves occasional very large gains but whose worst losses are only moderate, is dramatically better than Manager A, who exhibits the reverse pattern.

- **MAR and Calmar ratios.** In contrast to all the foregoing performance measures, these ratios are heavily influenced by the order of returns. A concentration of losses will have a much greater impact than the same losses dispersed throughout the track record. Both of these measures, however, focus on only the single worst equity drawdown. Therefore losses that occur outside the interim defined by the largest peak-to-valley equity drawdown will not have any impact on these ratios. Because the maximum drawdown for Manager A is much greater than for Manager B, these ratios show a dramatic difference between the two managers.

- **Return retracement ratio (RRR).** The RRR is the only return/risk measure that both penalizes *all* downside deviations and also penalizes consecutive or proximate losses. In contrast to the MAR and Calmar ratios, which reflect only those losses that define the maximum drawdown, the RRR calculation incorporates all losses.

Table 20.5 summarizes and compares the properties of the different risk-adjusted return measures.

Property	Sharpe Ratio	SDR Sharpe Ratio	Sortino Ratio	GPR	Tail Ratio	MAR and Calmar	RRR
Is impacted by upside volatility	X						
Is impacted only by downside volatility		X	X	X	X	X	X
Reflects *all* downside volatility	X	X	X	X			X
Gives more than proportionate weight to large losses	X	X	X		X		
Is impacted by proximity of losses						X	X
Focuses on extreme returns only					X		
Rankings remain consistent for net negative returns				X	X		

TABLE 20.5 Properties of Risk-Adjusted Performance Measures

Which Return/Risk Measure Is Best?

To some extent, the choice of which return/risk measures to use depends on the performance measure properties favored by the individual investor. The major advantages and disadvantages of these performance measures can be summarized as follows:

- **Sharpe ratio.** Although the Sharpe ratio is the most widely used risk-adjusted metric, it provides rankings that are least consistent with most people's intuitive sense of risk because it penalizes upside gains.

- **Sortino ratio.** This ratio corrects the main deficiency of the Sharpe ratio by focusing on downside risk instead of total volatility as the measure of risk. In addition, the Sortino ratio uses a compounded return, which matches actual return over the entire period, whereas the Sharpe ratio uses an arithmetic average return, which does not. One disadvantage of the Sortino ratio is that it is not directly comparable with the Sharpe ratio because its calculation is biased to delivering higher values.

- **SDR Sharpe ratio.** This ratio provides the same fix as the Sortino ratio, and it has the advantage of an additional adjustment that allows for direct comparisons of its values with Sharpe ratio values. Similar to the Sortino ratio, the SDR Sharpe ratio also uses the compounded return instead of the arithmetic average return. Since the SDR Sharpe ratio will provide nearly identical rankings as the Sortino ratio and has the advantage of allowing for comparisons with the Sharpe ratio for the same manager, it seems the better choice for any investor. Using both ratios would be redundant.

- **Gain-to-pain ratio (GPR).** Similar to the Sortino and SDR Sharpe ratios, the GPR penalizes a manager only for losses (zero percent is also a common choice for minimum acceptable return or benchmark in the Sortino and SDR Sharpe ratios). The GPR weights losses proportionately to their magnitude, whereas the Sortino and SDR Sharpe ratios magnify the weight of larger losses. Investors who view one 10 percent monthly loss the same as five 2 percent losses might prefer the GPR, whereas investors who consider the single 10 percent monthly loss to be worse might prefer the SDR Sharpe ratio.

- **Tail ratio.** Since, by definition, the tail ratio considers only a small percentage of all returns (20 percent or less), it is not intended as a stand-alone risk-adjusted return measure. Its focus on extreme returns, however, makes it a very useful supplemental metric to one of the other measures.

- **MAR and Calmar ratios.** These ratios will penalize for losses that occur with sufficient proximity to be part of the same drawdown. The other ratios (with the exception of the RRR) are unaffected by the sequence of returns. The drawback of these ratios is that the risk is defined by only a single event (the maximum drawdown), impeding their statistical significance and representativeness.

- **Return retracement ratio (RRR).** This ratio is both based on downside deviations and impacted by proximate losses. Its big advantage vis-à-vis the MAR and Calmar ratios is that it reflects all retracements, with the risk number based on all monthly numbers, rather than just a single event and single statistic: the maximum drawdown. Although the MAR and Calmar ratios might still be consulted as supplemental measures reflecting a worst-case situation, the RRR is preferable as a return/drawdown ratio.

■ Visual Performance Evaluation

Many people will find that the performance charts in this section provide a better intuitive sense of relative performance (in both return and risk terms) than do performance statistics.

Net Asset Value (NAV) Charts

An NAV chart, such as was illustrated in Figure 20.3, provides an extremely useful way of evaluating a track record. The NAV chart depicts the compounded growth of $1,000 over time. For example, an NAV of 2,000 implies that the original investment has doubled from its starting level as of the indicated time. The NAV chart can offer a good intuitive sense of past performance in terms of both return and risk. In fact, if an investor were to examine only a single performance gauge, the NAV chart would probably be the most informative.

The way we visually perceive conventionally scaled NAV charts that depict longer-term periods, however, may result in misleading inferences. Consider Figure 20.4, and answer the following three questions before reading on:

1. Was return higher in the first half of the track record or the second?
2. Was the manager riskier during the first half of the track record or the second?
3. Was the return/risk performance better during the first half of the track record or the second?

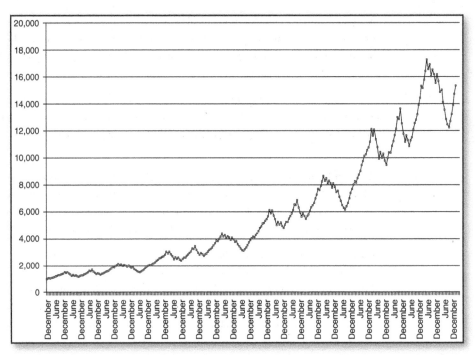

FIGURE 20.4 How Has Performance Changed over Time?

If you picked the first half as the answer to any of these three questions, you are wrong. If you picked the second half for any answer, you are also wrong. The two halves are exactly the same. In fact, all four quarters of the track record are the same. Figure 20.4 was created by copying the returns of Manager A in Figure 20.3 and pasting the sequence three times to the end to create an extended NAV that repeats the same return pattern, displaying it four times in all. Looking at Figure 20.4, however, it seems as if both the return and the volatility are increasing sharply over time. They are not. The illusion is an artifact of depicting NAV charts on a conventional arithmetic scale. On an arithmetic scale, an NAV decline of 1,000 when the NAV is at 16,000 looks the same as an NAV decline of 1,000 when the NAV is 2,000. The two declines, however, are radically different: a modest 6 percent decline in the first instance and a huge 50 percent drop in the second. The distortion on an arithmetic scale chart will get magnified when the NAV range is wide, which is frequently a serious problem for long-term charts.

The ideal way to depict an NAV chart is on a logarithmic scale. On a log scale chart, the increments for a fixed amount of movement (e.g., 1,000) become proportionately smaller as the level increases, and as a result, equal percentage price moves will appear as equal size moves on the vertical scale. Figure 20.5 depicts the same NAV as Figure 20.4, but on a log scale. The self-replicating nature of the chart is now evident as equal percentage changes now look identical wherever they appear. The moral is that a log scale is always the correct way to represent an NAV chart and is especially critical when there is a wide NAV range (more likely on long-term charts). A log scale was used for Figures 20.1 and 20.2 earlier in this chapter to allow for an accurate representation of relative volatility across time.

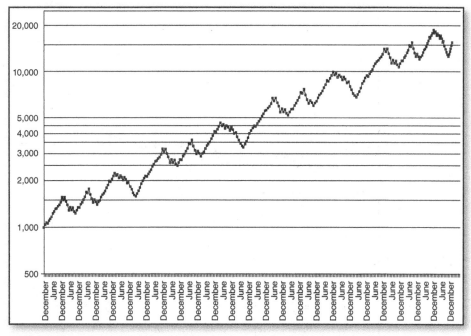

FIGURE 20.5　Log Scale: Equal Percentage Price Moves Appear Equal

Rolling Window Return Charts

The rolling window return chart shows the return for the specified time length ending in each month. For example, a 12-month rolling window return chart would show the 12-month return ending in each month (beginning with the 12th month of the track record). The rolling window return chart provides a clear visual summary of the results of investing with a manager for a specified length of time and answers such questions as: What would have been the range of outcomes with a manager for investments held for 12 months? 24 months? What was the worst loss for investments held for 12 months? 24 months?

For any December, the rolling 12-month return would be the same as the annual return. The important difference is that the rolling window return chart would show the analogous returns for all the other months as well. There is only a one-out-of-12 chance that December will be the worst 12-month return for the year. By showing all 12-month returns ending in any month, the rolling window chart will encompass worst-case events likely to be missed by annual returns and will provide a much more representative performance picture for one-year holding periods. The rolling window return chart can be calculated for other time intervals as well (e.g., 24 months, 36 months).

To illustrate the use of the rolling window return chart as a graphic analysis tool, we compare the two managers shown in Figure 20.6, who differ only moderately in terms of return (Manager E's annual compounded return is 1.3 percent higher), but differ widely in terms of the stability of returns. As shown in Figure 20.7, Manager E's 12-month returns range enormously from a severe

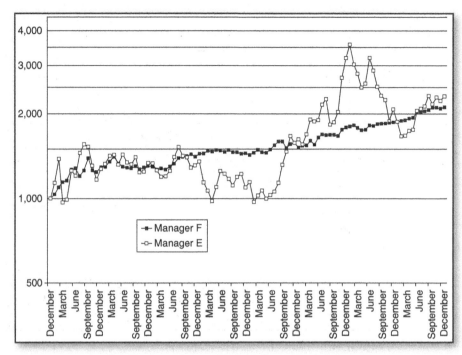

FIGURE 20.6 Small Difference in Return; Wide Difference in Stability of Return

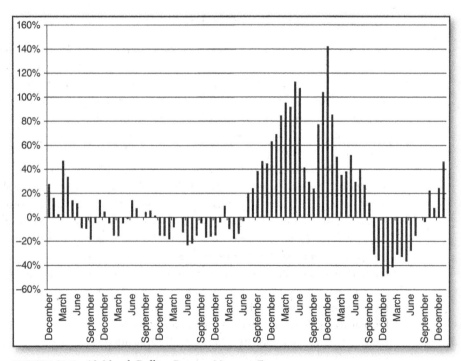

FIGURE 20.7 12-Month Rolling Return: Manager E

loss of 49 percent to a spectacular gain of 142 percent. In contrast, manager F's 12-month returns are contained in a far more moderate range of –10 percent to +29 percent (see Figure 20.8). Investors who were patient enough to stay with Manager F for at least 12 months would have experienced only a handful of investment initiation months that would have resulted in a net loss. Such patience, however, would not have provided any solace to investors with Manager E, who would have witnessed more than one-quarter of all 12-month holding periods resulting in net losses exceeding 15 percent, with several in excess of 40 percent. Even investors who committed to a 24-month holding period with Manager E would still have been subject to nearly one-fifth of all intervals with losses in excess of 15 percent (see Figure 20.9). In contrast, the worst-case outcome for investors with Manager F for a 24-month holding period would have been a positive return of 4 percent (see Figure 20.10).

Investors can use the rolling window return chart to assess the potential frequency and magnitude of worst-case outcomes as an aid in selecting investments consistent with their holding period tolerance for a losing investment. For example, an investor who is unwilling to maintain a losing investment for more than 12 months should avoid managers who have a meaningful percentage of negative 12-month returns, regardless of how favorable all the other performance statistics may be.

Rolling charts can also be used to depict other statistics besides return. For example, a rolling chart of annualized volatility (using daily data and a window of several months) can be used as a tool to monitor both managers and portfolios for early evidence of a possible increase in risk.

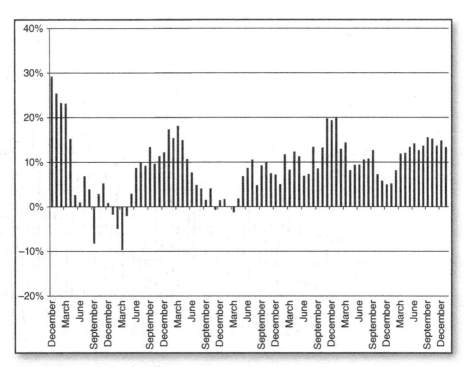

FIGURE 20.8   12-Month Rolling Return: Manager F

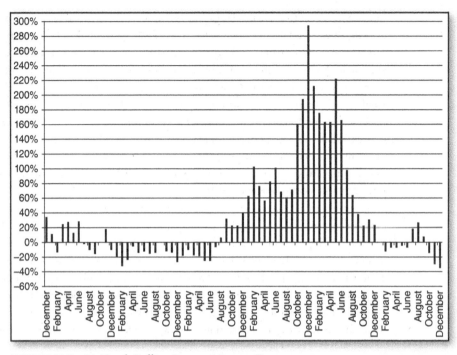

FIGURE 20.9 24-Month Rolling Return: Manager E

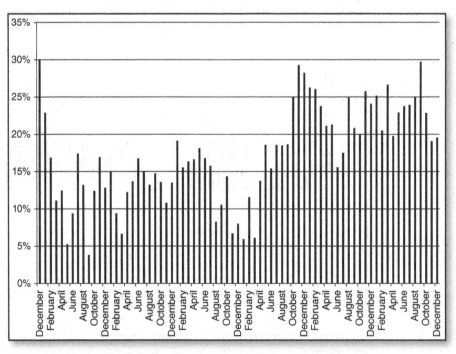

FIGURE 20.10 24-Month Rolling Return: Manager F

Underwater Curve and 2DUC Charts

The underwater chart shows the worst possible cumulative percentage loss any investor could have experienced as of the end of each month—an assumption that implies an investment started at the prior NAV peak. The low point in the NAV chart is the maximum retracement (the risk measure used in the MAR and Calmar ratios). The underwater chart, however, provides far more information because it shows not only the worst possible loss for the entire track record (the maximum retracement), but the worst possible loss as of the end of every other month in the track record as well. Figure 20.11 illustrates the underwater chart for the same two managers with widely disparate stability of returns depicted in Figure 20.6. The difference between the two could hardly be starker. Manager F's retracements are very shallow and relatively short-lived (a rise to the 0 percent level indicates a new NAV high); Manager E's retracements are both deep and protracted. The underwater chart provides an excellent visual representation of an investment's relative risk in a way that is very consistent with the way most investors perceive risk.

One shortcoming of the underwater curve is that it will understate risk for months in the early portion of the track record because there is an insufficient look-back period for a prior NAV peak. For these earlier months, there is no way of assessing a true worst-case loss representation, because a prior track record of sufficient length simply does not exist. Also, the underwater curve is constructed from the perspective of the worst cumulative loss that could have been

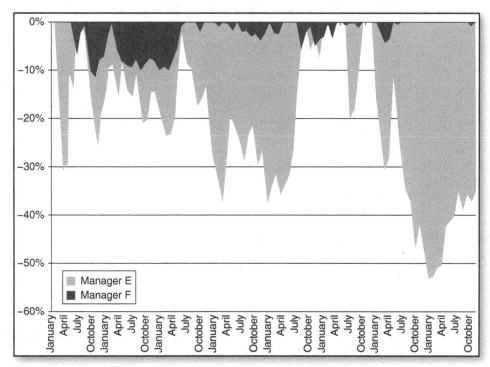

FIGURE 20.11 Underwater Curve: Manager E vs. Manager F

experienced by an existing investor. Arguably, the worst loss suffered by new investors may be an even more relevant measure. One solution to these inadequacies in the underwater curve calculation is to also consider the worst loss that could have been experienced by any investor starting in each month, assuming the investment was exited at the subsequent lowest NAV point. We can then create a two-direction underwater curve (2DUC) that for each month would show the maximum of the following two losses:

1. The cumulative loss of an existing investor starting at the prior NAV peak.
2. The cumulative loss of an investor starting that month-end and liquidating at the subsequent NAV low.

The average of all the points in the 2DUC chart would, in fact, be the risk measure used in the return retracement ratio (the average maximum retracement). The underwater excursions for Manager E become significantly more extreme in the 2DUC chart (Figure 20.12), widening from an average monthly value of 21 percent to 30 percent (the AMR). The underwater curve for Manager F remains subdued in the 2DUC chart with a still very low average value of 3 percent. The 2DUC chart implies that the average worst-case scenario for investors with Manager E is 10 times worse than with Manager F; that is a lot of extra risk for a 1.3 percent difference in the average annual compounded return. Based on performance, it would be difficult to justify choosing Manager E over Manager F, even for the most risk-tolerant investor.

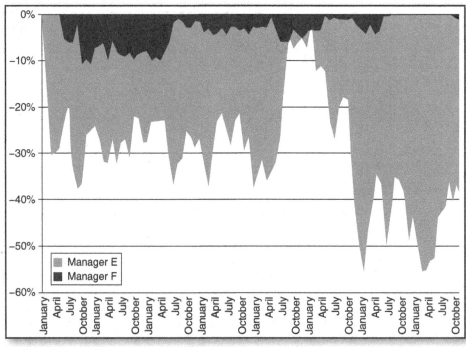

FIGURE 20.12 2DUC: Manager E vs. Manager F

■ Investment Insights

Many investors place too much emphasis on return. Since return can always be improved by increasing exposure (i.e., taking on greater risk), the return/risk ratio is a far more meaningful performance measure. An investment with higher return/risk and lower return than an alternative investment with the reverse characteristics can be brought up to the same higher return level with lower risk by using leverage.

The Sharpe ratio is by far the most widely used return/risk metric. The Sharpe ratio, however, penalizes upside volatility the same as downside volatility, which is not consistent with the way most investors view risk. Other return/risk measures detailed in this chapter, which focus on losses as the proxy for risk, more closely reflect the way most investors perceive risk. Investors can use Table 20.5, which summarizes the properties of different return/risk measures, to select the performance measures that best fit their criteria.

Return/risk statistics can be supplemented with the performance charts detailed in this chapter, which provide a tremendous amount of information in an intuitive and accessible format and should be at the core of any performance analysis. I recommend using the following performance charts in any manager or fund evaluation:

- An NAV chart

- Both 12-month and 24-month rolling window return charts

- A 2DUC chart

■ ■ ■

Note: Some of the statistics and chart analytics described in this chapter are my own invention and hence not yet available on any existing software. Many of these statistics and analytical charts can be accessed for free on FundSeeder.com.

PART V

FUNDAMENTAL ANALYSIS

CHAPTER 21

Fourteen Popular Fallacies, or What Not to Do Wrong

The fault, dear trader, is not in the fundamentals, but in ourselves.

(With apologies to Shakespeare)

■ Five Short Scenes

Scene 1

The U.S. Treasury announces a new plan to sell stockpiled gold. Not surprisingly, the market opens with near-limit losses the following day. You reason that the new gold sales will sharply increase supply and that, therefore, the market still offers a good selling opportunity, even given the decline. You are somewhat concerned about expectations for continued increasing inflation and dollar weakness but decide the gold sale will dominate market action over the near term.

After going short, the market hovers for two days and then, as you expected, breaks sharply. One week later, your trade is substantially in the plus column and convinced that you have caught a new bear market in its infancy, you resolve to hold the position as a long-term trade. The next week, however, the market begins to rally inexplicably, and your profits evaporate. Paradoxically, despite an absence of any meaningful bullish news, the rally continues and prices even surpass the levels they were at before the U.S. Treasury announcement. Your losses continue to grow, and finally you bail out, promising yourself, "That's the last time I trade on fundamentals."

Scene 2

You've done your homework and feel confident the U.S. Department of Agriculture's 50-state Hogs and Pigs report, which will be released in the afternoon, will reflect a large expansion in hog production. You anticipate that hog numbers will be up at least 7 percent over the year-ago level. Hog prices have already sold off sharply in recent weeks, but you reason that a report in line with your expectations will push prices still lower.

Although you are quite familiar with the dangers of riding a position into a major report, this is one time you cannot resist. At the report release time, eyes glued to your computer screen and your heart pounding, you read the critical figure. A smile crosses your face as you see the number. "I knew it!" you shout triumphantly. The report shows hog numbers up 8 percent.

The next day the market opens limit down, and you begin to calculate what your profits will be after three limit-down days—a conservative assumption. But before you can even finish calculating your profits, a strange thing happens: The market begins to rally. By the end of the session, hog prices are actually 100 points higher! The uptrend continues in subsequent trading sessions, and one week later you liquidate your position with a sizable loss. You feel cheated. You were right in your expectations: The report *was* bearish, wasn't it?

Scene 3

You've been long corn for three weeks and it's been one of your best trades ever. The market has moved steadily and sharply higher with export rumors flying in all directions. That evening on the news, the lead story is the official announcement of an additional large grain sale to Japan. Daydreaming, you wonder if this is the trade you will retire on.

Next morning you call your broker. "Corn is due 8 to 10 cents a bushel higher," he says. Not as good as you thought, but it will do. However, by the time corn is ready to open, the call has dropped to unchanged, and the market actually opens 2 cents lower. Several days later, corn has fallen more than 40 cents, and your profits have virtually evaporated.

Scene 4

Cattle futures have rallied to near all-time record highs. You are well aware that cattle supplies are down and expected to remain low, but upon closer examination, you have discovered that supplies were lower in a number of other past situations when prices were lower. You reason the current rally is overdone and go short.

When cattle rallies an additional 10¢/lb, you figure the market is an even better short, and add to your position. Prices are still moving higher when you finally throw in the towel on the trade.

Scene 5

You have read that sugar prices are below costs of production, a factor that seems to suggest that prices have overdone the down side. You go long. Not only does the price fail to rise, but it actually continues to slide steadily lower. You can't understand why producers continue to sell sugar at a loss. You are both confused and frustrated at the seemingly logic-defying market price action as your losses continue to mount.

▦   ▦   ▦

These five scenes appear to provide proof that fundamental analysis just does not work. At least, that is the conclusion a great many futures traders have drawn from such experiences.

The simple truth, however, is that much that passes for fundamental analysis is either incomplete or incorrect—and frequently both. The trader who ignores fundamentals completely is almost certainly better off than the trader who uses fundamentals incorrectly. However, this in no way alters the fact that good fundamental analysis is a useful, and even powerful, tool.

Before turning to how to do things right, it is essential to first cover what not to do wrong. We begin by exploring 14 common fallacies in fundamental analysis. Incidentally, these fallacies do not represent mistakes made solely by the novice trader. In fact, virtually all these errors have been repeated numerous times in the most respected financial news outlets and in myriad commodity research publications. There is no significance to the order of the list.

■ The Fourteen Fallacies

1. Viewing Fundamentals in a Vacuum

"The fundamentals are bearish" is often thought to be synonymous with an abundant supply situation. Such an interpretation might seem plausible, but it can lead to inaccurate conclusions.

For example, assume the sugar market is trading at 30¢/lb. and in transition from tightness to surplus. Given this scenario, the fundamentals can indeed be termed "bearish," and an expectation of lower prices would be reasonable. Assume that prices begin to move lower. Are the fundamentals still bearish at 25¢? Very likely. At 20¢? Maybe. At 15¢? At 10¢? At 5¢? The point is that at some price level, the fundamentals are no longer bearish, no matter how large the projected supply.

In fact, it is entirely possible that the fundamentals could be bullish in a surplus situation if prices have overdone the downside—a situation that is far from infrequent. Thus, fundamentals are not bullish or bearish in themselves; they are only bullish or bearish relative to price. The failure of many analysts to realize or acknowledge this fact is the reason why the fundamentals are so often termed *bullish* at market tops and *bearish* at market bottoms.

2. Viewing Old Information as New

Financial news outlets frequently report old information and new information in much the same manner. For example, a story with the headline "World Cotton Production Projected to Rise 10 Percent" may sound very bearish. However, what the story is not likely to indicate is that this may be the fourth or fifth such estimate released. Very likely, the previous month's estimate also projected an approximate 10 percent increase in world production. For that matter, the previous month's estimate might have forecast a 12 percent increase, and the current estimate actually represents a price-constructive development. The main point to keep in mind is that much information that sounds new is actually old news, long discounted by the market.

3. One-Year Comparisons

The use of one-year comparisons is fairly widespread, probably because it offers a simple means of instant analysis. This approach is overly simplistic, however, and should be avoided. For example, consider the following market commentary: "The December Hogs & Pigs Report indicates that large pork supplies are around the corner. Market hogs on all farms are up 10 percent. The projected 10 percent increase in hog slaughter should push prices lower. . . ." Although this type of analysis could be right on target in some situations, it will be susceptible to error if used consistently.

Sharp-eyed readers may already be citing fallacy number 1—that is, large supplies do not necessarily imply lower prices, since the market may already be discounting such a development. However, some additional potential errors pertain specifically to the one-year comparison. First, just because the December report indicated a 10 percent increase in hog numbers does not mean it implies large supplies. Perhaps hog numbers were extremely low the previous year. Second, the relationship between hog slaughter and market hogs can vary significantly. It is possible that the preceding year the ratio of slaughter to market hogs was abnormally high. In this case, a 10 percent increase in market hogs would imply a smaller increase in slaughter. Although one-year comparisons can be used sparingly for illustrative purposes, they should never represent the sole basis of fundamental analysis.

4. Using Fundamentals for Timing

If this list of fallacies were ordered on the basis of frequency of occurrence, this item would be a strong contender for the number 1 spot. Fundamental analysis is a method for gauging what price is right under given statistical conditions and can be used in constructing annual, quarterly, and in some instances monthly price projections. However, it is ludicrous to attempt to boil supply-demand statistics down to the point at which they provide an instantaneous price signal, which is exactly what some traders do when they rely on fundamentals for timing.

Trading on the basis of market websites, newspaper articles, and newswire stories, falls into this category. It is no surprise that speculators who base their trades on such items are usually spectacularly unsuccessful. The only major exception are those traders who use this type of information in a contrary way, such as viewing the failure of the market to rally after the release of a bullish newswire story as a signal to go short.

The fundamental researcher must also guard against the natural instinct of wanting to take a market position right after completing an analysis that indicates either an underpriced or overpriced situation. The market is not aware of the timing of a researcher's personal price discovery. Even if the analysis is correct, the right time may be three weeks or even three months off. In short, for purposes of timing, even the fundamental analyst should use some form of technical input.

5. Lack of Perspective

Assume the following scenario: Scanning the financial pages one day, you notice the following headline: "Government Officials Estimate 10,000 Head of Cattle Killed in Recent Midwest Winter Storm." Does such a large production loss suggest a major buying opportunity? Wait a minute. What large production loss? Ten thousand cattle might sound like a very big number if you were to picture them on your front lawn, but viewed in terms of a total U.S. cattle population of about 90 million head (and many times that globally), the loss does not even equal the proverbial drop in the bucket.

This example is based on supply, but cases involving domestic consumption or exports could be illustrated just as easily. In each instance, the same question should be asked: How important is the event (e.g., production loss, new export sales) in terms of the total picture?

6. Ignoring Relevant Time Considerations

True or false: Higher grain prices imply higher meat prices. No cheating—think before reading on.

Actually, this is not a fair question, because the answer depends on the time frame. Most people would probably answer true, since rising grain prices do suggest increased costs of production for feedlot operators, a development that would lead to reduced meat production and higher meat prices. (Cost of production is itself a primary source of misconception and is discussed separately.) However, this reasoning is true only for the very long run (2½ years plus).

Over the short to intermediate term—the time frame that is really of primary concern to futures traders—the effect might be exactly the opposite. If high grain prices are effective in influencing cattle feeders to reduce production, the preliminary impact will be increased marketings and lower prices as a result of breeding herd liquidation. Higher grain prices might reduce the weight to which cattle are fed, but this effect is relatively minor. Increased feeding costs would only imply a shift in the flow of supply (since cattle gain weight more slowly on grass) rather than a change in total actual supplies over the longer run.

In the world of economics, the cause-and-effect relationship is not necessarily instantaneous. In some cases, an event will trigger a very quick price response; in other instances, such as the cattle situation, the effect will not occur for many years.

7. Assuming That Prices Cannot Decline Significantly Below the Cost of Production

No matter how many times this old saw is disproved by actual events, it never seems to be laid to rest. The cost of production is not—repeat, not—a price-supporting factor, especially for nonstorable commodities.

Once a commodity is produced, the market does not care about the cost of production. Prices will be determined on the basis of existing supply and demand. If prices fall to the cost of production and there is still a surplus, prices will continue to decline until an equilibrium price level is reached.

Why should producers sell a commodity below the cost of production? The fact is they don't have much choice. Agricultural markets are highly competitive, with literally thousands of sellers. Consequently, any individual is powerless to pass on production costs to the marketplace. Instead, individuals must accept the price that the market will bear. After all, a low price is better than no price.

Of course, an unprofitable situation will lead to production cutbacks, but this will not happen overnight. The minimum time lag might be one year, but in many instances, it will take several years before prices below the cost of production actually result in reduced output. In this sense, fallacy number 7 is a corollary of fallacy number 6—ignoring relevant time considerations. Many commodity markets have witnessed periods in which prices have fallen and stayed below cost of production for years at a time. Keep this empirical reality in mind the next time you read a recommendation to purchase a commodity because it is at or below the cost of production.

8. Improper Inferences

Fallacy number 8 might be best explained by citing some examples. First, cattle-on-feed numbers do not necessarily provide an indication of potential future slaughter. Reason: cattle on feed do not include grass-fed cattle. As long as grass-fed cattle account for a stable percentage of total slaughter, there is no problem. But if the percentage varies widely over time (as has tended to be the case), the straightforward use of cattle-on-feed numbers to predict slaughter can lead to a totally erroneous conclusion. If, for instance, high feed prices influence a shift toward increased grass feeding of cattle, the total number of cattle could be higher, even if the cattle-on-feed figure shows a significant reduction.

Much market analysis and commentary naively ignores the preceding complication in projecting cattle slaughter. How bad is this error? Table 21.1 shows the relationship between percentage changes in cattle on feed and total slaughter. There is a great deal of variability between the two sets of figures. In fact, from 1995 through 2014 there were 34 quarters when the deviation in percentage changes between cattle on feed and total slaughter exceeded 5 percent and seven quarters with deviations greater than 10 percent! It is not an overstatement to say that one can achieve *far* more accurate slaughter projections using the naive assumption that slaughter in any given quarter will equal the corresponding previous year's level. This is a clear example of no information being far preferable to incorrectly used information.

TABLE 21.1	Percentage Changes in Cattle on Feed Numbers Versus Percentage Changes in Slaughter		
Quarter	Cattle on Feed as Percentage of Previous Year	Cattle Slaughter as Percentage of Previous Year	Discrepancy between Two Percentages[a]
Jan-2015	94.48%	100.98%	6.50%
Oct-2014	91.17%	99.49%	8.31%
Jul-2014	91.72%	97.61%	5.89%
Apr-2014	94.14%	99.53%	5.39%
Jan-2014	94.77%	94.79%	0.02%
Oct-2013	97.01%	92.31%	−4.70%
Jul-2013	99.85%	96.81%	−3.05%
Apr-2013	100.19%	95.01%	−5.18%
Jan-2013	96.95%	94.37%	−2.58%
Oct-2012	98.66%	97.40%	−1.26%
Jul-2012	95.37%	102.66%	7.28%
Apr-2012	96.18%	102.00%	5.82%

TABLE 21.1   (*Continued*)

Quarter	Cattle on Feed as Percentage of Previous Year	Cattle Slaughter as Percentage of Previous Year	Discrepancy between Two Percentages[a]
Jan-2012	96.53%	103.02%	6.49%
Oct-2011	97.00%	104.86%	7.85%
Jul-2011	99.84%	103.74%	3.90%
Apr-2011	99.54%	104.92%	5.39%
Jan-2011	101.85%	104.83%	2.99%
Oct-2010	105.02%	102.91%	−2.10%
Jul-2010	102.74%	103.26%	0.52%
Apr-2010	100.89%	96.46%	−4.42%
Jan-2010	102.36%	97.99%	−4.37%
Oct-2009	100.78%	100.57%	−0.22%
Jul-2009	96.14%	94.73%	−1.41%
Apr-2009	94.99%	95.53%	0.54%
Jan-2009	96.44%	92.90%	−3.53%
Oct-2008	95.30%	94.97%	−0.33%
Jul-2008	101.84%	95.88%	−5.96%
Apr-2008	102.58%	100.34%	−2.24%
Jan-2008	101.42%	101.03%	−0.39%
Oct-2007	103.22%	96.33%	−6.89%
Jul-2007	99.60%	98.76%	−0.84%
Apr-2007	100.25%	98.58%	−1.67%
Jan-2007	103.97%	101.44%	−2.53%
Oct-2006	103.73%	108.61%	4.89%
Jul-2006	102.94%	104.60%	1.66%
Apr-2006	106.22%	108.64%	2.41%
Jan-2006	103.25%	104.47%	1.22%
Oct-2005	100.45%	99.81%	−0.64%
Jul-2005	101.69%	102.57%	0.88%
Apr-2005	97.22%	100.99%	3.77%
Jan-2005	96.43%	100.41%	3.98%
Oct-2004	98.28%	102.73%	4.45%
Jul-2004	87.31%	101.96%	14.65%
Apr-2004	90.09%	100.33%	10.24%
Jan-2004	94.33%	105.58%	11.26%
Oct-2003	91.22%	98.05%	6.83%
Jul-2003	103.14%	94.62%	−8.51%
Apr-2003	103.37%	92.45%	−10.92%
Jan-2003	99.29%	91.60%	−7.70%
Oct-2002	100.62%	93.63%	−6.99%

(*Continued*)

TABLE 21.1 *(Continued)*

Quarter	Cattle on Feed as Percentage of Previous Year	Cattle Slaughter as Percentage of Previous Year	Discrepancy between Two Percentages[a]
Jul-2002	103.08%	95.24%	−7.84%
Apr-2002	101.37%	100.47%	−0.90%
Jan-2002	98.93%	98.03%	−0.91%
Oct-2001	100.65%	100.99%	0.34%
Jul-2001	97.13%	105.89%	8.76%
Apr-2001	98.22%	102.87%	4.65%
Jan-2001	94.41%	102.81%	8.40%
Oct-2000	98.64%	107.20%	8.56%
Jul-2000	99.18%	108.61%	9.43%
Apr-2000	100.26%	107.58%	7.33%
Jan-2000	103.09%	107.57%	4.48%
Oct-1999	102.15%	104.96%	2.81%
Jul-1999	102.89%	104.30%	1.41%
Apr-1999	102.03%	102.63%	0.60%
Jan-1999	100.62%	95.63%	−4.99%
Oct-1998	98.42%	97.83%	−0.59%
Jul-1998	97.99%	102.27%	4.28%
Apr-1998	96.69%	97.27%	0.58%
Jan-1998	97.54%	105.65%	8.11%
Oct-1997	99.57%	112.69%	13.12%
Jul-1997	101.46%	114.26%	12.80%
Apr-1997	97.00%	105.90%	8.90%
Jan-1997	99.19%	102.05%	2.86%
Oct-1996	100.12%	96.94%	−3.17%
Jul-1996	98.32%	85.05%	−13.27%
Apr-1996	105.91%	99.50%	−6.42%
Jan-1996	106.58%	107.92%	1.34%
Oct-1995	103.04%	101.63%	−1.41%
Jul-1995	105.14%	106.00%	0.85%
Apr-1995	105.48%	100.17%	−5.31%
Jan-1995	103.14%	94.61%	−8.53%
		Avg. (abs)	4.73%
		Med. (abs)	4.40%
		Max. (abs)	14.65%
		Min. (abs)	0.02%
Qtrs. w/ abs discrepancy ≥ 5%			34
Qtrs. w/ abs discrepancy ≥ 10%			7

[a]Column 2 minus column 3 percentages.

Another example of an improper inference is provided by the projection of production from acreage figures. A given percentage change in acreage does not necessarily imply a similar change in production (even assuming equivalent yields). For most crops, the distribution of production is a critically important variable. For example, average cotton yields in some states, such as California, are approximately three times as high as average yields in other states, such as Texas. Although considerably more time consuming, production projections should be based on a breakdown of acreage by area (region or state) rather than on a total acreage figure.

9. Comparing Nominal Price Levels

It is inaccurate to compare current prices with the actual recorded prices of previous years. In drawing comparisons with past seasons, it is necessary to adjust historical prices for inflation. Even though U.S. inflation has been subdued since the mid-1980s, over broad periods of time, even low inflation can have a significant cumulative effect. Moreover, in the future, higher inflation levels could recur, making this factor a critical consideration.

As an example, assume that an exhaustive survey of the statistical data for commodity x in past years indicates that 1997 and 2003 were very similar to the current season in terms of overall fundamentals. Does this observation imply that current-season prices will be about in line with the price levels of 1997 and 2003? Of course not. In real dollar terms, the prices may be roughly equivalent, but because of the impact of inflation, current nominal prices are likely to be higher.

Inflation cannot be considered in a vacuum, however. For example, a protracted downshift in demand for most physical commodities (resulting from reduced inventory requirements) beginning around 1980 provided a counterbalancing force to inflation. Because demand is very difficult to quantify—as will be discussed in detail in Chapter 22—the net effect is that inflation-adjusted forecasts can be biased to the high side. In other words, ironically, in some cases it is possible that a naive analyst who ignores both demand shifts and inflation adjustments may derive a more accurate forecast than the analyst who adjusts for inflation. Such accidental accuracy is likely to be a temporary phenomenon. The correct procedure would be to incorporate inflation adjustments in the model and then infer and include demand shifts in the model as well.

10. Ignoring Expectations

Markets often place greater emphasis on expectations for the following year (or season) than on prevailing fundamentals. This pattern is especially true in transitional periods when the supply situation is moving from surplus to tightness, or vice versa.

The 1990 wheat market provided an excellent example. In the 1989–1990 season, the winter wheat crop proved very disappointing because of below-average yields. As a result, carryover stocks (measured as a percent of utilization) fell to their lowest level in 15 years. Moreover, winter wheat seedings for the 1990 crop increased only slightly, thereby seeming to suggest the extension of a tight supply situation into the new season.

Despite the apparent bullish scenario, wheat prices moved steadily and sharply lower from the very beginning of 1990. This price slide cannot be explained in terms of prevailing fundamentals, but only in terms of expectations. As the year progressed, it became increasingly evident that the

1990–1991 hard red winter wheat crop would result in extremely good yields. As it turned out, the yield of the 1990–1991 winter wheat crop increased by an imposing 16 percent over the previous season's level, and the percentage of planted acreage harvested rose from 75 percent to 88 percent. As a result of excellent yields and sharply lower acreage abandonment, 1990–1991 winter wheat production increased by a huge 39 percent, despite the fact that planted acreage was only marginally higher, and carryover stocks returned to comfortable levels.

Although the fundamental transition just described was reflected by data available after mid-spring 1990, during early 1990 such changes would have fallen into the category of expectations. Thus, price action in the wheat market during the first half of 1990 provided a classic example of expectations dominating prevailing fundamentals.

11. Ignoring Seasonal Considerations

Almost every commodity exhibits one or more seasonal patterns. Ignoring seasonal factors can easily lead to the misinterpretation of fundamental data. For example, a 5 percent increase in hog slaughter during the fourth quarter relative to the third-quarter level would actually be indicative of a trend toward reduced production—not expanded production. The explanation behind this apparent paradoxical statement lies in the fact that hog production is highly seasonal. Producers breed hogs so that the largest pig crop is born during the spring and the smallest in winter. Because it takes approximately six months for hogs to reach market weight, slaughter tends to be heaviest during the fall and lightest during the summer. Thus, it is essential to adjust for the seasonal production pattern in drawing slaughter comparisons between the current period and the preceding month or quarter.

Comparisons of production and consumption figures with the corresponding figures of previous years obviously do not require any consideration of seasonal factors. However, if comparisons of fundamental data involve different time periods during the year, it is essential to examine historical data carefully for possible seasonal behavior and to make any necessary adjustments.

12. Expecting Prices to Conform to Target Levels in World Trade Agreements

The history of commodities is replete with examples of world trade agreements that totally failed to achieve their stated goals. Trade agreements typically attempt to support prices through export controls and stockpiling plans. Although these provisions provide some underlying support to the market and occasionally even spark temporary rallies, they are usually not sufficiently restrictive to maintain prices significantly above equilibrium levels for any extended period of time. The International Sugar Agreement and the International Cocoa Agreement are two examples of world trade agreements that ultimately failed to support prices above the lower end of their respective stated target ranges (in the years when these agreements attempted to support prices; they no longer even attempt to do so). Perhaps the most effective price-supporting organization has been the Organization of the Petroleum Exporting Countries (OPEC), but even the oil cartel has frequently seen prices fall below their target level—often by a wide margin.

It should be noted that world trade agreements are even more impotent in terms of restraining a price advance. In the case in which prices approach the upper end of a target range, the most powerful action that any agreement could take would be the elimination of all restrictions—in other words, a return to a free market.

13. Drawing Conclusions on the Basis of Insufficient Data

Sometimes it is virtually impossible to construct a fundamental forecasting model for a market because of a lack of sufficient comparative historical data. A perfect case in point was provided in the August 1972 issue of *Commodities* magazine (now called *Modern Trader*), which ran a detailed study of fundamentals in the cotton market. The article ultimately came to the valid conclusion that only two seasons since 1953 could truly be termed *free markets*. As the article explained, during the 1950s and 1960s, government programs had maintained cotton prices above the levels that would have been realized had prices been determined by the interaction of supply and demand. So far, so good.

The proper and very worthwhile conclusion would have been that existing data were insufficient to permit the use of fundamentals in forecasting prices. After all, how can you interpret the price implications of a projected statistical balance if there are only two previous years to use as a comparison?

Unfortunately, the author went on to sketch an entire set of price forecasting conclusions on the basis of admittedly very limited relevant information. Quoting the first item, "Final stock levels under 3½ million bales imply a very tight supply situation and suggest a likelihood of a price rise well above 30¢ in such seasons."

Although this statement certainly proved true, by implication it severely understated the upside potential in the cotton market. Only a little more than one year after the article was published, cotton prices reached an all-time peak of 99¢/lb. Incidentally, I was the author of that article.

14. Confusing the Concepts of Demand and Consumption

Demand is probably one of the two most misused words in futures literature and analysis (parameter being the other; see Chapter 19). The confusion between demand and consumption is not a matter of semantics; the two terms represent very different concepts, and their frequent interchangeable use leads to many major analytical errors. An adequate explanation of this statement requires a diversion into a short review of basic supply-demand theory, which is the subject of the next chapter.

At this point, it might be instructive to return to the five scenes depicted at the beginning of this chapter to try to determine which of the 14 fallacies were responsible for the incorrect trading conclusions. Note that each scene reflects two or more fallacies. The answers can be found in Table 21.2.

TABLE 21.2	Fallacies Committed in the Five Scenes
Scene	Fallacies[a]
1	4, 5, 10
2	1, 3, 4
3	2, 4
4	9, 10
5	7

[a]The inclusion of additional items is not necessarily incorrect. Other fallacies might also be applicable (e.g., fallacy number 1 in any of the scenes), but are not listed because the text provides insufficient information to make such a determination.

CHAPTER 22

Supply-Demand Analysis: Basic Economic Theory

There are in the fields of economics no consistent relations, and consequently, no measurement is possible.

—Ludwig Edler von Mises

■ Supply and Demand Defined

Supply curves slope upward, meaning more is offered to the market at higher prices (Figure 22.1).[1] Assuming that the time unit shown on the horizontal axis in Figure 22.1 equals one season, the supply that can be offered to the market will be limited to total production plus stocks, regardless of the price. At high prices, however, producers will be willing to hold smaller inventories and therefore offer greater quantities to the market. Conversely, at lower prices, producers will prefer to store

---

[1] The supply and demand curves in this section are drawn as straight lines for simplicity of exposition. It also seemed desirable to avoid the unnecessary digression of discussing the factors that determine the precise shapes of these curves. Although the straight-line assumption may often be adequate within normal boundaries, supply and demand curves will not be linear over the entire price range. For example, as prices rise and the quantity consumed declines, it will usually take greater and greater increases in price to induce a given further reduction in the amount consumed. As another example, over the short run, at some point the supply curve must begin to rise asymptotically, since the supply offered to the market cannot exceed the existing total supply (i.e., stocks plus current production).

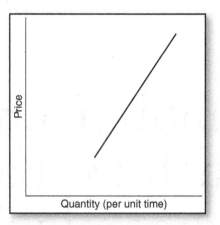

FIGURE 22.1 Supply Curve

larger quantities rather than marketing their goods at prevailing depressed levels. The slope of the supply curve will reflect this tradeoff between the options of sale and storage.[2]

For perishable (e.g., eggs, potatoes[3]) or nonstorable (e.g., cattle, hogs) commodities, supply is approximately fixed and can be represented by a vertical line (Figure 22.2). For example, if a supply curve is drawn for the hog market for a time unit of one-half year, the amount offered to the market during that period will be relatively independent of market prices. Low prices will not reduce the quantity supplied, because once hogs reach market weight, with the exception of temporary delays, producers have little choice but to bring those hogs to market, regardless of the price. However, since there is a lag of nearly one year between producers' breeding decisions and the time that resulting

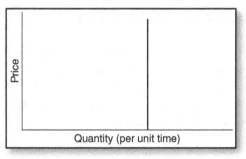

FIGURE 22.2 Fixed Supply

---

[2] For longer time units (e.g., 10 years), the supply curve will also reflect the potential for an expansion in production beyond current levels. For example, high prices may encourage shifts in acreage to the high-priced commodity and increased usage of fertilizer in new crops. From the vantage point of futures trading, however, it is most useful to limit the discussion of supply and demand to short time units (i.e., season or fraction of a season).

[3] These commodities are no longer traded as futures markets, but provide perfect illustrations of perishable goods.

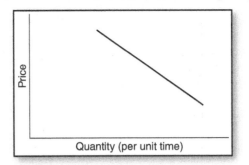

FIGURE 22.3 Demand Curve

offspring reach market weight, high prices cannot induce an increase in the quantity supplied. In fact, if anything, the supply curve in such a market exhibits a perverse behavior; that is, high prices will reduce the quantity supplied. The reason is that high prices will influence producers to withhold hogs from the market for breeding, thereby reducing current supplies. However, for simplicity's sake, we will assume a vertical supply curve in the case of perishable or nonstorable commodities.

Demand can be defined as a schedule of the various quantities of a commodity that will be consumed at each price level. In a sense, demand is a barometer of consumer buying pressure. Demand curves slope downward, meaning more will be demanded at lower prices (Figure 22.3).

Elasticity of demand can be defined as the percentage increase in the amount demanded divided by the percentage decrease in price. If the demand for a commodity is inelastic, it means that a relatively large percentage change in price will only induce a small percentage change in the amount demanded. Figure 22.4 presents illustrations of elastic and inelastic demand curves.[4]

The elasticity of demand is primarily determined by two basic factors:

1. **Availability of substitutes.** The elasticity of demand will vary directly with the availability of substitutes. For example, the demand for salt is highly inelastic, but the demand for a given brand of salt is very elastic.

2. **Percentage of total income spent on the good.** The elasticity of demand will vary directly with the percentage of expenditures allocated to a good. For example, the demand for automobiles is far more elastic than the demand for salt, even though there are no close substitutes for either item.

Generally speaking, the demand curves for most commodities tend to be inelastic; that is, a given percentage change in price will induce a smaller opposite percentage change in the amount demanded. This is a significant consideration, since prices of goods with inelastic demand curves are more subject to wide price swings in times of shortage.

---

[4] Elasticity is not constant along each demand curve. Elasticity is a concept that relates to a given point, not to the entire curve. As we move rightward along a line or demand curve (in both the elastic and inelastic cases), the elasticity of demand will decrease, since any given change in price will represent a larger percentage change, and will influence the same absolute, but smaller percentage, change in the quantity demanded. In other words, as can be verified in Figure 22.4, rightward movement along the demand curve will increase the denominator and decrease the numerator of the elasticity of demand.

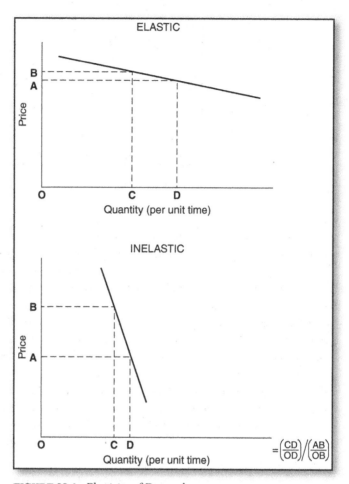

FIGURE 22.4 Elasticity of Demand

■ The Problem of Quantifying Demand

As all students of Economics 101 know, price is determined by the intersection of the supply and demand curves (Figure 22.5). However, there is one major problem in using supply-demand analysis to project prices: Demand is not readily quantifiable—that is, there is no way of determining how much will be consumed at any given price level. Whereas in most cases supply can be either approximately fixed as in the case of perishable and nonstorable commodities, or at least roughly estimated using production and stock statistics,[5] demand is entirely intangible. It is hardly feasible to query all

------

[5] The precious metal markets provide an important exception. See the section, Why Traditional Fundamental Analysis Doesn't Work in the Gold Market, at the end of this chapter.

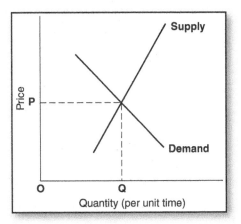

FIGURE 22.5 Equilibrium

potential consumers as to the amount of a good they would purchase at various price levels. Even if a sampling procedure were used—presumably an impractical and prohibitively expensive approach for the analyst—there is no reason to assume that consumers could even describe their demand curves.

The only theoretically acceptable means of quantifying demand is to infer demand curves through a detailed analysis of historical consumption and price data. Although this is an easy task if demand is relatively stable, unfortunately, it is either difficult or impossible if demand is subject to frequent wide shifts.

Understanding the Difference between Consumption and Demand

Perhaps the most commonly employed solution to the problem of quantifying demand is the use of consumption as a proxy for demand. This approach, however, has one major drawback: It is totally incorrect. The synonymous use of consumption and demand represents a confusion of two entirely different concepts. *Consumption* is the amount of a good used and is determined by price, which in turn is determined by supply and demand factors. *Demand* refers to the amount of a good that will be used at any given price level and, along with supply, determines price.

An increase in demand means that more will be consumed at any given price level (Figure 22.6). Factors that might affect demand include disposable income, consumer tastes, and the price of substitute goods but, by definition, not price. For most commodities, a rise in disposable income will result in an increase in demand; that is, at each given price, more will be consumed than before. A price decline will lead to increased consumption, showing movement along the same demand curve, but it does not imply anything about demand. In other words, all else being equal, the same amount will be consumed at each given price level unless there is a change in demand.

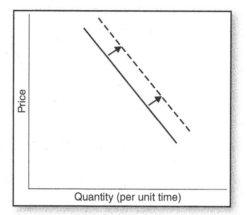

FIGURE 22.6 Increase in Demand

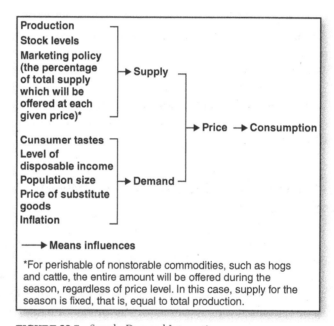

Production
Stock levels
Marketing policy
(the percentage
of total supply
which will be
offered at each
given price)*] → Supply]

→ Price → Consumption

Cunsumer tastes]
Level of
disposable income
Population size → Demand]
Price of substitute
goods
Inflation]

⟶ Means influences

*For perishable of nonstorable commodities, such as hogs
and cattle, the entire amount will be offered during the
season, regardless of price level. In this case, supply for the
season is fixed, that is, equal to total production.

FIGURE 22.7 Supply-Demand Interaction

Figure 22.7 summarizes the relationship between demand and consumption. Consumption (i.e., the amount consumed) is directly dependent on price, where price is determined by the interaction of supply and demand. The key point to keep in mind: Consumption is a consequence of price, not a determinant of price. Thus the concept that consumption mirrors demand is totally erroneous; consumption is determined by *both* supply and demand.

In fact, for perishable and nonstorable commodities, consumption primarily reflects supply, not demand. For example, assume that pork consumption has increased sharply. Does this mean that pork demand has suddenly improved dramatically? Absolutely not. The consumption increase is merely the result of increased hog slaughter. Recalling that the supply curve for hogs (and therefore pork) can be approximated by a vertical line, Figure 22.8 demonstrates the consumption level will be determined by supply and will be the same, no matter which demand curve prevails. Thus, an increase in consumption would merely reflect an increase, or rightward shift, in supply—a bearish development—and not an increase in demand, which would be a bullish development.

It is entirely possible for a demand increase and a consumption decrease to occur simultaneously. Figure 22.9 illustrates how this is possible for both the variable supply and fixed supply cases. At the

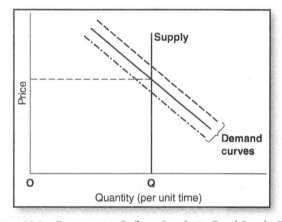

FIGURE 22.8   Consumption Reflects Supply (in Fixed Supply Case)

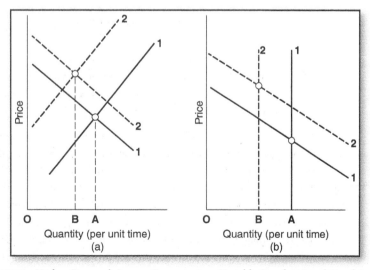

FIGURE 22.9   Higher Demand, Lower Consumption: Variable Supply (a) and Fixed Supply (b)

start, in period 1, the equilibrium consumption level is at point A. Although demand increases in period 2, the equilibrium consumption level declines to B as a result of the decline in supply.

Even the U.S. Department of Agriculture (USDA), one of the nation's leading employers of economists, has misused the term *demand*. The popularly termed *supply-demand* reports are in reality supply-disappearance reports (with *disappearance* defined as total domestic consumption plus exports).

Quite frequently, when the USDA changes its estimates for items that are sometimes discussed under the label of "demand" (domestic consumption, exports),[6] the revision reflects a change in supply, not demand. For example, if the projected carryover for a commodity is already at estimated minimum pipeline requirements, a reduced production forecast will mean that the USDA has to lower either the domestic consumption estimate, the export estimate, or both. Otherwise, the USDA might find itself in the absurd position of projecting a near-zero or even negative carryover. However, the key point is that such revisions do not imply that demand has been reduced—a bearish conclusion—but rather that high prices will ration scarce supplies, thereby resulting in reduced usage.

■ The Need to Incorporate Demand

Because of the difficulties involved in quantifying demand, there is often a temptation to concentrate solely on supply factors in constructing a fundamental price-forecasting model. This can be a grave error, because a demand shift can often be the dominant force in a major price move. The 1980–1982 copper market provided a classic example of the dangers of ignoring demand. To focus in on this example, we will examine a 21-year segment of the copper market (1973–1993) that contains three major bull-bear price cycles, with the bear phase of the middle cycle containing the 1980–1982 market that is the center of our attention.

Consider the following copper price-forecasting model:

$$P = f\left(\frac{S}{C}\right)$$

where P = average deflated copper price during the period

S = copper stock level (U.S. plus foreign refined copper stocks)

C = copper consumption level during the period (annualized refined copper deliveries, United States plus foreign)

$f(\ )$ is read as "is a function of," which basically means "is dependent on."

At surface glance, this model seems reasonably plausible. In essence, the model implies that prices will be low when copper stocks are large relative to the usage level and high in the reverse case. This model certainly seems logical enough. Figure 22.10, which illustrates the relationship between copper prices and the stock/consumption ratio during a 21-year segment (1973–1993) that is centered near the 1980–1982 bear market that we wish to focus on, appears to confirm this expected market behavior. The strong inverse correlation between the stock/consumption ratio and copper prices is

---

[6] USDA report tables, however, correctly label these items as components of "disappearance."

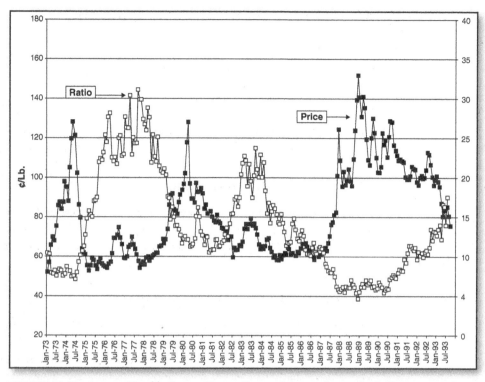

FIGURE 22.10 Average Monthly Copper Nearest Futures Price vs. Copper Stock/Consumption Ratio

broadly evident across the entire period shown. However, note the seemingly puzzling 1980 to mid-1982 price behavior. During this period, prices plunged dramatically despite a slide in the stock/consumption ratio to a major low. How can this counter-to-expected price action be explained?

There is no mystery. Although the stock/consumption ratio is an important price-influencing factor, it only reflects supply. The apparent paradoxical behavior from 1980 to mid-1982 is explained by the fact that the model does not incorporate demand. During this period, the anticipation and ultimate realization of a severe recession combined with high real interest rates (interest rate minus inflation rate) drastically reduced the inventories users wished to hold at each given price level. In other words, there was a sharp downward shift in the demand curve. This crucial fundamental development simply could not be reflected by the model just described.

The moral is that it is always necessary to take demand into account. The next section discusses several methods for incorporating demand in the price-forecasting model. But even when this type of analysis is not possible, demand must still be considered. If demand is not part of the model because of the inherent difficulties in quantifying demand, then the analysis should be divided into two steps:

1. Model projection
2. Informal evaluation of the potential impact of demand factors

■ Possible Methods for Incorporating Demand

How can the problem of nonquantifiable demand be circumvented? The answer depends on the market. The following types of markets permit various solutions to the problem of quantifying demand:

Stable Demand

For some markets, the supposition that demand is stable is a reasonable simplifying assumption. In effect, in this type of market, fundamental price forecasts can be based strictly on supply statistics.

Growth Pattern in Demand Change

For other markets, although demand changes from year to year, the pattern of change can be described by a simplified assumption (e.g., demand increases by 3 percent annually). For markets of this type, demand can be represented by an index that changes in a manner consistent with the assumed growth pattern for demand.

Identification of Demand-Influencing Variables

For some markets, although changes in demand cannot be described by any consistent growth pattern, the factors that affect demand can be identified. For example, beef demand increases in some years and decreases in others. Nevertheless, it can easily be demonstrated that these shifts are dependent on other identifiable factors, such as availability of competitive meat supplies. In such cases, one can bypass the problem of precisely specifying the demand curve by directly formulating a price-forecasting model that uses supply statistics and the factors determining demand as inputs. An example of such a model is given by the following equation:

$$QCP = f(CS, HS, BS, T)$$

where QCP = average quarterly cattle price
CS = quarterly cattle slaughter
HS = quarterly hog slaughter
BS = quarterly broiler slaughter
T = time trend

In the preceding example, CS represents a supply variable, while $HS, BS,$ and T represent variables that affect demand. Trend affects demand through inflation (more will be demanded at each nominal price level because of inflation) and possible other factors that have a trending characteristic.

As another example, in attempting to forecast copper prices, one of the ways we could incorporate the demand effect would be by focusing on the level of activity in the key copper-using industries. Figure 22.11 illustrates the relationship between copper prices and an index of new housing for the same 21-year period that was surveyed in Figure 22.10. Figure 22.12 illustrates the relationship between copper prices and domestic auto sales during the same period. Note how the

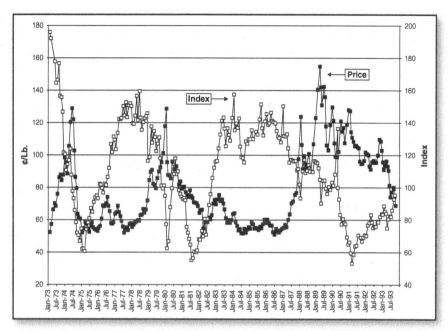

FIGURE 22.11 Average Monthly Copper Nearest Futures Price vs. Index of New Private Housing

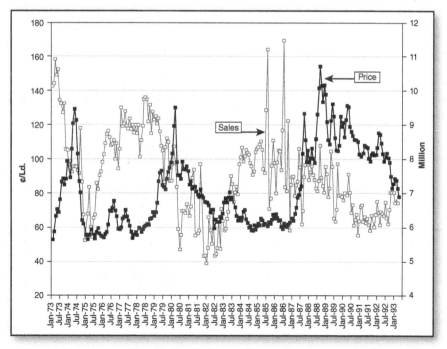

FIGURE 22.12 Average Monthly Copper Nearest Futures Price vs. Annualized Seasonally Adjusted Auto Sales

declines in housing starts and automobile sales *preceded* downturns in copper prices, including the 1980 to mid-1982 decline. Recall from the previous section that the imposing 1980 to mid-1982 bear market seemed somewhat puzzling when viewed solely relative to the stock/consumption ratio. Figure 22.11 and 22.12 illustrate how this seeming paradox can be resolved once demand factors are considered. Of course, the specific demand factors included would change over time. For example, our copper illustration focused on the 1973–1993 time segment. In a current copper price model, indicators of emerging market demand would be far more critical than they were then.

Highly Inelastic Demand (and Supply Elastic Relative to Demand)

Although conceptually incorrect, practically speaking, for markets of this type it is possible to use consumption as a proxy for demand. Since by definition in these markets consumption in a given year will not vary widely, regardless of price level, one can assume the prevailing consumption level roughly reflects the demand level. For example, Figure 22.13 illustrates a series of inelastic demand curves and two different supply curves. Note how the quantity consumed at the equilibrium price level is primarily dependent on the prevailing demand curve. Hence, consumption can serve as a proxy indicator for the unknown demand curve.

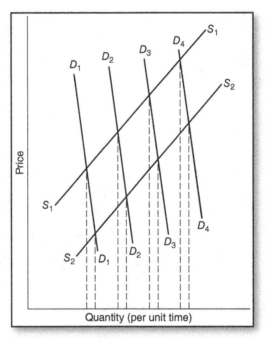

FIGURE 22.13   Consumption as Proxy for Inelastic Demand

An example of this approach is provided by the following model:

$$DASP = f\left(\frac{IS + P}{C}\right)$$

where $DASP$ = deflated average annual sugar price
  IS = initial stocks
  P = production
  C = consumption

Note that initial stocks plus production is a proxy for supply, and consumption is a proxy for demand.

■ Why Traditional Fundamental Analysis Doesn't Work in the Gold Market

Unfortunately, the approaches we have enumerated for dealing with the elusiveness of demand do not encompass all cases. For some markets, not only is demand highly erratic, it is also difficult or nearly impossible to define a stable relationship that describes the precise dependence of demand on other variables.

Gold is a perfect example of such a market. Gold demand is basically dependent on the market's psychological perception of the value of gold, which in turn is dependent on a myriad of interrelated variables, including relative inflation rates, world interest rates, currency fluctuations, trade balance figures, OPEC actions, and political turmoil. The problem of specifying gold demand is further complicated by the fact that the relative importance of any of these factors in influencing gold demand is subject to considerable variation. For example, during some periods, currency fluctuations may become the pivotal price-influencing factor, while at other times developments in this area exert only a minor price impact.

In the case of gold, even the supply side of the equation cannot be readily approximated. Similar to demand, supply is subject to wide, erratic shifts that are also dependent on market psychology. This instability of the supply curve is primarily attributable to shifts in dishoarding rather than to changes in commercial supply.

The combination of highly erratic, intangible supply and demand curves makes the gold market a fundamental analyst's nightmare. Some analysts attempt to construct a fundamental model for gold by focusing on such statistics as mine production and industrial usage. This approach represents true folly, since these figures are equal to only a minuscule fraction of total gold supply. Gold prices are dependent on the psychological considerations detailed earlier, and there is no way to avoid this fact.

In effect, for a market such as gold, the traditional fundamental approach just does not work. Constructing an econometric model to predict gold prices is like trying to write a computer program that will predict a photographer's next picture on the basis of her past shots—the answer may be somewhat better than a blind guess but is hardly worth the effort.

CHAPTER 23

Types of Fundamental Analysis

When you can measure what you are speaking about, and express it in numbers, you know something about it; but when you cannot measure it, when you cannot express it in numbers, your knowledge is of a meager and unsatisfactory kind: it may be the beginnings of knowledge, but you have scarcely, in your thoughts, advanced to the stage of science.

—William Thomson, Lord Kelvin

■ The "Old Hand" Approach

The "old hand" approach refers to the analytical method used by analysts whose familiarity with the market is so finely honed that they have developed a virtual sixth sense with respect to its price fluctuations. By talking to a variety of commercial participants, they get a feel for market tone. They are also well tuned in to the flow of market news and are constantly assessing the market's behavior in response to this information. This is strictly a nonscientific approach, with the individual acting as the computer. It is not intrinsically inferior to more sophisticated approaches; its value is strictly dependent on the skills and intuition of the practitioner. In fact, it is hardly unusual for some analysts of this school to consistently outperform their econometrically oriented counterparts. This approach is strictly individualistic, however, and by definition can only be acquired by personal experience.

■ The Balance Table

The balance table summarizes the key components of current-season supply and disappearance, along with prior-season comparisons. The balance between supply and disappearance will indicate a season-ending carryover; it is the relative magnitude of this figure that is considered the primary price-determining statistic. Table 23.1 illustrates a U.S. Department of Agriculture (USDA) balance table

TABLE 23.1	U.S. Wheat Supply/Disappearance Balance, June–May Crop Year (million bushels)					
	1988–1989	1989–1990	1990–1991	1991–1992	1992–1993	1993–1994[a]
Beginning stocks	1,261	702	536	366	472	529
Imports	23	23	37	41	70	75
Production	1,812	2,037	2,736	1,981	2,459	2,493
Total supply	**3,096**	**2,762**	**3,309**	**2,888**	**3,001**	**3,097**
Food use	726	749	786	789	829	845
Seed use	103	100	90	94	93	94
Feed/Residual	146	143	500	254	196	325
Total domestic use	975	992	1,376	1,137	1,118	1,264
Exports	1,419	1,233	1,068	1,280	1,354	1,125
Total disappearance	**2,394**	**2,225**	**2,444**	**2,416**	**2,472**	**2,389**
Ending stocks	**702**	**536**	**866**	**472**	**529**	**708**
Ending stocks as % of total use	29	24	35	20	21	30

[a]Projected.

Source: USDA.

for the wheat market. The analyst who relies heavily on the balance table will focus on possible shifts in the various components of supply and disappearance in an effort to anticipate the probable direction of price change.

The balance table is a valuable aid that succinctly summarizes the key market statistics. By itself, however, the balance table is insufficient in answering the critical question of what price is right under the given conditions. In fact, the analyst who uses only the balance-table approach to forecast prices will be guilty of fallacy number 1 detailed in Chapter 21 (i.e., viewing fundamentals in a vacuum).

■ The Analogous Season Method

In the *analogous season method,* the analyst finds past seasons that shared the same fundamental characteristics of a current season and then uses the price profiles of those analogous seasons as a "road map" in projecting current season price swings. For example, if in the current season production is up, usage is down, and the ending stocks/usage ratio is down, the analyst might find all past seasons that also exhibited these conditions. Next, the analyst would identify key price turning points in the analogous seasons (e.g., harvest low, postharvest high, winter low, crop-scare high). The timing and relative magnitude of price swings between these key turning points would then be calculated for each past analogous season. Finally, price swing ranges and turning point time windows would be projected for the current season, based on the assumption that the current season price patterns would be at least roughly similar to the price action of prior analogous seasons.

■ Regression Analysis

How can you determine which fundamental factors are most important in determining price levels? Even assuming you can make a reasonable conjecture as to what are the key fundamental factors influencing prices, how can you translate the current levels of these factors into a price forecast? Say, for example, you are trying to forecast hog futures prices. You assume that hog prices will be inversely correlated with hog slaughter levels and also inversely correlated with competitive meat supplies (e.g., broiler slaughter, cattle slaughter). You also assume that for any combination of supply levels for these various meats, prices will be higher in the current year than in past years because of the influence of inflation. Even if all these assumptions are correct, how can you determine the price implications for any given combination of the various meat supplies?

Simply comparing current supply levels to past year levels will not yield any price forecast. For example, what are the price implications of hog slaughter being 3 percent lower than in some prior year while broiler slaughter and cattle slaughter are each 2 percent higher? How does one reconcile the multiple comparisons of the current year to each of the past years examined? How much difference does a given time separation make when drawing comparisons between different years? All of these questions seem impossible to answer by simply comparing current and past data.

Regression analysis provides a statistical procedure that can be used to translate fundamental data into price projections. The assumptions we just made regarding the plausible key influences on hog prices could be formalized into the following equation:

$$P = a + b_1H + b_2B + b_3C + b_4T$$

where P = average price
H = hog slaughter
B = broiler slaughter
C = cattle slaughter
T = time trend

The values of a, b_1, b_2, b_3, and b_4 are determined by the regression analysis procedure (explained in the appendices). Given projections for hog slaughter, broiler slaughter, and cattle slaughter, we can plug those values and the time trend value for the current year into the preceding equation and obtain a precise price forecast.

Even if you are not mathematically inclined, think twice before dismissing the regression-analysis approach. Regression analysis embeds a number of important attributes:

1. Regression analysis makes it possible to combine multiple fundamental inputs, compared across multiple years, to derive a price forecast.
2. Regression analysis can be used to test the relative significance of each of the price-influencing variables (called *independent* variables) as well as the forecasting equation as a whole.
3. Regression analysis provides an efficient learning tool for understanding the interrelationships between various fundamental factors and price.

Regression analysis is probably the single most useful analytical tool in fundamental analysis. Appendices A through F provide an in-depth discussion of regression analysis.

■ Index Models

Sometimes we may wish to construct a fundamental model that uses scores of explanatory variables as indicators of a market's price. For example, we might postulate that bond prices are inversely related to a variety of inflation indicators (e.g., gold prices, S&P Goldman Sachs Commodity Index, consumer price index), economic indicators (e.g., employment, industrial production, housing starts), and monetary indicators (e.g., yield spread). Given the wide range of such indicators, and allowing that each indicator can be used with multiple time lags (as the relationship between bond rates and an indicator will frequently not be contemporaneous), it is easy to see how the number of possible explanatory variables could reach 50 or even higher.

Regression analysis cannot handle situations that involve large numbers of explanatory (independent) variables. Typically, a regression equation will employ five or fewer independent variables. There are two primary reasons why regression analysis cannot be applied to cases involving a multitude of variables:

1. If large numbers of independent variables are used, there is a great danger of overfitting (i.e., deriving a model that is tailored to fit past data but will be useless as a tool for projecting future prices or price trends).
2. When large numbers of independent variables are employed it is virtually inevitable that a number of such variables will be closely related to each other. High correlations among independent variables in a regression model will result in a statistical problem called *multicollinearity,* which destroys the reliability of the derived forecasting equation. (This problem is discussed in greater detail in Appendix E.)

One method of handling a large number of explanatory variables is to combine them all in an index model. The following step-by-step approach illustrates one possible procedure:

1. Assign each indicator a value of +1 if its current status is considered bullish for the price of the given market and a value of −1 if it is considered bearish. (How such a determination is made will be discussed momentarily.)
2. Add all the *assigned* indicator values to obtain an index value.
3. Normalize the index by multiplying by 100 divided by number of indicators. This step will yield an index with a theoretical range of −100 (if all the indicators are bearish) to +100 (if all the indicators are bullish). For example, if there are 50 indicators, and 30 are bullish and 20 bearish, the preceding procedure would yield a normalized index value of +20. Of course, an equal split between bullish and bearish indicators would yield an index value of 0, as is intuitively desirable.

This procedure sounds simple enough. The key question, however, is: how does one determine if a current indicator value is bullish or bearish? Deciding on some value as the division line between bullish and bearish values is highly undesirable for two key reasons: (1) many variables trend over time; and (2) due to structural changes over time, the definition of "high" and "low" will tend to shift for many, if not most, variables. Hence, it is far more practical to categorize a variable as bullish or bearish based on its *direction* of movement (i.e., trend) rather than its *level*. Trend categorization, however, falls more within the realm of technical analysis than fundamental analysis. Indeed, some of the very basic tools of technical analysis (e.g., crossover moving average) can be applied to defining the assigned indicator values in an index model of the type described in this section. For example, if using a crossover moving average to define the trend direction of the indicators, an indicator would be assigned a value of $+1$ if the short-term moving average was greater than the long-term moving average, and a value of -1 in the reverse case.

CHAPTER 24

The Role of Expectations

What we anticipate seldom occurs; what we least expect generally happens.

——Benjamin Disraeli

■ Using Prior-Year Estimates Rather Than Revised Statistics

Historical data are based on final revised estimates rather than the estimates that were available at the time. For example, the historical levels of U.S. corn production are revised throughout the season with the final revision occurring after the end of the season. These final revised estimates for each season (the *actual* levels) can differ substantially from the crop estimates that prevailed during each season (the *expected* levels). Similarly, historical corn consumption and export levels (the actual levels based on final revised estimates) can be very different from the expected levels that prevailed during each season.

Typically, fundamental models would use actual historical data as inputs. But is this default approach the best procedure? A strong argument can be made that the data levels expected at the time are more relevant to explaining price behavior than actual data levels that only became known after the price forecast period in question. Thus, it may be possible to build a more accurate model using past estimates rather than actual statistics as the price-explanatory variables. For example, if we are trying to construct a model to explain and predict September–November corn prices, we might well find that the past production and usage estimates released during the September–November period are more helpful than the actual supply statistics in explaining the year-to-year historical variation in September–November prices. Such price behavior would merely reflect that what the market thought was true in the past was more important in determining prices than what was actually true (as defined by the final revised estimates)—a reasonable outcome given that market participants have no way of determining actual statistics and must rely on prevailing estimates for their marketing, purchasing, and trading decisions.

The key point is that using past expected data rather than actual statistics might be theoretically sounder and may well yield better price-forecasting models. Of course, using past expected statistics in a model will require considerably more work in terms of data gathering, which may explain why such data are far less frequently used than the final revised numbers. As is true for most of life's endeavors, creating a better product (price-forecasting model in this case) requires more effort. There are no shortcuts in doing things right.

■ Adding Expectations as a Variable in the Price-Forecasting Model

Thus far, we have discussed the choice between using anticipated versus actual data for explaining past price variation. Regardless of which is used, one can also consider adding a variable to represent expectations for a key statistic in a following season. To clarify this distinction, we list the four possible variations in the extent to which expectations are incorporated in a model:

1. Price is a function of concurrent-season actual statistics (no use of expectations).
2. Price is a function of estimates for concurrent-season statistics (expectations used for concurrent-season data).
3. Price is a function of concurrent-season actual statistics and expectations for the following season (expectations used for following-season data).
4. Price is a function of concurrent-season estimates and expectations for the following season (expectations used for both concurrent- and following-season data).

The expectations for a coming season can often exert a more pronounced price impact than do prevailing fundamentals. This observation is especially true during the latter half of a season—a time at which the fundamentals for the given season are usually well defined and not subject to large variation. In fact, frequently, when there is a dichotomy between the implications of old-crop fundamentals and new-crop expectations, the latter tend to dominate the price picture.

Why should expectations for a coming season affect current-season prices? Expectations influence current selling and buying psychology. For example, if supplies are burdensome and a shift toward supply tightness is anticipated, sellers will have an incentive to hold back the commodity and will offer less to the market at each given price level (the supply curve will shift upward in response to reduced supply). At the same time, buyers will attempt to build inventories and therefore will purchase increased quantities at any given price level (the demand curve will shift upward). These two effects reinforce each other, and the net result will be higher prices in the current season.

■ The Influence of Expectations on Actual Statistics

Ironically, bullish new-crop expectations can actually cause current-season fundamentals to appear more bearish. The following cause-and-effect diagram illustrates this point:

Bullish expectations for new crop $\rightarrow$ price during old-crop season $\uparrow$ $\rightarrow$
old-crop consumption and exports $\downarrow$ $\rightarrow$ old-crop stocks $\uparrow$

As a result of this string of events, seasons that experience bullish new-crop expectations are likely to appear inexplicably overpriced based on old-crop fundamentals—another reason why new-crop expectations should be incorporated in the price-forecasting model wherever possible.

■ Defining New-Crop Expectations

On the supply side, new-crop expectations can be based on planting intentions and subsequently on acreage estimates. In using these estimates to define expectations, one usually assumes a trend yield (the yield implied by a regression-derived best-fit line of past yields) or an average yield (e.g., five-year average for each state or region) if there is no pronounced trend. Such neutral projections would then be adjusted upward in the case of very favorable growing weather, or downward if conditions were adverse.

On the usage side, expectations are defined by the historical behavior pattern. For example, if in recent years consumption changes for a given commodity have tended to range from −2 percent to +4 percent, as a function of the direction and magnitude of price change, in the absence of any additional information, one might use a 1 percent consumption increase as a representative figure for expected new-crop consumption.

Historical expectation statistics can be generated in a similar manner or by surveying past commentaries in U.S. Department of Agriculture situation reports, trade reports, and industry market reports. Unfortunately, there is some unavoidable arbitrariness in the latter approach, since the expectation figures depend on the sources chosen and on the weights assigned to each source. However, this ambiguity is not a critical drawback, since at any given time, new-crop projections by various sources tend to cluster in the same general area.

CHAPTER 25

Incorporating Inflation

Nothing so weakens government as persistent inflation.

—John Kenneth Galbraith

In designing price-forecasting models, it is essential to keep in mind that the measure of prices—the dollar—is itself a variable. Thus, using nominal prices to compare widely separated years makes as much sense as comparing the dollar price of a commodity in one season to the euro price in another season. It is safe to say that any model that does not adjust for inflation is critically flawed.

Figures 25.1 through 25.4 illustrate the difference between nominal and inflation-adjusted prices in different futures markets from 1995 to 2015. These charts illustrate that adjusting for the effect of inflation can alter the relationship between past highs and lows, as well as the relative magnitudes of prior past moves. For example, in Figure 25.1, the 2004 highs in lumber nearest futures were above the 1996 and 1999 highs in nominal terms (solid line), but lower than these previous peaks on an inflation-adjusted basis (dashed line). In Figure 25.2, in March 2004 soybean nearest futures eclipsed their March 1997 high on a nominal basis, but the inflation-adjusted series made a lower high in March 2004.

Figure 25.3 compares nominal and inflation-adjusted copper nearest futures. Successively higher highs in 2007 and 2008 in the nominal series were slightly lower highs in the deflated series. Also note that although nominal prices were substantially higher at the end of the period than at the start, inflation-adjusted prices were near unchanged for period as a whole.

Finally, in Figure 25.4, the nominal price graph reflects a strong uptrend in live cattle prices during 1995 through 2011 (the sharp correction in 2008 notwithstanding), while the inflation-adjusted

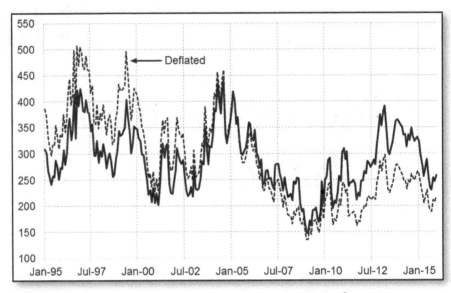

FIGURE 25.1 Lumber: Nearest Futures, Nominal vs. Deflated by PPI*
*Monthly closing prices deflated by PPI indexed to June 2005 = 100.

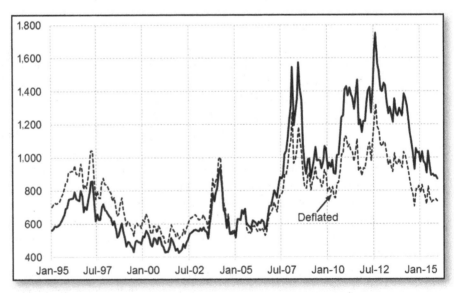

FIGURE 25.2 Soybeans: Nearest Futures, Nominal vs. Deflated by PPI*
*Monthly closing prices deflated by PPI indexed to June 2005 = 100.

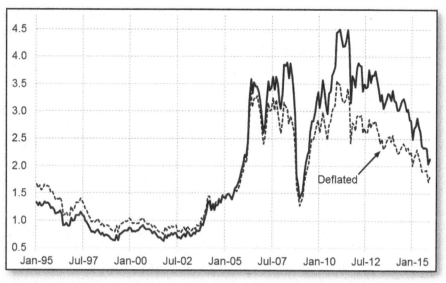

FIGURE 25.3 Copper: Nearest Futures, Nominal vs. Deflated by PPI*
*Monthly closing prices deflated by PPI indexed to June 2005 = 100.

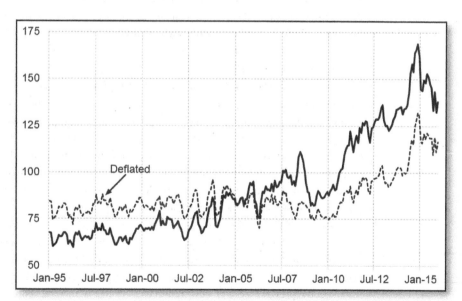

FIGURE 25.4 Live Cattle: Monthly Nearest Futures, Nominal Versus Deflated by PPI*
*Monthly closing prices deflated by PPI indexed to June 2005 = 100.

price series moved essentially sideways during the same period, with little net change for the period as a whole. In other words, the entire rise in nominal prices during this 17-year period was nothing more than the inflation effect.

Some of the ways inflation can be incorporated into the price-forecasting model include the following:

1. A representative inflation index is chosen, such as the producer price index (PPI), consumer price index (CPI), or the gross domestic product (GDP) deflator, and each historical price is divided by the contemporaneous index value, yielding a deflated price series. (Actually, the reported index value is divided by 100, since the index figures are quoted as a percent of a base of 100.) The inflation-adjusted price series in Figure 25.1 through 25.4 were deflated in this manner, using monthly PPI data with June 2005 as the base month (i.e., June 2005 PPI = 100). Table 25.1 applies this method to corn futures price data. A price forecast derived using this approach would be translated into current dollar terms by multiplying the projection by an estimate of the inflation index for the forecast period.

2. Alternately, all historical prices can be transformed into current dollar equivalents by multiplying each past price by the ratio of the estimated inflation index for the forecast period to the index value during the given past period. Table 25.2 illustrates this approach for a September–November 2015 forecast period, based on the assumption that PPI numbers are available only through August 2015. The table estimates the average September–November 2015 PPI by assuming the year-to-year percentage PPI change for this period will be the same as the known year-to-year percentage change in the June–August 2015 average PPI. (The estimated 7.5 percent decrease in PPI using this approach compared with an actual decrease of 7.3 percent.)

   Note that even when the PPI estimate used for the forecast period proves somewhat out of line, the distortion to the price analysis will be limited for two reasons. First, any reasonable inflation estimate will almost invariably be within a few percentage points of the actual figure and usually much closer. Second, all past prices will be overstated or understated equivalently (in percentage terms), thereby maintaining their relative relationship and leaving any price-explanatory model virtually unaffected. In any case, the forecast error attributable to an inaccurate inflation projection would be minuscule compared with the distortion that would result from the use of nominal rather than inflation-adjusted prices.

3. The inflation influence can be incorporated through its impact on the demand curve. Inflation implies an upward shift in the demand curve. All else being equal, the amount consumed at each given price level will increase over time, since each nominal price level represents a lower real price. However, because of the previously discussed problems in quantifying demand curves, this method represents more of a theoretical concept than a practical approach.

The actual method used to adjust for inflation is of secondary importance. The key point is that inflation is a critical input that should be incorporated in any fundamental price-forecasting model.

TABLE 25.1	Corn Monthly Nearest Futures Prices: Nominal and Deflated		
Year	Avg. Dec Futures Price, Sep–Nov	Avg. Sep–Nov PPI[a]	Inflation-Adjusted Avg. Price
1995	325.00	81.21	400.20
1996	277.83	83.04	334.57
1997	269.67	82.78	325.77
1998	215.58	80.23	268.70
1999	198.42	82.96	239.18
2000	204.17	87.51	233.31
2001	209.42	84.99	246.41
2002	246.42	86.11	286.17
2003	237.50	90.02	263.83
2004	200.17	97.02	206.32
2005	196.42	106.31	184.76
2006	320.08	106.33	301.03
2007	377.67	113.89	331.61
2008	412.83	121.00	341.19
2009	370.92	113.78	325.99
2010	535.92	120.80	443.63
2011	613.58	130.96	468.54
2012	753.33	131.71	571.95
2013	428.33	131.26	326.33
2014	357.75	131.93	271.17

[a]Reported index values would be divided by 100.0, since reported figures are quoted as a percentage of June 2005 base = 100.0.

Ironically, in the post-1979 period there were some instances when naïve price-forecasting models that totally ignored the effect of inflation may actually have provided more accurate projections than models incorporating this important factor. This apparent paradox can be explained by the extraordinarily high real interest rates (nominal rates minus inflation) witnessed in 1979–1980, which triggered a permanent change in inventory psychology. The high cost of holding commodity inventories provided a strong incentive to reduce inventories all along the pipeline (from raw product to retail). In effect, this widespread decision to hold lower inventories represented a classic example of a downshift in the demand curve. Once set in motion by the shock of the high inflation/high interest rate environment of 1979–1980, and abetted by technological advances and new inventory theories (e.g., "just-in-time"), inventory demand continued to contract even when inflation and interest rates fell sharply. The resulting sustained downshift in demand tended to counterbalance the influence of inflation.

The preceding discussion certainly is not intended to imply that inflation can be safely ignored, but rather that major shifts in the demand for commodities, which can run counter to the inflation

TABLE 25.2 Average September–November Price of December Corn Futures: Nominal and Estimated 2015 Dollar Equivalent Terms

Year	Avg. Dec Futures Price, Sep–Nov	Avg. Sep–Nov PPI[a]	Estimated Avg. Sep–Nov 2015 PPI	Multiplier to Convert Past Season Prices into 2015 Terms	Dec Futures Avg. Sep–Nov Price in 2015 $ Terms
1995	325.00	81.31	120.16	1.478	480.35
1996	277.83	83.24	120.16	1.444	401.19
1997	269.67	82.63	120.16	1.454	392.10
1998	215.58	80.02	120.16	1.502	323.80
1999	198.42	82.91	120.16	1.449	287.51
2000	204.17	87.84	120.16	1.368	279.30
2001	209.42	83.86	120.16	1.433	300.10
2002	246.42	86.24	120.16	1.393	343.26
2003	237.50	90.24	120.16	1.332	316.35
2004	200.17	97.56	120.16	1.232	246.61
2005	196.42	106.48	120.16	1.128	221.56
2006	320.08	106.37	120.16	1.130	361.69
2007	377.67	114.99	120.16	1.045	394.67
2008	412.83	115.38	120.16	1.041	429.76
2009	370.92	114.65	120.16	1.048	388.72
2010	535.92	121.84	120.16	0.986	528.42
2011	613.58	130.11	120.16	0.923	566.33
2012	753.33	131.09	120.16	0.917	690.80
2013	428.33	130.85	120.16	0.918	393.21
2014	357.75	129.90	120.16	0.925	330.92

[a]PPI indexed to June 2005 = 100.

effect, as was the case for the pronounced downward shift in demand evident in the 1980s and early 1990s, must also be incorporated. Some examples of ways the latter factor can be included (assuming a regression model) are the addition of a trend variable[1] and the use of a dummy variable to segment the data by different periods. (Dummy variables are discussed in Appendix E.)

_____

[1] Note that a trend variable need not increase for the entire period used in the analysis, but can be assumed to level off if the trending variable (the downward shift in demand in our example) is assumed to dissipate at some point.

CHAPTER 26

Seasonal Analysis

The freeze may come in winter, but the seasonal rally comes in fall.

—Jack D. Schwager

■ The Concept of Seasonal Trading

Various markets exhibit seasonal tendencies. Sometimes these seasonal patterns can be attributed to obvious fundamental causes, such as harvest selling or buying in front of potential freeze danger periods for some agricultural markets. Financial markets can also exhibit seasonal patterns tied to fundamental causes (e.g., Treasury refundings, year-end book squaring). Sometimes, however, seasonal patterns will not be associated with any apparent fundamental factors.

The concept of utilizing seasonal patterns in making trading decisions is based on the assumption that seasonal influences will cause biases in the movements of market prices. Of course, such correlations will be far from perfect. It is hardly uncommon for markets to move opposite to their normal seasonal trends. The key question is whether, on balance, there is enough positive correlation between future price movements and past seasonal patterns for such information to be useful. Because (as will be detailed later) apparent seasonal patterns would be expected to appear even in random series, it is difficult to determine to what extent seasonal price patterns reflect true biases as opposed to random occurrences. Hence, there is an unavoidable degree of subjectivity in deciding how much weight to give past seasonal patterns. A reasonable approach is to use seasonal analysis as a supplement to fundamental and technical analysis in making trading decisions, but never as a sole input.

■ Cash versus Futures Price Seasonality

It is important to understand that seasonal patterns in futures and cash prices may not be equivalent. For example, even if cash prices move lower for a given crop during harvest time with great consistency, it doesn't mean this pattern will provide a trading opportunity. It is entirely possible the futures market will discount harvest-time weakness in the cash market, thereby eliminating any profit opportunity. Because we are concerned with trading futures, not the cash commodities or financial instruments, the key question is whether a seasonal pattern exists in futures. Therefore, futures data should be used for all seasonality calculations.

■ The Role of Expectations

Because markets tend to discount expected events, such as changes in the seasons, true seasonal patterns often differ radically from conventional beliefs regarding such patterns. For example, it is widely believed that markets that are vulnerable to severe cold weather, such as heating oil, frozen concentrated orange juice, and coffee, exhibit strength during the winter. (For coffee, the relevant winter period is June through August.) However, these markets often exhibit seasonal strength *prior* to the advent of winter and tend to decline with the onset of winter.

■ Is It Real or Is It Probability?

Even if a market exhibits a seemingly pronounced seasonal pattern, this does not mean a true seasonal pattern exists. If enough markets are examined for enough periods of time, the emergence of some apparent seasonal patterns will be a virtual certainty *even if all the examined price series are random.* In other words, past seasonal patterns could simply be due to normal probability and not suggest any potential bias for future price behavior.

To illustrate how patterns can occur—in fact, are likely to occur—even if the distribution of price movements is random, we can use coin tosses to represent up or down price changes: heads represents a week with a net price gain; tails a week with a net price loss. Assume we flip a coin 10 times to represent the price movement in a given market in each of the past 10 years. We then repeat this 10-flip trial for a total of 52 times (one corresponding to each week in the year).

Although an equal number of heads and tails (i.e., an equal number of years of up and down price movement) will be the most common event, more than 75 percent of the trials will yield an unequal number of heads and tails (an unequal number of up and down years). In fact, some of these trials will result in a highly unbalanced number of heads and tails. It can be shown through probability theory that in 52 trials (weeks) there is a better than 75 percent chance of getting one or more 10-flip trials with at least 9 out of 10 heads or tails (one or more weeks with at least 9 out of 10 years of up or down price movements).

If the preceding process of 52 ten-flip trials is repeated a total of 25 times (to represent 25 different markets), then the probability of getting one or more 10-flip trials with at least 9 of 10 heads or tails is a virtual certainty (99.999999998 percent). In fact, there is a better than 99 percent probability there will be more than 15 ten-flip trials with at least 9 out of 10 heads or tails. To state this in market equivalent terms, even if the distribution of up and down price movements is random in all markets, in a group of 25 markets, there is a better than 99 percent chance of finding more than 15 instances in which a market moved higher (or lower) in at least 9 out of the past 10 years during a given week. Thus, it is important to understand that a certain number of apparent seasonal patterns are inevitable even if the distribution of price movements is random.

Calculating a Seasonal Index

There are many methods for calculating a seasonal index. This section examines two basic approaches.

Average Percentage Method

The average percentage method is by far the simplest way to calculate a seasonal index. This method involves the following steps:

1. Calculate an annual average for each year or season.
2. Express each data item (daily, weekly, or monthly value) as a percentage of the corresponding annual average. Either daily, weekly, or monthly data can be used in constructing seasonal indices. A daily or weekly seasonal index is obviously preferable to a monthly index, particularly for trading purposes, but it also requires far more data manipulation. This section uses monthly indices solely for simplicity of illustration.
3. Average the percentage values for each period (month, week, or day). The resulting figures are the seasonal index.

To illustrate this method, we will calculate the seasonal index for heating oil. Table 26.1 lists the average monthly prices for the 1996–2015 December heating oil contracts (which expire in November). Note the first column of data (November) is listed for later use and is not included in calculating the annual average. The final column in Table 26.1 indicates the 12-month average for each contract. Table 26.2 expresses each monthly price as a percentage of the annual average. These percentage figures are then averaged for each month to yield a seasonal index at the bottom of the table.

In calculating a seasonal index, it is wise to check for any extreme years that might distort the results. The question of what constitutes an extreme year can only be answered subjectively. With regard to the heating oil market from 1996 through 2015, one year stands out: 2008. As Table 26.1 shows, the December 2008 heating oil contract traversed an extraordinarily wide range. It is usually best to exclude such uncharacteristic years when calculating a seasonal index, unless some adjustment scheme is used to modify their exaggerated influence. However, there are no concrete rules, and the ultimate decision must depend on the judgment of the researcher.

Although a sense of the seasonal pattern can be gained by examining the seasonal index at the bottom of Table 26.2, a graphic presentation is far more convenient and informative. Figure 26.1 shows the seasonal index, both with and without the inclusion of 2008. In this case, the extreme year does not have a significant impact on the basic seasonal pattern. As is readily apparent, there is a seasonal tendency for prices to reach relative highs around September–October and to bottom around December–January.

It is important to note the average percentage method does not remove any trend from the data. Thus, what appears to be a seasonal pattern might partially reflect a long-term trend in prices. In fact,

TABLE 26.1 December Heating Oil Contract: Average Monthly Prices

Year of Contract Expiration	Nov[a]	Dec	Jan	Feb	Mar	Apr	May	Jun	Jul	Aug	Sep	Oct	Nov	Dec–Nov Avg
1996	0.507	0.515	0.510	0.509	0.527	0.543	0.538	0.543	0.572	0.601	0.672	0.711	0.701	0.579
1997	0.587	0.591	0.610	0.586	0.584	0.574	0.591	0.574	0.567	0.573	0.575	0.600	0.564	0.582
1998	0.572	0.553	0.528	0.514	0.495	0.500	0.489	0.458	0.435	0.398	0.417	0.416	0.358	0.463
1999	0.444	0.418	0.411	0.386	0.427	0.469	0.466	0.475	0.535	0.570	0.609	0.589	0.641	0.500
2000	0.563	0.570	0.601	0.651	0.686	0.647	0.720	0.794	0.794	0.877	0.977	1.016	1.004	0.778
2001	0.771	0.725	0.722	0.750	0.734	0.754	0.803	0.789	0.733	0.760	0.739	0.643	0.568	0.727
2002	0.600	0.596	0.597	0.596	0.665	0.702	0.707	0.685	0.709	0.735	0.787	0.778	0.720	0.690
2003	0.669	0.702	0.748	0.805	0.779	0.722	0.738	0.781	0.808	0.841	0.780	0.842	0.841	0.782
2004	0.760	0.785	0.828	0.841	0.899	0.916	1.018	1.036	1.120	1.219	1.272	1.491	1.402	1.069
2005	1.282	1.189	1.225	1.324	1.533	1.622	1.498	1.655	1.789	1.956	2.047	1.992	1.716	1.629
2006	1.807	1.857	1.934	1.959	1.949	2.128	2.135	2.171	2.239	2.177	1.916	1.729	1.725	1.993
2007	1.940	1.943	1.788	1.861	1.947	2.004	2.011	2.072	2.156	2.065	2.192	2.352	2.604	2.083
2008	2.445	2.477	2.531	2.624	2.897	3.115	3.634	3.902	3.917	3.383	3.001	2.438	1.926	2.987
2009	2.140	1.695	1.710	1.481	1.528	1.575	1.685	1.961	1.810	1.951	1.818	1.963	1.985	1.763
2010	2.261	2.213	2.209	2.118	2.231	2.378	2.234	2.162	2.090	2.140	2.163	2.279	2.343	2.213
2011	2.441	2.521	2.700	2.984	3.115	3.299	3.123	3.027	3.076	2.987	2.937	2.904	3.059	2.978
2012	2.971	2.919	3.000	3.160	3.276	3.214	2.988	2.657	2.811	3.019	3.139	3.122	3.014	3.027
2013	2.966	2.974	3.015	3.065	2.977	2.912	2.875	2.911	2.983	3.073	3.047	2.982	2.950	2.980
2014	2.904	2.963	2.915	2.921	2.937	2.917	2.921	2.986	2.952	2.879	2.763	2.558	2.374	2.840
2015	2.375	2.073	1.813	1.903	1.897	1.922	2.015	1.959	1.791	1.583	1.613	1.547	1.452	1.797

[a]November of year preceding the contract year. This column is needed to calculate Table 26.3.

TABLE 26.2 December Heating Oil Contract: Monthly Price as a Percentage of the December–November Average

Year of Contract Expiration	Dec	Jan	Feb	Mar	Apr	May	Jun	Jul	Aug	Sep	Oct	Nov
1996	88.98	88.23	88.03	91.14	93.87	92.90	93.92	98.87	103.79	116.20	122.85	121.21
1997	101.58	104.71	100.63	100.21	98.54	101.46	98.50	97.29	98.46	98.71	103.09	96.82
1998	119.36	113.98	111.00	106.75	107.83	105.46	98.76	93.94	85.97	89.97	89.80	77.18
1999	83.77	82.32	77.32	85.38	93.79	93.27	95.04	107.05	114.11	121.92	117.81	128.22
2000	73.26	77.23	83.67	88.15	83.09	92.53	102.08	102.05	112.71	125.60	130.58	129.07
2001	99.76	99.44	103.16	101.02	103.82	110.46	108.63	100.83	104.54	101.72	88.50	78.11
2002	86.40	86.59	86.45	96.42	101.80	102.44	99.28	102.74	106.53	114.13	112.80	104.43
2003	89.80	95.63	102.86	99.60	92.25	94.41	99.82	103.24	107.49	99.76	107.59	107.56
2004	73.41	77.43	78.72	84.08	85.72	95.26	96.92	104.80	114.03	119.00	139.49	131.12
2005	72.99	75.22	81.29	94.12	99.56	91.94	101.64	109.82	120.06	125.69	122.28	105.39
2006	93.16	97.01	98.28	97.76	106.75	107.12	108.92	112.35	109.23	96.14	86.73	86.54
2007	93.28	85.82	89.37	93.47	96.21	96.54	99.48	103.50	99.13	105.23	112.94	125.01
2008	82.92	84.73	87.84	96.98	104.28	121.65	130.65	131.13	113.26	100.47	81.63	64.47
2009	96.14	96.95	83.98	86.64	89.31	95.56	111.19	102.64	110.63	103.11	111.31	112.57
2010	100.00	99.80	95.71	100.82	107.42	100.93	97.69	94.44	96.68	97.71	102.96	105.84
2011	84.67	90.67	100.21	104.60	110.78	104.88	101.66	103.31	100.33	98.62	97.54	102.73
2012	96.44	99.13	104.41	108.23	106.17	98.74	87.79	92.87	99.76	103.71	103.16	99.58
2013	99.77	101.17	102.83	99.89	97.72	96.47	97.68	100.08	103.11	102.25	100.05	98.98
2014	104.33	102.61	102.82	103.38	102.69	102.83	105.12	103.91	101.36	97.29	90.06	83.59
2015	115.31	100.86	105.88	105.53	106.95	112.14	108.97	99.66	88.07	89.77	86.08	80.77
Averages:												
All Years	92.77	92.98	94.22	97.21	99.43	100.85	102.19	103.23	104.46	105.35	105.36	101.96
Excl. 2008	93.28	93.41	94.56	97.22	99.17	99.75	100.69	101.76	104.00	105.61	106.61	103.93

393

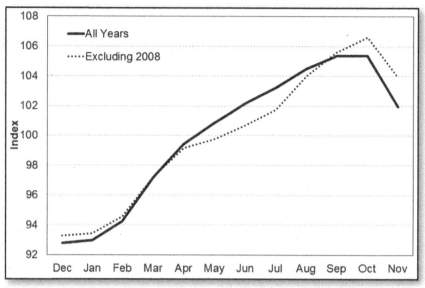

FIGURE 26.1 December Heating Oil Contract Seasonal Index: Average Percentage Method

for data exhibiting a strong trend, the effect of the trend will often totally swamp any true seasonal pattern. (By this we mean the seasonal pattern that remains after the trend has been removed from the data.) An unadjusted seasonal index, such as the average percentage method, is relevant because it more directly reflects the past results of implementing a position on a given date and exiting it on another given date. However, because secular trends may change, it can be argued that the *detrended seasonal index* might be more relevant in reflecting seasonal patterns. The next section describes one method for deriving a detrended seasonal index.

Link Relative Method

The link relative method involves the following steps:

1. Express each data value as a percentage of the previous month's value.
2. Average these percentage values for each month.
3. Set the first month's value at 100.0 and reexpress all the other monthly averages as relative percentages of the first month's value.
4. Adjust the resulting values for trend.
5. Multiply each of these values by the appropriate common factor so that the average monthly seasonal index value equals 100.0.

These steps will be clearer if we work through an example. Table 26.3 indicates each month's price as a percentage of the previous month's price. (These figures are derived from Table 26.1.) The monthly averages for all these percentages are listed at the bottom of the table.

TABLE 26.3 December Heating Oil Contract: Monthly Average Price as a Percentage of the Previous Month's Price

Year of Contract Expiration	Dec	Jan	Feb	Mar	Apr	May	Jun	Jul	Aug	Sep	Oct	Nov
1996	101.51	99.16	99.77	103.53	103.00	98.97	101.10	105.26	104.98	111.95	105.73	98.66
1997	100.70	103.09	96.10	99.58	98.33	102.96	97.08	98.78	101.20	100.25	104.44	93.92
1998	96.74	95.50	97.39	96.17	101.01	97.80	93.65	95.11	91.52	104.65	99.82	85.94
1999	94.23	98.27	93.93	110.42	109.85	99.45	101.90	112.64	106.59	106.84	96.63	108.84
2000	101.21	105.43	108.33	105.35	94.26	111.37	110.31	99.97	110.45	111.43	103.97	98.84
2001	93.95	99.68	103.74	97.93	102.77	106.39	98.35	92.82	103.68	97.30	87.01	88.26
2002	99.38	100.23	99.83	111.53	105.59	100.63	96.91	103.49	103.68	107.13	98.84	92.58
2003	104.99	106.50	107.56	96.82	92.62	102.34	105.74	103.43	104.12	92.80	107.85	99.97
2004	103.24	105.47	101.67	106.81	101.95	111.13	101.74	108.14	108.81	104.36	117.22	94.00
2005	92.72	103.06	108.07	115.79	105.77	92.35	110.54	108.05	109.33	104.69	97.29	86.18
2006	102.77	104.13	101.31	99.48	109.20	100.34	101.69	103.15	97.22	88.02	90.21	99.78
2007	100.16	92.01	104.13	104.58	102.94	100.34	103.05	104.04	95.78	106.15	107.33	110.69
2008	101.31	102.18	103.67	110.41	107.52	116.65	107.40	100.37	86.38	88.71	81.24	78.98
2009	79.23	100.84	86.63	103.16	103.08	106.99	116.36	92.31	107.78	93.21	107.95	101.13
2010	97.90	99.80	95.91	105.33	106.55	93.96	96.79	96.67	102.38	101.06	105.38	102.79
2011	103.30	107.09	110.52	104.38	105.91	94.67	96.93	101.62	97.11	98.29	98.91	105.32
2012	98.24	102.79	105.32	103.66	98.10	92.99	88.92	105.79	107.41	103.97	99.47	96.52
2013	100.26	101.40	101.64	97.14	97.84	98.72	101.25	102.46	103.03	99.17	97.85	98.93
2014	102.05	98.35	100.21	100.54	99.33	100.13	102.23	98.85	97.55	95.98	92.57	92.82
2015	87.27	87.46	104.98	99.67	101.34	104.85	97.18	91.46	88.37	101.93	95.88	93.84
Average	98.06	100.62	101.54	103.61	102.35	101.65	101.46	101.22	101.37	100.89	99.78	96.40

TABLE 26.4 December Heating Oil Contract 1996–2015: Monthly Average Price as a Percentage of the Prior December Average Price

Dec	Jan	Feb	Mar	Apr	May	Jun	Jul	Aug	Sep	Oct	Nov	Dec
100	100.62	102.17	105.86	108.35	110.14	111.74	113.10	114.65	115.67	115.42	111.26	109.10

As the next step, in Table 26.4 we express each month's value relative to the first month (December), which is set at 100.0. Thus, since the average ratio of January to December prices is 100.62 percent from Table 26.3, its value is set to 100.62 (i.e., 100.62 percent of 100.0). Similarly, since the average ratio of February to January prices is 101.54 percent, the February value would be set to 101.54 percent of 100.62 or 102.17. The value for March would be 103.61 percent of 102.17, or 105.86, and so on. Note that the entry for the second value of December is equal to 98.06 percent of the November value (98.06 is the average December value from Table 26.3).

The higher value for the second December entry reflects the trend in the data. To remove this trend, we must find the constant factor that will increase to 109.10 (the ratio of the second December value to the first) when multiplied by itself 12 times. In other words, we want to find a constant monthly growth factor X. This can be expressed as $X^{12} = 109.10$. The derivation of this value requires the use of logarithms (readers unfamiliar with logarithms can skip to the immediately following description of an alternative approach for detrending the data):

$$X^{12} = (1.091)$$
$$12 \log X = \log(1.091)$$
$$\log X = 1/12 \log(1.091)$$
$$\log X = 0.003152$$
$$\text{antilog of } 0.003152 = 1.007284, \text{ rounded to } 1.0073$$

In other words, $(1.0073)^{12} = 1.091$.

We assume a constant growth trend. The first month's (December) value will still equal 100.0; the second month's value will be divided by 1.0073; the third month's value will be divided by $(1.0073)^2$; the fourth by $(1.0073)^3$, and so on. These calculations are illustrated in Table 26.5. The final month (the second December entry) will be divided by $(1.0073)^{12}$, thereby transforming its value to 100.0. Since both December values are equal after the adjustment of the data by the constant growth factor, the trend has been removed from the data.

Alternative Approach

The following steps, which do not require the use of logarithms, can be used to derive a reasonably good approximation of the last column in Table 26.5.

TABLE 26.5 Trend Adjustment for Monthly Index Values

Month	Values from Table 26.4	Trend-Adjustment Divisor	Trend-Adj. Divisor Numerical Equivalent	Adjusted Value
Dec	100			100
Jan	100.62	$(1.007284)^1$	1.007284	99.89
Feb	102.17	$(1.007284)^2$	1.014621	100.69
Mar	105.86	$(1.007284)^3$	1.022012	103.58
Apr	108.35	$(1.007284)^4$	1.029456	105.25
May	110.14	$(1.007284)^5$	1.036954	106.21
Jun	111.74	$(1.007284)^6$	1.044508	106.98
Jul	113.10	$(1.007284)^7$	1.052116	107.50
Aug	114.65	$(1.007284)^8$	1.059779	108.18
Sep	115.67	$(1.007284)^9$	1.067499	108.36
Oct	115.42	$(1.007284)^{10}$	1.075275	107.34
Nov	111.26	$(1.007284)^{11}$	1.083107	102.73
Total				1256.71

1. Find the difference between the two December values in Table 26.4 (9.10).
2. Multiply this difference by 1/12 and subtract the product from the second month's (January) value $(100.62 - 0.76 = 99.86)$.
3. Multiply the difference found in step 1 by 2/12 and subtract the product from the third month's value. Multiply the difference found in step 1 by 3/12 and subtract the product from the fourth month's value. Continue this progression for the remaining months. Using this method, the adjusted values would be:

Dec	Jan	Feb	Mar	Apr	May	Jun	Jul	Aug	Sep	Oct	Nov
100	99.86	100.65	103.59	105.32	106.35	107.19	107.79	108.58	108.85	107.84	102.92

These approximated figures are very close to the precise adjusted values shown in Table 26.5.

For the sake of uniformity, it is desirable that the average of the monthly seasonal index values equal 100, or equivalently, that the sum of the monthly index values equal 1200. Table 26.5 shows the sum of the index values in this case is more than 1200, which makes it necessary to adjust the figures by a multiplier:

$$\text{Multiplier} = \frac{1200}{1256.71} = 0.9549$$

Dividing each of the values in Table 26.5 by 0.9549 produces the seasonal index values in Table 26.6, which are plotted in Figure 26.2. The average percentage method and link relative method indices are compared in Figure 26.3. Note there is a great deal of similarity between the two methods. The basic

TABLE 26.6	Seasonal Index for December Heating Oil Contract Using the Link Relative Method										
Dec	Jan	Feb	Mar	Apr	May	Jun	Jul	Aug	Sep	Oct	Nov
95.49	95.38	96.15	98.91	100.50	101.42	102.15	102.65	103.30	103.47	102.50	98.09

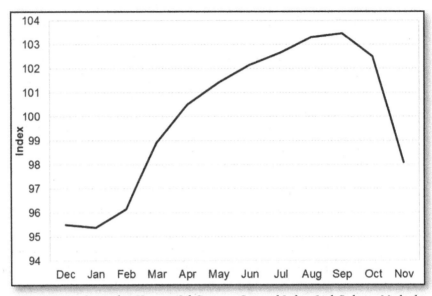

FIGURE 26.2 December Heating Oil Contract Seasonal Index: Link Relative Method

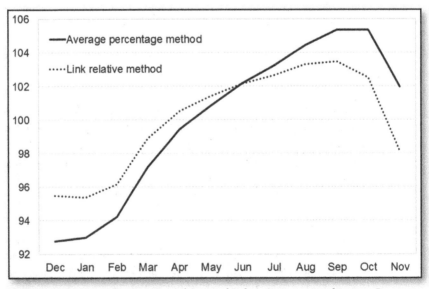

FIGURE 26.3 December Heating Oil Seasonal Index: Comparison of Average Percentage Method and Link Relative Method

difference is that the average percentage method index reflects the long-term trend, whereas the link relative method does not. Both approaches indicate a relative low in the December–January period and a relative high in September.

Figures 26.4 through 26.9 Illustrate the seasonal graphs for specific contract months in several futures markets, both unadjusted (average percentage method) and detrended (link relative method),

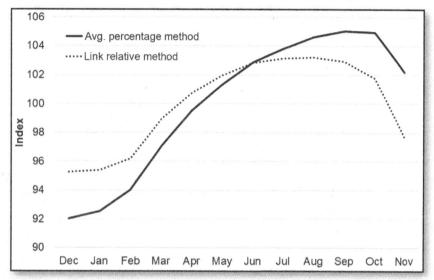

FIGURE 26.4 December WTI Crude Oil Seasonal Index: Comparison of Average Percentage Method and Link Relative Method

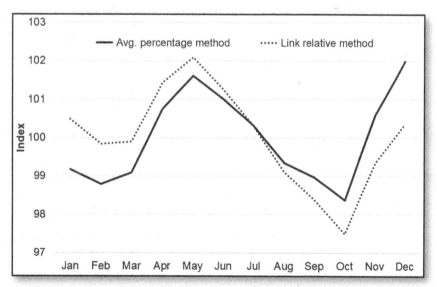

FIGURE 26.5 December E-Mini S&P 500 Seasonal Index: Comparison of Average Percentage Method and Link Relative Method

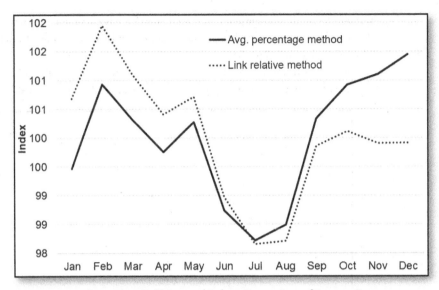

FIGURE 26.6 December Gold Seasonal Index: Comparison of Average Percentage Method and Link Relative Method

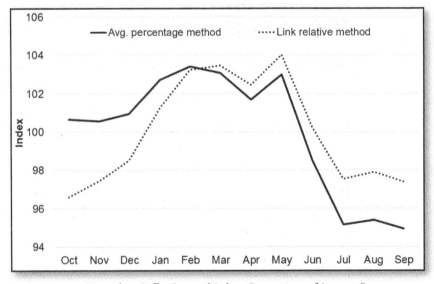

FIGURE 26.7 September Coffee Seasonal Index: Comparison of Average Percentage Method and Link Relative Method

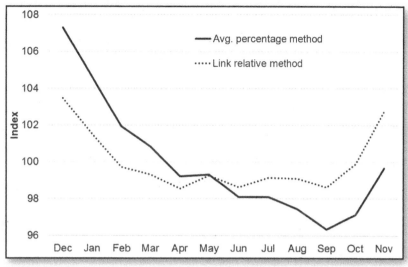

FIGURE 26.8   November Frozen Concentrated Orange Juice Seasonal Index: Comparison of Average Percentage Method and Link Relative Method

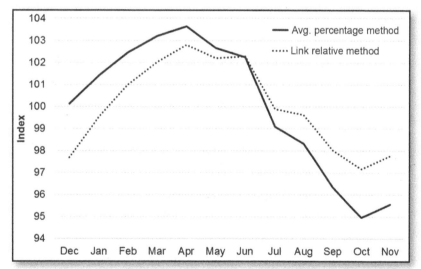

FIGURE 26.9   December Corn Seasonal Index: Comparison of Average Percentage Method and Link Relative Method

based on data from 1996 through 2015 (with the exception of the E-mini S&P 500 in Figure 26.6, which used data from 1998 through 2015).

It should be stressed that seasonal patterns should never be used as the sole basis for making trading decisions, as they are only one influence and can easily be swamped by fundamental and technical forces impacting the market.

CHAPTER 27

Analyzing Market Response

Markets are never wrong—opinions often are.

—Jesse Livermore

■ Evaluating Market Response for Repetitive Events

A market's response to key fundamental developments can provide important clues about the probable future price direction. When these developments are repetitive, such as the release of key economic numbers or U.S. Department of Agriculture (USDA) reports, a systematic approach can be used to analyze the implications of market response. The general analytic procedure would involve the following steps:

1. Identify the event to be studied (e.g., the Treasury market's response to the monthly employment report).
2. Construct a table comparing the market's immediate reaction to a report's release to subsequent price trends.
3. Search for consistent patterns.

There is no single correct format for analyzing market response. The objective of this chapter is to illustrate the analysis process rather than to provide specific market-response models for trading the markets. The observed responses in the following examples are moderate and there is not enough data to rule out that the results could simply be due to chance. The reader can apply a similar methodology for analyzing market reaction for other situations that may be of interest.

Example A: T-Note Futures Response to Monthly U.S. Employment Report

The U.S. employment situation report released by the Bureau of Labor Statistics is the most closely watched monthly economic release, capable of triggering volatile moves in a wide range of markets. Let's say our goal is to check whether the direction (and magnitude) of the price move in U.S. Treasury futures on the day the monthly employment report is released is indicative of the price action in subsequent weeks. In other words, we want to check the hypothesis that a "bullish" or "bearish" market response to the employment report is an indicator of probable near-term price direction. We might proceed as follows:

1. Determine the threshold to determine a bullish or bearish initial response to the employment report.
2. Measure the market's price action in the N days following employment report days that satisfy this criterion.

Table 27.1 shows how the U.S. 10-year-T-note futures traded in the first 10 trading days (two weeks) after the monthly employment report between 2006 and 2015 based on whether the move from the close of the day prior to the report to the report day's close was bullish or bearish. In this case, a bullish initial response was defined as a closing gain (measured from the previous day's close) of 0.50 points (16/32) or more on the day of the employment report, while a bearish initial response was defined as a 0.50-point or larger decline. (This nominal amount was selected solely for illustration purposes and has no special significance.)

Twenty-six employment report days fulfilled the bullish criteria from 2006 through 2015 (top half of table), while 33 fulfilled the bearish criteria (bottom half of table). Table 27.1 shows the cumulative average and median gains from the close of the employment report day to the closes of the next 10 days. For comparison, the table also includes the average price changes for all 1- to 10-day periods during the 10-year analysis window. The table also shows the percentage of times the T-note futures contract closed higher than the employment report day close after bullish and bearish initial responses to the report, along with the percentage of higher closes for all 1- to 10-day periods. For example, on the first day after bullish initial reactions to the employment report, 10-year T-note futures closed, on average, −0.054 points lower (−0.039 points median), compared to an average 0.021-point one-day gain for all days. The market closed higher 42.31 percent of the time one day after initial bullish responses, compared to 51.93 percent for all days.

Because it is often easier to digest such data visually, Figure 27.1 graphs the results for the bullish initial responses, while Figure 27.2 graphs the results for the bearish initial responses. Surprisingly, the analysis suggests that, if anything, there was a tendency for T-note price action in the near-term period following employment reports to move in the opposite direction of the market's initial response. Specifically, there seems to be a notable tendency for contrarian price action in the two days following a bullish initial response to the unemployment report (after which trading was mixed), while the price action was more consistently bullish after an initial bearish response. Figure 27.1 shows that after two days T-notes closed below the close of the employment report day 73 percent of the time, with an average decline of 0.205 points (around 6/32nds). This observation suggests that those seeking to enter a position in the direction of the market's bullish response to the report might

| TABLE 27.1 | 10-Year T-Note Futures Response to Monthly Employment Report: Cumulative Change as of Indicated Day (2006–2015) |

Bullish

26 instances	Day 1	Day 2	Day 3	Day 4	Day 5	Day 6	Day 7	Day 8	Day 9	Day 10
Median Post-Report Change	-0.039	-0.172	0.016	0.164	0.211	0.063	0.117	0.344	-0.055	0.117
Average Post-Report Change	-0.054	-0.205	-0.035	-0.030	0.119	0.214	0.093	0.189	0.082	0.111
Average Change All Days	0.021	0.042	0.063	0.084	0.105	0.126	0.147	0.168	0.188	0.208
Higher Close than Report Day (%Times)	42.31%	26.92%	50.00%	53.85%	65.38%	53.85%	53.85%	53.85%	46.15%	57.69%
All Days Higher Close (%Times)	51.93%	53.85%	55.09%	55.24%	54.94%	55.04%	56.09%	57.14%	56.79%	56.79%

Bearish

33 instances	Day 1	Day 2	Day 3	Day 4	Day 5	Day 6	Day 7	Day 8	Day 9	Day 10
Median Post-Report Change	0.031	0.219	0.141	0.328	0.484	0.422	0.406	0.609	0.313	0.484
Average Post-Report Change	0.081	0.285	0.306	0.401	0.474	0.605	0.707	0.649	0.622	0.603
Average Change All Days	0.021	0.042	0.063	0.084	0.105	0.126	0.147	0.168	0.188	0.208
Higher Close than Report Day (%Times)	51.52%	57.58%	57.58%	63.64%	63.64%	72.73%	69.70%	66.67%	72.73%	63.64%
All Days Higher Close (%Times)	51.93%	53.85%	55.09%	55.24%	54.94%	55.04%	56.09%	57.14%	56.79%	56.79%

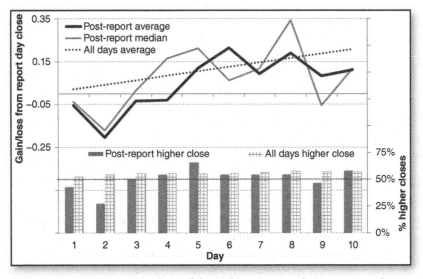

FIGURE 27.1 10-Year T-Note after Bullish Initial Response to Jobs Report (Cumulative)

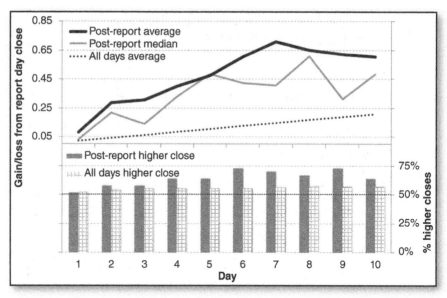

FIGURE 27.2 10-Year T-Note after Bearish Initial Response to Jobs Report (Cumulative)

be better off waiting a couple of days before entering a position. In contrast, Figure 27.2 highlights the market's tendency to move higher after bearish initial responses. It should be noted that the period surveyed was one that witnessed a long-term uptrend. Therefore, the appropriate comparison is to the corresponding changes for all days.

Figures 27.3 and 27.4 present a slightly different perspective of the performance of 10-year T-note futures after bullish and bearish initial responses to the monthly employment report. Instead of showing the cumulative performance from the close of the employment report day, these charts show each day's gain or loss. Figure 27.3 highlights the negative average returns in the first two days after bullish initial responses, while Figure 27.4 shows a tendency for higher prices in the first two days after bearish report responses.

In examining historical patterns (e.g., market response, seasonal tendencies), it is usually impossible to say whether apparent proclivities reflect true market biases (or inefficiencies) or whether such results are strictly a function of chance. Even clearly random events with a 50 percent expected outcome will sometimes deviate significantly from 50 percent simply by chance. For example, if you flipped 10 coins 1,000 times, approximately 17 percent of the time you would get seven or more heads. Getting seven or more heads on any individual toss of 10 coins certainly wouldn't imply the coins have a tendency to land on heads. Two factors should be considered in trying to assess whether a past pattern might be meaningful rather than due to chance:

1. **Number of observations.** The greater the number of observations, the more likely a past pattern might be significant.
2. **Theoretical explanation.** If there is a logical reason why a past pattern might have occurred, it enhances the potential significance of the observed tendency.

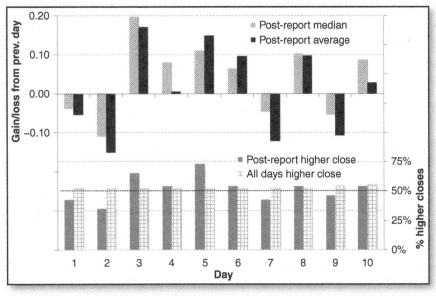

FIGURE 27.3   10-Year T-Note after Bullish Initial Response to Jobs Report (Daily)

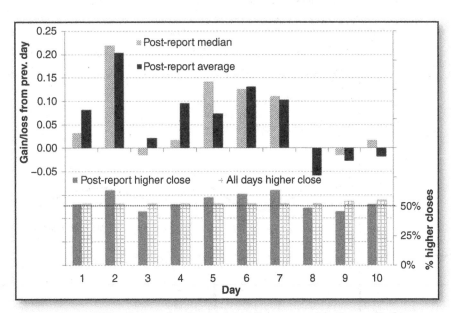

FIGURE 27.4   10-Year T-Note after Bearish Initial Response to Jobs Report (Daily)

Example B: Stock Index Futures Response to Employment Reports

Stock index futures also are prone to volatile moves in response to monthly employment reports. Figures 27.5 and 27.6 show the results of an analysis of the E-mini S&P 500 futures contract's performance in the first 10 trading days following bullish and bearish initial responses to employment reports from 2006 through 2015. In this case, however, bullish and bearish are defined not by the price change on the report day, but rather the location of the closing price within the report day's range:

1. A close within the upper 25 percent of the day's range is defined as a bullish initial response.
2. A close in the bottom 25 percent of the day's range is defined as a bearish initial response.

Of the 120 employment reports from 2006 through 2015, 42 satisfied the bullish response criteria, while 26 satisfied the bearish response criteria. Figure 27.5 shows the E-mini S&P's average and median cumulative gain/loss from the close of bullish response report days to the closes of the next 10 consecutive days, while Figure 27.6 provides an analogous chart for bearish response days. The most noticeable pattern is the tendency for follow-through weakness in the week following bearish response days (Figure 27.6). The chart for bullish response days (Figure 27.5) is fairly inconclusive.

Table 27.2 shows the results of a related analysis. In this case, an initial bullish reaction was defined as a close 1.35 percent or more above the previous day's close and a bearish reaction as a close 1.35 percent or more below the previous day's close. Initial responses between these thresholds were classified as neutral. These initial responses were then compared to the subsequent moves from the report day's close to the close of the day immediately preceding the next month's employment report (approximately 20 days, but ranging from 18 to 25 days for any given month). In this example, the cumulative price changes after bullish and neutral initial reactions were similar (and positive), while the

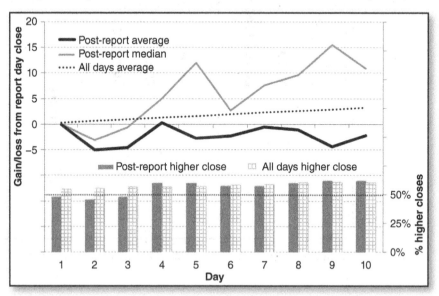

FIGURE 27.5 E-Mini S&P Change 500 after Bullish Initial Response to Jobs Report (Cumulative)

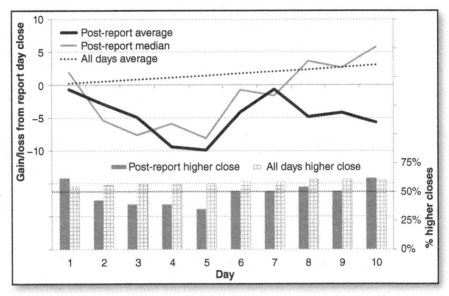

FIGURE 27.6 E-Mini S&P 500 Change after Bearish Initial Response to Jobs Report (Cumulative)

performance after bearish initial responses tended to be negative. Because there was a decisive uptrend in place during the survey period, there is a bias toward getting bullish price behavior following any defined event—a tendency reflected by the bullish result following neutral response days. Therefore, the bullish price action following bullish response days may be more a matter of reflecting the prevailing long-term trend than any meaningful pattern, particularly since the price responses following bullish and neutral response days were similar. The negative price action following bearish response days, however, seems potentially more significant since it runs counter to the prevailing long-term trend. Still, even here, there is the caveat that the results are based on a small number of observations.

Isolated Events

Expectations are the key to evaluating market response for any single event. In other words, the failure of a market to respond to a fundamental development as decisively as might have been anticipated could provide an important signal regarding the market's inherent strength or weakness.

TABLE 27.2	E-Mini S&P 500 Cumulative Change in Month Following Intitial Response to Employment Report, 2006–2015		
	Bullish Initial Response	**Bearish Initial Response**	**Neutral Initial Response**
Average	5.54	−16.05	7.88
Median	18.13	−8.75	14.25
% Higher Close	64.29%	35.71%	65.91%

A classic example of this principle was the counter-to-anticipated response of the gold market during the 1991 Gulf War. As the United States' January 17 deadline for starting air strikes approached without any concessions from Iraq, gold prices firmed. The start of the air war during nighttime hours in the United States saw gold surge to a three-month high of $410/oz. in the overnight market. But this rally abruptly fizzled, and gold prices began to sink rapidly. By the time the gold market opened in the United States the next morning, prices were actually $28/oz. lower than the previous evening's close. This extremely weak price action in response to an event that could have been expected to rally prices—even allowing for what proved to be the market's correct anticipation for a quick U.S. victory—suggested that gold prices were vulnerable to further erosion. As can be seen in Figure 27.7, prices did indeed continue to slide in the ensuing months, falling to new contract lows.

The basic principle is that a price response to an important event that is radically different from what might normally have been anticipated may provide an important clue as to the market's probable near-term direction.

Limitations of Market Response Analysis

The following are some of the ambiguities that arise in conducting market response analysis:

1. In any type of market response analysis, the answers we obtain are dependent on the parameters used in the analysis. For example, the various thresholds used to define bullish and bearish response days in this chapter were representative values selected to illustrate the analysis process; they were not the result of any attempt to find optimal definitions of what constitutes strong (bullish) or weak (bearish) reactions. The choice of analysis parameters, which will often

FIGURE 27.7 April 1991 Gold

be subjective, can have a large impact on the results—a reality that provides a strong argument for analyzing a range of parameters.

2. When dealing with market events that occur relatively infrequently, there is the problem of determining the significance of results based on samples that might be too small (or spread out across too long and varied an analysis period) to be considered statistically valid. For example, some of the examples in this chapter were based on only 13 or 14 observations.

3. Response patterns may shift over time. A market's response to a particular report or event might be consistent for an extended period during one type of economic environment or market regime, but that tendency could diminish or disappear if conditions change—for example, in the change from a rising interest rate environment to a declining rate environment.

In view of the foregoing limitations, market response patterns should be viewed as one potential indicator of near-term market direction, which could be combined with other analysis to support a trading opinion, as opposed to being used as a stand-alone market signal.

CHAPTER 28

Building a Forecasting Model: A Step-by-Step Approach

Economics as a positive science is a body of tentatively accepted generalizations about economic phenomena that can be used to predict the consequences of changes in circumstances.

—Milton Friedman

Because of the heterogeneous nature of commodity markets, there is no such thing as a standard fundamental model. Among the key substantive characteristics that differentiate markets are degree of storability, availability of substitutes, importance of imports and exports, types of government intervention, and sensitivity to general economic conditions. Consequently, in contrast to technical analysis, in which a specific system or methodology can often be applied to a broad spectrum of markets, the fundamental approach requires a separate analysis for each market.

The time-consuming nature of fundamental analysis makes it virtually impossible to cover a large number of markets adequately using this approach. Thus, as a practical matter, a trader wishing to employ fundamental inputs in trading decisions must resort to one of the following alternatives:

1. Restrict fundamental analysis to a superficial examination of the key statistics in a broad range of markets.
2. Employ in-depth fundamental analysis for only a few markets and trade all other markets based on technical input only.
3. Rely on published fundamental analysis.

The first alternative is usually a poor compromise. Market knowledge based on a cursory examination of fundamentals is often worse than total ignorance. In fact, next to poor money management, perhaps the most common reason that nonprofessional traders lose money in commodities is that they base their trading decisions on superficial fundamental information (e.g., market blogs, online forums, brokers' two-sentence market summaries). The analytic approach outlined in this chapter implicitly assumes alternative 2. It is a good idea to start by analyzing and following only one or two markets fundamentally, expanding this list only after all research ideas on previously chosen markets have been investigated. The third alternative is a reasonable supplement to individual research, as long as one is selective. Unfortunately, a significant portion of published research is analytically unsound. However, if you have fully grasped the concepts of this section, you should have no difficulty in evaluating the analytic merit of available published research.

Once a market has been selected for fundamental study, the following step-by-step approach can be employed:

1. **Read background material.** The first step in any analysis must be a familiarization with the given market. Before beginning, an analyst must have a good idea of the key fundamentals that affect the market, as well as the primary sources of statistical information.

2. **Gather statistics.** Once you have a good understanding of the basic mechanics of a market, list all the statistics that might be relevant in formulating a price analysis. The U.S. Department of Agriculture (USDA), which publishes a wide variety of reports on domestic and foreign agricultural products, is an excellent source of information. Another major source of statistics is the *CRB Commodity Yearbook*, which contains extensive data for the complete range of commodity markets. For many markets, special statistical sources will have to be consulted. The familiarization process described in step 1 should provide the information regarding the primary statistical sources for a given market.

3. **Adjust price data for inflation.** This adjustment is an essential step in fundamental price forecasting. As a caveat, though, if there is a prevailing downward-shifting trend in demand (a circumstance that will offset inflation), then unadjusted prices could yield more accurate forecasts.

4. **Construct a model.** Select one or more of the approaches discussed in Chapter 23 and attempt to construct a price-explanatory model. Regression analysis, which is perhaps the most powerful and efficient of these approaches, is covered comprehensively in the Appendices.

5. **Modify model.** After identifying which past years, or seasons, failed to fit the general pattern, try to determine the factors that were responsible for the aberrant behavior. Attempt to incorporate these factors into the general model. In some cases, highly unusual price action in a past year might reflect the impact of isolated events (e.g., price controls, export embargoes, forced liquidation by huge speculators) that are not relevant to the current market. In such situations, it is often preferable to delete the abnormal year from the model. It should be emphasized, however, that the expedient deletion of a year simply because it does not fit the pattern constitutes improper methodology. The practical decision-making process in the deletion of years from a model is discussed in much greater detail in Appendix E.

6. **Incorporate expectations.** Check to see whether expectation-based statistics improve the model.

7. **Estimate the independent variables.** The independent variables are the factors used to explain and forecast prices in the model. These inputs must be estimated for the forecast period. For example, the coming season's corn crop, which would obviously be a key input in any corn price-forecasting model, could be estimated on the basis of planting intentions, historical yields, and weather conditions to date.

8. **Forecast a price range.** Allowing for a plausible range of values for each of the independent variables, use the model to forecast a price range for the upcoming period.

9. **Evaluate the potential impact of government regulations.** Consider whether existing government programs or international agreements are likely to interfere with the normal free market mechanism.

10. **Examine seasonal patterns.** Using the methods discussed in Chapter 26, determine whether there are any pronounced seasonal patterns for the given market. Furthermore, it is essential to check whether recent price action has violated normal seasonal patterns, since such behavior might reflect underlying weakness or strength.

11. **Search for market response patterns.** As detailed in Chapter 27, a market response to key fundamental information (e.g., major government reports) might provide important clues regarding the impending price direction.

12. **Assess the trade opportunity.** Compare the potential price range implied by the foregoing analytic steps with the prevailing price level. A trading opportunity is only indicated if the current price is outside the projected range. (This step will not be applicable for analytical approaches designed to forecast the *direction* of the market rather than the price *level*.)

13. **Time trade entry.** Some elements of the fundamental approach, such as seasonal analysis and market response patterns, and some fundamental methods, such as index models, might provide timing clues. Generally speaking, however, the timing of a trade entry should be based on technical input (e.g., chart analysis, technical model). Otherwise, the timing of fundamentally oriented trades is apt to be based on the date on which the analysis is completed—a ludicrous proposition. Furthermore, it should be emphasized that even if the fundamental analysis is correct, prices can always get more out of line before the trend is reversed. The practical aspects of combining fundamental analysis and trading are the subject of Chapter 29.

Fundamental Analysis and Trading

All our knowledge brings us nearer to our ignorance.

—T. S. Eliot

417

■ Fundamental versus Technical Analysis: A Greater Need for Caution

Virtually every market student who has ever relied on fundamental analysis as the basis of a market opinion can recall instances in which his conclusions proved dead wrong. The same, of course, can be said for the technical analyst. However, there is a critical distinction between them. If the technical analyst's methodology leads to erroneous projections, the same analytic tools will eventually point to an opposite conclusion. In effect, technical analysis is a self-correcting approach. In contrast, the fundamental analyst treads on far more dangerous ground. If the fundamental analyst's assessment indicates wheat prices should be $7.00 when the market price is $6.00, by definition, he would be even more bullish if prices were to decline to $5.50—assuming the key economic statistics have remained unchanged.

Therein lies the great danger in using fundamental analysis: The more inaccurate the projection, the more adamant practitioners are apt to become regarding the current attractiveness of market positions in line with their original prognostications. Thus, traders who base their decisions strictly on fundamental considerations might find themselves pyramiding positions in those situations they are most incorrect—a blueprint for disaster. In other words, there is a real danger that a sole or near-exclusive reliance on fundamentals will sooner or later transform an error into a major trading loss.

In fact, this very experience has caused many fundamentalists to renounce their former analytic beliefs. One is reminded of Mark Twain's observation: "The cat that sits down on a hot stove lid will never sit down on a hot stove lid again . . . [nor on] a cold one." The problem lies not in the validity of fundamental analysis as a valuable analytic tool, but rather in the failure to recognize the limitations of this approach. This chapter focuses on these limitations.

■ Three Major Pitfalls in Fundamental Analysis

Even fundamental analysts who do everything right will eventually find themselves reaching the wrong conclusion. There are three possible reasons this could occur:

1. **The unexpected development.** In this case, the model is right, but the assumptions are wrong. The 1972–1973 cotton market provides a classic historical example of such a development. Before that time, the United States did not export any cotton to China. This situation changed dramatically during the 1972–1973 season, when the United States exported more than one-half million bales, or approximately 11 percent of its total shipments, to the People's Republic of China (PRC). Table 29.1 shows exports to the PRC further expanded in the 1973–1974 season. The sudden emergence of the PRC as a major importer of U.S. cotton was one of the key factors behind the historic 1972–1973 bull market in cotton.

Weather often plays the role of the unexpected development in agricultural markets. Figure 29.1 depicts the price impact of the 1989 freeze on the frozen concentrated orange juice (FCOJ) market. Figure 29.2 illustrates the price impact of the 2012 drought on the corn market. Although such developments in the weather are hardly extraordinary, they cannot be anticipated, since allowing for their possible occurrence would lead to inflated price projections in most other years.

An example of an impossible-to-predict sequence of events causing a major market reaction was the March 2011 Japanese earthquake, which triggered a tsunami that caused core meltdowns in three of the Fukushima Daiichi nuclear reactors. (Although the possibility that a tsunami could result in a major accident was anticipated by some, the timing of such a tsunami was, of course, unpredictable.) Figure 29.3 shows this disaster resulted in a 20 percent plunge in the Nikkei index futures over the course of four days.

TABLE 29.1	Early 1970s Shift in U.S. Cotton Exports to the People's Republic of China (1,000 bales)		
Season	Exports to PRC	Total Exports	Exports to PRC as Percentage of Total
1971–1972	0	3,385	0
1972–1973	585	5,311	11.0
1973–1974	898	6,123	14.7
1974–1975	307	3,926	7.8
1975–1976	9	3,311	0.2
1976–1977	0	4,784	0

FIGURE 29.1 March 1990 FCOJ

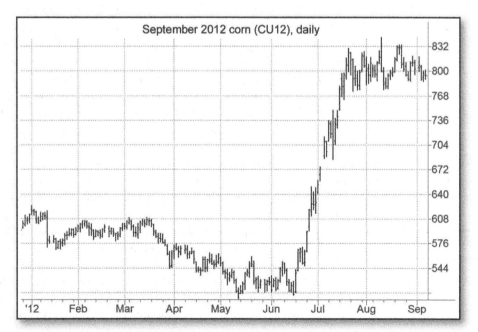

FIGURE 29.2 September 2012 Corn

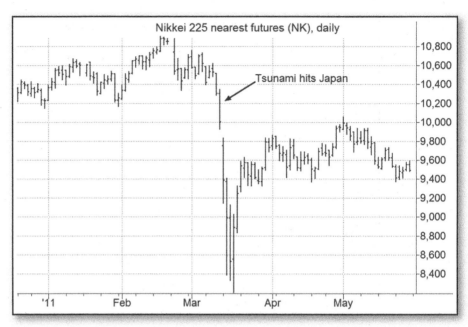

FIGURE 29.3 Nikkei 225 Continuous Futures

Chart created using TradeStation. ©TradeStation Technologies, Inc. All rights reserved.

Iraq's August 1990 invasion of Kuwait is another example of how an unanticipated event can dramatically alter the supply-demand balance and trigger a huge price shift. As depicted in Figure 29.4, this event was followed by a huge advance in crude oil prices, as the market's perceptions about available oil supplies shifted in response to interrupted Kuwaiti output, the embargo against Iraqi crude, and fears that the conflict would extend to threaten critical Saudi Arabian supplies.

Figure 29.5 shows the dramatic impact of the unexpected decision by Switzerland's central bank to remove a price cap on the Swiss franc that had been in place for approximately three years. This shock event caused an almost immediate 25 percent leap in the Swiss franc's value on January 15, 2015. Although this price surge was largely reversed over the subsequent two months, the sudden market move had a devastating impact on currency traders with short positions in the Swiss franc.

Surprises in government reports, which can trigger sharp price reactions, are a common source of unexpected developments. However, because the release dates of these reports are known, as are the reports that are apt to cause large price moves (typically, the initial planting and production estimates in agricultural markets), the resulting price moves are not completely unexpected in the way an unscheduled event might be (e.g., freeze, nuclear accident, invasion). Sometimes, however, a report that does not typically trigger a major price impact may do so. One such instance was the U.S. Department of Agriculture's (USDA) quarterly corn stocks report released on March 28, 2013. During what was perceived to be an exceptionally tight corn market (as a result of the drought referenced by Figure 29.2), the report indicated corn stocks were nearly 8 percent (387 million bushels) higher than previously estimated. In response, corn futures dropped more than 5 percent the next trading day, and more than 8 percent the day after that (see Figure 29.6).

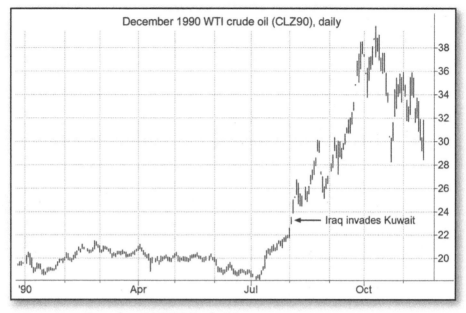

FIGURE 29.4 December 1990 WTI Crude Oil

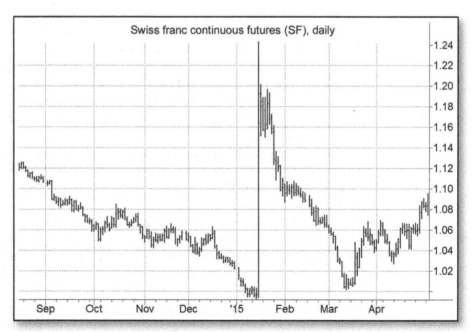

FIGURE 29.5 Swiss Franc Continuous Futures

FUNDAMENTAL ANALYSIS AND TRADING

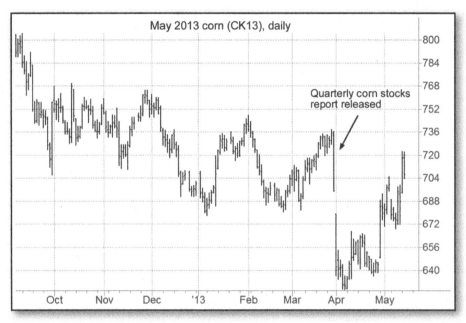

FIGURE 29.6 May 2013 Corn

2. **The missing variable.** Quite often, a market whose price behavior has been adequately described by a set of variables for an extended period of time will suddenly be dramatically affected by an entirely new factor. The 1972–1973 inflationary boom, and its associated hoarding psychology, provides an excellent example of a missing key factor. During this period, price behavior in different markets became far more interdependent, and a wide variety of markets far exceeded the price levels suggested by their intrinsic fundamentals. Any fundamental analysis of a specific market that failed to take into account the potential price impact of the overall bullish wave would have yielded sharply understated price projections.

The 1981–1982 period provided an almost exact opposite example of a missing key variable. In this instance, failure to take into account the pronounced impact of simultaneous deflation and high real interest rates on inventory psychology would have resulted in overstated price forecasts for virtually any commodity market.

It is tempting to think that pivotal events such as the two aforementioned major shifts in commodity demand curves were so readily apparent they would have been quickly incorporated into any fundamental model. Such major transitions, however, tend to be far more conspicuous in retrospect than at the time of their occurrence. Often by the time such structural changes become evident, prices have already witnessed a major move.

3. **Poor timing.** Even if fundamental analysis is accurate and the assumptions are correct, a market can still move counter to the fundamental price projection over the short term—or even the intermediate term. In other words, generally speaking, fundamental models do not provide reliable timing information.

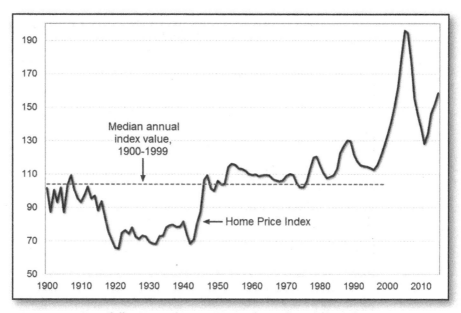

FIGURE 29.7 Case-Shiller National Home Price Index, Inflation Adjusted
Source: www.econ.yale.edu/~shiller/data.htm. Data reflect December values for each calendar year.
Chart created using TradeStation. ©TradeStation Technologies, Inc. All rights reserved.

The 2008 financial meltdown and the subsequent Great Recession provide an excellent illustration of the disconnect between changes in the fundamentals and the timing of price moves. There were many reasons for the 2008 financial crisis but certainly chief among them was the bursting of the housing bubble that had seen housing prices far exceed historical norms. For more than a century since the starting year of the Case-Shiller Home Price Index, the inflation-adjusted index level fluctuated in a range of approximately 65 to 130. At the peak of the 2003–2006 housing bubble, the index had nearly doubled its long-term median level (see Figure 29.7).

The extremes of the housing bubble were fueled by excesses in subprime mortgage lending: Loans were made to borrowers with poor credit, requiring little or no money down, and in its later phases no verification of income or assets. An insatiable demand for mortgages to bundle into mortgage-backed securities (MBSs) incentivized mortgage lenders to write as many mortgages as possible. These lenders were unconcerned about whether borrowers could pay back the loans because they passed on the ownership of mortgages to other financial institutions for use in securitizations. The competition among mortgage lenders to find new borrowers seemed like a race to issue the poorest quality mortgages possible.

The S&P Case-Shiller Home Price Index peaked in the spring of 2006 (see Figure 29.8). At the same time, the rate of delinquencies on subprime adjusted rate mortgages (ARMs) rose steadily throughout 2006 and accelerated in 2007 (see Figure 29.9). Despite these ominous developments, U.S. stock prices continued to move higher, ultimately extending to new record levels, as shown in Figures 29.8 and 29.9. In fact, the extension of the equity bull market after the peak in housing prices in mid-2006 occurred in the face of a more than doubling of sub-

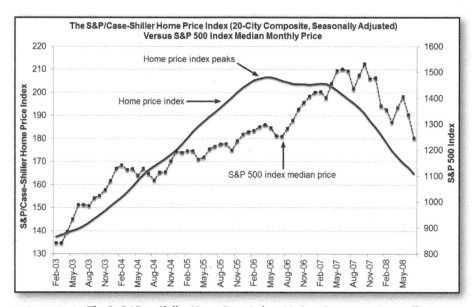

FIGURE 29.8 The S&P/Case-Shiller Home Price Index (20-City Composite, Seasonally Adjusted) vs. S&P 500 Index Median Monthly Price

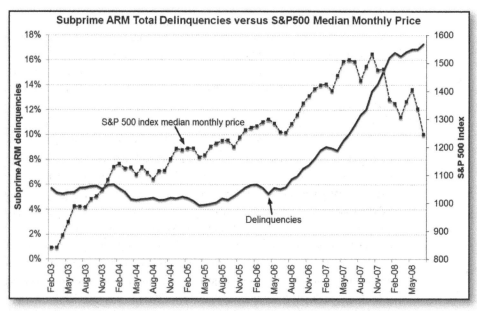

FIGURE 29.9 Subprime Arm Total Delinquencies vs. S&P 500 Median Monthly Price

Source: OTS (delinquency data)

prime delinquencies—a fundamental development that not only had very negative implications for housing prices and the economy, but also seriously imperiled the literally trillions of dollars of subprime MBS that had been issued. All these factors were bearish for the stock market. Nonetheless, it was not until 18 months after housing prices had peaked and a similar interim of sharply rising delinquencies on subprime mortgages that the stock market finally topped out in October 2007.

Assume a fundamental analyst came to the conclusion the prevailing bull market in equities during the mid-2000s was critically dependent on an ongoing housing bubble, which could not be sustained, and whose inevitable reversal would lead to a stock market collapse—a prognostication that would ultimately prove spectacularly correct. Further assume this analyst interpreted the reversal in the Case-Shiller Home Price Index in mid-2006 and the concurrent emerging uptrend in subprime mortgage delinquencies as early evidence that the housing bubble was unraveling—another correct assessment. Now consider the outcome if the analyst acted on this market assessment by implementing a short position in stock index futures in September 2006—the month after subprime delinquencies reached a new multiyear high. A short S&P position initiated at the median price in September 2006 would have been exposed to a 20 percent rise in the index before the stock market ultimately peaked in October 2007. Although the stock market subsequently collapsed, it is highly unlikely the analyst could have survived such a large adverse price move before giving up and liquidating the position at a large loss.

The point is not that fundamentally oriented traders should adamantly hold on to positions if they have a strong conviction in their market analysis—a mental attitude that would be almost certain to result in financial ruin, as it would take only one wrong forecast to lead to a devastating loss. Rather, the point is that even accurate fundamental analysis can lead to poor trading results *if fundamentals are used for timing.*

Crude oil prices in 1985 offer another classic example of a market that continued to extend its prior trend after an important fundamental change, only to witness a belated major reversal many months later. In March 1985 the Saudis announced they would no longer be the Organization of the Petroleum Exporting Countries' (OPEC) "swing supplier" (i.e., the producer that adjusted its output to keep supply and demand in balance). Their decision to abandon their price-supportive role had bearish implications. The Saudis implemented this policy by introducing netback crude oil pricing during the summer of 1985, or guaranteeing buyers of Saudi oil a profit margin. In essence, the Saudis were pricing their oil at whatever price was necessary to move all their production. Despite this ominous action, prices still continued to climb (see Figure 29.10). Prices did not collapse until OPEC officially decided to "pursue market share" at their December 1985 meeting, six months after the de facto implementation of such a policy by Saudi Arabia.

A fundamental analyst who decided in the summer of 1985 that the world oil market was vulnerable to a collapse would have been absolutely right—eventually. In the interim, any short positions implemented on this analysis would have been subject to a protracted, large loss. Thus, poor timing of trade entry based on the timing of fundamental events could have transformed a potential windfall trade into a major loss. The simple fact is that the timing of price moves is often out of sync with the timing of fundamental developments.

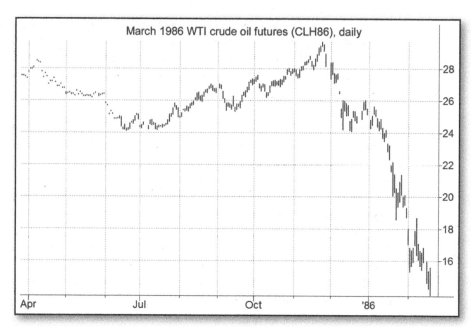

FIGURE 29.10 March 1986 WTI Crude Oil Futures

■ Combining Fundamental Analysis with Technical Analysis and Money Management

As a result of the three pitfalls in fundamental analysis, a buy-and-hold or sell-and-hold trading strategy will eventually prove disastrous for virtually any fundamental analyst. Even assuming a price-forecasting model always managed to include all key variables, a fundamental analyst would still be vulnerable to large trading losses as a result of unexpected developments and poor timing. The observations in the previous section suggest the following important trading rule:

RULE: Never hold a fundamental opinion with complete rigidity.

Clearly, fundamental analysis alone is insufficient for making trading decisions. The two missing ingredients are technical analysis and money management. These various inputs can be combined in the following manner. Fundamental analysis is used as the initial step in the decision-making process in order to determine whether the market is underpriced, overpriced, or in line.

RULE: View fundamental analysis as a tool for gauging whether the market is out of line.

Once a fundamental indication is obtained, technical factors are checked for possible confirmation. This technical input can be in the form of charts or a mechanical system. The main point is that it is necessary to check whether the fundamentally suggested trade appears reasonable in terms of market action. For example, if fundamentals suggest the market is overpriced at a time when prices are in an unbroken uptrend, it would usually be best to delay the implementation of any short position. However, such a fundamental projection might still provide the motivation for initiating shorts on the first signs the market is faltering.

Occasionally, it is reasonable to implement a fundamental trade counter to the prevailing price trend if the market is approaching a major resistance area. For example, assume corn prices are currently $6/bushel and in a virtually unbroken uptrend, while fundamental analysis suggests an equilibrium price level of only $5. If the market is approaching a major resistance area (e.g., a previous high, or the low end of a prior trading range), one might use fundamental analysis as the justification for anticipating a top. However, the trade should only be considered if the trader chooses a predetermined exit point.

This point introduces the third major element in making trading decisions: money management. Of course, the control of losses is essential even when the trading implications of fundamental and technical analysis are in full agreement. However, money management is particularly critical when one is anticipating a market turn.

RULE: An effective trading approach should combine fundamental analysis with technical analysis and money management.

■ Why Bother with Fundamentals?

At this point, the reader might well ask: If fundamental input must be used in conjunction with technical analysis, why should the trader even bother with fundamental analysis in the first place? There are several answers to this question:

1. Fundamental analysis provides an extra dimension of information not available to the purely technical trader. Knowing why a market is acting the way it is can be invaluable in trading decisions. For example, a rally in a declining market might be attributable to a news item that does not meaningfully alter a bearish fundamental outlook, or it might reflect that the market is oversold relative to the fundamentals. Technical analysts cannot distinguish between these two situations—they must treat all similar patterns alike, regardless of the underlying causes. The fundamental analyst, however, can use an awareness of existing market conditions and potential developments as an aid in assessing whether a rally is likely to be the beginning of a new bull market or a bull trap. Of course, such value judgments will not always be accurate, but this consideration is not a problem. For fundamental input to be of value, it is only necessary that profits (or reduced losses) tied to correct decisions exceed the losses (or reduced gains) resulting from incorrect decisions.

2. Fundamentals might sometimes portend a major price move well in advance of any technical signals. The trader who is aware of such a potential transition could have an important advantage over traders who are only following technical signals.

3. A knowledge of fundamentals would permit a trader to adopt a more aggressive stance when the fundamentals suggest the potential for a major move. The strictly technical trader, however, would have to treat all trading signals the same.

4. An understanding of the underlying fundamentals can provide the incentive to stay with a winning trade.
5. The way in which a market responds to fundamental news can be used as a trading tool, even by the technical trader.

■ Are Fundamentals Instantaneously Discounted?

One aspect of the *efficient market hypothesis*, a popular theory subscribed to by many economists, can be paraphrased as follows: At any given time, the market discounts all known information. Of course, if this premise were true, all market analysts—and readers of this book as well—would be suffering from mass delusion. However, there are more compelling reasons for contesting this hypothesis. One reason is the fundamental information responsible for a major price transition is frequently available well before the price trend actually develops. Another reason is that price moves often reflect a reaction to a preceding price swing that had carried the market well beyond fundamentally sustainable equilibrium levels. In both cases, dramatic price moves may materialize in the apparent absence of any significant *concurrent* change in the basic fundamentals. In fact, in the case in which a market has sharply overshot its equilibrium level, it is not unusual for prices to respond in the opposite direction one would anticipate for certain fundamental news (e.g., a rally following a bearish news item).

The aforementioned types of price behavior are inexplicable only if one assumes the market discounts all known information at any given time. However, a far more plausible view of market behavior is that prices sometimes lag or anticipate the levels implied by existing information.

Copper during 2002 through 2006 provides a good example of a market in which price moves occurred well after the fundamental changes responsible for those moves. In 2002, copper inventories reached enormous levels. Not surprisingly, the copper market languished at low prices. Inventories then embarked upon a long decline, but prices failed to respond for more than a year (see Figure 29.11). Beginning in late 2003, prices finally adjusted upward to a higher plateau, as inventories continued to slide. Prices then continued to move sideways at this higher level for about one year (early 2004 to early 2005), even though inventories fell still further. This sideways drift was followed by an explosive rally, which saw prices nearly triple in just over one year's time. Ironically, this enormous price advance occurred at a time when inventories had actually begun to increase moderately. A fundamental analyst who correctly anticipated both the peak and low in copper inventories and traded based on the timing of shifting fundamentals could well have fared poorly.

Price responses followed major changes in the fundamentals (inventory levels) with long lags. The market in 2006 traded at dramatically higher price levels on the same fundamentals as it did in early 2005. These long lags between changes in fundamentals and price adjustments contradict the immediate price adjustments implied by the efficient market hypothesis. The more plausible explanation is that the shift in market psychology from complacency regarding ample supply availability to heightened sensitivity over supply shortages occurred gradually over time rather than as an immediate response to changing fundamentals.

FIGURE 29.11 LME Copper Inventories vs. LME Copper Prices

CQG, Inc. ©

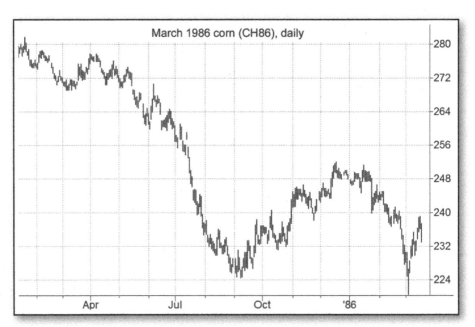

FIGURE 29.12 March 1986 Corn

The 1985–1986 corn market provides another excellent illustration of the nonsynchronous relationship between fundamental information and price movements. Corn prices rose steadily from September through December 1985 (see Figure 29.12), despite repeated increases in the production estimate and reductions in the total usage projection, which resulted in a consistent expansion in the forecasted ending stock/usage ratio (see Table 29.2). This price action would be completely inexplicable if one assumed that prices always responded instantaneously to new fundamental information, a popular academic premise that is subject to frequent empirical contradiction in the real world. Rather, it makes far more sense to view the subsequent price collapse in January/February 1986 as a belated response to the steady deterioration in the fundamental picture in late 1985.

TABLE 29.2 Corn: USDA Supply/Disappearance Estimates During 1985–1986 Season (million bushels)

Month	Production	Total Use	Ending Stocks	Stock/Use Ratio (%)
August 1985	8,266	7,145	2,364	33.1
September 1985	8,469	7,070	2,717	38.4
October 1985	8,603	7,070	2,851	40.3
November 1985	8,717	7,045	3,052	43.3
December 1985	8,717	7,045	3,052	43.3
January 1986	8,717	7,045	3,052	43.3
February 1986	8,865	6,845	3,403	49.7

■ Fitting the News to Price Moves

Although day-to-day price moves often reflect ongoing adjustments to background fundamentals and shifting expectations rather than reactions to concurrent events, the media will usually seek to fit the news to market price movements. If the market is up sharply on a given day, some economic news will be found to explain the price strength. Similarly, if the market breaks precipitously, it's a safe bet that some bearish fundamental explanation will be found. This tailoring of news to fit the price action can sometimes reach absurd lengths, as exemplified by the following two excerpts. The first selection is from an article with the headline, "Strong Economic Reports Give a Lift to the Dollar":

> The dollar closed mostly higher yesterday after what currency traders saw as stronger-than-expected economic reports. "There was good reaction to surprisingly strong numbers," said . . . "The biggest one was retail sales." . . . The Commerce Department reported that retail sales rose three-tenths of 1 percent in November, after remaining unchanged in October. A fall in new weekly claims for unemployment also helped the dollar.

The next quotation comes from a story with the headline, "Long-Term Rates Fall on Reports":

> . . . bond prices benefited from a Commerce Department report that showed the Christmas buying season got off to a slow start in November. . . . At first blush, the numbers seemed to suggest that consumer activity had begun to pick up. But analysts said the increase was tainted because of the downward revisions in sales figures for September and October. "The revisions showed that consumers are still struggling," said . . .

Both of these stories come from the same newspaper, on the same day, on facing pages!

Of course, major unexpected developments will have an immediate market impact when they become known, but for the most part, the efficient market hypothesis assumption that prices instantaneously adjust to fundamental news has it exactly backwards. It is far more accurate to say the financial news will instantaneously adjust to price changes. Whether the market is up or down on a given day, financial reporters have to find an explanation for the price move. Therefore, an explanation will be drawn from the coincident news developments on that day, whether they are pertinent or not. This routine process can lead to the comical situation of the same development being used as both a bullish and bearish explanation on days where the market traverses widely between up and down or vice versa.

August 26, 2011, was a perfect example. On that day, the market sold off in the morning, and then rallied sharply into the afternoon. The key focus of market attention was a speech by Federal Reserve Chairman Ben Bernanke. The following two headlines announced stock market news stories issued by the *same* newswire service on the same day:

Wall Street Slides after Bernanke Comments
Wall Street Bounces as Bernanke Keeps Hopes Alive

The first story read, "Major indexes fell more than 1 percent after Federal Reserve Chairman Ben Bernanke said the U.S. economic recovery was much less robust than hoped but stopped short of signaling further action to boost growth." The second story saw things a bit differently: "Bernanke raised hope the Fed could consider further stimulus measures for the economy at an extended policy meeting in September."

Now, you could believe the same event was bearish before it was bullish. It seems considerably more plausible, though, to believe that the interpretation of the event was altered to fit the market price action. I can assure you that if the market had failed to rebound, there would not have been any stories about how the market ignored Bernanke's constructive comments. The market action determines the interpretation of the news, not the other way around.

Quite frequently prices move higher on the same longer-term fundamentals that have been known for some time or in reaction to a prior decline that took prices too low based on the underlying fundamentals. But while these types of longer-term underlying factors are what really move prices, rather than the often minor or irrelevant developments that are coincident on the same day, they apparently do not make acceptable news copy. When was the last time you saw a financial page headline that read, "Market Rallies Sharply because Bullish Fundamentals Unchanged" or "Market Plunges as Prices Correct Recent Speculative Mania"?

■ Fundamental Developments: Long-Term Implications versus Short-Term Response

In interpreting new developments, it is necessary to make a distinction between the long term and the short term. The long-term interpretation is fairly straightforward: All else being equal, a bullish news item suggests higher prices. However, the short-term interpretation of new developments is entirely different: The essential consideration is how the market responds to the news. In this regard, as summarized by the following rule, the significant occurrence is a divergence between fundamental news and subsequent price action.

> **RULE:** A bullish fundamental development that is followed by a decline or that prompts a rally well below expectations should be viewed as a bearish signal. A bearish fundamental development that is followed by a rally or that prompts a significantly smaller-than-anticipated decline should be viewed as a bullish signal.

By no means is this rule sufficient by itself to allow trading decisions. But in conjunction with other market information, such as background fundamentals and the technical picture, an awareness of this rule should help improve a trader's performance.

Some examples of interpreting market response were provided in Chapter 27. Still, another example might help clarify this approach in using fundamental developments as a trading tool. The time was December 24, 1980, and the cotton market finished the holiday-shortened week just below contract highs and only a few cents below record highs. Despite the pronounced price advance over the previous six-month period, the fundamental picture still appeared bullish because supply and usage trends suggested the potential for the lowest ending carryover since the early 1950s. The weekly export report released after the close indicated a huge net sales figure in excess of one-half million bales. This export figure confirmed rumors of potential large sales to China and virtually assured a very low season ending carryover.

On the basis of her analysis, Stephanie Statistics had been long for some time. After the release of the strikingly bullish December 24 export figure, Stephanie had to virtually restrain herself from calculating the potential increase in her open equity as a result of this latest news item. Monday morning the market opened with near limit gains. "Not bad," she thought, but the fact that the market did not open locked limit-up was disconcerting. As the day progressed, prices began to ease and warning bells went off in her mind. Something was wrong—the market was not really acting right, given the export news. On the basis of this input, Stephanie liquidated one-third of her position that day, one-third the next day, and the remaining third one week later. This scaled liquidation reflected her reluctance to give up a long position in the cotton market, given what she still perceived to be an extremely bullish fundamental outlook.

Stephanie's fundamental view of the market at that time could not have been more off target. As subsequent events would prove, that Monday was the top of the market (see Figure 29.13) and the start of a yearlong slide—the impending extremely low carryover notwithstanding. Eventually, the fundamental explanations for the market's weakness became evident: high interest rates, a deep recession, and expectations for a large new crop. However, by that time, prices had already moved substantially lower (albeit a large portion of the bear move still remained to be realized). The crucial point is that a contrarian interpretation of a bullish news item provided a long liquidation signal at the

433

FUNDAMENTAL ANALYSIS AND TRADING

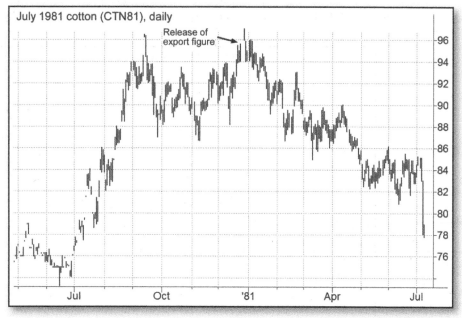

FIGURE 29.13 July 1981 Cotton

Chart created using TradeStation. ©TradeStation Technologies, Inc. All rights reserved.

market top and prevented an incorrect fundamental market evaluation from transforming a profitable position into a large loss.

The preceding story was not a recreation based on artificial hindsight. The events described are true, only the names have been changed to protect the guilty.

A large price move in response to a seemingly neutral event can also be significant. The FCOJ market's response to the October 1993 Crop Production report, which was initially interpreted as "neutral," provides an excellent example. This situation and its implications are nicely described *from a trader's perspective* in the following excerpt of an interview of Russell Sands that appeared in *Commodity Traders Consumers Report*:

> Yesterday there was a crop report. They were expecting between 165 and 180 million boxes of orange juice. The number came out at 172—right in the middle. The early call this morning was unchanged to slightly lower. A few minutes before the open they changed the call to 300 lower. The market opened 700 lower. Now it's down 900.
>
> I have no idea what the fundamentals are. I read the crop report yesterday afternoon, and I thought it would be a quiet day. Maybe the estimates were wrong. Maybe somebody didn't believe the estimates. I have no clue as to why this happened. All I know is there was a neutral report, there was a close-to-unchanged call, but all of a sudden the market is sharply lower and I didn't get out. All the fundamental knowledge in the world is not going to save me. I'm scrambling to get out and cut my losses.

As readers can ascertain in Figure 29.14, getting out of longs even 900 points lower on the day in question looked awfully good a few days or a few weeks later. The preceding quotation, which

FIGURE 29.14   November 1993 FCOJ

apparently was recorded at the moment of the market event being described, provides a good real-life illustration of how market response to fundamental news can be utilized as an aid in making trading decisions.

■ Summary

An awareness of the potential limitations of fundamental analysis is essential to its successful application. Perhaps the key point to keep in mind is that fundamental analysis is primarily a tool for forecasting intermediate or long-term price swings and should not be used as a timing indicator. The only exception to this basic premise is that a counter-to-anticipated market response to fundamental information could be viewed as a contrarian trading signal (e.g., a bullish fundamental development would have bearish near-term implications if it failed to elicit the anticipated positive price response).

PART VI

Futures Spreads and Options

CHAPTER 30

The Concepts and Mechanics of Spread Trading

There was a one-lot trader named Fred,
who tried to reduce risk with a spread.
But the spread was his demise—
He overdid position size,
trading not 1 but 10 instead.

■ Introduction

Despite widespread publicity and extensive information, spreads still remain an often misunderstood and relatively little-used trading vehicle. There is nothing inordinately complicated about spread trading; many traders simply lack the familiarity with the concepts involved. Ironically, it is usually the novice trader, for whom spreads can be a particularly useful trading vehicle, who shuns them as an esoteric operation confined to the "pros." Furthermore, even experienced traders often exhibit a bias against trading spreads, preferring to trade in outright positions because of their greater potential. These traders fail to realize that, at times, spreads may offer a more attractive reward/risk ratio than outright positions. In other words, at a given time, X number of spreads may offer equal potential to a one-contract outright position but imply a smaller risk. (Of course, such a judgment will always be subjective.)

■ Spreads—Definition and Basic Concepts

A spread trade involves the simultaneous purchase of one futures contract against the sale of another futures contract either in the same market or in a related market. Normally, the spread trader will initiate a position when he considers the price difference between two futures contracts to be out of line rather than when he believes the absolute price level to be too high or too low. In essence, the spread trader is more concerned with the *difference* between prices than the *direction* of price. For example, if a trader buys October cattle and sells February cattle, it would not make any difference to him whether October rose by 500 points and February by only 400 points or October fell by 400 and February fell by 500. In either case, October would have gained 100 points relative to February, and the trader's profit would be completely independent of the overall market direction.

However, this is not to say the spread trader will initiate a trade without having some definitive bias as to the future outright market direction. In fact, very often the direction of the market will determine the movement of the spread. In some instances, however, a spread trader may enter a position when he has absolutely no bias regarding future market direction but views a given price difference as being so extreme that he believes the trade will work, or at worst allow only a modest loss, regardless of market direction. We will elaborate on the questions of when and how market direction will affect spreads in later sections.

■ Why Trade Spreads?

The following are some advantages to not exclusively restricting one's trading to outright positions:

1. **In highly volatile markets, the minimum outright commitment of one contract may offer excessive risk to small traders.** In such markets, one-day price swings in excess of $1,500 per contract are not uncommon, and holding a one-contract position may well be overtrading for many traders. Ironically, it is usually these highly volatile markets that provide the best potential trading opportunities. Spreads offer a great flexibility in reducing risk to a desirable and manageable level, since a spread trade usually presents only a fraction of the risk involved in an outright position.[1] For example, assume a given spread is judged to involve approximately one-fifth the risk of an outright position. In such a case, traders for whom a one-contract outright position involves excessive risk may instead choose to initiate a one-, two-, three-, or four-contract spread position, depending on their desired risk level and objectives.

2. **There are times when spreads may offer better reward/risk ratios than outright positions.** Of course, the determination of a reward/risk ratio is a subjective matter. Nevertheless, given a trader's market bias, in a given situation spreads may sometimes offer a better means of approaching the market.

---

[1] For some markets, reduced-size contracts are available on one or more exchanges.

3. **Spreads often offer some protection against sudden extreme losses due to dramatic events that may spark a string of limit-up or limit-down moves counter to one's position (e.g., freeze, large export deal).** Such situations are not all that infrequent, and traders can sometimes lose multiples of the maximum loss they intended to allow (i.e., as reflected by a protective stop) before they can even liquidate their positions. In contrast, during a time of successive limit moves, the value of a spread might not even change as both months may move the limit. Of course, eventually the spread will also react, but when it does, the market may well be past its frenzied panic stage, and the move may be gradual and moderate compared with the drastic price change of the outright position.

4. **A knowledge and understanding of spreads can also be a valuable aid in trading outright positions.** For example, a failure of the near months to gain sufficiently during a rally (in those commodities in which a gain can theoretically be expected) may signal the trader to be wary of an upward move as a possible technical surge vulnerable to retracement. In other words, the spread action may suggest that no real tightness exists. This scenario is merely one example of how close observation of spreads can offer valuable insights into outright market direction. Naturally, at times, the inferences drawn from spread movements may be misleading, but overall they are likely to be a valuable aid to the trader. A second way an understanding of spreads can aid an outright-position trader is by helping identify the best contract month in which to initiate a position. The trader with knowledge of spreads should have a distinct advantage in picking the month that offers the best potential versus risk. Over the long run, this factor alone could significantly improve trading performance.

5. **Trading opportunities may sometimes exist for spreads at a time when none is perceived for the outright commodity itself.**

■ Types of Spreads

There are three basic types of spreads:

1. **The intramarket (or interdelivery) spread** is the most common type of spread and consists of buying one month and selling another month in the same commodity. An example of an intramarket spread would be long December corn/short March corn. The intramarket spread is by far the most widely used type of spread and will be the focus of this chapter's discussion.

   The **intercrop spread** is a special case of the intramarket spread involving two different crop years (e.g., long an old crop month and short a new crop month). The intercrop spread requires special consideration and extra caution. Intercrop spreads can often be highly volatile, and price moves in opposite directions by new and old crop months are not particularly uncommon. The intercrop spread may often be subject to price ranges and patterns that distinctly separate it from the intracrop spread (i.e., standard intramarket spread).

2. **The intercommodity spread** consists of a long position in one commodity and a short position in a related commodity. In this type of spread the trader feels the price of a given

commodity is too high or low relative to a closely related commodity. Some examples of this type of spread include long December cattle/short December hogs and long July wheat/short July corn. *The source/product spread*, which involves a commodity and its by-product(s)—for example, soybeans versus soybean meal and/or soybean oil—is a specific type of intercommodity spread that is sometimes classified separately.

Usually, an intercommodity spread will involve the same month in each commodity, but this need not always be the case. Ideally, traders should choose the month they consider the strongest in the market they are buying and the month they consider the weakest in the market they are selling. Obviously, these will not always be the same month. For example, assume the following price configuration:

	December	February	April
Cattle	120.00	116.00	118.00
Hogs	84.00	81.00	81.00

Given this price structure, a trader might decide the premium of cattle to hogs is too small and will likely increase. This trading bias would dictate the initiation of a long cattle/short hog spread. However, the trader may also believe February cattle is underpriced relative to other cattle months and that December hogs are overpriced relative to the other hog contracts. In such a case, it would make more sense for the trader to be long February cattle/short December hogs rather than long December cattle/short December hogs or long February cattle/short February hogs.

One important factor to keep in mind when trading intercommodity spreads is that contract sizes may differ for each commodity. For example, the contract size for euro futures is 125,000 units, whereas the contract size for British pound futures is 62,500 units. Thus, a euro/British pound spread consisting of one long contract could vary even if the price difference between the two markets remained unchanged. The difference in price levels is another important factor relevant to contract ratios for intercommodity spreads. The criteria and methodology for determining appropriate contract ratios for intercommodity spreads are discussed in the next chapter.

3. **The intermarket spread.** This spread involves buying a commodity at one exchange and selling the same commodity at another exchange, which will often be another country. An example of this type of spread would be long New York March cocoa/short London March cocoa. Transportation, grades deliverable, distribution of supply (total and deliverable) relative to location, and historical and seasonal basis relationships are the primary considerations in this type of spread. In the case of intermarket spreads involving different countries, currency fluctuations become a major consideration. Intermarket spread trading is often referred to as arbitrage. As a rule, the intermarket spread requires a greater degree of sophistication and comprehensive familiarity with the commodity in question than other types of spreads.

The General Rule

For many commodities, the intramarket spread can often, but not always, be used as a proxy for an outright long or short position. As a general rule, near months will gain ground relative to distant months in a bull market and lose ground in a bear market. The reason for this behavior is that a bull market usually reflects a current tight supply situation and often will place a premium on more immediately available supplies. In a bear market, however, supplies are usually burdensome, and distant months will have more value because they implicitly reflect the cost involved in storing the commodity for a period of time. Thus, if a trader expects a major bull move, he can often buy a nearby month and sell a more distant month. If he is correct in his analysis of the market and a bull move does materialize, the nearby contract will likely gain on the distant contract, resulting in a successful trade. It is critical to keep in mind that this general rule is just that, and is meant only as a rough guideline. There are a number of commodities for which this rule does not apply, and even in those commodities where it does apply, there are important exceptions. We will elaborate on the question of applicability in the next section.

At this point the question might legitimately be posed, "If the success of a given spread trade is contingent upon forecasting the direction of the market, wouldn't the trader be better off with an outright position?" Admittedly, the potential of an outright position will almost invariably be considerably greater. But the point to be kept in mind is that an outright position also entails a correspondingly greater risk. Sometimes the outright position will offer a better reward/risk ratio; at other times the spread will offer a more attractive trade. A determination of which is the better approach will depend upon absolute price levels, prevailing price differences, and the trader's subjective views of the risk and potential involved in each approach.

The General Rule—Applicability and Nonapplicability

Commodities to Which the General Rule Can Be Applied

Commodities to which the general rule applies with some regularity include corn, wheat, oats, soybeans, soybean meal, soybean oil, lumber, sugar, cocoa, cotton, orange juice, copper, and heating oil. (The general rule will also usually apply to interest rate markets.) Although the general rule will usually hold in these markets, there are still important exceptions, some of which include:

1. At a given point in time the premium of a nearby month may already be excessively wide, and consequently a general price rise in the market may fail to widen the spread further.
2. Since higher prices also increase carrying costs (see section entitled "The Limited-Risk Spread"), it is theoretically possible for a price increase to widen the discount of nearby months in a surplus market. Although such a spread response to higher prices is atypical, its probability of occurrence will increase in a high-interest-rate environment.

3. Spreads involving a spot month near expiration can move independently of, or contrary to, the direction implied by the general rule. The reason is that the price of an expiring position is critically dependent upon various technical considerations involving the delivery situation, and wide distortions are common.
4. A bull move that is primarily technical in nature may fail to influence a widening of the nearby premiums since no real near-term tightness exists. (Such a price advance will usually only be temporary in nature.)
5. Government intervention (e.g., export controls, price controls, etc.), or even the expectation of government action, can completely distort normal spread relationships.

Therefore, it is important that when initiating spreads in these commodities, the trader keep in mind not only the likely overall market direction, but also the relative magnitude of existing spread differences and other related factors.

Commodities Conforming to the Inverse of the General Rule

Some commodities, such as gold and silver, conform to the exact inverse of the general rule: In a rising market distant months gain relative to more nearby contracts, and in a declining market they lose relative to the nearby positions. *In fact, in these markets, a long forward/short nearby spread is often a good proxy for an outright long position, and the reverse spread can be a substitute position for an outright short.* In each of these markets nearby months almost invariably trade at a discount, which tends to widen in bull markets and narrow in bear markets.

The reason for the tendency of near months in gold and silver to move to a wider discount in a bull market derives from the large worldwide stock levels of these metals. Generally speaking, price fluctuations in gold and silver do not reflect near-term tightness or surplus, but rather the market's changing perception of their value. In a bull market, the premium of the back months will increase because higher prices imply increased carrying charges (i.e., interest costs will increase as the total value of the contract increases). Because the forward months implicitly contain the cost of carrying the commodity, their premium will tend to widen when these costs increase. Although the preceding represents the usual pattern, there have been a few isolated exceptions due to technical factors.

Commodities Bearing Little or No Relationship to the General Rule

Commodities in which there is little correlation between general price direction and spread differences usually fall into the category of nonstorable commodities (cattle and live hogs). We will examine the case of live cattle to illustrate why this there is no consistent correlation between price and spread direction in nonstorable markets.

Live cattle, by definition, is a completely nonstorable commodity. When feedlot cattle reach market weight, they must be marketed; unlike most other commodities, they obviously cannot be placed in storage to await better prices. (To be perfectly accurate, cattle feeders have a small measure of flexibility, in that they can market an animal before it reaches optimum weight or hold it for a while after. However, economic considerations will place strong limits on the extent of such marketing shifts.) As a consequence of the intrinsic nature of this commodity, different months in live cattle are, in a sense, different commodities. June live cattle is a very different commodity from December live cattle. The price of each will be dependent on the market's perception of the supply-demand picture that it expects to prevail at each given time period. It is not unusual for a key cattle on feed report to carry bullish implications for near months and bearish connotations for distant months, or vice versa. In such a case, the futures market can often react by moving in opposite directions for the near and distant contracts. The key point is that in a bullish (bearish) situation, the market will sometimes view the near-term supply/demand balance as being more bullish (bearish) and sometimes it will view the distant situation as being more bullish (bearish). A similar behavioral pattern prevails in hogs. Thus, the general rule would not apply in these types of markets.

In these markets, rather than being concerned about the overall price direction, the spread trader is primarily concerned with how he thinks the market will perceive the fundamental situation in different time periods. For example, at a given point in time, June cattle and December cattle may be trading at approximately equal levels. If the trader believes that marketings will become heavy in the months preceding the June expiration, placing pressure on that contract, and further believes the market psychology will view the situation as temporary, expecting prices to improve toward year-end, he would initiate a long December/short June cattle spread. Note that if he is correct in the development of near-term pressure but the market expects even more pronounced weakness as time goes on, the trade will not work even if his expectations for improved prices toward year-end also prove accurate. One must always remember that a spread's life span is limited to the expiration of the nearer month, and substantiation of the spread idea after that point will be of no benefit to the trader. Thus, the trader is critically concerned, not only with the fundamentals themselves, but also with the market's perception of the fundamentals, which may or may not be the same.

■ Spread Rather Than Outright—An Example

Frequently, the volatility of a given market may be so extreme that even a one-contract position may represent excessive risk for some traders. In such instances, spreads offer the trader an alternative approach to the market. For example, in early 2014, coffee futures surged dramatically, gaining more than 75 percent from late January to early March, with average daily price volatility more than tripling during that period. Prices swung wildly for the next several months—pushing to a higher high in April, giving back more than half of the rally in the sell-off to the July low, and then rallying to yet another new high in October (see Figure 30.1). At that juncture, assume a low-risk trader believed that prevailing nearest futures prices near $2.22 in mid-October 2014 were unsustainable, but based on the market's volatility (which was still around three times what it had been early in the year) and his money management rules felt he could not assume the risk of an outright position. Such a trader could instead have entered a bear spread (e.g., short July 2015 coffee/long December 2015 coffee) and profited handsomely from the subsequent price slide. Figure 30.1 illustrates the close correspondence between the spread and the market. The fact that an outright position would have garnered a much larger profit is an irrelevant consideration, since the trader's risk limitations would have prevented him from participating in the bear move altogether had his market view been confined to outright trades.

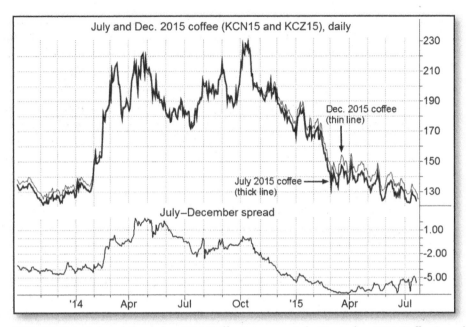

FIGURE 30.1 July and December 2015 Coffee Futures vs. July/December 2015 Coffee Spread

Chart created using TradeStation. ©TradeStation Technologies, Inc. All rights reserved.

The Limited-Risk Spread

The limited-risk spread is a type of intracommodity spread involving the buying of a near month (relatively speaking) and the selling of a more distant month in a storable commodity in which the process of taking delivery, storing, and redelivering at a later date does not require reinspection or involve major transportation or storage complications. This definition would exclude such commodities as live cattle, which by definition are nonstorable, and sugar, which involves major complications in taking delivery and storing. Commodities that fall into the limited-risk category include corn, wheat, oats, soybeans, soybean oil, copper, cotton, orange juice, cocoa, and lumber.[2]

In a commodity fulfilling the above specifications, the maximum premium that a more distant month can command over a nearby contract is roughly equal to the cost of taking delivery, holding the commodity for the length of time between the two expirations, and then redelivering. The cost for this entire operation is referred to as *full carry*. The term *limited risk* will be used only when the nearby month is at a discount. For example, assuming full carry in the October/December cotton

---

[2] Although precious metals can easily be received in delivery, stored, and redelivered, they are not listed here because spreads in precious metals are almost entirely determined by carrying charges. Thus, the only motivation for implementing an intramarket precious metals spread is an expectation for a change in carrying charges. In contrast, the purpose of a limited-risk spread is to profit from an expected narrowing of the spread relative to the level implied by carrying charges (which are assumed to remain constant).

spread is equal to 200 points, a long October/short December spread initiated at October 100 points under might be termed a limited-risk spread. However, the same long October/short December cotton spread would not be termed limited risk if, for example, October were at a 300-point premium. Nevertheless, it should be noted that even in this latter case, the maximum risk would still be defined—namely, 500 points—and in this respect the spread would still differ from spreads involving the selling of the nearby contract, or spreads in markets that do not fulfill the limited-risk specifications detailed above.

The best way to understand why it is unlikely for the premium of a distant month to exceed carrying costs is to assume the existence of a situation where this is indeed the case. In such an instance, a trader who bought a nearby month and sold a more distant month would have an opportunity for speculative gain and, at worst, would have the option of taking delivery, storing, and redelivering at a likely profit (since we assumed a situation in which the premium of the distant month exceeded carrying charges). Sounds too good to be true? Of course, and for this reason differences beyond full carry are quite rare unless there are technical problems in the delivery process. In fact, it is usually unlikely for a spread difference to even approach full carry since, as it does, the opportunity exists for a speculative trade that has very limited risk but, theoretically, no limit on upside potential. In other words, as spreads approach full carry, some traders will initiate long nearby/short forward spreads with the idea that there is always the possibility of gain, but, at worst, the loss will be minimal. For this reason, spreads will usually never reach full carry.

At a surface glance, limited-risk spreads seem to be highly attractive trades, and indeed they often are. However, it should be emphasized that *just because a spread is relatively near full carry does not necessarily mean it is an attractive trade*. Very often, such spreads will move still closer to full carry, resulting in a loss, or trade sluggishly in a narrow range, tying up capital that could be used elsewhere. However, if the trader has reason to believe the nearby month should gain on the distant, the fact that the spread has a limited risk (the difference between full carry and the current spread differential) makes the trade particularly attractive.

The components of carrying costs include interest, storage, insurance, and commission. We will not digress into the area of calculating carrying charges. (Such information can be obtained either through the exchanges themselves or through commodity brokers or analysts specializing in the given commodity.) However, we would emphasize that the various components of carrying charges are variable rather than fixed, and consequently *carrying charges can fluctuate quite widely over time*. Interest costs are usually the main component of carrying charges and are dependent on interest rates and price levels, both of which are sometimes highly volatile. It is critical to keep changes in carrying costs in mind when making historical comparisons.

Can a trader ever lose more money in a limited-risk spread than the amount implied by the difference between full carry and the spread differential at which the trade was initiated? The answer is that although such an occurrence is unlikely, it is possible. For one thing, as we indicated above, carrying charges are variable, and it is possible for the theoretical maximum loss of a spread trade to increase as a result of fluctuations in carrying costs. For example, a trader might enter a long October/short December cotton spread at 100 points October under, at a time when full carry approximates 200 points—implying a maximum risk of 100 points. However, in ensuing months, it is possible higher prices and rising interest rates could cause full carry to move beyond 200 points, increasing the trader's risk correspondingly. In such an instance, it is theoretically possible for the given spread to move significantly beyond the point the trader considered the maximum risk point. Although such an event can occur, it should be emphasized that it is rather unusual, since in a limited-risk spread increased carrying costs due to sharply higher price levels will usually imply larger gains for the nearby months. As for interest rates, changes substantial enough to influence marked changes in carrying costs will usually take time to develop.

Another example of a limited-risk spread that might contain hidden risk is the case in which the government imposes price ceilings on nearby contracts but not on the more distant contracts. Although highly unusual, this situation has happened before and represents a possible risk that the spread trader should consider in the unlikely event that the prevailing political environment is conducive to the enactment of price controls.

Also, for short intervals of time, spread differences may well exceed full carry due to the absence of price limits on the nearby contract. For a number of commodities, price limits on the nearby contract are removed at some point before its expiration (e.g., first notice day, first trading day of the expiring month, etc.). Consequently, in a sharply declining market, the nearby month can move to a discount exceeding full carry as the forward month is contained by price limits. Although this situation will usually correct itself within a few days, in the interim, it can generate a substantial margin call for the spread trader. It is important that spread traders holding their positions beyond the removal of price limits on the nearby contract are sufficiently capitalized to easily handle such possible temporary spread aberrations.

As a final word, it should be emphasized that *although there is a theoretical limit on the premium that a distant month can command over a nearby contract in carrying-charge markets, there is no similar limit on the premium that a nearby position can command.* Nearby premiums are usually indicative of a tight current supply situation, and there is no way of determining an upper limit to the premium the market will place on more immediately available supplies.

The Spread Trade—Analysis and Approach

Step 1: Straightforward Historical Comparison

A logical starting point is a survey of the price action of the given spread during recent years. Historical spread charts, if available, are ideal for this purpose. If charts (or historical price data that can be downloaded into a spreadsheet) are unavailable, the trader should, if possible, scan historical price data, checking the difference of the given spread on a biweekly or monthly basis for at least the past 5 to 10 years. This can prove to be a time-consuming endeavor, but a spread trade initiated without any concept of historical patterns is, in a sense, a shot in the dark. Although spreads can deviate widely from historical patterns, it is still important to know the normal range of a spread, as well as its "average" level.

Step 2: Isolation of Similar Periods

As a rule, spreads will tend to act similarly in similar situations. Thus, the next step would be a refinement of step 1 by means of isolating roughly similar periods. For example, in a high-priced year, we might be interested in considering the spread action only in other past bull seasons, or we can cut the line still sharper and consider only bull seasons that were demand oriented or only those that were supply oriented. An examination of the spread's behavior during different fundamental conditions in past years will usually reveal the relative comparative importance of similar and dissimilar seasons.

Step 3: Analysis of Spread Seasonality

This step is a further refinement of step 1. Sometimes a spread will tend to display a distinct seasonal pattern. For example, a given spread may tend to widen or narrow during a specific period. Knowledge of such a seasonality can be critically important in deciding whether or not to initiate a given spread. For example, if in nine of the past 10 seasons the near month of a given spread lost ground to the distant month during the March–June period, one should think twice about initiating a bull spread in March.

Step 4: Analysis and Implications of Relevant Fundamentals

This step would require the formulation of a concept of market direction (in commodities where applicable), or equivalent appropriate analysis in those commodities where it is not. This approach is fully detailed in the sections entitled "The General Rule" and "The General Rule—Applicability and Nonapplicability."

Step 5: Chart Analysis

A key step before initiating a spread trade should be the examination of a current chart of the spread (or the use of some other technical input). As in outright positions, charts are an invaluable informational tool and a critical aid to timing.

■ Pitfalls and Points of Caution

- Do not automatically assume a spread is necessarily a low-risk trade. In some instances, a spread may even involve greater risk than an outright position. Specifically, in the case of intercommodity spreads, intercrop spreads, and spreads involving nonstorable commodities, the two legs of the spread can sometimes move in opposite directions.

- Be careful not to overtrade a spread because of its lower risks or margin. A 5- to 10-contract spread position gone astray can often prove more costly than a bad one-contract outright trade. Overtrading is a very common error in spread trading.

- As a general rule, traders should avoid trading spreads in markets in which they are unfamiliar with the fundamentals.

- Check the open interest of the months involved to ensure adequate liquidity, especially in spreads involving distant back months. A lack of liquidity can significantly increase the loss when getting out of a spread that has gone awry. At times, of course, a given spread may be sufficiently attractive despite its less-than-desirable liquidity. Nevertheless, even in such a case, it is important that traders be aware of the extra risk involved.

- Place a spread order on a spread basis rather than as two separate outright orders. Some traders place their spread orders one leg at a time in the hopes of initiating their position at a better price than the prevailing market level. Such an approach is inadvisable not only because it will often backfire, but also because it will increase commission costs.

- When the two months of the spread are very close in price, extra care should be taken to specify clearly which month is the premium month in the order.

- Do not assume that current price quotations accurately reflect actual spread differences. Time lags in the buying and selling of different contracts, as well as a momentary concentration of orders in a given contract month, can often result in outright price quotations implying totally unrepresentative spread values.

- Do not liquidate spreads one leg at a time. Failing to liquidate the entire spread position at one time is another common and costly error, which has caused many a good spread trade to end in a loss.

- Avoid spreads involving soon-to-expire contracts. Expiring contracts, aside from usually being free of any price limits, are subject to extremely wide and erratic price moves dependent on technical delivery conditions.

- Do not assume the applicability of prior seasons' carrying charges before initiating a limited-risk spread. Wide price swings and sharply fluctuating interest costs can radically alter carrying costs.

- Try to keep informed of any changes in contract specifications, since such changes can substantially alter the behavior of a spread.

- Properly implemented intercommodity and intermarket spreads often require an unequal number of contracts in each market. The methodology for determining the proper contract ratio between different markets is discussed in the next chapter.

- Do not use spreads to protect an outright position that has gone sour—that is, do not initiate an opposite direction position in another contract as an alternative to liquidating a losing position. In most cases such a move amounts to little more than fooling oneself and often can exacerbate the loss.

■ Because it is especially easy to procrastinate in liquidating a losing spread position, the spread trader needs to be particularly vigilant in adhering to risk management principals. It is advisable that the spread trader determine a mental stop point (usually on the basis of closing values) prior to entering a spread and rigidly stick to liquidating the spread position if this mental stop point is reached.

■ Avoid excessively low-risk spreads because transaction costs (slippage as well as commission) will represent a significant percentage of the profit potential, reducing the odds of a net winning outcome. In short, the odds are stacked against the very-low-risk spread trader.

■ As a corollary to the prior item, a trader should choose the most widely spaced intramarket spread consistent with the desired risk level. Generally speaking, the wider the time duration in an intramarket spread, the greater the volatility of the spread. This observation is as true for markets conforming to the general rule as for markets unrelated or inversely related to the general rule. Traders implementing a greater-than-one-unit intramarket spread position should be sure to choose the widest liquid spread consistent with the trading strategy. For example, it usually would make little sense to implement a two-unit March/May corn spread, since a one-unit March/July corn spread would offer a very similar potential/risk trade at half the transaction cost.

CHAPTER 31

Intercommodity Spreads: Determining Contract Ratios

. . . many more people see than weigh.

—Philip Dormar Stanhope, Earl of Chesterfield

By definition, the intention of the spread trader is to implement a position that will reflect changes in the price *difference* between contracts rather than changes in outright price levels. To achieve such a trade, the two legs of a spread must be equally weighted. As an obvious example, long 2 December corn/short 1 March corn is a spread in name only. Such a position would be far more dependent on fluctuations in the price level of corn than on changes in the price difference between December and March.

The meaning of *equally weighted,* however, is by no means obvious. Many traders simply assume that a balanced spread position implies an equal number of contracts long and short. Such an assumption is usually valid for most intramarket spreads (although an exception will be discussed later in this chapter). However, for many intermarket and intercommodity[1] spreads, the automatic presumption of an equal number of contracts long and short can lead to severe distortions.

Consider the example of a trader who anticipates that demand for lower quality Robusta coffee beans (London contract) will decline relative to higher quality Arabica beans (New York contract) and

---

[1] The distinction between intermarket and intercommodity spreads was defined in Chapter 30. An intermarket spread involves buying and selling the same commodity at two different exchanges (e.g., New York vs. London cocoa); the intercommodity spread involves buying and selling two different but related markets (e.g., wheat vs. corn, cattle vs. hogs).

attempts to capitalize on this forecast by initiating a 5-contract long New York coffee/short London coffee spread. Assume the projection is correct, and London coffee prices decline from $0.80/lb to $0.65/lb, while New York coffee prices simultaneously decline from $1.41/lb to $1.31/lb. At surface glance, it might appear this trade is successful, since the trader is short London coffee (which has declined by $0.15/lb) and long New York coffee (which has lost only $0.10/lb). However, the trade actually loses money (even excluding commissions). The explanation lies in the fact that the contract sizes for the New York and London coffee contracts are different: The size of the New York coffee contract is 37,500 lb, while the size of the London coffee contract is 10 metric tonnes, or 22,043 lb. (*Note:* In practice, the London coffee contract is quoted in dollars/tonne; the calculations in this section reflect a conversion into $/pound for easier comparison with the New York coffee contract.) Because of this disparity, an equal contract position really implies a larger commitment in New York coffee. Consequently, such a spread position is biased toward gaining in bull coffee markets (assuming the long position is in New York coffee) and losing in bear markets. The long New York/short London spread position in our example actually loses $2,218 plus commissions, despite the larger decline in London coffee prices:

$$\text{Profit/loss} = \# \text{ of contracts} \times \# \text{ of units per contract} \times \text{gain/loss per unit}$$
$$\text{Profit/loss in long New York coffee position} = 5 \times 37,500 \times (-\$0.10/\text{lb}) = -\$18,750$$
$$\text{Profit/loss in short London coffee position} = 5 \times 22,043 \times (+\$0.15/\text{lb}) = +\$16,532$$
$$\text{Net profit/loss in spread} = -\$2,218$$

The difference in contract size between the two markets could have been offset by adjusting the contract ratio of the spread to equalize the long and short positions in terms of units (lb). The general procedure would be to place $U1/U2$ contracts of the smaller-unit market (i.e., London coffee) against each contract of the larger-unit contract (i.e., New York coffee). ($U1$ and $U2$ represent the number of units per contract in the respective markets—$U1 = 37,500$ lb and $U2 = 22,043$ lb.) Thus, in the New York coffee/London coffee spread, each New York coffee contract would be offset by 1.7 (37,500/22,043) London coffee contracts, implying a minimum equal-unit spread of five London coffee versus three New York coffee (rounding down the theoretical 5.1-contract London coffee position to 5 contracts.) This unit-equalized spread would have been profitable in the above example:

$$\text{Profit/loss} = \# \text{ of contracts} \times \# \text{ of units per contract} \times \text{gain/loss per unit}$$
$$\text{Profit/loss in long New York coffee position} = 3 \times 37,500 \times (-\$0.10/\text{lb}) = -\$11,250$$
$$\text{Profit/loss in short London coffee position} = 5 \times 22,043 \times (+\$0.15/\text{lb}) = +\$16,532$$
$$\text{Net profit/loss in spread} = +\$5,282$$

The unit-size adjustment, however, is not the end of our story. It can be argued that even the equalized-unit New York coffee/London coffee spread is still unbalanced, since there is another significant difference between the two markets: London coffee prices are lower than New York coffee prices. This observation raises the question of whether it is more important to neutralize the spread against equal price moves or equal-percentage price moves. The rationale for the latter approach is that, all else being equal, the magnitude of price changes is likely to be greater in the higher-priced market.

The fact that percentage price change is a more meaningful measure than absolute price change is perhaps best illustrated by considering the extreme example of the gold/silver spread. The equal-unit approach, which neutralizes the spread against equal-dollar price changes in both markets, would imply the rather ludicrous spread position of 50 gold contracts versus 1 silver contract. (The contract size of silver is 5,000 oz; the contract size of gold is 100 oz.) Obviously, such a position would be almost entirely dependent upon changes in the price of gold rather than any movement in the gold/silver spread. The disparity is due to the fact that since gold is far higher priced than silver (by a ratio of 32-101:1 based on the past 30-year range), its price swings will also be far greater. For example, if gold is trading at \$1,400/oz and silver at \$20/oz, a \$2 increase in silver prices is likely to be accompanied by far more than a \$2 increase in gold prices. Clearly, the relevant criterion in the gold/silver spread is that the position should be indifferent to equal percentage price changes rather than equal absolute price changes. Although less obvious, the same principle would also appear preferable, even for intercommodity or intermarket spreads between more closely priced markets (e.g., New York coffee/London coffee).

Thus we adopt the definition that a *balanced spread* is a spread that is indifferent to equal percentage price changes in both markets. It can be demonstrated this condition will be fulfilled if the spread is initiated so the dollar values of the long and short positions are equal.[2] An equal-dollar-value spread

---

[2] If the spread is implemented so that dollar values are equal, then:

$$N_1 U_1 P_{1,t=0} = N_2 U_2 P_{2,t=0}$$

where N_1 = number of contracts in market 1
N_2 = number of contracts in market 2
U_1 = number of units per contract in market 1
U_2 = number of units per contract in market 2
$P_{1,t=0}$ = price of market 1 at spread initiation
$P_{2,t=0}$ = price of market 2 at spread initiation

An equal-percentage price change implies that both prices change by the same factor k. Thus,

$$P_{1,t=1} = k\, P_{1,t=0} \quad \text{and} \quad P_{2,t=1} = k\, P_{2,t=0}$$

where $P_1, t = 1$ = price of market 1 after equal-percentage price move
$P_{2,t=1}$ = price of market 2 after equal-percentage price move

And the equity changes (in absolute terms) are:

Equity change in market 1 position $= N_1 U_1 \mid kP_{1,t=0} - P_{1,t=0} \mid = N_1 U_1 P_{1,t=0} \mid k - 1 \mid$
Equity change in market 2 position $= N_2 U_2 \mid kP_{2,t=0} - P_{2,t=0} \mid = N_2 U_2 P_{2,t=0} \mid k - 1 \mid$

Since, by definition, an equal-dollar-value spread at initiation implies that $N_1 U_1 P_{1,t=0} = N_2 U_2 P_{2,t=0}$, the equity changes in the positions are equal.

It should be noted that the equal-dollar-value spread only assures that equal-percentage price changes will not affect the spread if the percentage price changes are measured relative to the initiation price levels. However, equal-percentage price changes from subsequent price levels will normally result in different absolute dollar changes in the long and short positions (since the position values are not necessarily equal at any post-initiation points of reference).

can be achieved by using a contract ratio that is inversely proportional to the contract value (CV) ratio. This can be expressed as follows (see footnote 2 for symbol definitions):

$$\frac{N_2}{N_1} = \frac{CV_1}{CV_2} = \frac{U_1 P_{1,t=0}}{U_2 P_{2,t=0}}$$

$$\text{or, } N_2 = N_1 \left(\frac{CV_1}{CV_2} \right)$$

For example, if New York coffee is trading at $1.41/lb and London coffee at $.80/lb, the equal-dollar-value spread would indicate a contract ratio of 1 New York coffee/3 London coffee:

$$N_2 = N_1 \left(\frac{CV_1}{CV_2} \right) = N_1 \left(\frac{U_1 P_{1,t=0}}{U_2 P_{2,t=0}} \right)$$

If $N_1 = 1$ New York coffee contract,

$$N_2 = 37,500 \times \$1.41 / 22,043 \times \$.080 = 3 \text{ London contracts}$$

Thus, in an equal-dollar-value spread position, 3 New York coffee contracts would be balanced by 9 (not 5) London contracts.

It may help clarify matters to compare the just-defined equal-dollar-value approach to the equal-unit approach for the case of the New York coffee/London coffee spread. Although the equal-unit spread is indifferent to equal absolute price changes, it will be affected by equal-percentage price changes (unless, of course, the price levels in both markets are equal, in which case the two approaches are equivalent). For example, given initiation price levels of New York coffee = $1.41/lb and London coffee = $.80/lb, consider the effect of a 25 percent price decline on a long 3 New York/ short 5 London coffee (equal unit) spread:

Profit/loss in long New York coffee position = $3 \times 37,500 \times (-\$0.3525) = -\$39,656$
Profit/loss in short London coffee position = $5 \times 22,043 \times (-\$0.20) = +\$22,043$
Profit/loss in spread = $-\$17,613$

The equal-dollar-value spread, however, would be approximately unchanged:

Profit/loss in long New York coffee position = $3 \times 37,500 \times (-\$0.3525) = -\$39,656$
Profit/loss in short London coffee position = $9 \times 22,043 \times (+\$0.20) = +\$39,677$
Profit/loss in spread = $+\$21$

Returning to our original example, if the trader anticipating price weakness in London coffee relative to New York coffee had used the equal-dollar-value approach (assuming a 3-contract position for New York coffee), the results would have been as follows:

Profit/loss in long New York coffee position = $3 \times 37,500 \times (-\$0.10) = -\$11,250$
Profit/loss in short London coffee position = $9 \times 22,043 \times (+\$0.15) = +\$29,758$
Profit/loss in spread = $+\$18,508$

Thus, while the naive placement of an equal contract spread actually results in a $2,218 loss despite the validity of the trade concept, the more appropriate equal-dollar-value approach results in a $18,508 gain. This example emphasizes the critical importance of determining appropriate contract ratios in intercommodity and intermarket spreads.

An essential point to note is that if intercommodity and intermarket spreads are traded using an equal-dollar-value approach—as they should be—the price difference between the markets is no longer the relevant subject of analysis. Rather, such an approach is most closely related to the price *ratio* between the two markets. This fact means that chart analysis and the definition of historical ranges should be based on the price ratio, not the price difference. Figures 31.1, 31.2, and 31.3 illustrate this point. Figure 31.1 depicts the September 2013 wheat/September 2013 corn spread in the standard form as a price difference. Figure 31.2 illustrates the price ratio of September 2013 wheat to September 2013 corn during the same period. Finally, Figure 31.3 plots the equity fluctuations of the approximate equal-dollar-value spread: 3 wheat versus 4 corn. Note how much more closely the equal dollar position is paralleled by the ratio than by the price difference.[3]

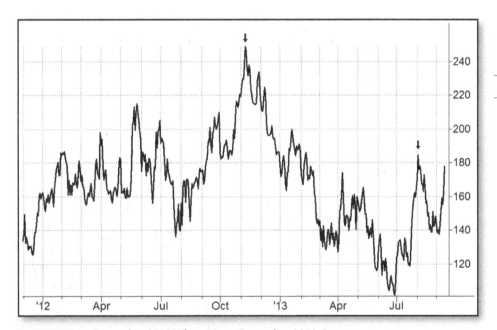

FIGURE 31.1   September 2013 Wheat Minus September 2013 Corn
Chart created using TradeStation. ©TradeStation Technologies, Inc. All rights reserved.

---

[3] The equal-dollar-value spread would be precisely related to the price ratio only if the contract ratios in the spread were continuously adjusted to reflect changes in the price ratio. (An analogous complication does not exist in equal-unit spreads, since the contract weightings are determined independent of price levels.) However, unless price levels change drastically during the holding period of the spread, the absence of theoretical readjustments in contract ratios will make little practical difference. In other words, equity fluctuations in the equal-dollar-value spread will normally closely track the movements of the price ratio.

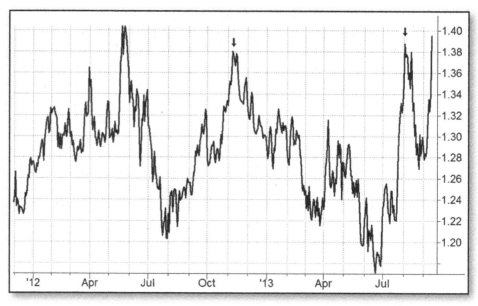

FIGURE 31.2   Price Ratio of September 2013 Wheat to September 2013 Corn

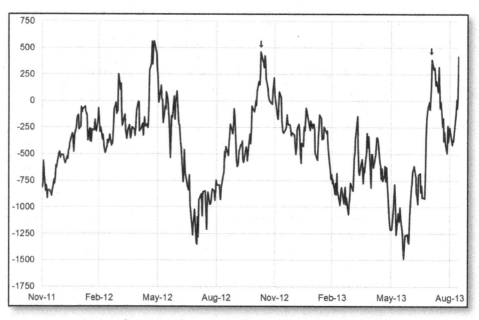

FIGURE 31.3   3 September 2013 Wheat Minus 4 September 2013 Corn

In the preceding example, because wheat is a larger contract than corn (in dollar-value terms), a long 1 wheat/short 1 corn spread would be biased in the direction of the general price trend of grains. For example, during November 2012–August 2013, a period of declining grain prices (see Figure 31.4), the equal contract spread seems to suggest that wheat prices weakened significantly relative to corn prices (see Figure 31.1). In reality, as indicated by Figures 31.2 and 31.3, the wheat/corn relationship during this period was best characterized by a trading range. To illustrate the trading implications of the spread ratio, consider a long wheat/short corn spread initiated at the late-November 2012 relative high and liquidated at the August 2013 peak. This trade would have resulted in a near breakeven trade if the spread were implemented on an equal-dollar-value basis (see Figure 31.2 or 31.3), but a significant loss if an equal contract criterion were used instead (see Figure 31.1).

It should now be clear why the standard assumption of an equal contract position is usually valid for intramarket spreads. In these spreads, contract sizes are identical, while price levels are normally close. Thus, the equal-dollar-value approach suggests a contract ratio very close to 1:1.

If, however, two contracts in an intramarket spread are trading at significantly different price levels, the argument for using the equal-dollar-value approach (as opposed to equal contract positions) would be analogous to the intercommodity and intermarket case. Wide price differences between contracts in an intramarket spread can occur in extreme bull markets that place a large premium on

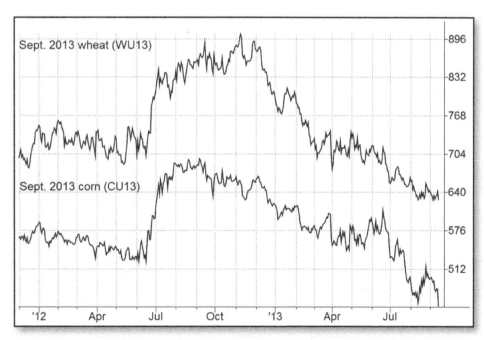

FIGURE 31.4 September 2013 Wheat and September 2013 Corn

nearby supplies (i.e., in markets conforming to the "general rule" defined in Chapter 30). Intercrop spreads (which are a subset of intramarket spreads) can also exhibit wide price differences. In these cases, the greater dollar volatility implicit in the higher-priced month suggests that the spread be initiated with a larger number of contracts in the lower-priced month.

It should be noted that the concept of equal dollar value is meaningless for interest rate futures. For example, a $1 million eurodollar contract is certainly not 10 times as large as a $100,000 T-bond contract. In fact, because of its much longer maturity, and, hence, much greater volatility, the T-bond contract is a substantially "larger" contract by any reasonable definition.

CHAPTER 32

Spread Trading in Stock Index Futures

The stock market is but a mirror which . . . provides an image of the underlying or fundamental economic situation.

—John Kenneth Galbraith

■ Intramarket Stock Index Spreads

Spreads in carrying charge markets, such as gold, provide a good starting point for developing a theoretical behavioral model for spreads in stock index futures. As is the case for gold, there can never be any near-term shortage in stock indexes, which means spreads will be entirely determined by carrying charges. As was explained in Chapter 30, gold spreads are largely determined by short-term interest rates. For example, since a trader could accept delivery of gold on an expiring contract and redeliver it against a subsequent contract, the price spread between the two months would primarily reflect financing costs and, hence, short-term rates. If the premium of the forward contract were significantly above the level implied by short-term rates, the arbitrageur could lock in a risk-free profit by performing a cash-and-carry operation. And if the premium were significantly lower, an arbitrageur could lock in a risk-free profit by implementing a short nearby/long forward spread, borrowing gold to deliver against the nearby contract and accepting delivery at the expiration of the forward contract. These arbitrage forces will tend to keep the intramarket spreads within a reasonably well-defined band for any given combination of short-term interest rates and gold prices.

The same arguments could be duplicated substituting a stock index for gold. In a broad sense this is true, but there is one critical difference between stock index spreads and gold spreads: Stocks pay dividends. Thus, the interest rate cost of holding a stock position is offset (partially, or more than totally) by dividend income. The presence of dividends is easily incorporated into the framework of calculating a theoretical spread level. The spread would be in equilibrium if, based on current prices, interest rates, and dividends, there would be no difference between holding the actual equities in the index for the interim between the two spread months versus buying the forward index futures contract. Holding equities would incur an interest rate cost that does not exist in holding futures, but would also accrue the dividend yield the holder of futures does not receive. The theoretical spread level ($P_2 - P_1$) at the expiration of P_1 at which these two alternative means of holding a long equity position—equity and stock index futures—would imply an equivalent outcome can be expressed symbolically as follows:

$$P_2 - P_1 = P_1 \left(\frac{t}{360} \right)(i - d)$$

where P_1 = price of nearby (expiring) futures contract

P_2 = price of forward futures contract

t = number of days between expiration of nearby contract and expiration of forward contract

i = short-term interest rate level at time of P_1 expiration

d = annualized dividend yield (%)

As is evident from this equation, if short-term interest rates exceed dividend yields, forward futures will trade at a premium to nearby contracts. Conversely, if the dividend yield exceeds short-term interest rates, forward futures will trade at a discount.

Since the dividend yield is not subject to sharp changes in the short run, for any given index (price) level, intramarket stock index spreads would primarily reflect expected future short-term rates (similar to gold spreads). If short-term interest rates exhibit low volatility, as characterized by the near-zero interest rate environment that prevailed in the years following the 2008 financial crisis, stock index spreads will tend to trade in relatively narrow range—a consequence of both major drivers of stock index spreads (interest rates and dividend yield) being stable.

■ Intermarket Stock Index Spreads

As is the case with intercommodity and intermarket spreads trading at disparate price levels, stock index spreads should be traded as ratios rather than differences—an approach that will make the spread position indifferent to equal percentage price changes in both markets (indexes). As a reminder, to trade a ratio, the trader should implement each leg of the spread in approximately equal contract value positions, which, as was shown in Chapter 31, can be achieved by using a contract ratio that is inversely proportional to the contract value ratio.

For example, if the E-mini Nasdaq 100 futures contract, which has a contract value of 20 times the index, is trading at 4,300 (a contract value of $86,000), and the Russell 2000 Mini futures contract, which has a contract value of 100 times the index, is trading at 1,150 (a contract value of $115,000), the contract value ratio (CVR) of Nasdaq to Russell futures would be equal to:

$$CVR = (20 \times 4{,}300)/(100 \times 1{,}150) = 0.7478$$

Therefore, the contract ratio would be equal to the inverse of the contract value ratio: $1/0.7478 = 1.337$. Thus, for example, a spread with 3 long (short) Russell contracts would be balanced by 4 Nasdaq short (long) contracts: $3 \times 1.337 = 4.01$.

Because some stock indexes are inherently more volatile than other indexes—for example, smaller-cap indexes tend to be more volatile than larger-cap indexes—some traders may wish to make an additional adjustment to the contract ratio to neutralize volatility differences. If this were done, the contract ratio defined by the inverse of the contract value ratio would be further adjusted by multiplying by the inverse of some volatility measure ratio. One good candidate for such a volatility measure is the average true range (ATR), which was defined in Chapter 17. As an illustration, if in the aforementioned example of the Nasdaq 100/Russell 2000 ratio, the prevailing ATR of the Nasdaq 100 is 0.8 times the ATR of the Russell 2000, then the Nasdaq/Russell 2000 contract ratio of 1.337 would be further adjusted by multiplying by the inverse of the ATR ratio ($1 / 0.8 = 1.25$), yielding a contract ratio of 1.671 instead of 1.337. If this additional adjustment is made, then a spread with 3 long (short) Russell contracts would be balanced by 5 short (long) Nasdaq contracts: $3 \times 1.671 = 5.01$.

It is up traders to decide whether they wish to further adjust the contract ratio for volatility. For the remainder of this chapter, we assume the more straightforward case of contract ratios being adjusted only for contract value differences (i.e., without any additional adjustment for volatility differences).

The four most actively traded stock index futures contracts are the E-mini S&P 500, E-mini Nasdaq 100, E-mini Dow, and the Russell 2000 Mini. There are six possible spread pairs for these four markets:

- E-mini S&P 500 / E-mini Dow

- E-mini S&P 500 / E-mini Nasdaq 100

- E-mini S&P 500 / Russell 2000 Mini

- E-mini Nasdaq 100 / E-mini Dow

- E-mini Nasdaq 100 / Russell 2000 Mini

- E-mini Dow / Russell 2000 Mini

Traders who believe a certain group of stocks will perform better or worse than another group can express this view through stock index spreads. For example, a trader who expected large-cap stocks to outperform small-cap stocks could initiate long E-mini S&P 500/short Russell 2000 Mini spreads or long E-mini Dow/short Russell 2000 Mini spreads. A trader expecting relative outperformance by small-cap spreads would place the reverse spreads. As another example, a trader expecting relative outperformance by technology stocks might consider spreads that are long the tech-heavy Nasdaq 100 index and short another index, such as long E-mini Nasdaq 100/short E-mini S&P 500 spreads. Again, to trade these types of spreads as price ratios, the spreads would be implemented so the contract values of each side are approximately equal, a condition that will be achieved when the contract ratio between the indexes is equal to the inverse of the contract value ratio.

Figures 32.1 through 32.6 illustrate the contract value ratios for these six spread pairs during 2002–2015. In some cases, such as the S&P 500/Dow spread, the contract value ratio does not vary much. As can be seen in Figure 32.1, the contract value ratio for this pair ranged by a factor of only about 1.2 from low to high over the entire period. For other index pairs, however, the contract value ratio ranged widely. For example, Figure 32.4 shows that during the same period, the high Nasdaq/ Dow contract value ratio was nearly 2.5 times the low ratio. Since the contract ratio required to keep the trade neutral to equal percentage price changes in both markets is equal to the inverse of the prevailing contract value ratio, the appropriate contract ratio for these spreads can range widely over time. For example, for the aforementioned Nasdaq 100/Dow ratio, a three-contract Dow position would have been balanced by a seven-contract Nasdaq position when the contract value ratio was at its low versus only a three-contract position (rounding up) when the ratio was at its high.

Figures 32.7 through 32.12 illustrate the price ratios for the six stock index pairs during the same period, along with an overlay of one of the indexes to facilitate visually checking of the relationships between the index price ratio and the overall stock market direction. Note that the price ratios in Figures 32.7 through 32.12 are identical in pattern to the contract value ratios in Figures 32.1 through 32.6, which is a consequence of the contract value ratio being equal to the price ratio times a constant—the constant being equal to the ratio of the multipliers for the indexes.

FIGURE 32.1   Contract Value Ratio: S&P 500/Dow E-Mini Futures

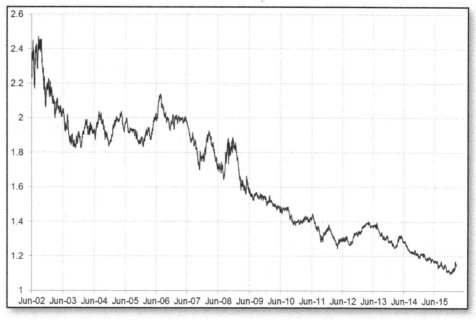

FIGURE 32.2 Contract Value Ratio: S&P 500/Nasdaq 100 E-Mini Futures

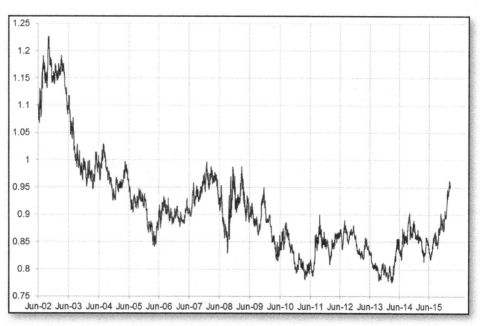

FIGURE 32.3 Contract Value Ratio: S&P 500/Russell 2000 Mini Futures

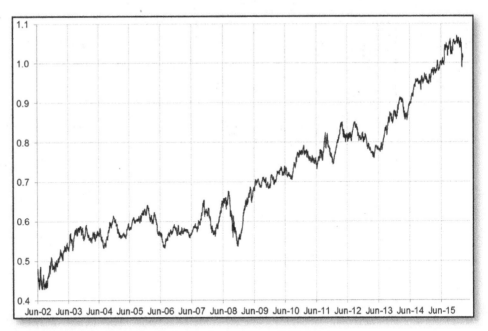

FIGURE 32.4   Contract Value Ratio: Nasdaq 100/Dow E-Mini Futures

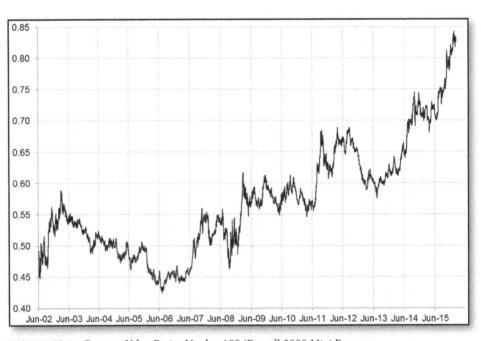

FIGURE 32.5   Contract Value Ratio: Nasdaq 100/Russell 2000 Mini Futures

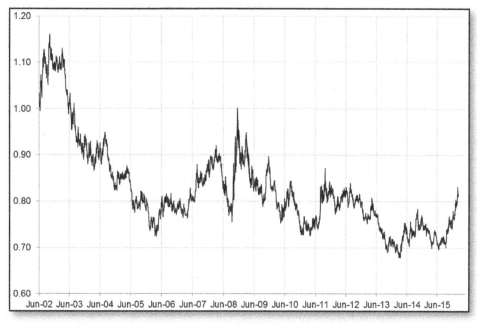

FIGURE 32.6 Contract Value Ratio: Dow/Russell 2000 Mini Futures

467

SPREAD TRADING IN STOCK INDEX FUTURES

FIGURE 32.7 S&P 500/Dow E-Mini Futures Ratio vs. S&P

FIGURE 32.8 S&P 500/Nasdaq 100 E-Mini Futures Ratio vs. S&P

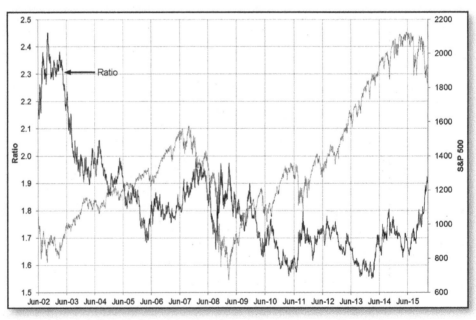

FIGURE 32.9 S&P 500/Russell 2000 Mini Futures Ratio vs. S&P

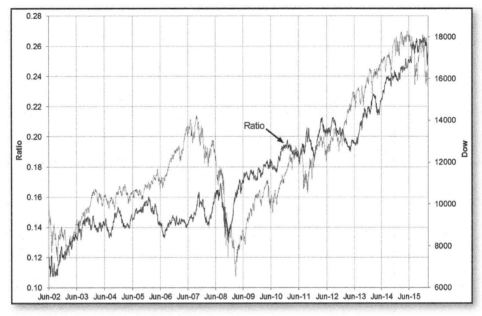

FIGURE 32.10 Nasdaq 100/Dow E-Mini Futures Ratio vs. Dow

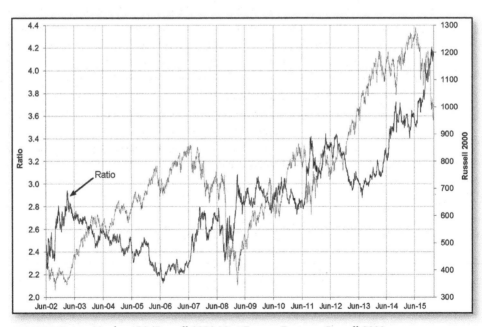

FIGURE 32.11 Nasdaq 100/Russell 2000 Mini Futures Ratio vs. Russell 2000

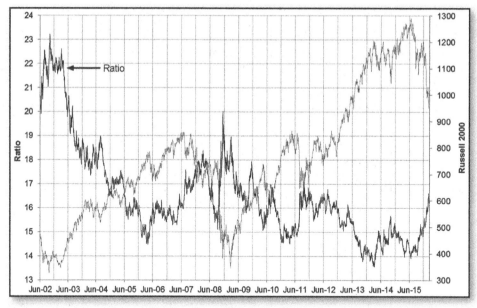

FIGURE 32.12 Dow/Russell 2000 Mini Futures Ratio vs. Russell 2000

Generally speaking, at least during the 14-year period depicted in these charts, Figures 32.7 through 32.12 reflect a tendency for larger-cap indexes to lose ground to smaller-cap indexes during market uptrends and to outperform (i.e., decline less) during market downtrends. For example, Figure 32.12 compares the index ratio of the largest cap of the four indexes (Dow) to the smallest cap of the four indexes (Russell 2000) with the Russell 2000 index. On balance, there is a clear inverse correlation between the index ratio and the market direction. As another example, in Figure 32.7, in which both indexes in the spread are large-cap, but in which the smaller-cap of the two (S&P) is in the numerator of the ratio, the ratio is clearly positively correlated with the market direction. Another interesting aspect of Figure 32.7 is that there appears to be some tendency for the S&P/Dow ratio to lead major trend reversals in the outright market.

CHAPTER 33

Spread Trading in Currency Futures

Lenin was certainly right. There is no subtler, no surer means of overturning the existing basis of society than to debauch the currency. The process engages all the hidden forces of economic law on the side of destruction, and does it in a manner which not one man in a million is able to diagnose.

—John Maynard Keynes

471

■ Intercurrency Spreads

Conceptually, intercurrency spreads are identical to outright currency trades. After all, a net long or short currency futures position is also a spread in that it implies an opposite position in the dollar. For example, a net long Japanese yen (JY) position means that one is long the JY versus the U.S. dollar (USD). If the JY strengthens against the USD, the long JY position will gain. If the JY strengthens against the Swiss franc (SF) and euro but remains unchanged against the USD, the long JY position will also remain unchanged.

In an intercurrency spread, the implied counterposing short in the USD is replaced by another currency. For example, in a long JY/short euro spread, the position will gain when the JY strengthens relative to the euro, but will be unaffected by fluctuations of the JY relative to the dollar. The long JY/short euro spread is merely the combination of a long JY/short USD and a long USD short euro position, in which the opposite USD positions offset each other. (To be precise, the implied USD positions will only be completely offset if the dollar values of the JY and euro positions are exactly equal.)

There are two possible reasons for implementing an intercurrency spread:

1. The trader believes currency 1 will gain against the USD, while currency 2 will lose against the USD. In this case, a long currency 1/short currency 2 spread is best thought of as two separate outright trades.
2. The trader believes that one foreign currency will gain on another, but has no strong opinion regarding the movement of either currency against the USD. In this case, the intercurrency spread is analogous to an outright currency trade, with the implied short or long in the USD replaced by another currency. If, however, the two currencies are far more closely related to each other than to the USD, the connotation normally attributed to a spread might be at least partially appropriate.

If an intercurrency spread is motivated by the second of these factors, the position should be balanced in terms of equal dollar values. (This may not always be possible for the small trader.) Otherwise, equity losses can occur, even if the exchange rate between the two currencies remains unchanged.

For example, consider a long 4 December SF/short 4 December euro spread position implemented when the December SF = $1.000 and the December euro = $1.250. At the trade initiation, the exchange rate between the SF and euro is 1 euro = 1.25 SF. If the SF rises to $1.100 and the euro climbs to $1.375, the exchange rate between the SF and euro is unchanged: 1 euro = 1.25 SF. However, the spread position will have lost $12,500:

$$\text{Equity change} = \text{number of contracts} \times \text{number of units per contract} \times \text{gain/loss per unit}$$
$$\text{Equity change in long SF} = 4 \times 125,000 \times \$0.10 = \$50,000$$
$$\text{Equity change in short euro} = 4 \times 125,000 \times -\$0.125 = -\$62,500$$
$$\text{Net profit/loss} = -\$12,500$$

The reason the spread loses money even though the SF/euro exchange rate remains unchanged is that the original position was unweighted. At the initiation prices, the spread represented a long SF position of $500,000 but a short euro position of $625,000. Thus, the spread position was biased toward gaining if the dollar weakened against both currencies and losing if the dollar strengthened. If, however, the spread were balanced in terms of equal dollar values, the equity of the position would have been unchanged. For example, if the initial spread position were long 5 December SF/short 4 December euro (a position in which the dollar value of each side = $625,000), the aforementioned price shift would not have resulted in an equity change:

$$\text{Equity change in long SF} = 5 \times 125,000 \times \$0.10 = \$62,500$$
$$\text{Equity change in short euro} = 4 \times 125,000 \times (-\$0.125) = \underline{-\$62,500}$$
$$\text{Net profit/loss} = 0$$

The general formula for determining the equal-dollar-value spread ratio (number of contracts of currency 1 per contract of currency 2) is:

$$\text{Equal-dollar-spread ratio} = \frac{\left(\begin{array}{c}\text{number of units per}\\\text{contract of currency 2}\end{array}\right)\left(\begin{array}{c}\text{price of}\\\text{currency 2}\end{array}\right)}{\left(\begin{array}{c}\text{number of units per}\\\text{contract of currency 1}\end{array}\right)\left(\begin{array}{c}\text{price of}\\\text{currency 1}\end{array}\right)}$$

For example, if currency 1, the British pound (BP) = $1.50, and currency 2, the euro = $1.20, and the BP futures contract consists of 62,500 units, while the euro futures contract consists of 125,000 units, the implied spread ratio would be:

$$\frac{(125,000)(\$1.20)}{(62,500)(\$1.50)} = 1.6$$

Thus, the equal dollar value spread would consist of 1.6 BP contracts per euro contract, or 8 BP to 5 euro.

Equity fluctuations in an equal-dollar-value intercurrency spread position will mirror the price ratio (or exchange rate) between currencies. It should be emphasized that price ratios (as opposed to price spreads) are the only meaningful means of representing intercurrency spreads. For example, if the BP = \$1.50 and SF = \$1.00, an increase of \$0.50 in both the currencies will leave the price spread between the BP and SF unchanged, even though it would drastically alter the relative values of the two currencies: a decline of the BP vis-à-vis the SF from 1.5 SF to 1.33 SF.

■ Intracurrency Spreads

An intracurrency spread—the price difference between two futures contracts for the same currency—directly reflects the implied forward interest rate differential between dollar-denominated accounts and accounts denominated in the given currency. For example, the June/December euro spread indicates the expected relationship between six-month eurodollar and euro rates in June.[1]

To demonstrate the connection between intracurrency spreads and interest rate differentials, we compare the alternatives of investing in dollar-denominated versus euro-denominated accounts:

S = spot exchange rate (\$/euro)
F = current forward exchange rate for date at end of investment period (\$/euro)
r_1 = simple rate of return on dollar-denominated account for investment period (nonannualized)
r_2 = simple rate of return on euro-denominated account for investment period (nonannualized)

Alternative A: Invest in Dollar-Denominated Account	Alternative B: Invest in Euro-Denominated Account
1. Invest \$1 in dollar-denominated account.	1. Convert \$1 to euro at spot.
2. Funds at end of period = \$1 $(1 + r_1)$	Exchange rate is S, which yields $1/S$ euro. (By definition, if S equals dollars per euro, $1/S$ = euro per dollar.)
	2. Invest $1/S$ euro in euro-denominated account at r_2.
	3. Lock in forward exchange rate by selling the anticipated euro proceeds at end of investment period at current forward rate F.[2]
	4. Funds at end of period = $1/S (1 + r_2)$ euro.
	5. Converted to dollars at rate F, funds at end of period = $\$F/S (1 + r_2)$ (since F = dollars per euro).

---

[1] The eurocurrency rates are interest rates on time deposits for funds outside the country of issue and hence free of government controls. For example, interest rates on dollar-denominated deposits in London are eurodollar rates, while rates on sterling-denominated deposits in Frankfurt are eurosterling rates. The quoted eurocurrency rates represent the rates on transactions between major international banks.

[2] A short forward position can be established in one of two ways: (1) selling futures that are available for forward dates at three-month intervals; and (2) initiating a long spot/short forward position in the foreign exchange (FX) swap market and simultaneously selling spot.

If the proceeds of the two above alternatives are to be equivalent, then:

$$1 + r_1 = \frac{F}{S}(1 + r_2)$$

Thus, at this equilibrium level, given values for S, r_1, and r_2, F would be automatically determined. For example, if $S = \$0.80/\text{euro}$, $r_1 = 2$ percent per six-month period (4.04 percent annualized), and $r_2 = 1$ percent per six-month period (2.01 percent annualized), at equilibrium, the six-month forward rate would be:

$$F = \frac{S(1 + r_1)}{(1 + r_2)} = \frac{0.8(1.02)}{(1.01)} = 0.80792$$

At forward rate of $F = 0.80792$, both alternatives will yield \$1.02. This result is obvious for the dollar-denominated account; for the euro-denominated account:

$$\$F / S(1 + r_2) = \frac{\$0.80792(1.01)}{0.80} = \$1.02$$

Consider what would happen if the forward exchange rate F were greater than the equilibrium level (i.e., greater than \$0.80792/euro in the above example). For instance, using an assumed value of $F = \$0.82/\text{euro}$, the proceeds of Alternative B would be:

$$\frac{\$0.82(1.01)}{0.80} = \$1.03525$$

Thus, if $F = \$0.82/\text{euro}$, arbitrageurs could borrow dollars at r_1 convert the dollars into euro, invest the euro at r_2, and hedge the anticipated six-month forward euro proceeds at \$0.82/euro. In doing so, they would pay \$1.02 for the dollar loan, but would earn \$1.03525, thereby netting a risk-free profit of \$0.01525 per dollar borrowed. If such a wonderful opportunity existed (and it will soon be clear why it could not), all arbitrageurs who were awake and could add would rush to implement the above set of transactions. This activity by arbitrageurs would impact both the spot and forward exchange rates. In the spot market, the concentration of conversions of dollars into euros would cause the euro to gain against the dollar, and hence the spot rate S would rise. Similarly, in the forward market, heavy sales of euro against the dollar would cause the euro to weaken against the dollar and hence the forward rate F would fall.[3] These market forces would narrow the gap between the forward and spot rates until:

$$\frac{F}{S} = \frac{1 + r_1}{1 + r_2}$$

---

[3] In the futures market, such sales would occur directly. In the cash FX market, downward pressure on the implied forward rate would manifest itself through the initiation of long spot/short forward swaps (spreads).

Of course, the market forces just described would come into play well before the forward/spot ratio increased to $0.82/0.80 = 1.025$. The intervention of arbitrageurs will assure the six-month forward/spot ratio would not rise significantly above $1 + r_1/1 + r_2 = 1.0099$. A similar argument could be used to demonstrate that arbitrage intervention would keep the forward/spot ratio from declining significantly below 1.0099. In short, arbitrage activity will assure that the forward/spot ratio will be approximately defined by the above equation. This relationship is commonly referred to as the *interest rate parity theorem*.

Since currency futures must converge with spot exchange rates at expiration, the price spread between a forward futures contract and a nearby expiring contract must reflect the prevailing interest rate ratio (between the eurodollar rate and the given eurocurrency rate).[4] Hence, a spread between two forward futures contracts can be interpreted as reflecting the market's expectation for the interest rate ratio at the time of the nearby contract expiration. Specifically, if P_1 = price of the more nearby futures expiring at t_1 and P_2 = price of the forward futures contract expiring at time t_2, then P_2/P_1 will equal the expected interest rate ratio (expressed as $1+r_1/1+r_2$) for term rates of duration $t_2 - t_1$ at time t_1. It should be stressed that the forward interest rate ratio implied by spreads in futures will usually differ from the prevailing interest rate ratio.

If the market expects the eurodollar rate to be greater than the foreign eurocurrency rate, forward futures for that currency will trade at a premium to more nearby futures—the wider the expected differential, the wider the spread. Conversely, if the foreign eurocurrency rate is expected to be greater than the eurodollar rate, forward futures will trade at a discount to nearby futures.

The above relationships suggest that intracurrency spreads can be used to trade expectations regarding future interest rate differentials between different currencies. If a trader expected eurodollar rates to gain (move up more or down less) on a foreign eurocurrency rate (relative to the expected interest rate ratio implied by the intracurrency futures spread), this expectation could be expressed as a long forward/short nearby spread in that currency. Conversely, if the trader expected the foreign eurocurrency rate to gain on the eurodollar rate, the implied trade would be a long nearby/short forward intracurrency spread.

As a technical point, a 1:1 spread ratio would fluctuate even if the implied forward interest rate ratio were unchanged. For example, if $P_2 = \$0.81/\text{euro}$ and $P_1 = \$0.80/\text{euro}$, a 10-percent increase in both rates would result in a 810-point price gain in the forward contract and only a 800-point gain in the nearby contract, even though the implied forward interest rate ratio would be unchanged (since an equal percentage change in each month would leave F/S unchanged). In order for the spread position to be unaffected by equal percentage price changes in both contracts, a development that would not affect the implied forward interest rate ratio, the spread would have to be implemented so that the dollar value of the long and short positions were equal. This parity will be achieved when the contract ratio is equal to the inverse of the price ratio. For example, given the above case of $P_2 = \$0.81$ and

---

[4] All references to interest rate ratios in this section should be understood to mean $(1 + r_1)/(1 + r_2)$ where r_1 and r_2 are the nonannualized rates of return for the time interim between S and F. Thus, in the above example, the interest rate ratio for the six-month period given annualized rates of 4.04 percent and 2.01 percent is equal to $1.02/1.01 = 1.0099$. The reader should be careful not to misconstrue the intended definition of interest rate ratio with a literal interpretation, which in the above example would suggest a figure of $0.02/0.01 = 2$.

$P_1 = \$0.80$, an 80-contract forward/81-contract nearby spread would not be affected by equal price changes (e.g., a 10-percent price increase would cause a total 64,800-point change in both legs of the spread). As can be seen in this example, a balanced spread will only be possible for extremely large positions. This fact, however, does not present a problem, since the distortion is sufficiently small so that a 1:1 contract ratio spread serves as a reasonable approximation.

Intracurrency spreads can also be combined to trade expectations regarding two foreign eurocurrency rates. In this case, the trader would implement a long nearby/short forward spread in the currency with the expected relative rate gain, and a long forward/short nearby spread in the other currency. For example, assume that in February the June/December euro spread implies that the June six-month eurodollar rate will be 1 percent above the euro rate, while the June/December JY spread implies that the June eurodollar rate will be 2 percent above the euroyen rate. In combination, these spreads imply that the June euro rate will be higher than the June euroyen rate. If a trader expected euroyen rates to be higher than euro rates in June, the following combined spread positions would be implied: long June JY/short December JY plus long December euro/short June euro.

To summarize, intracurrency spreads can be used to trade interest rate differentials in the following manner:

Expectation	Indicated Trade
Eurodollar rate will gain on given eurocurrency rate (relative to rate ratio implied by spread).	Long forward/short nearby spread in given currency
Eurodollar rate will lose on given eurocurrency rate (relative to rate ratio implied by spread).	Long nearby/short forward spread in given currency
Eurocurrency rate 1 will gain on eurocurrency rate 2 (relative to rate ratio implied by spreads in both markets).	Long nearby/short forward spread in market 1 and long forward/short nearby spread in market 2

CHAPTER 34

An Introduction to Options on Futures

A put might more properly be called a stick. For the whole point of a put—its purpose, if you will—is that it gives its owner the right to force 100 shares of some godforsaken stock onto someone else at a price at which he would very likely rather not take it. So what you are really doing is sticking it to him.

—Andrew Tobias
Getting By on $100,000 a Year (and Other Sad Tales)

■ Preliminaries

There are two basic types of options: calls and puts. The purchase of a *call option* on futures[1] provides the buyer with the right, but not the obligation, to purchase the underlying futures contract at a specified price, called the *strike* or *exercise price,* at any time up to and including the *expiration date.*[2] A *put option* provides the buyer with the right, but not the obligation, to sell the underlying futures contract at the strike price at any time prior to expiration. (Note, therefore, that buying a put is a *bearish* trade, while selling a put is a *bullish* trade.) The price of an option is called the *premium,* and is quoted in

---

[1] Chapters 34 and 35 deal specifically with options on futures contracts. However, generally speaking, analogous concepts would apply to options on cash (physical) goods or instruments (e.g., bullion versus gold futures). Some of the advantages of basing an option contract on futures as opposed to the cash asset are discussed in the next section.

[2] For some markets, the expiration date on the option and the underlying futures contract will be the same; for other markets, the expiration date on the option will be a specified date prior to the expiration of the futures contract.

TABLE 34.1 Determining the Dollar Value of Option Premiums

Contracts Quoted on an Index

Option premium (in points)	×	$ value per point	=	$ value of the option premium
Examples:				
E-mini S&P 500 options				
8.50 (option premium)	×	$50 per point	=	$425 (option premium $ value)
U.S. dollar index options				
2.30 (option premium)	×	$1,000 per point	=	$2,300 (option premium $ value)

Contracts Quoted in Dollars

Option premium (in dollars or cents per unit)	×	No. of units in futures contract	=	$ value of the option premium
Examples:				
Gold options				
$42 (option premium)	×	100 (ounces in futures contract)	=	$4,200 (option premium $ value)
WTI crude oil options				
$1.24 (option premium)	×	1,000 (barrels in futures contract)	=	$1,240 (option premium $ value)

either dollars (or cents) per unit or points. Table 34.1 illustrates how to calculate the dollar value of a premium. As a specific example, a trader who buys a $1,000 August gold call at a premium of $50 pays $50/oz ($5,000 per contract) for the right to buy an August gold futures contract at $1,000 (regardless of how high its price may rise) at any time up to the expiration date of the August option.

Because options are traded for both puts and calls and a number of strike prices for each futures contract, the total number of different options traded in a market will far exceed the number of futures contracts—often by a factor of 10 to 1 or more. This broad variety of listed options provides the trader with myriad alternative trading strategies.

Like their underlying futures contracts, options are exchange-traded, standardized contracts. Consequently, option positions can be offset prior to expiration simply by entering an order opposite to the position held. For example, the holder of a call could liquidate his position by entering an order to sell a call with the same expiration date and strike price.

The buyer of a call seeks to profit from an anticipated price rise by locking in a specific purchase price. His maximum possible loss will be equal to the dollar amount of the premium paid for the option. This maximum loss would occur on an option held until expiration if the strike price were above the prevailing futures price. For example, if August gold futures were trading at $990 upon the expiration of the August option, a $1,000 call would be worthless because futures could be purchased more cheaply at the existing market price.[3] If the futures were trading above the strike price at expiration, then the option would have some value and hence would be exercised. However, if the difference

---

[3] However, it should be noted that even in this case, the call buyer could have recouped part of the premium if he had sold the option *prior* to expiration. This is true since the option will maintain some value (i.e., premium greater than zero) as long as there is some possibility of the futures price rising above the strike price prior to the expiration of the option.

between the futures price and the strike price were less than the premium paid for the option, the net result of the trade would still be a loss. In order for the call buyer to realize a net profit, the difference between the futures price and the strike price would have to exceed the premium at the time the call was purchased (after adjusting for commission cost). The higher the futures price, the greater the resulting profit. Of course, if the futures reach the desired objective, or the call buyer changes his market opinion, he could sell his call prior to expiration.[4]

The buyer of a put seeks to profit from an anticipated price decline by locking in a sales price. Similar to the call buyer, his maximum possible loss is limited to the dollar amount of the premium paid for the option. In the case of a put held until expiration, the trade would show a net profit if the strike price exceeded the futures price by an amount greater than the premium of the put at purchase (after adjusting for commission cost).

While the buyer of a call or put has limited risk and unlimited potential gain,[5] the reverse is true for the seller. The option seller ("writer") receives the dollar value of the premium in return for undertaking the obligation to assume an opposite position at the strike price if an option is exercised. For example, if a call is exercised, the seller must assume a short position in futures at the strike price (since by exercising the call, the buyer assumes a long position at that price). Upon exercise, the exchange's clearinghouse will establish these opposite futures positions at the strike price. After exercise, the call buyer and seller can either maintain or liquidate their respective futures positions.

The seller of a call seeks to profit from an anticipated sideways to modestly declining market. In such a situation, the premium earned by selling a call will provide the most attractive trading opportunity. However, if the trader expected a large price decline, he would usually be better off going short futures or buying a put—trades with open-ended profit potential. In a similar fashion, the seller of a put seeks to profit from an anticipated sideways to modestly rising market.

Some novices have trouble understanding why a trader would not always prefer the buy side of an option (call or put, depending on his market opinion), since such a trade has unlimited potential and limited risk. Such confusion reflects the failure to take probability into account. Although the option seller's theoretical risk is unlimited, the price levels that have the greatest probability of occurring (i.e., prices in the vicinity of the market price at the time the option trade occurs) would result in a net gain to the option seller. Roughly speaking, the option buyer accepts a large probability of a small loss in return for a small probability of a large gain, whereas the option seller accepts a small probability of a large loss in exchange for a large probability of a small gain. In an efficient market, neither the consistent option buyer nor the consistent option seller should have any advantage over the long run.[6]

---

[4] Even if the call is held until the expiration date, it will usually still be easier to offset the position in the options market rather than exercising the call.

[5] Technically speaking, the gains on a put would be limited, since prices cannot fall below zero; but for practical purposes, it is entirely reasonable to speak of the maximum possible gain on a long put position as being unlimited.

[6] To be precise, this statement is not intended to imply that the consistent option buyer and consistent option seller would both have the same expected outcome (zero excluding transactions costs). Theoretically, on average, it is reasonable to expect the market to price options so there is some advantage to the seller to compensate option sellers for providing price insurance—that is, assuming the highly undesirable exposure to a large, open-ended loss. So, in effect, option sellers would have a more attractive return profile and a less attractive risk profile than option buyers, and it is in this sense that the market will, on average, price options so that there is no net advantage to the buyer or seller.

■ Factors That Determine Option Premiums

An option's premium consists of two components:

$$\text{Premium} = \text{intrinsic value} + \text{time value}$$

The intrinsic value of a call option is the amount by which the current futures price is above the strike price. The intrinsic value of a put option is the amount by which the current futures price is below the strike price. In effect, the intrinsic value is that part of the premium that could be realized if the option were exercised and the futures contract offset at the current market price. For example, if July crude oil futures were trading at $74.60, a call option with a strike price of $70 would have an intrinsic value of $4.60. The intrinsic value serves as a floor price for an option. Why? Because if the premium were less than the intrinsic value, a trader could buy and exercise the option, and immediately offset the resulting futures position, thereby realizing a net gain (assuming this profit would at least cover the transaction costs).

Options that have intrinsic value (i.e., calls with strike prices below the current futures price and puts with strike prices above the current futures price) are said to be *in-the-money*. Options with no intrinsic value are called *out-of-the-money* options. An option whose strike price equals the futures price is called an *at-the-money* option. The term *at-the-money* is also often used less restrictively to refer to the specific option whose strike price is closest to the futures price.

An out-of-the-money option, which by definition has an intrinsic value of zero, nonetheless retains some value because of the possibility the futures price will move beyond the strike price prior to the expiration date. An in-the-money option will have a value greater than the intrinsic value because a position in the option will be preferred to a position in the underlying futures contract. Reason: Both the option and the futures contract will gain equally in the event of favorable price movement, but the option's maximum loss is limited. The portion of the premium that exceeds the intrinsic value is called the *time value*.

It should be emphasized that because the time value is almost always greater than zero, one should avoid exercising an option before the expiration date. Almost invariably, the trader who wants to offset his option position will realize a better return by selling the option, a transaction that will yield the intrinsic value plus some time value, as opposed to exercising the option, an action that will yield only the intrinsic value.

The time value depends on four quantifiable factors[7]:

1. **The relationship between the strike price and the current futures price.** As illustrated in Figure 34.1, the time value will decline as an option moves more deeply in-the-money or out-of-the-money. Deeply out-of-the-money options will have little time value, since it is unlikely the futures will move to (or beyond) the strike price prior to expiration. Deeply in-the-money options have little time value because these options offer very similar positions to the underlying futures contracts—both will gain and lose equivalent amounts for all but an extreme adverse price move. In other words, for a deeply in-the-money option, the fact that the

---

[7]Theoretically, the time value will also be influenced by price expectations, which are a non-quantifiable factor.

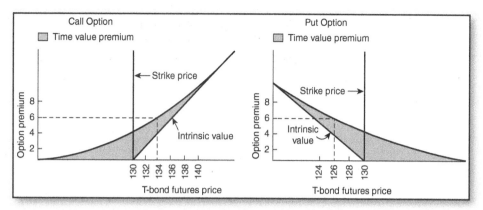

FIGURE 34.1 Theoretical Option Premium Curve
Source: Chicago Board of Trade, Marketing Department.

risk is limited is not worth very much, because the strike price is so far away from the prevailing futures price. As Figure 34.1 shows, the time value will be at a maximum at the strike price.

2. **Time remaining until expiration.** The more time remaining until expiration, the greater the time value of the option. This is true because a longer life span increases the probability of the intrinsic value increasing by any specified amount prior to expiration. In other words, the more time until expiration, the greater the probable price range of futures. Figure 34.2 illustrates the standard theoretical assumption regarding the relationship between time value and time remaining until expiration for an at-the-money option. Specifically, the time value is

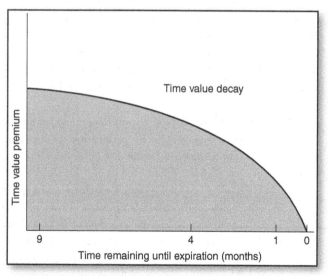

FIGURE 34.2 Time Value Decay
Source: Options on Comex Gold Futures, published by Commodity Exchange, Inc. (COMEX), 1982.

TABLE 34.2	Option Prices as a Function of Volatility in E-Mini S&P 500 Futures Prices[a]	
Annualized Volatility	**Put or Call Premium**
10	22.88 ($1,144)
20	45.75 ($2,288)
30	68.62 ($3,431)
40	91.46 ($4,573)
50	114.29 ($5,715)

[a] At-the-money options at a strike price of 2000 with 30 days to expiration.

assumed to be a function of the square root of time. (This relationship is a consequence of the typical assumption regarding the shape of the probability curve for prices of the underlying futures contract.) Thus, an option with nine months until expiration would have 1.5 times the time value of a four-month option with the same strike price ($\sqrt{9} = 3$; $\sqrt{4} = 2$; $3 \div 2 = 1.5$) and three times the time value of a one-month option ($\sqrt{9} = 3$; $\sqrt{1} = 1$; $3 \div 1 = 3$).

3. **Volatility.** Time value will vary directly with the *estimated* volatility of the underlying futures contract for the remaining lifespan of the option. This relationship is the result of the fact that greater volatility raises the probability the intrinsic value will increase by any specified amount prior to expiration. In other words, the greater the volatility, the larger the probable range of futures prices. As Table 34.2 shows, volatility has a strong impact on theoretical option premium values.

Although volatility is an extremely important factor in determining option premium values, it should be stressed that the future volatility of the underlying futures contract is never precisely known until after the fact. (In contrast, the time remaining until expiration and the relationship between the current price of futures and the strike price can be exactly specified at any juncture.) Thus, volatility must always be estimated on the basis of historical volatility data. As will be explained, this factor is crucial in explaining the deviation between theoretical and actual premium values.

4. **Interest rates.** The effect of interest rates on option premiums is considerably smaller than any of the above three factors. The specific nature of the relationship between interest rates and premiums was succinctly summarized by James Bowe[8]:

> The effect of interest rates is complicated because changes in rates affect not only the underlying value of the option, but the futures price as well. Taking it in steps, a buyer of any given option must pay the premium up front, and of course the seller receives the money. If interest rates go up and everything else stays constant, the opportunity cost to the option buyer of giving up the use of his money increases, and so he is willing to bid less. Conversely, the seller of options can make more on the premiums by

[8] James Bowe, *Option Strategies Trading Handbook* (New York, NY: Coffee, Sugar, and Cocoa Exchange, 1983).

investing the cash received and so is willing to accept less; the value of the options fall. However, in futures markets, part of the value of distant contracts in a carry market reflects the interest costs associated with owning the commodity. An increase in the interest rate might cause the futures price to increase, leading to the value of *existing* calls going up. The net effect on calls is ambiguous, but puts should decline in value with increasing interest rates, as the effects are reinforcing.

Theoretical versus Actual Option Premiums

There is a variety of mathematical models available that will indicate the theoretical "fair value" for an option, given specific information regarding the four factors detailed in the previous section. Theoretical values will approximate, but by no means coincide with, actual premiums. Does the existence of such a discrepancy necessarily imply that the option is mispriced? Definitely not. The model-implied premium will differ from the actual premium for two reasons:

1. The model's assumption regarding the mathematical relationship between option prices (premiums) and the factors that affect option prices may not accurately describe market behavior. This is always true because, to some extent, even the best option-pricing models are only theoretical approximations of true market behavior.
2. The volatility figure used by an option-pricing model will normally differ somewhat from the market's expectation of future volatility. This is a critical point that requires further elaboration.

Recall that although volatility is a crucial input in any option pricing formula, its value can only be estimated. The theoretical "fair value" of an option will depend on the specific choice of a volatility figure. Some of the factors that will influence the value of the volatility estimate are the length of the prior period used to estimate volatility, the time interval in which volatility is measured, the weighting scheme (if any) used on the historical volatility data, and adjustments (if any) to reflect relevant influences (e.g., the recent trend in volatility). It should be clear that any specific volatility estimate will implicitly reflect a number of unavoidably arbitrary decisions. Different assumptions regarding the best procedure for estimating future volatility from past volatility will yield different theoretical premium values. Thus, there is no such thing as a single, well-defined fair value for an option.

All that any option pricing model can tell you is what the value of the option should be given the specific *assumptions* regarding expected volatility and the form of the mathematical relationship between option prices and the key factors affecting them. If a given mathematical model provides a close approximation of market behavior, a discrepancy between the theoretical value and the actual premium means the market expectation for volatility, called the *implied volatility,* differs from the historically based volatility estimate used in the model. The question of whether the volatility assumptions of a specific pricing model provide more accurate estimates of actual volatility than the implied volatility figures (i.e., the future volatility suggested by actual premiums) can only be answered empirically. A bias toward buying "underpriced" options (relative to the theoretical model fair value) and selling "overpriced" options would be justified only if empirical evidence supported the contention that, on balance, the model's volatility assumptions proved to be better than implied volatility in predicting actual volatility levels.

If a model's volatility estimates were demonstrated to be superior to implied volatility estimates, it would suggest, from a strict probability standpoint, a bullish trader would be better off selling puts than buying calls if options were overpriced (based on the fair value figures indicated by the model), and buying calls rather than selling puts if options were underpriced. Similarly, a bearish trader would be better off selling calls than buying puts if options were overpriced, and buying puts rather than selling calls if options were underpriced. The best strategy for any individual trader, however, would depend on the specific profile of his price expectations (i.e., the probabilities the trader assigns to various price outcomes).

■ Delta (the Neutral Hedge Ratio)

Delta, also called the *neutral hedge ratio,* is the expected change in the option price given a one-unit change in the price of the underlying futures contract. For example, if the delta of an August gold call option is 0.25, it means that a $1 change in the price of August futures can be expected to result in a $0.25 change in the option premium. Thus, the delta value for a given option can be used to determine the number of options that would be equivalent in risk to a single futures contract *for small changes in price.* It should be stressed that delta will change rapidly as prices change. Thus, the delta value cannot be used to compare the relative risk of options versus futures for large price changes.

Table 34.3 illustrates the estimated delta values for out-of-the-money, at-the-money, and in-the-money call options for a range of times to expiration. Where did these values come from? They are derived from the same mathematical models used to determine a theoretical value for an option premium given the relationship between the strike price and the current price of futures, time remaining

TABLE 34.3	Change in the Premium of an E-Mini S&P 500 Call Option for 20.00 ($1000) Move in the Underlying Futures Contract[a]					
	Increase in the 2000 call option premium if the futures price rises:					
	From 1900 to 1920		From 2000 to 2020		From 2100 to 2120	
Time to expiration	$	Delta	$	Delta	$	Delta
1 week	$10	0.01	$500	0.5	$1,000	1
1 month	$120	0.12	$510	0.51	$870	0.87
3 months	$260	0.26	$510	0.51	$750	0.75
6 months	$330	0.33	$520	0.52	$690	0.69
12 months	$390	0.39	$520	0.52	$650	0.65

[a]Assumed volatility: 15 percent; assumed interest rate: 2 percent per year.

Source: CME Group (www.cmegroup.com).

until expiration, estimated volatility, and interest rates. For any given set of values for these factors, delta will equal the absolute difference between the option premium indicated by the model and the model-indicated premium if the futures price changes by one point. Table 34.3 illustrates a number of important observations regarding theoretical delta values:

1. **Delta values for out-of-the-money options are low.** This relationship is a result of the fact that there is a high probability that any given price increase[9] will not make any actual difference to the value of the option at expiration (i.e., the option will probably expire worthless).

2. **Delta values for in-the-money options are relatively high, but less than one.** In-the-money options have high deltas because there is a high probability that a one-point change in the futures price will mean a one-point change in the option value at expiration. However, since this probability must always be equal to less than one, the delta value will also always be equal to less than one.

3. **Delta values for at-the-money options will be near 0.50.** Since there is a 50/50 chance that an at-the-money option will expire in-the-money, there will be an approximately 50/50 chance that a one-point increase in the price of futures will result in a one-point increase in the option value at expiration.

4. **Delta values for out-of-the-money options will increase as time to expiration increases.** A longer time to expiration will increase the probability that a price increase in futures will make a difference in the option value at expiration, since there is more time for futures to reach the strike price.

5. **Delta values for in-the-money options will decrease as time to expiration increases.** A longer time to expiration will increase the probability that a change in the futures price will not make any difference to the option value at expiration since there is more time for futures to fall back to the strike price by the time the option expires.

6. **Delta values for at-the-money options are not substantially affected by time to maturity until near expiration.** This behavioral pattern is true because the probability that an at-the-money option will expire in-the-money remains close to 50/50 until the option is near expiration.

---

[9]This section implicitly assumes that the option is a call. If the option is a put, read "price decrease" for all references to "price increase."

CHAPTER 35

Option Trading Strategies

Brokers are fond of pointing out to possible buyers of options that they are a splendid thing to buy, and pointing out to sellers that they are a splendid thing to sell. They believe implicitly in this paradox. Thus the buyer does well, the seller does well, and it is not necessary to stress the point that the broker does well enough. Many examples can be cited showing all three of them emerging from their adventures with a profit. One wonders why the problem of unemployment cannot be solved by having the unemployed buy and sell each other options, instead of mooning around on those park benches.

—Fred Schwed
Where Are the Customers' Yachts?

■ Comparing Trading Strategies

The existence of options greatly expands the range of possible trading strategies. For example, in the absence of an option market, a trader who is bullish can either go long or initiate a bull spread (in those markets in which spread movements correspond to price direction). However, if option-related trading approaches are included, the bullish trader can consider numerous alternative strategies including: long out-of-the-money calls, long in-the-money calls, long at-the-money calls, short out-of-the-money puts, short in-the-money puts, short at-the-money puts, "synthetic" long positions, combined positions in futures and options, and a variety of bullish option spreads. Frequently, one of these option-related strategies will offer significantly better profit potential for a given level of risk than an outright futures position. Thus, the trader who considers both option-based strategies and outright positions should have a decided advantage over the trader who restricts his trades to only futures.

There is no single best trading approach. The optimal trading strategy in any given situation will depend on the prevailing option premium levels and the specific nature of the expected price scenario. How does one decide on the best strategy? This chapter will attempt to answer this critical question in two steps. First, we will examine the general profit/loss characteristics (profiles) of a wide range of alternative trading strategies. Second, we will consider how price expectations can be combined with these profit/loss profiles to determine the best trading approach.

The *profit/loss profile* is a diagram indicating the profit or loss implied by a position (vertical axis) for a range of market prices (horizontal axis). The profit/loss profile provides an ideal means of understanding and comparing different trading strategies. The following points should be noted regarding the profit/loss profiles detailed in the next section:

1. All illustrations are based on a single option series, for a single market, on a single date: the August 2015 gold options on April 13, 2015. This common denominator makes it easy to compare the implications of different trading strategies. The choice of April 13, 2015, was not arbitrary. On that date, the closing price of August futures (1,200.20) was almost exactly equal to one of the option strike prices ($1,200/oz), thereby providing a nearly precise at-the-money option—a factor that greatly facilitates the illustration of theoretical differences among out-of-the-money, in-the-money, and at-the-money options. The specific closing values for the option premiums on that date were as follows ($/oz):

Strike Price	August Calls	August Puts
1,050	155.2	5.1
1,100	110.1	10.1
1,150	70.1	19.9
1,200	38.8	38.7
1,250	19.2	68.7
1,300	9.1	108.7
1,350	4.5	154.1

Option pricing data in this chapter courtesy of OptionVue (www.optionvue.com).

The reader should refer to these quotes when examining each of the profit/loss profiles in the next section.

2. In order to avoid unnecessarily cluttering the illustrations, the profit/loss profiles do not include transaction costs and interest income effects, both of which are very minor. (Note the assumption that transaction costs equal zero imply that commission costs equal zero *and* that positions can be implemented at the quoted levels—in this case, the market close.)

3. The profit/loss profiles reflect the situation at the time of the option expiration. This assumption simplifies the exposition, since the value of an option can be precisely determined at that point in time. At prior times, the value of the option will depend on the various factors discussed in the previous chapter (e.g., time until expiration, volatility, etc.). Allowing for an evaluation of each option strategy at interim time stages would introduce a level of complexity that would place the discussion beyond the scope of this book. However, the key point to keep in mind

is that the profit/loss profile for strategies that include a net long options position will shift upward as the time reference point is further removed from the expiration date. The reason is that at expiration, options have only *intrinsic value;* at points prior to expiration, options also have *time value.* Thus, prior to expiration, the holder of an option could liquidate his position at a price above its intrinsic value—the liquidation value assumed in the profit/loss profile. Similarly, the profit/loss profile would be shifted downward for the option writer (seller) at points in time prior to expiration. This is true since at such earlier junctures, the option writer would have to pay not only the intrinsic value but also the time value if he wanted to cover his position.

4. It is important to keep in mind that a single option is equivalent to a smaller *position size* than a single futures contract (see section entitled "Delta—the Neutral Hedge Ratio" in the previous chapter). Similarly, an out-of-the-money option is equivalent to a smaller position size than an in-the-money option. Thus, the trader should also consider the profit/loss profiles consisting of various multiples of each strategy. In any case, the preference of one strategy over another should be based entirely on the relationship between reward and risk rather than on the absolute profit (loss) levels. In other words, strategy preferences should be totally independent of position size.

5. Trading strategies are evaluated strictly from the perspective of the speculator. Hedging applications of option trading are discussed separately at the end of this chapter.

■ Profit/Loss Profiles for Key Trading Strategies

Strategy 1: Long Futures

EXAMPLE. Buy August gold futures at $1,200. (See Table 35.1 and Figure 35.1.)

Comment. The simple long position in futures does not require much explanation and is included primarily for purposes of comparison to other less familiar trading strategies. As every trader knows, the long futures position is appropriate when one expects a significant price advance. However, as will

TABLE 35.1 Profit/Loss Calculations: Long Futures

Futures Price at Expiration ($/oz)	Futures Price Change ($/oz)	Profit/Loss on Position
1,000	−200	−$20,000
1,050	−150	−$15,000
1,100	−100	−$10,000
1,150	−50	−$5,000
1,200	0	$0
1,250	50	$5,000
1,300	100	$10,000
1,350	150	$15,000
1,400	200	$20,000

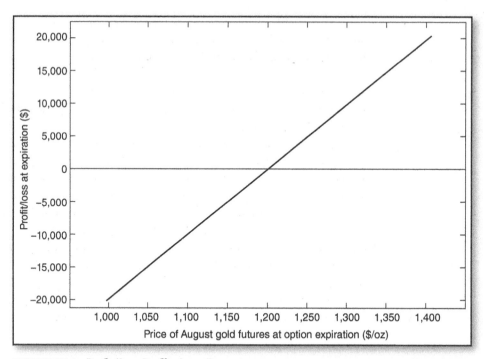

FIGURE 35.1 Profit/Loss Profile: Long Futures

be illustrated later in this section, for any given price scenario, some option-based strategy will often provide a more attractive trade in terms of reward/risk characteristics.

Strategy 2: Short Futures

EXAMPLE. Sell August gold futures at $1,200. (See Table 35.2 and Figure 35.2.)

TABLE 35.2   Profit/Loss Calculations: Short Futures

Futures Price at Expiration ($/oz)	Futures Price Change ($/oz)	Profit/Loss on Position
1,000	200	$20,000
1,050	150	$15,000
1,100	100	$10,000
1,150	50	$5,000
1,200	0	$0
1,250	−50	−$5,000
1,300	−100	−$10,000
1,350	−150	−$15,000
1,400	−200	−$20,000

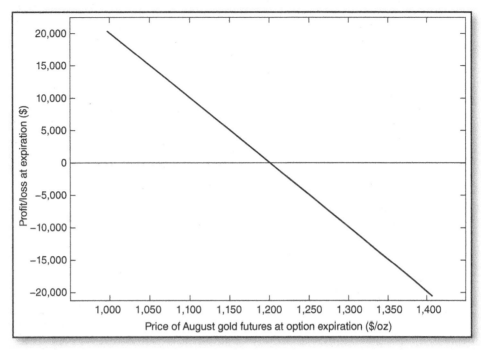

FIGURE 35.2   Profit/Loss Profile: Short Futures

Comment. Once again, this strategy requires little explanation and is included primarily for comparison to other strategies. As any trader knows, the short futures position is appropriate when one is expecting a significant price decline. However, as will be seen later in this chapter, for any given expected price scenario, some option-based strategy will often offer a more attractive trading opportunity in terms of reward/risk characteristics.

Strategy 3a: Long Call (At-the-Money)

EXAMPLE. Buy August $1,200 gold futures call at a premium of $38.80/oz ($3,880), with August gold futures trading at $1,200/oz. (See Table 35.3a and Figure 35.3a.)

Comment. The long call is a bullish strategy in which maximum risk is limited to the premium paid for the option, while maximum gain is theoretically unlimited. However, the probability of a loss is greater than the probability of a gain, since the futures price must rise by an amount exceeding the option premium (as of the option expiration) in order for the call buyer to realize a profit. Two specific characteristics of the at-the-money option are the following:

1. The maximum loss will only be realized if futures are trading at or below their current level at the time of the option expiration.
2. For small price changes, each $1 change in the futures price will result in approximately a $0.50 change in the option price. (At-the-money options near expiration, which will change by a greater amount, are an exception.) Thus, for small price changes, a net long futures position is equivalent to approximately two call options in terms of risk.

TABLE 35.3a Profit/Loss Calculations: Long Call (At-the-Money)

(1) Futures Price at Expiration ($/oz)	(2) Premium of August $1,200 Call at Initiation ($/oz)	(3) $ Amount of Premium Paid	(4) Call Value at Expiration	(5) Profit/Loss of Position [(4) – (3)]
1,000	38.8	$3,880	$0	–$3,880
1,050	38.8	$3,880	$0	–$3,880
1,100	38.8	$3,880	$0	–$3,880
1,150	38.8	$3,880	$0	–$3,880
1,200	38.8	$3,880	$0	–$3,880
1,250	38.8	$3,880	$5,000	$1,120
1,300	38.8	$3,880	$10,000	$6,120
1,350	38.8	$3,880	$15,000	$11,120
1,400	38.8	$3,880	$20,000	$16,120

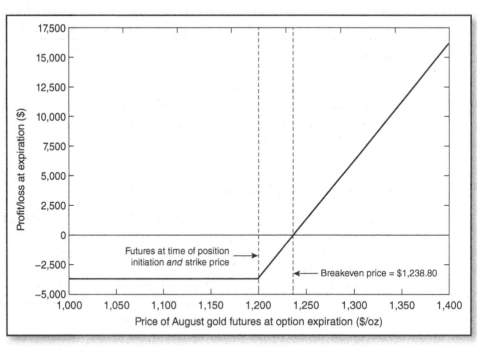

FIGURE 35.3a Profit/Loss Profile: Long Call (At-the-Money)

Strategy 3b: Long Call (Out-of-the-Money)

EXAMPLE. Buy August $1,300 gold futures call at a premium of $9.10/oz ($910), with August gold futures trading at $1,200/oz. (See Table 35.3b and Figure 35.3b.)

Comment. The buyer of an out-of-the-money call reduces his maximum risk in exchange for accepting a smaller probability that the trade will realize a profit. By definition, the strike price of an out-of-the-money call is above the current level of futures. In order for the out-of-the-money call position to realize a profit, the futures price (as of the time of the option expiration) must exceed the strike price by an amount greater than the premium ($9.10/oz in this example). Note that in the out-of-the-money call position, price increases that leave futures below the option strike price will still result in a maximum loss on the option. The long out-of-the-money call might be a particularly appropriate position for the trader expecting a large price advance, but also concerned about the possibility of a large price decline.

It should be emphasized that the futures price need not necessarily reach the strike price in order for the out-of-the-money call to be profitable. If the market rises quickly, the call will increase in value and hence can be resold at a profit. (However, this characteristic will not necessarily hold true for slow price advances, since the depressant effect of the passage of time on the option premium could more than offset the supportive effect of the increased price level of futures.)

For small price changes, the out-of-the-money call will change by less than a factor of one-half for each dollar change in the futures price. Thus, for small price changes, each long futures position will be equivalent to several long out-of-the-money calls in terms of risk.

TABLE 35.3b Profit/Loss Calculations: Long Call (Out-of-the-Money)

(1) Futures Price at Expiration ($/oz)	(2) Premium of August $1,300 Call at Initiation ($/oz)	(3) $ Amount of Premium Paid	(4) Call Value at Expiration	(5) Profit/Loss on Position [(4) − (3)]
1,000	9.1	$910	$0	−$910
1,050	9.1	$910	$0	−$910
1,100	9.1	$910	$0	−$910
1,150	9.1	$910	$0	−$910
1,200	9.1	$910	$0	−$910
1,250	9.1	$910	$0	−$910
1,300	9.1	$910	$0	−$910
1,350	9.1	$910	$5,000	$4,090
1,400	9.1	$910	$10,000	$9,090

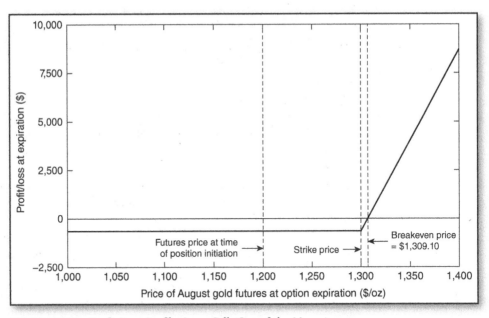

FIGURE 35.3b   Profit/Loss Profile: Long Call (Out-of-the-Money)

Strategy 3c: Long Call (In-the-Money)

EXAMPLE. Buy August $1,100 gold futures call at a premium of $110.10/oz ($11,010), with August gold futures trading at $1,200/oz. (See Table 35.3c and Figure 35.3c.)

Comment. In many respects, a long in-the-money call position is very similar to a long futures position. The three main differences between these two trading strategies are:

1. The long futures position will gain slightly more in the event of a price rise—an amount equal to the time value portion of the premium paid for the option ($1,010 in the above example).
2. For moderate price declines, the long futures position will lose slightly less. (Once again, the difference will be equal to the time value portion of the premium paid for the option.)
3. In the event of a large price decline, the loss on the in-the-money long call position would be limited to the total option premium paid, while the loss on the long futures position will be unlimited.

In a sense, the long in-the-money call position can be thought of as a long futures position with a built-in stop. This characteristic is an especially important consideration for speculators who typically employ protective stop-loss orders on their positions—a prudent trading approach. A trader using a protective sell stop on a long position faces the frustrating possibility of the market declining sufficiently to activate his stop and subsequently rebounding. The long in-the-money call position offers the speculator an alternative method of limiting risk that does not present this danger. Of course, this benefit does not come without a cost; as mentioned above, the buyer of an in-the-money call will gain slightly less than the outright futures trader if the market advances, and will lose slightly more if the market declines *moderately.* However, if the trader is anticipating volatile market conditions, he might very

TABLE 35.3c	Profit/Loss Calculations: Long Call (In-the-Money)			
(1) Futures Price at Expiration ($/oz)	(2) Premium of August $1,100 Call at Initiation ($/oz)	(3) $ Amount of Premium Paid	(4) Call Value at Expiration	(5) Profit/Loss on Position [(4) – (3)]
1,000	110.1	$11,010	$0	–$11,010
1,050	110.1	$11,010	$0	–$11,010
1,100	110.1	$11,010	$0	–$11,010
1,150	110.1	$11,010	$5,000	–$6,010
1,200	110.1	$11,010	$10,000	–$1,010
1,250	110.1	$11,010	$15,000	$3,990
1,300	110.1	$11,010	$20,000	$8,990
1,350	110.1	$11,010	$25,000	$13,990
1,400	110.1	$11,010	$30,000	$18,990

well prefer a long in-the-money call position to a long futures position combined with a protective sell stop order. In any case, the key point is that the trader who routinely compares the strategies of buying an in-the-money call versus going long futures with a protective sell stop should enjoy an advantage over those traders who never consider the option-based alternative.

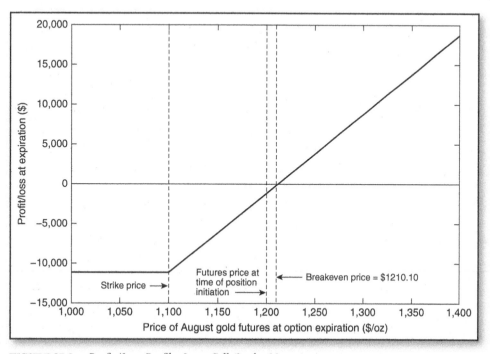

FIGURE 35.3c Profit/Loss Profile: Long Call (In-the-Money)

Table 35.3d summarizes the profit/loss implications of various long call positions for a range of price assumptions. Note that as calls move deeper in-the-money, their profit and loss characteristics increasingly resemble a long futures position. The very deep in-the-money $1,050 call provides an interesting apparent paradox: The profit/loss characteristics of this option are nearly the same as those of a long futures position for all prices above $1,050, but the option has the advantage of limited risk for lower prices. How can this be? Why wouldn't all traders prefer the long $1,050 call to the long futures position and, therefore, bid up its price so that its premium also reflected more time value? (The indicated premium of $15,520 for the $1,050 call consists almost entirely of intrinsic value.)

There are two plausible explanations to this apparent paradox. First, the option price reflects the market's assessment that there is a very low probability of gold prices moving to this deep in-the-money strike price, and therefore the market places a low value on the time premium. In other words, the market places a low value on the loss protection provided by an option with a strike price so far below the market. Second, the $1,050 call represents a fairly illiquid option position, and the quoted price does not reflect the bid/ask spread. No doubt, a potential buyer of the call would have had to pay a higher price than the quoted premium in order to assure an execution.

TABLE 35.3d   **Profit/Loss Matrix for Long Calls with Different Strike Prices**

		Dollar Amount of Premiums Paid						
		$1,050 Call	$1,100 Call[a]	$1,150 Call	$1,200 Call[a]	$1,250 Call	$1,300 Call[a]	$1,350 Call
		$15,520	$11,010	$7,010	$3,880	$1,920	$910	$450

		Position Profit/Loss at Expiration						
		In-the-Money			At-the-Money	Out-of-the-Money		
Futures Price at Expiration ($/oz)	Long Futures at $1,200	$1,050 Call	$1,100 Call[a]	$1,150 Call	$1,200 Call[a]	$1,250 Call	$1,300 Call[a]	$1,350 Call
1,000	−$20,000	−$15,520	−$11,010	−$7,010	−$3,880	−$1,920	−$910	−$450
1,050	−$15,000	−$15,520	−$11,010	−$7,010	−$3,880	−$1,920	−$910	−$450
1,100	−$10,000	−$10,520	−$11,010	−$7,010	−$3,880	−$1,920	−$910	−$450
1,150	−$5,000	−$5,520	−$6,010	−$7,010	−$3,880	−$1,920	−$910	−$450
1,200	$0	−$520	−$1,010	−$2,010	−$3,880	−$1,920	−$910	−$450
1,250	$5,000	$4,480	$3,990	$2,990	$1,120	−$1,920	−$910	−$450
1,300	$10,000	$9,480	$8,990	$7,990	$6,120	$3,080	−$910	−$450
1,350	$15,000	$14,480	$13,990	$12,990	$11,120	$8,080	$4,090	−$450
1,400	$20,000	$19,480	$18,990	$17,990	$16,120	$13,080	$9,090	$4,550

[a]These calls are compared in Figure 35.3d.

Figure 35.3d compares the three types of long call positions to a long futures position. It should be noted that in terms of absolute price changes, the long futures position represents the largest position size, while the out-of-the-money call represents the smallest position size. Figure 35.3d suggests the following important observations:

1. As previously mentioned, the in-the-money call is very similar to an outright long futures position.
2. The out-of-the-money call will lose the least in a declining market, but will also gain the least in a rising market.
3. The at-the-money call will lose the most in a steady market and will be the middle-of-the-road performer (relative to the other two types of calls) in advancing and declining markets.

Again, it should be emphasized that these comparisons are based upon single-unit positions that may differ substantially in terms of their implied position size (as suggested by their respective delta values). A comparison that involved equivalent position size levels for each strategy (i.e., equal delta values for each position) would yield different observations. This point is discussed in greater detail in the section entitled "Multiunit Strategies."

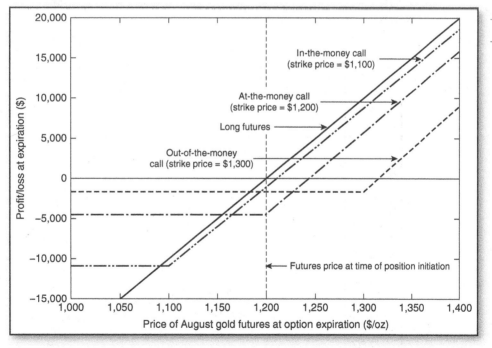

FIGURE 35.3d Profit/Loss Profile: Long Futures and Long Call Comparisons (In-the-Money, At-the-Money, and Out-of-the-Money)

Chart created using TradeStation. ©TradeStation Technologies, Inc. All rights reserved.

Strategy 4a: Short Call (At-the-Money)

EXAMPLE. Sell August $1,200 gold futures call at a premium of $38.80/oz ($3,880), with August gold futures trading at $1,200/oz. (See Table 35.4a and Figure 35.4a.)

TABLE 35.4a	Profit/Loss Calculations-Short Call (At-the-Money)			
(1)	(2)	(3)	(4)	(5)
	Premium of August			
Futures Price at	$1,200 Call at	$ Amount of	Call Value at	Profit/Loss on
Expiration ($/oz)	Initiation ($/oz)	Premium Received	Expiration	Position [(3) – (4)]
1,000	38.8	$3,880	$0	$3,880
1,050	38.8	$3,880	$0	$3,880
1,100	38.8	$3,880	$0	$3,880
1,150	38.8	$3,880	$0	$3,880
1,200	38.8	$3,880	$0	$3,880
1,250	38.8	$3,880	$5,000	–$1,120
1,300	38.8	$3,880	$10,000	–$6,120
1,350	38.8	$3,880	$15,000	–$11,120
1,400	38.8	$3,880	$20,000	–$16,120

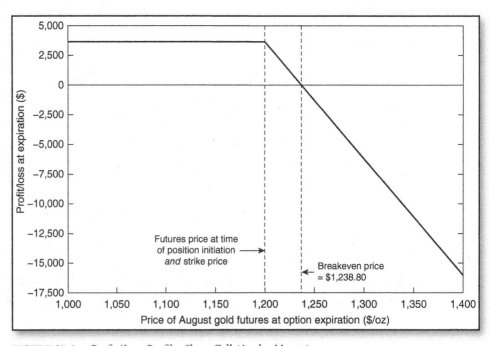

FIGURE 35.4a   Profit/Loss Profile: Short Call (At-the-Money)

Comment. The short call is a bearish position with a maximum potential gain equal to the premium received for selling the call and unlimited risk. However, in return for assuming this unattractive maximum reward/maximum risk relationship, the seller of a call enjoys a greater probability of realizing a profit than a loss. Note the short at-the-money call position will result in a gain as long as the futures price at the time of the option expiration does not exceed the futures price at the time of the option initiation by an amount greater than the premium level ($38.80/oz in our example). However, the maximum possible profit (i.e., the premium received on the option) will only be realized if the futures price at the time of the option expiration is below the prevailing market price at the time the option was sold (i.e., the strike price). The short call position is appropriate if the trader is *modestly* bearish and views the probability of a large price rise as being very low. If, however, the trader anticipated a large price decline, he would probably be better off buying a put or going short futures.

Strategy 4b: Short Call (Out-of-the-Money)

EXAMPLE. Sell August $1,300 gold futures call at a premium of $9.10/oz ($910), with August gold futures trading at $1,200/oz. (See Table 35.4b and Figure 35.4b.)

Comment. The seller of an out-of-the-money call is willing to accept a smaller maximum gain (i.e., premium) in exchange for increasing the probability of a gain on the trade. The seller of an out-of-the-money call will retain the full premium received as long as the futures price does not rise by an amount greater than the difference between the strike price and the futures price at the time of the option sale. The trade will be profitable as long as the futures price at the time of the option expiration is not above the strike price by more than the option premium ($9.10/oz in this example). The short out-of-the-money call represents a less bearish posture than the short at-the-money call position. Whereas the short at-the-money call position reflects an expectation that prices will either decline or increase only slightly, the short out-of-the-money call merely reflects an expectation that prices will not rise sharply.

TABLE 35.4b	Profit/Loss Calculations: Short Call (Out-of-the-Money)			
(1) Futures Price at Expiration ($/oz)	(2) Premium of August $1,300 Call at Initiation ($/oz)	(3) $ Amount of Premium Received	(4) Value of Call at Expiration	(5) Profit/Loss on Position [(3) – (4)]
1,000	9.1	$910	$0	$910
1,050	9.1	$910	$0	$910
1,100	9.1	$910	$0	$910
1,150	9.1	$910	$0	$910
1,200	9.1	$910	$0	$910
1,250	9.1	$910	$0	$910
1,300	9.1	$910	$0	$910
1,350	9.1	$910	$5,000	–$4,090
1,400	9.1	$910	$10,000	–$9,090

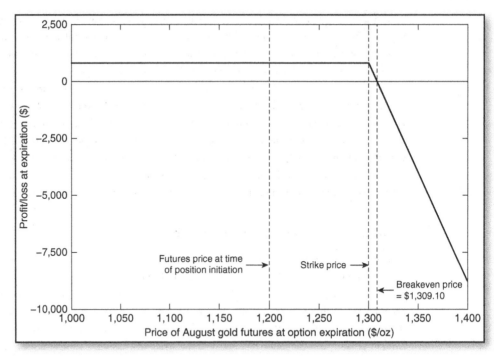

FIGURE 35.4b Profit/Loss Profile: Short Call (Out-of-the-Money)
Chart created using TradeStation. ©TradeStation Technologies, Inc. All rights reserved.

Strategy 4c: Short Call (In-the-Money)

EXAMPLE. Sell August $1,100 gold futures call at a premium of $110.10/oz ($11,010), with August gold futures trading at $1,200/oz. (See Table 35.4c and Figure 35.4c.)

TABLE 35.4c Profit/Loss Calculations: Short Call (In-the-Money)

(1) Futures Price at Expiration ($/oz)	(2) Premium of August $1,100 Call at Initiation ($/oz)	(3) Dollar Amount of Premium Received	(4) Value of Call at Expiration	(5) Profit/Loss on Position [(3) – (4)]
1,000	110.1	$11,010	$0	$11,010
1,050	110.1	$11,010	$0	$11,010
1,100	110.1	$11,010	$0	$11,010
1,150	110.1	$11,010	$5,000	$6,010
1,200	110.1	$11,010	$10,000	$1,010
1,250	110.1	$11,010	$15,000	−$3,990
1,300	110.1	$11,010	$20,000	−$8,990
1,350	110.1	$11,010	$25,000	−$13,990
1,400	110.1	$11,010	$30,000	−$18,990

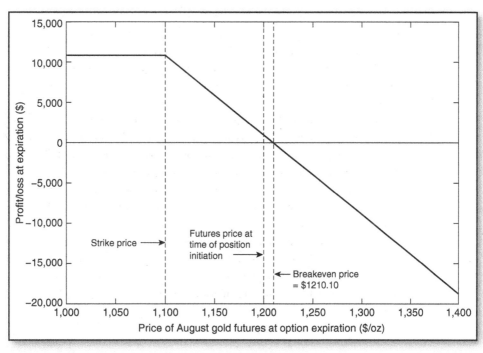

FIGURE 35.4c Profit/Loss Profile: Short Call (In-the-Money)
Chart created using TradeStation. ©TradeStation Technologies, Inc. All rights reserved.

Comment. For most of the probable price range, the profit/loss characteristics of the short in-the-money call are fairly similar to those of the outright short futures position. There are three basic differences between these two positions:

1. The short in-the-money call will lose modestly less than the short futures position in an advancing market because the loss will be partially offset by the premium received for the call.
2. The short in-the-money call will gain modestly more than the short futures position in a moderately declining market.
3. In a very sharply declining market, the profit potential on a short futures position is open-ended, whereas the maximum gain in the short in-the-money call position is limited to the total premium received for the call.

In effect, the seller of an in-the-money call chooses to lock in modestly better results for the probable price range in exchange for surrendering the opportunity for windfall profits in the event of a price collapse. Generally speaking, a trader should only choose a short in-the-money call over a short futures position if he believes that the probability of a sharp price decline is extremely small.

Table 35.4d summarizes the profit/loss results for various short call positions for a range of price assumptions. As can be seen, as calls move more deeply in-the-money, they begin to resemble a short futures position more closely. (Sellers of deep in-the-money calls should be aware that longs may choose to exercise such options well before expiration. Early exercise can occur if the potential interest income on the premium is greater than the theoretical time value of the option for a zero interest rate assumption.) Short positions in deep out-of-the-money calls will prove profitable for the vast range of prices, but the maximum gain is small and the theoretical maximum loss is unlimited.

Figure 35.4d compares each type of short call to a short futures position. The short at-the-money call position will be the most profitable strategy under stable market conditions and the middle-of-the-road strategy (relative to the other two types of calls) in rising and declining markets. The short out-of-the-money call will lose the least in a rising market, but it will also be the least profitable strategy if prices decline. The short in-the-money call is the type of call that has the greatest potential and risk and, as mentioned above, there is a strong resemblance between this strategy and an outright short position in futures.

It should be emphasized that the comparisons in Figure 35.4d are based upon single-unit positions. However, as previously explained, these alternative strategies do not represent equivalent position sizes. Comparisons based on positions weighted equally in terms of some risk measure (e.g., equal delta values) would yield different empirical conclusions.

TABLE 35.4d Profit/Loss Matrix for Short Calls with Different Strike Prices

	Dollar Amount of Premium Received						
	$1,050 Call	$1,100 Call	$1,150 Call	$1,200 Call	$1,250 Call	$1,300 Call	$1,350 Call
	$15,520	$11,010	$7,010	$3,880	$1,920	$910	$450

		Position Profit/Loss at Expiration						
Futures Price at Expiration ($/oz)	Short Futures at $1,200	In-the-Money			At-the-Money	Out-of-the Money		
		$1,050 Call	$1,100 Call[a]	$1,150 Call	$1,200 Call[a]	$1,250 Call	$1,300 Call[a]	$500 Call
1,000	$20,000	$15,520	$11,010	$7,010	$3,880	$1,920	$910	$450
1,050	$15,000	$15,520	$11,010	$7,010	$3,880	$1,920	$910	$450
1,100	$10,000	$10,520	$11,010	$7,010	$3,880	$1,920	$910	$450
1,150	$5,000	$5,520	$6,010	$7,010	$3,880	$1,920	$910	$450
1,200	$0	$520	$1,010	$2,010	$3,880	$1,920	$910	$450
1,250	−$5,000	−$4,480	−$3,990	−$2,990	−$1,120	$1,920	$910	$450
1,300	−$10,000	−$9,480	−$8,990	−$7,990	−$6,120	−$3,080	$910	$450
1,350	−$15,000	−$14,480	−$13,990	−$12,990	−$11,120	−$8,080	−$4,090	$450
1,400	−$20,000	−$19,480	−$18,990	−$17,990	−$16,120	−$13,080	−$9,090	−$4,550

[a]These calls are compared in Figure 35.4d.

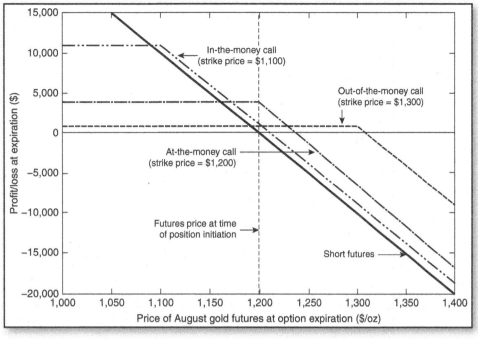

FIGURE 35.4d Profit/Loss Profile: Short Futures and Short Call Comparisons (In-the-Money, At-the-Money, and Out-of-the-Money)

Strategy 5a: Long Put (At-the-Money)

EXAMPLE. Buy August $1,200 gold futures put at a premium of $38.70/oz ($3,870), with August gold futures trading at $1,200/oz. (See Table 35.5a and Figure 35.5a.)

TABLE 35.5a Profit/Loss Calculations: Long Put (At-the-Money)

(1) Futures Price at Expiration ($/oz)	(2) Premium of August $1,200 Put at Initiation ($/oz)	(3) $ Amount of Premium Paid	(4) Put Value at Expiration	(5) Profit/Loss on Position [(4) − (3)]
1,000	38.7	$3,870	$20,000	$16,130
1,050	38.7	$3,870	$15,000	$11,130
1,100	38.7	$3,870	$10,000	$6,130
1,150	38.7	$3,870	$5,000	$1,130
1,200	38.7	$3,870	$0	−$3,870
1,250	38.7	$3,870	$0	−$3,870
1,300	38.7	$3,870	$0	−$3,870
1,350	38.7	$3,870	$0	−$3,870
1,400	38.7	$3,870	$0	−$3,870

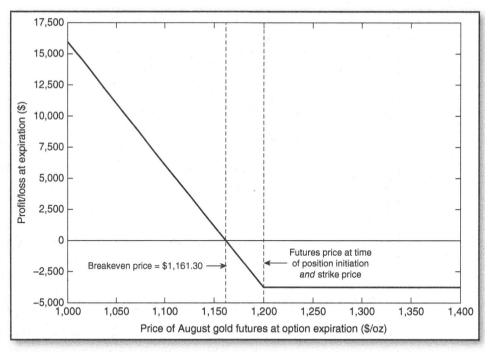

FIGURE 35.5a Profit/Loss Profile: Long Put (At-the-Money)

Comment. The long put is a bearish strategy in which maximum risk is limited to the premium paid for the option, while maximum gain is theoretically unlimited. However, the probability of a loss is greater than the probability of a gain, since the futures price must decline by an amount exceeding the option premium (as of the option expiration) in order for the put buyer to realize a profit. Two specific characteristics of the at-the-money option are:

1. The maximum loss will be realized only if futures are trading at or above their current level at the time of the option expiration.
2. For small price changes, each $1 change in the futures price will result in approximately a $0.50 change in the option price (except for options near expiration). Thus, for small price changes, a net short futures position is equivalent to approximately 2 put options in terms of risk.

Strategy 5b: Long Put (Out-of-the-Money)

EXAMPLE. Buy August $1,100 gold futures put at a premium of $10.10/oz ($1,010). (The current price of August gold futures is $1,200/oz.) (See Table 35.5b and Figure 35.5b.)

Comment. The buyer of an out-of-the-money put reduces his maximum risk in exchange for accepting a smaller probability that the trade will realize a profit. By definition, the strike price of an out-of-the-money put is below the current level of futures. In order for the out-of-the-money put position

TABLE 35.5b Profit/Loss Calculations: Long Put (Out-of-the-Money)

(1) Futures Price At Expiration ($/oz)	(2) Premium of August $1,100 Put at Initiation ($/oz)	(3) $ Amount of Premium Paid	(4) Value of Put at Expiration	(5) Profit/Loss on Position [(4) − (3)]
1,000	10.1	$1,010	$10,000	$8,990
1,050	10.1	$1,010	$5,000	$3,990
1,100	10.1	$1,010	$0	−$1,010
1,150	10.1	$1,010	$0	−$1,010
1,200	10.1	$1,010	$0	−$1,010
1,250	10.1	$1,010	$0	−$1,010
1,300	10.1	$1,010	$0	−$1,010
1,350	10.1	$1,010	$0	−$1,010
1,400	10.1	$1,010	$0	−$1,010

to realize a profit, the futures price (as of the time of the option expiration) must penetrate the strike price by an amount greater than the premium ($10.10/oz in the above example). Note that in the out-of-the-money put position, price decreases that leave futures above the option strike price will still result in a maximum loss on the option. The long out-of-the-money put might be a particularly appropriate position for the trader expecting a large price decline, but also concerned about the possibility of a large price rise.

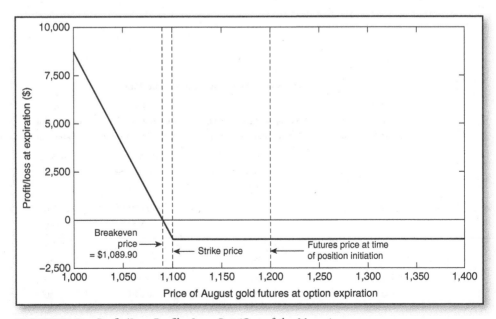

FIGURE 35.5b Profit/Loss Profile: Long Put (Out-of-the-Money)

It should be emphasized that the futures price need not necessarily reach the strike price in order for the out-of-the-money put to be profitable. If the market declines quickly, the put will increase in value, and hence can be resold at a profit. (However, this behavior will not necessarily hold for slow price declines, since the depressant effect of the passage of time on the option premium could well more than offset the supportive effect of the decreased price level of futures.)

For small price changes, the out-of-the-money put will change by less than a factor of one-half for each dollar change in the futures price. Thus, for small price changes, each short futures position will be equivalent to several short out-of-the-money puts in terms of risk.

Strategy 5c: Long Put (In-the-Money)

EXAMPLE. Buy August $1,300 gold futures put at a premium of $108.70/oz ($10,870), with August gold futures trading at $1,200/oz. (See Table 35.5c and Figure 35.5c.)

Comment. In many respects, a long in-the-money put option is very similar to a short futures position. The three main differences between these two trading strategies are:

1. The short futures position will gain slightly more in the event of a price decline—an amount equal to the time value portion of the premium paid for the option ($870 in this example).
2. For moderate price advances, the short futures position will lose slightly less. (Once again, the difference will be equal to the time value portion of the premium paid for the option.)
3. In the event of a large price advance, the loss on the in-the-money long put position would be limited to the total option premium paid, while the loss on the short futures position would be unlimited.

TABLE 35.5c	Profit/Loss Calculations: Long Put (In-the-Money)			
(1) Futures Price at Expiration ($/oz)	(2) Premium of August $1,300 Put at Initiation ($/oz)	(3) Dollar Amount of Premium Paid	(4) Value of Put at Expiration	(5) Profit/Loss on Position [(3) – (4)]
1,000	108.7	$10,870	$30,000	$19,130
1,050	108.7	$10,870	$25,000	$14,130
1,100	108.7	$10,870	$20,000	$9,130
1,150	108.7	$10,870	$15,000	$4,130
1,200	108.7	$10,870	$10,000	−$870
1,250	108.7	$10,870	$5,000	−$5,870
1,300	108.7	$10,870	$0	−$10,870
1,350	108.7	$10,870	$0	−$10,870
1,400	108.7	$10,870	$0	−$10,870

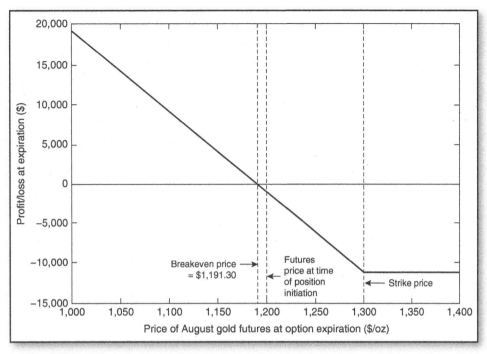

FIGURE 35.5c   Profit/Loss Profile: Long Put (In-the-Money)

In a sense, the long in-the-money put position can be thought of as a short futures position with a built-in stop. This characteristic is an especially important consideration for speculators who typically employ protective stop loss orders on their positions—a prudent trading approach. A trader using a protective buy stop on a short position faces the frustrating possibility of the market advancing sufficiently to activate his stop and subsequently breaking. The long in-the-money put position offers the speculator an alternative method of limiting risk that does not present this danger. Of course, this benefit does not come without a cost: as mentioned earlier, the buyer of an in-the-money put will gain slightly less than the outright short futures trader if the market declines and lose slightly more if the market advances *moderately*. However, if the trader is anticipating volatile market conditions, he might very well prefer a long in-the-money put position to a short futures position combined with a protective buy stop order. In any case, the key point is that the trader who routinely compares the strategies of buying an in-the-money put versus going short futures with a protective buy stop should enjoy an advantage over those traders who never consider the option-based alternative.

Table 35.5d summarizes the profit/loss implications of various long put positions for a range of price assumptions. Note that as puts move deeper in-the-money, their profit and loss characteristics increasingly resemble a short futures position.

TABLE 35.5d Profit/Loss Matrix for Long Puts with Different Strike Prices

		Dollar Amount of Premium Paid						
		$1,350 Put	$1,300 Put	$1,250 Put	$1,200 Put	$1,150 Put	$1,100 Put	$1,050 Put
		$15,410	$10,870	$6,870	$3,870	$1,990	$1,010	$510

		Position Profit/Loss at Expiration						
		In-the-Money			At-the-Money	Out-of-the-Money		
Futures Price at Expiration ($/oz)	Short Futures at $1,200	$1,350 Put	$1,300 Put[a]	$1,250 Put	$1,200 Put[a]	$1,150 Put	$1,100 Put[a]	$1,050 Put
1,000	$20,000	$19,590	$19,130	$18,130	$16,130	$13,010	$8,990	$4,490
1,050	$15,000	$14,590	$14,130	$13,130	$11,130	$8,010	$3,990	−$510
1,100	$10,000	$9,590	$9,130	$8,130	$6,130	$3,010	−$1,010	−$510
1,150	$5,000	$4,590	$4,130	$3,130	$1,130	−$1,990	−$1,010	−$510
1,200	$0	−$410	−$870	−$1,870	−$3,870	−$1,990	−$1,010	−$510
1,250	−$5,000	−$5,410	−$5,870	−$6,870	−$3,870	−$1,990	−$1,010	−$510
1,300	−$10,000	−$10,410	−$10,870	−$6,870	−$3,870	−$1,990	−$1,010	−$510
1,350	−$15,000	−$15,410	−$10,870	−$6,870	−$3,870	−$1,990	−$1,010	−$510
1,400	−$20,000	−$15,410	−$10,870	−$6,870	−$3,870	−$1,990	−$1,010	−$510

[a]These puts are compared in Figure 35.5d.

Figure 35.5d compares the three types of long put positions to a short futures position. It should be noted that in terms of absolute price changes, the short futures position represents the largest position size, while the out-of-the-money put represents the smallest position size. Figure 35.5d suggests the following important observations:

1. As previously mentioned, the in-the-money put is very similar to an outright short futures position.
2. The out-of-the-money put will lose the least in a rising market, but will also gain the least in a declining market.
3. The at-the-money put will lose the most in a steady market and will be the middle-of-the-road performer (relative to the other two types of puts) in declining and advancing markets.

Again, it should be emphasized that these comparisons are based on single-unit positions that may differ substantially in terms of their implied position size (as suggested by their respective delta values). A comparison that involved equivalent position size levels for each strategy (i.e., equal delta values for each position) would yield different observations.

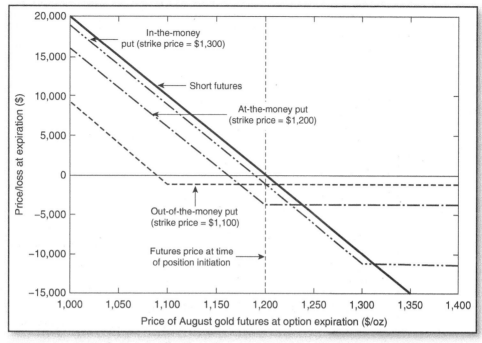

FIGURE 35.5d Profit/Loss Profile: Short Futures and Long Put Comparisons (In-the-Money, At-the-Money, and Out-of-the-Money)

EXAMPLE. Sell August $1,200 gold futures put at a premium of $38.70/oz ($3,870), with August gold futures trading at $1,200/oz. (See Table 35.6a and Figure 35.6a.)

TABLE 35.6a Profit/Loss Calculations: Short Put (At-the-Money)

(1) Futures Price at Expiration ($/oz)	(2) Premium of August $1,200 Put at Initiation ($/oz)	(3) $ Amount of Premium Received	(4) Put Value at Expiration	(5) Profit/Loss on Position [(3) – (4)]
1,000	38.7	$3,870	$20,000	−$16,130
1,050	38.7	$3,870	$15,000	−$11,130
1,100	38.7	$3,870	$10,000	−$6,130
1,150	38.7	$3,870	$5,000	−$1,130
1,200	38.7	$3,870	$0	$3,870
1,250	38.7	$3,870	$0	$3,870
1,300	38.7	$3,870	$0	$3,870
1,350	38.7	$3,870	$0	$3,870
1,400	38.7	$3,870	$0	$3,870

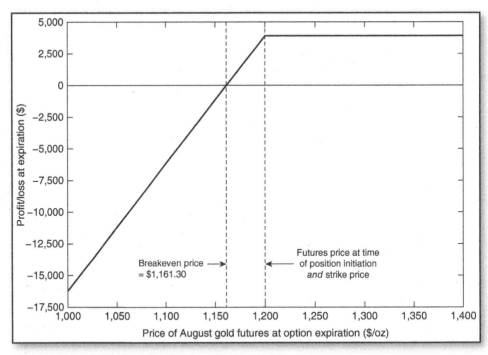

FIGURE 35.6a Profit/Loss Profile: Short Put (At-the-Money)

Comment. The short put is a bullish position with a maximum potential gain equal to the premium received for selling the put and unlimited risk. However, in return for assuming this unattractive maximum reward/maximum risk relationship, the seller of a put enjoys a greater probability of realizing a profit than a loss. Note that the short at-the-money put position will result in a gain as long as the futures price at the time of the option expiration is not below the futures price at the time of the option initiation by an amount greater than the premium level ($38.70/oz in our example). However, the maximum possible profit (i.e., the premium received on the option) will only be realized if the futures price at the time of the option expiration is above the prevailing market price at the time the option was sold (i.e., the strike price). The short put position is appropriate if the trader is *modestly* bullish and views the probability of a large price decline as being very low. If, however, the trader anticipated a large price advance, he would probably be better off buying a call or going long futures.

Strategy 6b: Short Put (Out-of-the-Money)

EXAMPLE. Sell August $1,100 gold futures put at a premium of $10.10/oz ($1,010), with August gold futures trading at $1,200/oz. (See Table 35.6b and Figure 35.6b.)

Comment. The seller of an out-of-the-money put is willing to accept a smaller maximum gain (i.e., premium) in exchange for increasing the probability of gain on the trade. The seller of an out-of-the-money put will retain the full premium received as long as the futures price does not decline by an

TABLE 35.6b	Profit/Loss Calculations: Short Put (Out-of-the-Money)			
(1) Futures Price at Expiration ($/oz)	(2) Premium of August $1,100 Put at Initiation ($/oz)	(3) Dollar Amount of Premium Received	(4) Value of Put at Expiration	(5) Profit/Loss on Position [(3) – (4)]
1,000	10.1	$1,010	$10,000	−$8,990
1,050	10.1	$1,010	$5,000	−$3,990
1,100	10.1	$1,010	$0	$1,010
1,150	10.1	$1,010	$0	$1,010
1,200	10.1	$1,010	$0	$1,010
1,250	10.1	$1,010	$0	$1,010
1,300	10.1	$1,010	$0	$1,010
1,350	10.1	$1,010	$0	$1,010
1,400	10.1	$1,010	$0	$1,010

amount greater than the difference between the futures price at the time of the option sale and the strike price. The trade will be profitable as long as the futures price at the time of the option expiration is not below the strike price by more than the option premium ($10.10/oz in this example). The short out-of-the-money put represents a less bullish posture than the short at-the-money put

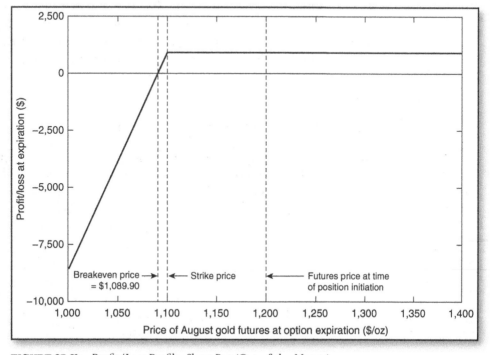

FIGURE 35.6b Profit/Loss Profile: Short Put (Out-of-the-Money)

position. Whereas the short at-the-money put position reflects an expectation that prices will either rise or decline only slightly, the short out-of-the-money put merely reflects an expectation that prices will not decline sharply.

Strategy 6c: Short Put (In-the-Money)

EXAMPLE. Sell August $1,300 gold futures put at a premium of $108.70/oz ($10,870), with August gold futures trading at $1,200/oz. (See Table 35.6c and Figure 35.6c.)

Comment. For most of the probable price range, the profit/loss characteristics of the short in-the-money put are fairly similar to those of the outright long futures position. There are three basic differences between these two positions:

1. The short in-the-money put will lose modestly less than the long futures position in a declining market because the loss will be partially offset by the premium received for the put.
2. The short in-the-money put will gain modestly more than the long futures position in a moderately advancing market.
3. In a very sharply advancing market, the profit potential on a long futures position is open-ended, whereas the maximum gain in the short in-the-money put position is limited to the total premium received for the put.

In effect, the seller of an in-the-money put chooses to lock in modestly better results for the probable price range in exchange for surrendering the opportunity for windfall profits in the event of a price explosion. Generally speaking, a trader should only choose a short in-the-money put over a long futures position if he believes that the probability of a sharp price advance is extremely small.

TABLE 35.6c Profit/Loss Calculations: Short Put (In-the-Money)

(1) Futures Price at Expiration ($/oz)	(2) Premium of August $1,300 Put at Initiation ($/oz)	(3) Dollar Amount of Premium Received	(4) Put Value at Expiration	(5) Profit/Loss on Position [(3) − (4)]
1,000	108.7	$10,870	$30,000	−$19,130
1,050	108.7	$10,870	$25,000	−$14,130
1,100	108.7	$10,870	$20,000	−$9,130
1,150	108.7	$10,870	$15,000	−$4,130
1,200	108.7	$10,870	$10,000	$870
1,250	108.7	$10,870	$5,000	$5,870
1,300	108.7	$10,870	$0	$10,870
1,350	108.7	$10,870	$0	$10,870
1,400	108.7	$10,870	$0	$10,870

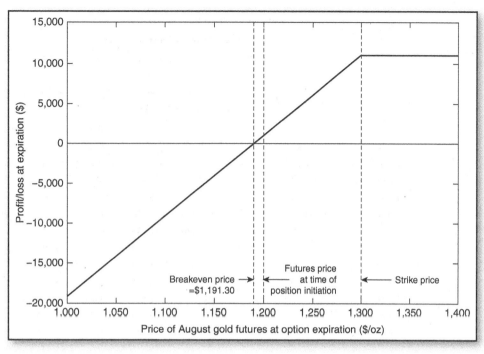

15,000

10,000

5,000

0

−5,000

−10,000

−15,000

−20,000

Profit/loss at expiration ($)

Breakeven price →
=$1,191.30

Futures price
at time of
position initiation

Strike price

1,000   1,050   1,100   1,150   1,200   1,250   1,300   1,350   1,400

Price of August gold futures at option expiration ($/oz)

FIGURE 35.6c   Profit/Loss Profile: Short Put (In-the-Money)

Table 35.6d summarizes the profit/loss results for various short put positions for a range of price assumptions. As can be seen, as puts move more deeply in the money, they begin to more closely resemble a long futures position. (As previously explained in the case of calls, sellers of deep in-the-money options should be cognizant of the real possibility of early exercise.) Short positions in deep out-of-the-money puts will prove profitable for the vast range of prices, but the maximum gain is small and the theoretical maximum loss is unlimited.

Figure 35.6d compares each type of short put to a long futures position. The short at-the-money put position will be the most profitable strategy under stable market conditions and the middle-of-the-road strategy (relative to the other two types of puts) in declining and rising markets. The short out-of-the-money put will lose the least in a declining market, but it will also be the least profitable strategy if prices advance. The short in-the-money put is the type of put that has the greatest potential and risk and, as mentioned above, there is a strong resemblance between this strategy and an outright long position in futures.

It should be emphasized that the comparisons in Figure 35.6d are based upon single-unit positions. However, as previously explained, these alternative strategies do not represent equivalent position sizes. Comparisons based on positions weighted equally in terms of some risk measure (e.g., equal delta values) would yield different empirical conclusions.

| TABLE 35.6d | Profit/Loss Matrix for Short Puts with Different Strike Prices |

		Dollar Amount of Premium Received						
		$1,350 Put	$1,300 Put	$1,250 Put	$1,200 Put	$1,150 Put	$1,100 Put	$1,050 Put
		$15,410	$10,870	$6,870	$3,870	$1,990	$1,010	$510

		Position Profit/Loss at Expiration						
		In-the-Money			At-the-Money		Out-of-the-Money	
Futures Price at Expiration ($/oz)	Long Futures at $1,200	$1,350 Put	$1,300 Put[a]	$1,250 Put	$1,200 Put[a]	$1,150 Put	$1,100 Put[a]	$1,050 Put
1,000	−$20,000	−$19,590	−$19,130	−$18,130	−$16,130	−$13,010	−$8,990	−$4,490
1,050	−$15,000	−$14,590	−$14,130	−$13,130	−$11,130	−$8,010	−$3,990	$510
1,100	−$10,000	−$9,590	−$9,130	−$8,130	−$6,130	−$3,010	$1,010	$510
1,150	−$5,000	−$4,590	−$4,130	−$3,130	−$1,130	$1,990	$1,010	$510
1,200	$0	$410	$870	$1,870	$3,870	$1,990	$1,010	$510
1,250	$5,000	$5,410	$5,870	$6,870	$3,870	$1,990	$1,010	$510
1,300	$10,000	$10,410	$10,870	$6,870	$3,870	$1,990	$1,010	$510
1,350	$15,000	$15,410	$10,870	$6,870	$3,870	$1,990	$1,010	$510
1,400	$20,000	$15,410	$10,870	$6,870	$3,870	$1,990	$1,010	$510

[a]These puts are compared in Figure 35.6d.

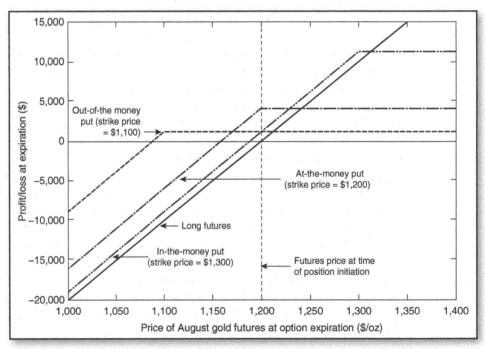

FIGURE 35.6d Profit/Loss Profile: Long Futures and Short Put Comparisons (In-the-Money, At-the-Money, and Out-of-the-Money)

Strategy 7: Long Straddle (Long Call + Long Put)

EXAMPLE. Buy August $1,200 gold futures call at a premium of $38.80/oz ($3,880) and simultaneously buy an August $1,200 gold futures put at a premium of $38.70/oz ($3,870). (See Table 35.7 and Figure 35.7.)

Comment. The long straddle position is a volatility bet. The buyer of a straddle does not have any opinion regarding the probable price direction; he merely believes that option premiums are underpriced relative to the potential market volatility. Andrew Tobias once offered a somewhat more cynical perspective of this type of trade[1]: "Indeed, if you haven't any idea of which way the [market] is headed but feel it is headed someplace, you can buy both a put and a call on it. That's called a straddle and involves enough commissions to keep your broker smiling all week."

As can be seen in Figure 35.7, the long straddle position will be unprofitable for a wide price range centered at the current price. Since this region represents the range of the most probable price outcomes, the long straddle position has a large probability of loss. In return for accepting a large probability of loss, the buyer of a straddle enjoys unlimited profit potential in the event of either a large price rise or a large price decline. The maximum loss on a long straddle position is equal to the total premium paid for both the long call and long put and will only be experienced if the expiration price is equal to the futures price at the time the options were purchased. (Implicit assumption: both the call and put are at-the-money options.)

515

OPTION TRADING STRATEGIES

TABLE 35.7	Profit/Loss Calculations: Long Straddle (Long Call + Long Put)					
(1)	(2)	(3)	(4)	(5)	(6)	(7)
Futures Price at Expiration ($/oz)	Premium of August $1,200 Call at Initiation ($/oz)	Premium of August $1,200 Put at Initiation ($/oz)	$ Amount of Total Premium Paid	Call Value at Expiration	Put Value at Expiration	Profit/Loss on Position [(5) + (6) − (4)]
1,000	38.8	38.7	$7,750	$0	$20,000	$12,250
1,050	38.8	38.7	$7,750	$0	$15,000	$7,250
1,100	38.8	38.7	$7,750	$0	$10,000	$2,250
1,150	38.8	38.7	$7,750	$0	$5,000	−$2,750
1,200	38.8	38.7	$7,750	$0	$0	−$7,750
1,250	38.8	38.7	$7,750	$5,000	$0	−$2,750
1,300	38.8	38.7	$7,750	$10,000	$0	$2,250
1,350	38.8	38.7	$7,750	$15,000	$0	$7,250
1,400	38.8	38.7	$7,750	$20,000	$0	$12,250

---

[1] Andrew Tobias, *Getting By on $100,000 a Year (and Other Sad Tales)* (New York, NY: Simon & Schuster, 1980).

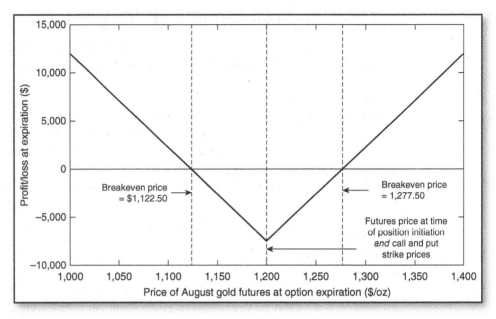

<figure> 15,000
10,000
5,000
0
Breakeven price = $1,122.50
Breakeven price = 1,277.50
−5,000
Futures price at time of position initiation and call and put strike prices
−10,000
1,000   1,050   1,100   1,150   1,200   1,250   1,300   1,350   1,400
Price of August gold futures at option expiration ($/oz)
Profit/loss at expiration ($) </figure>

FIGURE 35.7 Profit/Loss Profile: Long Straddle (Long Call + Long Put)

Strategy 8: Short Straddle (Short Call + Short Put)

EXAMPLE. Sell August $1,200 gold futures call at a premium of $38.80/oz ($3,880) and simultaneously sell an August $1,200 put at a premium of $38.70/oz ($3,870). (See Table 35.8 and Figure 35.8.)

TABLE 35.8 Profit/Loss Calculations: Short Straddle (Short Call + Short Put)

(1) Futures Price at Expiration ($/oz)	(2) Premium of August $1,200 Call at Initiation ($/oz)	(3) Premium of August $1,200 Put at Initiation ($/oz)	(4) $ Amount of Total Premium Received	(5) Call Value at Expiration	(6) Put Value at Expiration	(7) Profit/Loss on Position [(4) − (5) − (6)]
1,000	38.8	38.7	$7,750	$0	$20,000	−$12,250
1,050	38.8	38.7	$7,750	$0	$15,000	−$7,250
1,100	38.8	38.7	$7,750	$0	$10,000	−$2,250
1,150	38.8	38.7	$7,750	$0	$5,000	$2,750
1,200	38.8	38.7	$7,750	$0	$0	$7,750
1,250	38.8	38.7	$7,750	$5,000	$0	$2,750
1,300	38.8	38.7	$7,750	$10,000	$0	−$2,250
1,350	38.8	38.7	$7,750	$15,000	$0	−$7,250
1,400	38.8	38.7	$7,750	$20,000	$0	−$12,250

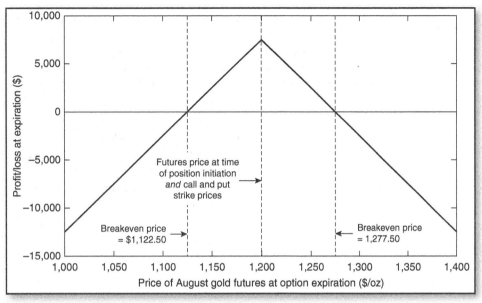

FIGURE 35.8 Profit/Loss Profile: Short Straddle (Short Call + Short Put)

Comment. The short straddle position will be profitable over a wide range of prices. The best outcome for a seller of a straddle is a totally unchanged market. In this circumstance, the seller will realize his maximum profit, which is equal to the total premium received for the sale of the call and put. The short straddle position will remain profitable as long as prices do not rise or decline by more than the combined total premium of the two options. The seller of the straddle enjoys a large probability of a profitable trade, in exchange for accepting unlimited risk in the event of either a very sharp price advance or decline.

This strategy is appropriate if the speculator expects prices to trade within a moderate range, but has no opinion regarding the probable market direction. A trader anticipating nonvolatile market conditions, but also having a price-directional bias, would be better off selling either calls or puts rather than a straddle. For example, a trader expecting low volatility and modestly declining prices should sell 2 calls instead of selling a straddle.

Strategy 9: Bullish "Texas Option Hedge" (Long Futures + Long Call)[2]

EXAMPLE. Buy August gold futures at $1,200 and simultaneously buy an August $1,200 gold futures call at a premium of $38.80/oz ($3,880). (See Table 35.9 and Figure 35.9.)

---

[2] By definition, a hedge implies a futures position opposite to an existing or anticipated actual position. In commodity trading, *Texas hedge* is a facetious reference to so-called "hedgers" who implement a futures position in the same direction as their cash position. The classic example of a Texas hedge would be a cattle feeder who goes long cattle futures. Whereas normal hedging reduces risk, the Texas hedge increases risk. There are many option strategies that combine offsetting positions in options and futures. This strategy is unusual in that it combines reinforcing positions in futures and options. Consequently, the term Texas option hedge seems to provide an appropriate label.

TABLE 35.9 **Profit/Loss Calculations: Bullish "Texas Option Hedge" (Long Futures + Long Call)**

(1) Futures Price at Expiration ($/oz)	(2) Premium of August $1,200 Call at Initiation ($/oz)	(3) $ Amount of Premium Paid	(4) Profit/Loss on Long Futures Position	(5) Call Value at Expiration	(6) Profit/Loss on Position [(4)+(5)−(3)]
1,000	38.8	$3,880	−$20,000	$0	−$23,880
1,050	38.8	$3,880	−$15,000	$0	−$18,880
1,100	38.8	$3,880	−$10,000	$0	−$13,880
1,150	38.8	$3,880	−$5,000	$0	−$8,880
1,200	38.8	$3,880	$0	$0	−$3,880
1,250	38.8	$3,880	$5,000	$5,000	$6,120
1,300	38.8	$3,880	$10,000	$10,000	$16,120
1,350	38.8	$3,880	$15,000	$15,000	$26,120
1,400	38.8	$3,880	$20,000	$20,000	$36,120

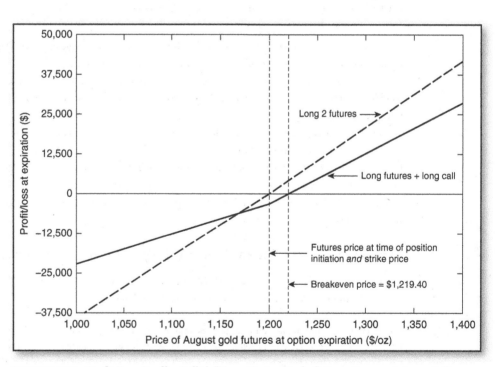

FIGURE 35.9 Profit/Loss Profile: Bullish "Texas Option Hedge" (Long Futures + Long Call)

Comment. This strategy provides an interesting alternative method of pyramiding—that is, increasing the size of a winning position. For example, a trader who is already long a futures contract at a profit and believes the market is heading higher may wish to increase his position without doubling his risk in the event of a price reaction—as would be the case if he bought a second futures contract. Such a speculator could choose instead to supplement his long position with the purchase of a call, thereby limiting the magnitude of his loss in the event of a price retracement, in exchange for realizing a moderately lower profit if prices continued to rise.

Figure 35.9 compares the alternative strategies of buying two futures versus buying a futures contract and a call. (For simplicity of exposition, the diagram assumes that both the futures contract and the call are purchased at the same time.) As can be seen, the long two futures position will always do moderately better in a rising market (by an amount equal to the premium paid for the call), but will lose more in the event of a significant price decline. The difference in losses between the two strategies will widen as larger price declines are considered.

Strategy 10: Bearish "Texas Option Hedge" (Short Futures + Long Put)

EXAMPLE. Sell August gold futures at $1,200 and simultaneously buy an August $1,200 gold put at a premium of $38.70/oz ($3,870). (See Table 35.10 and Figure 35.10.)

Comment. This strategy is perhaps most useful as an alternative means of increasing a short position. As illustrated in Figure 35.10, the combination of a short futures contract and a long put will gain moderately less than 2 short futures contracts in a declining market, but will lose a more limited amount in a rising market.

TABLE 35.10 | Profit/Loss Calculations: Bearish "Texas Option Hedge" (Short Futures + Long Put)

(1) Futures Price at Expiration ($/oz)	(2) Premium of August $1200 Put at Initiation ($/oz)	(3) $ Amount of Premium Paid	(4) Profit/Loss on Short Futures Position	(5) Put Value at Expiration	(6) Profit/Loss on Position [(4) + (5) – (3)]
1,000	38.7	$3,870	$20,000	$20,000	$36,130
1,050	38.7	$3,870	$15,000	$15,000	$26,130
1,100	38.7	$3,870	$10,000	$10,000	$16,130
1,150	38.7	$3,870	$5,000	$5,000	$6,130
1,200	38.7	$3,870	$0	$0	−$3,870
1,250	38.7	$3,870	−$5,000	$0	−$8,870
1,300	38.7	$3,870	−$10,000	$0	−$13,870
1,350	38.7	$3,870	−$15,000	$0	−$18,870
1,400	38.7	$3,870	−$20,000	$0	−$23,870

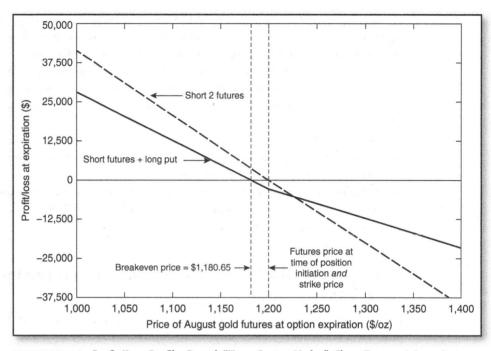

FIGURE 35.10 Profit/Loss Profile: Bearish "Texas Option Hedge" (Short Futures + Long Put)

Strategy 11a: Option-Protected Long Futures (Long Futures + Long At-the-Money Put)

EXAMPLE. Buy August gold futures at $1,200/oz and simultaneously buy an August $1200 gold put at a premium of $38.70/oz ($3,870). (See Table 35.11a and Figure 35.11a.)

Comment. A frequently recommended strategy is that the trader implementing (or holding) a long futures position can consider buying a put to protect his downside risk. The basic idea is that if the market declines, the losses in the long futures position will be offset dollar for dollar by the long put position. Although this premise is true, it should be stressed that such a combined position represents nothing more than a proxy for a long call. The reader can verify the virtually identical nature of these two alternative strategies by comparing Figure 35.11a to Figure 35.3a. If prices increase, the long futures position will gain, while the option will expire worthless. On the other hand, if prices decline, the loss in the combined position will equal the premium paid for the put. In fact, if the call and put premiums are equal, a long futures plus long put position will be precisely equivalent to a long call.

In most cases, the trader who finds the profit/loss profile of this strategy attractive would be better off buying a call, because the transaction costs are likely to be lower. However, if the trader already holds a long futures position, buying a put may be a reasonable alternative to liquidating this position and buying a call.

(1)	(2)	(3)	(4)	(5)	(6)
Futures Price at Expiration ($/oz)	Premium of August $1,200 Put at Initiation ($/oz)	$ Amount of Premium Paid	Profit/Loss on Long Futures Position	Put Value at Expiration	Profit/Loss on Position [(4) + (5) − (3)]
1,000	38.7	$3,870	−$20,000	$20,000	−$3,870
1,050	38.7	$3,870	−$15,000	$15,000	−$3,870
1,100	38.7	$3,870	−$10,000	$10,000	−$3,870
1,150	38.7	$3,870	−$5,000	$5,000	−$3,870
1,200	38.7	$3,870	$0	$0	−$3,870
1,250	38.7	$3,870	$5,000	$0	$1,130
1,300	38.7	$3,870	$10,000	$0	$6,130
1,350	38.7	$3,870	$15,000	$0	$11,130
1,400	38.7	$3,870	$20,000	$0	$16,130

TABLE 35.11a Profit/Loss Calculations: Option-Protected Long Futures—Long Futures + Long At-the-Money Put (Similar to Long At-the-Money Call)

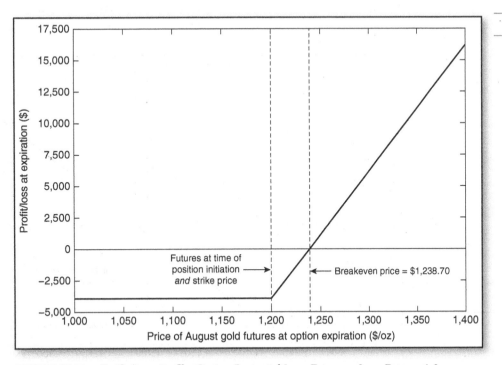

FIGURE 35.11a Profit/Loss Profile: Option-Protected Long Futures—Long Futures + Long at-the-Money Put (Similar to Long At-the-Money Call)

Strategy 11b: Option-Protected Long Futures (Long Futures + Long Out-of-the-Money Put)

EXAMPLE. Buy August gold futures at $1,200/oz and simultaneously buy an August $1,100 gold futures put at a premium of $10.10/oz ($1,010). (See Table 35.11b and Figure 35.11b.)

TABLE 35.11b	Profit/Loss Calculations: Option-Protected Long Futures—Long Futures + Long Out-of-the-Money Put (Similar to Long In-the-Money Call)				
(1)	(2)	(3)	(4)	(5)	(6)
Futures Price at Expiration ($/oz)	Premium of August $1,100 Put at Initiation ($/oz)	$ Amount of Premium Paid	Profit/Loss on Long Futures Position	Put Value at Expiration	Profit/Loss on Position [(4) + (5) − (3)]
1,000	10.1	$1,010	−$20,000	$10,000	−$11,010
1,050	10.1	$1,010	−$15,000	$5,000	−$11,010
1,100	10.1	$1,010	−$10,000	$0	−$11,010
1,150	10.1	$1,010	−$5,000	$0	−$6,010
1,200	10.1	$1,010	$0	$0	−$1,010
1,250	10.1	$1,010	$5,000	$0	$3,990
1,300	10.1	$1,010	$10,000	$0	$8,990
1,350	10.1	$1,010	$15,000	$0	$13,990
1,400	10.1	$1,010	$20,000	$0	$18,990

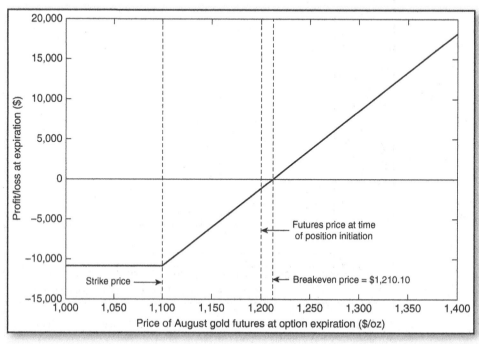

FIGURE 35.11b   Profit/Loss Profile: Option-Protected Long Futures—Long Futures + Long Out-of-the-Money Put (Similar to Long In-the-Money Call)

Comment. As can be verified by comparing Figure 35.11b to Figure 35.3c, this strategy is virtually equivalent to buying an in-the-money call. Supplementing a long futures position with the purchase of an out-of-the-money put will result in slightly poorer results if the market advances, or declines moderately, but will limit the magnitude of losses in the event of a sharp price decline. Thus, much like the long in-the-money call position, this strategy can be viewed as a long position with a built-in stop.

In most cases, it will make more sense for the trader to simply buy an in-the-money call since the transaction cost will be lower. However, if a speculator is already long futures, the purchase of an out-of-the-money put might present a viable alternative to liquidating this position and buying an in-the-money call.

Strategy 12a: Option-Protected Short Futures (Short Futures + Long At-the-Money Call)

EXAMPLE. Sell August gold futures at $1,200/oz and simultaneously buy an August $1,200 gold call at a premium of $38.80/oz ($3,880). (See Table 35.12a and Figure 35.12a.)

Comment. A frequently recommended strategy is that the trader implementing (or holding) a short futures position can consider buying a call to protect his upside risk. The basic idea is that if the market advances, the losses in the short futures position will be offset dollar for dollar by the long call position. Although this premise is true, it should be stressed that such a combined position represents nothing more than a proxy for a long put. The reader can verify the virtually identical nature of these two alternative strategies by comparing Figure 35.12a to Figure 35.5a. If prices decline, the short futures position will gain, while the option will expire worthless. And if prices advance, the loss in the combined position will equal the premium paid for the call. In fact, if the put and call premiums are equal, a short futures plus long call position will be precisely equivalent to a long put.

TABLE 35.12a	Profit/Loss Calculations: Option-Protected Short Futures—Short Futures + Long At-the-Money Call (Similar to Long At-the-Money Put)				
(1) Futures Price at Expiration ($/oz)	(2) Premium of August $1,200 Call at Initiation ($/oz)	(3) $ Amount of Premium Paid	(4) Profit/Loss on Short Futures Position	(5) Call Value at Expiration	(6) Profit/Loss on Position [(4)+ (5) − (3)]
1,000	38.8	$3,880	$20,000	$0	$16,120
1,050	38.8	$3,880	$15,000	$0	$11,120
1,100	38.8	$3,880	$10,000	$0	$6,120
1,150	38.8	$3,880	$5,000	$0	$1,120
1,200	38.8	$3,880	$0	$0	−$3,880
1,250	38.8	$3,880	−$5,000	$5,000	−$3,880
1,300	38.8	$3,880	−$10,000	$10,000	−$3,880
1,350	38.8	$3,880	−$15,000	$15,000	−$3,880
1,400	38.8	$3,880	−$20,000	$20,000	−$3,880

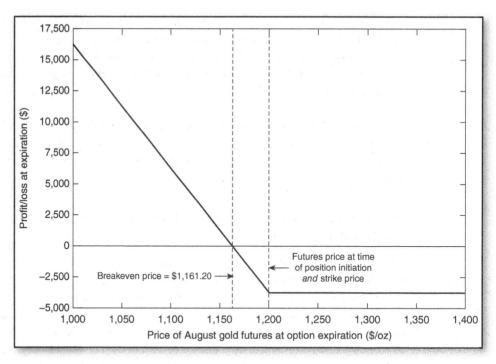

FIGURE 35.12a Profit/Loss Profile: Option-Protected Short Futures—Short Futures + Long At-the-Money Call (Similar to Long At-the-Money Put)

In most cases, the trader who finds the profit/loss profile of this strategy attractive would be better off buying a put, because the transaction costs are likely to be lower. However, if the trader already holds a short futures position, buying a call may be a reasonable alternative to liquidating this position and buying a put.

Strategy 12b: Option-Protected Short Futures (Short Futures + Long Out-of-the-Money Call)

EXAMPLE. Sell August gold futures at $1,200/oz and simultaneously buy an August $1,300 gold futures call at a premium of $9.10/oz ($910). (See Table 35.12b and Figure 35.12b.)

Comment. As can be verified by comparing Figure 35.12b to Figure 35.5c, this strategy is virtually equivalent to buying an in-the-money put. Supplementing a short futures position with the purchase of an out-of-the-money call will result in slightly poorer results if the market declines or advances moderately, but will limit the magnitude of losses in the event of a sharp price advance. Thus, much as with the long in-the-money put position, this strategy can be viewed as a short position with a built-in stop.

TABLE 35.12b Profit/Loss Calculations: Option-Protected Short Futures—Short Futures + Long Out-of-the-Money Call (Similar to Long In-the-Money Put)

(1) Futures Price at Expiration ($/oz)	(2) Premium of August $1,300 Call at Initiation ($/oz)	(3) $ Amount of Premium Paid	(4) Profit/Loss on Short Futures Position	(5) Call Value at Expiration	(6) Profit/Loss on Position [(4) + (5) − (3)]
1,000	9.1	$910	$20,000	$0	$19,090
1,050	9.1	$910	$15,000	$0	$14,090
1,100	9.1	$910	$10,000	$0	$9,090
1,150	9.1	$910	$5,000	$0	$4,090
1,200	9.1	$910	$0	$0	−$910
1,250	9.1	$910	−$5,000	$0	−$5,910
1,300	9.1	$910	−$10,000	$0	−$10,910
1,350	9.1	$910	−$15,000	$5,000	−$10,910
1,400	9.1	$910	−$20,000	$10,000	−$10,910

In most cases, it will make more sense for the trader simply to buy an in-the-money put since the transaction costs will be lower. However, if a speculator is already short futures, the purchase of an out-of-the-money call might present a viable alternative to liquidating this position and buying an in-the-money put.

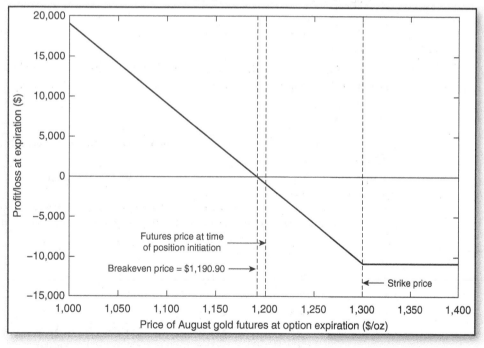

FIGURE 35.12b Profit/Loss Profile: Option-Protected Short Futures—Short Futures + Long Out-of-the-Money Call (Similar to Long In-the-Money Put)

Strategy 13: Covered Call Write (Long Futures + Short Call)

EXAMPLE. Buy August gold futures at $1,200/oz and simultaneously sell an August $1,200 gold futures call at a premium of $38.80/oz ($3,880). (See Table 35.13 and Figure 35.13.)

Comment. There has been a lot of nonsense written about covered call writing. In fact, even the term is misleading. The implication is that *covered call* writing—the sale of calls against long positions—is somehow a more conservative strategy than *naked call* writing—the sale of calls without any offsetting long futures position. This assumption is absolutely false. Although naked call writing implies unlimited risk, the same statement applies to covered call writing. As can be seen in Figure 35.13, the covered call writer merely exchanges unlimited risk in the event of a market advance (as is the case for the naked call writer) for unlimited risk in the event of a market decline. In fact, the reader can verify that this strategy is virtually equivalent to a "naked" short put position (see Strategy 35.6a).

One frequently mentioned motivation for covered call writing is that it allows the holder of a long position to realize a better sales price. For example, if the market is trading at $1,200 and the holder of a long futures contract sells an at-the-money call at a premium of $38.80/oz instead of liquidating his position, he can realize an effective sales price of $1,238.80 if prices move higher (the $1,200 strike price plus the premium received for the sale of the call). And, if prices move down by no more than $38.80/oz by option expiration, he will realize an effective sales price of at least $1,200. Presented in this light, this strategy appears to be a "heads you win, tails you win" proposition. However, there is no free lunch. The catch is that if prices decline by more than $38.80, the trader will realize a lower sales price than if he had simply liquidated the futures position. And, if prices rise substantially higher, the trader will fail to participate fully in the move as he would have if he had maintained his long position.

The essential point is that although many motivations are suggested for covered call writing, the trader should keep in mind that this strategy is entirely equivalent to selling puts.

	TABLE 35.13	Profit/Loss Calculations: Covered Call Write—Long Futures + Short Call (Similar to Short Put)				
(1) Futures Price at Expiration ($/oz)	(2) Premium of August $1,200 Call at Initiation ($/oz)	(3) $ Amount of Premium Received	(4) Profit/Loss on Long Futures Position	(5) Call Value at Expiration	(6) Profit/Loss on Position [(3) + (4) − (5)]
1,000	38.8	$3,880	−$20,000	$0	−$16,120
1,050	38.8	$3,880	−$15,000	$0	−$11,120
1,100	38.8	$3,880	−$10,000	$0	−$6,120
1,150	38.8	$3,880	−$5,000	$0	−$1,120
1,200	38.8	$3,880	$0	$0	$3,880
1,250	38.8	$3,880	$5,000	$5,000	$3,880
1,300	38.8	$3,880	$10,000	$10,000	$3,880
1,350	38.8	$3,880	$15,000	$15,000	$3,880
1,400	38.8	$3,880	$20,000	$20,000	$3,880

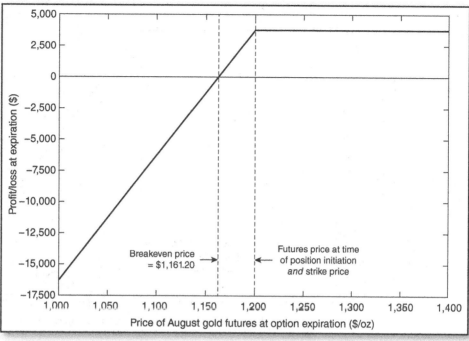

FIGURE 35.13 Profit/Loss Profile: Covered Call Write—Long Futures + Short Call (Similar to Short Put)

Strategy 14: Covered Put Write (Short Futures + Short Put)

EXAMPLE. Sell August futures at $1,200 and simultaneously sell an August $1,200 gold futures put at a premium of $38.70/oz ($3,870). (See Table 35.14 and Figure 35.14.)

	TABLE 35.14	Profit/Loss Calculations: Covered Put Write—Short Futures + Short Put (Similar to Short Call)				
(1)	(2)	(3)	(4)	(5)	(6)
Futures Price at Expiration ($/oz)	Premium of August $1,200 Put at Initiation ($/oz)	$ Amount of Premium Received	Profit/Loss on Short Futures Position	Put Value at Expiration	Profit/Loss on Position [(3) + (4) − (5)]
1,000	38.7	$3,870	$20,000	$20,000	$3,870
1,050	38.7	$3,870	$15,000	$15,000	$3,870
1,100	38.7	$3,870	$10,000	$10,000	$3,870
1,150	38.7	$3,870	$5,000	$5,000	$3,870
1,200	38.7	$3,870	$0	$0	$3,870
1,250	38.7	$3,870	−$5,000	$0	−$1,130
1,300	38.7	$3,870	−$10,000	$0	−$6,130
1,350	38.7	$3,870	−$15,000	$0	−$11,130
1,400	38.7	$3,870	−$20,000	$0	−$16,130

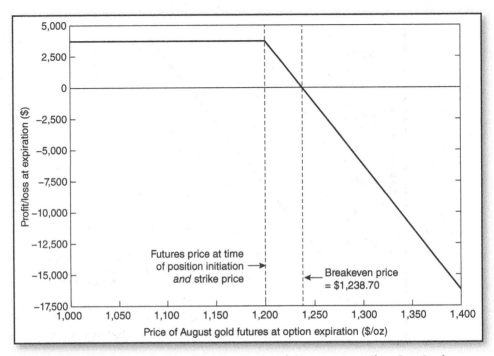

FIGURE 35.14 Profit/Loss Profile: Covered Put Write—Short Futures + Short Put (Similar to Short Call)

Comment. Comments analogous to those made for Strategy 13 would apply here. The sale of a put against a short futures position is equivalent to the sale of a call. The reader can verify this by comparing Figure 35.14 to Figure 35.4a. The two strategies would be precisely equivalent (ignoring transaction cost differences) if the put and call premiums were equal.

Strategy 15: Synthetic Long Futures (Long Call + Short Put)

EXAMPLE. Buy an August $1,150 gold futures call at a premium of $70.10/oz ($7,010) and simultaneously sell an August $1,150 gold futures put at a premium of $19.90/oz ($1,990). (See Table 35.15 and Figure 35.15.)

Comment. A synthetic long futures position can be created by combining a long call and a short put *for the same expiration date and the same strike price.* For example, as illustrated in Table 35.15 and Figure 35.15, the combined position of a long August $1,150 call and a short August $1,150 put is virtually identical to a long August futures position. The reason for this equivalence is tied to the fact that the difference between the premium paid for the call and the premium received for the put is approximately equal to the intrinsic value of the call. Each $1 increase in price will raise the intrinsic value of the call by an equivalent amount and each $1 decrease in price will reduce the intrinsic value of the

TABLE 35.15 Profit/Loss Calculations: Synthetic Long Futures (Long Call + Short Put)

(1) Futures Price at Expiration ($/oz)	(2) Premium of August $1,150 Call at Initiation ($/oz)	(3) $ Amount of Premium Paid	(4) Premium of August $1,150 Put at Initiation ($/oz)	(5) $ Amount of Premium Received	(6) Call Value at Expiration	(7) Put Value at Expiration	(8) Profit/Loss on Position $[(5) - (3) + (6) - (7)]$
1,000	70.1	$7,010	19.9	$1,990	$0	$15,000	−$20,020
1,050	70.1	$7,010	19.9	$1,990	$0	$10,000	−$15,020
1,100	70.1	$7,010	19.9	$1,990	$0	$5,000	−$10,020
1,150	70.1	$7,010	19.9	$1,990	$0	$0	−$5,020
1,200	70.1	$7,010	19.9	$1,990	$5,000	$0	−$20
1,250	70.1	$7,010	19.9	$1,990	$10,000	$0	$4,980
1,300	70.1	$7,010	19.9	$1,990	$15,000	$0	$9,980
1,350	70.1	$7,010	19.9	$1,990	$20,000	$0	$14,980
1,400	70.1	$7,010	19.9	$1,990	$25,000	$0	$19,980

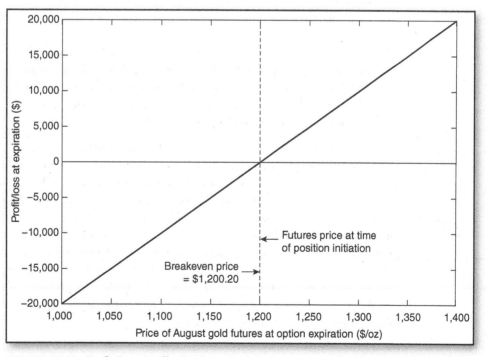

FIGURE 35.15 Profit/Loss Profile: Synthetic Long Futures (Long Call + Short Put)

call (or if prices decline below $1,150, increase the value of the put) by an equivalent amount. Thus, as long as the expiration date and strike price of the two options are identical, a long call/short put position acts just like a long futures contract.

The futures equivalent price implied by a synthetic position is given by the following formula:

$$\text{Synthetic futures position price} = \text{strike price} + \text{call premium} - \text{put premium}$$

It should be noted there will be one synthetic futures position price corresponding to each strike price for which options are traded for the given futures contract.

In this example, the synthetic long position is the same price as a long futures contract. (Synthetic futures position price = $1,150 + $70.10 − $19.90 = $1,200.20.) Thus, ignoring transaction costs and interest income effects, buying the August $1,150 call and simultaneously selling the August $1,150 put would be equivalent to buying an August futures contract. Of course, the trader considering this strategy as an alternative to an outright long futures position must incorporate transaction costs and interest income effects into the calculation. In this example, the true cost of the synthetic futures position would be raised vis-à-vis a long futures contract as a result of the following three factors:

1. Because the synthetic futures position involves two trades, in a less liquid market, it is reasonable to assume the execution costs will also be greater. In other words, the option-based strategy will require the trader to give up more points (relative to quoted levels) in order to execute the trade.
2. The synthetic futures position will involve greater commission costs.
3. The dollar premium paid for the call ($7,010) exceeds the dollar premium received for the put ($1,990). Thus, the synthetic futures position will involve an interest income loss on the difference between these two premium payments ($5,020). This factor, however, would be offset by the margin requirements on a long futures position.

Once the above differences are accounted for, the apparent relative advantage a synthetic futures position will sometimes seemingly offer will largely, if not totally, disappear. Nonetheless, insofar as some market inefficiencies may exist, the synthetic long futures position will sometimes offer a slight advantage over the direct purchase of a futures contract. In fact, the existence of such discrepancies would raise the possibility of pure arbitrage trades.[3] For example, if the price implied by the synthetic long futures position was less than the futures price, even after accounting for transaction costs and interest income effects, the arbitrageur could lock in a profit by buying the call, selling the put, and selling futures. Such a trade is called a *reverse conversion*. Alternately, if after adjusting for transaction costs and interest income effects, the implied price of the synthetic long futures position were greater than the futures price, the arbitrageur could lock in a profit by buying futures, selling the call, and buying the put. Such a trade is called a *conversion*.

---

[3] Pure arbitrage implies a risk-free trade in which the arbitrageur is able to lock in a small profit by exploiting temporary price distortions between two related markets.

It should be obvious that such risk-free profit opportunities will be limited in terms of both duration and magnitude. Generally speaking, conversion and reverse conversion arbitrage will normally only be feasible for professional arbitrageurs who enjoy much lower transaction costs (commissions plus execution costs) than the general public. The activity of these arbitrageurs will tend to keep synthetic futures position prices about in line with actual futures prices.

Strategy 16: Synthetic Short Futures (Long Put + Short Call)

EXAMPLE. Buy an August $1,300 gold futures put at a premium of $108.70/oz ($10,870) and simultaneously sell an August $1,300 gold futures call at a premium of $9.10/oz ($910). (See Table 35.16 and Figure 35.16.)

Comment. As follows directly from the discussion of the previous strategy, a synthetic short futures position can be created by combining a long put and a short call *with the same expiration date and the same strike price*. In this example, the synthetic futures position based upon the $1,300 strike price options is $0.40 higher priced than the underlying futures contract. (Synthetic futures position = $1,300 + $9.10 − $108.70 = $1,200.40.) However, for reasons similar to those discussed in the previous strategy, much of the advantage of an implied synthetic futures position price versus the actual futures price typically disappears once transaction costs and interest income effects are incorporated into the evaluation. An arbitrage employing the synthetic short futures position is called a *conversion* and was detailed in the previous strategy.

TABLE 35.16	Profit/Loss Calculations: Synthetic Short Futures (Long Put + Short Call)						
(1)	(2)	(3)	(4)	(5)	(6)	(7)	(8)
Futures Price at Expiration ($/oz)	Premium of August $1,300 Call at Initiation ($/oz)	Dollar Amount of Premium Received	Premium of August $1,300 Put at Initiation ($/oz)	Dollar Amount of Premium Paid	Value of Call at Expiration	Value of Put at Expiration	Profit/Loss on Position [(3) − (5) + (7) − (6)]
1,000	9.1	$910	108.7	$10,870	$0	$30,000	$20,040
1,050	9.1	$910	108.7	$10,870	$0	$25,000	$15,040
1,100	9.1	$910	108.7	$10,870	$0	$20,000	$10,040
1,150	9.1	$910	108.7	$10,870	$0	$15,000	$5,040
1,200	9.1	$910	108.7	$10,870	$0	$10,000	$40
1,250	9.1	$910	108.7	$10,870	$0	$5,000	−$4,960
1,300	9.1	$910	108.7	$10,870	$0	$0	−$9,960
1,350	9.1	$910	108.7	$10,870	$5,000	$0	−$14,960
1,400	9.1	$910	108.7	$10,870	$10,000	$0	−$19,960

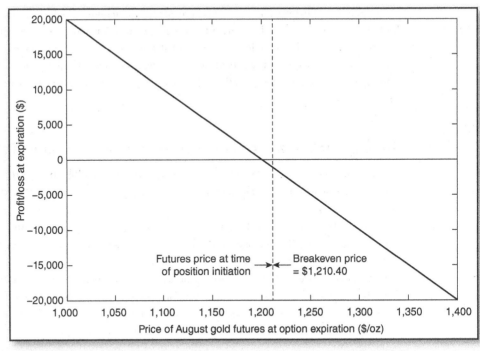

FIGURE 35.16 Profit/Loss Profile: Synthetic Short Futures (Long Put + Short Call).

Strategy 17: The Ratio Call Write (Long Futures + Short 2 Calls)

EXAMPLE. Buy August gold futures at $1,200 and simultaneously sell two August $1,200 gold futures calls at a premium of $38.80/oz. ($7,760). (See Table 35.17 and Figure 35.17.)

TABLE 35.17	Profit/Loss Calculations: Ratio Call Write—Long Futures + Short 2 Calls (Similar to Short Straddle)				
(1) Futures Price at Expiration ($/oz)	(2) Premium of August $1,200 Call at Initiation ($/oz)	(3) $ Amount of Total Premium Received	(4) Profit/Loss on Long Futures Position	(5) Value of 2 Calls at Expiration	(6) Profit/Loss on Position [(3) + (4) − (5)]
1,000	38.8	$7,760	−$20,000	$0	−$12,240
1,050	38.8	$7,760	−$15,000	$0	−$7,240
1,100	38.8	$7,760	−$10,000	$0	−$2,240
1,150	38.8	$7,760	−$5,000	$0	$2,760
1,200	38.8	$7,760	$0	$0	$7,760
1,250	38.8	$7,760	$5,000	$10,000	$2,760
1,300	38.8	$7,760	$10,000	$20,000	−$2,240
1,350	38.8	$7,760	$15,000	$30,000	−$7,240
1,400	38.8	$7,760	$20,000	$40,000	−$12,240

Comment. The combination of 1 long futures contract and 2 short at-the-money calls is a balanced position in terms of delta values. In other words, at any given point in time, the gain or loss in the long futures contract due to small price changes (i.e., price changes in the vicinity of the strike price) will be approximately offset by an opposite change in the call position. (Over time, however, a market characterized by small price changes will result in the long futures position gaining on the short call position due to the evaporation of the time value of the options.) The maximum profit in this strategy will be equal to the premium received for the 2 calls and will occur when prices are exactly unchanged. This strategy will show a net profit for a wide range of prices centered at the prevailing price level at the time the position was initiated. However, the position will imply unlimited risk in the event of very sharp price increases or declines.

The profit/loss profile for this strategy should look familiar—it is virtually identical to the short straddle position (see Strategy 35.8). The virtual equivalence of this strategy to the short straddle position follows directly from the previously discussed structure of a synthetic futures position:

$$\text{Ratio call write} = \text{long futures} + \text{short 2 calls}$$

However, from the synthetic futures position relationship, we know that:

$$\text{Long futures} \approx \text{long call} + \text{short put}$$

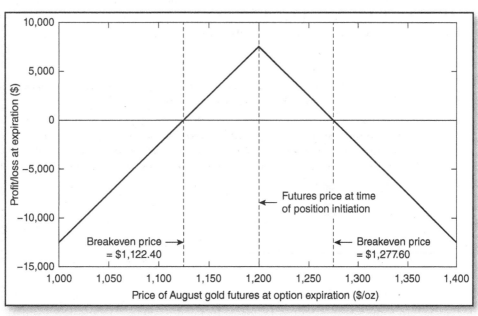

FIGURE 35.17 Profit/Loss Profile: Ratio Call Write—Long Futures + Short 2 Calls (Similar to Short Straddle)

Thus:

$$\text{Ratio call write} \approx \text{long call} + \text{short put} + \text{short 2 calls, or}$$
$$\text{Ratio call write} \approx \text{short put} + \text{short call}$$

The right-hand term of this last equation is, in fact, the definition of a short straddle. In similar fashion, it can be demonstrated that a short put write (short futures + short 2 puts) would also yield a profit/loss profile nearly identical to the short straddle position.

Strategy 18: Bull Call Money Spread (Long Call with Lower Strike Price/Short Call with Higher Strike Price)

EXAMPLE. Buy an August $1,250 gold futures call at a premium of $19.20/oz ($1,920) and simultaneously sell an August $1,300 call at a premium of $9.10 ($910). (See Table 35.18 and Figure 35.18.)

Comment. This type of spread position is also called a debit spread because the amount of premium paid for the long call is greater than the amount of the premium received for the short call. The maximum risk in this type of trade is equal to the difference between these two premiums. The maximum possible gain in this spread will be equal to the difference between the two strike prices minus the net difference between the two premiums. The maximum loss will occur if prices fail to rise at least beyond the lowest strike price. The maximum gain will be realized if prices rise above the higher strike price. Note that although the maximum profit exceeds the maximum risk by a factor of nearly 4 to 1, the probability of a loss is significantly greater than the probability of a gain. This condition is true since prices must rise $60.10/oz before the strategy proves profitable.

TABLE 35.18 Profit/Loss Calculations: Bull Call Money Spread (Long Call with Lower Strike Price/Short Call with Higher Strike Price)

(1) Futures Price at Expiration ($/oz)	(2) Premium of August $1,250 Call ($/oz)	(3) $ Amount of Premium Paid	(4) Premium of August $1,300 Call ($/oz)	(5) Dollar Amount of Premium Received	(6) $1,250 Call Value at Expiration	(7) $1,300 Call Value at Expiration	(8) Profit/Loss on Position [(5) − (3) + (6) − (7)]
1,000	19.2	$1,920	9.1	$910	$0	$0	−$1,010
1,050	19.2	$1,920	9.1	$910	$0	$0	−$1,010
1,100	19.2	$1,920	9.1	$910	$0	$0	−$1,010
1,150	19.2	$1,920	9.1	$910	$0	$0	−$1,010
1,200	19.2	$1,920	9.1	$910	$0	$0	−$1,010
1,250	19.2	$1,920	9.1	$910	$0	$0	−$1,010
1,300	19.2	$1,920	9.1	$910	$5,000	$0	$3,990
1,350	19.2	$1,920	9.1	$910	$10,000	$5,000	$3,990
1,400	19.2	$1,920	9.1	$910	$15,000	$10,000	$3,990

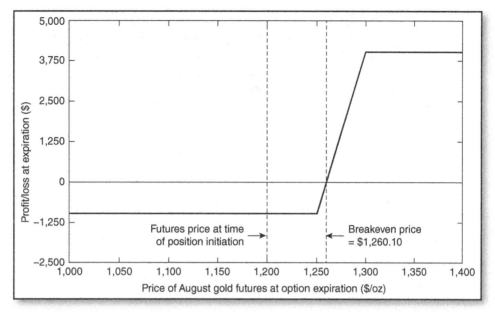

FIGURE 35.18 Profit/Loss Profile: Bull Call Money Spread (Long Call with Lower Strike Price/ Short Call with Higher Strike Price)

This strategy can perhaps be best understood by comparing it to the long call position (e.g., long August $1,250 gold futures call). In effect, the spread trader reduces the premium cost for the long call position by the amount of premium received for the sale of the more deeply out-of-the-money call. This reduction in the net premium cost of the trade comes at the expense of sacrificing the possibility of unlimited gain in the event of a large price rise. As can be seen in Figure 35.18, in contrast to the outright long call position, price gains beyond the higher strike price will cease to affect the profitability of the trade.

Strategy 19a: Bear Call Money Spread (Short Call with Lower Strike Price/Long Call with Higher Strike Price)—Case 1

EXAMPLE. Buy August $1,150 gold futures call at a premium of $70.10/oz ($7,010) and simultaneously sell an August $1,100 gold futures call at a premium of $110.10/oz ($11,010), with August gold futures trading at $1,200/oz. (See Table 35.19a and Figure 35.19a.)

Comment. This type of spread is called a *credit spread,* since the amount of premium received for the short call position exceeds the premium paid for the long call position. The maximum possible gain on the trade is equal to the net difference between the two premiums. The maximum possible loss is equal to the difference between the two strike prices minus the difference between the two premiums. The maximum gain would be realized if prices declined to the lower strike price. The maximum loss would occur if prices failed to decline to at least the higher strike price. Although

TABLE 35.19a	Profit/Loss Calculations: Bear Call Money Spread (Short Call with Lower Strike Price/ Long Call with Higher Strike Price); Case 1—Both Calls In-the-Money						
(1) Futures Price at Expiration ($/oz)	(2) Premium of August $1,150 Call ($/oz)	(3) $ Amount of Premium Paid	(4) Premium of August $1,100 Call ($/oz)	(5) $ Amount of Premium Received	(6) $1,150 Call Value at Expiration	(7) $1,100 Call Value at Expiration	(8) Profit/Loss on Position [(5) − (3) + (6) − (7)]
1,000	70.1	$7,010	110.1	$11,010	$0	$0	$4,000
1,050	70.1	$7,010	110.1	$11,010	$0	$0	$4,000
1,100	70.1	$7,010	110.1	$11,010	$0	$0	$4,000
1,150	70.1	$7,010	110.1	$11,010	$0	$5,000	−$1,000
1,200	70.1	$7,010	110.1	$11,010	$5,000	$10,000	−$1,000
1,250	70.1	$7,010	110.1	$11,010	$10,000	$15,000	−$1,000
1,300	70.1	$7,010	110.1	$11,010	$15,000	$20,000	−$1,000
1,350	70.1	$7,010	110.1	$11,010	$20,000	$25,000	−$1,000
1,400	70.1	$7,010	110.1	$11,010	$25,000	$30,000	−$1,000

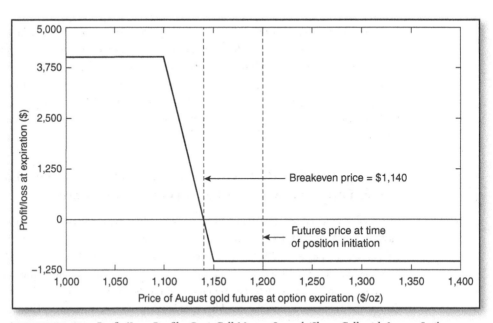

FIGURE 35.19a Profit/Loss Profile: Bear Call Money Spread (Short Call with Lower Strike Price/Long Call with Higher Strike Price); Case 1—Both Calls In-the-Money

in the above example the maximum gain exceeds the maximum risk by a factor of 4 to 1, there is a greater probability of a net loss on the trade, since prices must decline by $60/oz before a profit is realized.

In this type of spread, the trader achieves a bearish position at a fairly low premium cost at the expense of sacrificing the potential for unlimited gains in the event of a very sharp price decline. This strategy might be appropriate for the trader expecting a price decline but viewing the possibility of a very large price slide as being very low.

Strategy 19b: Bear Call Money Spread (Short Call with Lower Strike Price/Long Call with Higher Strike Price)—Case 2

EXAMPLE. Buy an August $1,300 gold futures call at a premium of $9.10/oz ($9.10) and simultaneously sell an August $1,200 gold futures call at a premium of $38.80/oz ($3,880), with August gold futures trading at $1,200/oz. (See Table 35.19b and Figure 35.19b.)

Comment. In contrast to the previous strategy, which involved two in-the-money calls, this illustration is based on a spread consisting of a short at-the-money call and a long out-of-the-money call. In a sense, this type of trade can be thought of as a short at-the-money call position with built-in stop-loss protection. (The long out-of-the-money call will serve to limit the risk in the short at-the-money call position.) This risk limitation is achieved at the expense of a reduction in the net premium received by the seller of the at-the-money call (by an amount equal to the premium paid for the out-of-the-money call). This trade-off between risk exposure and the amount of net premium received is illustrated in Figure 35.19b, which compares the outright short at-the-money call position to the above spread strategy.

| TABLE 35.19b | Profit/Loss Calculations: Bear Call Money Spread (Short Call with Lower Strike Price/Long Call with Higher Strike Price); Case 2—Short At-the-Money Call/Long Out-of-the-Money Call |

(1) Futures Price at Expiration ($/oz)	(2) Premium of August $1,300 Call ($/oz)	(3) $ Amount of Premium Paid	(4) Premium of August $1,200 Call ($/oz)	(5) $ Amount of Premium Received	(6) Value of $1,300 Call at Expiration	(7) Value of $1,200 Call at Expiration	(8) Profit/Loss on Position [(5) − (3) + (6) − (7)]
1,000	9.1	$910	38.8	$3,880	$0	$0	$2,970
1,050	9.1	$910	38.8	$3,880	$0	$0	$2,970
1,100	9.1	$910	38.8	$3,880	$0	$0	$2,970
1,150	9.1	$910	38.8	$3,880	$0	$0	$2,970
1,200	9.1	$910	38.8	$3,880	$0	$0	$2,970
1,250	9.1	$910	38.8	$3,880	$0	$5,000	−$2,030
1,300	9.1	$910	38.8	$3,880	$0	$10,000	−$7,030
1,350	9.1	$910	38.8	$3,880	$5,000	$15,000	−$7,030
1,400	9.1	$910	38.8	$3,880	$10,000	$20,000	−$7,030

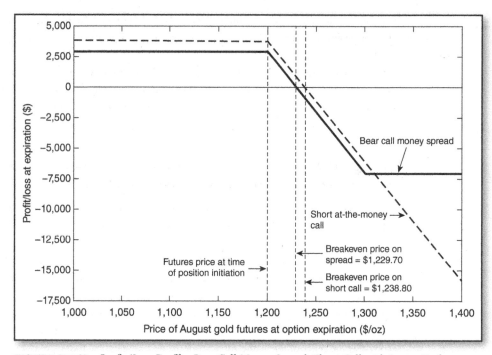

FIGURE 35.19b Profit/Loss Profile: Bear Call Money Spread (Short Call with Lower Strike Price/Long Call with Higher Strike Price); Case 2—Short At-the-Money Call/Long Out-of-the-Money Call with Comparison to Short At-the-Money Call

Strategy 20a: Bull Put Money Spread (Long Put with Lower Strike Price/Short Put with Higher Strike Price)—Case 1

EXAMPLE. Buy an August $1,250 gold futures put at a premium of $68.70/oz ($6,870) and simultaneously sell August $1,300 put at a premium of $108.70/oz ($10,870), with August gold futures trading at $1,200/oz. (See Table 35.20a and Figure 35.20a.)

Comment. This is a net credit bull spread that uses puts instead of calls. The maximum gain in this strategy is equal to the difference between the premium received for the short put and the premium paid for the long put. The maximum loss is equal to the difference between the strike prices minus the difference between the premiums. The maximum gain will be achieved if prices rise to the higher strike price, while the maximum loss will occur if prices fail to rise at least to the lower strike price. The profit/loss profile of this trade is very similar to the profile of the net debit bull call money spread illustrated in Figure 35.18.

(1) Futures Price at Expiration ($/oz)	(2) Premium of August $1,250 Put ($/oz)	(3) $ Amount of Premium Paid	(4) Premium of August $1,300 Put ($/oz)	(5) $ Amount of Premium Received	(6) $1,250 Put Value at Expiration	(7) $1,300 Put Value at Expiration	(8) Profit/Loss on Position [(5) − (3) + (6) −(7)]
1,000	68.7	$6,870	108.7	$10,870	$25,000	$30,000	−$1,000
1,050	68.7	$6,870	108.7	$10,870	$20,000	$25,000	−$1,000
1,100	68.7	$6,870	108.7	$10,870	$15,000	$20,000	−$1,000
1,150	68.7	$6,870	108.7	$10,870	$10,000	$15,000	−$1,000
1,200	68.7	$6,870	108.7	$10,870	$5,000	$10,000	−$1,000
1,250	68.7	$6,870	108.7	$10,870	$0	$5,000	−$1,000
1,300	68.7	$6,870	108.7	$10,870	$0	$0	$4,000
1,350	68.7	$6,870	108.7	$10,870	$0	$0	$4,000
1,400	68.7	$6,870	108.7	$10,870	$0	$0	$4,000

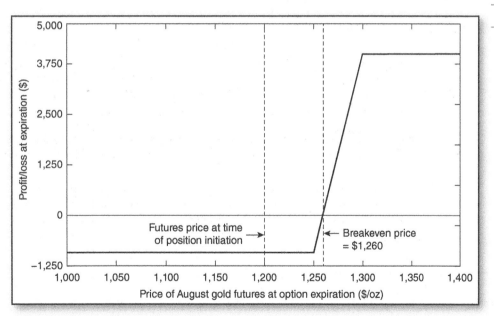

FIGURE 35.20a Profit/Loss Profile: Bull Put Money Spread (Long Put with Lower Strike Price/ Short Put with Higher Strike Price); Case 1—Both Puts In-the-Money

Strategy 20b: Bull Put Money Spread (Long Put with Lower Strike Price/Short Put with Higher Strike Price)—Case 2

EXAMPLE. Buy an August $1,100 gold futures put at a premium of $10.10/oz ($1,010) and simultaneously sell an August $1,200 put at a premium of $38.70/oz ($3,870), with August gold futures trading at $1,200/oz. (See Table 35.20b and Figure 35.20b.)

Comment. In contrast to Case 1, which involved two in-the-money puts, this strategy is based on a long out-of-the-money put versus a short at-the-money put spread. In a sense, this strategy can be viewed as a short at-the-money put position with a built-in stop. (The purchase of the out-of-the-money put serves to limit the maximum possible loss in the event of a large price decline.) This risk limitation is achieved at the expense of a reduction in the net premium received. This trade-off between risk exposure and the amount of premium received is illustrated in Figure 35.20b, which compares the outright short at-the-money put position to this spread strategy.

Strategy 21: Bear Put Money Spread (Short Put with Lower Strike Price/Long Put with Higher Strike Price)

EXAMPLE. Sell an August $1,100 gold futures put at a premium of $10.10/oz ($1,010) and simultaneously buy an August $1,150 put at a premium of $19.90/oz ($1,990), with August gold futures trading at $1,200/oz. (See Table 35.21 and Figure 35.21.)

Comment. This is a debit bear spread using puts instead of calls. The maximum risk is equal to the difference between the premium paid for the long put and the premium received for the short put. The maximum gain equals the difference between the two strike prices minus the difference between the premiums. The maximum loss will occur if prices fail to decline to at least the higher strike price. The maximum gain will be achieved if prices decline to the lower strike price. The profit/loss profile of this spread is approximately equivalent to the profile of the bear call money spread (see Figure 35.19a).

| TABLE 35.20b | Profit/Loss Calculations: Bull Put Money Spread (Long Put with Lower Strike Price/Short Put with Higher Strike Price); Case 2—Long Out-of-the-Money Put/Short At-the-Money Put |

(1) Futures Price at Expiration ($/oz)	(2) Premium of August $1,100 Put ($/oz)	(3) Dollar Amount of Premium Paid	(4) Premium of August $1,200 Put ($/oz)	(5) Dollar Amount of Premium Received	(6) Value of $1,100 Put at Expiration	(7) Value of $1,200 Put at Expiration	(8) Profit/Loss on Position $[(5)-(3)+(6)-(7)]$
1,000	10.1	$1,010	38.7	$3,870	$10,000	$20,000	−$7,140
1,050	10.1	$1,010	38.7	$3,870	$5,000	$15,000	−$7,140
1,100	10.1	$1,010	38.7	$3,870	$0	$10,000	−$7,140
1,150	10.1	$1,010	38.7	$3,870	$0	$5,000	−$2,140
1,200	10.1	$1,010	38.7	$3,870	$0	$0	$2,860
1,250	10.1	$1,010	38.7	$3,870	$0	$0	$2,860
1,300	10.1	$1,010	38.7	$3,870	$0	$0	$2,860
1,350	10.1	$1,010	38.7	$3,870	$0	$0	$2,860
1,400	10.1	$1,010	38.7	$3,870	$0	$0	$2,860

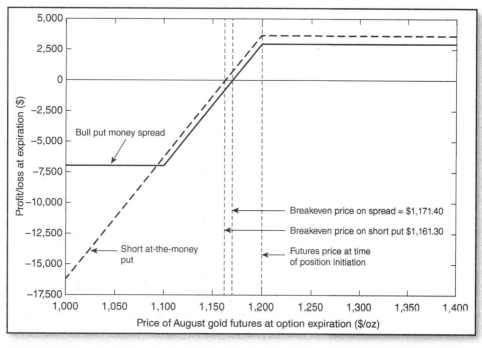

FIGURE 35.20b Profit/Loss Profile: Bull Put Money Spread (Long Put with Lower Strike Price/Short Put with Higher Strike Price); Case 2—Long Out-of-the-Money Put/Short At-the-Money Put with Comparison to Short At-the-Money Put

TABLE 35.21 Profit/Loss Calculations: Bear Put Money Spread (Short Put with Lower Strike Price/Long Put with Higher Strike Price)

(1) Futures Price at Expiration ($/oz)	(2) Premium of August $1,150 Put ($/oz)	(3) $ Amount of Premium Paid	(4) Premium of August $1,100 Put ($/oz)	(5) $ Amount of Premium Received	(6) Value of $1,150 Put	(7) Value of $1,100 Put	Profit/Loss on Position [(5) − (3) + (6) − (7)]
1,000	19.9	$1,990	10.1	$1,010	$15,000	$10,000	$4,020
1,050	19.9	$1,990	10.1	$1,010	$10,000	$5,000	$4,020
1,100	19.9	$1,990	10.1	$1,010	$5,000	$0	$4,020
1,150	19.9	$1,990	10.1	$1,010	$0	$0	−$980
1,200	19.9	$1,990	10.1	$1,010	$0	$0	−$980
1,250	19.9	$1,990	10.1	$1,010	$0	$0	−$980
1,300	19.9	$1,990	10.1	$1,010	$0	$0	−$980
1,350	19.9	$1,990	10.1	$1,010	$0	$0	−$980
1,400	19.9	$1,990	10.1	$1,010	$0	$0	−$980

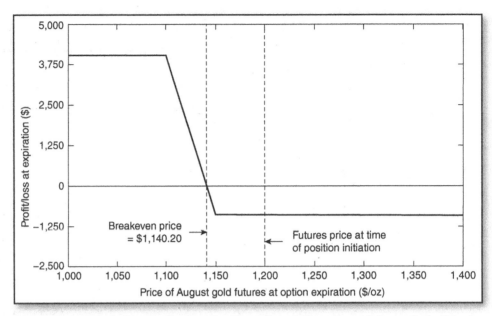

FIGURE 35.21   Profit/Loss Profile; Bear Put Money Spread (Short Put with Lower Strike Price/ Long Put with Higher Strike Price)

Other Spread Strategies

Money spreads represent only one class of option spreads. A complete discussion of option spread strategies would require a substantial extension of this section—a degree of detail beyond the scope of this presentation. The following are examples of some other types of spreads.

> **Time spread.** A time spread is a spread between two calls or two puts with the same strike price, but a different expiration date. An example of a time spread would be: long 1 August $1,300 gold futures call/short 1 December $1,300 gold futures call. Time spreads are more complex than the other strategies discussed in this section, because the profit/loss profile at the time of expiration cannot be precisely predetermined, but rather must be estimated on the basis of theoretical valuation models.

> **Diagonal spread.** This is a spread between two calls or two puts that differ in terms of both the strike price and the expiration date. An example of a diagonal spread would be: long 1 August $1,200 gold futures call/short 1 December $1,250 gold futures call. In effect, this type of spread combines the money spread and the time spread into one trade.

> **Butterfly spread.** This is a three-legged spread in which the options have the same expiration date but differ in strike prices. A butterfly spread using calls consists of two short calls at a given strike price, one long call at a higher strike price, and one long call at a lower strike price.

The list of types of option spreads can be significantly extended, but the above examples should be sufficient to give the reader some idea of the potential range of complexity of spread strategies. One critical point that must be emphasized regarding option spreads is that these strategies are normally subject to a major disadvantage: the transaction costs (commissions plus cumulative bid/asked spreads) for these trades are relatively large compared to the profit potential. This consideration means that the option spread trader must be right a large percentage of the time if he is to come out ahead of the game. The importance of this point cannot be overemphasized. In short, as a generalization, other option strategies will usually offer better trading opportunities.

Multiunit Strategies

The profit/loss profile can also be used to analyze multiple-unit option strategies. In fact, multiple-unit option positions may often provide the more appropriate strategy for purposes of comparison. For example, as previously detailed, a long futures position is more volatile than a long or short call position. In fact, for small price changes, each $1 change in a futures price will only result in approximately a $0.50 change in the call price (the delta value for an at-the-money call is approximately equal to 0.5). As a result, in considering the alternatives of buying futures and buying calls, it probably makes more sense to compare the long futures position to two long calls (see Table 35.22) as opposed to one long call.

Figure 35.22 compares the strategies of long futures versus long two calls, which at the time of initiation are approximately equivalent in terms of delta values. Note this comparison indicates that the long futures position is preferable if prices change only moderately, but that the long two-call position will gain more if prices rise sharply, and lose less if prices decline sharply. In contrast, the comparison between long futures and a long one-call position would indicate that futures provide the better strategy in the event of a price advance of any magnitude (see Figure 35.3d). For most purposes, the comparison employing two long calls will be more meaningful because it comes much closer to matching the risk level implicit in the long futures position.

TABLE 35.22	**Profit/Loss Calculations: Long Two At-the-Money Calls**			
(1) Futures Price at Expiration ($/oz)	(2) Premium of August $1,200 Call ($/oz)	(3) $ Amount of Total Premium Paid	(4) Value of 2 Calls at Expiration	(5) Profit/Loss on Position [(4) − (3)]
1,000	38.8	$7,760	$0	−$7,760
1,050	38.8	$7,760	$0	−$7,760
1,100	38.8	$7,760	$0	−$7,760
1,150	38.8	$7,760	$0	−$7,760
1,200	38.8	$7,760	$0	−$7,760
1,250	38.8	$7,760	$10,000	$2,240
1,300	38.8	$7,760	$20,000	$12,240
1,350	38.8	$7,760	$30,000	$22,240
1,400	38.8	$7,760	$40,000	$32,240

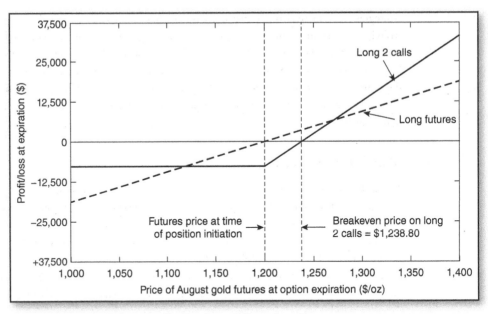

FIGURE 35.22 Profit/Loss Profile: Two Long Calls vs. Long Futures

Choosing an Optimal Strategy

It the previous sections we examined a wide range of alternative trading strategies. Now what? How does a trader decide which of these alternatives provides the best trading opportunity? This question can be answered only if probability is incorporated into the analysis. The selection of an optimal option strategy will depend entirely on the trader's price and volatility expectations. Insofar as these expectations will differ from trader to trader, the optimal option strategy will also vary, and the success of the selected option strategy will depend on the accuracy of the trader's expectations. In order to select an optimal option strategy, the trader needs to translate his price expectations into probabilities.

The basic approach requires the trader to assign estimated probability levels for the entire range of feasible price intervals. Figure 35.23 illustrates six different types of probability distributions for August gold futures. These distributions can be thought of as representing six different hypothetical expectations. (The charts in Figure 35.23 implicitly assume that the current price of August gold futures is $1,200.) Several important points should be made regarding these probability distributions:

1. The indicated probability distributions only represent approximations of traders' price expectations. In reality, any reasonable probability distribution would be represented by a smooth curve. The stair-step charts in Figure 35.23 are only intended as crude models that greatly simplify calculations. (The use of smooth probability distributions would require integral calculus in the evaluation process.)

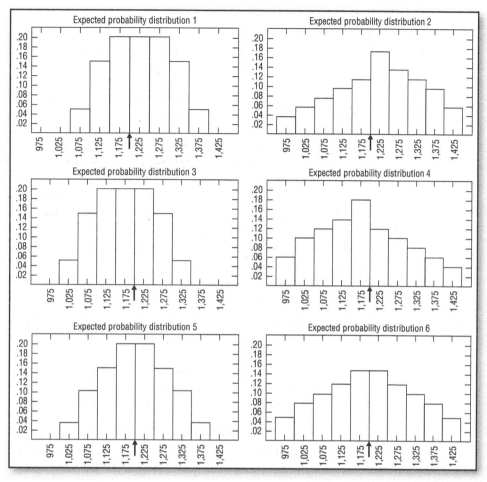

FIGURE 35.23 Probability of Futures Price within Given Range of Option Expiration for Various Expected Probability Distributions (Arrow Indicates Current Price of Futures)

2. The sum of all the probabilities is equal to 1.0.

3. The stair-step type of graph used in Figure 35.23 implicitly assumes an equal probability for each price in the interval.

4. The high and low intervals in each diagram are intended as summary descriptions for all prices beyond the internal border of that interval. For example, in Expected Probability Distribution 1, the assumption of a 5 percent probability of a price between $1,050 and $1,099.90 (with all prices in that range having an equal probability of occurrence) and a zero probability of a lower price is equivalent to the more realistic assumption of a 5 percent probability of a price below $1,100, with the probability-weighted average of such prices equal to $1,075.

5. The probability distributions in Figure 35.23 represent sample hypothetical illustrations of personal price expectations. The indicated optimal strategy in any given situation will depend upon the specific shape of the expected price distribution, *an input that will differ from trader to trader.*

The general nature of the price expectations implied by each of the distributions in Figure 35.23 can be summarized as follows:

Expected Probability Distribution 1. Higher prices and low volatility. This interpretation follows from the fact that there is a greater probability of higher prices and that the probabilities are heavily weighted toward intervals close to the current price level.

Expected Probability Distribution 2. Higher prices and high volatility. This distribution reflects the same 60/40 probability bias toward higher prices as was the case for Distribution 1, but the assumed probability of a substantially higher or lower price is much greater.

Expected Probability Distribution 3. Lower prices and low volatility. This distribution is the bearish counterpart of Distribution 1.

Expected Probability Distribution 4. Lower prices and high volatility. This distribution is the bearish counterpart of Distribution 2.

Expected Probability Distribution 5. Neutral price assumptions and low volatility. This distribution is symmetrical in terms of higher and lower prices, and probability levels are heavily weighted toward prices near the current level.

Expected Probability Distribution 6. Neutral price assumptions and high volatility. This distribution is also symmetrical in terms of high and low prices, but substantially higher and lower prices have a much greater probability of occurrence than in Distribution 5.

Figure 35.24 combines Expected Probability Distribution 1 with three alternative bullish strategies. (Since it is assumed that there is a greater probability of higher prices, there is no need to consider bearish or neutral trading strategies.) Insofar as the assumed probability distribution is very heavily weighted toward prices near the current level, the short put position appears to offer the best strategy. Figure 35.25 combines the same three alternative bullish strategies with the bullish/volatile price scenario suggested by Expected Probability Distribution 2. In this case, the long call position appears to be the optimal strategy, since it is by far the best performer for large price advances and declines—price outcomes that account for a significant portion of the overall probability distribution.

In analogous fashion, Figure 35.26 suggests the preferability of the short call position given the bearish/nonvolatile price scenario assumption, while Figure 35.27 suggests that the long put position is the optimal strategy given the bearish/volatile price scenario. Finally, two alternative neutral strategies are compared in Figures 35.28 and 35.29 for two neutral price distributions that differ in terms of assumed volatility. The short straddle appears to offer the better strategy in the low volatility distribution assumption, while the reverse conclusion is suggested in the volatile price case.

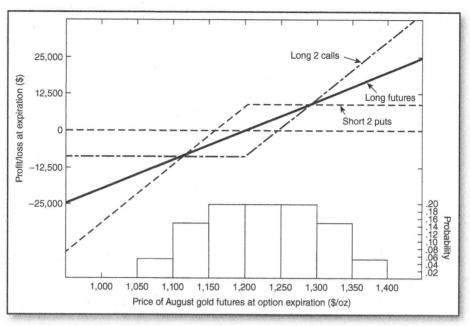

FIGURE 35.24 "Bullish/Nonvolatile" Expected Probability Distribution and Profit/Loss Profiles for Three Alternative Bullish Strategies

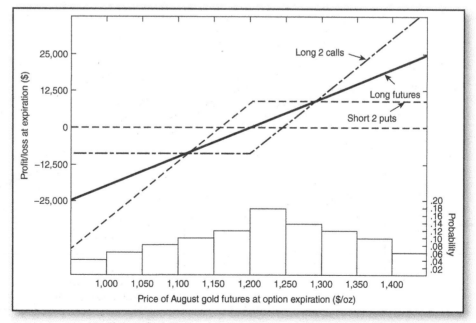

FIGURE 35.25 "Bullish/Volatile" Expected Probability Distribution and Profit/Loss Profiles for Three Alternative Bullish Strategies

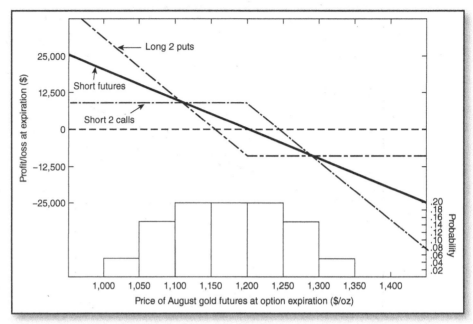

FIGURE 35.26 "Bearish/Nonvolatile" Expected Probability Distribution and Profit/Loss Profiles for Three Alternative Bearish Strategies

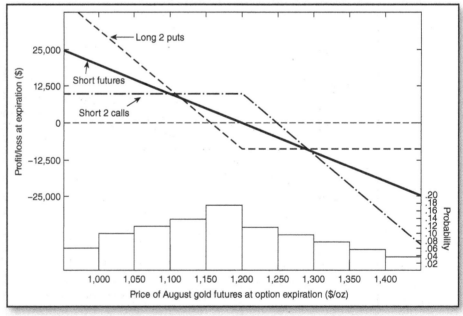

FIGURE 35.27 "Bearish/Volatile" Expected Probability Distribution and Profit/Loss Profiles for Three Alternative Bearish Strategies

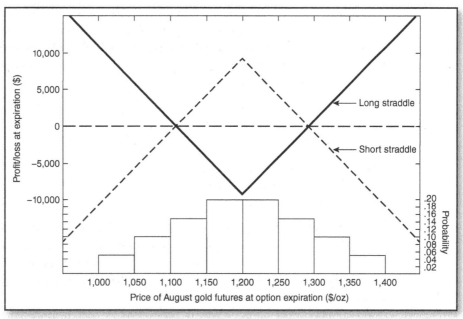

FIGURE 35.28 "Neutral/Nonvolatile" Expected Probability Distribution and Profit/Loss Profiles for Two Alternative Neutral Strategies

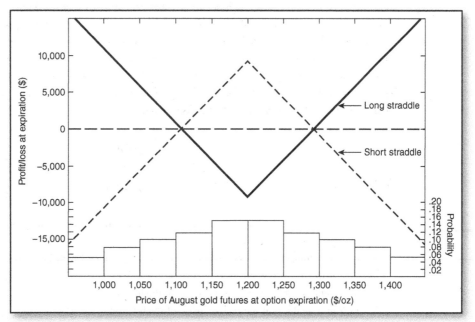

FIGURE 35.29 "Neutral/Volatile" Expected Probability Distribution and Profit/Loss Profiles for Two Alternative Neutral Strategies

One problem with the graphic approach described thus far is that it may not always be visually clear which is the best strategy for the given price distribution assumption. Obviously, a more precise method of determining the optimal trading strategy would be desirable. Intuitively, it might appear that expected gain would provide such a relative measure. Expected gain is the expected gain (or loss) on a trade and can be expressed as follows:

$$\text{Expected gain} = \sum_{i=1}^{n} (P_i)(X_i)$$

where P_i = probability of price interval i
   X_t = average gain (or loss) of interval i
   n = number of intervals

Unfortunately, expected gain has a major defect as a relative measure: it is dependent upon position size. The expected gain of any strategy that has a positive expected gain could always be improved by trading a multiple of the position. Thus, in comparing alternative strategies with positive expected gains, the indicated optimal strategy would vary depending on the assumed position sizes. Such arbitrariness in a relative measure is obviously unacceptable.

The use of expected gain as a relative measure can lead to some ludicrous conclusions. For example, a strategy that had a 50 percent probability of a $1,000 gain and a 50 percent probability of a $900 loss would be judged better than an alternative strategy with a 50 percent chance of a $100 gain and a 50 percent chance of a $10 loss (an expected gain of $50 vs. an expected gain of $45). Obviously, virtually any trader would prefer the second strategy, despite its lower expected gain.

The dependency of expected gain on position size actually reflects a more fundamental flaw in this measure: expected gain does not incorporate a measure of risk. A measure that included risk would not be dependent upon position size, since doubling the position would not only double the expected gain, but would also double the risk. One such possible measure is the probability-weighted profit/loss ratio (PWPLR), which can be defined as follows:

$$PWPLR = -\frac{\sum_{i=1}^{m} (P_i)(G_i)}{\sum_{j=1}^{n} (P_j)(L_j)}$$

where P_i = probability of interval i, where i represents an interval with a net gain at the average price of the interval
   P_j = probability of interval j, where j represents an interval with a net loss at the average price of the interval
   G_i = indicated gain at the average price of the interval
   L_j = indicated loss at the average price of the interval
   m = number of intervals with net gain at average price of interval
   n = number of intervals with net loss at average price of interval

An implicit assumption in the formulation of the probability-weighted profit/loss ratio is that each price in a given interval has an equal probability of occurrence.[4]

Note that the PWPLR will be totally unaffected by position size. This is true because increasing the position will affect the numerator and denominator of the PWPLR equally, thereby leaving the ratio unchanged. Tables 35.23 through 35.28 evaluate the strategies graphically analyzed in Figure 35.24 through 35.29. The conclusions are equivalent, but the advantage of this method is that it yields precise, unambiguous results. To select an optimal strategy, the trader would merely define his estimate of the probability distribution for prices and then calculate the PWPLRs for each alternative trading approach.

TABLE 35.23 Probability-Weighted Profit/Loss Ratio Comparisons for "Bullish/Nonvolatile" Expected Probability Distribution

			Long Futures		Long Call		Short Put	
Price Range ($/oz)	Average Price ($/oz)	Assumed Probability	Gain/Loss at Average Price ($)	Probability-Weighted Gain/Loss ($)	Gain/Loss at Average Price ($)	Probability-Weighted Gain/Loss ($)	Gain/Loss at Average Price ($)	Probability-Weighted Gain/Loss ($)
1,050–1,099.9	1,075	0.05	−12,500	−625	−3,880	−194	−8,630	−431.5
1,100–1,149.9	1,125	0.15	−7,500	−1,125	−3,880	−582	−3,630	−544.5
1,150–1,199.9	1,175	0.2	−2,500	−500	−3,880	−776	1,370	274
1,200–1,249.9	1,225	0.2	2,500	500	−1,380	−276	3,870	774
1,250–1,299.9	1,275	0.2	7,500	1,500	3,620	724	3,870	774
1,300–1,349.9	1,325	0.15	12,500	1,875	8,620	1,293	3,870	580.5
1,350–1,399.9	1,375	0.05	17,500	875	13,620	681	3,870	193.5
Probability-weighted profit/loss ratio:			4,750/2,250 = 2.11		2,698/1,828 = 1.48		2,596/976 = 2.66	

[4] It is worth noting that the probability-weighted profit/loss ratio will yield the same ordering of strategies as the ratio of the expected gain to the expected loss on losing trades, where the expected loss on losing trades is defined as: $\sum_{j=1}^{n}(P_j)(L_j)$. This can be demonstrated as follows:

$$\text{Expected gain} = \sum_{i=1}^{m}(P_i)(G_i) - \sum_{j=1}^{n}(P_j)(L_j)$$

$$\frac{\text{Expected gain}}{\text{Expected loss on losing trades}} = \frac{\sum_{i=1}^{m}(P_i)(G_i)}{\sum_{j=1}^{n}(P_j)(L_j)} - 1$$

$$= PWPLR - 1$$

TABLE 35.24 Probability-Weighted Profit/Loss Ratio Comparisons for "Bullish/Volatile" Expected Probability Distribution

Price Range ($/oz)	Average Price ($/oz)	Assumed Probability	Long Futures		Long Call		Short Put	
			Gain/Loss at Average Price ($)	Probability-Weighted Gain/Loss ($)	Gain/Loss at Average Price ($)	Probability-Weighted Gain/Loss ($)	Gain/Loss at Average Price ($)	Probability-Weighted Gain/Loss ($)
950–999.9	975	0.04	−22,500	−900	−3,880	−155	−18,630	−745.2
1,000–1,049.9	1,025	0.06	−17,500	−1,050	−3,880	−233	−13,630	−817.8
1,050–1,099.9	1,075	0.08	−12,500	−1,000	−3,880	−310	−8,630	−690.4
1,100–1,149.9	1,125	0.1	−7,500	−750	−3,880	−388	−3,630	−363
1,150–1,199.9	1,175	0.12	−2,500	−300	−3,880	−466	1,370	164.4
1,200–1,249.9	1,225	0.18	2,500	450	−1,380	−248	3,870	696.6
1,250–1,299.9	1,275	0.14	7,500	1,050	3,620	507	3,870	541.8
1,300–1,349.9	1,325	0.12	12,500	1,500	8,620	1,034	3,870	464.4
1,350–1,399.9	1,375	0.1	17,500	1,750	13,620	1,362	3,870	387
1,400–1,449.9	1,425	0.06	22,500	1,350	18,620	1,117	3,870	232.2
Probability-weighted profit/loss ratio:			6,100/4,000 = 1.53		4,020/1,800 = 2.23		2,486/2,616 = 0.95	

TABLE 35.25 Probability-Weighted Profit/Loss Ratio Comparisons for "Bearish/Nonvolatile" Expected Probability Distribution

Price Range ($/oz)	Average Price ($/oz)	Assumed Probability	Short Futures		Short Call		Long Put	
			Gain/Loss at Average Price ($)	Probability-Weighted Gain/Loss ($)	Gain/Loss at Average Price ($)	Probability-Weighted Gain/Loss ($)	Gain/Loss at Average Price ($)	Probability-Weighted Gain/Loss ($)
1,000–1,049.9	1,025	0.05	17,500	875	3,880	194	13,630	681.5
1,050–1,099.9	1,075	0.15	12,500	1,875	3,880	582	8,630	1,294.5
1,100–1,149.9	1,125	0.2	7,500	1,500	3,880	776	3,630	726
1,150–1,199.9	1,175	0.2	2,500	500	3,880	776	−1,370	−274
1,200–1,249.9	1,225	0.2	−2,500	−500	1,380	276	−3,870	−774
1,250–1,299.9	1,275	0.15	−7,500	−1,125	−3,620	−543	−3,870	−580.5
1,300–1,349.9	1,325	0.05	−12,500	−625	−8,620	−431	−3,870	−193.5
Probability-weighted profit/loss ratio:			4,750/2,250 = 2.11		2,604/974 = 2.67		2,702/1,822 = 1.48	

| TABLE 35.26 | Probability-Weighted Profit/Loss Ratio Comparisons for "Bearish/Volatile" Expected Probability Distribution | | | | | | | |

Price Range ($/oz)	Average Price ($/oz)	Assumed Probability	Short Futures		Short Call		Long Put	
			Gain/Loss at Average Price ($)	Probability-Weighted Gain/Loss ($)	Gain/Loss at Average Price ($)	Probability-Weighted Gain/Loss ($)	Gain/Loss at Average Price ($)	Probability-Weighted Gain/Loss ($)
950–999.9	975	0.06	22,500	1,350	3,880	233	18,630	1,117.8
1,000–1,049.9	1,025	0.1	17,500	1,750	3,880	388	13,630	1,363
1,050–1,099.9	1,075	0.12	12,500	1,500	3,880	466	8,630	1,035.6
1,100–1,149.9	1,125	0.14	7,500	1,050	3,880	543	3,630	508.2
1,150–1,199.9	1,175	0.18	2,500	450	3,880	698	−1,370	−246.6
1,200–1,249.9	1,225	0.12	−2,500	−300	1,380	166	−3,870	−464.4
1,250–1,299.9	1,275	0.1	−7,500	−750	−3,620	−362	−3,870	−387
1,300–1,349.9	1,325	0.08	−12,500	−1,000	−8,620	−690	−3,870	−309.6
1,350–1,399.9	1,375	0.06	−17,500	−1,050	−13,620	−817	−3,870	−232.2
1,400–1,449.9	1,425	0.04	−22,500	−900	−18,620	−745	−3,870	−154.8
Probability-weighted profit/loss ratio:			6,100/4,000 = 1.53		2,494/2,614 = 0.95		4,025/1,795 = 2.24	

| TABLE 35.27 | Probability-Weighted Profit/Loss Ratio Comparisons for "Neutral/Nonvolatile" Expected Probability Distribution | | | | | |

Price Range ($/oz)	Average Price ($/oz)	Assumed Probability	Long Straddle		Short Straddle	
			Gain/Loss at Average Price ($)	Probability-Weighted Gain/Loss ($)	Gain/Loss at Average Price ($)	Probability-Weighted Gain/Loss ($)
1,000–1,049.9	1,025	0.05	9750	488	−9,750	−488
1,050–1,099.9	1,075	0.1	4,750	475	−4,750	−475
1,100–1,149.9	1,125	0.15	−250	−38	250	38
1,150–1,199.9	1,175	0.2	−5,250	−1,050	5,250	1,050
1,200–1,249.9	1,225	0.2	−5,250	−1,050	5,250	1,050
1,250–1,299.9	1,275	0.15	−250	−38	250	38
1,300–1,349.9	1,325	0.1	4,750	475	−4,750	−475
1,350–1,399.9	1,375	0.05	9,750	488	−9,750	−488
Probability-weighted profit/loss ratio:			1,925/2,175 = 0.89		2,175/1,925 = 1.13	

			Long Straddle		Short Straddle	
Price Range ($/oz)	Average Price ($/oz)	Assumed Probability	Gain/Loss at Average Price ($)	Probability-Weighted Gain/Loss ($)	Gain/Loss at Average Price ($)	Probability-Weighted Gain/Loss ($)
950–999.9	975	0.05	14,750	738	−14,750	−738
1,000–1,049.9	1,025	0.08	9,750	780	−9,750	−780
1,050–1,099.9	1,075	0.1	4,750	475	−4,750	−475
1,100–1,149.9	1,125	0.12	−250	−30	250	30
1,150–1,199.9	1,175	0.15	−5,250	−788	5,250	788
1,200–1,249.9	1,225	0.15	−5,250	−788	5,250	788
1,250 1,299.9	1,275	0.12	−250	−30	250	30
1,300–1,349.9	1,325	0.1	4,750	475	−4,750	−475
1,350–1,399.9	1,375	0.08	9,750	780	−9,750	−780
1,400–1,449.9	1,425	0.05	14,750	738	−14,750	−738
Probability-weighted profit/loss ratio:			3,985/1,635 = 2.44		1,635/3,985 = 0.41	

TABLE 35.28 Probability-Weighted Profit/Loss Ratio Comparisons for "Neutral/Volatile" Expected Probability Distribution

Hedging Applications

The entire discussion in this chapter has been approached from the vantage point of the speculator. However, option-based strategies can also be employed by the hedger. To illustrate how options can be used by the hedger, we compare five basic alternative strategies for the gold jeweler who anticipates a requirement for 100 ounces of gold in August. The assumed date in this illustration is April 13, 2015, a day on which the relevant price quotes were as follows: spot gold = $1,198.90, August gold futures = $1,200, August $1,200 gold call premium = $38.80, August $1,200 gold put premium = $38.70. The five purchasing alternatives are:[5]

1. **Wait until time of requirement.** In this approach, the jeweler simply waits until August before purchasing the gold. In effect, the jeweler gambles on the interim price movement of gold. If gold prices decline, he will be better off. However, if gold prices rise, his purchase price will increase. If the jeweler has forward-contracted for his products, he may need to lock in his raw material purchase costs in order to guarantee a satisfactory profit margin. Consequently, the price risk inherent in this approach may be unacceptable.

---

[5] There is no intention to imply that the following list of alternative hedging strategies is all-inclusive. Many other option-based strategies are also possible. For example, the jeweler could buy a call and sell a put at the same strike price—a strategy similar to buying a futures contract (see Strategy 15).

2. **Buy spot gold.** The jeweler can buy spot gold and store it until August. In this case, he locks in a purchase price of $1,198.90/oz plus carrying costs (interest, storage, and insurance). This approach eliminates price risk, but also removes the potential of benefiting from any possible price decline.

3. **Buy gold futures.** The jeweler can purchase one contract of August gold futures, thereby locking in a price of $1,200/oz. The higher price of gold futures vis-à-vis spot gold reflects the fact that futures embed carrying costs. Insofar as the price spread between futures and spot gold will be closely related to the magnitude of carrying costs, the advantages and disadvantages of this approach will be very similar to those discussed in the above strategy.

4. **Buy an at-the-money call.** Instead of purchasing spot gold or gold futures, the jeweler could instead buy an August $1,200 gold futures call at a premium of $38.80/oz. The disadvantage of this approach is that if prices advance the jeweler locks in a higher purchase price: $1,238.80/oz. However, by purchasing the call, the jeweler retains the potential for a substantially lower purchase price in the event of a sharp interim price decline. Thus, if, for example, spot prices declined to $1,050/oz by the time of the option expiration, the jeweler's purchase price would be reduced to $1,088.80/oz (the spot gold price plus the option premium).[6] In effect, the purchase of the call can be viewed as a form of price risk insurance, with the cost of this insurance equal to the "premium."[7]

5. **Buy an out-of-the-money call.** As an example, the jeweler could purchase an August $1,300 gold futures call at a premium of $9.10/oz. In this case, the jeweler forgoes protection against moderate price advances in exchange for reducing the premium costs. Thus, the jeweler assures he will have to pay no more than $1,309.10/oz. The cost of this price protection is $910 as opposed to the $3,880 premium for the at-the-money call. In a sense, the purchase of the out-of-the-money call can be thought of as a price risk insurance policy with a "deductible." As in the case of purchasing an at-the-money call, the jeweler would retain the potential of benefiting from any interim price decline.

As should be clear from the above discussion, options meaningfully expand the range of choices open to the hedger. As was the case for speculative applications, the choice of an optimal strategy will depend on the trader's (hedger's) individual expectations and preferences. It should be stressed that this section is only intended as an introduction to the concept of using options for hedging. A comprehensive review of hedging strategies would require a far more extensive discussion.

---

[6] Technically speaking, since gold futures options expire before the start of the contract month, the effective purchase price would be raised by the amount of carrying costs for the remaining weeks until August.

[7] The use of futures for hedging is also often described as "insurance." However, in this context, the term is misapplied. In standard application, the term insurance implies protection against a catastrophic event for a cost that is small relative to the potential loss that is being insured. In using futures for hedging, the potential cost is equivalent to the loss protection. For example, if the jeweler buys gold futures, he will protect himself against a $10,000 increase in purchase cost if prices increase by $100/oz, but he will also realize a $10,000 loss on his hedge if prices decline by $100/oz. In this sense, the use of the call for hedging comes much closer to the standard concept of insurance: the magnitude of the potential loss being insured is much greater than the cost of the insurance.

PART VII

PRACTICAL TRADING GUIDELINES

CHAPTER 36

The Planned Trading Approach

If making money is a slow process, losing it is quickly done.

—Ihara Saikaku

If the amount of money you risk in futures trading represents a minuscule fraction of your net worth, and your major motivation for speculation is entertainment, the shoot-from-the-hip approach might be fine. However, if your major objective in futures trading is to make money, an organized trading plan is essential. This assertion is not just a platitude. Search out successful futures speculators, and you will no doubt find that they all use a well-defined, disciplined trading approach.

The following seven steps provide general guidelines for constructing an organized trading plan.

▪ Step 1: Define a Trading Philosophy

How do you plan to make your trading decisions? If your answer is something vague like, "When my friend gets a hot tip from his broker," "When I get a trade idea from reading a blog," or "On market feel while watching the trading screen," you're not ready to begin trading. A meaningful strategy would be based on either chart analysis, technical trading systems, fundamental analysis, or some combination of these approaches. The same method will not necessarily be used in all markets. For example, in some markets a trader might use a synthesis of fundamental and chart analyses to make trading decisions, while in other markets decisions may be based on chart analysis only.

The more specific the trading strategy, the better. For example, a trader who plans to base his trades on chart analysis should be able to specify the types of patterns that would signal trades, as well as other details, such as confirmation rules. Of course, the most specific trading strategy would be one based on a mechanical trading system; however, such a fully automated approach may not appeal to all traders.

Step 2: Choose Markets to Be Traded

After deciding how to pick trades, you must choose which markets to follow. For most traders, constraints on time and available funds will significantly limit the number of markets that can be monitored and traded. Three factors might be considered in selecting markets.

Suitability to Trading Approach

Traders should choose those markets that appear to have the best potential for satisfactory performance, given their planned approach. Of course, such a determination can be made only on the basis of either past trading experience or historical testing of a specific trading strategy.

Diversification

The multiple benefits of diversification were fully discussed in Chapter 16. However, the essential point here is that diversification provides one of the most effective means of reducing risk. Diversification can be enhanced by choosing markets that are not closely related. For example, if you knew that you wanted to trade gold, then silver and platinum would be poor choices for additional markets, unless your available funds were sufficient to permit you to trade many other markets as well.

Volatility

A trader with limited funds should avoid extremely volatile markets, since the inclusion of such markets in a portfolio will severely limit the total number of markets that can be traded. (Volatility here refers to dollar volatility per contract. Consequently, high volatility could imply relatively large price swings, large-size contracts, or both.) Unless your approach is better suited to a given volatile market, you will be better off trading a wider variety of less volatile markets (diversification again).

Step 3: Specify Risk Control Plan[1]

The rigid control of losses is perhaps the most critical prerequisite for successful trading. A risk control plan should include the following elements.

Maximum Risk per Trade

Traders can substantially increase their probability of long-term success by restricting the percentage of total funds allocated to any given trade.[2] The maximum risk on any trade should be limited to

---

[1] Risk control is typically referred to as "money management," although I believe the former represents the more descriptive label.

[2] The implicit assumption here is that the trader's expected net profit per trade (ENPPT) is positive. If a trader's ENPPT is negative, the laws of probability will assure failure if he trades long enough. Such a situation would be analogous to the roulette player whose expected gain per bet is negative.

2 percent of total equity and, ideally, 1 percent or less. For smaller accounts, adhering to such a guideline will require restricting trading to less volatile markets, mini contracts, and spreads. Speculators who find that they must risk 3 percent or more of their equity on individual trades should seriously reconsider their financial suitability for futures trading.

The maximum risk per trade can be used to determine the number of contracts that can be initiated in any given trade. For example, if the maximum risk per trade is 1 percent of equity, and the trader's account size is $200,000, a crude oil trade that required a stop point $1/barrel below the market would imply a maximum position size of two contracts. (The crude oil contract represents 1,000 barrels, so each $1 move equates to $1,000 per contract.)

Stop-Loss Strategy

Know where you're going to get out before you get in. The importance of this rule cannot be over-emphasized. Without a predetermined exit point, you can find yourself vulnerable to procrastinating in the liquidation of a losing position. At the wrong time, one such lapse of trading discipline could literally knock you out of the game.

Ideally, you should place a good-till-canceled (GTC) stop order when entering a trade. However, if you are fairly certain you can trust yourself, a mental stop point can be determined at trade entry, and thereafter adjusted only to reduce risk. For a more detailed discussion of stop-order placement strategies, see Chapter 13.

It should be noted that a system trader does not necessarily need to employ stop-loss rules in order to achieve risk control. For example, if a trading system automatically reverses the position given a sufficient trend reversal, the system will inherently perform the major function of a stop-loss rule—the prevention of catastrophic losses on individual trades—without such a rule being explicit. Of course, large cumulative losses can still occur over many trades, but the same vulnerability would also apply if stops were used.

Diversification

Because different markets will experience adverse moves at different times, trading multiple markets will reduce risk. As a very simple example, assume you have a $100,000 account and you are using a system that experiences average drawdowns of $5,000 in both gold and euro futures. If you traded two contracts of either market, the average drawdown would be equal to 10 percent ($10,000 ÷ $100,000), whereas if you traded one contract of each, the average drawdown would invariably be less (possibly even less than for *one* contract of a *single* market if the markets were inversely correlated). In fact, the average drawdown could reach 10 percent (assuming average drawdowns remain at $5,000 for each market) only if the drawdowns in the two markets proved to be exactly synchronized, which is exceedingly unlikely. Of course, the risk-reduction benefit of diversification would increase if more unrelated markets were added to the portfolio. Also, as noted in Chapter 16, the concept of diversification applies not only to trading multiple markets but also multiple systems (or approaches) and multiple system variations (i.e., parameter sets) for each market, assuming equity is sufficient to do so.

Although our focus in this section is risk control, it should be noted that diversification can also increase return by allowing the trader to increase the average exposure in each market without increasing overall risk. In fact, the addition of markets with a lower average return than other markets in an existing portfolio can actually *increase the return* of the portfolio if the risk reduction gained by diversification is greater than the decline in return and the trader adjusts exposure accordingly. Two other benefits of diversification—ensuring participation in major trends and "bad luck insurance"—were discussed in Chapter 16.

Reduce Leverage for Correlated Markets

Although adding markets to a portfolio allows a trader to increase leverage, it is important to make adjustments for highly correlated markets. For example, a currency portfolio, consisting of the eight most active currency futures contracts (euro, Japanese yen, British pound, Australian dollar, Canadian dollar, U.S. dollar index, Mexican peso, Swiss franc), would be subject to much greater risk than a more broadly diversified eight-market portfolio because of the very strong correlations between some of these markets. Consequently, the exposure level (as measured by the margin-to-equity ratio or other risk metric) of such an all-currency portfolio should be adjusted downward vis-à-vis a more diversified eight-market portfolio with equivalent individual market volatilities.

Market Volatility Adjustments

The number of contracts traded in each market for any given equity size should be adjusted to account for volatility differences. There are two aspects of this rule. First, fewer contracts would be traded in more volatile markets. Second, even for a single market, the number of contracts would vary in conjunction with fluctuations in volatility. Of course, since contracts can't be traded in fractions, traders with small accounts will be unable to make such volatility adjustments, which is one reason why small accounts will be subject to greater risk. (Other reasons include the unavoidability of the maximum risk per trade exceeding desired levels and an inability to diversify sufficiently.)

Adjusting Position Size to Equity Changes

Position size should also be adjusted in accordance with major fluctuations in equity. For example, if a trader's position size in the corn market was equal to four contracts when the account equity was at $200,000, then a $50,000 decline in the account equity should result in the corn position size being reduced to three contracts. (Of course, if equity rose instead, the position size should be increased.)

Losing Period Adjustments (Discretionary Traders Only)

When a trader's confidence is shaken because of an ongoing losing streak, it is often a good idea to temporarily cut back position size or even take a complete trading break until confidence returns. In this way, the trader can keep a losing phase from steamrolling into a disastrous retracement. This advice would not apply to a system trader, however, since for most viable systems, a losing period enhances the potential for favorable performance in the ensuing period. Or to put it another way, confidence and frame of mind are critical to the performance of a discretionary trader but are not relevant to the performance of a system.

■ Step 4: Establish a Planning Time Routine

It is important to set aside some time each evening for reviewing markets and updating trading strategies. In most cases, once the trader has established a specific routine, 30–60 minutes should be sufficient (less if only a few markets are being traded). The primary tasks performed during this time would be:

1. **Update trading systems or review charts.** At least one of these should be employed as an aid in making trading decisions. In those markets in which fundamental analysis is employed, the trader will also have to reevaluate the fundamental picture periodically after the release of important new information (e.g., government crop report).
2. **Plan new trades.** Determine whether any new trades are indicated for the next day, which could be defined as either including or excluding the preceding night session. If new trades are indicated, decide on a specific entry plan. (This step applies to discretionary trading only, since any systematic approach should include a specific trade entry approach.) In some cases, a trading decision may be contingent on an evaluation of market behavior on the following day. For example, assume a trader is bearish on corn, and a modestly bullish crop report is received after the close. Such a trader might decide to go short *if* the market is trading lower on the day at any point within one hour of the close.
3. **Update exit points for existing positions.** The trader should review the stops and objectives on existing positions to see whether any revisions appear desirable in light of the current day's price action. In the case of stops, such changes should be made only to reduce trade risk.

■ Step 5: Maintain a Trader's Spreadsheet

The planning routine discussed in the previous section implies some systematic form of record keeping. Figure 36.1 provides one sample of a format that might be used for a trader's spreadsheet.

The first four columns simply identify the trade. Column 5 would be used to indicate the intended stop point at time of entry. Revisions of this stop would be entered in column 6. The reason for maintaining the initial stop point as a separate item is that this information may be useful in any subsequent trade analysis. For example, traders may wish to check whether their initial stops tend to be too wide or too close.

Columns 7 through 10 provide a summary of the implied risk on open positions. By adding these entries for all open positions, a trader can assess current total exposure—information critical in controlling risk and determining whether new positions can be initiated.

(1) Trade Entry Date	(2) Long or Short	(3) Units	(4) Market	(5) Entry Price	(6) Stops Initial	(6) Stops Current	(7) Cumulative Implied Risk Initial	(8) Cumulative Implied Risk Current	(9) As Percentage of Equity Initial	(10) As Percentage of Equity Current	(11) Objective Initial	(12) Objective Current	(13) Exit Date	(14) Exit Price	(15) Net Profit or Loss	(16) Reasons for Entering Trade	(17) Comment

FIGURE 36.1 Sample Page from a Trader's Spreadsheet

The use of objectives (columns 11 and 12) is a matter of individual preference. Although in some cases the use of objectives will permit a better exit price, in other circumstances objectives will result in the premature liquidation of a trade. Consequently, some traders may prefer to forgo the use of objectives, allowing the timing of liquidation to be determined by either a trailing stop or a change of opinion.

Liquidation information is contained in columns 13 through 15. The reason for maintaining the exit date is that it can be used to calculate the duration of the trade, information that may be useful in trade analysis. Column 15 would indicate the profit or loss on the trade *after* deducting commissions.

Columns 16 and 17 provide room for capsule comments regarding the reasons for entering the trade (made at that time) and a hindsight evaluation of the trade. (Of course, entries for these two columns would require much greater space than shown in Figure 36.1.) The observations noted in these two columns can be particularly helpful in detecting any patterns in successes and failures. Furthermore, a more extensive description of the trade would be contained in a trader's diary, which is discussed in the next section.

The novice will usually benefit from a period of paper trading before plunging into actual trading. The trader's spreadsheet is ideally suited to this purpose, since it would not only provide an indication of potential trading success, but it would also get the new trader into the habit of approaching speculation in a systematic and disciplined fashion. Thus, when the transition is made to actual trading, the decision process will have become routine. Of course, the difficulty of trading decisions will increase dramatically once real money is at stake, but at least new traders who have established a routine of maintaining a trader's spreadsheet will have a decisive advantage over their typically ill-prepared counterparts.

Step 6: Maintain a Trader's Diary

The trader's diary should contain the following basic information for each trade:

1. **Reasons for trade.** It is important that the reasons for the trade are entered *at the time the trade is taken* so that this summary provides an accurate description of the original trade rationale, unbiased by hindsight and trade outcome. Over time, this information can help traders determine whether any of their trading strategies are particularly prone to success or failure.

2. **Trade exit comments.** Trade exit is as important as trade entry. Here, the trader would note both good and bad decisions made in exiting trades. For example, if a close stop was used on the trade, did it result in getting stopped out of a good trade, or did it reduce the loss on what would have been a losing trade even with a wider stop? As another example, if a trailing stop was used, did it result in premature exit or did it avoid a larger surrender of open profits? Comments in this section can help the trader determine whether the exit strategies employed are benefiting or hurting performance.

3. **Lessons.** A trader should itemize the mistakes or correct decisions made in the course of the trade. The mere act of keeping such a written record can greatly help a trader to both reinforce good trading habits and avoid repeating past mistakes—particularly if repeated errors are denoted in bold or in capital letters. The trader's diary should be reviewed periodically to help reinforce these observations. After a while, the lessons will sink in. Speaking from personal experience, this approach can be instrumental in eradicating frequently repeated mistakes.

It may also be very useful to augment the written diary with charts illustrating trade entry and exit points.

Step 7: Analyze Personal Trading

Traders must not only analyze the markets, but also their own past trades in order to isolate the strengths and weaknesses of their approach. Besides the trader's diary, two useful tools in such an analysis are analysis of segmented trades and the equity chart.

Analysis of Segmented Trades

The idea behind segmenting trades into different categories is to help identify any patterns of substantially above- or below-average performance. For example, a trader who makes decisions based on chart patterns could segment trades by the type of chart pattern that signaled the trade. This exercise could potentially reveal that some patterns provide much more reliable signals than others, allowing the trader to make appropriate strategy adjustments.

As another example, by breaking down trades into buys and sells, a trader might discover a predilection toward taking long side trades, even though past short trades have a higher average profit. Such a combined observation would obviously imply the desirability of correcting a bias toward the long side.

As a third example, after breaking down performance results by market, a trader might discover a tendency to consistently lose money in a specific market. Such evidence might suggest the trader could improve overall performance by not trading this market. Segmenting trading results by market can be an extremely important exercise, since many traders have a poor intuitive sense of their relative degree of success in various markets. The cessation of trading in poorer performing markets need not be permanent. The trader could attempt to identify the reasons for the disappointing results in these markets and then research and test possible trading adjustments.

As a fourth example, a trader who combines day trading and position trading might find it particularly instructive to compare the net results of each category. My suspicion is that if such analysis were performed by all traders to whom the exercise is relevant, the population of day traders would shrink by 50 percent overnight.

Of course, there are many other criteria that can be used to segment trades. Two other examples of relevant comparisons are fundamentally versus technically oriented trades, and trades that were in agreement with the position of a given trading system versus those that were not. In each case, the trader would be searching for patterns of success or failure. The process of analyzing segmented trades can be greatly simplified by utilizing the previously described trader's spreadsheet.

Equity Chart

The equity chart is a close-only type of chart in which the indicated value for each day represents the account equity (including the equity on open positions). The primary purpose of such a chart is to alert the trader when there is a precipitous deterioration of performance. For example, if after an extended, steady climb, the account equity experiences a sudden, steep decline, a trader might well be advised to lighten positions and take time to reassess the situation. Such an abrupt shift in performance might reflect a transformation of market conditions, a current vulnerability in the trader's approach, or a recent predilection toward poor trading decisions. A determination of the actual cause is not essential, since any of these factors could be viewed as strong cautionary signals to reduce risk exposure. In short, the equity chart can be an important tool in mitigating equity retracements.

Traders can create equity charts for their accounts, as well as access other performance charts and statistics, cost-free at fundseeder.com.[3]

---

[3] For the sake of full disclosure, I have a financial interest in FundSeeder.

CHAPTER 37

Seventy-Five Trading Rules and Market Observations

Live long enough and you will eventually be wrong about everything.

—Russell Baker

Few things are easier to ignore than trading advice. Many of the most critical trading rules have been so widely circulated that they have lost their ability to provoke any thought in the new trader. Thus, valid market insights are often dismissed as obvious clichés.

Consider the rule "Cut your losses short"—perhaps the single most important trading maxim. Lives there a speculator who has not heard this advice? Yet there is certainly no shortage of speculators who have ignored this rule. Not surprisingly, there is also no shortage of speculators whose accounts were virtually obliterated by one or two losing trades.

The truth is that most speculators will ignore advice until they have "rediscovered the wheel" through their own trading experience. Moreover, most traders will repeat a mistake many times before the lesson finally sinks in. Thus, I have no illusions that the advice presented in this and the next chapter will spare the reader from committing basic trading errors. However, it is hoped that several readings of these chapters (particularly following periods of negative trading results) will at least help some novice traders reduce the number of times these mistakes are repeated—hardly a trivial achievement.

The observations in this chapter are based on personal experience. Thus, the following list of rules should be viewed in their proper perspective: empirically based opinions as opposed to proven facts. Overall, there will be substantial overlap with other published expositions of trading guidelines. This is hardly surprising, since a wide range of rules (many of them mundane) are based on such sound principles that they are almost universally accepted as trading truths. For example, I have never met a successful trader who did not believe that risk control was essential to profitable trading. However, some of the rules listed below reflect a subjective view that is contradicted by other writers (e.g., using market orders instead of limit orders). In the final analysis, traders must discover their own trading truths. It is hoped that the following list will help speed the process.

■ Entering Trades

1. Differentiate between major position trades and short-term trades. Focus on major position trades, since these are usually far more critical to trading success. The average risk allocated to short-term trades (as implied by number of contracts in position and stop point) should be significantly smaller. A mistake made by many traders is that they become so involved in trying to catch the minor market swings (generating lots of commissions and slippage in the process) that they miss the major price moves.

2. If you believe a major trading opportunity exists, don't be greedy in trying to get a slightly better entry price. The lost profit potential of one missed price move can offset the savings from 50 slightly better execution prices.

3. Entry into any major position should be planned and carefully thought out—never an intraday impulse.

4. Find a chart pattern that says the timing is right—*now.* Don't initiate a trade without such a confirming pattern. (Of course, this rule applies only to traders who base their trading decisions on charts.)

5. Place orders determined by daily analysis. If the market is not close to the desired entry level, either enter a good-till-canceled (GTC) order at the appropriate price or record the trade idea and review it each day until the trade is entered or the trade idea is no longer deemed attractive. Failure to adhere to this rule can result in missing good trades. One common occurrence is that a trade idea is recalled once the market has moved beyond the intended entry, and it is then difficult to do the same trade at a worse price.

6. When looking for a major reversal in a trend, it is usually wiser to wait for some pattern that suggests that the timing is right rather than fading the trend at projected objectives and support/ resistance points. This rule is particularly important in the case of a market in which the trend has carried prices to long-term highs/lows (e.g., highs/lows beyond a prior 100-day range). Remember, in most cases of an extended trend, the market will not form V-type reversals. Instead prices will normally pull back to test highs and lows—often a number of times. Thus, waiting for a top or bottom to form can prevent getting chopped to pieces during the topping or bottoming process—not to mention the losses that can occur if you are highly premature in picking the top or bottom. Even if the market does form a major V top or V bottom, subsequent consolidations (e.g., flags) can allow favorable reward/risk entries.

7. If you have an immediate instinctive impression when looking at a chart (particularly, if you are not conscious about which market you are looking at), go with that feeling.

8. Don't let the fact that you missed the first major portion of a new trend keep you from trading with that trend (as long as you can define a reasonable stop-loss point).

9. Don't take positions counter to recent price failure patterns (e.g., a long position after a bull trap or a short position after a bear trap), even if there are many other reasons for the trade.

10. Don't trade counter to the first wide-ranging day (i.e., day with a range far exceeding the recent average range) of a price move. For example, if you are waiting to enter a trade on a correction, and the correction then forms on a wide-ranging day, don't enter the trade.

11. In most cases, use market orders rather than limit orders. This rule is especially important when liquidating a losing position or entering a perceived major trading opportunity—situations in which traders are apt to be greatly concerned about the market getting away from them. Although limit orders will provide slightly better fills for a large majority of trades, this benefit will usually be more than offset by the substantially poorer fills, or missed profit potential, in those cases in which the initial limit order is not filled.

12. Never double up near the original trade entry point after having been ahead. Often, the fact that the market has completely retraced is a negative sign for the trade. Even if the trade is still good, doubling up in this manner will jeopardize holding power due to overtrading.

■ Exiting Trades and Risk Control (Money Management)

13. Decide on a specific protective stop point *at the time of trade entry.*

14. Exit any trade as newly developing patterns or market action are contrary to trade—even if stop point has not been reached. Ask yourself, "If I had to have a position in this market, which way would it be?" If the answer is not the position you hold, get out! In fact, if contradictory indications are strong enough, reverse the position.

15. Always get out *immediately* once the original premise for a trade is violated.

16. If you are dramatically wrong the first day trade is on, abandon trade immediately.

17. In the event of a major breakout counter to the position held, either liquidate immediately or use a very close stop.

18. If a given market suddenly trades far in excess of its recent volatility in a direction opposite to the position held, liquidate your position immediately. For example, if a market that has been trading in approximate 50-point daily ranges opens 100 to 150 points higher, cover immediately if you are short.

19. If you sell into resistance or buy into support, and the market then consolidates instead of reversing, get out.

20. For analysts and market advisors: If your gut feeling is that a recent recommendation or written report is wrong, reverse your opinion.

21. If you're unable to watch markets for a period of time (e.g., when traveling), either liquidate all positions or be sure to have GTC stop orders on all open positions. (Also, in such situations, limit orders can be used to ensure getting into the market on planned buys at lower prices or planned sells at higher prices.)

22. Do not get complacent about an open position. Always know where you are getting out even if the point is far removed from the current price. Also, an evolving pattern contrary to the trade may suggest the desirability of an earlier-than-intended exit.

23. Fight the desire to immediately get back into the market following a stopped-out trade. Getting back in will usually supplement the original loss with additional losses. The only reason to get back in on a stopped out trade is if the timing seems appropriate based on evolving price patterns—that is, only if it meets all the conditions and justifications of any new trade.

■ Other Risk-Control (Money Management) Rules

24. When trading is going badly: (a) reduce position size (keep in mind that positions in strongly correlated markets are similar to one larger position); (b) use tight stop-loss points; (c) slow up in taking new trades.

25. When trading is going badly, reduce risk exposure by liquidating losing trades, not winning trades. This observation was memorably related by Edwin Lefèvre in *Reminiscences of a Stock Operator*: "I did precisely the wrong thing. The cotton showed me a loss and I kept it. The wheat showed me a profit and I sold it out. Of all the speculative blunders there are few greater than trying to average a losing game. Always sell what shows you a loss and keep what shows you a profit."

26. Be extremely careful not to change trading patterns after making a profit:
    a. Do not initiate any trades that would have been deemed too risky at the start of the trading program.
    b. Do not suddenly increase the number of contracts in a typical trade. (However, a gradual increase as equity grows is OK.)

27. Treat small positions with the same common sense as large positions. Never say, "It's only one or two contracts."

28. Avoid holding very large positions into major reports or the release of important government statistics.

29. Apply the same money management principles to spreads as to outright positions. It is easy to be lulled into thinking that spreads move gradually enough so that it is not necessary to worry about stop-loss protection.

30. Don't buy options without planning at what outright price the trade is to be liquidated.

■ Holding and Exiting Winning Trades

31. Do not take *small*, quick profits in major position trades. In particular, if you are dramatically right on a trade, never, never take profits on the first day.

32. Don't be too hasty to get out of a trade with a wide-ranging day in your direction. The wide-ranging day, however, can be used to reset stop to closer point.

33. Try to use trailing stops, supplemented by developing market action, instead of objectives as a means of getting out of profitable trades. Using objectives will often work against fully realizing the potential of major trends. Remember, you need the occasional big winners to offset losers.

34. The preceding rule notwithstanding, it is still useful to set an initial objective at the time of trade entry to allow the application of the following rule: If a very large portion of an objective is realized very quickly (e.g., 50 to 60 percent in one week or 75 to 80 percent in two or three weeks), take partial profits, with the idea of reinstating liquidated contracts on a reaction. The idea is that it is OK to take a quick, *sizable* profit. Although this rule may often result in missing the remainder of the move on the liquidated portion of the position, holding the entire position, in such a case, can frequently lead to nervous liquidation on the first market correction.

35. If an objective is reached, but you still like the trade, stay with it using a trailing stop. This rule is important in order to be able to ride a major trend. Remember, patience is not only important in waiting for the right trades, but also in staying with trades that are working. The failure to adequately profit from correct trades is a key profit-limiting factor.

36. One partial exception to the previous rule is that if you are *heavily* positioned and equity is surging straight up, consider taking scale-up profits. Corollary rule: *When things look too good to be true—watch out!* If everything is going right, it is probably a good time to begin taking scale-up (scale-down) profits and using close trailing stops on a portion of your positions.

37. If taking profits on a trade that is believed to still have long-term potential (but is presumably vulnerable to a near-term correction), have a game plan for reentering the position. If the market doesn't retrace sufficiently to allow for reentry, be cognizant of patterns that can be used for timing a reentry. Don't let the fact that the reentry point would be worse than the exit point keep you from getting back into a trade in which the perception of both the long-term trend and current timing suggest reentering. The inability to enter at a worse price can often lead to missing major portions of large trends.

38. If trading multiple contracts, avoid the emotional trap of wanting to be 100 percent right. For example, if tempted to take profits on a trade that is still acting well, try to keep at least a partial position for the duration of the move—until the market forms a convincing reversal pattern or reaches a meaningful stop-loss point.

■ Miscellaneous Principles and Rules

39. Always pay more attention to market action and evolving patterns than to objectives and support/resistance areas. The latter can often cause you to reverse a correct market bias very prematurely.

40. Whenever you feel action should be taken either entering or exiting a position—act, don't procrastinate.

41. Never go counter to your own opinion of the long-term trend of the market. In other words, don't try to dance between the raindrops.

42. Winning trades tend to be ahead right from the start. Along the same line of thought, Peter Brandt, a successful trader with four decades of experience advises: "Never take a losing trade home on a Friday."

43. Correct timing of entry and exit (e.g., timing entry on a reliable pattern, getting out immediately on the first sign of trade failure), can often keep a loss small even if the trade is dead wrong.

44. Intraday decisions are usually wrong. Most traders would be better off keeping their screens turned off during the day and reviewing markets once daily after the close of the main trading session.

45. Be sure to check markets before the close on Friday. Often, the situation is clearer at the end of the week. In such cases, a better entry or exit can usually be obtained on Friday near the close than on the following Monday opening. This rule is particularly important if you are holding a significant position.

46. Act on market dreams (that are recalled unambiguously). Such dreams are often right because they represent your subconscious market knowledge attempting to break through the barriers established by the conscious mind (e.g., "How can I buy here when I could have gone long $2,000 lower last week?")

47. You are never immune to bad trading habits—the best you can do is to keep them latent. As soon as you get lazy or sloppy, they will return.

■ Market Patterns

48. If the market sets new historical highs and holds, the odds strongly favor a move very far beyond the old highs. Selling a market at new record highs is probably one the amateur trader's worst mistakes.

49. Narrow market consolidations near the upper end of broader trading ranges are bullish patterns. Similarly, *narrow* consolidations near the low end of trading ranges are bearish.

50. Play the breakout from an extended, narrow range with a stop against the other side of the range.

51. Breakouts from trading ranges that hold 1 to 2 weeks, or longer, are among the most reliable technical indicators of impending trends.

52. A common and particularly useful form of the above rule is: Flags or pennants forming right above or below prior extended and broad trading ranges tend to be fairly reliable continuation patterns.

53. If the market breaks out to a new high or low and then pulls back to form a flag or pennant in the pre-breakout trading range, assume that a top or bottom is in place. A position can be taken using a protective stop beyond the flag or pennant consolidation.

54. A breakout from a trading range followed by a pullback deep into the range (e.g., three-quarters of the way back into the range or more) is yet another significant bull- or bear-trap formation.

55. If an apparent V bottom is followed by a nearby congestion pattern, it may represent a bottom pattern. However, if this consolidation is then broken on the downside and the V bottom

is approached, the market action can be read as a sign of an impending move to new lows. In the latter case, short positions could be implemented using protective stops near the top of the consolidation. Analogous comments would apply to V tops followed by nearby consolidations.

56. V tops and V bottoms followed by multimonth consolidations that form in close proximity to the reversal point tend to be major top or bottom formations.

57. Tight flag and pennant consolidations tend to be reliable continuation patterns and allow entry into an existing trend, with a reasonably close, yet meaningful, stop point.

58. If a tight flag or pennant consolidation leads to a breakout in the wrong direction (i.e., a reversal instead of a continuation), expect the move to continue in the direction of the breakout.

59. Curved consolidations tend to suggest an accelerated move in the direction of the curve.

60. The breaking of a short-term curved consolidation, in the direction opposite of the curve pathway, tends to be a good trend-reversal signal.

61. A wide-ranging day that closes counter to the main trend can often provide a reliable early signal of a trend change—particularly if it also triggers a reversal signal (e.g., complete penetration of prior consolidation).

62. Near-vertical, large price moves over a period of 2 to 4 days (coming off of a relative high or low) tend to be extended in the following weeks.

63. Spikes are good short term reversal signals. The extreme of the spike can be used as a stop point.

64. In spike situations, look at chart both ways—with and without spike. For example, if a flag is evident when a spike is removed, a penetration of that flag is a meaningful signal.

65. The ability of a market to hold relatively firm when other correlated markets are under significant pressure can be viewed as a sign of intrinsic strength. Similarly, a market acting weak when correlated markets are strong can be viewed as a bearish sign.

66. If a market trades consistently higher for most of the daily trading session, anticipate a close in the same direction.

67. Two successive flags with little separation can be viewed as a probable continuation pattern.

68. View a curved bottom, followed by a shallower, same-direction curved consolidation near the top of this pattern, as a bullish formation (cup-and-handle). A similar pattern would apply to market tops.

69. A failed signal is more reliable than the original signal. Go the other way, using the high (low) before the failure signal as a stop. Some examples of such failure patterns are rule numbers 53, 54, 58, and 60.

70. The failure of a market to follow through on significant bullish or bearish news (e.g., a major U.S. Department of Agriculture report) is often a harbinger of an imminent trend reversal. Pay particular attention to such a development if you have an existing position.

■ Analysis and Review

71. Review charts every day—especially if you are too busy.

72. Periodically review long-term charts (e.g., every 2 to 4 weeks).

73. Religiously maintain a *trader's diary*, including a chart for *each* trade taken and noting the following: reasons for trade; intended stop and objective (if any); follow-up at a later point indicating how the trade turned out; observations and lessons (mistakes, things done right, or noteworthy patterns); and net profit/loss. It is important that the trade sheet be filled out when a trade is entered so that the reasons for the trade accurately reflect your actual thinking rather than a reconstruction.

74. Maintain a *patterns chart book* whenever you notice a market pattern that is interesting and you want to note how you think it will turn out, or you want to record how that pattern is eventually resolved (in the case where you don't have any bias concerning the correct interpretation). Be sure to follow each chart up at a later date to see the actual outcome. Over time, this process may improve skills in chart interpretation by providing some statistical evidence of the forecasting reliability of various chart patterns (as recognized in real time).

75. Review and update trading rules, trader's diary, and patterns chart book on a regular schedule (e.g., three-month rotation for the three items). Of course, any of these items can be reviewed more frequently, whenever it is felt such a review would be useful.

CHAPTER 38

50 Market Wizard Lessons*

There is no such thing as being right or beating the market. If you make money, it is because you understood the same thing the market did. If you lose money, it is simply because you got it wrong. There is no other way of looking at it.

—Musawer Mansoor Ijaz

The methods employed by exceptional traders are extraordinarily diverse. Some are pure fundamentalists; others employ only technical analysis; and still others combine the two methodologies. Some traders consider two days to be long term, while others consider two months to be short term. Yet despite the wide gamut of styles, I have found that certain principles hold true for a broad spectrum of successful traders. This chapter contains a list of 50 observations regarding success in trading drawn from the lessons I learned and insights I developed in the process of interviewing great traders over several decades—an endeavor chronicled in four *Market Wizards* books.

1. **First things first.** First, be sure that you really want to trade. It is common for people who think they want to trade to discover that they really don't.
2. **Examine your motives.** Think about why you really want to trade. If you want to trade for the excitement, you might be better off riding a roller coaster or taking up hang gliding. If you are drawn to trading because you think it is an easy way to make a lot of money, the markets are likely to disabuse you of that assumption.

---

*This chapter is adapted from the following two sources: Jack Schwager, *The New Market Wizards* (New York, NY: Harper Business, 1989), pp. 461–478; © 1989 by Harper Collins Publishers. Used with permission. Jack Schwager, *Hedge Fund Market Wizards* (New York, NY: John Wiley & Sons, 2012), pp. 489–499; © 2012 by John Wiley & Sons Publishers. Used with permission.

3. **There is no holy grail in trading.** Many traders mistakenly believe there is some single solution to defining market behavior. Not only did the methods used by highly successful traders I interviewed vary widely, they were sometimes polar opposites of each other.

4. **Match the trading method to your personality.** Trading success is not about finding the one true method but rather about finding the one method that is right for you. It is critical to choose a method that is consistent with your own personality and comfort level. If you can't stand to give back significant profits, then a long-term trend-following approach—even a very good one—will be a disaster, because you will never be able to follow it. If you don't want to watch the quote screen all day (or can't), don't try a day-trading method. If you can't stand the emotional strain of making trading decisions, then try to develop a mechanical system for trading the markets. The importance of finding an approach that fits you cannot be overemphasized. Randy McKay, who met success as both an on-the-floor and off-the-floor trader, asserted: "Virtually every successful trader I know ultimately ended up with a trading style suited to his personality."

   Incidentally, the mismatch of trading style and personality is one of the key reasons why purchased trading systems rarely make profits for those who buy them, even if the system is a good one. Why? Because every system will have periods of poor performance. And if you are trading someone else's system, particularly a "black box" system where you have no idea why signals are being generated, you will likely abandon it the first time it does poorly.

5. **It is absolutely necessary to have an edge.** You can't win without an edge, even with the world's greatest discipline and money management skills. If you could, then it would be possible to win at roulette (over the long run) using perfect discipline and risk control. Of course, that is an impossible task because of the laws of probability. If you don't have an edge, all that money management and discipline will do for you is to guarantee that you will bleed to death gradually. Incidentally, if you don't know what your edge is, you don't have one.

6. **Derive a method.** To have an edge, you must have a method. The type of method is irrelevant. Some of the supertraders are pure fundamentalists; some are pure technicians; and some are hybrids. Even within each group, there are tremendous variations. For example, within the group of technicians, there are tape readers (or their modern-day equivalent—screen watchers), chartists, mechanical system traders, Elliott Wave analysts, Gann analysts, and so on. The type of method is not important, but having one is critical—and, of course, the method must have an edge.

7. **Developing a method is hard work.** Shortcuts rarely lead to trading success. Developing your own approach requires research, observation, and thought. Expect the process to take lots of time and hard work. Expect many dead ends and multiple failures before you find a successful trading approach that is right for you. Remember that you are playing against tens of thousands of professionals. Why should you be any better? If it were that easy, there would be a lot more millionaire traders.

8. **Skill versus hard work.** Is trading success dependent on innate skills, or is hard work sufficient? There is no question in my mind that many of the supertraders have a special talent for trading. Marathon running provides an appropriate analogy. Virtually anyone can run a

marathon, given sufficient commitment and hard work. Yet, regardless of the effort and desire, only a small fraction of the population will ever be able to run a 2:12 marathon (or 2:25 for women). Similarly, anyone can learn to play a musical instrument. But again, regardless of work and dedication, only a handful of individuals possess the natural talent to become concert soloists. The general rule is that exceptional performance requires both natural talent and hard work to realize its potential. If the innate skill is lacking, hard work may provide proficiency, but not excellence.

In my opinion, the same principles apply to trading. Virtually anyone can become a net profitable trader, but only a few have the inborn talent to become supertraders. For this reason, it may be possible to teach trading success, but only up to a point. Be realistic in your goals.

9. **Good trading should be effortless.** Wait a minute. Didn't I just list hard work as an ingredient to successful trading? How can good trading require hard work and yet be effortless?

There is no contradiction. Hard work refers to the preparatory process—the research and observation necessary to become a good trader—not to the trading itself. In this respect, hard work is associated with such qualities as vision, creativity, persistence, drive, desire, and commitment. Hard work certainly does not mean that the process of trading itself should be filled with exertion. It certainly does not imply struggling with or fighting against the markets. On the contrary, the more effortless and natural the trading process, the better the chances for success. One trader quoting *Zen and the Art of Archery* made the following analogy: "In trading, just as in archery, whenever there is effort, force, straining, struggling, or trying, it's wrong. You're out of sync; you're out of harmony with the market. The perfect trade is one that requires no effort."

Visualize a world-class distance runner, clicking off mile after mile at a five-minute pace. Now picture an out-of-shape, 250-pound couch potato trying to run a mile at a 10-minute pace. The professional runner glides along gracefully—almost effortlessly—despite the long distance and fast pace. The out-of-shape runner, however, is likely to struggle, huffing and puffing like a Yugo going up a 1 percent grade. Who is putting in more work and effort? Who is more successful? Of course, the world-class runner puts in his hard working during training, and this prior effort and commitment are essential to his success.

10. **Trade within your comfort zone.** If a position is too large you will be prone to exit good trades on inconsequential corrections because fear will dominate the decision process.

11. **Money management and risk control.** Almost all the great traders I interviewed felt that money management was even more important than the trading method. Many potentially successful systems or trading approaches have led to disaster because the trader applying the strategy lacked a method of controlling risk. You don't have to be a mathematician or an expert in portfolio theory to manage risk. Risk control can be as easy as the following four-step approach:

1. Never risk more than 1 to 2 percent of your capital on any trade. (Risking less than 1 percent per trade is even better if this restriction can be met while still being consistent with your methodology.)

2. Predetermine your exit point *before* you get into a trade. Many of the traders I interviewed cited *exactly* this rule.

3. Start with a deliberately small trading stake that you can afford to lose without it causing any significant financial or emotional impact. If this equity is lost, stop trading. Once you feel confident and ready to start trading again, begin with another small stake. By rigorously limiting the worst case in this manner, you will never be knocked out of the game because of one disastrous trading experience, as happens to so many novice traders.

4. If you are in an equity drawdown and feel you are out of sync with the markets or your trading confidence is shaky, take a breather, analyze what went wrong, and wait until you feel confident and have a high-probability idea before you begin trading again. For traders with large accounts, trading very small is a reasonable alternative to a complete trading hiatus. The strategy of cutting trading size down sharply during losing streaks is one mentioned by many of the traders I interviewed.

12. **The trading plan.** Trying to win in the markets without a trading plan is like trying to build a house without blueprints—costly (and avoidable) mistakes are virtually inevitable. A trading plan simply requires combining a personal trading method with specific money management and trade entry rules. Robert Krausz, a hypnotist who made a specialty of working with traders, considered the absence of a trading plan the root of all the principal difficulties traders encounter in the markets. Richard Driehaus, a very successful mutual fund manager I interviewed, stresses that a trading plan should reflect a personal core philosophy. He explains that without a core philosophy, you are not going to be able to hold on to your positions or stick with your trading plan during really difficult times.

13. **Don't confuse the concepts of winning and losing trades with good and bad trades.** A good trade can lose money, and a bad trade can make money. Even the best trading process will lose a certain percentage of the time. There is no way of knowing *a priori* which individual trade will make money. As long as a trade adheres to a process with a positive edge, it is a good trade, regardless of whether it wins or loses, because if similar trades are repeated multiple times, they will come out ahead. Conversely, a trade that is taken as a gamble is a bad trade, regardless of whether it wins or loses, because over time such trades will lose money.

14. **Discipline.** *Discipline* was probably the most frequent word used by the exceptional traders that I interviewed. Often, it was mentioned in an almost apologetic tone: "I know you've heard this a million times before, but believe me, it's really important."

There are two basic reasons why discipline is critical. First, it is a prerequisite for maintaining effective risk control. Second, you need discipline to apply your method without second-guessing and choosing which trades to take. I guarantee that you will almost always pick the wrong ones. Why? Because you will tend to pick the comfortable trades, and as Bill Eckhardt, a mathematician turned successful commodity trading advisor (CTA), explained, "What feels good is often the wrong thing to do."

15. **Understand that you are responsible.** Whether you win or lose, you are responsible for your own results. Even if you lost on your broker's tip, an advisory service recommendation, or a bad signal from the system you bought, you are responsible because you made the decision to listen and act. I have never met a successful trader who blamed others for his losses.

16. **The need for independence.** You need to do your own thinking. Don't get caught up in mass hysteria. Ed Seykota, a futures trader who multiplied the equity in his accounts a thousandfold over an 18-year period, pointed out that by the time a story is making the cover of national periodicals, the trend is probably near an end.

Independence also means making your own trading decisions. Never listen to other opinions. Even if it occasionally helps on a trade or two, listening to others invariably seems to end up costing you money—not to mention confusing your own market view. As Michael Marcus, a spectacularly successful futures trader, stated in *Market Wizards,* "You need to follow your own light. If you combine two traders, you will get the worst of each."

A related personal anecdote concerns another trader I interviewed in *Market Wizards.* Although he could trade better than I if he were blindfolded and placed in a trunk at the bottom of a pool, he still was interested in my view of the markets. One day he called and asked, "What do you think of the yen?"

The yen was one of the few markets about which I had a strong opinion at the time. It had formed a particular chart pattern that made me very bearish. "I think the yen is going straight down, and I'm short," I replied.

He proceeded to give me 51 reasons why the yen was oversold and due for a rally. After he hung up, I thought: "I'm leaving on a business trip tomorrow. My trading has not been going very well during the last few weeks. The short yen trade is one of the only positions in my account. Do I really want to fade one of the world's best traders given these considerations?" I decided to close out the trade.

By the time I returned from my trip several days later, the yen had fallen 150 points. As luck would have it, that afternoon the same trader called. When the conversation rolled around to the yen, I couldn't resist asking, "By the way, are you still long the yen?"

"Oh no," he replied, "I'm short."

The point is not that this trader was trying to mislead me. On the contrary, he firmly believed each market opinion at the time he expressed it. However, he was a very short-term trader and his timing was good enough so that he probably made money on both sides of the trade. In contrast, I ended up with nothing, even though I had the original move pegged exactly right. The moral is that even advice from a much better trader can lead to detrimental results.

17. **Confidence.** An unwavering confidence in their ability to continue to win in the markets, was a nearly universal characteristic among the traders I interviewed. Dr. Van Tharp, a psychologist who has done a great deal of research on traders and was interviewed in *Market Wizards,* claims that one of the basic traits of winning traders is that they believe "they've won the game before they start."

The trader who has confidence will have the courage to make the right decisions and the strength not to panic. There is a passage in Mark Twain's *Life on the Mississippi* that I find remarkably apropos, even though it has nothing to do with trading. In it, the protagonist—an apprentice steamboat river pilot—is tricked by his mentor and the crew into panicking in a stretch of river he *knows* to be the easiest in the entire run. The following exchange then ensues with his mentor:

"Didn't you know there was no bottom in that crossing?"

"Yes sir, I did."

"Very well then, you shouldn't have allowed me or anybody else to shake your confidence in that knowledge. Try to remember that. And another thing, when you get into a dangerous place, don't turn coward. That isn't going to help matters any."

18. **Losing is part of the game.** The great traders fully realize that losing is an intrinsic element in the game of trading. This attitude seems linked to confidence. Because exceptional traders are confident that they will win over the long run, individual losing trades no longer seem horrible; they simply appear inevitable—which is what they are. As Linda Raschke, a futures trader with a high ratio of winning to losing trades, explained, "It never bothered me to lose because I always knew I would make it right back."

There is no more certain recipe for losing than having a fear of losing. If you can't stand taking losses, you will either end up taking large losses or missing great trading opportunities—either flaw is sufficient to sink any chance for success.

19. **Lack of confidence and time-outs.** Trade only when you feel confident and optimistic. I have often heard traders say: "I just can't seem to do anything right." Or "I bet I get stopped out right near the low again." If you find yourself thinking in such negative terms, it is a sure sign that it is time to take a break from trading. Get back into trading slowly. Think of trading as a cold ocean. Test the water before plunging in.

20. **The urge to seek advice.** The urge to seek advice betrays a lack of confidence. As Linda Raschke said, "If you ever find yourself tempted to seek out someone else's opinion on a trade, that's usually a sure sign that you should get out of your position."

21. **The virtue of patience.** Waiting for the right opportunity increases the probability of success. You don't always have to be in the market. As Edwin Lefèvre put it in his classic *Reminiscences of a Stock Operator*, "There is the plain fool who does the wrong thing at all times anywhere, but there is the Wall Street fool who thinks he must trade all the time."

One of the more colorful descriptions of patience in trading was offered by well-known investor Jim Rogers in *Market Wizards*: "I just wait until there is money lying in the corner, and all I have to do is go over there and pick it up." In other words, until he is so sure of a trade that it seems as easy as picking money off the floor, he does nothing.

Mark Weinstein, who was interviewed in *Market Wizards,* provided the following apt analogy: "Although the cheetah is the fastest animal in the world and can catch any animal on the plains, it will wait until it is absolutely sure it can catch its prey. It may hide in the bush for a week, waiting for just the right moment. It will wait for a baby antelope, and not just any baby antelope, but preferably one that is also sick or lame. Only then, when there is no chance it can lose its prey, does it attack. That, to me, is the epitome of professional trading."

22. **The importance of sitting.** Patience is important not only in waiting for the right trades, but also in staying with trades that are working. The failure to adequately profit from correct trades is a key profit-limiting factor. Quoting again from Lefèvre in *Reminiscences,* "It never was my

thinking that made big money for me. It was always my sitting. Got that? My sitting tight!" Bill Eckhardt offered a particularly memorable comment on this subject: "One common adage . . . that is completely wrongheaded is: You can't go broke taking profits. That's precisely how many traders *do* go broke. While amateurs go broke by taking large losses, professionals go broke by taking small profits."

23. **Developing a low-risk idea.** One of the exercises Dr. Van Tharp uses in his seminars is having the participants take the time to write down their ideas on low-risk trades. The merit of a low-risk idea is that it combines two essential elements: patience (because only a small portion of ideas will qualify) and risk control (inherent in the definition). Taking the time to think through low-risk strategies is a useful exercise for all traders. The specific ideas will vary greatly from trader to trader, depending on the markets traded and methodologies used. At the seminar I attended, the participants came up with a long list of descriptions of low-risk ideas. As one example: a trade in which the market movement required to provide convincing proof that you are wrong is small. Although it had nothing to do with trading, my personal favorite of the low-risk ideas mentioned was: "Open a doughnut shop next door to a police station."

24. **The importance of varying bet size.** All traders who win consistently over the long run have an edge. However, that edge may vary significantly from trade to trade. It can be mathematically demonstrated that in any wager game with varying probabilities, winnings are maximized by adjusting the bet size in accordance with the perceived chance for a successful outcome. Optimal blackjack betting strategy provides a perfect illustration of this concept.

   If the trader has some idea as to which trades have a greater edge—say, for example, based on a higher confidence level (assuming that it is a reliable indicator)—then it makes sense to be more aggressive in these situations. As Stanley Druckenmiller, one of the most consistently profitable hedge fund managers ever, expressed it, "The way to build [superior] long-term returns is through preservation of capital and home runs. . . . When you have tremendous conviction on a trade, you have to go for the jugular. It takes courage to be a pig." For a number of Market Wizards, keen judgment as to when to really step on the accelerator and the courage to do so have been instrumental to their achieving exceptional (as opposed to merely good) returns.

   Some of the traders I interviewed mentioned that they varied their trading size in accordance with how they were doing. For example, McKay indicated that it was not uncommon for him to vary his position size by as much as a factor of one hundred to one. He finds this approach helps him reduce risk during losing periods while enhancing profits during the winning periods.

25. **Scaling in and out of trades.** You don't have to get in or out of a position all at once. Scaling in and out of positions provides the flexibility of fine-tuning trades and broadens the set of alternative choices. Most traders sacrifice this flexibility without a second thought because of the innate human desire to be completely right. (By definition, a scaling approach means that some portions of a trade will be entered or exited at worse prices than other portions.) Some traders also noted that scaling out enabled them to stay with at least a portion of long-term winning trades much longer than would otherwise have been the case.

26. **Trading around a position can be beneficial.** Most traders tend to view trading as a two-step process: a decision when to enter and a decision when to exit. It may be better to

view trading as a dynamic rather than static process between entry and exit points. The basic idea is that as a trade moves in the intended direction, the position exposure would be gradually reduced. The larger the move and the closer the market gets to a target objective, the more the position would be decreased. After reducing exposure in this manner, the position would be reinstated on a market correction. Any time the market retraced to a correction reentry point, a net profit would be generated that otherwise would not have been realized. The choppier the market, the more excess profits trading around the position will generate. Even a trade in which the market fails to move in the intended direction, on balance, could still be net profitable as a result of gains generated by lightening the total position on favorable trend moves and reinstating liquidated portions of the position on corrections. This strategy will also reduce the chances of being knocked out of a favorable position on a market correction, because if the position has already been reduced, the correction will have less impact and may even be desired to reinstate the liquidated portion of the position. The only time this strategy will have a net adverse impact is if the market keeps going in the intended direction without ever retracing to correction reentry levels. This negative outcome, however, simply means that the original trade was profitable, but the total profits are smaller than they would have been otherwise. In a nutshell, trading around a position will generate extra profits and increase the chances of staying with a good trade the at expense of sometimes giving up a portion of profits when the market moves smoothly in the intended direction.

27. **Being right is more important than being a genius.** I think one reason why so many people try to pick tops and bottoms is that they want to prove to the world how smart they are. Think about winning rather than being a hero. Forget trying to judge trading success by how close you can come to picking major tops and bottoms, but rather by how well you can pick individual trades with favorable return/risk characteristics. Go for consistency on a trade-to-trade basis, not perfect trades.

28. **Don't worry about looking stupid.** Last week, you told everyone at the office, "My analysis has just given me a great buy signal in the S&P. The market is going to a new high." Now as you examine the market action since then, something appears to be wrong. Instead of rallying, the market is breaking down. Your gut tells you that the market is vulnerable. Whether you realize it or not, your announced prognostications are going to color your objectivity. Why? Because you don't want to look stupid after telling the world that the market was going to a new high. Consequently, you are likely to view the market's action in the most favorable light possible. "The market isn't breaking down, it's just a pullback to knock out the weak longs." As a result of this type of rationalization, you end up holding a losing position far too long. There is an easy solution to this problem: Don't talk about your position.

What if your job requires talking about your market opinions (as mine once did)? Here the rule is: Whenever you start worrying about contradicting your previous opinion, view that concern as reinforcement to reverse your market stance. As a personal example, in early 1991, I came to the conclusion that the dollar had formed a major bottom. I specifically remember one talk in which an audience member asked me about my outlook for currencies. I responded by boldly predicting that the dollar would head higher for years. Several months later, when the dollar surrendered the entire gain it had realized following the news of the August 1991 Soviet coup before the coup's failure was confirmed, I sensed that something was wrong. I recalled my many predictions over the preceding months in which I had stated that the dollar would go up for years. The discomfort and embarrassment I felt about these previous forecasts told me it was time to change my opinion.

In my earlier years in the business, I invariably tried to rationalize my original market opinion in such situations. I was burned enough times so that I eventually learned a lesson. In the preceding example, the abandonment of my original projection was fortunate because the dollar collapsed in the ensuing months.

29. **Sometimes action is more important than prudence.** Waiting for a price correction to enter the market may sound prudent, but it is often the wrong thing to do. When your analysis, methodology, or gut tells you to get into a trade at the market instead of waiting for a correction—do so. Caution against the influence of knowing that you could have gotten in at a better price in recent sessions, particularly in those situations when the market witnesses a sudden, large move (often due to an important surprise news item). These types of trades often work because they are so hard to do.

30. **Catching part of the move is just fine.** Just because you missed the first major portion of a new trend, don't let that keep you from trading with that trend (as long as you can define a reasonable stop-loss point). McKay commented that the easiest part of a trend is the middle portion, which implies always missing part of the trend prior to entry.

31. **Don't try to be 100 percent right.** Almost every trader has had the experience of the market moving against the position sufficiently to raise significant concern regarding the potential additional loss, while still believing the position is correct. Staying in the trade risks an uncomfortably large loss, but liquidating the trade risks abandoning a good position at nearly the worst possible point. In such circumstances, instead of making an all-or-nothing decision, traders can choose to liquidate part of the position. Taking a partial loss is much easier than liquidating the entire position and will avoid the possibility of riding the entire position for a large loss. It will also preserve the potential for a partial recovery if the market turns around.

32. **Maximize gains, not the number of wins.** Eckhardt explains that human nature does not operate to maximize gain but rather the chance of a gain. The problem with this is that it implies a lack of focus on the magnitudes of gains (and losses)—a flaw that leads to nonoptimal performance results. Eckhardt bluntly concludes: "The success rate of trades is the least important performance statistic and may even be inversely related to performance." Jeff Yass, a very successful options trader, echoes a similar theme: "The basic concept that applies to both poker and option trading is that the primary object is not winning the most hands, but rather maximizing your gains."

33. **Learn to be disloyal.** Loyalty may be a virtue in family, friends, and pets, but it is a fatal flaw for a trader. Never have loyalty to a position. The novice trader will have lots of loyalty to his original position. He will ignore signs that he is on the wrong side of the market, riding his trade into a large loss while hoping for the best. The more experienced trader, having learned the importance of money management, will exit quickly once it is apparent he has made a bad

trade. However, the truly skilled trader will be able to do a 180-degree turn, *reversing* his position at a loss if market behavior points to such a course of action. Druckenmiller made the awful error of reversing his stock position from short to long on the very day before the October 19, 1987, crash. His ability to quickly recognize his error and, more important, to unhesitatingly act on that realization by reversing back to short at a large loss helped transform a potentially disastrous month into a net profitable one.

34. **Pull out partial profits.** Pull a portion of winnings out of the market to prevent trading discipline from deteriorating into complacency. It is far too easy to rationalize overtrading and procrastination in liquidating losing trades by saying, "It's only profits." Profits withdrawn from an account are much more likely to be viewed as real money.

35. **Hope is a four-letter word.** Hope is a dirty word for a trader, not only in regards to procrastinating in a losing position, hoping the market will come back, but also in terms of hoping for a reaction that will allow for a better entry in a missed trade. If such trades are good, the hoped-for reaction will not materialize until it is too late. Often, the only way to enter such trades is to do so as soon as a reasonable stop-loss point can be identified.

36. **Don't do the comfortable thing.** Eckhardt offers the rather provocative proposition that the human tendency to select comfortable choices will lead most people to experience worse than random results. In effect, he is saying that natural human traits lead to such poor trading decisions that most people would be better off flipping coins or throwing darts. Some of the examples Eckhardt cites of the comfortable choices people tend to make that run counter to sound trading principles include gambling with losses, locking in sure winners, selling on strength and buying on weakness, and designing (or buying) trading systems that have been overfitted to past price behavior. The implied message to the trader is: do what is right, not what feels comfortable.

37. **You can't win if you have to win.** There is an old Wall Street adage: "Scared money never wins." The reason is quite simple: If you are risking money you can't afford to lose, all the emotional pitfalls of trading will be magnified. Early in his career, when the bankruptcy of a key financial backer threatened the survival of his fledgling investment firm, Druckenmiller "bet the ranch" on one trade, in a last-ditch effort to save his firm. Even though he came within one week of picking the absolute bottom in the T-bill market, he still lost all his money. The need to win fosters trading errors (e.g., excessive leverage and a lack of planning in the example just cited). The market seldom tolerates the carelessness associated with trades born of desperation.

38. **The road to success is paved with mistakes.** Learning from mistakes is essential to improvement and ultimate success. Each mistake, if recognized and acted on, provides an opportunity for improving a trading approach. Most traders would benefit by writing down each mistake, the important lesson, and the intended change in the trading process. Such a trading log can be periodically reviewed for reinforcement. Trading mistakes cannot be avoided, but repeating the same mistakes can be, and doing so is often the difference between success and failure.

39. **Think twice when the market lets you off the hook easily.** Don't be too eager to get out of a position you have been worried about if the market allows you to exit at a much better price than anticipated. If you had been worried about an adverse overnight (or over-the-weekend)

price move because of a news event or a technical price failure on the previous close, it is likely that many other traders shared this concern. The fact that the market does not follow through much on these fears strongly suggests that there must be some very powerful underlying forces in favor of the direction of the original position. This concept, which was first proposed in *Market Wizards* by Marty Schwartz, who compiled an astounding track record trading stock index futures, was illustrated by the manner in which Lipschutz, a large-scale currency trader, exited the one trade he admitted had scared him. In that instance, on Friday afternoon, a time when the currency markets are particularly thin (after Europe's close), Lipschutz found himself with an enormous short dollar position in the midst of a strongly rallying market. He had to wait over the weekend for the Tokyo opening on Sunday evening to find sufficient liquidity to exit his position. When the dollar opened weaker than expected in Tokyo, he didn't just dump his position in relief; rather, his trader's instincts told him to delay liquidation—a decision that resulted in a far better exit price.

40. **A mind is a terrible thing to close.** Open-mindedness seems to be a common trait among those who excel at trading. For example, Gil Blake, a mutual fund timer who has made incredibly consistent profits, actually fell into a trading career by attempting to demonstrate to a colleague that prices were random. When he realized he was wrong, he became a trader. In the words of Driehaus, "The mind is like a parachute—it's only good when it's open."

41. **The markets are an expensive place to look for excitement.** Excitement has a lot to do with the image of trading, but nothing to do with success in trading (except in an inverse sense). In *Market Wizards*, Larry Hite, the founder of Mint Management, one of the largest CTA firms, described his conversation with a friend who couldn't understand his absolute adherence to a computerized trading system. His friend asked, "Larry, how can you trade the way you do? Isn't it boring?" Larry replied, "I don't trade for excitement; I trade to win."

42. **Beware of trades born of euphoria.** Take caution against placing impulsive trades influenced by being caught up in market hysteria. Excessive euphoria in the market should be seen as a cautionary flag of a potential impending reversal.

43. **If you are on the right side of euphoria or panic, lighten up.** Parabolic price moves tend to end abruptly and sharply. If you are fortunate enough to be on the right side of the market in which the price move turns near vertical, consider scaling out of the position while the trend is still moving in your direction. If you would be petrified to be on the other side of the market, that is probably a good sign that you should be lightening your position.

44. **The calm state of a trader.** If there is an emotional state associated with successful trading, it is the antithesis of excitement. Based on his observations, Charles Faulkner, a neuro-linguistic programming (NLP) practitioner who works with traders, stated that exceptional traders are able to remain calm and detached regardless of what the markets are doing. He describes Peter Steidlmayer's (a successful futures trader who is best known as the inventor of the Market Profile trading technique) response to a position that is going against him as being typified by the thought, "Hmmm, look at that."

45. **Identify and eliminate stress.** Stress in trading is a sign that something is wrong. If you feel stress, think about the cause, and then act to eliminate the problem. For example, let's say you

determine that the greatest source of stress is indecision in getting out of a losing position. One way to solve this problem is simply to enter a protective stop order every time you put in a position.

I will give you a personal example. When I was a research director, one of the elements of my job was providing trading recommendations to brokers in my company. This task is very similar to trading, and, having done both, I believe it's actually more difficult than trading. At one point, after years of net profitable recommendations, I hit a bad streak. I just couldn't do anything right. When I was right about the direction of the market, my buy recommendation was just a bit too low (or my sell price too high). When I got in and the direction was right, I got stopped out—frequently within a few ticks of the extreme of the reaction.

I responded by developing a range of computerized trading programs and technical indicators, thereby widely diversifying the trading advice I provided to the firm. I still made my day-to-day subjective calls on the market, but everything was no longer riding on the accuracy of these recommendations. By widely diversifying the trading-related advice and information, and transferring much of this load to mechanical approaches, I was able to greatly diminish a source of personal stress—and improve the quality of the research product in the process.

46. **Pay attention to intuition.** As I see it, intuition is simply experience that resides in the subconscious mind. The objectivity of the market analysis done by the conscious mind can be compromised by all sorts of extraneous considerations (e.g., one's current market position, a resistance to change a previous forecast). The subconscious, however, is not inhibited by such constraints. Unfortunately, we can't readily tap into our subconscious thoughts. However, when they come through as intuition, the trader needs to pay attention. As the Zen-quoting trader mentioned earlier expressed it, "The trick is to differentiate between what you *want* to happen and what you *know* will happen."

47. **Life's mission and love of the endeavor.** In talking to the traders interviewed in *Market Wizards,* I had the definite sense that many of them felt that trading was what they were meant to do—in essence, their mission in life. In this context, Charles Faulkner quoted NLP cofounder John Grinder's description of mission: "What do you love so much that you would pay to do it?" Throughout my interviews, I was struck by the exuberance and love the Market Wizards had for trading. Many used gamelike analogies to describe trading. This type of love for the endeavor may indeed be an essential element for success.

48. **The elements of achievement.** Faulkner has a list of six key steps to achievement based on Gary Faris's study of successfully rehabilitated athletes, which appears to apply equally well to the goal of achieving trading success. These strategies include the following:
    1. Using both "Toward" and "Away From" motivation;
    2. Having a goal of full capability plus, with anything less being unacceptable;
    3. Breaking down potentially overwhelming goals into chunks, with satisfaction garnered from the completion of each individual step;
    4. Keeping full concentration on the present moment—that is, the single task at hand rather than the long-term goal;

5. Being personally involved in achieving goals (as opposed to depending on others); and

6. Making self-to-self comparisons to measure progress.

49. **Prices are nonrandom = the markets can be beat.** In reference to academicians who believe market prices are random, Monroe Trout, a commodity trading advisor with one of the best risk/return records in the industry, says, "That's probably why they're professors and why I'm making money doing what I'm doing." The debate over whether prices are random is not yet over. However, my experience in interviewing scores of great traders left me with little doubt that the random walk theory is wrong. It is not the magnitude of the winnings registered by the Market Wizards, but the consistency of these winnings in some cases, that underpin my belief. As a particularly compelling example, in his first fund, Edward Thorp, a mathematician best known for his best-selling book *Beat the Dealer*, compiled a track record of 227 winning months and only 3 losing months (all under 1 percent)—an extraordinary 98.7 winning percentage. The odds of getting such a result by chance (as would be the case if the markets were random) are less than 1 out of 10^{63}. To put this probability in context, the odds of randomly selecting a specific atom in the earth would be about a trillion times better. Certainly, winning at the markets is not easy—and, in fact, it is getting more difficult as professionals account for a constantly growing proportion of the activity—but it can be done!

50. **Keep trading in perspective.** There is more to life than trading.

Introduction to Regression Analysis

Theory helps us bear our ignorance of fact.

—George Santayana

Basics

Regression analysis is concerned with describing and evaluating the relationship between a given variable and one or more other variables. For example, we might be interested in describing the relationship between the pig crop (number of pigs born during a given period) and the hog slaughter level in the following six-month period.[1] The relationship between these variables is illustrated in Figure A.1. Each point in Figure A.1 represents a single observation or year. The location of a point along the horizontal axis is determined by the December–May pig crop, while its placement along the vertical axis is determined by the June–November hog slaughter level. Note that there is a clear

---

[1] Readers may notice that a predominant number of the examples in the Appendices will be drawn from the hog market. There are three basic reasons for this: (1) Such comparisons will illustrate the advantages of regression analysis in terms of preciseness, efficiency, flexibility, and ease of application. (2) The exposition will be clearer if a limited number of markets are used to provide illustrative examples. (3) Because hogs are nonstorable, the hog market can be represented adequately by simple fundamental models. In any event, it should be stressed that chosen examples are merely intended as vehicles to illustrate the general concepts and techniques of regression analysis, and not as a description of the methodology for analyzing any specific market. Consequently, the illustrations should be as relevant to the reader interested in applying regression analysis to the interest rate markets as to the reader whose primary focus is the livestock sector.

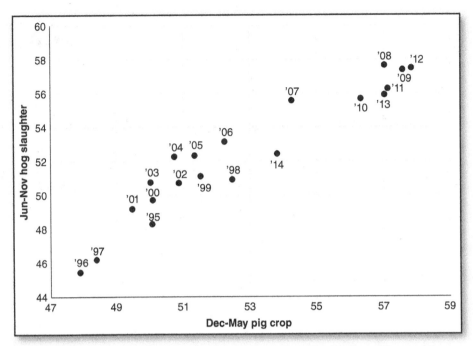

FIGURE A.1 June–November Hog Slaughter vs. December–May Pig Crop (Thousands)

relationship between these two variables: large hog slaughter levels correspond to large pig crop levels. In this example, hog slaughter is the *dependent* variable in that hog slaughter depends on the pig crop, but not vice versa, and the pig crop is the *independent*, or *explanatory*, variable. The primary goal of regression analysis is to define a mathematical relationship between the dependent variable and the independent variable(s).

Perhaps the most basic underlying assumption in the standard regression analysis approach is that the relationship between the dependent and independent variables is linear. In the case in which there is only one explanatory variable, the regression equation will be a straight line and can be expressed as

$$Y = a + bX$$

where a and b are constants determined by the regression procedure.[2] The values derived for a and b by the regression procedure are termed the *regression coefficients* (a is sometimes simply referred to as the *constant term*). By convention, Y is the variable that we are trying to explain or predict—the dependent variable—while X is the explanatory or independent variable.

---

[2] To be precise, a and b are parameters. A parameter can be thought of as a hybrid between a variable and a constant. If the focus is on the variation of the equation as a whole, then a and b are variables. Given the equation, $Y = a + bX$, each set of values for a and b will define a different line. However, if we are concerned with the relationship between the variables X and Y, given a specific set of values for a and b, as is the case in regression analysis, then a and b can be termed constants.

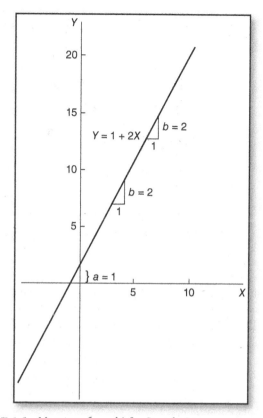

FIGURE A.2 Meaning of *a* and *b* for Straight Line

The constants *a* and *b* in the regression equation have special meanings. Constant *b* is the amount variable *Y* (e.g., hog slaughter) will change given a one-unit change in variable *X* (e.g., pig crop). For example, in the simple linear equation $Y = 1 + 2X$ each unit change in *X* will result in a two-unit change in *Y*. Note this relationship will hold regardless of the level of *X*. In fact, the constancy of the change in *Y* given a fixed change in *X* is a basic characteristic of a linear equation. Constant *a* is called the *Y* intercept because it is the value of *Y* at which the line crosses the *Y* axis—that is, the value of *Y* when *X* equals zero. (See Figure A.2 for a graphic depiction of the preceding points.)

Given a set of data points such as those illustrated in Figure A.1, regression analysis will seek to find the values of *a* and *b* in the regression equation that result in the line that best fits the observed points.

■ Meaning of Best Fit

Using Figure A.1 as an example, how would we define the best-fit line to the scatter of points? Intuitively, it seems that we would want to pick the line that minimizes the deviations from the individual points to the line. The *deviation* of any single point or observation can be defined as the difference

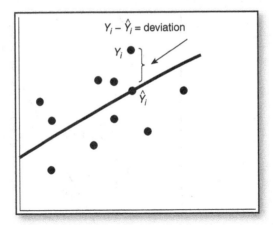

FIGURE A.3 Deviation for a Single Observation

between Y_i, the observed value, and $\hat{Y}_i$, the Y value predicted by the line for the same value of X. The deviation of a single point is thus equal to $Y_i - \hat{Y}_i$ (see Figure A.3).

These deviations are also called *residuals.* We cannot derive a summary deviation figure for a group of points by adding all the individual deviations. Why? Because deviations above and below the line will tend to cancel each other out. Thus, the sum of the residuals can be small even if the line fits the data points poorly. In fact, if the deviations below the line are greater than the deviations above the line, the sum of the residuals will be negative—an absurd value for a measure of total deviation. How would one interpret a negative total deviation? In other words, the sum of the residuals does not offer a criterion for determining best fit.

One possible solution is to find the line that minimizes the sum of the *absolute* deviations, that is, the sum of the residuals measured without regard to sign. Another possible approach would be to square each of the deviations before adding them, thereby assuring that they will all be positive, and then to find the line that minimizes the sum of these squared deviations[3]:

$$\sum_{i=1}^{n} (Y_i - \hat{Y}_i)^2$$

This *least-squares* approach represents the method employed by regression analysis, and is preferable to the sum of the absolute deviations for several reasons:

1. Theoretically, the least-squares approach will yield the best estimates.[4]
2. The least-squares method will place greater weight on large errors as a result of the squaring operation in its computation. This approach is usually advantageous, since it is desirable to avoid large deviations.

---

[3] The symbol Σ means "the sum of." The superscript n indicates the number of observations, and the subscript $i = 1$ indicates the observation number at which the summation begins. In other words, in this term, all the squared deviations are summed, and there are a total of n observations.

[4] The least-squares estimates will be both *unbiased* and *efficient.* These terms are defined in Appendix C.

3. The sum of the absolute deviations is computationally far more unwieldy than the sum of the squared deviations.

4. The least-squares approach permits many useful tests of the reliability of the equation.

It can be demonstrated by straightforward calculus proofs the values of a and b that minimize the sum of the squared deviations are:

$$b = \frac{n \cdot \sum\limits_{i=1}^{n} X_i Y_i - \sum\limits_{i=1}^{n} X_i \cdot \sum\limits_{i=1}^{n} Y_i}{n \sum\limits_{i=1}^{n} X_i^2 - \left(\sum\limits_{i=1}^{n} X_i \right)^2}$$

$$a = \frac{\sum\limits_{i=1}^{n} Y_i}{n} - b \frac{\sum\limits_{i=1}^{n} X_i}{n} = \overline{Y} - b\overline{X}$$

where n = number of observations
$\overline{Y}$ = mean of Y_i, and
$\overline{X}$ = mean of X_i

A Practical Example

As a practical example, we will find the best-fit line using the least-squares approach for the set of observations in Figure A.1. Table A.1 summarizes the necessary computations. The resulting best-fit line is illustrated in Figure A.4. To obtain a specific forecast, we would merely plug the estimated pig crop value into the regression equation. For example, if the December–May pig crop estimate were 51 million, the forecast for hog slaughter in the subsequent June–November period would be 50.51 million ($-3.6279 + (1.0615 * 51)$).

Reliability of the Regression Forecast

It is essential to understand that, by itself, a point price projection derived from a regression equation is of little use. One must first consider how well the model describes the data and the expected variability of forecasts based upon the regression equation. We can get an intuitive answer to this question by examining how closely the observations fall to the fitted regression line (Figure A.4).

But we should be able to assess a model's accuracy more precisely. Simply examining a scatter chart leaves many unanswered questions. How close do the observations have to be to the regression line for the model to be judged satisfactory? How do we check whether a model provides an undistorted representation of the real world? How closely can we expect the model's forecasts to anticipate actual results?

TABLE A.1 Computation of Least-Squares Best-Fit Line

Year	Pig Crop (Dec–May, millions) X_i	Hog Slaughter (Jun–Nov, millions) Y_i	X_i^2	X_iY_i
1995	50.077	48.294	2,507.71	2,418.40
1996	47.888	45.453	2,293.26	2,176.64
1997	48.394	46.201	2,341.98	2,235.85
1998	52.469	50.929	2,753.00	2,672.20
1999	51.519	51.111	2,654.21	2,633.20
2000	50.087	49.689	2,508.71	2,488.76
2001	49.472	49.169	2,447.48	2,432.50
2002	50.858	50.709	2,586.54	2,578.94
2003	50.029	50.758	2,502.90	2,539.38
2004	50.737	52.265	2,574.24	2,651.76
2005	51.33	52.333	2,634.77	2,686.23
2006	52.242	53.150	2,729.23	2,776.68
2007	54.266	55.569	2,944.80	3,015.52
2008	57.019	57.648	3,251.17	3,287.05
2009	57.564	57.391	3,313.61	3,303.68
2010	56.326	55.681	3,172.62	3,136.26
2011	57.118	56.264	3,262.47	3,213.69
2012	57.818	57.478	3,342.92	3,323.23
2013	57.02	55.914	3,251.28	3,188.23
2014	53.821	52.418	2,896.70	2,821.17
	$\Sigma X_i = 1{,}056.05$	$\Sigma Y_i = 1{,}048.42$	$\Sigma X_i^2 = 55{,}969.58$	$\Sigma X_iY_i = 55{,}579.37$

$b = (20 * 55{,}579.37) - (1{,}056.05 * 1{,}048.42) / (20 * 55{,}969.58) - (55{,}969.58)^2 = 1.0615$

$a = (1{,}048.42/20) - 1.0615 * (1{,}056.05/20) = -3.6279$

$Y_i = -3.6279 + 1.0615X_i$

Another problem with the graphic analysis depicted in Figure A.4 is that it just isn't feasible for regression equations that include two or more explanatory variables—a situation that is the rule rather than the exception.

These considerations lead us to one of the primary benefits of regression analysis: The approach permits a wide variety of scientific tests of a model's adequacy. Such tests are essential to the successful application of regression analysis. An understanding of these tests, as opposed to a mere cookbook application, requires a synopsis of some key statistical concepts. Appendix B provides an abridged crash course in elementary statistics. We will return to regression analysis in Appendix C.

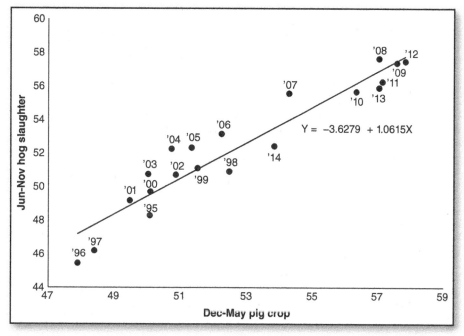

FIGURE A.4 Best-Fit Line for June–November Hog Slaughter vs. December–May Pig Crop

A Review of Elementary Statistics

The theory of probabilities is at bottom nothing but common sense reduced to Calculus.

—Pierre Simon de Laplace

▇ Measures of Dispersion

For any data series there are two basic types of descriptive statistics: (1) some measure of central tendency (e.g., arithmetic mean, median, mode, geometric mean, harmonic mean); and (2) a measure of dispersion. The intuitive meaning of dispersion is quite clear. For example, consider the following two sets of numbers:

A. 30, 53, 3, 22, 16, 104, 71, 41
B. 42, 40, 42, 46, 39, 45, 42, 44

Although both series have the same arithmetic mean, it is clear that series A would have a high dispersion measure and series B a low dispersion measure. The concept of dispersion is extremely important in forecasting. For example, if we were told there was a ninth number in each of the series that was not listed, we would be far more certain about our guess being close to the mark in series B than in series A. Thus, it is extremely desirable to have a measure that describes the dispersion of a set of numbers, much as the mean describes the central tendency of a set of numbers.

The basic question is: How do we measure dispersion? In a sense, we have already answered this question. Deriving a dispersion measure for a set of numbers is entirely analogous to the computation of a single deviation measure for a group of points from a line. In the case of a set of numbers, the deviations would be measured relative to some central point. For theoretical reasons, the arithmetic mean is the most desirable measure of central tendency. To derive a single deviation measure for a set of numbers, we cannot simply add the individual deviations, because they will tend to cancel each other out. Once again, two possible solutions are the sum of the absolute deviations or the sum of the squared deviations. The latter measure is far more convenient to use and is preferable for theoretical reasons.

However, the sum of the squared deviations is not a representative measure of dispersion since it is dependent on how many numbers are in the series. For example, if series B contained 1,000 sets of the indicated string of numbers, the sum of the squared deviations for the series would be greater than the corresponding figure for series A. This measure is therefore quite misleading because series A would still reflect greater dispersion by any intuitive definition of that term. This problem is solved simply by dividing the sum of the squared deviations by the number of items in the series. The resulting measure is called the *variance,* which can be expressed as:

$$\text{Variance} = \sigma^2 = \frac{\sum_{i=1}^{N}(X_i - \bar{X})^2}{N}$$

where $\bar{X}$ = mean
X_i = individual data values
N = number of observations

Note the variance is not stated in the same units as the original data series. For example, if the units of the original set of numbers were tons, the variance would be expressed in tons squared.

The dispersion measure can be expressed in the same units as the original data series by simply taking the square root of the variance. This computation also makes intuitive sense since it reverses the original squaring process applied to the individual terms. The resulting figure is called the *standard deviation* and can be expressed as:

$$\text{Standard deviation} = \sigma = \sqrt{\frac{\sum_{i=1}^{N}(X_i - \bar{X})^2}{N}}$$

In a rough sense, the standard deviation is a type of average deviation (of the individual data points from the mean), in which the data points that are further from the mean have greater than proportionate impact on the calculation. (This greater weight is the result of the squaring process.)[1]

---

[1] These definitions for the variance and standard deviation are applicable when the entire set of data elements is known, in which case the set of numbers is called the *population*. However, in actual practice, available sets of numbers will often represent *samples* from a population. In fact, this assumption appears to be implied for series A and B. For reasons that will be explained later, the variance and standard deviation calculations for a sample are slightly different. Specifically, for samples, the variance and standard deviation would be expressed as follows:

$$\text{Variance (sample)} = s^2 = \frac{\sum_{i=1}^{n}(X_i - \bar{X})^2}{n-1}$$

$$\text{Standard deviation (sample)} = s = \sqrt{\frac{\sum_{i=1}^{n}(X_i - \bar{X})^2}{n-1}}$$

where n = number of observations in the sample.

TABLE B.1 Standard Deviation Computations

Series A: 30, 53, 3, 22, 16, 104, 71, 41			Series B: 42, 40, 42, 46, 39, 45, 42, 44		
X_i	$X_i - \bar{X}$	$(X_i - \bar{X})^2$	X_i	$X_i - \bar{X}$	$(X_i - \bar{X})^2$
30	−12.5	156.25	42	−0.5	0.25
53	+10.5	110.25	40	−2.5	6.25
3	−39.5	1,560.25	42	−0.5	0.25
22	−20.5	420.25	46	+3.5	12.25
16	−26.5	702.25	39	−3.5	12.25
104	+61.5	3,782.25	45	+2.5	6.25
71	+28.5	812.25	42	−0.5	0.25
41	−1.5	2.25	44	+1.5	2.25

$\sum_{i=1}^{n} X_i = 340$		$\sum_{i=1}^{N}\left(X_i - \bar{X}\right)^2 = 7,546.00$	$\sum_{i=1}^{N} X_i = 340$		$\sum_{i=1}^{N}\left(X_i - \bar{X}\right)^2 = 40.00$

$$\bar{X} = \frac{\sum X_i}{N} = 42.5 \qquad\qquad \bar{X} = \frac{\sum X_i}{N} = 42.5$$

$$\text{Variance} = \sigma^2 = \frac{\sum_{i=1}^{N}\left(X_i - \bar{X}\right)^2}{N} = \frac{7,546}{8} = 943.25 \qquad \text{Variance} = \sigma^2 = \frac{\sum_{i=1}^{N}\left(X_i - \bar{X}\right)^2}{N} = \frac{40}{8} = 5$$

$$\text{Standard deviation} = \sigma = \sqrt{\frac{\sum_{i=1}^{n}\left(X_i - \bar{X}\right)^2}{N}} = 30.712 \qquad \text{Standard deviation} = \sigma = \sqrt{\frac{\sum_{i=1}^{n}\left(X_i - \bar{X}\right)^2}{N}} = 2.236$$

Note: These computations apply to a population. For samples, the computation would be slightly different (see footnote 1).

The greater the standard deviation, the greater the degree of variability in a set of numbers. To get a better sense of this statistic, Table B.1 calculates the standard deviation for series A and B. It is essential to have a clear understanding of the standard deviation before proceeding, since this term will play a pivotal role in defining the *normal distribution* and in probability testing.

■ Probability Distributions

A *random variable* is a variable with a value that depends on a statistical experiment in which each outcome (or range of outcomes) has a specific probability of occurrence. For example, if trading decisions were based on the toss of a coin, the number of winning trades, excluding commissions, in 10 trades would be a random variable. A *probability distribution* indicates the probability associated with different values of a random variable. Figure B.1 indicates the probabilities for different numbers of gains in 10 trades if trading decisions are based on chance. The highest probability of 0.246 is associated with five gains in 10 trades. The probability of alternative events decreases as the number of gains moves

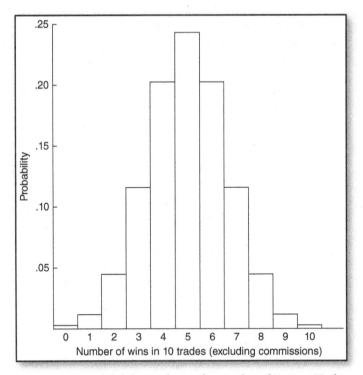

FIGURE B.1 Probability Distribution for Number of Winning Trades in 10 Trades If Decision Based on Chance

away from five. The probability of 10 out of 10 winning trades is only 0.001. (By definition, the sum of all the probabilities equals 1.0.)

This example of a probability distribution was based on a *discrete* variable, which is a variable that can take on only certain fixed values—for example, we can have six winning trades or seven winning trades, but not 6.3 winning trades. Frequently, we will be concerned with random variables that are *continuous,* which are variables that can assume any value. An example of a continuous variable would be the reaction time of drivers in stepping on the brake when a stop sign is flashed on a screen in a simulation test. For continuous variables, the probability of each event (e.g., probability of the reaction time being exactly 0.41237 second) is not meaningful or even definable. Instead, the relevant consideration is the probability of events in a certain range (e.g., the probability of a reaction time between 0.4 and 0.5 seconds).

A *continuous distribution* describes the probability associated with a continuous random variable. The total area under a continuous distribution curve will equal 1.0 (100 percent) since there is 100 percent probability an event will take on some value, and the sum of all the probabilities of mutually exclusive events cannot exceed 100 percent.[2] A continuous distribution is characterized by the

---

[2] *Mutually exclusive* means that only one event can occur at a time. For example, in the reaction time test, only one time value can be associated with any given test.

fact that the area between any two given values is equal to the probability the random variable will fall in the interval between these two values. For example, in Figure B.2 the total area under the curve would be equal to 1.0, and the shaded area would indicate the probability of the continuous variable having a value between X_1 and X_2. If the shaded area represented 20 percent of the total area under the curve, the probability of the continuous variable falling in a range between X_1 and X_2 would be 20 percent.

Figure B.2 represents the familiar bell-shaped *normal distribution* curve. Empirically, the normal distribution has been shown to serve as a good approximation of the probability distribution for an extremely wide range of random variables. For example, it can be demonstrated that as the number of trades in Figure B.1 increases, the distribution will begin to approach a normal distribution. For a large number of trades (e.g., 1,000), the probability distribution would be almost exactly represented by a normal distribution. Probabilities for continuous random variables such as reaction time frequently will also be well described by the normal distribution.

Figure B.3 shows how the probability of an event falling within a fixed interval increases as the interval moves closer to the mean. The probability of an event occurring in the range X_1–X_2 (i.e., the area under the curve between X_1 and X_2) is greater than the probability of an event in the range

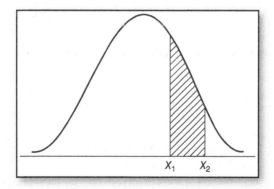

FIGURE B.2   Continuous Probability Distribution

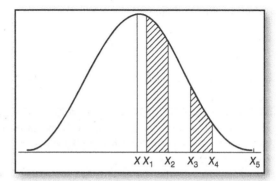

FIGURE B.3   Fixed Interval Probability Increases with Proximity to Mean

$X_3 - X_4$. Note the probability of an event occurring in a range distant from the mean is near zero, even if it is a very broad range. For example, in Figure B.3, the probability of the variable having a value between X_5 and infinity is near zero.

The formula for the normal distribution is:

$$Y = \frac{1}{\sigma\sqrt{2\pi}}\, e^{-(1/2)\left[(X-\bar{X})/\sigma\right]^2}$$

This seemingly intimidating formula is not as frightening as it might initially appear. Like any other equation describing a relationship between X and Y, it tells us the value of Y given a value for X. The key point to realize about this equation is the precise relationship between X and Y will be determined entirely by the mean of $X(\bar{X})$ and the variance of X (σ).[3] All the other values in the formula are constants ($\pi = 3.1416$, $e = 2.7183$). Thus, once $\bar{X}$ and σ are determined, the normal distribution for a particular set of numbers is completely defined. Note the value of Y will reach a maximum when X equals $\bar{X}$, at which point the formula reduces to

$$Y = \frac{1}{\sigma\sqrt{2\pi}}$$

At any other value of X, the value of the term

$$\frac{1}{2}\left(\frac{X-\bar{X}}{\sigma}\right)^2$$

will be greater than 0, resulting in a lower value of Y. The further any given value X is from $\bar{X}$, the larger this term and the lower the value of Y.[4]

Because the normal distribution will differ for any given set of values for $\bar{X}$ and σ, it is desirable to choose a given set of values upon which to base a standard table of probability values. For simplicity, this table is based on $\bar{X} = 0$ and $\sigma = 1$. To be able to use this standard table, we have to transform the numbers in a series into Z values, where

$$Z_i = \frac{X_i - \bar{X}}{\sigma_x}$$

---

[3] $\bar{X}$ and σ are parameters. As explained in footnote 2 in Appendix A, a parameter can be thought of as a hybrid between a variable and a constant. In this instance, $\bar{X}$ and σ will assume different values for different distributions of X (i.e., different sets of numbers); however, for any given distribution (set of numbers), $\bar{X}$ and σ will be fixed (i.e., constants).

[4] e^{-k} is equivalent to $1/e^k$, therefore the larger $1/2[(X-\bar{X})/\sigma]^2$ gets, the smaller the value of $e^{-(1/2)[(X-\bar{X})/\sigma]^2}$, hence the smaller the value of Y.

and X_i is a given value in a set of numbers.[5] The numerator of this term is the distance of the given number from the mean; the denominator is the standard deviation of the set of numbers. Thus, the Z value is simply the distance of a given value from the mean in terms of standard deviations. For example, if the mean of a set of numbers is 10, and the standard deviation is 2, the Z value for a

[5] The fact that the distribution of Z values will always have a mean equal to zero ($\bar{Z} = 0$) and a standard deviation equal to 1 ($\sigma_z = 1$) given that any set of X values is easy to demonstrate:

$$Z = \frac{X_i - \bar{X}}{\sigma_X} \qquad \bar{Z} = \frac{\displaystyle\sum_{i=1}^{N}\left(\dfrac{X_i - \bar{X}}{\sigma_X}\right)}{N} = \frac{\dfrac{1}{\sigma_X}\left(\displaystyle\sum_{i=1}^{N} X_i - \sum_{i=1}^{N}\bar{X}\right)}{N}$$

Keeping in mind that $\bar{X} = \left(\displaystyle\sum_{i=1}^{N} X_i\right)/N$.

$$\bar{Z} = \frac{1}{N\sigma_X}\left(N\bar{X} - N\bar{X}\right) = 0$$

The standard deviation of Z (σ_z) can be expressed as

$$\sigma_z = \sqrt{\frac{\displaystyle\sum_{i=1}^{N}\left(Z_i - \bar{Z}\right)^2}{N}}$$

But we have just proved that $\bar{Z} = 0$, so

$$\sigma_Z = \sqrt{\frac{\displaystyle\sum_{i=1}^{N} Z_i^2}{N}} = \sqrt{\frac{\displaystyle\sum_{i=1}^{n}\left(\dfrac{X_i - \bar{X}}{\sigma_X}\right)^2}{N}} = \sqrt{\frac{1}{\sigma_x^2}\cdot\frac{\displaystyle\sum_{i=1}^{N}\left(X_i - \bar{X}\right)^2}{N}}$$

$$\sigma_Z = \frac{1}{\sigma_X}\sqrt{\frac{\displaystyle\sum_{i=1}^{N}\left(X_i - \bar{X}\right)^2}{N}}$$

Since

$$\sqrt{\frac{\displaystyle\sum_{i=1}^{N}\left(X_i - \bar{X}\right)^2}{N}}$$

is the definition for σ_x,

$$\sigma_Z = \frac{1}{\sigma_X}\cdot\sigma_X = 1$$

number $X = 6$ would be -2 (i.e., X is 2 standard deviations removed from the mean). This standardized distance of a number from its mean will allow us to gauge the probabilities of a given value being higher or lower than a given number.

■ Reading the Normal Curve (Z) Table

Remember, a Z value indicates how many standard deviations a given observation lies above or below its mean, with the sign indicating whether the number is above or below the mean. Table B.2 lists the probabilities corresponding to different Z values. These numbers represent the probabilities of an observation of a normally distributed random variable falling in the range between zero and the given Z value. For example, there is a .4332 (43.32 percent) probability the Z value will be between zero and $+1.5$. To determine the probability of a Z value being less than a given number, simply add .50 (the probability of a value below the mean) to the probability listed in Table B.2. Thus, the probability of a Z value less than $1.5 = .9332$. The probability of a Z value greater than 1.5 would be .0668 (i.e., $1 - .9332$). To find the probability of a Z value being more than $+1.5$ or less than -1.5 (in other words, more than 1.5 standard deviations removed from the mean), we would merely double this figure and get .1336.

From Table B.2, we can verify that for a normal distribution there is a .6826 probability that an observation will fall within one standard deviation of the mean, a .9554 probability that it will be within two standard deviations, and a .9974 probability that it will be within three standard deviations.

An example may help clarify some of these ideas. ABC is a brokerage house that has a long-running program to train new brokers. In addition to interviews, the firm administers a test to decide which candidates will be accepted into the program. After testing thousands of candidates over the years they have found the scores are approximately normally distributed, with a mean of 70 and a standard deviation of 10. Given these facts, try the following questions:

1. What is the probability a new applicant taking the test will get a score above 92 (assuming we are not given any additional information about the person)?
2. What is the probability the applicant will get a score between 50 and 80?

Give it a try before reading on.

Answers

1. $Z = \dfrac{X - \bar{X}}{\sigma}$

$$Z = \frac{92 - 70}{10} = 2.2$$

Checking Table B.2, we see that the probability value corresponding to $Z = 2.2$ is .4861. Thus, there is a .9861 probability that a candidate will score 92 or less, or equivalently, a .0139 (1.39 percent) probability that the score will be higher.

An entry in the table is the proportion under the entire curve that is between $z = 0$ and a positive value of z. Areas for negative values of z are obtained by symmetry.

Second Decimal Place of Z

z	.00	.01	.02	.03	.04	.05	.06	.07	.08	.09
0.0	.0000	.0040	.0080	.0120	.0160	.0199	.0239	.0279	.0319	.0359
0.1	.0398	.0438	.0478	.0517	.0557	.0596	.0636	.0675	.0714	.0753
0.2	.0793	.0832	.0871	.0910	.0948	.0987	.1026	.0164	.1103	.1141
0.3	.1179	.1217	.1255	.1293	.1331	.1368	.1406	.1443	.1480	.1517
0.4	.1554	.1591	.1628	.1664	.1700	.1736	.1772	.1808	.1844	.1879
0.5	.1915	.1950	.1985	.2019	.2054	.2088	.2123	.2157	.2190	.2224
0.6	.2257	.2291	.2324	.2357	.2389	.2422	.2454	.2486	.2517	.2549
0.7	.2580	.2611	.2642	.2673	.2703	.2734	.2764	.2794	.2823	.2852
0.8	.2881	.2910	.2939	.2967	.2995	.3023	.3051	.3078	.3106	.3133
0.9	.3159	.3186	.3212	.3238	.3264	.3289	.3315	.3340	.3365	.3389
1.0	.3413	.3438	.3461	.3485	.3508	.3531	.3554	.3577	.3599	.3621
1.1	.3643	.3665	.3686	.3708	.3729	.3749	.3770	.3790	.3810	.3830
1.2	.3849	.3869	.3888	.3907	.3925	.3944	.3962	.3980	.3997	.4015
1.3	.4032	.4049	.4066	.4082	.4099	.4115	.4131	.4147	.4162	.4177
1.4	.4192	.4207	.4222	.4236	.4251	.4265	.4279	.4292	.4306	.4319
1.5	.4332	.4345	.4357	.4370	.4382	.4394	.4406	.4418	.4429	.4441
1.6	.4452	.4463	.4474	.4484	.4495	.4505	.4515	.4525	.4535	.4545
1.7	.4554	.4564	.4573	.4582	.4591	.4599	.4608	.4616	.4625	.4633
1.8	.4641	.4649	.4656	.4664	.4671	.4678	.4686	.4693	.4699	.4706
1.9	.4713	.4719	.4726	.4732	.4738	.4744	.4750	.4756	.4761	.4767
2.0	.4772	.4778	.4783	.4788	.4793	.4798	.4803	.4808	.4812	.4817
2.1	.4821	.4826	.4830	.4834	.4838	.4842	.4846	.4850	.4854	.4857
2.2	.4861	.4864	.4868	.4871	.4875	.4878	.4881	.4884	.4887	.4890
2.3	.4893	.4896	.4898	.4901	.4904	.4906	.4909	.4911	.4913	.4916
2.4	.4918	.4920	.4922	.4925	.4927	.4929	.4931	.4932	.4934	.4936
2.5	.4938	.4940	.4941	.4943	.4945	.4946	.4948	.4949	.4951	.4952
2.6	.4953	.4955	.4956	.4957	.4959	.4960	.4961	.4962	.4963	.4964
2.7	.4965	.4966	.4967	.4968	.4969	.4970	.4971	.4972	.4973	.4974
2.8	.4974	.4975	.4976	.4977	.4977	.4978	.4979	.4979	.4980	.4981
2.9	.4981	.4982	.4982	.4983	.4984	.4984	.4985	.4985	.4986	.4986
3.0	.4987	.4987	.4987	.4988	.4988	.4989	.4989	.4989	.4990	.4990

Source: Donald J. Koosis, *Business Statistics* (New York, NY: John Wiley & Sons, 1997). Copyright © 1997 by John Wiley & Sons; reprinted by permission.

2. This question is not as easy. It would be incorrect to proceed as follows:

$$Z = \frac{80 - 50}{10} = 3.0$$

Why? Because Z values must be measured relative to the mean. So the solution requires two steps: First, the probability of getting a score between 70 and 80 must be calculated. This can be done as follows:

$$Z = \frac{80 - 70}{10} = 1.0$$

Checking Table B.2, we find that this probability equals .3413. Next, to calculate the probability of a score between 50 and 70, we proceed as follows:

$$Z = \frac{50 - 70}{10} = -2.0$$

This corresponds to a probability of .4772. Thus, the probability of a score between 50 and 80 is the sum of these two values:

.3413 + .4772 = .8185 (81.85 percent)

■ Populations and Samples

If a data set contains all possible observations, it is called a *population*. If it consists of only a portion of these observations, it is called a *sample*. Whether a data set represents a population or a sample depends on the intended use. For example, if we are interested in the average income of all the employed people in Manhattan, the population would consist of all workers in Manhattan, and a sample would be only a portion of those workers. However, if we wish to estimate the average income of all U.S. workers, all workers in Manhattan would be a sample.

Intuitively, it should be clear that all workers in Manhattan would not be a very good sample of all U.S. workers. The problem in this case is that the sample is not representative of the population. In order for a sample to be representative of a population, it must be a *random sample*. A random sampling process is one in which each sample that can be drawn from the population has an equal chance of being selected. Samples that are not random will be *biased*, and a sampling approach that is not random will yield biased estimates. The mean of sample means that are biased will deviate from the population mean. Ironically, for a biased sample, the larger the sample size, the more certain its mean will deviate from the population mean.

In standard terminology, when a measure refers to the population, it is called a *parameter*.[6] A measure that refers to a sample is called a *statistic*. Thus, the standard deviation for a population (σ) is a parameter, and the standard deviation of a sample (s) is a statistic.

---

[6]The meaning of the term *parameter* when used in this context should not be confused with the distinction among *parameters*, *variables*, and *constants* explained in footnote 2 of Appendix A.

Estimating the Population Mean and Standard Deviation from the Sample Statistics

Although the intention of probability testing is to draw inferences about a population, it is usually impractical to collect data for the entire population. In fact, it is frequently impossible, since some populations are infinite. For example, the number of heads in 10 tosses of a coin is an infinite population, since there is no limit to how many times this event can be repeated. In practice, most applications of probability testing, including those in regression analysis, are based on samples rather than on populations.

Thus far, we have avoided the troublesome fact that the population mean and standard deviation are usually not known. We must now turn to the question of how the population mean and standard deviation can be estimated from a sample. It can be demonstrated that the mean of a random sample is an unbiased estimate of the population mean, even if the population does not show a normal distribution. This is equivalent to saying that, on average, the mean of randomly selected samples will equal the population mean. The sample standard deviation, however, is not an unbiased estimate of the population standard deviation, since it tends to slightly underestimate the population parameter. It has been proved that an unbiased estimate of the population variance (once again, variance is the square of the standard deviation) is given by the following equation[7]:

$$s^2 = \frac{\sum \left(X - \bar{X} \right)^2}{n - 1}$$

Taking the square root to translate this variance into a standard deviation, we get

$$s = \sqrt{\frac{\sum \left(X - \bar{X} \right)^2}{n - 1}}$$

This formula is almost identical to the population standard deviation. The only difference is the use of the divisor $n - 1$ instead of N.[8] For large samples, the difference between the formulas will be nearly negligible.

Finally, although the sample mean is an unbiased estimate of the population mean, this does not suggest the sample mean is necessarily close to the population mean. Thus, in addition to the point estimate provided by the sample mean, it would be highly desirable to determine a probable range for the population mean. But before we consider how such a range might be determined, we must first grasp the concept of a sampling distribution.

---

[7] When a standard deviation refers to a sample rather than a population, it is designated by an s instead of σ.
[8] The quantity $n - 1$ is called the number of degrees of freedom. We will define this term later.

■ Sampling Distribution

Fast Fred is a relatively active day trader. Being meticulous—but old-fashioned—at the end of every trading day he records the details of each of his trades in a notebook because he feels doing so helps him better absorb the lessons of his successes and failures in the markets. He eventually realizes that he should have kept his entries in an Excel spreadsheet so he could make calculations on his performance, but being a creature of habit, he continues to enter his trades in his notebook.

Fast Fred varies the number of contracts per trade based on the volatility of the market. He does all his trades using market orders. Recently, he has noticed that his average slippage per trade has increased significantly. (Slippage is the difference between the actual execution price and the market price at the time of trade entry.) Being concerned that his trading approach may no longer be viable, Fast Fred begins monitoring his slippage and notices that it is running around $75 per trade, which he believes is roughly $50 higher than it has averaged in the past. He reasons that if his average net profit (profit after gross commission and slippage) is not at least $60 per trade, it is probably not worthwhile continuing to trade. Unfortunately, he has never bothered to compile summary statistics from his many trades. The thought of going through all his trade records, which he estimates at more than 3,000 for the past year alone, seems worse than just taking his chances. Instead, he decides to draw a sample.

Knowing a little about statistics, Fred creates a random sample of 30 trade entries and calculates the average net profit per trade of this sample is $85 and the standard deviation of the sample is $100. He believes a 95 percent probability of an expected gain of at least $60 per trade is necessary to justify his continued trading activity. (An implicit assumption is that the past mean gain can be used as an estimate of his future expected gain per trade.) Given this information, is Fred's day trading method still viable? Unfortunately, we are not quite ready to answer this question without some additional theoretical background.

We will eventually return to Fred's dilemma, but first let us consider what might happen if Fred took another random sample of all his trades (including those selected for the first sample).[9] The mean net profit per trade of this sample would be different. If he repeated this process many times, Fred would generate list of different means, each corresponding to a different sample. However, it should be apparent these sample means would be much less spread out (i.e., have a smaller standard deviation) than the individual observations in a single sample. As will be detailed shortly, the standard deviation of observations within a sample and the standard deviation of sample means are related in a specific way.

In Figure B.4, hypothetical sample means for the net profit per trade are grouped by class (ranges of $10), with the y axis indicating the frequency of occurrences in each class. If the

---

[9] The assumption that trades that were picked for a prior sample can be picked again is important. Remember, the definition of a random sample is that each sample must have an equal chance of being selected. If the trade entries are not replaced, all possible samples that included any of the original trades will no longer be able to be picked—violating the random sample assumption. If the population is very large, the absence of replacement will not be significant, since combinations involving the selected sample will account for only a minute fraction of all possible combinations.

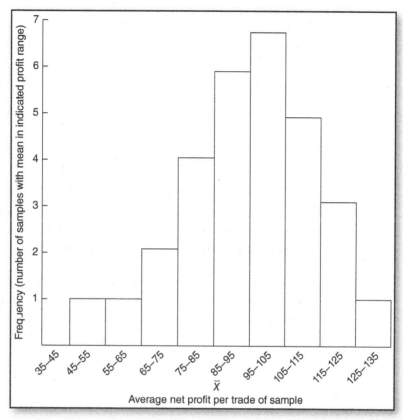

FIGURE B.4 Sampling Distribution of Mean

number of samples was repeated infinitely, and the class sizes were reduced correspondingly, Figure B.4 would approach a continuous curve known as a sampling distribution. The key point to realize is that the sampling distribution is a probability distribution curve related to sample statistics (e.g., sample means). Looking at Figure B.4, we might guess the sampling distribution would be similar to a normal distribution. In fact, if the sample size (i.e., standard size of each sample, not number of samples) is large enough, the sampling distribution will precisely approach a normal distribution.

■ Central Limit Theorem

The preceding illustration leads us to the *central limit theorem,* one of the most important concepts in statistical testing. The central limit theorem can be paraphrased as follows: The distribution of sample means from a population will approach a normal distribution as the sample size increases even if the population is not normally distributed.

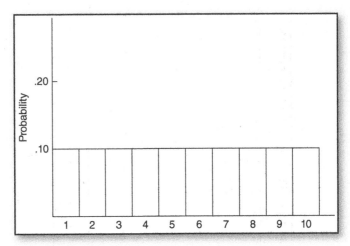

FIGURE B.5   Probability Distribution for Spinning Wheel

To illustrate the central limit theorem, consider the probability distribution for the number that turns up when spinning a wheel numbered 1 through 10. The probability distribution for this random variable is depicted in Figure B.5. Assuming an *honest* wheel, each number has an equal 0.10 probability of turning up. This illustration is obviously well removed from a normal probability

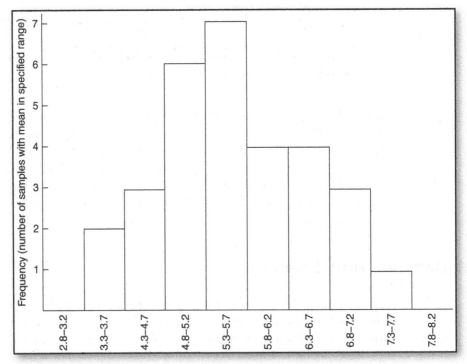

FIGURE B.6   Sampling Distribution of Mean for Spinning Wheel Trials

TABLE B.3 30 Samples on Spinning Wheel ($N = 10$)

Sample Number	Numbers on Wheel (10 spins)										Mean ($\bar{X}$)
1	8	10	5	6	6	2	4	6	8	10	6.5
2	5	7	1	1	4	3	8	9	5	3	4.5
3	8	5	4	10	7	5	5	4	10	10	6.8
4	3	1	8	5	7	1	6	5	9	10	5.5
5	1	9	10	9	3	2	6	5	2	10	5.7
6	9	1	6	2	1	3	5	7	3	1	3.8
7	4	6	6	10	8	4	4	9	5	2	5.8
8	4	10	10	2	4	5	6	3	8	1	5.3
9	8	7	8	10	6	6	10	3	1	9	6.8
10	7	4	9	8	6	9	7	6	8	10	7.4
11	7	9	2	10	3	7	10	5	10	9	7.2
12	6	4	1	3	8	8	1	1	10	7	4.9
13	5	7	2	7	9	6	4	8	8	9	6.5
14	1	2	6	10	3	5	10	9	1	4	5.1
15	7	4	10	6	8	2	4	5	4	3	5.3
16	5	3	1	10	3	10	7	4	7	5	5.5
17	6	2	4	8	8	5	8	5	4	8	5.8
18	6	3	9	2	4	9	9	6	1	10	5.9
19	2	5	3	6	9	3	4	6	6	9	5.3
20	6	2	1	8	6	1	5	2	9	7	4.7
21	4	4	5	7	8	7	5	10	8	6	6.4
22	2	9	10	6	9	1	4	5	3	5	5.4
23	5	4	7	1	10	1	4	7	3	3	4.5
24	9	4	5	2	6	9	6	4	2	2	4.9
25	4	5	8	5	7	6	8	5	9	7	6.4
26	8	2	1	2	8	6	8	7	1	6	4.9
27	7	8	7	6	6	5	1	7	9	6	6.2
28	9	7	7	5	9	4	3	3	2	1	4.9
29	2	3	5	7	9	1	6	1	8	9	5.1
30	4	3	2	9	2	1	8	4	1	6	4.0

distribution. Table B.3 summarizes the means of 30 samples of 10 spins each.[10] These samples are grouped by class in Figure B.6. Note the sample means roughly approximate a normal distribution, even though the parent population bears no resemblance to a normal distribution. Our sample size of 10 was fairly small. If a larger sample size had been used, the approximation of a normal distribution would have been better.

---

[10] These numbers were constructed using a random numbers table, an approach precisely equivalent to the example given.

Before moving on, bear in mind the examples involving repeated samplings were intended only as illustrations to elucidate the concepts of sampling distributions and the central limit theorem. In practice, however, we would always select only a single sample. Accuracy could be improved by simply increasing the size of this single sample.

■ Standard Error of the Mean

The standard deviation of sample means is usually smaller than the standard deviation of any given sample. The standard deviation of sample means is called the standard error of the mean and is represented by the symbol: $\sigma_{\bar{x}}$. (*Standard error* is a frequently used statistical term and can be interpreted as the standard deviation of the sampling distribution of the given statistic. In this case, the given statistic is the mean. Other types of standard error related to regression analysis are considered in Appendix C.) Given a distribution with a standard deviation σ, it can be proved that a random sample of size n has the following standard error of the mean:[11]

$$\sigma_{\bar{x}} = \frac{\sigma}{\sqrt{n}}$$

Of course, we usually will not know the value of σ and will have to use s as an unbiased estimate of σ. (Recall that the two are very similar for all but very small samples.) Thus, in practice we would use

$$\sigma_{\bar{x}} = \frac{s}{\sqrt{n}}$$

For example, if the standard deviation of the sample (s) is 20 and the sample size is 25, then $\sigma_{\bar{x}}$ would equal 4. The larger the sample, the smaller $\sigma_{\bar{x}}$. However, note that the accuracy of the sample increases much more slowly than the sample size. For instance, a 25-fold increase in the sample size would reduce $\sigma_{\bar{x}}$ only by a factor of 5.

■ Confidence Intervals

Recall that assuming a data set is normally distributed, the probability of an observation falling within a given range can be determined from Table B.2. For example, the $\pm Z$ values that include 95 percent of observations are ± 1.96, since 2.5 percent of the distribution lies above $+1.96$ and 2.5 percent below -1.96. (Table B.2 indicates that .4750 of the area lies between $Z = 0$ and $Z = +1.96$; so, given

---

[11] This formula applies to infinite populations or samples in which the sample size is relatively small compared with the population. Although we will not be concerned with such cases, the precise formula when the sample size represents a significant percent of the population is

$$(\sigma / \sqrt{n})\sqrt{(N - n)/(N - 1)}$$

where n = sample size and N = population size.

the symmetry of the normal distribution, 95 percent of observations could be expected to fall within the range of -1.96 to $+1.96$.)

The formula for the Z value was formerly stated as

$$Z = \frac{X - \bar{X}}{\sigma}$$

In the case of a distribution of sample means (which the central limit theorem assures us will approximate a normal distribution), we have

$$Z = \frac{\bar{X} - \mu}{\sigma_{\bar{x}}}$$

where $\bar{X}$ = sample mean

μ = population mean

$\sigma_{\bar{x}}$ = standard error of the mean (i.e., the standard deviation of sample means)

From the previous section, we know that $\sigma_{\bar{x}}$ can be approximated by $s/\sqrt{n}$. Thus,

$$Z = \frac{\bar{X} - \mu}{s/\sqrt{n}}$$

or

$$\mu = \bar{X} - Z \cdot \frac{s}{\sqrt{n}}$$

If we were interested in the area that enclosed 95 percent of sample means, $Z = \pm 1.96$, the previous formula could be expressed as

$$\mu = \bar{X} \pm 1.96 \frac{s}{\sqrt{n}}$$

$$\bar{X} - 1.96 \cdot \frac{s}{\sqrt{n}} < \mu < \bar{X} + 1.96 \cdot \frac{s}{\sqrt{n}}$$

This calculation can be interpreted as follows. In repeated samplings the true population mean could be expected to lie between $\bar{X} - 1.96 \cdot s/\sqrt{n}$ and $\bar{X} + 1.96 \cdot s/\sqrt{n}$ 95 percent of the time. Such a range is called a *confidence interval*.

The confidence interval can be used to test hypotheses about the population mean.[12] The standard approach involves testing the null hypothesis, which states there is no difference between the sample mean and the hypothesized population mean. Typically, we want to reject the null hypothesis, or, equivalently, demonstrate the sample mean is different from the hypothesized population mean at

------

[12] This discussion refers to population and sample means. However, it applies more generally to any sample statistic used to test an hypothesis about the population parameter.

some specified level of significance. The most commonly used level of significance is 0.05 (5 percent), which means that the sample mean lies outside the 95 percent confidence interval of the hypothesized population mean.[13] A statistical rejection of the null hypothesis demonstrates, with a probability at the stated level, that the sample could not have been drawn from a parent population with the hypothesized mean.

Sometimes, however, it is more critical to minimize the chance of rejecting the null hypothesis when in fact it is true (i.e., accepting that the sample mean is statistically different from the hypothesized population mean when it is not).[14] In such a case we might use a 0.01 level of significance. Of course, there is a tradeoff, because the lower the value for the level of significance (the more stringent the test), the wider (less specific) the confidence interval.

■ The *t*-Test

The *Z*-test is appropriate when the sampling distribution is normal, a condition that can be assumed true when the sample size is large.[15] However, for small samples the sampling distribution is better approximated by the *t*-distribution, and hence the *t*-test is more accurate. The *t* distribution is very similar to the normal distribution for all but very small samples. As the sample size increases, the normal and *t* distributions become increasingly similar. For example, at a 0.05 level of significance for a one-tailed test, the *t* value is 10 percent greater than the *Z* value for a sample of 10, 3 percent greater for a sample of 30, and 1 percent greater for a sample of 100. For an infinite sample, the normal and *t* distributions will be identical.

Similar to the standardized normal distribution, the *t* distribution is symmetrical, with a mean equal to zero and a standard deviation equal to 1. The formula for the *t* value of a sample statistic (e.g., mean) is totally analogous to the *Z* value:

$$t = \frac{\bar{X} - \mu}{s/\sqrt{n}}$$

[13] This statement assumes that there is no a priori reason for assuming a value above or below the hypothesized mean. Such a situation is referred to as a two-tailed test. If, however, there is reason to believe that the sample mean would be above the null hypothesis population mean, the relevant question would be whether the sample mean was significantly *higher* than the population mean, not whether it was significantly *different from* the population mean. Such a situation is called a *one-tailed test*. The 0.05 significance level for a one-tailed test would correspond to the probability that a value was outside the 90 percent confidence interval. The distinction between one-tailed and two-tailed tests is discussed in greater detail in subsequent sections.

[14] An incorrect decision of this type is called a *type 1 error*. The probability of making a type 1 error is indicated by the level of significance. Accepting the null hypothesis when it is false is called a *type 2 error*. It should be stressed that the acceptance of the null hypothesis does not prove it is true, but only indicates that the null hypothesis could not be rejected at the stated level of significance. Thus, the acceptance of the null hypothesis does not prove that the sample was drawn from a population with the hypothesized mean, but rather that the sample and hypothesized population means are not statistically different at the specified level of significance.

[15] The meaning of *large* depends on the distribution of the underlying population. Roughly speaking, 30 is usually sufficiently large.

The t-test uses the t distribution for probability testing and is entirely analogous to the Z-test.[16]

The specific t distribution will depend on the *degrees of freedom (df)*—the number of observations (sample size) minus the number of constraints. For example, in tests of the sampling distribution of the mean, $df = n - 1$. There is one constraint, since given the mean, only $n - 1$ terms can be freely assigned. To see this, assume we have 10 observations with a mean of 50. If the sum of the first nine items equals 400, the value of the last term must be 100. Thus we say there are only $n - 1$ *df.* In a two-variable regression line, there are two parameters: *a* and *b.* Once these are fixed, only $n - 2$ terms can be assigned freely. Thus, t-tests of regression coefficients in the two-variable model are based on $n - 2$ degrees of freedom.

The application of the t-test is almost totally analogous to the Z-test. The only difference between the two is that the specific value used in the t-test depends on the degrees of freedom. Table B.4 provides a list of t values. The appropriate row is determined by the number of degrees of freedom, and the column by the desired level of significance in testing. Given the great similarity between the Z-test and the t-test, it would probably be redundant to provide a detailed description of the use of Table B.4. However, to check that you understand how to use this table, try the following questions:

1. If you are testing the hypothesis that the population mean is not significantly *greater than* the null hypothesis, what value must t exceed to reject this hypothesis at a 0.05 level of significance (i.e., to conclude that the true population mean is significantly greater than the null hypothesis)? The sample size is 20.

2. If you are testing the hypothesis that the population mean is not significantly *different from* the null hypothesis, what value must t exceed in order to reject this hypothesis at the 0.05 level of significance (i.e., to conclude that the true population mean is significantly different from the null hypothesis)? Once again, the sample size is 20.

3. a. Given a four-unit sample with a mean equal to 40 and a standard deviation equal to 10, what is the 95 percent confidence interval for the population mean?
   b. Now try it for a sample size equal to 30.

Answers

1. 1.729. For $df = 19$, Table B.4 indicates that there is only a 5 percent probability that this level will be exceeded. This type of test is called a one-tailed test.

2. 2.093. A 5 percent probability of being significantly different from the null hypothesis is equivalent to determining the t values that will define the boundaries for the upper and lower 2.5 percent of the distribution. This is an example of a two-tailed test.

---

[16] The astute reader may well wonder why we bother describing the Z-test in the first place, since the t-test would be more accurate for samples. The reason is that the mathematics underlying the t distribution assume that the population of the data series is normally distributed. This is a much stronger assumption than was necessary for the application of the Z-test, which only required that the sampling distribution be normal—a condition that the central limit theorem guaranteed would be approximately fulfilled for a sufficiently large sample. Thus, the Z-test provides the justification for probability testing of non-normally distributed populations. This is a critical fact, since the assumption of a normally distributed population is often not warranted.

TABLE B.4   Student's *t* Distribution

The first column lists the number of degrees of freedom (*k*). The headings of the other columns give probabilities (*P*) for *t* to exceed the entry value. Use symmetry for negative *t* values.

df	.10	.05	.025	.01	.005
			P		
1	3.078	6.314	12.706	31.821	63.657
2	1.886	2.920	4.303	6.965	9.925
3	1.638	2.353	3.182	4.541	5.841
4	1.533	2.132	2.776	3.747	4.604
5	1.476	2.015	2.571	3.365	4.032
6	1.440	1.943	2.447	3.143	3.707
7	1.415	1.895	2.365	2.998	3.499
8	1.397	1.860	2.306	2.896	3.355
9	1.383	1.833	2.262	2.821	3.250
10	1.372	1.812	2.228	2.764	3.169
11	1.363	1.796	2.201	2.718	3.106
12	1.356	1.782	2.179	2.681	3.055
13	1.350	1.771	2.160	2.650	3.012
14	1.345	1.761	2.145	2.624	2.977
15	1.341	1.753	2.131	2.602	2.947
16	1.337	1.746	2.120	2.583	2.921
17	1.333	1.740	2.110	2.567	2.898
18	1.330	1.734	2.101	2.552	2.878
19	1.328	1.729	2.093	2.539	2.861
20	1.325	1.725	2.086	2.528	2.845
21	1.323	1.721	2.080	2.518	2.831
22	1.321	1.717	2.074	2.508	2.819
23	1.319	1.714	2.069	2.500	2.807
24	1.318	1.711	2.064	2.492	2.797
25	1.316	1.708	2.060	2.485	2.787
26	1.315	1.706	2.056	2.479	2.779
27	1.314	1.703	2.052	2.473	2.771
28	1.313	1.701	2.048	2.467	2.763
29	1.311	1.699	2.045	2.462	2.756
30	1.310	1.697	2.042	2.457	2.750
40	1.303	1.684	2.021	2.423	2.704
60	1.296	1.671	2.000	2.390	2.660
120	1.289	1.658	1.980	2.358	2.617
∞	1.282	1.645	1.960	2.326	2.576

Source: Donald J. Koosis, *Business Statistics* (New York, NY: John Wiley & Sons, 1997). Copyright © 1997 by John Wiley & Sons; reprinted by permission.

3. a. $\bar{X} \cdot t \cdot \dfrac{s}{\sqrt{n}} < \mu < \bar{X} + t \cdot \dfrac{s}{\sqrt{n}}$

$40 - 3.182 \cdot \dfrac{10}{\sqrt{4}} < \mu < 40 + 3.182 \cdot \dfrac{10}{\sqrt{4}}$

$24.09 < \mu < 55.91$

   b. $40 - 2.045 \cdot \dfrac{10}{\sqrt{30}} < \mu < 40 + 2.045 \cdot \dfrac{10}{\sqrt{30}}$

$36.27 < \mu < 43.73$

Note how dramatically the larger sample size increases the precision of the estimated confidence interval at the same probability level.

The choice of whether to employ a one-tailed or two-tailed test is not always clear-cut. Normally, a two-tailed test is used when we do not have any preconceived conclusion about the sample. In this case, the probability test for significance must allow for variation in either direction of the statistic being estimated (e.g., population mean). However, sometimes there are strong reasons to believe the sample statistic will be above or below the hypothesized population value—the only question being whether the difference will be significant. This type of situation will often apply in testing the significance of regression coefficients, as will be detailed in Appendix C.

It is finally time to return to our beleaguered day trader. We now see the solution to Fred's dilemma is fairly straightforward. You might wish to return to the section, "Sampling Distribution," to try to determine the correct decision before reading on.

Given the previously stated assumptions, the confidence interval for the expected net profit per trade would be

$$\$85 - 1.699 \cdot \dfrac{\$100}{\sqrt{30}} < \text{expected net profit per trade} < \$85 + 1.699 \cdot \dfrac{\$100}{\sqrt{30}}$$
$$\$53.98 < \text{expected net profit per trade} < \$116.02$$

Thus, it is not possible to say that there is a 95 percent probability the expected net profit per trade is greater than $60.

A few comments are in order. First, a one-tailed test is used because Fred is only concerned about testing the statistical significance of the expected net profit per trade being *greater than* $60 rather than the statistical significance of it being *different from* $60. Second, it should be stressed the confidence interval merely failed to demonstrate with a 95 percent or higher probability that the population expected net profit per trade was more than $60; it in no way proved that this figure was less than $60. Such a proof would have required a sample mean of $28.97 (or less), which would have implied a confidence interval of −$2.05 to $59.99. Third, if Fred had chosen a less-restrictive probability requirement, such as 90 percent, the confidence interval would have been

$$\$85 - 1.311 \cdot \dfrac{\$100}{\sqrt{30}} < \text{expected net profit per trade} < \$85 + 1.311 \cdot \dfrac{\$100}{\sqrt{30}}$$
$$\$61.06 < \text{expected net profit per trade} < \$108.94$$

implying the opposite decision.

The arbitrariness of the preceding example might seem unsettling. However, it should be emphasized the tester is free to choose the criterion that is deemed most important. If Fred is very concerned about continuing to trade when in fact such a decision would be unwarranted by the true population expected net profit per trade (type 1 error), he would choose a low (restrictive) value for the level of significance for testing. If he was less concerned about this type of error, he would use a higher value for the level of significance. In fact, if Fred's primary concern was to avoid terminating his trading when the true expected net profit per trade was actually more than $60, he might continue to trade even if the sample mean was less than $60, constructing a confidence interval to test whether the sample mean was significantly below the hypothesized $60 population mean.

Checking the Significance of the Regression Equation

Factual evidence can never "prove" a hypothesis; it can only fail to disprove it, which is what we generally mean when we say, somewhat inexactly, that the hypothesis is "confirmed" by experience.

—Milton Friedman

■ The Population Regression Line

In Appendix A we discussed the derivation of a regression line on the basis of empirical data. While it was premature to raise the subject then, the fitted line provided by the regression formula is actually a sample of the true population line, which is not known. For example, the regression line relating hog slaughter to the pig crop was a sample of the true relationship between the two variables. The fitted line is a sample because it represents only one realization of an entire series of possible regression lines. The actual regression line realized will depend on measurement error in the data and the unknown influence of variables not included in the model.

The population or true regression model can be expressed as

$$Y_i = a + \beta X_i + e$$

where e is a randomly distributed *error* or *disturbance term*.

Even if we knew the true population regression line, the actual observed values Y_i would still deviate from the predicted level by an amount equal to the error term e. The key reason for this is that a regression equation is a highly simplified model for the behavior of the dependent variable. In reality, the number of hogs slaughtered will depend on many more variables than just the pig crop— for example, the distribution of pigs born during the period, weather conditions, feed prices, and hog prices. Although the magnitude of the disturbance term can be reduced by including other relevant variables in the regression model (this anticipates multiple regression, discussed in Appendix D), it is impossible to introduce enough variables to eliminate these deviations completely.[1]

In addition, even if all relevant variables were included in the model, observations would still deviate from the regression line due to measurement errors. This is not a trivial consideration, since data items that can be precisely measured (e.g., temperature) are by far the exception. Most data can only be estimated from samples (e.g., pig crop, hog slaughter).

Basic Assumptions of Regression Analysis

Appendix A explained that a basic assumption of regression analysis is that the relationship between the dependent variable Y and the independent variable X is linear. Several other key assumptions are related to the error terms:

1. The mean value of the error terms equals zero.
2. The error terms have a constant variance equal to σ^2.
3. The error terms are independent random variables. This assumption has two important implications:
   a. The error terms are uncorrelated.
   b. The error terms and the independent variable X are uncorrelated.
4. The error terms are normally distributed.

These assumptions underlie the various tests used to assess a regression model's reliability.

Testing the Significance of the Regression Coefficients

The empirically derived values of a and b will not equal the population values of α and β except by chance (Figure C.1). It can be shown, however, that a is an unbiased estimate of α and b is an unbiased estimator of β.[2] Actually, it can be demonstrated that a and b are not only unbiased estimators, but

---

[1] Even if all such variables were known and could be precisely determined—two extraordinarily unlikely assumptions—the regression computation would still limit the number of variables that could be introduced, since each additional variable would reduce the degrees of freedom by 1. The significance of the regression equation is reduced as the degrees of freedom decline, and the equation becomes totally trivial when the number of variables is equal to the number of observations.

[2] An unbiased estimator is one that on the average will equal the population parameter. In other words, the mean of the sampling distribution for an unbiased estimator will be equal to the population parameter value.

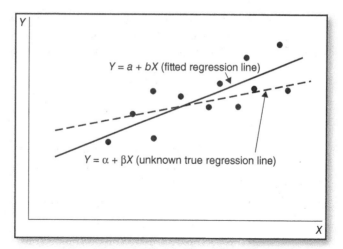

FIGURE C.1 Fitted vs. True Regression Line

that they are the "best linear unbiased estimators" (BLUE). This means that a and b will have the lowest variance (i.e., are the most "efficient") among all possible unbiased *linear* estimators of α and β.

Although b provides an unbiased point estimate for the population regression coefficient β, we would like to know the variability of this estimate. In other words, we are interested in the standard error of b. Recall from Appendix B that the standard error is the standard deviation of a sampling distribution of a statistic. In this case, the relevant statistic is the regression coefficient b.

A diagram can help clarify this point. Figure C.2 shows a distribution with a mean equal to β—the population regression coefficient. Figure C.2 illustrates the distribution that will be formed by the estimated values of b if an infinite number of samples were drawn. In other words, Figure C.2 is a sampling distribution of b. The standard deviation of this distribution is called the standard error of b.

In Appendix B we indicated that the t value for a sample mean could be expressed as

$$t = \frac{\overline{X} - \mu}{s/\sqrt{n}}.$$

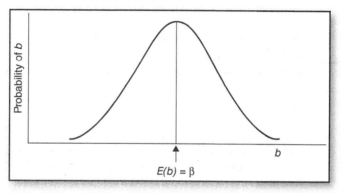

FIGURE C.2 Sampling Distribution of Regression Coefficient

The only difference now is that we are trying to make judgments about the population regression coefficient β from the sample coefficient b, rather than making decisions about the population mean μ from the sample mean $\overline{X}$. In general terms, the t value could be expressed as

$$t = \frac{\text{sample statistic} - \text{population parameter}}{\text{standard error (s.e.) of sample statistic}}$$

In other words, in all applications, the t values indicate the number of standard deviations between the sample statistic and the hypothesized population parameter. A large t value (approximately 2 or more) will indicate there is only a small probability the hypothesized population parameter could be correct. The higher the t value, the less likely the sample came from a parent population with the hypothesized parameter value. In the case of the regression coefficient, the preceding general formula for the t value could be expressed as follows[3]:

$$t = \frac{b - \beta}{\text{s.e.}(b)}$$

Frequently, we will be interested in testing the hypothesis that $\beta = 0$. The reason? In the absence of any information, the best estimate for a variable is the mean, or equivalently, the regression line

$$Y = a + bX$$

where $a = \overline{Y}$
$\quad b = 0$

If, however, the independent variable has some explanatory power, then a regression line with a nonzero slope would offer a better fit to the observations (Y_i). Thus, a key question to be considered in any regression analysis is whether the regression coefficient b is significantly different from zero.

In order to answer this question, we test the assumption that the population regression coefficient $\beta = 0$. In this case the t value reduces to

$$t = \frac{b}{\text{s.e.}(b)}$$

Thus, the t value is the regression coefficient divided by the standard error of the regression coefficient. In other words, the t value indicates how many standard deviations the regression coefficient is from the population coefficient if our hypothesis that $\beta = 0$ were true. If the t value is high (e.g., an

---

[3] Strictly speaking, the distribution of b is not generally normal except in the limit of a large number of observations. Although this implies that the use of the t distribution for calculating confidence intervals is imprecise, from a practical standpoint, the t distribution will yield satisfactory results because the exact boundaries of the confidence interval are not critically dependent on the actual distribution of b.

absolute value approximately greater than 2.0),[4] it suggests that the population regression coefficient is not equal to zero.

In order to apply the preceding formula, we need to know the value of s.e.(b). Given the previously detailed assumptions of regression analysis, it can be demonstrated that

$$\text{s.e.}(b) = \sqrt{\frac{s^2}{\sum_{i=1}^{n}\left(X_i - \overline{X}\right)^2}}$$

where s^2 is an unbiased estimator of the population variance σ^2. (σ^2 is the variance of the error terms, or equivalently, the variance of the observations from the unknown population regression line.[5]) Since the true regression line is not known, σ^2 must be estimated. It can be proved that s^2 is an unbiased estimator of σ^2 where[6]

$$s^2 = \frac{\sum_{i=1}^{n}\left(Y_i - \hat{Y}_i\right)^2}{n - 2} = \frac{\sum_{i=1}^{n}\left(Y_i - a + bX_i\right)^2}{n - 2}$$

where Y_i = the individual observations

$\hat{Y}_i$ = fitted values (i.e., values implied by regression line) at X_i (the values of the independent variable corresponding to the observations Y_i)

Assuming that we are testing the hypothesis $b = 0$, we can now express the regression coefficient t value:

$$t = \frac{b}{\text{s.e.}(b)} = \frac{b}{\dfrac{s}{\sqrt{\sum_{i=1}^{n}\left(X_i - \overline{X}\right)^2}}} = (b)\frac{\sqrt{\sum_{i=1}^{n}\left(X_i - \overline{X}\right)^2}}{\sqrt{\dfrac{\sum_{i=1}^{n}\left(Y_i - \hat{Y}_i\right)^2}{n - 2}}}$$

---

[4] For example, if there are 5 degrees of freedom, a t value of 2.0 would imply that a coefficient at least as much greater than 0 than the one measured would occur only 5 percent of the time, if the true population regression coefficient were equal to 0 (Table B.4). If there are 60 degrees of freedom, such an event would occur only 2.5 percent of the time. These figures assume that a one-tailed test is employed. (See discussion at end of this section.)

[5] Note that error terms refer to the differences between the observed values (Y_i) and the true population regression line (not the fitted regression line). *Terminology note:* The term *error* or *disturbance* describes the difference between an observation and the true population regression line (which is usually not known), while the term *residual* or *deviation* refers to the difference between an observation and the fitted regression line. This theoretical distinction is obscured by the rather commonplace use of error terms to refer to the residuals (the deviations between the observations and the fitted regression line).

[6] The reason for dividing by $n - 2$ is that 2 degrees of freedom are lost because of the constraints imposed by fitting a and b. In other words, for any given set of values for a and b, once $n - 2$ observations are specified, the remaining 2 observations can no longer be freely assigned. In general, the number of degrees of freedom will equal the number of observations minus the total number of parameters (see footnote 2 in Appendix A).

Note the following three facts:

1. The sign of the t value will depend upon the regression coefficient. If X and Y are inversely correlated, the regression coefficient and t will be negative. The sign of the t value is insignificant. We are only concerned with the absolute value of t in testing the significance of the regression coefficient b.
2. As seems intuitively desirable, the s term in the previous equation will ensure that the t value will decline as the sum of the squared deviations increases.
3. The narrower the range of X values for the observations, the lower the t value, since

$$\sum_{i=1}^{n}\left(X_i - \bar{X}\right)^2$$

will be smaller, hence the less reliable the regression coefficient estimate. This concept is illustrated in Figure C.3. Note that when the observations correspond to a small range of the independent variable (Figure C.3a), the influence of the deviations can easily swamp the effect of the slope, and the estimated regression line will not be very reliable. Conversely, when the observations correspond to a wide range of X values (Figure C.3b) the estimated regression line will be far more reliable.

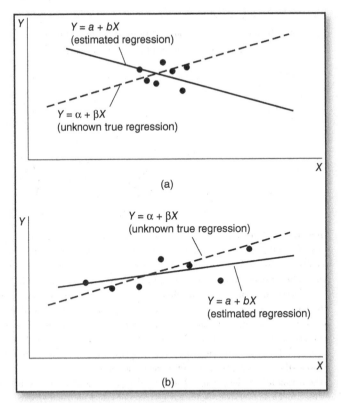

FIGURE C.3 Effect of Range of X_t on Reliability of the Regression Coefficient
Source: T. H. Wonnacott and R. J. Wonnacott. *Econometrics,* John Wiley & Sons, New York, 1980.
Copyright © 1980 by John Wiley & Sons; reprinted by permission.

In testing the significance of the regression coefficient b, it is often more appropriate to use a one-tailed test. The reason for this is that the direction of the relationship between the dependent and explanatory variable(s) is usually known a priori. In such cases it is more relevant to test whether the coefficient value is significantly *greater than* or *less than* zero rather than whether it is significantly *different from* zero. For example, we know that a larger pig crop will result in higher hog slaughter. The only relevant question is if the relationship is statistically significant. Thus, the appropriate question is not whether *b* is significantly different from zero, but whether it is significantly greater than zero, since we do not entertain the possibility that a larger pig crop will result in lower hog slaughter. If, however, we wanted to test whether there was a relationship between the dependent variable and the independent variable, without any bias about the direction of the relationship, a two-tailed test would be used.

The *t*-test can also be applied to the constant or intercept term, *a*. In this case, the *t* value to test the hypothesis that the population regression line intercept is equal to zero would be

$$ t = \frac{a}{\text{s.e.}(a)} = \frac{a}{s \sqrt{\dfrac{1}{n} + \dfrac{\overline{X}^2}{\sum\limits_{i=1}^{n}\left(X_i - \overline{X}\right)^2}}} $$

In practice, there is usually little reason to be overly concerned about the significance of the constant term, and *t*-tests of the constant term can be omitted without any great loss.

As an example of how the *t*-test might be applied, consider the regression equation

$$ Y = 1.1094X - 6.8276 $$

derived in Appendix A. Table C.1 illustrates how to compute the *t* value for the regression coefficient *b*. Although it will not be necessary to compute the *t* value in practice, since the availability of a standard computer regression program is presumed, it is important to have a feel for the computations that underlie the key regression statistics. Checking the *t* value derived in Table C.1, we find that it far exceeds 1.734—the *t* value at a 0.05 level of significance for a one-tailed test with 18*df* (see Table B.4). We conclude the December–May pig crop is indeed significant in explaining the June–November slaughter.

The conclusion that the regression coefficient in the previous example is statistically significant might seem somewhat trivial. After all, the same conclusion would seem to be intuitively obvious by examining the scatter chart for the observations (see Figure A.4). In fact, as a generalization, unless one demonstrates an extraordinarily poor sense of intuition in choosing the independent variable in a *simple regression*, that is, a regression equation with only one explanatory variable, the *t*-test will usually prove significant. However, the *t*-test becomes critically important in evaluating a *multiple regression model*—a regression equation with two or more explanatory variables. In this case, a simple graphic depiction of the regression fit is no longer possible, and the significance of additional variables is often not intuitively apparent. The *t*-test is one of the most important statistical tests in regression analysis and will be considered further in the multiple regression case.

TABLE C.1 (*a*) Computing the *t*-Value for the Regression Coefficient

Year	Jun–Nov Hog Slaughter Y_i	Dec–May Pig Crop X_i	$X_i - \bar{X}$	$(X_i - \bar{X})^2$	Fitted Value $\hat{Y}_i$	Residual $Y_i - \hat{Y}_i$	$(Y_i - \hat{Y}_i)^2$	$Y_i - \bar{Y}$	$(Y_i - \hat{Y})$
1995	50.077	48.2936	−2.726	7.429	49.529	−1.235	1.526	−4.128	17.037
1996	47.888	45.4527	−4.915	24.154	47.205	−1.753	3.071	−6.968	48.559
1997	48.394	46.2009	−4.409	19.437	47.742	−1.541	2.376	−6.220	38.692
1998	52.469	50.9291	−0.334	0.111	52.068	−1.139	1.297	−1.492	2.226
1999	51.519	51.1112	−1.284	1.648	51.060	0.052	0.003	−1.310	1.716
2000	50.087	49.6888	−2.716	7.375	49.539	0.149	0.022	−2.732	7.466
2001	49.472	49.1693	−3.331	11.094	48.887	0.283	0.080	−3.252	10.575
2002	50.858	50.7086	−1.945	3.782	50.358	0.351	0.123	−1.713	2.933
2003	50.029	50.7581	−2.774	7.693	49.478	1.280	1.639	−1.663	2.766
2004	50.737	52.2648	−2.066	4.267	50.229	2.035	4.143	−0.156	0.024
2005	51.33	52.3326	−1.473	2.169	50.859	1.474	2.172	−0.089	0.008
2006	52.242	53.1504	−0.561	0.314	51.827	1.323	1.751	0.729	0.532
2007	54.266	55.5693	1.463	2.141	53.975	1.594	2.540	3.148	9.911
2008	57.019	57.6483	4.216	17.777	56.898	0.751	0.563	5.227	27.323
2009	57.564	57.3914	4.761	22.670	57.476	−0.085	0.007	4.970	24.703
2010	56.326	55.6805	3.523	12.414	56.162	−0.482	0.232	3.259	10.623
2011	57.118	56.2641	4.315	18.622	57.003	−0.739	0.546	3.843	14.768
2012	57.818	57.4775	5.015	25.153	57.746	−0.268	0.072	5.056	25.567
2013	57.02	55.9142	4.217	17.786	56.899	−0.985	0.969	3.493	12.201
2014	53.821	52.4176	1.018	1.037	53.503	−1.085	1.178	−0.004	0.000

$\Sigma Y_i = 1{,}056.05 \quad \Sigma X_i = 1{,}048.42 \qquad \Sigma (X_i - X)^2 = 207.073 \qquad \Sigma (Y_i - Y_i)^2 = 24.311 \qquad \Sigma (Y_i - Y)^2 = 257.630$

$\bar{Y} = 52.803 \quad \bar{X} = 52.421$

Fitted regression line (from Table A.1): $Y = -3.6279 + 1.0615X$

$$ t = \frac{b}{\text{s.e.}(b)} = \frac{b \cdot \sqrt{\sum_{i=1}^{n}(X_i - \bar{X})^2}}{\sqrt{\dfrac{\sum_{i=1}^{n}(Y_i - \hat{Y}_i)^2}{n-2}}} = \frac{1.0615\sqrt{207.073}}{\sqrt{\dfrac{24.311}{18}}} = 13.144 $$

(*b*) Computing r^2

Note: Ignore this section of the table until reaching the appropriate section later in this appendix.

$$ r^2 = 1 - \frac{\sum_{i=1}^{n}(Y_i - \hat{Y}_i)^2}{\sum_{i=1}^{n}(Y_i - \bar{Y})^2} = 1 - \frac{24.311}{257.63} = 0.9056 $$

Standard Error of the Regression

The *standard error of the regression* (SER) is the standard deviation of the residuals, or equivalently, the standard deviation of the observations from the fitted regression line:[7]

$$\text{SER} = \sqrt{\frac{\sum_{i=1}^{n}\left(Y_i - \hat{Y}_i\right)^2}{n-2}}$$

This formula should look familiar. The SER was previously denoted by an s and appeared in the calculation of the standard error of the regression coefficient, s.e.(b). The name *standard error of the regression* merely highlights the fact that this figure is a measure of dispersion for the entire equation. Note that the wider the scatter of points from the regression line, the larger the SER.

It should be emphasized that the SER can only be interpreted relative to the range of the dependent variable. For example, in price-forecasting equations, an SER figure of 10¢ would be indicative of an excellent fit if the given price series ranged between $6 and $12, and an extremely poor fit if the price range were $0.30 to $0.60. For this reason, as long as the mean of the dependent variable $\bar{Y}$ is greater than the range between the high and low values, it may be useful to consider the percent (%SER) where[8]

$$\%\text{SER} = \frac{\text{SER}}{\bar{Y}}$$

In effect, the %SER is a dispersion measure normalized by the magnitude of the underlying data. When comparing different equations with the *same dependent variable*, over the same time interval, the %SER will yield the same conclusions as the SER, with the advantage of being stated in terms that are intuitively more meaningful.[9]

Confidence Interval for an Individual Forecast

Assume that we used our regression equation to forecast a future value of the dependent variable Y, given a specific value of the independent variable X. What forecast range would have a 95 percent probability of containing the true value of Y? (*Implicit assumption:* The estimated value for the

---

[7] The SER is also often referred to as the standard error of the estimate (SEE), or simply as the standard error (SE).

[8] If $\bar{Y}$ is less than the range, the %SER could be very misleading. For example, if the dependent variable included values that were both positive and negative, its mean could be close to 0. In this case, the %SER could approach infinity.

[9] Caution should be exercised in drawing any conclusions from comparisons that involve equations with different dependent variables, since the %SER would be sensitive to the dependent variable chosen. For an example of why this is undesirable, see the discussion in the section "Coefficient of Determination (r^2)."

independent variable is either known or precisely projected; that is, there is no forecast error involved in the X value.) In answering this question, we note that even if all the regression assumptions are fulfilled, there are three sources of potential error:

1. **Error of the mean.** The true population regression line is unknown and is estimated from the observations. The resulting fitted line passes through $(\overline{X}, \overline{Y})$, while the population line passes through $(\overline{X}, \overline{Y}_{\overline{X}})$, where in general, $\overline{Y}_{\overline{X}}$, the unknown population mean at $\overline{X}$, will not equal the sample mean $\overline{Y}$. As indicated in Figure C.4a, this type of error will result in all forecasts (i.e., projections of Y for any value of X) being too high or low by the difference between the value of $\overline{Y}$ and $\overline{Y}_{\overline{X}}$. (Figure C.4a depicts the case of a positive error of the mean; a symmetric image would apply for a negative error.)

2. **Error of the slope.** There will also be some difference between the true regression coefficient β and the fitted line slope b. Figure C.4b illustrates the combined effect of this source of error and the error of the mean for the forecasted value $\hat{Y}_f$ at X_f. Note that the error of the slope will be zero at $\overline{X}$ since the fitted regression must pass through $(\overline{X}, \overline{Y})$, but will increase steadily as X values are further removed from $\overline{X}$. (The illustration in Figure C.4b depicts the case of a positive error of the mean and an estimated regression coefficient that is too high; a symmetric image would apply for the reverse case.)

3. **Random error.** For reasons previously explained, even if the true population line were precisely known, there would still be error terms. The confidence interval for the population line is illustrated in Figure C.4c. Note that the interval is independent of the value of X.

The forecast error for any individual prediction would reflect the combined effect of all three of the influences just discussed (Figure C.4d). The shape of the confidence interval depicted in Figure C.4d is a consequence of the fact that, although the error of the mean and the random error components will be equal for all values of X, the error of the slope increases for values further removed from $\overline{X}$. If the independent variable value for the forecast period is denoted by X_f, the standard error for the forecasted value of Y_f is given by

$$\text{s.e.}(\hat{Y}_f) = s \sqrt{1 + \frac{1}{n} + \frac{\left(X_f - \overline{X}\right)^2}{\sum_{i=1}^{n}\left(X_i - \overline{X}\right)^2}}$$

Note that when X_f, equals $\overline{X}$, and n is large, this term reduces to approximately s—the standard deviation of the residuals. (Once again, s is more commonly called the standard error of the regression.) Also note that the further X_f is from $\overline{X}$, the larger the s.e. $(\hat{Y}_f)$

The confidence interval for Y_f would be

$$\hat{Y}_f - t \sum \text{s.e.}(\hat{Y}_f) < Y_f < \hat{Y}_f + t \cdot \text{s.e.}(\hat{Y}_f)$$

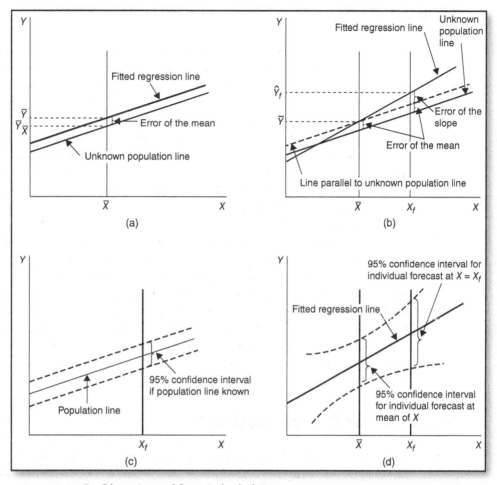

FIGURE C.4 Confidence Interval for an Individual Forecast

where $t = t$ value at the specified level of significance for the given number of degrees of freedom. At $X = \overline{X}$, this interval would reduce to

$$\hat{Y}_f - t \cdot s\sqrt{1 + \frac{1}{n}} < Y_f < \hat{Y}_f + t \cdot s\sqrt{1 + \frac{1}{n}}$$

■ Extrapolation

Extrapolation refers to predictions beyond the range of observations, that is, forecasts for Y_f where X_f is greater than or less than any observed value X_i. As should be apparent from the preceding formula for s.e. (Y_f), predictions in the extrapolated range will be particularly subject to uncertainty, since s.e. $(\hat{Y}_f)$ increases as the X value moves farther away from $\overline{X}$. However, there is an even more important reason why extrapolation-based forecasts should be viewed with great skepticism. Basically, it is never safe to assume that the relationship between the dependent and independent variables exhibited in the observed range would continue to hold in the extrapolated range. For example, consider a market in which there is a rough inverse linear relationship between price and the final stock/consumption ratio during the observation period. This relationship would likely break down in a record shortage situation, since prices frequently begin to rise at an accelerated rate once an expected shortage reaches a critically low level.

What should be done in the case in which the expected value for the explanatory variable falls beyond the observed range? Many professional analysts faced with such a dilemma will apprehensively extrapolate and hope for the best (probably because of implicit pressure to provide forecasts, whether the necessary data exists or not). Such hopes are often misplaced. This does not mean to imply that the analyst must resign herself to a yearlong hibernation before she ventures any market forecast—few firms are that enlightened. Rather, the intended point is that in such a situation, the analyst must rely almost totally on her intuitive fundamental sense of the market and technical analysis to generate forecasts, rather than naively continuing to use a formal fundamental model that is no longer relevant.

■ Coefficient of Determination (r^2)

If the regression model were unavailable or, equivalently, if the independent variable were useless in explaining the dependent variable Y, the best forecast for a value of Y would be its mean $\overline{Y}$. We define the difference between an individual observation and the mean, $Y_i - \overline{Y}$, as the total deviation. Now if X is of any use in explaining Y, the deviations between the observed points and the fitted regression line should tend to be smaller than the total deviation. For any given observation Y_i, the portion of the total deviation explained by the regression equation would equal the fitted value minus the mean, $\hat{Y}_i - \overline{Y}$. The portion that remains unexplained will equal the observed value minus the fitted value $Y_i - \hat{Y}_i$. The relationship among the *explained*, *unexplained*, and *total deviations* is illustrated in Figure C.5. For any given observation, this relationship can be expressed as follows:

$$
\begin{array}{ccccc}
\text{Total deviation} & = & \text{explained deviation} & + & \text{unexplained deviation} \\
\text{for } Y_i & & \text{for } Y_i & & \text{for } Y_i \\
\left(Y_i - \overline{Y} \right) & = & \left(\hat{Y}_i - \overline{Y} \right) & + & \left(Y_i - \hat{Y}_i \right)
\end{array}
$$

If we are interested in deriving a relationship between *total variation*, a measure of the deviation of all points, and *explained* and *unexplained variation*, we cannot simply sum the terms, because opposite

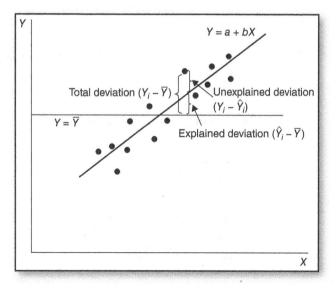

FIGURE C.5 Explained, Unexplained, and Total Deviation

deviations will offset each other, yielding a tautological relationship.[10] Thus, we square both sides of the equation before summing. This step is analogous to the approach used to get around the same problem in trying to find the best-fit line:

$$\sum_{i=1}^{n}\left(Y_i - \overline{Y}\right)^2 = \sum_{i=1}^{n}\left[\left(\hat{Y}_i - \overline{Y}\right) + \left(Y_i - \hat{Y}_i\right)\right]^2$$

$$= \sum_{i=1}^{n}\left(\hat{Y}_i - \overline{Y}\right)^2 + \sum_{i=1}^{n}\left(Y_i - \hat{Y}_i\right)^2 - 2\sum_{i=1}^{n}\left(Y_i - \hat{Y}_i\right)\left(\hat{Y}_i - \overline{Y}\right)$$

Given the previously stated assumption that the independent variable X and the error terms are uncorrelated, it can be algebraically demonstrated that

$$2\sum_{i=1}^{n}\left(Y_i - \overline{Y}_i\right)\left(Y_i - \overline{Y}\right) = 0$$

---

[10] $\sum_{i=1}^{n}\left(Y_i - \overline{Y}\right) = \sum_{i=1}^{n}\left(\hat{Y}_i - \overline{Y}\right) + \sum_{i=1}^{n}\left(Y_i - \hat{Y}_i\right)$

$$= \sum_{i=1}^{n}\hat{Y}_i - \sum_{i=1}^{n}\overline{Y} + \sum_{i=1}^{n}Y_i - \sum_{i=1}^{n}\hat{Y}_i$$

$$= \sum_{i=1}^{n}\left(Y_i - \overline{Y}\right) = \sum_{i=1}^{n}Y_i - n\overline{Y}$$

$$0 = 0$$

Thus, we have

$$\text{Total variation} = \text{explained variation} + \text{unexplained variation}$$

$$\sum_{i=1}^{n}(Y_i - Y)^2 = \sum_{i=1}^{n}(\hat{Y}_i - \overline{Y})^2 + \sum_{i=1}^{n}(Y_i - \hat{Y}_i)^2$$

where variation is defined as the sum of the squared deviations.

Dividing both sides by $\sum_{i=1}^{n}(Y_i - \overline{Y})^2$

$$1 = \frac{\sum_{i=1}^{n}(\hat{Y}_i - \overline{Y})^2}{\sum_{i=1}^{n}(Y_i - \overline{Y})^2} + \frac{\sum_{i=1}^{n}(Y_i - \hat{Y}_i)^2}{\sum_{i=1}^{n}(Y_i - \overline{Y})^2}$$

$$1 = \frac{\text{explained variation}}{\text{total variation}} + \frac{\text{unexplained variation}}{\text{total variation}}$$

We define r^2 as the

$$\frac{\text{Explained variation}}{\text{Total variation}} = \frac{\sum_{i=1}^{n}(\hat{Y}_i - \overline{Y})^2}{\sum_{i=1}^{n}(Y_i - \overline{Y})^2}$$

or equivalently,

$$r^2 = 1 - \frac{\text{unexplained variation}}{\text{total variation}} = 1 - \frac{\sum_{i=1}^{n}(Y_i - \hat{Y}_i)^2}{\sum_{i=1}^{n}(Y_i - \overline{Y})^2}$$

The second form is more convenient because the analysis of the regression equation focuses on the unexplained variation (residuals). Note that $0 \leq r^2 \leq 1$. If X does not explain any of the variation in Y, then $r^2 = 0$. If X explains all of the variation in Y (i.e., all the observations fall precisely on the fitted line), $r^2 = 1$. The r^2 calculation is an extremely useful summary statistic because of the significance of what it measures—the percentage of variation explained by the regression equation—and the intuitive clarity with which the r^2 figure can be interpreted. Table C.1b illustrates the calculation of r^2 for the regression line derived in Table A.1.

The statistic r^2 is extremely useful in comparing alternative models, as long as they all have the same dependent variable, that is, they differ only in the explanatory variables. However, when regression equations have different dependent variables, inferences based on r^2 can prove very misleading. For example, consider the following two models:

$$\text{Model I:} \quad P_t = a + bP_{t-1}, \quad r^2 = 0.98$$
$$\text{Model II:} \quad \Delta P_t = a + bX, \quad r^2 = 0.50$$

where P_t = closing price on day t
      P_{t-1} = closing price on day $t - 1$
      $\Delta P_t = P_t - P_{t-1}$
      X = an explanatory variable known on day $t - 1$ and used to predict price changes

Despite the fact that Model I has a much higher r^2, Model II represents the better forecasting equation. If the survey period is sufficiently long, an equation such as Model I will merely tell us that the price on a given day will be almost equal to the preceding day's price. (In such an equation, b is likely to be very close to 1.0.) The reason for the high r^2 value is that although prices for the entire period may range widely, prices on adjacent days must be closely correlated (at most, they can be separated by the daily price limit). Model I, however, is totally useless in forecasting the next day's price. In contrast, the independent variable in Model II explains 50 percent of the price *change* on a given day and might be an extremely important aid in day trading. This illustration is intended to highlight the potential folly of making value judgments about regression equations with different dependent variables.[11]

---

[11] An even more extreme example is possible. If we used hogs not slaughtered (HNS) instead of hog slaughter (HS) as the dependent variable regressed against the pig crop (PC), where HNS = PC − HS, the sum of the squared residuals and hence SER would be exactly the same, but r^2 would be different. Why? Because r^2 would be affected by the dependent variable chosen

$$r^2 = 1 - \frac{\text{unexplained variation}}{\text{total variation}} = 1 - \frac{\sum_{i=1}^{n}\left(Y_i - \hat{Y}_i\right)^2}{\sum_{i=1}^{n}\left(Y_i - \overline{Y}\right)^2}$$

In this example,

$$\sum_{i=1}^{n}\left(Y_i - \hat{Y}_i\right)^2$$

will be the same whether HS or HNS is the dependent variable, but

$$\sum_{i=1}^{n}\left(Y_i - \overline{Y}\right)^2$$

will be different, hence r^2 will be different.

■ Spurious ("Nonsense") Correlations

It is important to understand that cause and effect in the regression procedure are in the eyes of the beholder. The r^2 value derived in Table C.1*b* merely tells us that there is a strong correlation between hog slaughter and the preceding pig crop. The way we interpret the cause and effect of this statistic emanates only from our theoretical understanding of the underlying process. In this particular example, it is quite obvious the pig crop in one period affects slaughter in the next period rather than vice versa. However, if enshrouded in ignorance, we set out to prove the level of hog slaughter determines the number of pigs born in the preceding period, the resulting equation would yield the identical r^2 value. Thus, r^2 only reflects the degree of correlation between two variables; it in no way proves a cause-and-effect relationship.

The potential folly of drawing cause-and-effect inferences from an r^2 figure is demonstrated by Figure C.6. Note what appears to be a striking relationship between the number of hedge funds and U.S. wine consumption. In fact, the r^2 value between the number of hedge funds and U.S. wine consumption during the period depicted is a remarkably high 0.99! What conclusions are we to draw from this chart?

■ Increased wine consumption encourages people to invest in hedge funds.

■ Hedge funds drive people to drink.

■ The hedge fund industry should promote wine consumption.

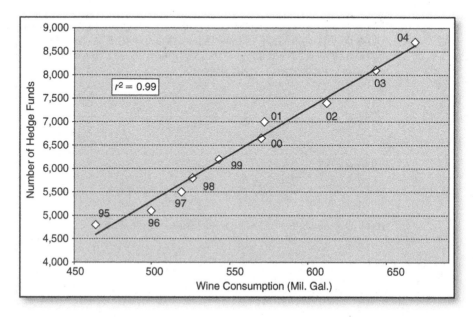

FIGURE C.6 Number of Hedge Funds vs. U.S. Wine Consumption

- Wine growers should promote hedge fund investing.

- All of the above.

- None of the above.

Actually, the striking correlation between wine consumption and the number of hedge funds is very easily explained. Both variables were affected by a common third variable during the period depicted: time. In other words, both the number of hedge funds and wine consumption witnessed pronounced growth trends during this time period. The apparent relationship arises from the fact that these trends were simultaneous. This type of coincident linear relationship is called "spurious" or "nonsense" correlation. Actually, the correlation is real enough; only the interpretation of cause and effect is nonsense.

The Multiple Regression Model

In our description of nature the purpose is not to disclose the real essence of the phenomena but only to track down, so far as it is possible, relations between the manifold aspects of our experience.

—Niels Bohr

Basics of Multiple Regression

In practice, it is rarely possible to explain the behavior of a dependent variable adequately with only one explanatory variable. For example, hog slaughter alone will provide only a rough indication of hog prices. A more satisfactory model would also incorporate other independent variables, such as broiler slaughter. The *multiple regression equation* is a straightforward extension of simple regression and describes the linear relationship between the dependent variable and two or more independent variables.

The meaning of *linear*, which might not be intuitively obvious beyond the two-dimensional case, is that all the variables are of the first degree and are combined only by addition or subtraction. For example, in terms of Z as a function of X and Y, $Z = 2X + Y + 3$ is a linear equation, while $Z = X^2 + 2y^2 + 4$, $Z = XY$, and $Z = \log X + \log Y$ are nonlinear equations. A basic characteristic of a linear equation is that a one-unit change in an independent variable will result in a *constant* magnitude change in the dependent variable, regardless of the independent variable value. In other words, in a linear equation, the slope in each dimension is constant. When there are only two variables, as is the case in simple regression, the linear equation can be depicted by a straight line. When there are three variables, the linear equation can be represented by a plane in three-dimensional space. Linear equations involving more than three variables can no longer be simply represented in three-dimensional Euclidean space.

As in the simple regression case, regression analysis is only appropriate if the relationship between the variables is approximately linear. This is not as strict a limitation as it may sound, since many non-linear equations can be transformed into linear equations.

The general form of the multiple regression equation is

$$Y = \alpha + \beta_1 X_1 + \beta_2 X_2 \ldots \beta_k X_k + e$$

The preceding equation represents the unknown population or true regression. The general form of the fitted regression is

$$Y = a + b_1 X_1 + b_2 X_2 \ldots b_k X_k$$

where $a, b_1, b_2, \ldots, b_k$ are chosen so as to minimize the sum of the squared residuals. A regression coefficient b_i can be interpreted as follows: If all other independent variables are held constant, a one-unit change in X_i will cause the dependent variable Y to change by b_i. A residual can still be interpreted as the difference between an observed value of the dependent variable (Y_i) and the fitted value (Y_i). Regardless of how many variables there are in the equation, the residuals still represent a single-dimensional difference.

These concepts can perhaps be clarified by considering a practical example. Assume that we have derived a regression equation relating hog prices to hog slaughter and broiler slaughter:

$$Y = a_1 + b_1 X_1 + b_2 X_2$$

where Y = deflated hog prices
X_1 = hog slaughter
X_2 = broiler slaughter

This relationship is depicted in Figure D.1. Each combination of values for X_1 and X_2 will fix a location in the (X_1, X_2) plane. The regression equation will indicate the value of Y (the height of the y axis) at that point. In other words, the regression equation defines the price level that corresponds to any combination of hog and broiler slaughter.

For any given value of X_2 (broiler slaughter), increases in hog slaughter will reduce Y (hog prices) at a constant rate. Similarly, for any given value of X_1 (hog slaughter), increases in broiler slaughter will reduce Y. Thus, as can be seen, the highest prices will occur when hog slaughter and broiler slaughter are low, and the lowest prices when these explanatory variables are high.

Each observation will represent a combination of values for X_1 and X_2 and the corresponding value of Y during the given period. Of course, the actual observed Y_i values, which are indicated by solid dots in Figure D.1, will rarely fall exactly on the plane. The vertical distance between any point and the plane (i.e., the difference between the actual hog price and the price predicted by the regression plane) is the residual and is indicated by an arrow. As in the simple regression case, the residual is measured along a single axis (y). The regression procedure will specify the values for a, b_1, and b_2, which will minimize the sum of the squares of these residuals.

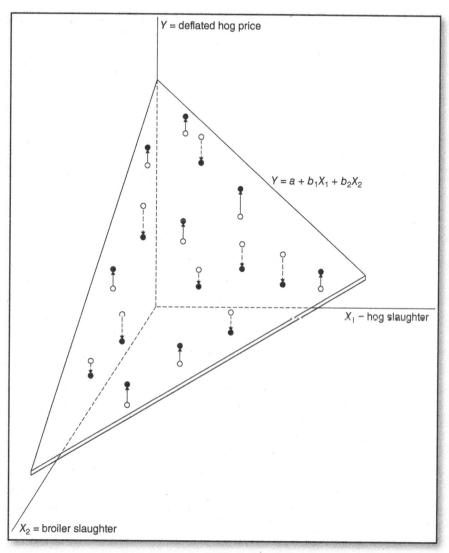

FIGURE D.1 Scatter of Observed Points About the Regression Plane

We deliberately avoid indicating the computational formulas for deriving the regression coefficients, or for that matter, any of the statistics for the multiple regression case. The reason for this is that multiple regression computations are far too cumbersome to be reasonably considered without the aid of a computer. The assumptions underlying multiple regression are completely analogous to those detailed for the simple regression model. In the multiple regression case, there is one additional assumption: that there is no linear relationship among any two or more independent variables. If this assumption is not met, it will lead to a problem called *multicollinearity*.

Applying the *t*-Test in the Multiple Regression Model

The t values in the multiple regression output can be used to evaluate the significance of the regression coefficients. The t values from any standard computer regression analysis assume the hypothesis being tested is that the regression coefficient equals zero. In this case, the t value for b_i is provided by

$$t = \frac{b_i}{\text{s.e.}(b_i)}$$

This relationship can be expressed as follows:

$$\text{T-STAT} = \frac{\text{COEFF}}{\text{ST ER}}$$

where T-STAT $= t$ value for given regression coefficient
COEFF[1] $=$ value of given regression coefficient
ST ER $=$ standard error of given regression coefficient (not to be confused with the standard error of the regression, SER, which is described in the next section)

Frequently, these statistics will be listed in three adjacent columns with each row providing statistics for the constant term or specified regression coefficient. The interpretation of the t statistic is identical to the simple regression case. The t value indicates the number of standard deviations between the indicated coefficient value and the true population coefficient if the latter were actually equal to zero. The higher the t value, the more significant the regression coefficient. To use the t table (Table B.4), one would check the row corresponding to $n-k$ degrees of freedom (df) where n equals the total number of observations and k equals the number of variables in the equation. Roughly speaking, t values above 2.0 are clearly significant and indicate that the given independent variable should be retained in the model. It should be noted that the t value does not definitively prove significance; rather it establishes significance at a specific probability level. The higher the t value, the more unlikely a regression coefficient would be assumed to be significant when it is not.

What if the t statistic is less than the t value at the 0.05 level of significance (e.g., less than 1.812 for a one-tailed test with 10 df)?[2] Here there is no clear-cut answer. The choice depends on the priorities of the analyst. If she is more concerned about retaining an insignificant variable in the model, she might lean to dropping any variable whose regression coefficient is not significant at the 0.05 level. On the other hand, if she is more concerned about deleting a meaningful variable, she would retain the variable unless the t value was very low.

A reasonable criterion is that any theoretically meaningful variable with a t value greater than 1.0 should usually be retained,[3] although it should be noted that many analysts prefer to use a cutoff

---

[1] Frequently also called VALUE.

[2] It is assumed that the regression coefficient has the anticipated sign (e.g., negative for hog slaughter in an equation in which hog prices are the dependent variable). Situations in which the sign is opposite to expectations are discussed later in this appendix.

[3] There is a special meaning to t values > 1.0. It has been demonstrated that if explanatory variables are retained if their t-value > 1.0 and deleted otherwise, the "Corrected R^2" (which is discussed later) will be maximized.

level of 2.0. The key words are *theoretically meaningful*. A low *t* value does not contradict the assumed relationship between the dependent and explanatory variable. Remember, a *t* value below the level of statistical significance does not indicate that the independent variable is not meaningful in explaining the dependent variable. It only means that its significance has not been demonstrated at the desired probability level. As long as the variable has the anticipated sign, the results are still consistent with theoretical expectations, albeit the relationship is not as strong as would be desired. Furthermore, even a *t* value of 1.0 would still be significant at the 0.20 level (i.e., 80 percent probability) for any regression equation in which $df > 2$. Variables with *t* values below 1.0 should usually be dropped.

There is one exception to the decision process just detailed. Occasionally, the analyst might try including all the independent variables she believes should significantly affect the dependent variable, only to find that the resulting regression equation is disappointing. At this point, in desperation she might try a variety of independent variables in the hopes that perhaps one or more of these are significantly related to the dependent variable. Such a method could be termed a "shotgun" or "kitchen sink" approach and is not recommended unless all theoretically plausible variables have been exhausted. In any event, in this case one should apply stricter requirements for retaining a variable. First, a two-tailed rather than one-tailed test should be used (see section "Testing the Significance of the Regression Coefficients" in Appendix C). Second, variables with *t* values below the 0.05 level of significance should be rejected. In fact, one can argue that a more restrictive significance level should be adopted (e.g., 0.01), since the probability of accepting a meaningless variable increases with the number of variables tested.

Thus far, we have assumed that a theoretically chosen variable has the correct sign. However, in equations with many variables, a coefficient with the wrong sign is not uncommon. Such an occurrence usually indicates the presence of multicollinearity—a linear dependence between two or more explanatory variables. (A discussion of how to handle such variables is presented in the section on multicollinearity in Appendix E.) At this point, suffice it to say that the *t* values of such variables are usually irrelevant.

■ Standard Error of the Regression

The standard error of the regression (SER) is a measure of the unexplained variation. The definition of the SER is almost totally analogous to the simple regression case. The only difference is that the sum of the squared residuals is divided by the appropriate degrees of freedom, instead of $n-2$. Thus, for the more general multiple regression case, the SER could be expressed as

$$SER = \frac{\sum_{i=1}^{n}\left(Y_i - \hat{Y}_i\right)^2}{n-k}$$

where k = number of parameters in equation (which is equal to the number of independent variables plus 1, assuming there is a constant term in the equation). Note in the simple regression case that $k = 2$.

As in the simple regression case, the % SER is equal to the SER divided by $\bar{Y}$. Where appropriate (see Appendix C), the % SER may be more convenient to use, because it is stated in a form that is intuitively meaningful.

■ Confidence Intervals for an Individual Forecast

In the multiple regression case, the calculation of a confidence interval for an individual forecast is somewhat complicated. As a simplification, the confidence interval can be calculated for the situation in which all of the independent variables are equal to their means. In this specialized case, the formula for the confidence interval would be analogous to the simple regression case in which $X = \bar{X}$:

$$\hat{Y}_f - t \cdot s \sqrt{1 + \frac{1}{n}} < Y_f < \hat{Y}_f + t \cdot \sqrt{1 + \frac{1}{n}}$$

where $s = \text{SER}$

$t = t$ value at specified level of significance for the given degrees of freedom

This represents a minimum confidence interval, and the further removed the independent variables are from their respective means, the wider the actual confidence interval.

■ R^2 and Corrected R^2

The term R^2 is the multiple regression counterpart of r^2 and is defined in exactly the same way. Thus, the entire discussion related to r^2 in Appendix C applies here as well and need not be duplicated.

In the multiple regression case, it is important to realize that the addition of another independent variable can only increase R^2. Remember that R^2 is the ratio of explained variation to total variation. The introduction of a new variable will not affect total variation, and it can only increase explained variation. Even the introduction of a totally irrelevant variable will probably result in a small increase in explained variation. For example, it is a safe bet that adding a variable for the number of ducks in Belgium would increase the R^2 of a regression equation for forecasting U.S. interest rates.

The point that the addition of a meaningless explanatory variable will raise R^2 is more than an esthetic consideration. Recall that each additional variable will decrease the degrees of freedom by 1, thereby reducing the significance of the equation on the basis of other measures such as the t-test and SER, all else being equal. For this reason, it is desirable to modify the R^2 measure so that it is penalized for the addition of irrelevant variables. This alternative measure is called the *Corrected* R^2 (CR^2), or sometimes the *Adjusted* R^2. The problem with R^2 is that it is based on *variation*, which does not account for the number of degrees of freedom. The CR^2 avoids this defect, because it is based on variance. The variance is simply the variation divided by the number of degrees of freedom. It will be recalled that R^2 can be defined as[4]

$$R^2 = 1 - \frac{\text{unexplained variation}}{\text{total variation}}$$

---

[4]The formulas for R^2 and r^2 are identical.

We now define CR^2 as

$$CR^2 = 1 - \frac{\text{unexplained variance}}{\text{total variance}}$$

where

$$\text{Variance} = \frac{\text{variation}}{df}$$

Thus,

$$CR^2 = 1 - \frac{\dfrac{\sum\limits_{i=1}^{n}(Y_1 - \widehat{Y}_i)^2}{n - k}}{\dfrac{\sum\limits_{i=1}^{n}(Y_1 - \overline{Y})^2}{n - 1}}$$

The numerator of the ratio term is based on n observations, but there are k constraints in finding the regression line used to calculate Y_i. Thus $df = n - k$. The denominator is also based on n observations, but there is only one constraint, $\overline{Y}$; thus $df = n - 1$. The preceding equation can be rewritten as

$$CR^2 = 1 - (1 - R^2) \cdot \frac{n - 1}{n - k}$$

As is readily apparent in this form of the equation, when n is large relative to k, the CR^2 will almost equal R^2.

Typical regression runs will provide the CR^2 (corrected R square or adjusted R square) along with R^2 (R square). As a general rule, the CR^2 is a more useful measure for comparing different regression equations for the same dependent variable.

■ F-Test

Whereas the t distribution is used to test the significance of the individual regression coefficients, the F distribution is used to test the significance of the regression equation as a whole. In other words, the F statistic tests the hypothesis that none of the regression coefficients is significant. The F statistic can be expressed as

$$F = \frac{\text{explained variance}}{\text{unexplained variance}}$$

Note that the F value is based on variance, not variation. Once again, variance = variation $\div$ df.

$$F = \frac{\dfrac{\displaystyle\sum_{i=1}^{n}\left(Y_i - \overline{Y}\right)^2}{k-1}}{\dfrac{\displaystyle\sum_{i=1}^{n}\left(Y_i - \hat{Y}_i\right)^2}{n-k}} = \frac{\displaystyle\sum_{i=1}^{n}\left(\hat{Y}_i - \overline{Y}\right)^2}{\displaystyle\sum_{i=1}^{n}\left(Y_i - \hat{Y}_i\right)^2} \cdot \frac{n-k}{k-1}$$

The degrees of freedom for the explained variance $= k - 1$, since k values are employed in defining the regression line used to calculate $\hat{Y}_i$, but one df is lost because of the constraint imposed by $\overline{Y}$. As for the unexplained variance, there are n observations, but k constraints are imposed in finding the regression line upon which Y_i is based. Recalling the alternative definitions for R^2, we can re-express F as[5]

$$F = \frac{R^2}{1 - R^2} \cdot \frac{n-k}{k-1}$$

The appropriate degrees of freedom will be specified in the notation for the F statistic. For example, $F(2/8) = 23.5$ indicates an F value for a regression equation in which $k - 1 = 2$ and $n - k = 8$. To check for significance, the F statistic is compared to the listed values in the F table for the corresponding number of degrees of freedom. For example, checking Table D.1, it can be determined that at the 0.01 level of significance, $F(2/8) = 8.65$; thus, a value of 23.5 would be significant.

In practice, the F-test is not particularly critical, since it will almost invariably prove significant. This should not be surprising, because the F-test checks whether all the regression coefficients combined have any predictive value—a very weak criterion. In any case, for comparisons of regression equations with the same dependent variable, higher F values would indicate a better model (assuming none of the regression assumptions are violated). However, similar information could be gathered by comparing CR^2 values.

■ Analyzing a Regression Run

Table D.2 presents the results for a sample regression run. At this juncture, most of Table D.2 should be comprehensible. However, it may be helpful to interpret the key statistics of this table.

1. The regression equation is $Y = 49.06899 - 1.07049\,(X1) + 0.35775\,(X2)$. To get a point forecast for Y, one would merely plug in the estimated values of $X1$ and $X2$. For example, if $X1 = 20$

---

[5] $\displaystyle\sum_{i=1}^{n}\left(\hat{Y}_i - \overline{Y}\right)^2 = R^2 \cdot \sum_{i=1}^{n}\left(Y_i - \overline{Y}\right)^2$ and $\displaystyle\sum_{i=1}^{n}\left(Y_i - \hat{Y}_i\right)^2 = (1 - R^2)\sum_{i=1}^{n}(Y_i - \overline{Y})^2$

Values of $F_{n1,n2,\alpha}$ on the $F_{(n1,n2,\alpha)}$-distribution

$$\Pr\{F_{(n1,n2)}\text{-variable} \geq F_{n1,n2,\alpha}\} = \alpha = 0.01$$

$\alpha = .01$

$F(n_1, n_2)$-distribution

n^2 (denominator df)	\multicolumn{9}{c}{n_1 (numerator df)}
	1	2	4	6	8	10	12	24	∞
	$[t_{n2,.005}]^2$	Values of $F_{n1,n2,\alpha}$							
1	4,052	5,000	5,625	5,859	5,982	6,056	6,106	6,235	6,366
2	98.50	99.00	99.25	99.33	99.37	99.40	99.42	99.46	99.50
3	34.12	30.82	28.71	27.91	27.49	27.23	27.05	26.60	26.13
4	21.20	18.00	15.98	15.21	14.80	14.55	14.37	13.93	13.46
5	16.26	13.27	11.39	10.67	10.29	10.05	9.89	9.47	9.02
6	13.75	10.92	9.15	8.47	8.10	7.87	7.72	7.31	6.88
7	12.25	9.55	7.85	7.19	6.84	6.62	6.47	6.07	5.65
8	11.26	8.65	7.01	6.37	6.03	5.81	5.67	5.28	4.86
9	10.56	8.02	6.42	5.80	5.47	5.26	5.11	4.73	4.31
10	10.04	7.56	5.99	5.39	5.06	4.85	4.71	4.33	3.91
11	9.65	7.21	5.67	5.07	4.74	4.54	4.40	4.02	3.60
12	9.33	6.93	5.41	4.82	4.50	4.30	4.16	3.78	3.36
13	9.07	6.70	5.21	4.62	4.30	4.10	3.96	3.59	3.17
14	8.86	6.51	5.04	4.46	4.14	3.94	3.80	3.43	3.00
15	8.68	6.36	4.89	4.32	4.00	3.80	3.67	3.29	2.87
20	8.10	5.85	4.43	3.87	3.56	3.37	3.23	2.86	2.42
25	7.77	5.57	4.18	3.63	3.32	3.13	2.99	2.62	2.17
30	7.56	5.39	4.02	3.47	3.17	2.98	2.84	2.47	2.01
40	7.31	5.18	3.83	3.29	2.99	2.80	2.66	2.29	1.80
60	7.08	4.98	3.65	3.12	2.82	2.63	2.50	2.12	1.60
120	6.85	4.79	3.48	2.96	2.66	2.47	2.34	1.95	1.38
∞	6.63	4.61	3.32	2.80	2.51	2.32	2.18	1.79	1.00

Source: Abridged from Table 18 of Pearson and Hartley, *Biometrika Tables for Statisticians,* Third Edition, Volume 1, 1976, with kind permission of the *Biometrika* Trustees (http://biomet.oxfordjournals.org).

The diagram, and this presentation of the table, are taken from Table 4b of S. R. Searle, *Linear Models* (New York, NY: John Wiley & Sons, 1997). Copyright © 1997 by John Wiley & Sons; reprinted by permission.

Variable	Coefficient	Standard Error	T-Stat	Mean
CONSTANT	49.06899	9.67267	5.07	41.16071 (dependent variable)
X1	−1.07049	0.23464	−4.56	21.00714
X2	0.35775	0.13400	2.67	40.75357
Observation	Actual	Fitted	Residual	% Deviation
1	35.90000	35.25925	0.64075	1.82
2	52.70000	54.54910	−1.84910	−3.39
3	46.30000	50.74680	−4.44680	−8.76
4	34.20000	36.98609	−2.78609	−7.53
5	51.30000	46.15574	5.14426	11.15
6	44.20000	44.02220	0.17780	0.40
7	33.90000	29.70675	4.19325	14.12
8	31.30000	30.54304	0.75696	2.48
9	31.70000	32.74207	−1.04207	−3.18
10	29.90000	31.58795	−1.68795	−5.34
11	51.10000	49.76981	1.33019	2.67
12	56.10000	51.62468	4.47532	8.67
13	43.90000	45.56465	−1.66465	−3.65
14	33.7500	36.99187	−3.24187	−8.76

$Y = \text{CONSTANT} + C1 \cdot X1 + C2 \cdot X2$

RSQ = 0.8953   SER = 3.2338 $F_{(2,11)} = 47.0$

RSQC = 0.8762   % SER = 7.86   DW = 1.69

and $X2 = 40$, the predicted Y value would be 41.969. In practice, it will be more convenient to use mnemonic symbols for the variables instead of Y, $X1$, and $X2$.

2. $R^2 = 0.8953$, which means that $X1$ and $X2$ explain 89.53 percent of the total variation in Y. The CR^2, which is adjusted downward for lost degrees of freedom, is 0.8762.

3. SER = 3.2338. This would be a key figure of merit in comparisons with alternative models. The SER could also be used to construct a crude confidence interval for an individual forecast based on the assumption that all the independent variable values are equal to their respective means. This confidence interval would be[6]

$$\hat{Y}_f - t \cdot s \sqrt{1 + \frac{1}{n}} < Y_f < \hat{Y}_f + t \cdot s \sqrt{1 + \frac{1}{n}}$$

---

[6] See the section, "Confidence Intervals for an Individual Forecast."

where $s = \text{SER} = 3.23$

$n = 14$

$t = 2.201$ (t value for two-sided test at 0.05 level of significance for 11 df)

$$\hat{Y}_f - 2.201\,(3.23)\,(1.0351) < Y_f < \hat{Y}_f + 2.201\,(3.23)\,(1.0351)$$
$$\hat{Y}_f - 7.3588 < Y_f < \hat{Y}_f + 7.3588$$

Using the point estimate for Y_f of 41.969 derived in 1, the 95 percent confidence interval would be

$$34.610 < Y_f < 49.328$$

This would mean a 95 percent probability the actual value will fall in the stated range if the forecast is based on independent variables equal to their respective means. Of course, this will never be the case. Consequently, the actual confidence interval will always be wider. Nevertheless, given this understanding, the simplified confidence interval provides at least a rough sense of the potential variability of the forecast.

4. The %SER $= \text{SER} \div \overline{Y}$. The %SER provides a figure that is intuitively meaningful and can be used instead of the SER if all model comparisons involve the same dependent variable.

5. The F value for 2 df in the numerator and 11 df in the denominator $= 47.0$, which is well above the listed F value of 7.21 at the 0.01 significance level. Again, the F test will almost invariably verify that the equation is significant.

6. DW stands for Durbin-Watson, a measure discussed in Appendix E..

7. The t statistic is equal to the coefficient values divided by the respective standard error. In this example, all the coefficients are significant (t value at the 0.05 level of significance for a one-tailed test with 11 df is 1.796).

8. The Actual column in Table D.2 lists the actual observations of Y, and the Fitted (also called Predicted) column lists the corresponding values indicated by the regression equation. The difference between these two figures for each observation is listed in the Residual column. The Percent Deviation column is equal to the residual divided by the fitted value. (In some cases, the residuals are normalized by dividing the residuals by the SER—that is, expressing residuals in standard deviation units. Residuals normalized in this manner are termed *standardized residuals* or *standard residuals* and are discussed in Appendix E.)

Thus far, we have only discussed the meaning of the overall summary statistics for the regression equation. As will be detailed in Appendix E, the individual residual values also contain extremely important information and should be carefully analyzed.

Analyzing the Regression Equation

It is a test of true theories not only to account for but to predict phenomena.

—William Whewell

Outliers

An outlier is an observation with a large residual—that is, a large deviation between the observed value and fitted value. Outliers reflect one of the following conditions:

1. An error in collecting or manipulating the data for the given point.
2. The existence of a significant extraneous causal factor that only affected the outlier(s).
3. The omission of an important explanatory variable from the equation.
4. A structural flaw in the model.

The presence of outliers indicates a deficiency in the model. After verifying that an outlier is not the result of error, one should try to identify possible factors responsible for the aberrant behavior. If the outlier can be explained by a missing variable that affected all observations, then this variable should be included in the equation. If, however, the outlier was a consequence of an isolated event that is not expected to reoccur, then it should be viewed as an unrepresentative point, and the regression should be rerun with the outlier deleted. This recalculation is important, since the method of least squares used to derive the regression coefficients will give greater weight to outliers. Thus, one or two such points could seriously distort the regression equation fit. However, unless the isolated causes of the outlier have been identified, one should avoid the temptation of deleting such points simply because it will improve the regression fit.

■ The Residual Plot

The scatter diagram, such as the one depicted in Figure A.4, is of limited use in detecting outliers, since it can only be applied in the simple regression case. The residual plot provides a graphic technique for detecting outliers that is as easy to apply in multiple regression as it is in simple regression. In constructing residual plots, it is more convenient to use standardized residuals rather than the actual residuals, which vary widely from case to case. The *standardized residual* for the *i*th observation is defined as

$$sr_i = \frac{Y_i - \hat{Y}_i}{s}$$

where

$$s = \text{SER} = \sqrt{\frac{\sum\limits_{i=1}^{n}\left(Y_i - \hat{Y}_i\right)^2}{n - k}}$$

where n = number of observations

k = number of parameters (which is equal to the number of independent variables plus 1, assuming there is a constant term in the equation)

In effect, the standardized residual can be thought of as indicating how many standard deviations a residual is from the assumed residual mean of zero. If the regression assumptions are valid, the standardized residuals should be randomly distributed and fall primarily in a range between +2 and −2. One great advantage of using standardized residuals is that the interpretation of a residual plot is the same for all types of data. There are three basic types of residual plots:

1. sr_i versus the fitted Y values ($\hat{Y}_i$).
2. sr_i versus the independent variables (in multiple regression, there can be one such plot for each independent variable).
3. sr_i versus time (i.e., the sr_i values are plotted in time order).

The preceding plots are available on some computer packages. However, even when they are not, they can easily be constructed from the printout of residual values. Since virtually all applications of regression analysis in forecasting futures involve time series data, the third type of residual plot will normally be the most useful.

Figure E.1 provides an example of a residual plot plotted against time. As is readily visible, 2011 and 2014 are outliers. Also note the predominance of negative residuals in the remaining years—a consequence of the two positive outliers pulling up the regression line. (Remember, the least-squares procedure will tend to place greater weight on outliers.)

One essential attribute of the residual plot is that it can be applied just as easily when a model contains three or more variables, a situation in which a scatter diagram cannot be constructed. Perhaps even more importantly, the residual plot can be used to check for autocorrelation. Before turning to this critical application of the residual plot, it is first necessary to discuss autocorrelation and the most commonly used method for its detection, the Durbin-Watson (DW) statistic.

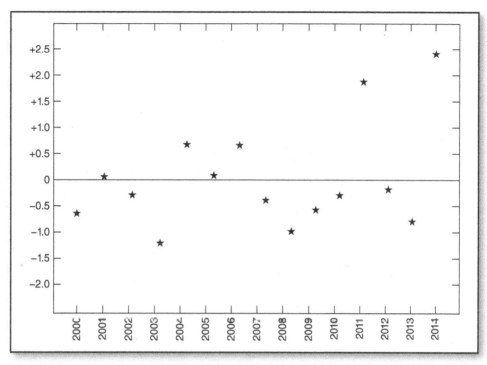

FIGURE E.1 Standardized Residuals Plotted Against Time

■ Autocorrelation Defined

Autocorrelation refers to the situation in which the error terms are correlated. The existence of autocorrelation indicates that there is a pattern in the data that has not yet been captured by the explanatory variables. For this reason, the presence of autocorrelation suggests that the model is still inadequate. Furthermore, it should be recalled that one of the basic assumptions underlying the statistics of regression analysis is that the error terms are randomly distributed. If autocorrelation exists, then the standard error of the coefficients and the SER may all be severely understated. Thus, the normal tests of significance may yield a very distorted picture of the equation's precision.

■ The Durbin-Watson Statistic as a Measure of Autocorrelation

Autocorrelation refers to a linear dependency in the error terms. In the simplest case, the error terms are correlated to the error terms of the preceding period. This type of condition is called *first-order autocorrelation* and is reflected by the DW statistic, which is a standard measure included in the regression summary printout.

Although ideally a test for autocorrelation would be based on the population error terms, these are unavailable. The DW test is based on the residuals (denoted here by $\hat{e}_t$) and defined as:

$$DW = \frac{\sum\limits_{t=2}^{n}\left(\hat{e}_t - \hat{e}_{t-1}\right)^2}{\sum\limits_{t=2}^{n}\hat{e}_t^2}$$

where $\hat{e}_t$ = residual value in time period t

$\hat{e}_t - 1$ = residual value in time period immediately preceding period t

The following approximate relationship, however, is more useful for an intuitive explanation of the Durbin-Watson statistic:

$$DW \approx 2(1 - r)$$

where

$$r = \frac{\sum\limits_{t=2}^{n}\hat{e}_t \cdot \hat{e}_{t-1}}{\sum\limits_{t=2}^{n}\hat{e}_t^2}$$

If there is no first-order autocorrelation, the positive values for the product $\hat{e}_t \cdot \hat{e}_{t-1}$ will tend to offset the negative values, and $\sum \hat{e}_t \cdot \hat{e}_{t-1}$ should approximate zero. In this case, r will approach zero and DW will approach 2. If adjacent residuals are positively correlated, then $\hat{e}_t \cdot \hat{e}_{t-1}$ and $\sum \hat{e}_t \cdot \hat{e}_{t-1}$ will tend to be positive. The greater the correlation between adjacent residuals, the more positive $\sum \hat{e}_t \cdot \hat{e}_{t-1}$ will be. In the extreme, $\sum \hat{e}_t \cdot \hat{e}_{t-1}$ will approach $\sum \hat{e}_t^2$, causing r to approach 1 and DW to approach 0. Similarly, if the adjacent residuals are negatively correlated (i.e., positive residuals tending to follow negative residuals), $\sum \hat{e}_t \cdot \hat{e}_{t-1}$ will be negative. If the negative correlation is extreme, $\sum \hat{e}_t \cdot \hat{e}_{t-1}$ will approach $-\sum \hat{e}_t^2$, causing r to approach -1 and DW to approach 4. In summary, the DW has a possible range between 0 and 4. Values near 2 indicate no first-order autocorrelation, values significantly below 2 indicate positive autocorrelation, and values significantly above 2 indicate negative autocorrelation.

Table E.1 contains a list of DW values that can be used to test for autocorrelation at the 0.05 level of significance. The appropriate values will depend on the number of observations, n, and the number of independent variables in the regression equation, k. Note that unlike the other tests discussed so far, there are two values listed for each category. In a test for positive autocorrelation, the interpretation would be as follows (for negative autocorrelation use $4 - DW$ instead of DW):

1. $DW < d_L$ Positive autocorrelation exists
2. $DW > d_U$ No positive autocorrelation exists
3. $d_L < DW < d_U$ Test is inconclusive

TABLE E.1 The Distribution of Durbin-Watson d 5 Percent Significance Points of d_l and d_u

n	k = 1 d_L	k = 1 d_U	k = 2 d_L	k = 2 d_U	k = 3 d_L	k = 3 d_U	k = 4 d_L	k = 4 d_U	k = 5 d_L	k = 5 d_U
15	1.08	1.36	0.95	1.54	0.82	1.75	0.69	1.97	0.56	2.21
16	1.10	1.37	0.98	1.54	0.86	1.73	0.74	1.93	0.62	2.15
17	1.13	1.38	1.02	1.54	0.90	1.71	0.78	1.90	0.67	2.10
18	1.16	1.39	1.05	1.53	0.93	1.69	0.82	1.87	0.71	2.06
19	1.18	1.40	1.08	1.53	0.97	1.68	0.86	1.85	0.75	2.02
20	1.20	1.41	1.10	1.54	1.00	1.68	0.90	1.83	0.79	1.99
21	1.22	1.42	1.13	1.54	1.03	1.67	0.93	1.81	0.83	1.96
22	1.24	1.43	1.15	1.54	1.05	1.66	0.96	1.80	0.86	1.94
23	1.26	1.44	1.17	1.54	1.08	1.66	0.99	1.79	0.90	1.92
24	1.27	1.45	1.19	1.55	1.10	1.66	1.01	1.78	0.93	1.90
25	1.29	1.45	1.21	1.55	1.12	1.66	1.04	1.77	0.95	1.89
26	1.30	1.46	1.22	1.55	1.14	1.65	1.06	1.76	0.98	1.88
27	1.32	1.47	1.24	1.56	1.16	1.65	1.08	1.76	1.01	1.86
28	1.33	1.48	1.26	1.56	1.18	1.65	1.10	1.75	1.03	1.85
29	1.34	1.48	1.27	1.56	1.20	1.65	1.12	1.74	1.05	1.84
30	1.35	1.49	1.28	1.57	1.21	1.65	1.14	1.74	1.07	1.83
31	1.36	1.50	1.30	1.57	1.23	1.65	1.16	1.74	1.09	1.83
32	1.37	1.50	1.31	1.57	1.24	1.65	1.18	1.73	1.11	1.82
33	1.38	1.51	1.32	1.58	1.26	1.65	1.19	1.73	1.13	1.81
34	1.39	1.51	1.33	1.58	1.27	1.65	1.21	1.73	1.15	1.81
35	1.40	1.52	1.34	1.58	1.28	1.65	1.22	1.73	1.16	1.80
36	1.41	1.52	1.35	1.59	1.29	1.65	1.24	1.73	1.18	1.80
37	1.42	1.53	1.36	1.59	1.31	1.66	1.25	1.72	1.19	1.80
38	1.43	1.54	1.37	1.59	1.32	1.66	1.26	1.72	1.21	1.79
39	1.43	1.54	1.38	1.60	1.33	1.66	1.27	1.72	1.22	1.79
40	1.44	1.54	1.39	1.60	1.34	1.66	1.29	1.72	1.23	1.79
45	1.48	1.57	1.43	1.62	1.38	1.67	1.34	1.72	1.29	1.78
50	1.50	1.59	1.46	1.63	1.42	1.67	1.38	1.72	1.34	1.77
55	1.53	1.60	1.49	1.64	1.45	1.68	1.41	1.72	1.38	1.77
60	1.55	1.62	1.51	1.65	1.48	1.69	1.44	1.73	1.41	1.77
65	1.57	1.63	1.54	1.66	1.50	1.70	1.47	1.73	1.44	1.77
70	1.58	1.64	1.55	1.67	1.52	1.70	1.49	1.74	1.46	1.77
75	1.60	1.65	1.57	1.68	1.54	1.71	1.51	1.74	1.49	1.77
80	1.61	1.66	1.59	1.69	1.56	1.72	1.53	1.74	1.51	1.77
85	1.62	1.67	1.60	1.70	1.57	1.72	1.55	1.75	1.52	1.77
90	1.63	1.68	1.61	1.70	1.59	1.73	1.57	1.75	1.54	1.78
95	1.64	1.69	1.62	1.71	1.60	1.73	1.58	1.75	1.56	1.78
100	1.65	1.69	1.63	1.72	1.61	1.74	1.59	1.76	1.57	1.78

Note: DW values below d_L indicate that positive autocorrelation exists; values above d_U indicate that no positive autocorrelation exists. DW values between d_L and d_U are inconclusive. To test for negative correlation use $4 - DW$ instead of DW.

Source: S. Chatterjee and B. Price, *Regression Analysis by Example*, 3rd ed. (New York, NY: John Wiley & Sons, 1999). Copyright © 1999 by John Wiley & Sons; reprinted with permission.

For example, assume we are testing a regression equation with 18 observations and three variables. Positive autocorrelation would be indicated if $DW < 0.93$, no autocorrelation if $DW > 1.69$, and the test would be inconclusive if $0.93 < DW < 1.69$. The test for negative autocorrelation would be analogous, using $4 - DW$ instead of DW.

A routine check of summary statistics for a regression equation should include the DW. A particularly low or high DW would indicate a definite need for further analysis and model modification. However, it should be emphasized that even a perfect DW value (2.0) does not guarantee that autocorrelation does not exist. The DW only tests for first-order autocorrelation. If the interrelationship between the error terms is more complex, the DW might not pick it up. For this reason, it is also advisable to check a residual plot for autocorrelation. Furthermore, as will be illustrated in subsequent sections, the residual plot can also be used to provide important clues for improving the regression model.

■ The Implications of Autocorrelation

The presence of a pattern in the residuals suggests a potential inadequacy in the regression equation. Specifically, autocorrelation may reflect one of the two following flaws:

1. The omission of significant explanatory variables in the regression equation.
2. The use of the linear regression method to describe a nonlinear relationship between the dependent and independent variables.

If the autocorrelation is due to one of these factors, it is clear why autocorrelation is undesirable. These conditions indicate that a better model can be constructed, either by adding variables to the equation or by trying different functional relationships. However, even when this is not the case, an equation that exhibits autocorrelation is still undesirable, because the violation of the assumption that the error terms are randomly distributed will lead to distortions.[1] For this reason, as a last resort, transformations designed to remove the autocorrelation should be considered.

To summarize, the DW and residual plot should be checked for autocorrelation. If residuals are found to be correlated, the following steps should be taken:

1. Try to find any significant variables that may have been omitted from the equation.
2. If all feasible variables have been tried and autocorrelation still exists, experiment to see whether alternative functional forms (other than the linear form assumed in the regression procedure) are more appropriate.
3. If both of the preceding steps are unsuccessful, transformations to remove autocorrelation might be tried.

---

[1] If autocorrelation exists, the standard regression approach, which is called *ordinary least squares (OLS)*, will still yield unbiased estimates (i.e., estimates that on average will equal the population parameters). However, the estimates will no longer be *efficient* (i.e., they will not be the minimum variance estimates). Even worse, the standard error estimates of the regression coefficients and the equation as a whole may be severely understated. Consequently, the true confidence interval may be much wider than suggested, and the regression equation may be too imprecise to be used for forecasting.

The first of these steps will be illustrated by an example in the next section. Methods to address the second two steps are discussed in the addendum to this appendix.

■ Missing Variables and Time Trend

A pattern in the residual plot (or the presence of autocorrelation) can be viewed as an indication that significant explanatory variables are missing from the equation. For example, Figure E.2 shows the residual plot for the simple regression model of the average December hog futures price during July–November as a function of per capita June–November hog slaughter. Note the obvious nonrandom distribution of the residuals: There seems to be a definite trending pattern in the residuals with large negative values predominating in the earlier years and large positive values predominating in the later years.

Given this strong trending pattern in the residuals, we add a time trend as one of the explanatory variables. A time trend is simply a set of successive integers. Normally, the first observation would be assigned a value of 1, the second a value of 2, and so on. However, since the regression model is linear, any set of consecutive integers would serve equally well.

It is not surprising that the fitted values of the original equation tend to be too high in the earlier years and too low in the later years since our model used nominal rather than deflated prices. The reader may well wonder why we didn't first change the model by using deflated prices instead of adding a time trend. In fact, this alternative approach is entirely reasonable as the first change to try,

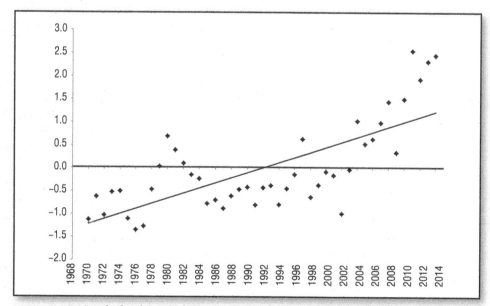

FIGURE E.2 Standardized Residuals for Average Price of December Hog Futures (July–November) vs. June–November Hog Slaughter

and we did run this model (not shown), but the results were substantially inferior to the model that added a time trend.

Table E.2 compares the summary statistics of this two-independent-variable regression equation with those of the original one-independent-variable model. Note the dramatic improvement in all the summary statistics and the significance of the time trend as reflected by its t statistic. In fact, the time trend is statistically even more significant in explaining hog prices than hog slaughter! In addition, the strong trend evident in the residual plot for the original simple regression (Figure E.2) has been eliminated in the residual plot for the new equation (Figure E.3). Although the trend in the residuals has been eliminated, Figure E.3 still exhibits a non-random pattern. Specifically, the residuals now conform to a broad "U" pattern, with positive residuals predominating in the early and late years and negative residuals predominating in the middle years. The existence of this pattern suggests other significant variables are still missing from the equation.

Next we add per capita broiler slaughter to the model, since poultry is an important competitive meat to pork. Table E.3 compares the key statistics for this new equation (Model 3) with the corresponding values for the first two models. As can be seen, the addition of poultry slaughter provides a large improvement in all the key statistics. For example, the corrected R^2 jumps from 0.66 in Model 2 to 0.82 in Model 3. Moreover, not only is the t statistic for broiler slaughter highly significant but the addition of this variable also increases the t statistics for the other explanantory variables (hog slaughter and trend). The addition of broiler slaughter to the equation also eliminates the pattern in the residuals. As can be seen in Figure E.4, which shows the residual plot corresponding to Model 3, the scatter of residuals now seems random.

Achieving a random residual plot doesn't necessarily mean the model is complete. It may well be possible to further improve the model by adding other variables. Model 4 in Table E.3 illustrates

TABLE E.2 Regression Summary Statistics for Hog-Price-Forecasting Models

Statistic	Model 1: Hog Price vs. Per Capita Hog Slaughter	Model 2: Hog Price vs. Per Capita Hog Slaughter and Trend
R^2	0.21	0.66
CR^2	0.20	0.64
SER	13.95	9.30
%SER	27.2	18.16
F	11.72	40.62
t-stat (constant)	5.19	4.57
t-stat (hog slaughter)	−3.42	−3.12
t-stat (trend)	NA	7.41
t-stat (broiler slaughter)	NA	NA
t-stat (cattle slaughter)	NA	NA

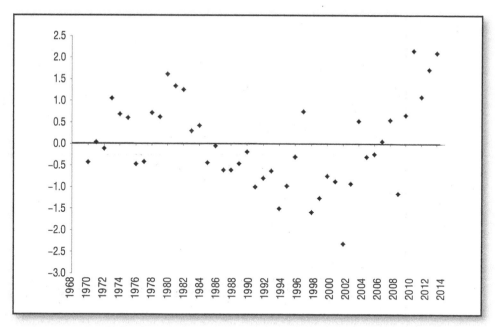

FIGURE E.3   Standardized Residuals for Average Price of December Hog Futures (July–November) vs. June–November Hog Slaughter, and Trend

TABLE E.3   Regression Summary Statistics for Hog-Price-Forecasting Models

Statistic	Model 1: Hog Price vs. Per Capita Hog Slaughter	Model 2: Hog Price vs. Per Capita Hog Slaughter and Trend	Model 3: Hog Price vs. Per Capita Hog Slaughter, Broiler Slaughter, and Trend	Model 4: Hog Price vs. Per Capita Hog Slaughter, Broiler Slaughter, Cattle Slaughter, and Trend
R^2	0.21	0.66	0.84	0.85
CR^2	0.20	0.64	0.82	0.84
SER	13.95	9.30	6.53	6.24
%SER	27.2	18.16	12.76	12.18
F	11.72	40.62	69.51	58.40
t-stat (constant)	5.19	4.57	8.45	6.02
t-stat (hog slaughter)	−3.42	−3.12	−4.39	−5.11
t-stat (trend)	NA	7.41	10.29	5.88
t-stat (broiler slaughter)	NA	NA	−6.64	−7.23
t-stat (cattle slaughter)	NA	NA	NA	−2.22

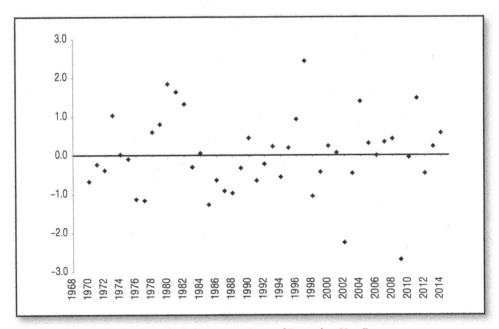

FIGURE E.4 Standardized Residuals for Average Price of December Hog Futures (July–November) vs. June–November Hog Slaughter, Broiler Slaughter, and Trend

one such attempt: adding per capita cattle slaughter to the model on the premise that beef is another competitive meat to pork. The t statistic for cattle slaughter is statistically significant and adding this variable modestly increases the corrected R^2 and lowers the SER.

■ Dummy Variables

In Appendix A we derived a regression equation for forecasting June–November hog slaughter from the prior December–May pig crop. Consider what happens when we attempt to make the equation more general by forecasting hog slaughter during a six-month period from the pig crop of the previous six-month period. In this case, half the observations are those of the original equation, while the other half relate December–May slaughter to the June–November pig crop. Figure E.5 illustrates the residual plot for this equation. We have used two different symbols to distinguish between the residuals for June–November slaughter and the residuals for December–May slaughter. Note the striking pattern of the predominance of positive residuals for June–November slaughter and negative residuals for December–May slaughter. As Figure E.5 dramatically indicates, our equation is missing some important information: the seasonal period of the slaughter forecast. Clearly, we want our equation to distinguish between the two periods. In other words, it is necessary to include a seasonal indicator.

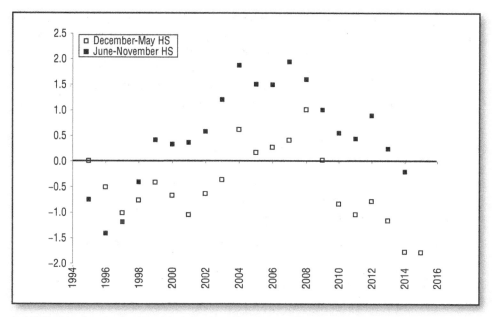

FIGURE E.5   Standardized Residuals for Hog Slaughter vs. Previous Six-Month Pig Crop

A simple method for handling such a situation would be to add a *dummy variable* to the equation, which has a value of 1 for one season and a value of 0 for the other season. The regression equation adding a dummy variable could be written as

$$HS = a + bPC + cS$$

where HS = hog slaughter
   PC = pig crop
   S = dummy variable, which equals 0 during December–May and 1 during June–November

The dummy variable can be thought of as a switch that is set to off (0) during the base period (December–May) and on (1) during June–November. The dummy variable will have the effect of shifting the intercept by an amount c for the June–November observations. Note that this adjustment will be exactly equivalent to finding two separate equations with the same slope, one for each period. That is, $HS = a + bPC + cS$ for all periods is equivalent to:

$$HS = a_1 + bPC \text{ for December-May slaughter}$$
$$HS = a_2 + bPC \text{ for June-November slaughter}$$

where $a_2 = a_1 + c$

Typically, most users of regression analysis will only employ a dummy variable to shift the intercept, while the slope is assumed to remain constant from period to period. However, in most instances there is no reason to impose an *a priori* restriction that the slopes be equal in different periods. Rather, it seems preferable to begin by using dummy variables for both the intercept and the slopes.[2] Once this full version of dummy variables is run, we can check the t statistics to see which of the dummy variables are significant and then choose the appropriate model accordingly. Thus, in our example, we would begin with:

$$HS = a + bPC + cS + d \cdot S \cdot PC$$

where $S = 0$ during December–May

$S = 1$ during June–November

The form of the equation used will depend on which of the dummy variables proves significant. Some examples:

1. If neither c or d is significant, we would use:

$$HS = a + bPC$$

2. If only c is significant, we would use:

$$HS = a + bPC + cS$$

3. If both c and d are significant, we would use the full-version equation:

$$HS = a + bPC + cS + d \cdot S \cdot PC$$

---

[2] There are two important exceptions: (1) When one of the periods contains only a few observations, the slope estimate for this period might be unreliable, and it would be better to pool the data in terms of assuming a common slope coefficient for all observations. For example, consider an annual price-forecasting model with 15 observations, three of which coincided with a government program that distorted normal market behavior. In this case, we would definitely only use the dummy variable for the constant term (with the aforementioned three years having a dummy variable value equal to 1), thereby implicitly imposing the restriction of a common slope. The reason for this is that a slope estimate based on only three observations would not be very reliable. This example illustrates one of the advantages of using dummy variables, as opposed to separate equations for each set of observations. (2) When the number of all possible dummy variables is large compared with the number of observations, it may be desirable to conserve degrees of freedom by limiting the number of dummy variables.

Note that in this last case, when both c and d are significant, the resulting equation is equivalent to the following two separate equations for each period:[3]

$$HS = a + bPC \quad \text{for December–May}$$
$$HS = (a + c) + (b + d)PC \quad \text{for June–November}$$

Why, then, do we not just run separate equations for each period? There are several reasons:

1. By pooling the data, we increase the number of degrees of freedom and add to the statistical reliability of the equation.
2. We do not know beforehand which, if any, of the dummy variables will be significant. The single-equation approach will allow us to eliminate the dummy variables that appear insignificant, thereby providing a better model. In contrast, the two-equation approach is equivalent to automatically assuming that all the dummy variables are significant.
3. In terms of the various tasks of checking alternative models, testing for significance, and forecasting, it is more convenient to have a single equation that is applicable to all periods than a separate equation for each period.
4. As mentioned in footnote 2, there are times when it is definitely preferable to impose slope restrictions—an approach that requires the use of dummy variables.

Since in our example of hog slaughter versus the prior six-month pig crop the dummy variable for the slope is statistically significant, we use the full form of the equation:

$$HS = a + bPC + cS + d \cdot S \cdot PC$$

Figure E.6 shows the residual plot for the regression equation that adds dummy variables for the slope and intercept. Note that the positive bias for June–November residuals and the negative bias for December–May residuals has been eliminated.

The failure to include dummy variables when they are appropriate will bias the regression coefficient estimates. In Figure E.7 we provide a hypothetical example where the points associated with two different periods are best described by best-fit lines with different constant terms. Note how the slope of a single regression equation line without inclusion of dummy variables is biased by the failure to distinguish between the two periods.

Although our example involved only two periods (one period other than the base period), the dummy variable approach can be extended to more period divisions. For example, if we were using a quarterly model, there would be one dummy variable for each quarter other than the base quarter.

$$Y = a + bX + c_1 S_1 + c_2 S_2 + c_3 S_3 + d \cdot S_1 \cdot X + e \cdot S_2 \cdot X + f \cdot S_3 \cdot X$$

[3] Although the intercept and slopes will be identical in the one- and two-equation versions, there is a minor technical difference between the two models. The single equation implicitly assumes a common variance for all periods, while the two-equation version allows for different variances in each period. This difference could theoretically affect the various tests of significance.

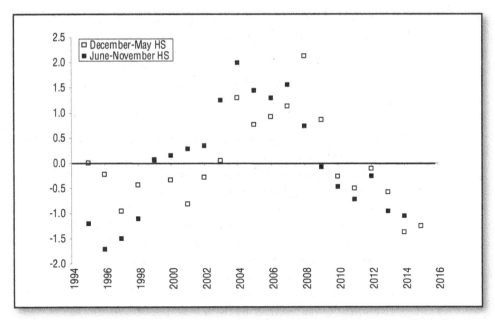

FIGURE E.6 Standardized Residuals for Hog Slaughter vs. Previous Six-Month Pig Crop after Including Dummy Variables

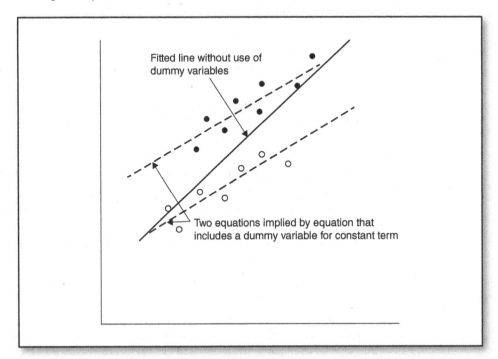

Fitted line without use of dummy variables

Two equations implied by equation that includes a dummy variable for constant term

FIGURE E.7 Bias in Regression Line Due to Omission of Dummy Variables

where S_1 = dummy variable for the first quarter

S_2 = dummy variable for the second quarter

S_3 = dummy variable for the third quarter

Note that the number of dummy variables is always equal to one less than the number of periods, since the base period conditions, assumed to be the fourth quarter in our example, are captured by the original constant and regression coefficient.[4]

If there are two independent variables, the full-version equation would be

$$Y = a + b_1 X_1 + b_2 X_2 + c_1 S_1 + c_2 S_2 + c_3 S_3 + d_1 \cdot S_1 \cdot X_1$$
$$+ d_2 \cdot S_1 \cdot X_2 + e_1 \cdot S_2 \cdot X_1 + e_2 \cdot S_2 \cdot X_2 + f_1 \cdot S_3 \cdot X_1 + f_2 \cdot S_3 \cdot X_2$$

Note that:

b values are regression coefficients for regular independent variables.

c values are regression coefficients for dummy constants.

d values are regression coefficients for dummy slope for the first period (S_1).

e values are regression coefficients for dummy slope for the second period (S_2).

f values are regression coefficients for dummy slope for the third period ($S3$).

As should be quite apparent, when the number of periods is increased, the number of dummy variables increases like rabbits. Since the researcher might wish to avoid beginning with an equation that contains a large number of dummy variables, she might prefer to only include constant dummy variable terms in the starting equation and then experiment with the addition of selected slope dummy variable terms if she believes that her initial equation needs improvement.

■ Multicollinearity

The reader may recall that the extension to the multiple regression model required the additional assumption that the independent variables be linearly independent. *Multicollinearity* is a term used to describe the presence of significant correlation between two or more independent variables.

To see why multicollinearity is a problem, consider a hog-slaughter-forecasting model that includes both the pig crop during the prior six-month period and the number of market hogs at the start of the period as explanatory variables. In this case, the independent variables would be extremely highly correlated, that is, large market hog figures would coincide with large pig-crop numbers. As illustrated in Figure E.8, a three-dimensional representation is really unnecessary for this model, as

---

[4] In fact, including a dummy variable for the base period would actually result in perfect multicollinearity—a totally undesirable situation (see next section).

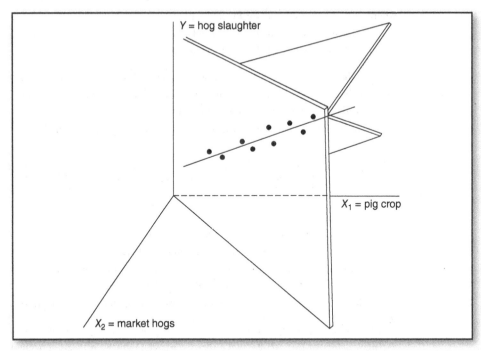

FIGURE E.8 Multicollinearity
Source: Adapted from T. H. Wonnacott and R. J. Wonnacott, *Econometrics*, John Wiley & Sons, New York, 1980.

demonstrated by the proximity of the points to a straight line. Actually, either the $X1$, Y plane or the $X2$, Y plane alone would have been adequate. The first plane would be a two-dimensional representation of the relationship between hog slaughter and the pig crop, and the second, a two-dimensional representation of the relationship between hog slaughter and market hogs. In effect, the inclusion of both the pig crop and market hogs forces the use of a three-dimensional model to represent a relationship that can be adequately described by two dimensions.

The problem lies not in the fact that multicollinearity implies the inclusion of superfluous information, but rather that this redundancy can severely affect the regression equation's reliability. Multicollinearity is a perfect example of the phrase "more is less." As can be seen in Figure E.8, when multicollinearity is present, there may be very divergent planes that closely approximate the fit of points. For any given set of observations, the regression procedure will choose one plane that best fits the observations. However, the real problem in multicollinearity lies in the fact that if the observations were only slightly altered, a totally different plane might be chosen as the best fit. Thus, if multicollinearity exists, the regression coefficients are no longer reliable indicators of how the dependent variable will change when each of the independent variables is changed (while all the other independent variables are held constant). This fact will be reflected by high standard errors, and hence low t statistics, for the regression coefficients of highly correlated explanatory variables.

What about the reliability of the equation in forecasting? If the values of the independent variables for the forecast period lie in the neighborhood of past observations, then the multicollinear model can still provide adequate forecasts. This situation describes the preceding example, since presumably the pig crop and market hogs will continue to remain highly correlated. In other circumstances, however, if the two correlated independent variables cease to be correlated in the future, then the forecast provided by the multicollinear equation could be distorted because the model is only valid for points in the neighborhood of past observations. At other locations, there is no historical evidence to provide any clues regarding the expected relationship between the variables. In geometric terms, all planes passing through a line provide accurate forecasts in the vicinity of the line, but drastically different projections at points removed from the line (Figure E.8).

To summarize, there are two major drawbacks to a multicollinear equation:

1. The regression coefficients lose their meaning (i.e., are no longer statistically reliable).
2. If the equation is used for forecasts in which the independent variables do not lie in the neighborhood of past observations, the projection could be severely distorted.

Clearly, then, it is always desirable to avoid multicollinearity. The presence of multicollinearity can be detected in a number of ways:

1. **Check the regression coefficients.** The regression coefficients of an equation can provide a number of clues indicating that multicollinearity is present:
   a. Low t statistics for coefficients that were expected to be highly significant.
   b. In more extreme cases, a regression coefficient sign that may actually be counter to theoretical expectations.
   c. Large changes in the coefficient values when variables are added or deleted from the equation.
   d. Large changes in coefficient values when data points are added or deleted from the equation. Any of these patterns would suggest that the independent variables should be examined for signs of correlation.
2. **Compare the independent variables.** Sometimes common sense will dictate when the independent variables are likely to be correlated. By being aware of the problem, one can often avoid multicollinearity by carefully selecting the independent variables. For example, if the researcher thought that gross national product (GNP) and disposable income might help explain the variation of the dependent variable, she would use either one, or try both successively, but she would not include them in the same equation simultaneously. Beyond intuition, one can check for correlation between the independent variables statistically. High absolute values of the *correlation coefficients*[5] between any two independent variables would indicate a potential

---

[5] The correlation coefficient, denoted by the symbol r, reflects the degree of relationship between two variables and can range between -1 and $+1$. Values close to $+1$ indicate a strong positive relationship, while values close to -1 indicate a strong inverse relationship. If r is close to 0, it means that there is little, if any, correlation between the two variables. The square of the correlation coefficient is equal to the r^2 of the simple regression equation in which one of the variables is a dependent variable and the other an independent variable.

multicollinearity problem. The *correlation matrix*—an output feature in some software packages—offers a summary array of all the paired correlation values.

What should be done if multicollinearity is discovered in an equation? One solution is simply to delete one of the correlated independent variables.

■ Addendum: Advanced Topics

Transformations to Achieve Linearity[6]

Perhaps the most basic assumption in a regression analysis is that the relationship between the dependent and independent variables is approximately linear. If, in fact, the relationship is decisively nonlinear, the error terms might appear to be correlated. For example, consider what happens when we try to fit a regression line to the scatter points in Figure E.9a. Forcing these points into a linear fit would result in the residual pattern illustrated in Figure E.9b, in which the residuals would tend to be positive at high and low values of the independent variable X and negative in the middle range of values. (In Figure E.9b, the standardized residuals are plotted against the independent variable not time.)

Fortunately, many nonlinear relationships can be transformed into linear equations. For example, the scatter of points in Figure E.9a suggests a hyperbolic function, or an equation of the general form

$$Y = a + \frac{b}{X + c}$$

This can be transformed into a linear relationship by setting

$$X' = \frac{1}{X + c}$$

then

$$Y = a + bX'$$

In this form, the equation can be solved in straightforward fashion using ordinary least squares (OLS), the standard regression procedure. To get a specific forecast for Y, one would merely plug in the value $1/(X + c)$ for X'. For example, if $a = 2$, $b = 16$, $c = 4$, and $X = 4$, the forecast for Y is 4.

---

[6] Although still involving nothing more mathematically complex than algebra, the remainder of this appendix covers material that is somewhat more advanced.

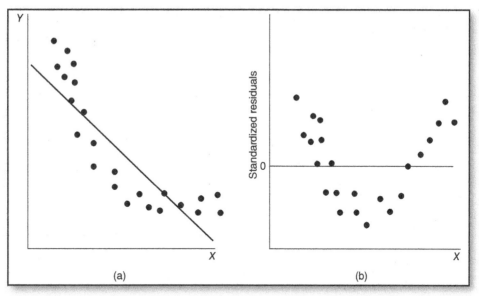

FIGURE E.9 Distortion in Applying Linear Regression to Nonlinear Function

Many other types of functions can be transformed into linear equations. Let us consider a few more examples:

1. $Y = a + b_1 X + b_2 X^2 + b_3 X^3$

   Let $X_1 = X$; $X_2 = X^2$; $X_3 = X^3$; then

   $Y = a + b_1 X_1 + b_2 X_2 + b_3 X_3$

   This is a linear equation and OLS can be applied. Note that although the independent variables are related, the relationship is nonlinear, so that the regression assumption regarding linear independence among the explanatory variables is not violated.

2. $Y = ae^{bX}$

   Taking the natural logarithm of both sides:

   $$\ln Y = \ln a + bX$$

   Let $Y' = \ln Y$; $a' = \ln a$; then

   $$Y' = a' + bX$$

   This is a linear equation and OLS can be applied. Note that in this case, plugging a value for X into the derived regression equation will yield a forecast for $\ln Y$. To get a forecast for Y, it would be necessary to find the antilog value. Figure E.10 illustrates the shapes of the function $Y = ae^{bX}$ for different values of b.

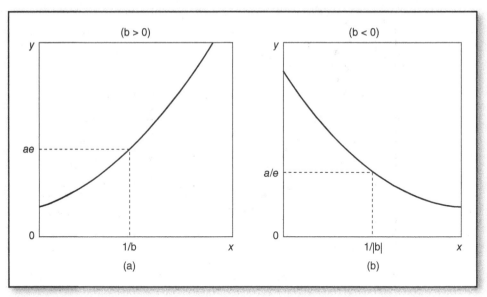

FIGURE E.10 $Y = ae^{bX}$

Source: S. Chatterjee and B. Price, *Regression Analysis by Example,* 3rd ed. (New York, NY: John Wiley & Sons 1999). Copyright © 1999 by John Wiley & Sons; reprinted with permission.

3. $Y = a \cdot X^b$

    Taking logs of both sides:

$$\log Y = \log a + b \log X$$

    Let $Y' = \log Y$; $a' = \log a$; $X' = \log X$; then

$$Y' = a' + bX'$$

    This is a linear equation and OLS can be applied. Here we would plug the value for log X, not X, into the regression equation to get a forecast of log Y. To get a forecast for Y, it would then be necessary to find the antilog value. Figure E.11 illustrates the shape of the function $Y = aX^b$ for different values of a and b.

    If a residual plot still reflects autocorrelation after all feasible variables have been tried, the possibility of nonlinearity should be considered. In the simple regression case, a scatter diagram can be constructed in order to check whether a linear assumption is warranted or whether another functional form is more appropriate, just as Figure E.9a suggested the equation form $Y = a + b/(X + c)$. In a multiple regression, if nonlinearity is expected for one of the independent variables, a regression could be run using only the other independent variables. The residuals of this equation would then be plotted against the unused independent variable. The presence of any nonlinearity would be apparent in the resulting scatter diagram.

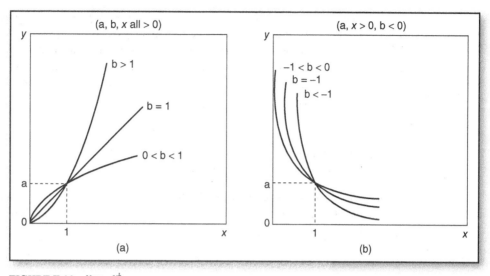

FIGURE E.11 $Y = aX^b$

Source: S. Chatterjee and B. Price, *Regression Analysis by Example*, 3rd ed. (New York, NY: John Wiley & Sons, 1999). Copyright © 1999 by John Wiley & Sons; reprinted with permission.

Transformation to Remove Autocorrelation

The simplest assumption one can make about autocorrelation is that a current period's error term will be equal to the previous period's error term plus a random disturbance. This can be expressed as

$$e_t = e_{t-1} + \upsilon_t,$$

where υ_t = a random disturbance term.

Since $Y_t = \alpha + \beta X_t + e_t$ and $Y_{t-1} = \alpha + \beta X_{t-1} + e_{t-1}$, then

$$Y_t - Y_{t-1} = \beta(X_t - X_{t-1}) + \upsilon_t$$

Let $Y_t^* = Y_t - Y_{t-1}$ and $X_t^* = X_t - X_{t-1}$; then

$$Y_t^* = \beta X_t^* + \upsilon_t$$

For a k-variable multiple regression equation, these steps would yield

$$Y_t^* = \beta_1 X_{1t}^* + \beta_2 X_{2t}^* + \cdots + \beta_k X_{kt}^* + \upsilon_t$$

Since by definition υ_t is randomly distributed, OLS can now be applied to this equation.

The preceding method, which is perhaps the most commonly used transformation for removing autocorrelation, is known as *first differences*. In effect, the first difference regression equation states that the change in Y will be linearly dependent on the change in X. Equations of this type will tend to have much lower R^2 values. This is only to be expected, since forecasting the *change* from one period to the next is much more difficult than forecasting the *level*. Once again, consider the following daytrading price-forecasting model:

$$P_t = a + bP_{t-1}$$

where P_t = closing price on day t
P_{t-1} = closing price on day $t - 1$

Such an equation would have an extremely high R^2 since it would give us a close approximation of the price level for a given day. However, it would be useless in forecasting the change in price from day to day. The model

$$P_t^* = a + bX_t^*$$

where $P_t^* = P_t - P_{t-1}$

$X_t^* = X_t - X_{t-1}$

in which X_t is some explanatory variable the value of which is known before day t, would be far preferable, even if its R^2 value were low (e.g., $R^2 = 0.30$).

The first difference approach is easy to use, but it does involve an extreme simplifying assumption regarding the nature of the autocorrelation. A more realistic assumption would be

$$e_t = \rho e_{t-1} + \upsilon_t$$

where $|\rho| < 1$. Note that the larger the value of ρ, the more the error term in a given period will be dependent upon the previous period's error term. A generalized transformation is analogous to the first difference transformation:

$$Y_t = \alpha + \beta X_t + e_t$$
$$Y_{t-1} = \alpha + \beta X_{t-1} + e_{t-1}$$

If we multiply the equation for $Y_t - 1$ by ρ

$$\rho Y_{t-1} = \rho\alpha + \rho\beta X_{t-1} + \rho e_{t-1}$$

Thus, $Y_t - \rho Y_{t-1} = \alpha(1 - \rho) + \beta(X_t - \rho X_{t-1}) + \upsilon_t$.
Let $Y_t^* = Y_t - \rho Y_{t-1}$ and $X_t^* = X_t - \rho X_{t-1}$.
Then $Y_t^* = \alpha(1 - \rho) + \beta X_t^* + \upsilon_t$.

For a k-variable equation, these steps would yield

$$Y^* = \alpha(1 - \rho) + \beta_1 X_{1t}^* + \beta_2 X_{2t}^* + \cdots + \beta_k X_{kt}^* + \upsilon_t$$

Since by definition υ_t is randomly distributed, OLS can once again be used. The only problem with this procedure is that we do not know the value of ρ. We very briefly describe two approaches for estimating ρ.

1. **The Hildreth-Lu procedure.** This procedure specifies a set of spaced values for ρ. If positive autocorrelation is assumed, these values might be 0, 0.1, 0.2, 0.3, 0.4, 0.5, 0.6, 0.7, 0.8, 0.9, 1.0. A regression is then run for the transformed equation:

$$Y_t^* = \alpha(1 - \rho) + \beta_1 X_{1t}^* + \beta_2 X_{2t}^* + \cdots + \beta_k X_{kt}^*$$

using each of the specified values. The procedure will select the equation that results in the lowest SER. If desired, the process can be repeated using a closer spacing of ρ values in the vicinity of the ρ selected in the initial step.

2. **The Cochrane-Orcutt procedure.** This iterative procedure estimates a ρ value from the residuals of the original equation, and a regression is then run on the transformed equation using this estimate of ρ. If the resulting equation still indicates autocorrelation, the process is repeated using the residuals of the new equation.

■ Heteroscedasticity

One of the assumptions that justifies the use of ordinary least squares (OLS) is that the error terms are homoscedastistic, that is, they have an approximate constant variance. When this condition is not met, the problem is called *heteroscedasticity*. Figure E.12 illustrates a case of heteroscedasticity. Note that the relationship between the dependent and independent variables becomes increasingly variable as X increases, resulting in higher absolute residual values at higher values of X. The wider variability between the dependent and independent variables in a given region will make the resulting regression equation less reliable.

Weighted least squares (WLS) is a method used to circumvent this problem. For the relationship depicted in Figure E.12, the WLS approach would give greater weight to the observations for lower values of X, since these offer a more precise indication of the location of the true regression line. Rather than describe the WLS procedure, suffice it to say that there is a simpler approach using a transformation that achieves exactly equivalent results. This transformation assumes that the standard deviation of the error terms is proportional to the independent variable. Specifically,

$$\sigma_i = kX_i$$

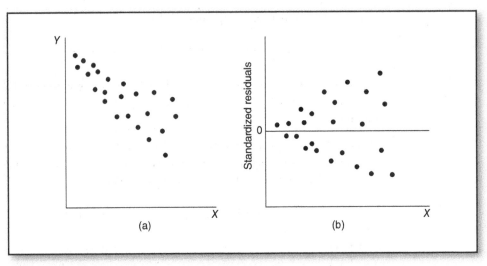

FIGURE E.12 Heteroscedasticity

where σ_i = standard deviation of the error terms (e_i). Starting with the standard regression equation

$$Y_i = \alpha + \beta X_i + e_i$$

we divide by X_i,

$$\frac{Y_i}{X_i} = \frac{a}{X_i} + \beta + \frac{e_i}{X_i}$$

The standard deviation of e_i / X_i. is equal to the standard deviation of e_i divided by X_i. Since the standard deviation of e_i is σ_i, which equals kX_i, the standard deviation of $e_i / X_i = k$, a constant. Thus, this transformation removes the heteroscedasticity of the original equation. Now if we let

$$Y_i' = \frac{Y_i}{X_i} \quad X_i' = \frac{1}{X_i} \quad \alpha' = \beta \quad \beta' = \alpha \quad \text{and} \quad e' = \frac{e_i}{X_i}$$

then

$$Y_i' = \alpha' + \beta' X_i' + e_i'$$

This equation can be solved by using OLS, yielding

$$Y_i' = a + bX_i'$$

where a is an estimator of β in the original equation and b is an estimator of α in the original equation.

Practical Considerations in Applying Regression Analysis

I remember the rage I used to feel when a prediction went awry. I could have shouted at the subjects of my experiments, "Behave, damn you, behave as you ought!" Eventually I realized that the subjects were always right. It was I who was wrong. I had made a bad prediction.

—Burrhus Frederic Skinner

■ Determining the Dependent Variable

The title of this section might sound trivial. After all, the dependent variable is what we wish to fore-cast. However, in a price-forecasting equation, the selection of a dependent variable is by no means obvious. The following choices must be made:

1. Should the price be stated in nominal or deflated terms?
2. Should the price be based on cash or futures?

3. If the price is based on futures, should it be based on a nearest futures price series or a single contract?

4. Should the price represent the entire season or only a specified segment of the season?

The answer to question 1 would typically be deflated prices, unless a trend variable is included in the equation, in which case nominal prices may be a better choice. If, however, the equation does not include a trend variable, then the use of nominal prices implicitly assumes that equivalent fundamental conditions in two widely spaced years should result in approximately equal price levels. Obviously, this assumption is wrong. All else being equal, inflation will result in considerably higher prices in the more recent year. The subject of adjusting prices for inflation is covered in greater detail in Chapter 25.

The answers to questions 2 and 3 depend primarily on the particular price you wish to forecast. Although this consideration is also a factor in answering question 4, the choice of the time period should depend more heavily on the fundamental characteristics of the market. Of course, if the initial choice is inappropriate, the misjudgment will become apparent in analyzing the regression results. However, by giving some thought to the intrinsic market fundamentals before selecting the forecast period, it is possible to minimize unnecessary trial and error in the regression-analysis process.

For example, in most agricultural markets, the statistical balance for a given season will have a far greater impact on price levels during the first half of the season than on price levels during the second half. This typical market behavioral pattern reflects the fact that by the second half of the season, the prevailing fundamental situation is well-defined and frequently largely discounted. More often than not, major price shifts during the latter part of a season reflect developments affecting new crop expectations (e.g., drought and freeze). Consequently, for a fundamental model that does not include new crop expectations as an explanatory variable, it would generally make more sense to select a price forecast period that approximates the first half of the season rather than the full season. This approach does not mean that we ignore the other six months. Rather, the implication is that it will be necessary to develop other models to forecast prices in those months. For example, the latter months of a season might be grouped with the early months of the following season in a model that employed new-crop statistics to forecast prices.

In some markets, intrinsic fundamental considerations will not dictate a specific observation period. In such cases, the choice will involve only the time frame of the individual observations (e.g., annual, semiannual, quarterly, monthly).[1] Here a general rule might apply: start with the longest period (i.e., annual or semiannual), and if the regression model is satisfactory, work toward a shorter period. Although the shortest time frame projection is most useful for trading purposes, the difficulty of forecasting is inversely proportional to the length of the time period. Also, the shorter the time frame, the more likely the problem of autocorrelation. For example, in a monthly model there is a high probability that a high positive residual in one month will be followed by a positive residual in the next month. Thus, for monthly and even quarterly models, transformations to remove autocorrelation may be necessary (e.g., first differences).

---

[1] The choice of the length of the period must also be made for markets in which the structure of the model depends on the forecast period. For example, a model based solely on old-crop statistics (i.e., a model that does not incorporate new-crop expectations) could use a six-month forecast period (coinciding with the first half of the season) or it could be applied to two separate three-month periods.

■ Selecting the Independent Variables

General Considerations

There is more to selecting the independent variables than choosing the factors that intuitively appear to be good candidates for explanatory variables. Perhaps the pivotal question to be considered is whether the regression equation is intended for explaining or forecasting the dependent variable. Sometimes, a regression equation is only intended as an explanatory model. For example, a wheat producer might be interested in determining the relationship between yield and the quantity of fertilizer applied. In this case, his goal is not to forecast yield, a projection that will also depend heavily on other factors, such as weather conditions, but to understand the implications of various management choices. Furthermore, he need not worry about estimating the independent variable (quantity of fertilizer), since it is entirely under his control.

In contrast, most applications of regression analysis in the futures markets will be concerned with forecasting. If an equation is intended primarily for prediction, it is critical to choose explanatory variables that can be determined with relative reliability. For example, if we were to construct a copper price-forecasting model in which the concurrent gross domestic product (GDP) was an important input, the equation would be useless if GDP levels were no more predictable than copper prices, even if $R^2 - 1.00$. Thus, in selecting independent variables, the researcher should keep in mind the precision with which these variables can be estimated *before* the forecast period.

If they prove statistically significant, *lagged variables* are the ideal choice for explanatory variables. A lagged variable is one whose value is determined during a period before the period for the corresponding dependent variable. For example, the average GDP during the prior six months would be a lagged variable. Thus, even if the lagged value of GDP were substantially less significant in explaining copper prices than the concurrent value, it might still be a preferable choice.

Unfortunately, the analyst will rarely be lucky enough to construct a regression equation that uses only lagged variables. Concurrent variables that can be forecast with reasonable accuracy provide an acceptable alternative. In fact, some variables, such as population, can be forecast with such accuracy that they are similar to lagged variables. Other variables can be projected within a reasonable range. For example, in the hog model, hog slaughter is much easier to project than hog prices, since it depends on lagged variables (e.g., prior pig crop, market hogs at start of period). In short, the essential question to consider is whether the values for a potential explanatory variable are known before the forecast period or are at least substantially easier to project than the values for the dependent variable.

Another criterion in selecting the independent variables is that they should not be correlated, in order to avoid the problem of multicollinearity. If several correlated variables seem to be good choices for explanatory variables, they should be tested individually.

■ Should the Preforecast Period Price Be Included?

An important question to be decided in a price-forecasting equation is whether to include the preforecast period (PFP) price as an explanatory variable. One reason for including the PFP price is that it is usually an important factor. For example, consider the following two situations in which the PFP price was not taken into account by the model:

Situation A Projected average price for forecast period = 60¢;
      price on day before forecast period = 40¢.

Situation B Projected average price for forecast period = 60¢;
      price on day before forecast period = 80¢.

Would it be reasonable to expect the same price level in both cases? Definitely not! Some textbook theories notwithstanding, in the real world, prices do not adjust instantaneously to changing fundamentals. In situation A, a major uptrend would be required for prices merely to reach the forecasted equilibrium level. Such an advance will not occur overnight. Furthermore, it is not sufficient for prices to reach 60¢ in order to achieve the projected 60¢ average. Prices would have to go far beyond .60¢ in order to make up for all the days of sub-60¢ prices during the early part of the period. Similarly, in situation B, prices would have to go far below 60¢ to achieve a 60¢ average. In practice, prices may well reach 60¢ in both situations A and B, but the average price is likely to be well below 60¢ in situation A and well above 60¢ in situation B.

The preceding example illustrates that the PFP price may often be an important explanatory variable. Then why not always include it in the model? Ironically, the answer is that it may sometimes be too good in explaining price behavior. In other words, if the PFP price swamps the effect of the other independent variables, the price projection will primarily reflect current price levels. Thus, if the PFP price accounts for a large percentage of the R^2, the model may be good at explaining prices, but will be ineffective at predicting price changes, which after all is the primary goal in price projection. However, in some cases, the other independent variables may explain a major portion of total variation, even when the PFP price is included. In these situations, including the PFP price may help eliminate a significant portion of the unexplained variation that would exist if it were omitted, while still yielding a model that is capable of predicting price changes.

The decision of whether to include the PFP price as an independent variable must be made empirically on a case-by-case basis. A reasonable procedure would be to use a stepwise regression approach (see the section titled "Stepwise Regression" in this appendix) both with and without including the PFP price on the list of independent variables. Although the model that includes the PFP price will always exhibit better summary statistics, it should only be chosen if the effect of the PFP price is significant without being overwhelming.

■ Choosing the Length of the Survey Period

Ideally, it is desirable to use the longest feasible survey period, since more data points will increase the accuracy of the regression statistics. However, in the real world, there is a tradeoff between the length of the survey period and the relevance of the earliest data points to current conditions. For example, it would be ludicrous to include data before 1973 in a fundamental forecasting model for currency rates, since exchange rates were fixed before that point.

As the preceding example illustrates, fundamental considerations will often limit the number of observations that can be included without distorting the model. Basically, the longest survey period consistent with current market conditions should be used. Scatter diagrams for the dependent variable plotted against each of the explanatory variables may be helpful in making this decision. It will often be necessary to run several regressions for periods of different lengths in order to decide on the optimum number of observations to be included. Occasionally, it may be possible to include earlier nonrepresentative years through the use of dummy variables.

■ Sources of Forecast Error

In order to build the best model as well as understand its potential limitations, it is important to be aware of the potential sources of forecast error. These include:

1. Random errors for true population regression. Any regression equation is only a simplification that cannot include all possible influences on the dependent variable. Thus, even if we knew the true population regression equation, which we never do, and the explanatory variables were precisely determined, this source of error would still exist. In other words, this type of error can never be avoided.

2. Random errors in the estimated regression coefficients. Since the data used to run a regression represents only a sample from the population, the estimated regression coefficients will deviate from the true population values.

3. Regression equation may be misspecified. The regression model may not represent the true underlying model because of the following reasons:

    a. Omission of significant variables;

    b. True model is nonlinear or wrong functional form is assumed in a linear transformation;

    c. Error terms are autocorrelated[2].

4. Errors in independent variable values. Often, the independent variables must themselves be projected, thereby introducing another tier of potential forecasting error. Sometimes, unexpected events (e.g., droughts, freezes, export embargoes) can result in the actual values of the explanatory variables deviating sharply from the estimated levels. In these situations, the regression projections can prove wide of the mark, even when the model would have provided an accurate forecast if the input had been correct.

5. Data errors. Lagged variable data and the data used to forecast the independent variables may be inaccurate because of sampling or compilation errors.

6. Structural changes. Structural change accounts for perhaps the most serious vulnerability of the regression forecast. Regression analysis is a static approach to a dynamic process; that is, the structure and behavior of a market are constantly changing. Thus, even if a model offers a good representation of the past, it may fail to describe a market adequately in the future. Any major structural change in a market can lead to large forecast errors.

---

[2] Of course, conditions 3(a) and 3(b) could also result in autocorrelation; the implication here is autocorrelation that exists without the presence of 3(a) and 3(b).

As an example, consider the plight of the unfortunate fundamental analyst using historical regressions to forecast prices for the 1981–1982 period, when the unprecedented combination of severe recession and high interest rates resulted in a dramatic downward shift in demand for many commodities. As a result, prices in a broad spectrum of markets declined to well below the levels that might have been anticipated on the basis of fundamental models that worked well in prior years, but did not include these effects. As a more recent example, the late 2008 financial crisis had such a huge depressant impact on commodity prices across the board that virtually any viable fundamental model for any commodity market would have been likely to yield price forecasts for the late 2008, early 2009 period that were far too high.

The preceding examples illustrated structural changes simultaneously affecting a broad range of markets. A structural change can also be confined to a single market. One example of such a change was the dramatic shift in corn usage for ethanol production. Corn use for fuel went from one-tenth the feed-use level before 2000 to greater than feed usage by 2010.

It is important to realize the standard error measures in regression analysis only account for the first two sources of error just listed. Perhaps even more sobering is the fact that with the exception of a misspecified equation (3), all these sources or error are beyond the control of the analyst. However, the potential variability attributable to errors in estimating the independent variables (4) can at least be defined by allowing for a range of possibilities. For example, in addition to generating a price forecast based on a set of best estimates for the explanatory variables, projections can also be derived for sets of bearish and bullish assumptions. In this way, it is at least possible to gauge the potential impact of inaccurate estimates for the independent variables. Furthermore, some solace can be drawn from the fact that the various types of errors listed here are not necessarily cumulative; that is, they may partly offset each other.

As a final word, it should be emphasized that this list of potential errors is not intended to discourage the potential user of regression analysis, but rather to instill a sense of realism in interpreting regression results.

■ Simulation

As the previous section demonstrated, comparisons between the fitted values of the regression equation and actual observations may severely understate potential forecasting errors. The process of determining how forecasts based on the given model would have compared with reality is called *simulation,* which is an extremely useful technique for testing a model under near real-life conditions. Simulation should only be undertaken once the choice of a model has been finalized, or at least reduced to a small number of possibilities. Ideally, the simulation period should be long enough to include a variety of conditions (e.g., at least one bull, one bear, and one neutral market in a price-forecasting equation).

For example, assume it is 2015 and we have decided the past 20 years of data are relevant to the current market structure. Given the constraint that each forecast must be based on at least 10 years of data, a 10-year simulation of a calendar-year forecast could be constructed as follows:

1. Using only data available on January 1, 2005, derive a regression equation for the same model for 1995 through 2004.

2. Using only data available on January 1, 2005, estimate the independent variables.
3. Plug these values into the 1995–2004 regression equation to obtain a forecast for 2005.
4. Repeat an analogous procedure for each subsequent year (2006–2014).
5. Compare simulations to actual values and calculate the root mean square (defined later in this section).

For a quarterly model, the simulation procedure would be analogous. However, with a quarterly model, very little would be lost by revising the regression equation only once every four times (each year) in order to reduce the amount of computation.

It may be instructive to compare the differences between the simulation forecasts and actual values with the residuals of the current regression equation. Of course, the former will almost invariably be higher, since simulation results are based on forecasts, while the regression equation is a best fit of past values.

A measure that may be useful in comparing the simulation results of different models is the *root mean square* (RMS):

$$\text{rms} = \sqrt{\frac{\sum_{t=1}^{N}\left(Y_t^F - Y_t^A\right)^2}{N}}$$

where

$\quad Y_t^F$ = forecasted value of Y for period t

$\quad Y_t^A$ = actual value of Y for period t

$\quad N$ = number of simulated observations

Note that the RMS calculation is analogous to the formula for the standard error of the regression (SER) (except for the number of degrees of freedom) and reflects the same underlying meaning.

■ Stepwise Regression

Ideally, having selected a list of explanatory variables, regression equations would be generated for each possible equation form. For example, given a dependent variable Y and three independent variables X_1, X_2, and X_3 there would be eight possible equations:

1. Y vs. X_1, X_2, and X_3 (all independent variables included)
2. Y vs. X_1, X_2
3. Y vs. X_1, X_3
4. Y vs. X_2, X_3
5. Y vs. X_1
6. Y vs. X_2
7. Y vs. X_3
8. $Y = \overline{Y}$ (no independent variables included)

Such a procedure, however, is not very efficient. The total number of possible equations doubles with the addition of each independent variable (e.g., 16 for four variables, 32 for five).

Stepwise regression is a highly useful and efficient procedure for isolating and providing summary results for the most statistically interesting equations. There are two basic types of stepwise regression:

1. **Forward selection.** The program selects the single independent variable that provides the highest r^2 value to form the first equation. Explanatory variables are then added one at a time to form subsequent equations, with the choice depending on which variable will result in the highest R^2 equation. The program terminates with an equation that includes all of the specified explanatory variables.

2. **Backward elimination.** The program begins by listing the equation that includes all the specified independent variables. The program then deletes the variable with the lowest t value to form the second equation. Subsequent equations are formed by continuing to delete variables, one at a time, with the elimination decision dependent on which remaining variable has the lowest t value.

The two methods will not necessarily yield the same subset of equations. Overall, the backward elimination process is preferable, particularly if the PFP price is one of the explanatory variables. In the forward selection process, the PFP price will usually be chosen first, since it is likely to explain more variation in the dependent variable than any other single variable. However, once more explanatory variables are added, the significance of the PFP price may drop sharply, as other variables in combination explain a portion of the variation originally attributed to the PFP price. Thus, in the backward elimination process, at some stage the PFP price might have a lower t value than any of the remaining variables.

Although the PFP price is effective as an explanatory variable, its inclusion may yield equations that are less useful for forecasting purposes. With the forward selection process, there is a higher probability that all of the chosen equations will include the PFP price, since the first variable chosen remains in all subsequent equations.

Once the stepwise regression results have been analyzed, detail should be generated for the equations that appear to be the most promising.[3] Minimum detail would include a listing of actual observations, predicted values, and residuals. Residual plots should also be constructed for these equations and modification implemented as suggested by these plots.

■ Sample Step-by-Step Regression Procedure

There is no single right order in which to perform the various elements of regression analysis. The following order merely represents one suggested sequence:

1. Determine the dependent variable.
2. List all possible choices for explanatory variables.

---

[3] The summary statistics would not be the only criteria for making this choice. For example, an equation that did not include the PFP price as a dependent variable might be preferable to one that did if the summary statistics were only modestly less favorable.

3. Choose a subset of these (usually no more than five), taking care to avoid selecting correlated independent variables. Scatter diagrams can be used as an aid in this selection process.
4. Choose the length of the survey period. Scatter diagrams can also be used as an aid in this step.
5. Apply a stepwise regression program to the selected variables.
6. Analyze the results by examining the various key statistics: t values, SER, CR^2, F, and DW. If there is any evidence of multicollinearity, check out this possibility and rerun stepwise regression with a different set of variables if necessary.
7. Generate detail and construct residual plots for the most promising equations in the stepwise regression run.
8. Check residual plots for outliers. Decide whether outliers should be deleted.
9. Check residual plots for autocorrelation.
10. If outliers or autocorrelation exist, try to correct through the addition of variables or transformations to achieve linearity.
11. If autocorrelation is still a problem, try a transformation to eliminate autocorrelation (e.g., first differences).
12. Check the correlation matrix or R^2 values for various combinations of equations based on the explanatory variables in order to verify that multicollinearity is not a problem.
13. Repeat steps 3–12 for other selections of explanatory variables.
14. *Optional:* After narrowing the number of possible models to three or less, generate simulations.

■ Summary

Regression analysis is an extremely efficient and powerful tool; it is a virtual necessity for fundamental analysis. The foregoing appendices were intended to provide the necessary background to interpret and analyze the results available on standard regression software packages. Regression analysis provides the means for precisely answering the question: What is the approximate equilibrium level, *given the specified conditions and assumptions*? The italicized qualification is essential. There is a danger of viewing regression results with great rigidity because of the scientific manner in which they are derived. This would be a mistake. As explained in the section "Sources of Forecast Error," a variety of factors are capable of causing the regression projection to be inaccurate. Therefore, the trader must always be open to the possibility the regression forecast might be wrong. However, given such a sense of realistic awareness, fundamental regression models can provide valuable insight into a market's current state and its potential future direction.

Wonnacott, R. J., and T. H. Wonnacott. *Econometrics* (New York, NY: John Wiley & Sons, 1980). This is an extraordinarily lucid treatment of an abstruse subject and is an excellent choice for readers interested in a more in-depth understanding of regression analysis. One of the outstanding features of this book is that it is divided into two separate parts, which cover essentially the same material but on different levels of difficulty. As a result, Part I, which provides a comprehensive and insightful overview of the key concepts of regression analysis, is fully accessible to a reader with only limited mathematical background.

Chatterjee, Samprit, and Ali S. Hadi. *Regression Analysis by Example,* 5th edition (New Delhi: Wiley India, 2012). This may be the best book available on the practical application of regression analysis. As promised in the title, the essential concepts are demonstrated by example. Perhaps the book's best feature is its thorough exposition of the use and interpretation of residual plots, an extremely effective yet easy-to-apply method for analyzing regression results.

Pindyck, R. S., and D. L. Rubinfeld. *Econometric Models and Econometric Forecasts,* 4th edition (New York, NY: McGraw-Hill/Irwin, 1997). The first of the three sections in this book covers single-equation regression analysis. (The other two sections are Multi-Equation Simulation Models and Time Series Models.) This book offers a clear exposition of theoretical concepts, as well as many useful insights into the practical application of regression analysis. Readers with limited mathematical background will find the presentation more difficult than Part I of Wonnacott and Wonnacott.

Makridakis, S., and S. C. Wheelwright. *Forecasting Methods and Applications,* 3rd edition (New York, NY: John Wiley & Sons, 1997). This text provides a broad overview of forecasting techniques, with regression analysis accounting for one of six sections. The presentation is aimed at an audience interested in practical applications rather than theory. This book is clearly written, covers a wide range of topics, and provides a plethora of examples to illustrate the discussion.

Freund, J. E., and F. J. Williams. *Elementary Business Statistics: The Modern Approach*, 6th sub edition (Upper Saddle River, NJ: Prentice Hall College Div., 1992). This book provides a good general overview of elementary statistics for the nonmathematical reader. The text is clearly written and replete with examples.

Kimble, G. A. *How to Use (and Misuse) Statistics* (Englewood Cliffs, NJ: Prentice-Hall, 1978). This introduction to elementary statistics is written with style and a sense of humor. Although it may be hard to believe, this is one statistics book that can actually be read for entertainment value alone.